W9-BKN-308

INSIDERS' GUIDE® SERIES

Insiders' Guide®
to
Atlanta

SIXTH EDITION

John and Bonnie McKay

Guilford, Connecticut
An imprint of The Globe Pequot Press

The prices and rates listed in this guidebook were confirmed at press time. We recommend, however, that you call establishments before traveling to obtain current information.

Copyright © 2001, 2004 by The Globe Pequot Press
A previous edition of this book was published by Falcon Publishing, Inc. in 2000.

Insiders' Guide is a registered trademark of The Globe Pequot Press.

Cover photos: front: © Didier Dorval/Masterfile www.masterfile.com; back: © 2003 www.clipart.com

Maps created by XNR Productions Inc. © The Globe Pequot Press

ISSN 1537-0569
ISBN 0-7627-2812-4

Manufactured in the United States of America
Sixth Edition/First Printing

Publications from the Insiders' Guide® series are available at special discounts for bulk purchases for sales promotions, premiums, or fund-raisings. Special editions, including personalized covers, can be created in large quantities for special needs. For more information, please contact The Globe Pequot Press at (800) 962-0973.

Contents

Preface ix

Acknowledgments xi

How to Use This Book 1

Getting Here, Getting Around 3

History 27

International Atlanta 39

Accommodations 47

Bed-and-Breakfasts 65

Restaurants 71

Nightlife 115

Shopping 129

Attractions 149

Kidstuff 187

Festivals and Events 201

The Arts 216

Parks and Recreation 236

Spectator Sports 262

Day Trips and Weekend Getaways 285

Relocation 320

Education 341

Health Care 364

Media 387

Worship and Spirituality 398

Index 400

About the Authors 416

Directory of Maps

Atlanta iv

Greater Atlanta v

Atlanta's Surrounding Counties vi

Hartsfield Atlanta International Airport vii

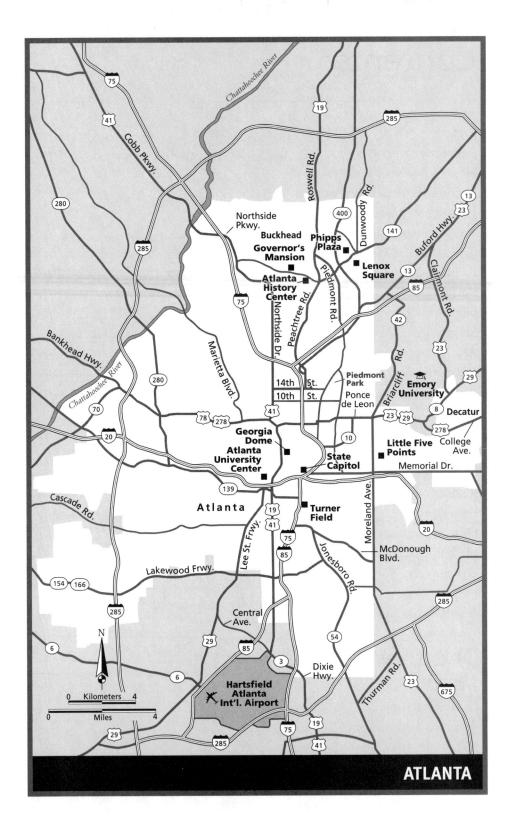

ATLANTA

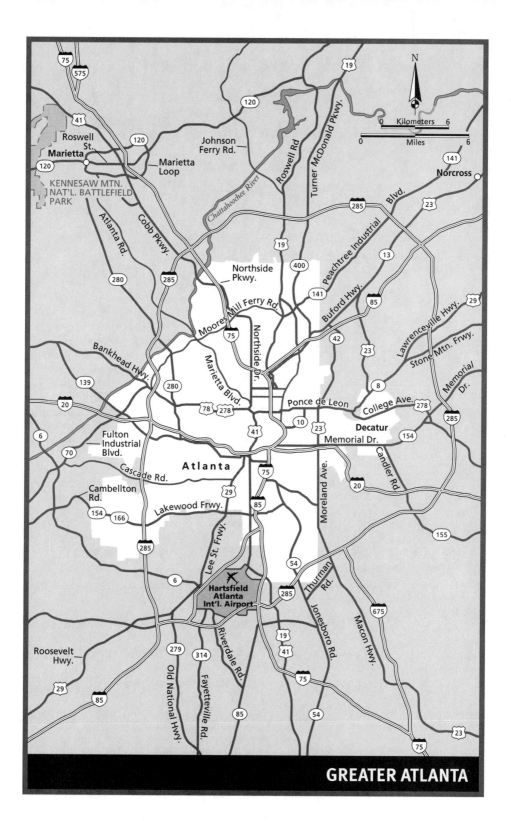

GREATER ATLANTA

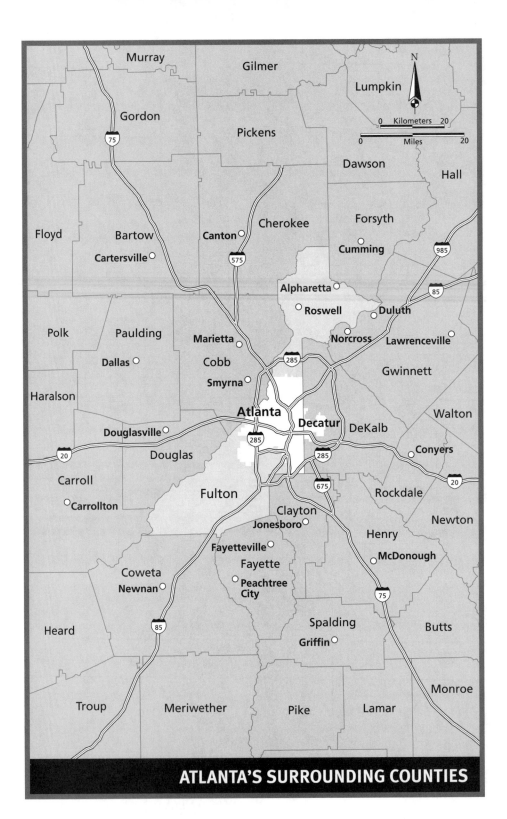

ATLANTA'S SURROUNDING COUNTIES

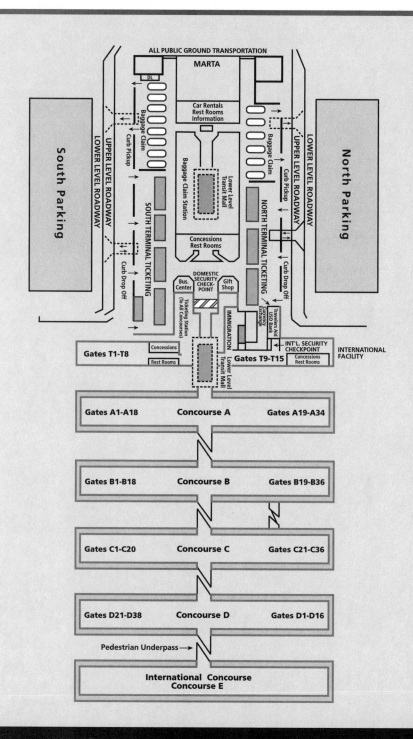

HARTSFIELD ATLANTA INTERNATIONAL AIRPORT

Preface

Welcome to Atlanta!

Over the years, new ideas and new people—people like you—have made Atlanta the social, cultural, and economic capital of the American South. From its earliest days as Terminus, Atlanta's soundtrack has been the music of motion: Unceasing change has been its one constant. Its chief product has always been a service—transportation and distribution—that, by its nature, provokes endless renewal.

From the day in 1835 when the Whitehall Tavern opened at a wagon crossroads in what is today the intersection of Lee and Gordon Streets in the West End neighborhood, Atlantans have looked toward the future, excited about the arrival of the next stagecoach, train, automobile, or jet plane. Atlanta was created from the wilderness; it grew into a major railroad center; it found itself a prime military target in the Civil War; and it was deliberately and almost utterly destroyed—all before the 17th anniversary of its incorporation as a city!

In 1865, with nearly its entire population displaced, 90 percent of its buildings in ruins, and its rail system systematically destroyed, that might have been the end of the story—but for what we call the Atlanta spirit. Somehow, though humbled and broken by the Civil War, Atlanta rose from its ashes like the mythical phoenix whose image graces the city's seal.

In the days and decades following the Civil War, ongoing upheaval and continuous infusions of new people, money, and ideas created an outlook unique among Southern cities. Here the focus is the future, not the past. Here what is old may be respected, but what is new is adored. Here is a city that seems to reinvent itself every year: Streets get new names; office complexes, residential communities, and strip malls pop up seemingly overnight.

It is here that bold innovations have flourished. An Atlanta pharmacist invented the world's most popular soft drink. An Atlanta journalist wrote the world's most popular novel. It was here, too, that an Atlanta minister would lead the South and the United States from the cruel vestiges of segregation toward the true realization of the ideals of the Declaration of Independence: "that all men are created equal."

From its earliest days, Atlanta was a crossroads, and it still is that today, sitting solidly in the center of a network of roads, rails, and air routes. But it has also become a new kind of crossroads, this time on the information superhighway. Twenty-four hours a day, every day of the year, satellites beam news, weather, sports, and entertainment programming from Atlanta to the rest of the world. Atlanta is home base for the mega services offered by media mogul Ted Turner through his company's merger with Time Warner: Cable News Network (CNN), CNN International, CNN en Español, CNNSI (*Sports Illustrated*), CNNFN (Financial News), CNN Airport Network, Headline News, Cartoon Network, Cartoon Network in Latin America, Cartoon Network in Europe, Cartoon Network in Japan, Turner Network Television (TNT), TNT in Latin America, TNT in Europe, TNT & Cartoon Network in Asia Pacific, and SuperStation TBS. The 24-hour Weather Channel beams up-to-the-minute worldwide weather forecasts from Atlanta.

Modern Atlanta is composed of many parts. There's downtown, with its soaring skyscrapers and big-city pace. Southwest Atlanta is home to Atlanta University Center, the nation's largest consortium of historically African-American colleges. Along the tree-lined streets of Midtown, Virginia-Highland, and Inman Park, renovators have breathed new life into fine old homes. In the shops and clubs of eclectic Little Five Points and high-style Buckhead, trendsetters are ever on the prowl for the new and different.

And Atlanta just keeps right on growing, with new residential areas popping up farther and farther from the city proper. Tens of thousands of Atlantans commute from homes once so remote they would have been a long day's or even several days' buggy ride away.

Atlanta's a party town, with an all-encompassing variety of nightclubs, from booming discos to intimate jazz clubs to cozy neighborhood pubs. When it's chow time, your choices include the world's largest drive-in, classic Southern restaurants, and barbecue joints, exquisite five-star dining rooms, and everything in between. And with attractions such as Six Flags Over Georgia, White Water, the Atlanta Cyclorama, Zoo Atlanta, Fernbank Science Center, SciTrek, and the World of Coca-Cola, there's plenty of excitement for younger visitors, too.

Almost everything about Atlanta has changed in the 170 years since the first drink was poured in the old Whitehall Tavern. Little Terminus went from the end of the line to the center of the South; from a smoldering, war-ravaged ruin to the premier Southern city of the United States; from complete obscurity to the host of the 1996 Olympics.

How'd we do it? Through the one constant that remained through all of our changes—the adventurous spirit of that spunky little rail crossroads. Atlanta is well known internationally as a bustling business center, with a somewhat inaccurate reputation as being "the city too busy to care about its past." There is seemingly no place to sit still or to dwell on days and things gone by. However, most native (and even some transplanted!) Atlantans are proud of the city's past, and we jealously guard our remaining old landmarks. In fact, because so much of our history was swept away during the Civil War, we try to hold onto even our recent past, as an outcry over the 1997 demolition of the Omni and Atlanta–Fulton County Stadium demonstrated. But once we've voiced our objections, usually without riots or demonstrations, we're quite pragmatic people. The old, established country and driving clubs still play host to debuts of young Southern belles, but white-gloved ladies' lunches at Rich's Magnolia Room have given way to two-income families.

That adventurous spirit—and the ability to attract people who share it—remains Atlanta's abiding strength. Whether you're a longtime resident, a new Atlantan, a first-time visitor, or a frequent guest in town, we're glad to see you. And just like our 19th-century predecessors watching the trains pull in, we're eager to hear your news and ideas, for they help us keep our city fresh and exciting and ready for the future.

Thank you for coming—and welcome to Atlanta!

Acknowledgments

While there are many kind people who helped us with this project, first and foremost we must thank our friend and editor at Insiders' Guides, Erin Turner, for offering us this project and endlessly helping us through a difficult transition period. Our colleague Tom Alexander was most helpful in a number of areas, not the least of which has been his good-natured and humorous sharing of the trials and tribulations of high school teaching, while our good friends Brian and Sherrie Johnston, Debbie Hunsinger, Bill and Debra Kinsland, Anne van Prooyen, Lesley Bowman, Ellen Balk, Rabbi Mordechai Pollock, and Howard Clark were all very helpful in making suggestions and recommendations for this book. As always, this and other projects benefited from the kind professionalism of Travis Clark of Wolf Camera, in Alpharetta. Last but decidedly not least, we thank our friends, colleagues, and students for their understanding and gracious assistance in many aspects of this project.

Atlanta Vital Statistics

Important dates in history:
Georgia founded as the 13th original British colony, 1732; fourth state to ratify the Constitution, 1788; Atlanta founded 1837 as Terminus; name changed to Atlanta, 1845; important center for civil rights activities through the 1960s; host of the XXVI Olympic Games, 1996.

Military:
Dobbins Air Reserve Base, Marietta; Fort Gillem, Forest Park; Fort McPherson, Atlanta; Naval Air Station Atlanta, Marietta.

Alcohol:
Drinking age: 21
DUI: 0.08 for persons age 21 and older; 0.02 for under 21; 0.04 for commercial drivers.
Sunday sales: local ordinance applies, but generally no sales of beer, wine, or liquor by the bottle or by the glass in bars; can be sold by the glass in restaurants.
Bars open: by local ordinance, but generally until 2:00 A.M.
Sales locations: by local ordinance, but generally, beer and wine available in supermarkets; beer in convenience stores; beer, wine, and liquor in private package stores.

Capital of Georgia: Atlanta

Major metropolitan area cities:
Jonesboro, Clayton County; Acworth, Austell, Kennesaw, Marietta, Smyrna, Vinings, Cobb County; Chamblee, Decatur, Lithonia, DeKalb County; Douglasville, Douglas County; Fayetteville, Peachtree City, Fayette County; Alpharetta, Roswell, East Point, College Park, Fulton County; Lawrenceville, Lilburn, Norcross, Snellville, Gwinnett County; McDonough, Stockbridge, Henry County.

Outlying counties:
Barrow, Bartow, Carroll, Cherokee, Coweta, Forsyth, Hall, Newton, Paulding, Pickens, Rockdale, Spalding, Walton.

Population:
City of Atlanta: 431,500
Metro area: 4.1 million
State of Georgia: 7.64 million

Metropolitan area (sq. miles): 6,150

Nickname: "The city too busy to hate"

Average temperatures:
Average July: 79 degrees
Average January: 42 degrees

Average rainfall:
14 inches, spring; 12 inches, summer; 10 inches, fall; 14 inches, winter. Average monthly precipitation, 4 inches.

Major universities:
Emory University, Georgia Institute of Technology, Georgia State University.

Major area employers:
Delta Air Lines, BellSouth, Emory University, Wal-Mart, Gwinnett County Public Schools, AT&T, Lockheed Martin Aeronautical Systems, Fulton County Schools, Kroger (grocery stores), Home Depot, IBM.

Atlanta area's famous sons and daughters:
Hank Aaron, baseball great; Joel Chandler Harris, author; Bobby Jones, golf great; Martin Luther King, civil rights leader; Margaret Mitchell, author; Julia Roberts, actress; Ted Turner, founder of CNN; Andrew Young, first black U.S. ambassador to the United Nations, first black elected to Congress since Civil War, former Atlanta mayor, 1981–1989.

State/city holidays:
January: New Year's Day, Martin Luther King Jr. birthday, Robert E. Lee birthday
February: Presidents' Day
April: Confederate Memorial Day
May: Memorial Day
July: Independence Day
September: Labor Day
November: Veterans' Day, Thanksgiving
December: Christmas

Toll roads: GA 400, 50 cents

Major airports:
Hartsfield Atlanta International Airport; DeKalb-Peachtree Airport.

Major interstates:
I–20, I–75, I–85, I–285, I–575, I–675

Public transportation:
Metropolitan Atlanta Rapid Transit Authority (MARTA); Cobb Community Transit (CCT).

Driving laws:
Car seats: required for children younger than four.
HOV lanes: operate 24 hours a day on I–75, I–85, and I–20 on Atlanta's east side inside the I–285 Perimeter.
Right turn on red: after a complete stop, unless posted otherwise.
Seatbelts: required for all passengers ages 4 to 18 as well as front-seat riders.
Speed limits: maximum, 55 mph; some interstates range from 55 to 70; residential districts, 30 unless posted otherwise.
Headlights: required in fog, rain, snow, and smoke.

Daily newspapers:
Atlanta Journal-Constitution; Gwinnett Daily Post; Marietta Daily Journal; La Vision de Georgia (bilingual).

Sales tax:
Varies by county. Ranges from 5 to 7 percent on everything except basic food items; bed tax: 7 percent.

Annual visitors to metro Atlanta:
In 2001, 17.32 million, who spent $8.93 billion in the city.

Unceasing change has made Atlanta the social, cultural, and economic capital of the South.

How to Use This Book

We've planned this book so it gives you quick and easy access to everyday, practical information. All chapters are independent and can be read in any order: If you're famished and your first priority is finding a place to eat, turn immediately to our Restaurants chapter. If you're reading this on an Atlanta-bound flight and need to know how to get out of the airport and into town, flip right to our Getting Around chapter and read the sections on Hartsfield Atlanta International Airport and MARTA.

We've organized our information to make it easy for you to explore areas that interest you and breeze by those that don't. But we hope you'll find time to look over those chapters you might initially skip. You don't have to be a history buff to be enthralled by the story of Atlanta's birth, near destruction, and rebirth, which you'll find in our History chapter. And even if you're not shopping for a home, our Relocation chapter will help you understand the locations and characteristics of city districts you'll hear people talking about every day.

This is no coffee-table book: It's designed to be used. Don't leave it in your hotel room! Keep it in your glove compartment, briefcase, or backpack; make notes in it. No matter where you travel in the Atlanta area, take this book with you to find the best food, entertainment, lodging, attractions, places, activities, and events.

While we have made every effort to ensure accuracy and to include all the best of Atlanta, we're only human. Atlanta is a city characterized by ceaseless change, and no one can keep up with every single aspect of life here. If you find mistakes in our book, if you disagree with something we've said, if you'd like to see additions or changes in future editions, or if you'd like to pat us on the back, we would appreciate your taking the time to write to us:

Insiders' Guide to Atlanta
Globe Pequot Press
P.O. Box 480
Guilford, CT 06437

How This Book Is Organized

Atlanta's city limits have not been revised since 1952, when they were expanded to take in another 92 square miles and more than 100,000 people.

More than 60 city and county governments share authority over the Atlanta metro area. In a practical sense, central Atlanta's "real" boundary is defined by I-285—what we call "the Perimeter." Within the Perimeter is the vast majority of the city itself, along with large portions of Fulton and DeKalb Counties and small slices of Cobb and Clayton Counties. In addition, "bedroom" communities and suburbs extend into counties far outside I-285. This can get confusing: One person may live in Atlanta city and DeKalb County, another in Decatur in DeKalb County, another in College Park in Fulton County (and pay taxes to both!), and another might live in a northern Forsyth County suburb, a good 45 miles out from the central part of downtown. But to avoid confusion, all four people would probably give the short answer "Atlanta" when asked where they're from because there is some panache to being from a big city.

The term "metro Atlanta" refers to Atlanta, the city, as well as a number of outlying counties in (relative) close proximity. Just what exactly constitutes the "Atlanta metro area" is in itself somewhat of a controversy; one official agency, the Atlanta Regional Commission (a state government agency charged with planning and development guidelines for the region), defines the metro area as the City of Atlanta and 10 encompassing counties: Cherokee, Clayton, Cobb, DeKalb, Douglas, Fayette, Fulton, Gwinnett, Henry, and Rockdale. Other groups, including the Metro Atlanta Chamber of Commerce and most residents here, expand the "metro" area to include up to 20 counties, encompassing an area from near metro Chattanooga, Tennessee, to the north, Macon to the south, the Alabama border to the west, and Athens to the east. The entire 20-county metro area boasts a population of over four million souls, out of a population of over eight million for the entire 159-county state of Georgia!

So, to help keep life simple, we've organized our book along the following lines: We've used "Atlanta" and "Beyond Atlanta" to geographically arrange many chapters and categories within chapters. Any restaurant, shop, theater, etc. that falls under "Atlanta" lies within the I–285 Perimeter. Anything under "Beyond Atlanta" lies outside the I–285 Perimeter, and we've often organized those attractions and businesses by county. Within the entries, we've often indicated in which neighborhood or area you'll find the eatery, nightspot, or attraction since most folks in town can at least point you in the direction of Buckhead, Morningside, or Inman Park, even if a particular address is not familiar to them.

Two small portions of the city of Atlanta are actually outside the Perimeter: the Ben Hill section in the southwest and the Adamsville section in the west. Consistent with our use of the Perimeter as Atlanta's practical boundary, we will consider these areas to be "Beyond Atlanta."

Know the New Code

For years, Atlanta has enjoyed the nation's largest toll-free calling zone. In 1995, that zone was greatly expanded to include more than 7,000 square miles. Now many outlying areas that had previously been pricey long-distance calls from Atlanta are free calls.

In the process, however, driven by the demand for new phone numbers for fax machines, cellular phones, and pagers, the Atlanta calling zone required three more area codes: 770, 678, and 470. This may seem a little confusing, but we'll try to make it simple.

The center of the Atlanta region—an area that corresponds approximately (but not exactly) to the inside of I–285—is primarily the area code 404. For the most part, the area surrounding Atlanta is the 770 area code. But all new phone numbers, be they inside or outside of the Perimeter, get the 678 or 470 area code.

It is not necessary to dial 1 before local area codes; just dial the area code and the number. But you must dial the area code—all 10 numbers—even if you're just calling across the street. Calls between the 404, 770, and 678 area codes are toll-free local calls. While some areas considered to be part of the more outlying Atlanta metro area have the 706, 912, and the new 229 and 478 area codes, these are long-distance toll calls.

And here's a bit of trivia: Because small portions of two Alabama counties (with the area codes 205 and 256) are now part of the local Atlanta calling zone, our zone can truthfully be said to contain parts of four area codes, two states, and two time zones. Happy calling!

Getting Here, Getting Around

By now you probably know that transportation—in the form of railroads, highways, and airports—built Atlanta. But it might surprise you to learn that our area was a transportation center long before the advent of modern travel.

Atlanta stands at the convergence of three giant granite ridges, and these were used by Native Americans as land bridges between the coastal, Piedmont, and mountain regions of southeastern North America. As European settlers drove out the native population, wagon roads, railroads, and finally highways followed the same routes as those old trails.

Modern Atlanta towers at the center of a vast network of roads, rails, and air routes. With so many people and packages arriving, leaving, and passing through, a certain amount of chaos is unavoidable, and most Atlantans are good-humored about it. But as the city has grown to accommodate thousands of new residents and businesses each year, getting around Atlanta has become more challenging—and a lot less convenient.

This chapter is planned to help you understand the basics of finding your way into, around, and back out of Atlanta. Read it; spend a little time studying the maps we've included; and soon you'll be buzzing around town like a native. (OK, you'll be sitting in traffic jams like a native.)

First, let's talk about Atlanta's highways and streets.

Roadways

Interstates and Highways

Atlanta is served by three interstate highways. On radio traffic reports, these are frequently identified by their location relative to downtown instead of by number.

Interstate 85 North (the Northeast Expressway) connects Atlanta with Greenville, South Carolina, and Charlotte, North Carolina, before merging with I-95 near Richmond, Virginia. South of the city, I-85 South (the Southwest Expressway) continues on to Montgomery, Alabama.

Interstate 75 North (the Northwest Expressway) extends from Atlanta to Chattanooga and Knoxville in Tennessee; Cincinnati, Ohio; Detroit, Michigan; and the Canadian border. Below Atlanta, I-75 South (the Southeast Expressway) is the route to Florida via the Georgia cities of Macon and Valdosta.

Interstate 20 West (the West Expressway) goes from Atlanta to Birmingham, Alabama; Jackson, Mississippi; Dallas, Texas; and beyond. I-20 East (the East Expressway) continues to Augusta, Georgia, and Columbia, South Carolina, connecting with I-95 in Florence, South Carolina.

There are two connecting interstate highways that are important to understand:

Interstate 285 (the Perimeter) is the 62.77-mile ring road encircling Atlanta. Very frequently, you can hear traffic reporters talking about the "inner" and "outer" loops. This can be somewhat confusing in terms of specific directions of traffic flow, but the "inner" loop is simply the lanes of I-285 that are closer to the city's center. For example, the "inner" loop is almost always jammed up near "Spaghetti Junction"—this simply means the south/east lanes of I-285 near the intersection with I-85 on the northeast side

3

of town (a very good place to avoid during rush hours!).

I-75 and I-85 merge just north of Georgia Tech and become the same road, curving around the downtown business district. This section is called the Downtown Connector and is marked on maps as 75/85. The interchange connecting the combined 75/85 with I-20 is near Turner Field, the former Olympic Stadium and home of the Atlanta Braves. Interstates 75 and 85 go their separate ways just north of Hartsfield Atlanta International Airport; I-85 goes to the airport and on to Montgomery, and I-75 continues south to Macon and Florida.

Another bit of shorthand you're likely to hear on radio reports is Spaghetti Junction, as we mentioned above. This is not a favorite spot for pasta, but rather the looping, futuristic interchange that connects the Northeast Expressway with I-285 and several nearby side streets. As we said, this intersection is subject to near paralysis on a daily basis during both rush hours, even without the added delay caused by frequent accidents on the high, looping ramps. During the infrequent ice and snow days, avoid the exit ramps of this intersection at all costs, as they are some of the first in the entire metro area to develop sometimes lethal and always impassible icing of the roadway.

Interstate 675 is a short stretch that connects the southeast side of I-285 with I-75 about 10 miles south of town. It's hard to find—some maps cover it up with ads or a street index—but it's a real timesaver. If you're heading south from the east side of town, take Moreland Avenue south until it crosses I-285; I-675 is on your left. It's handy for hooking up with

I-75 South during rush hour, since it lets you steer clear of the Downtown Connector and the congested section of I-285 between the interchanges for I-75 and I-85.

On the northwest side of town, Interstate 575 branches off from I-75 above Marietta, cuts through rapidly growing Cherokee County, and heads into the north Georgia mountains. A heavily traveled commuter route, I-575 is regularly snarled during rush hours as it feeds into and exits from I-75. The section of I-75 from its intersection with I-575 to the intersection with I-285 is notorious for featuring multiple accidents and very uncomfortable driving conditions.

North of the city, Georgia Highway 400 travels by the west side of Lake Lanier, and ends just outside the northeast mountain town of Dahlonega some 60 miles away. Southbound GA 400 connects to the Northeast Expressway near the Lindbergh MARTA station. GA 400's extension inside I-285 to I-85 is a toll road (50 cents). The toll plaza is just north of the Buckhead/Lenox Road exit.

On the toll portion of GA 400, have your 50 cents ready. As you drive north, some booths have attendants to make change, others take exact change only, and the two left lanes are for "cruise card" holders only. (A cruise card is an electronic device attached to your sun visor; it automatically debits your account each time you pass through the toll plaza. A camera photographs the license plate of anyone who zips through the cruise lanes without a card; freeway freeloaders will shortly receive a ticket and a fine by mail.) It varies from day to day (sometimes hour to hour) which booths are manned and which are not, but one useful tip is that the manned booths usually have shorter lines, and you are free to just smile at the attendant, throw your exact change in the basket, and drive on.

The Freedom Parkway is a 3.1-mile limited access road in the downtown area that can keep drivers moving from the Downtown Connector at International Boulevard to Ponce De Leon Avenue (just east of Midtown) and Moreland Avenue (just south of North Avenue), after dividing at the Carter Presidential Center. Before its completion in 1994, the road was the center of a legal battle between the Georgia Department of Transportation and area residents, who did not like the initially proposed larger highway's potential impact on their neighborhoods. In the end, the neighbors won significant changes in the parkway, which now has jogging trails, bike paths, and a 35-mph speed limit.

HOV Lanes

For several decades Atlanta has been redesigning and widening its freeways, causing residents to wonder whether the work will ever be finished. Some longtime Atlantans admit they've forgotten what it was like not to have orange barrels blocking off lanes for road construction.

The most recent highway projects have centered around the addition of express car pool lanes, also known as HOV (High Occupancy Vehicles) lanes. The completed first phase resurfaced and restriped 330 lane miles of existing roadway and added 60 new express-lane miles to the interstates inside the Perimeter. Still, work continues on some areas beyond that boundary as the need for traffic relief continues to grow.

Why add HOV lanes? As Atlanta's population and traffic woes continue to grow, the Environmental Protection Agency rates Atlanta as a "serious" non-attainment area for ozone smog pollution. Car pool lanes encourage folks to ride together and help reduce the city's output of auto exhausts. And during rush hour, they're frequently less congested and move more smoothly than other bumper-to-bumper lanes. (Also, the DOT committed to build the lanes as part of a deal that secured federal funds to improve Atlanta's freeways in the 1970s and '80s. So it had to be done.)

In addition to the HOV project, it seems there's always some section of roadway under construction. The speed limit in the vicinity of all DOT work sites is 45 mph, and Georgia Highway Patrol officers come out in abundance to enforce it. Speeding in construction sites has caused numerous deadly accidents; slow down and take it easy.

Express lanes extend along I–75, I–85, the Downtown Connector (75/85), and I–20 east of the city. An express lane will not be added to the less congested stretch of I–20 west of the city. Express lanes are marked with a diamond symbol and a sign reading LEFT LANE—BUSES AND CAR POOLS ONLY. Only buses, vehicles with two or more persons, and motorcycles may use the express lanes during their hours of operation. The express lanes on I–75, I–85, and the Downtown Connector operate at all times, 24 hours a day, seven days a week. On I–20 east of the city, the inbound express lane operates during morning rush hour, from 6:30 to 9:30 A.M.; the outbound express lane operates from 4:00 to 7:00 P.M.

For information on the latest lane and ramp openings and closings, the locations of construction crews each day, and road conditions, call the DOT at (404) 656–5267.

Interstate Tips

Now that we've given you the rundown of the various interstates and their aliases, here are a few tips to bear in mind as you're merging into traffic.

Every day, Atlanta's interstates are the scenes of horrible multicar collisions caused by people driving too fast. The Georgia Highway Patrol and local law enforcement agencies prowl the freeways constantly, trolling for drivers zipping along over the speed limit and cheerfully shattering the commonly held false perception that you won't get a ticket unless you're more than 10 mph over the limit. Be aware also that troopers patrol more heavily on big travel holidays and when large numbers of people are expected to drive into the city from out of state. This said, however, the problems of "road rage" and generally lethal driving habits are most definitely on the increase, with few plans or measures being instituted to deal with the problems. A series of high-profile, multifatality accidents caused by unsafe driving early in 2001 and during the summer of 2002 have put more pressure on the state legislature and police agencies to do something to reduce the daily body count, but until stricter traffic control measures can be developed, it is important to pay attention to your own driving, know the route you are planning to take, and listen to traffic reports on any of the metro radio and TV stations to stay abreast of the road conditions.

In theory and according to the Georgia Driver's Manual, slower traffic is supposed to keep right, and always stay within the posted limits. In reality, the slowest traffic on the metro interstates is usually in the lane second from the left, and the general flow of traffic is habitually anywhere from 10 to 20 miles per hour over the posted limit. Frequent accidents, especially during rush hour, can lead to the need to abruptly slow down or stop, and can make a 20-minute commute (say from Holcomb Bridge Road to I-285 on GA 400) take well over an hour to complete.

One new driving habit that has caught on like wildfire in the metro area is the use of cellular telephones while driving in heavy traffic. This dangerous habit has led to many accidents and near-misses, and has resulted in bills presented in the state legislature to ban the practice. (The latest such bill stands a good chance of passing in the 2003 legislative session.)

Driving north on the Downtown Connector, I-75 and I-85 split just after you pass Downtown. You must take one or the other. The division comes up only 1.25 miles after the first sign announcing it, so you have to be prepared to act fast. This seemingly straightforward stretch of interstate has confused many a driver, and it's easy to see why. The three lanes for I-85 (the Northeast Expressway) are on the left; the three lanes for I-75 (the Northwest Expressway) are on the right—exactly backwards from what you'd instinctively expect. (However, in the same vicinity, the I-75 northbound HOV lane shares the same space as the I-85 northbound HOV on the far left. It snakes below I-85 and rejoins the flow of I-75 traffic farther along.) Begin to move into the appropriate lanes as soon as you safely can after seeing the first signs for the upcoming split, or you may get caught on the wrong side. And, even if you've paid attention and found your lane early, be alert for other drivers frantically switching sides at the last minute.

As you approach Atlanta by interstate, be particularly cautious around I-285, as its interchanges with the expressways are frequently the sites of accidents. All 18-wheel vehicles traveling the interstates are required by law to take the Perimeter, unless their destination is inside Atlanta. Many a trucker has jackknifed on I-285's ramps after failing to slow down. And even seasoned Atlanta drivers find themselves braking or changing lanes at the last minute because they're baffled by the signage, which is particularly confusing on the west side of town. There, as they try to enter I-285 from I-75 on the north side, the roads crisscross, with left lanes heading west and right lanes heading east.

Traffic on the north side of I-285 has gone way beyond the road's capacity. Morning and afternoon rush hours on this highway are when Atlanta most resembles Los Angeles—or worse. East of I-75 across the top of the Perimeter, past I-85, through Spaghetti Junction, and sometimes all the way over to I-20 East, the northside Perimeter at rush hour can be totally maddening. It often seems there are only two speeds on this highway: 65 mph and stopped. If you must travel to or from the north/northeast Perimeter area on a daily basis, it's worth your while to investigate alternate routes or travel times.

The GA 400 extension has won raves from those commuting from Roswell, Alpharetta, and Lake Lanier. It's also very popular with Atlantans, who can travel the fast lanes to new shopping malls and sites on the northside. The reason has to do with the location of the toll plaza: It's just north of the exit for Lenox Road/Buckhead. This is a real break for in-towners: It means you can ride for free from the beginning of GA 400 directly up to mega-malls Lenox Square and Phipps Plaza. From downtown, take I-85 North to the GA 400-Cumming-Buckhead toll road exit 29; get off at exit 2 LENOX ROAD-BUCKHEAD, LAST EXIT BEFORE TOLL. Turn right at the TO PEACHTREE ROAD sign: Phipps Plaza will be on your left; the Ritz-Carlton Buckhead will be on your right; Lenox Square is just across Peachtree.

Within the past few years, rapid population growth on the northside has made GA 400 just another jammed-up frustration during both the morning and evening rush hours. It is very much worth your time to investigate possible side-street alternatives (at least they are moving, most of the time!), or better yet, take advantage of the MARTA stations adjacent to GA 400 north of the Perimeter (for more information see the section on MARTA later in this chapter).

The HOV lanes heading into Downtown on I–75 South have made life a little easier for car pool drivers. Instead of fighting the congestion as I–75 and I–85 merge into the Downtown Connector, these cars can follow the HOV lane on the far left as it glides under the traffic and resurfaces past the jam on the Connector.

Surface Streets

Something like 55 streets in Atlanta have the word "Peachtree" in their names. How did this mania begin?

The first Peachtree was a Creek Indian village on the Chattahoochee River called Standing Peachtree (it was near the present-day Atlanta Water Works facility on Hemphill Avenue). An army outpost built nearby took the name Fort Peachtree. The road that linked it to Fort Daniel in Gwinnett County was the first Peachtree Road. (The Old Peachtree Road exit on the Northeast Expressway has confused many a traveler heading into Atlanta, since it's more than 30 minutes outside town.)

From this has come a forest of Peachtrees. But even if you could keep this jumble straight, there are more hazards ahead.

It's not uncommon for the same street to have two, three, or even more names in different locations. You're driving on Juniper Street and suddenly it's Courtland; you head east on Decatur Street, and it turns into DeKalb Avenue. The same holds true even in the suburbs: In Marietta, Whitlock Avenue west of town turns into Dallas Highway. In Gwinnett County, Peachtree Parkway becomes Medlock Bridge Road just before it crosses the Chattahoochee River.

In town, the name changes reflect the way the city developed, block by block. In other places, the practice dates from the days of racial segregation, when it was meant to convey an unsubtle message of divided territory. This was the case at Ponce de Leon Avenue, once a racial dividing line. South of Ponce, Monroe becomes Boulevard and Briarcliff becomes Moreland.

In many suburban counties, the streets frequently change names depending on the direction you're headed: For instance, in Cobb County, the road west from Marietta to Powder Springs is Powder Springs Road. The same street in Powder Springs is called Marietta Street. Sometimes it's handy to think about where you want to go, and take the appropriately named road!

A favorite Atlanta City Hall activity is renaming streets, or sections of streets, to honor civic leaders or to recognize social

Insiders' Tip

Say what? The "L" in DeKalb (a county, an airport, an avenue, and then some) is silent: Say "de-CAB." And one of the main streets from Atlanta into DeKalb has a distinctly Southern accent. The noted Spanish explorer may have been Ponce de Le-ON, but the Atlanta street is Ponce de LE-on. If you just can't bring yourself to say it that way, do what the natives do and call it just "Ponce" or "Poncy." Natives frequently slur the name of this fair city, making it sound more like "Lanna" or "AT-lanna."

changes. Although a noble gesture in itself, this too causes confusion. Take Irwin, which at Peachtree becomes John Wesley Dobbs Avenue. Before it was renamed in 1994 for the distinguished businessman and activist, the final stretch was called Houston (pronounced "house-ton" in Atlanta-speak). Such changes typically take years to show up on most maps, however.

Furthermore, terms such as "street," "avenue," and "boulevard" are often used without apparent rhyme or reason. Peachtree Street runs north and south, but 10th Street runs east and west. North Avenue runs east and west (it used to mark the "north" boundary of the city), but Piedmont Avenue runs north and south. Ralph McGill Boulevard runs east and west, but Boulevard (south Monroe Drive) runs north and south. (Before it was renamed as a tribute to the progressive newspaper editor, Ralph McGill Boulevard was called Forrest Avenue, honoring Confederate cavalryman Lieutenant General Nathan Bedford Forrest.)

While driving around Atlanta, you'll find you have more options when traveling north and south than when traveling east and west. In the afternoon rush hour, you may move south along Peachtree at a brisk clip, then turn left onto Ponce de Leon to find traffic crawling east toward Decatur. Commuters trying to avoid crosstown traffic often work out curious diagonal routes through neighborhoods, keeping off the clogged main streets. This may not save time, but some folks prefer it to sitting still. But beware: To cut down on the number of commuters buzzing along the residential streets, many in-town neighborhoods have succeeded at restricting the times drivers may turn into their area. In some cases, they've made streets one-way to keep commuters out. Particularly in the Buckhead area, pay close attention to signs posted at neighborhood entrances that spell out the restrictions. Remember those ridges; that's why Atlanta's streets are not laid out in a grid pattern.

There's no overnight way to learn your way around Atlanta's streets, but here are a few suggestions that should help:

Concentrate on learning the main roads first. About Peachtree's various forms: It is first street, then road, and eventually boulevard. It is Peachtree Street from downtown to a point just north of the Midtown district, where it becomes Peachtree Road. Decades ago, this is where the paved city road ended and a country dirt road began.

Atlanta is a hilly town, and Peachtree Street runs along its highest ridge. Peachtree begins downtown (its short, southernmost stretch is called Whitehall, after Atlanta's first store and bar), then passes through the hotel district and Midtown, before becoming Peachtree Road and heading into Peachtree Battle and Buckhead. In Buckhead the street forks: To the right, Peachtree Road continues on past Lenox Square, Phipps Plaza, Oglethorpe University, and on to I-285, which it crosses as Peachtree Industrial Boulevard. The left fork in Buckhead becomes Roswell Road and travels north to Sandy Springs, Roswell, and Alpharetta. Peachtree is Atlanta's main street and, though often crowded, is always a dependable north/south route.

Piedmont Avenue can be a good alternative to Peachtree for traveling between Downtown, Midtown, and Buckhead.

Ponce de Leon Avenue is an easy route to Decatur and to Stone Mountain. Eastbound, Ponce forks just after the stone railroad overpass: To the left, Scott Boulevard continues out to the Lawrenceville Highway; to the right, East Ponce de Leon goes to downtown Decatur (where the speed limit is strictly enforced) and Stone Mountain.

Martin Luther King Jr. Drive is the direct route between Downtown and the Atlanta University Center area. Within the AU district, James P. Brawley Drive runs north and south between M. L. King Jr. Drive and Spelman College, near I-20.

U.S. Highway 41 (also known at different locations as Northside Drive, Northside Parkway, and Cobb Parkway) is a noninterstate route out to the Cumberland Mall/Galleria area and on to Dobbins Air Force Base and Marietta in Cobb County.

Five Points is the center of downtown Atlanta. It's formed by the intersection of Peachtree, Decatur/Marietta Streets, and Edgewood Avenue.

Little Five Points is 2.5 miles east of downtown at the convergence of Moreland, McLendon, and Euclid Avenues. It's one of Atlanta's most eclectic shopping areas and a multicultural mecca, a scaled-down version of New York's East Village.

Downtown is the area around Five Points. Midtown is the area around Piedmont Park; it's the first neighborhood bordering Peachtree north of Downtown. Uptown is Buckhead, filled with lots of upscale clubs, restaurants, and boutiques that draw shoppers by day and barhoppers by night. The heart of Buckhead is about 6 miles up Peachtree Street from Five Points.

Here are a few general pointers for getting your bearings on Atlanta's streets:

Start by studying the maps we've included in this book. Spend a little time getting to know the major streets and highways. Once you understand a few of the main north/south and crosstown routes, you'll feel more confident and find your knowledge of Atlanta's roads increasing rapidly. Then graduate to a good, larger street map. They're inexpensive, widely available, and always come in handy.

When possible, take MARTA. Riding MARTA's buses and trains (whose tracks are usually aboveground) is a great way to get your bearings and study the lay of the city without having to fight traffic.

When you're riding with friends (or a knowledgeable cabby), ask the driver what route he or she is taking. You'll find you're on the same streets again and again, though you may not always recognize them at first.

Ask veteran Atlantans for their favorite shortcuts. Most newcomers understandably stick to the busy main roads. Friends or coworkers may be able to give you tips about routes that bypass the worst jams.

For goodness sake, don't be shy about asking directions. You'll frequently hear longtime Atlantans having involved conversations about main routes and alternates, street openings, and closings. Many a conversation begins with "What's the best way to get from ____ to ____ now?" There's definitely no stigma attached to asking for directions; it may even make you seem more like a native.

When you're going somewhere new, always call ahead for directions. Simply locating the street on a map may not be good enough. Sometimes two streets share the same name and even the same directional indicator (such as NE), but they're miles apart in completely different parts of town. Many times, addresses apply to an entire shopping center, not just the particular establishment you're trying to locate, so it helps to know if your destination is part of a complex. Also, even the newest maps seldom reflect all the intricacies of Atlanta's often-changed street names. To add to the fun, street address numbering systems do not always follow a logical sequence, or even a simple numerical order!

In Atlanta, it's always hard to say today what route will be best tomorrow. This city's rebuilding began in 1865 and shows no sign of letting up, so road construction and utility work are always a part of life. No wonder some residents have lobbied to have those orange-and-white-striped construction barrels named the city's official symbol!

Rules of the Road

Because traffic laws differ from state to state, take a moment to look over the following rules. You may obtain a free copy of Georgia Driver, the official state handbook, at any driver's license renewal location. Call (404) 657–9300 or check out www.ganet.org/dps for more information.

The driver and all front-seat passengers of every car must wear a seat belt. Persons between 4 and 18 must wear a seat belt in the car at all times.

Children younger than four must ride in an approved child safety seat. (This law has exceptions: A seat belt is sufficient for kids between three and four, and the law does not apply to nonresidents of Georgia.)

After coming to a complete stop at an intersection, you may make a right turn on red, traffic permitting. Some intersections, however, are posted as no turn on red.

A left turn on red is permissible only when turning from the left lane of a one-way street on to another one-way street on which traffic is moving to the driver's left.

Your headlights must be on (day or night) when you are driving through rain, fog, snow, or smoke.

You must stop when approaching (from either direction) a school bus with its stop sign out and its lights flashing. On a highway divided by a median, you are required to stop when you are behind a stopped bus but not when you're coming from the opposite direction.

The maximum speed limit in Georgia typically is 55 mph. On rural interstates, where posted, the speed limit is 65 or 70 mph. In all business and residential districts, the speed limit is 30 mph unless otherwise posted.

If you can steer it, clear it. Drivers involved in a minor accident are required to remove the accident vehicles from the roadway immediately; then you can call for assistance. Most of the interstates have accident investigation sites for that purpose.

Drivers are considered drunk in Georgia when they register 0.08gm percent or more. Penalties are severe; don't drive drunk in Georgia. Drivers younger than the legal drinking age (21) are considered drunk if tests show they have consumed any amount of alcohol (the law actually states 0.02gm percent or more, but that is the sensitivity limit of most detection devices in use).

Motorcycle drivers and passengers must wear a helmet.

Bicycle riders younger than 16 must wear a bicycle helmet.

If you are moving to the state, you are required to get a Georgia license and to register your car in your county within 30 days.

It's Customary

From the moment you notice the interstate traffic speeding up (although the speed limit decreases) as you motor into Atlanta, you may find driving here intimidating. Rush hour never seems to end on some of our main roads. A significant clue

to the state of traffic these days is that the metro television stations have added traffic reports on weekends as well within the past few years.

But for most people, driving around Atlanta gets easier fast. The best drivers seem to develop an alert yet laid-back attitude. The alert part is essential, since traffic here is often quick and close and the streets are curvy and hilly. But the laid-back part, though harder to develop, is essential too. (It explains why some people never get speeding tickets and others get them over and over.) The worst thing is to take the traffic personally. And in the worst-case scenarios, road rage can be fatal.

Given that many of our thoroughfares are carrying far more cars than they were built to handle, Atlanta traffic would be an ongoing disaster were it not for our secret weapon: Most Atlanta drivers are actually quite courteous.

We're not suggesting for a moment that there are no hothead speed demons on the streets of Atlanta. There are some, but fortunately they're the exception, outnumbered by drivers who realize that a little neighborliness and cooperation can help get everybody home on time.

Here are a couple of other pointers along these lines:

Blowing your horn when you're stuck in traffic is not a custom here—and it won't help you make friends either. Here we consider excessive horn blowing—as well as flashing your high beams into the cars of slower drivers or riding on their rear bumper—downright rude.

Use your turn signals. Most drivers will be happy to let you maneuver through traffic if you give them a clue as to what you're trying to do.

Don't tailgate. Rear-ending someone is a terrible way to meet.

Don't run red lights, and don't speed. Going almost anywhere in Atlanta involves traveling through residential areas filled with kids, dogs, bicyclists, and people backing out of driveways. Zooming around neighborhoods at 55 mph can lead to a ticket or a tragedy.

MARTA buses make their way through many streets that are not really wide enough for them; this is especially a problem at sharp turns. When a bus is trying to turn a corner and its way is blocked by cars waiting at the light, all the cars must back up to make way for the bus. This is less likely to happen if you observe the stop-line at intersections.

Having cautioned you against excessive horn blowing, we should note that judicious use of your horn can definitely help prevent accidents. Keep one hand close to your horn, especially when you're driving in tight, fast-moving traffic. If your reaction time is quick, you can "beep" weaving drivers back into their lane before they bump into you.

Cruising

We freely admit Atlanta's worst shortcoming: no beaches. Deprived of an oceanside main drag, lots of young people take to cruising Peachtree between downtown and Midtown on warm weekend nights. The resulting traffic tie-ups can be annoying but are concentrated on and around Peachtree. The situation has improved greatly since no-cruising signs have been well posted and enforced. But if you find yourself in a jam, just get off Peachtree and pick up one of the other north/south streets, such as Piedmont, Courtland, West Peachtree, Spring, or Techwood.

MARTA

Atlanta's mass transit system is called MARTA (Metropolitan Atlanta Rapid Transit Authority). MARTA is one of the most advanced rapid transit systems in the United States.

Though approved by referendum in 1965, MARTA lacked money until 1971, when voters agreed to fund the system with a sales tax. To win approval of the tax, an arrangement was made to cut bus fares from 40 cents to 15 cents and to hold them there for seven years. The tax passed; the promise was kept; MARTA was on its way.

Today MARTA serves the 800-square-mile district at the heart of the metro area. The first MARTA rail stations opened in

June 1979. When the Airport station opened in 1988, Atlanta became one of the few U.S. cities to offer direct rail service from the airport to downtown. Another big year for MARTA was 1996, when the north line extension opened, along with the Buckhead, Medical Center, and Dunwoody rail stations. The latest stations to open were the Sandy Springs and North Springs stations on the north line, both opening on December 16, 2000. The opening of these stations, which help relieve traffic congestion on the booming northside, was an item of significance for quite another reason; for the first time since rail planning began, there are no stations either under construction or being planned to be built within the immediate future. A new study about adding rail service to the I-20 corridor is under way, but any construction start is years away.

The Buckhead station is 7.4 miles north of Five Points on a 1.35-acre site. It's on the median of GA 400 at Capital City Plaza on Peachtree Street in Buckhead. The subway station is near the Atlanta Financial Center complex; an underground tunnel lets patrons enter from either side of Peachtree. Built at a cost of $12 million, Buckhead station has a passenger drop-off area but no parking facility.

Just 12 miles north of Five Points, Medical Center station sits on a 9.6-acre site. A pedestrian walkway over Peachtree Dunwoody Road provides access to Northside Hospital. Other major facilities served by this station include St. Joseph's Hospital and Children's Healthcare of Atlanta Scottish Rite Hospital. It has no parking facility but provides for handicapped parking, bicycles, and taxis. Medical Center station, built at a cost of almost $23 million, is a 21-minute train ride from Five Points; getting to the airport from here will take about 36 minutes.

Dunwoody station at the corner of Hammond Drive and Perimeter Center Parkway serves workers and shoppers in the Perimeter Center area. Dunwoody station is an aboveground facility, 13.1 miles north of Five Points. The $21.6 million station includes a four-level, 572-car parking deck, as well as additional spaces that opened in late 1997.

Planning a night on the town? Remember, MARTA runs only until 1:00 A.M. PHOTO: MARTA

Two more north line stations, at Sandy Springs and North Springs, are facilities serving the northern suburbs; and North Springs has more than 2,000 spaces in a low cost ($3 per day) parking garage built specifically to hold long-term parking for those northsiders headed to Hartsfield Airport.

MARTA operates 248 electric rail cars on 48 miles of track with regular service to 38 rapid rail stations. In addition, 702 buses traverse 154 routes covering 1,500 miles. On an average weekday, the system records 550,000 passenger boardings.

Weekdays, trains run every four to eight minutes between 5:00 A.M. and 7:00 P.M.; from 7:00 P.M. until 1:00 A.M., they run every 10 minutes. On Saturday, trains run every 10 minutes between 5:00 A.M. and 7:00 P.M.; from 7:00 P.M. until 1:00 A.M., they run every 15 minutes. On Sunday and holidays, trains run every 15 minutes from 5:00 to 12:30 A.M. Extra trains are typically called into service during big downtown events.

Bus schedules vary, but there's a printed timetable for every route. You can get free schedules at Five Points station and at MARTA information kiosks. Each bus usually has a supply of its own schedule; ask your driver.

A single MARTA fare (required for each passenger older than three) is currently $1.75, including two free transfers. (This means you can take a bus to the train, change at Five Points to a train on the other line, ride to another station, and then take a bus from the station to your destination—all for a single fare. You can't, however, use a transfer as your return fare in a round trip.)

All buses and train stations accept the MARTA TransCard. For a flat fee ($13 for the Monday-through-Sunday weekly card, $52.50 for the monthly card, and $9 for a monthly weekends-only card) patrons get unlimited use of the entire system. TransCard users do not need transfers. Token packs (10 for $17.50 or the 20-pack for $30) and TransCards are sold at RideStore locations (at Five Points, Airport, and Lenox stations, at MARTA headquarters, beside Lindbergh station, and in many grocery and convenience stores throughout the service area).

The weekly TransCard is good for a calendar week (not for unlimited travel on any seven days); the monthly card is good for a calendar month. Weekly and monthly cards are both available before the date they take effect, so you can buy your next week's card before you start your weekend.

MARTA route and schedule information is available by phone from 6:00 A.M. to 10:00 P.M. Monday through Friday and from 8:00 A.M. to 4:00 P.M. Saturday; call (404) 848–4711. Tell the operator your location and destination; she or he will tell you which bus to take, where to catch it, whether you need to transfer, and when the bus runs.

MARTA also posts information about its service on its Web site, www.itsmarta.com.

(Please note: Every effort has been made to ensure accuracy, but MARTA's services, schedules, and fares are subject to change. The fares posted above reflect those in effect in the summer of 2003.)

Riding the Train

MARTA's rapid rail system is easy and fun to use.

Each MARTA station is different, with its own architectural style and works of art. Most spectacular is Peachtree Center station, which was blasted out of the solid-granite ridge under Peachtree Street. Getting here is half the fun! Access is by incredibly steep, 192-foot escalators. (Of course, you may take the elevator if you prefer.) Exposed rock forms a natural cave around the platforms, where you'll wait for your train some 12 stories below Peachtree Street!

MARTA's rail lines intersect at the huge Five Points station, where you can transfer between east/west and north/south lines. You can also pick up the north line to Dunwoody at the Lindbergh station. You don't need a transfer to go from one line to the other, as they're both inside the station. Five Points station has its own entrance to Underground Atlanta via a tunnel under Peachtree Street; it's on your right just before you exit the station on the Peachtree side.

Rail station turnstiles accept exact change in coin (but not pennies, half-dollars, or dollar bills) and MARTA to-kens, which are sold in vending machines at all stations. Token machines take $1, $5, $10, and $20 bills; and, although generally reliable, these machines can sometimes be excessively picky about wrinkled money. If this happens, try another machine. If no machine will cooperate (or if one eats your money), don't panic. Pick up the nearby white courtesy phone and tell your troubles to the MARTA employee who answers. She or he will give you permission to enter through the "Handicapped" gate (just ignore that loud alarm).

Take the appropriate escalator to the train boarding area. In stations where the platform is between the tracks, the escalator is marked TO ALL TRAINS. Other stations have two platforms with the tracks in between. In these, you must use the escalator marked with the direction in which you're traveling.

Signs on the front and side of each train indicate its final stop. The opening of the north line created some confusion, since every northbound train could no longer be counted on to go to Lenox Square. Here's how to tell where a train is headed:

An "Airport" train is southbound and will take you all the way to Hartsfield at the end of the south line. An "Indian Creek" train is eastbound and will take you through Decatur out to the end of the east line. The westbound "Hamilton East Holmes" trains go to the end of the west line, while "Bankhead" trains (also westbound) branch off on the northwest Proctor Creek line. A "Doraville" train goes on to the end of the northeast line (this is also

Insiders' Tip

The low-fare, long-term parking lots in some MARTA stations are excellent alternatives to parking at the airport.

MARTA train passes Grady Memorial Hospital on the south side of downtown Atlanta. PHOTO: MARTA

the train to Lenox station). "Dunwoody" trains service Buckhead, Medical Center, and Dunwoody (near Perimeter Mall) stations on the north line. "Doraville" and "Dunwoody" trains alternate in their service along the central portion of the north line. The northernmost station at which to transfer between these two trains is Lindbergh Center.

In the MARTA station, wait well behind the white strip at the edge of the platform until the arriving train has come to a complete stop. When the doors open, allow departing passengers the opportunity to exit the train before you board. MARTA's electric trains are speedy: As soon as you board, sit down or grab the nearest handrail to avoid losing your balance as the train whisks away.

When the train begins slowing down for your stop, gather up your belongings and your group and prepare to disembark. Atlanta is not Tokyo, but the trains are fast-paced. If you're in the middle of a crowded rail car and take your time get-

ting to the exit, the doors may close before you have a chance to get off.

Signs inside all MARTA stations indicate bus stops, surrounding streets, and major buildings. If you need directions, all you have to do is pick up a white courtesy phone and ask the operator for assistance.

Riding the Bus

To board a MARTA bus, wait at a bus stop (indicated by either a white concrete obelisk or a tricolor pole-mounted MARTA sign). The front of each bus is marked with the route number and route name. Different bus routes use the same bus stops—make sure to board the right bus. (Express bus routes include stretches along which passengers are neither picked up nor discharged. Before boarding a bus marked "express," ask the driver whether you'll be able to disembark at your desired stop.) When you see your bus approaching, raise your hand to signal to the driver that you wish to board.

Enter through the front door. Drop your fare into the fare box, hand your transfer to the driver, or pass your Trans-Card through the card reader. Fare boxes accept cash (including dollar bills and any combination of coins) and MARTA tokens, but drivers do not make change. If you'd like a transfer, you must request it when you pay your fare. Using the local shorthand, just say "train" if you'd like a rail transfer or "bus" if you're changing buses. Some bus routes terminate inside stations, where you won't need a transfer to board the train. Your driver will let you know if this is the case.

If you're unsure about directions, tell the driver your destination as you board; sit up front and you'll be let off at the closest stop. Pressing the yellow stop request strip or pulling the cord will signal the driver that you want off at the next scheduled stop. Use the rear door when exiting.

Special Events

Shuttle service from the Five Points station to Turner Field, home of the Braves, begins 90 minutes before games begin and runs continuously until an hour after the game. You'll need a transfer to board the shuttle, so remember to get one when you pay your fare as you enter the MARTA system.

When the weather is nice, lots of Braves fans take the train to the Georgia State station and walk to the stadium, less than three-quarters of a mile away. The extra effort really pays off after the game, when you'll be back in your car and on your way home long before traffic clears out around the stadium.

During the summer concert season, shuttle service from the Lakewood/Ft. McPherson station to the Lakewood Amphitheater begins 90 minutes before showtime and continues after the show until the venue is empty.

Special Services

For MARTA schedule information, call (404) 848-4711. To make a suggestion or report a problem, or for any other infor-

mation, call MARTA's customer service center at (404) 848-4800.

All MARTA buses and trains have seats designated as "reserved" for any elderly or those in wheelchairs. Disabled persons and those 65 and older are eligible for a special reduced 75-cent fare. The required half-fare card may be obtained free of charge at any RideStore. All MARTA stations have at least one entrance that is fully accessible to the elderly and those with disabilities.

Almost all of MARTA's buses are wheelchair accessible and have lifts. However, MARTA also operates L-VANS, which provide door-to-door service. A single fare on these buses is $3.50. For more information, call (404) 848-5389. Patrons in wheelchairs who make use of buses along MARTA's regular routes are not charged extra.

Deaf persons may use MARTA's TTY schedule information line, by calling (404) 848-5665.

Parking

MARTA has thousands of parking spaces for use by system passengers, including more than 25,000 spaces at rail stations and 3,000 spaces at park and ride lots. Parking is free at all times in all MARTA lots except the following.

For airport patrons, the Brookhaven, Lindbergh, Doraville, Lenox, College Park, North Springs, and Medical Center stations offer fenced parking lots with 24-hour security. Parking is $3.00 per day, payable upon exiting the lot.

MARTA to the Airport

Hartsfield Atlanta International Airport is the last stop on the south rail line; board the train marked "Airport." North/south train cars have a designated space where you may stow your luggage; of course, you should keep an eye on it at all times. The ride from Five Points station to the airport is about 15 minutes. As you exit Airport station, follow the signs to your airline's ticketing area. South terminal is to your right; north terminal is to your left. There is no extra charge for the trip to the airport; the fare is the same as any other line, $1.75. Taking MARTA back to the city after your trip is a breeze: The station is adjacent to baggage claim.

Security

MARTA maintains its own 290-member police force. Armed uniformed and plainclothes officers heavily patrol the system. Surveillance cameras are also used to deter vandals, gate-jumpers, and other criminals.

All stations include white-colored passenger-assistance telephones, which connect riders with helpful MARTA operators, and blue police emergency telephones, which connect callers to the MARTA police. Both are located near the fare gates and on the platforms. Every rail car has an intercom that connects passengers with the train conductor.

One word of caution: In spite of the vigilance of the MARTA police, crime does occur in the system. Especially when traveling alone or at night, keep your guard up. Access to many stations is by long stairways and pedestrian overpasses, which can be scary. If you feel you're being followed, avoid walking alone into these areas. If you're frightened, stay in the main part of the station, in plain view of the security cameras, and use the blue telephone to request assistance from the MARTA police. Avoid strangers in the parking lot; have your keys ready, and walk briskly to your car.

Rules

Be sure to observe the following rules:

On all buses and in all trains and rail stations, it is illegal to smoke, eat, drink, litter, or play radios or stereos without earphones.

Moving between train cars, unless directed to do so by MARTA personnel in an emergency, is forbidden.

MARTA's high-voltage tracks are extremely dangerous. Passengers must never climb onto the tracks or attempt to cross them.

Cobb Community Transit

Atlanta's northwest neighbor Cobb County operates its own bus system on local and express routes around Cobb and to Atlanta. CCT buses access MARTA regularly at the Arts Center station. The system operates both local (adult fare $1.25) and express (adult fare $3 one-way, $4 round-trip) routes. Kids less than 42 inches tall ride free; youth through high school fare is 80 cents; senior citizen and handicapped fare is 60 cents with ID. Although holiday schedules apply on most special days, CCT does not run on Thanksgiving, Christmas, New Year's Day, Memorial Day, Fourth of July, and Labor Day. For information on schedules and monthly passes, call (770) 427-4444.

Hartsfield Atlanta International Airport

Hartsfield Atlanta International Airport, the world's busiest passenger airport, is 10 miles south of downtown on I-85. It compares in size and population to a small city. Including airline, City of Atlanta, Federal Aviation Administration Airport, and concession tenants and employees, some 44,800 people work at 3,750-acre Hartsfield. The airport's direct and indirect impact on the Georgia economy is nearly $16.8 billion per year, making it the largest employment center in the state.

Hartsfield handled more than 75 million passengers in 2001 and is expecting volume to jump to 121 million annually by 2015. Hartsfield has 24 international gates and 146 domestic gates. Its four parallel runways are laid out east to west; the longest is 11,889 feet (more than 2.25 miles) long. In 2001, even with the interruptions caused by the 9/11 attacks, more than 890,000 aircraft took off and landed on these four runways.

In 70 years, Hartsfield went from a lonesome landing field to one of the world's major airports. Rail travel was king, and airplanes were little more than extravagant oddities in 1925 when the city leased an abandoned, 287-acre racetrack as Atlanta's first airport. But the popularity of flying grew quickly, and so did traffic at Candler Field. The airport began to grow, acquiring surrounding properties and increasing its aviation capacity.

In 1961 the airport boasted the largest single terminal in the country, but it wasn't big enough for long—booming Atlanta's huge demand for aviation services required a huge airport, and a massive new building project was undertaken.

For three and a half years in the late 1970s, the Atlanta airport was the biggest construction project in the South. When the new Hartsfield (the name honors former Atlanta mayor William B. Hartsfield, who was a tireless booster of aviation) opened in 1980, it was the largest airport in the world. But before long, Atlanta's growth again began to test its capacity.

In 1991 the city broke ground on the airport's sixth concourse, E, which opened in September 1994. Dedicated exclusively to international travel, the 1.3-million-square-foot, five-story addition is the largest international concourse in the nation. It has 24 gates (expandable to 34) and can handle 18 jumbo jets simultaneously, processing 6,000 arriving passengers an hour through Immigration and Customs.

Because of all the essential security, international concourses can sometimes look more like detention facilities than airports. Hartsfield's Concourse E is a stunning exception; its design is appropriate to the exciting and romantic idea of international travel. Light is beautifully used throughout, beaming from the broad skylights and the streamlined lighting fixtures. Since 1996, corridor walls, display cases, and gate areas at this concourse have showcased a collection of more than 32 pieces of art put together by the Bureau of Cultural Affairs.

In October 1995, Hartsfield unveiled its latest addition: a 225,000-square-foot, four-story atrium. Topped with a 60-foot-wide skylight and encompassing some 40 restaurants, shops, and services, the $24 million atrium provides an aesthetic focus for the airport as it connects the north and south terminals. The Atrium was envisioned as a place for people to rendezvous at the airport. Spaced throughout it are planters and comfortable living

Terminal building at the Hartsfield Atlanta International Airport. PHOTO: WILLIAM B. HARTSFIELD ATLANTA INTERNATIONAL AIRPORT

Aviation in Atlanta

Atlanta began as a railroad terminus (named Terminus at first, for some odd reason), and grew into the single most important transportation and logistics crossroads in the Confederacy. It rose from the Union army's desecrating fires to regain its status as a railroad and manufacturing center, helped the South rise again from the equally destructive invasion of the boll weevil (which nearly wiped out its agriculturally dependent economy) by restructuring the New South as one more dependent on high-tech manufacturing and tourism, and finally emerged into the 21st century pretty much what it was in the beginning: a center for trade and commerce that has literally become the crossroads of the nation. Depending on the source (and the year in question), the William B. Hartsfield Atlanta International Airport is either the world's busiest commercial airport, or at least the second or third busiest. An old joke frequently retold in these parts is that you can't go straight to either heaven or hell when you die—you first have to change planes in Atlanta.

Atlanta's Hartsfield Airport began in the most modest of manners, as a single short, bumpy dirt strip built over the remains of an abandoned racetrack. Local businessman William Berry Hartsfield (later the mayor of Atlanta) was persuaded in 1923 by two local pilots, Doug Davis and Beeler Blevins, that air travel would be vital to the growth of the City of Atlanta, and he soon found the abandoned racetrack owned by the Coca-Cola magnate Asa Candler. After two years of pleading and dealing, the Atlanta City Council agreed to grant him a five-year lease, rent free, to develop newly named Candler Field with the option for the city to buy the land and whatever was developed on it for $100,000 at the end of the lease period.

As was usual for that period of aviation history, the first use for the new airfield was strictly for the delivery of airmail, and the first contracted flight to do so took off

Atlanta Municipal Airport, during the "Golden Age" of air transport, 1948. PHOTO:
COURTESY OF THE TRACY W. O'NEAL PHOTOGRAPHIC COLLECTION, SPECIAL COLLECTIONS DEPT., PULLEN LIBRARY,
GEORGIA STATE UNIVERSITY

Eastern Airlines stewardesses wait to greet their passengers at the Atlanta Municipal Airport in 1946. PHOTO: COURTESY OF THE TRACY W. O'NEAL PHOTOGRAPHIC COLLECTION, SPECIAL COLLECTIONS DEPT., PULLEN LIBRARY, GEORGIA STATE UNIVERSITY

on September 15, 1926, bound for Macon and Jacksonville, Florida. Mail flights continued with some interruptions until October 15, 1930, when American Airlines inaugurated the first passenger service with initial flights to Dallas and Los Angeles. Within a few months scheduled service to New York and Florida began. In the early 1930s the federal government changed the way airmail contracts were awarded, and soon the tiny Delta Air Lines, from Monroe, Louisiana, won the Atlanta to Charlotte, North Carolina, mail contract. The first Delta flight from Atlanta, piloted by Charles Dolson, carried no passengers because the newly required airways navigation systems were not complete, and there were no suitable emergency landing fields between the two cities. Delta, of course, quickly grew into both one of the biggest commercial airline carriers and an Atlanta corporate icon.

The war years slowed Candler Field's growth, but after the airport was declared a government air base in 1940, it doubled in size and nearly quadrupled in the amount of air traffic almost overnight. In 1942 a record of 1,700 takeoffs and landings in a single day was set, and Candler Field for the first time was named the nation's busiest airport in terms of flight operation. As the nation's economy boomed in the postwar years, Atlanta's airport boomed right along. In 1946 the field was renamed Atlanta Municipal Airport, and on June 1, 1956, an Eastern Airlines flight to Montreal made the first international flight from the growing city.

In January 1977 work began on what was then to be the world's largest aviation-related construction project, what eventually grew into the present-day 3.8-million-square-foot facility, opening and renamed officially on September 21, 1980, to honor its most prominent supporter, the William B. Hartsfield Atlanta International Airport. This wasn't the end of growth for Atlanta's port, by any stretch, however, as ground was broken in April 2001 for a fifth runway, officially marking the beginning of a 10-year, $5.4 billion expansion and restoration project, now delayed for an unknown length of time by the 9/11 attacks.

room-style seating for approximately 100 people.

The Atrium's many amenities include a 20,000-square-foot conference center (with the capability to run 15 simultaneous meetings); offices of the United Service Organization, or USO, and Travelers' Aid; a 9,000-square-foot Houlihan's restaurant and piano bar; Paschal's (famous local soul food); fast-food restaurants; and more shops included in what is now known as The Shops of Hartsfield. Besides newsstands and gift shops, there are also currency exchanges, banks, the Coca-Cola Store, the Museum Company, golf stores, and the customary airport services. To book the conference facility, call the airport at (404) 761-6116, or toll-free at (800) 713-1359.

Throughout the airport, generic food concessions are being replaced with name-brand restaurants, such as Wendy's, Chick-fil-A, Burger King, Ben and Jerry's, and Starbuck's Coffee. There are also Disney Store locations on the concourses, as well as an ample number of ATMs. It's all part of the Hartsfield Improvement Project, a $170 million list of 60 different upgrade projects brought about by the 1996 Olympic Games presence in Atlanta.

The backbone of the airport is the 1.75-mile transportation mall, an underground walkway and train system that ferries passengers between the six concourses and terminal. Computer-operated trains (free of charge) run about every two minutes, traveling between all concourses and the terminal. Automated announcements will direct you onboard.

After the international gates were switched to Concourse E, their former concourse was moved to domestic use. Concourse T is the only concourse you access directly from the terminal without using the transportation mall connecting the terminal to the concourses.

To keep up with increasing air traffic, the airport plans future expansion.

Here's a brief walk-through of Hartsfield for arriving and departing domestic and international passengers. Further information is available on the airport's Web site, www.atlanta-airport.com.

Domestic Arrivals

Your domestic flight will taxi in to Concourse A, B, C, D, or T. Follow the signs for Terminal/Baggage Claim. You'll go down an escalator or elevator to the transportation mall. If you like, you may walk through the transportation mall or take the moving sidewalk, but we don't recommend this unless you are going only between adjacent concourses. If your plane comes in at the last domestic gate on Concourse D and you take the train, you'll be at baggage claim in less than 15 minutes. The moving sidewalk route, which also involves long stretches of nonmoving hallway, will take closer to 30 minutes.

At the last stop, "Terminal/Baggage Claim," go up the escalator or elevator to baggage claim and all ground transportation. Here you'll also find the rental car counters. Signs will direct you to the appropriate baggage area for your airline: North terminal baggage claim is to your right; south terminal (where the Delta Air Lines baggage goes) is to your left. Flight numbers flash over the various baggage carousels as the bags roll up the conveyor belt. There's also a big sign on the far wall telling you which carousel your flight's baggage is on. Passengers are required to present their half of the baggage check ticket for each checked bag before leaving baggage claim; uniformed employees near the exits will ask for your check tickets. If you don't have the check tickets, you'll be asked to show identification.

If you're being picked up by a friend, exit through the glass doors to the curbside area. Since there are two baggage claim areas (one on either side of the terminal), it's important to let your friend know what airline you're flying.

For all other transportation—taxi, limo, shuttle bus, or MARTA train—follow the signs to ground transportation at the west curb.

Passengers arriving on Concourse T won't need to ride the train to the terminal; you're already there. Special note for arriving American Airlines passengers: American Airlines flights use Concourse T. From your arriving gate, follow the signs downstairs to American baggage claim. Directly outside, American has its own curb where you can get a cab. If friends are picking you up, tell them to take the lanes for the north terminal, then follow the signs to American baggage claim.

Domestic Departures

As you approach Hartsfield by car from I-85, large signs will direct you to either the north or south terminal, depending on your airline. (All Delta flights use the south terminal.)

All airlines have ticket agents inside the terminal. If you have your boarding pass and no luggage to check, you can check your concourse and gate from one of the TV monitors near the ticket counters and in the transportation mall. However, not all airlines are listed on the monitors, so you may need to ask your airline's agent.

Everyone going from the terminal to any concourse must pass through the central security screening checkpoint. From security, take the train or moving sidewalk to your concourse; follow the signs to your gate. Nonticketed visitors are no longer allowed past the security checkpoint.

International Departures

International ticketing for Delta and a few international airlines is in the south terminal; ticketing for most other international carriers is in the north terminal. Check your bags at your airline's counter and proceed through security and the transportation mall to Concourse E, where signs will direct you to your gate.

Should your flight be delayed, you won't have to console yourself with an overcooked hot dog and yesterday's paper. Concourse E's food court includes Burger King, Starbuck's, and Mo' Better Chicken. Browse the excellent selection of U.S. and international publications at a bookstore or pick up a new tape or CD for that long flight. There is also a pair of duty-free shops.

Currency exchanges operate both on Concourse E and in the Atrium. Fees are

Insiders' Tip

Depending on the security levels in force on any given day, you may or may not be able to drop off passengers next to the airport terminal building. Check with Hartsfield's Web site or the local news for current information.

about $4 to $5, or 1 percent of the foreign exchange.

International Arrivals

As your international flight arrives at Concourse E, you'll first be directed to United States Immigration. From there you'll go downstairs to claim your bags and pass through Customs.

Once you've cleared Customs, you must recheck your bags at your airline's counter. If you're continuing to another city, they will be checked through to your final destination. But, even if Atlanta is your final destination, you are still required to recheck your bags. They will then be delivered to the terminal, where you can pick them up at baggage claim. This FAA-mandated policy is designed to alleviate overcrowding on the underground trains but caused lots of confusion when it was implemented.

Multilingual announcements describe the customs and baggage recheck procedures. In addition, most airlines now show an in-flight video that orients arriving passengers to the airport. Also, in the Immigration and Naturalization Service area, translators, whose badges indicate the languages they speak, assist non-English-speaking arriving passengers. Multilingual signs in the transportation mall tell passengers how to get around the airport.

Smoking

Smoking lounges are located throughout the airport; these are open to persons 18 and older. Feel free to smoke in the following lounges:

Concourse A near gates 14 and 23
Concourse B near gates 7 and 24
Concourse C near gates 17 and 26
Concourse T near gates 3 and 13
Concourse E near gates 33 and 34

Security

The terrorist attacks of 9/11 changed nearly the whole picture of security at Hartsfield (as well as the other 428 commercial airports across the nation). As one of the busiest airports in the world, Hartsfield is a high-profile target for those wishing to do evil, and as such, security concerns are equally high profile. The new Transportation Security Agency (TSA), the federal agency that assumed control of airport security across the nation in 2002, has maintained many of the features of pre-9/11 security checks, including X-raying carry-on baggage and requiring passengers to walk through metal detectors, but has increased screening in several other ways.

First, no one may pass through the security checkpoint without either a boarding pass or ticket, along with a photo ID. This means that friends and family can no longer meet or wave you off at the gate, and must remain back in the main terminal area of the airport. Secondly, 100 percent of all baggage going through Hartsfield now has to pass through newly installed bomb-detecting machines, which early reports have revealed considerably slows down an already slow process. Departing passengers now are subject to second or third levels of screening at random, which includes using more sensitive handheld metal detectors, special inspections of footwear, and "pat-down" searches done in a private room. Any food brought in through the checkpoint has to go through the X-ray machine. Lastly, there is an expanded list of "prohibited items" that are banned from being carried onto the airliner.

The TSA has a five-page document on its Web site (www.tsa.dot.gov) that details the items that are permitted to be brought onboard the plane, those that must be placed inside your checked-in luggage, and those items that are forbidden to be carried either way. The short version is: use common sense.

The most important thing to remember is that this security is very serious and the screeners are attempting to do their jobs in an efficient, businesslike manner. Atlanta was one of several airports across the nation where hidden weapons were found on grounded aircraft following the 9/11 attacks, and everyone is committed to preventing any further security breaches. Do not joke with the screeners, answer their questions directly, and do not resist any requested searches—at the very least you will be prevented from flying that day if you do.

During times of alerts or increased security, there may be additional restrictions on parking. Vans and large vehicles may be directed away from the close-in, short-term lots and told to park in the airport's other lots. Your vehicle also may be towed away if you leave it unattended in the drop-off/pickup lanes for even one minute.

Airport Parking

Hartsfield has more than 30,000 parking spaces. Lots near the terminal are for short-term parking ($1 an hour for the first and second hours; $2 per hour for each additional hour; maximum $24 for the first day and $48 per day after the first day). The economy lots are for long-term parking ($1 per hour; maximum $8 per 24 hours). Long-term deck parking is $1 per hour; maximum $12 per 24 hours. The park-and-ride lots at Hartsfield are $1 per hour; maximum $9 per 24 hours. You may access all these lots from either side (north or south) of the terminal. You may pay with cash, credit card, or check. If you have to lug your luggage very far, you may wish to rent a cart, but they are hard to come

From MARTA's station inside the Hartsfield Atlanta International Airport, it's an easy ride to the city.

by. They rent for $1.50 from the stands in baggage claim.

In addition, satellite lots around the airport have thousands more parking spaces. These lots run vans or buses to the airline curbsides and pick up returning passengers at ground transportation, eliminating that long walk back to the car when you're dead-tired from your trip.

Hartsfield's lots can fill up at peak travel times such as holidays, some weekends, and whenever the airlines slash fares to whip up business. If all the airport lots are filled, you'll have to backtrack and park at one of the satellites. To avoid this delay, call the airport parking office, (877) ATL-PARK (285-7275), before you leave and ask whether parking is adequate. Another good source for parking lot information is on Hartsfield's Web site, www.atlanta-airport.com, which updates lot information in near real-time.

Here are some companies that run satellite parking lots; call for directions and ask about return procedures. Some companies note your returning flight and meet you outside ground transportation; others require you to call when you arrive.

Park Air Express, $8.50 per day, (404) 762-0966.

Park N Fly, $11.00 per day, $9.75 for senior citizens, $66.00 weekly, (404) 763-3185.

Park N Fly Plus, daily rates: valet covered, $15.00; valet uncovered, $13.00; self-park, $10.25; $1.00 discount for senior citizens; (404) 761-0364.

Park N Go, daily rates: covered, $9.50; uncovered, $8.25; (404) 669-9300.

Park N Ticket, $9.00 per day uncovered, $12.00 covered, (404) 669-3800.

Rental Cars

Rental car counters are in the corridor between north and south baggage claim. The numbers given are for the airport offices unless otherwise noted. You'll find Alamo, (404) 768-4161; Dollar, (404) 766-0244, in College Park; Budget, (404) 530-3000; Hertz, (404) 530-2925; Avis, (800) 831-2847 nationwide reservation number; Thrifty, (770) 996-2350; and National, (404) 530-2800. Check with individual companies for car rental policies and procedures.

Ground Transportation Directory

A lighted directory listing ground transportation alternatives is at the west curb, just before you exit the terminal. As you exit at the west curb and walk away from the terminal, you'll encounter taxis, rental car shuttles, downtown and metro area buses, non-metro area buses, courtesy vehicles, and prearranged limousines.

MARTA

The easiest, fastest, and cheapest transportation into the city is the MARTA train. The station entrance is near baggage claim at the west curb, just before you reach the outside doors. You can enter the MARTA station from either the north or the south terminal. MARTA trains run from early in the morning until past midnight. The fare is $1.75, and an attendant is on hand to answer your questions. Stairs, escalators, and elevators are available for getting from the airport entrance up to the platform. (For detailed information, please see the previous MARTA section in this chapter.) Remember, if you're heading north beyond the Lindbergh station to North Springs or Doraville, make sure you get on the train marked for the proper line.

Taxis

Taxis line up in the first lane at the west curb at Hartsfield. Follow the ground transportation signs. If you like, an agent outside will arrange for you to share a cab into the city.

Atlanta's approximately 1,500 cabs operate under a limited flat-rate structure. From the airport to the downtown business and convention district, the fare is $25 for one passenger; $13 each for two; and $10 each for three or more passengers. Fares do not include sales tax (7 percent at this writing). The rate is not to exceed $40.

From the airport to the Buckhead business district, the fare is $35 for one passenger; $18 each for two; and $13 per person for three. Four or more is $11.25 per person, with an additional charge of $2.00 for every additional person.

A flat fare is also used for travel within the Downtown and Buckhead districts. The flat rate is $5.00 for one person; $1.00 for each additional person. At these rates, the fare adds up fast. If four people take a taxi from the Westin Peachtree Plaza to the Omni Hotel, the fare will be $8.00, even though they only traveled about five blocks.

The Downtown business and convention district is bounded by Boulevard, 14th Street, Northside Drive, and Memorial Drive (extended to Turner Field during Braves games). The Buckhead business district is harder to explain, but it's basically the heart of Buckhead, from Pharr Road up to Wieuca Road (that's just north of Lenox Square and Phipps Plaza).

For all other destinations, rates are $2.00 for the first seventh of a mile, 25 cents for each additional seventh of a mile, and $1.00 per each extra passenger. Per-hour waiting time is $18; use of additional space for luggage is $5.00. Add sales tax to all fares. Disabled persons and senior citizens with ID who are residents of the City of Atlanta are eligible for a 20 percent discount off the total fare, and they must purchase a $5.00 card that is renewed on their birthday.

For more information on Atlanta's taxis or to report a problem, call (404) 658-7600. Some cab company numbers are Atlanta Yellow Cab, (404) 521-0200; Buckhead Safety Cab, (404) 233-1152; Checker Cab, (404) 351-8255; and University Taxi, (404) 522-0200.

Hotel Courtesy Vehicles

Some 30 Atlanta hotels provide airport transportation for their guests. These hotels and their phone numbers are listed on the ground transportation directory.

Limousines and Hired Cars

If you'd prefer to arrive at your Atlanta destination in high style, you may wish to hire a limousine or sedan; some 138 limo companies serve Hartsfield Airport. Although it's best to reserve your car a day before your arrival, companies can often accommodate you with less notice.

Rates vary by company and by destination. Rates for a sedan to downtown are in the $50-to-$75 range; for a stretch limo, expect to pay about $65 to $100. Rates do not include tax and gratuity.

When you make your reservation, ask about pickup arrangements. Most drivers meet their arriving passengers outside in the ground transportation area. There's typically an additional charge of $15 to $20 to be met at your arrival gate; international gate service may add $20 to $30.

Among the hired car companies are Atlanta Limousine, (770) 432–LIMO, and Carey Limousine, (404) 223–2000. Most accept major credit cards. Check the Yellow Pages for a more complete listing.

Metro Area Shuttles

Here's a partial listing of airport shuttle services. Reservations may be required; call for complete information.

AAA Airport Express offers scheduled service to Northlake-Airport, $25 one-way; Norcross, Gwinnett, Suwanee, and Lawrenceville, $25; Lake Lanier, Gainesville, Château Élan, Braselton, and Athens, $30. Call for departure times and reservations, (800) 354–7874, local (404) 767–2000. Shuttles run from 6:00 A.M. to 11:30 P.M.

Atlanta Airport Shuttle offers scheduled service: from the airport (7:00 A.M. to 11:00 P.M.); to the airport (5:00 A.M. to 5:00 P.M.; later by reservation). Rates are $30 one-way to Norcross. Reservations are not required, and tickets may be purchased from the driver. Service departs on the half-hour to most locations. Hours are 7:00 A.M. to 11:00 P.M. Call for departure times and reservations, (404) 524–3400, (800) 842–2770. The Hartsfield Web site (www.atlanta-airport.com) has a lengthy list of other shuttle companies and destinations.

Non-Metro Shuttles

Other firms transport passengers out of town or out of state.

Groome Transportation offers service to Macon, $27, $50 round-trip; Warner Robins, $29, $55; and Columbus, $27, $50. On weekdays shuttles depart on the hour from 9:00 A.M. to 11:00 P.M. On Saturday they depart every hour between 9:00 A.M. and 10:00 P.M. On Sunday shuttles depart every hour between 9:00 A.M. and 10:00 P.M. Reservations are not accepted. Shuttles depart from the second island ground transportation. Call (800) 537–7903 or (912) 471–1616.

Other Area Airports

DeKalb-Peachtree Airport
3915 Clairmont Road
(770) 936–5440

DeKalb-Peachtree is a general aviation airport near I-85 in DeKalb County. Known by the initials PDK, the airport, built on the site of the World War II location of the Atlanta Naval Air Station (and World War I location of Camp Gordon), is the second busiest in Georgia and the 50th busiest of its kind in the United States. The airport has no commercial or scheduled flights; most users are corporate aircraft.

Private individuals can land at PDK; the tower telefrequency is 120.9. There is no landing fee, but ramp fees, if fuel is not purchased, and overnight fees, which vary by size of craft, are charged. Seven flight schools based at the airport provide lessons. For flight school numbers as well as the fixed base operator (FBO) numbers at PDK, call the number above.

Fulton County Airport–Brown Field
3952 Aviation Circle
(404) 699–4200

This 600-acre general aviation facility, known locally as Charlie Brown, is owned by Fulton County. It has three active runways and is used by many domestic and international corporate aircraft and also by state and federal government planes. Like DeKalb-Peachtree Airport, Brown Field is available to private aircraft and charges no landing fees. Ramp fees, if fuel is not purchased, and overnight fees apply. There is one flying school based at the airport. The tower telefrequency is 118.5. The airport's location is convenient to I–20, Martin Luther King Jr. Drive, and Fulton Industrial Boulevard.

McCollum Airport
1723 McCollum Parkway, Marietta
(770) 422–4300

Located at the foot of Kennesaw Mountain in Cobb County, McCollum Airport also serves general aviation and corporate aircraft. It charges no landing fees. Ramp fees, if fuel is not purchased, and overnight fees apply. There is one flying school based at the airport. The tower telefrequency is 125.9. The airport's location is convenient to I–75 and Cobb Parkway (U.S. 41) in the northwest section of the metro area.

Railways and Trailways

Amtrak
Brookwood Station
1688 Peachtree Street NW
(404) 881–3060

Amtrak's long, silver trains stop at Brookwood Station at the corner of Peachtree and Deering Road, just north of the Peachtree overpass across the Downtown Connector. Famous Atlanta architect Neel Reid designed the building, which was the smaller of Atlanta's two passenger rail terminals and was once considered to be in the suburbs. In 1925, 142 passenger trains rolled through Brookwood each day.

Today, Amtrak's Crescent line stops here. Atlanta enjoys daily service of one train each to and from New York's Penn Station and daily service to and from New Orleans.

Arriving passengers should note that the Amtrak station is at a very busy corner—take care crossing the streets, especially if you're lugging lots of overpacked bags. When you walk out of the Amtrak station and face Peachtree Street, downtown will be to your right; Buckhead will be to your left. If you're not being met and your destination is not nearby, you can take a cab (which you can easily get at the station) or take MARTA.

To take MARTA downtown from Brookwood Station, wait at the bus stop on the same side of the street and take the 23 Lenox/Arts Center MARTA bus southbound ($1.75 exact change; it runs frequently throughout the day and evening) to the Arts Center MARTA station. No transfer is necessary to board the train (southbound to Downtown; northbound to Buckhead). You'll find more information about MARTA detailed previously in the chapter.

Greyhound Bus Lines
232 Forsyth Street SW
(404) 584–1731, (800) 231–2222

Greyhound runs some 90 buses a day out of Atlanta. In addition to the main terminal, which is downtown near the Garnett Street MARTA station, the company operates bus stations in Decatur, Gainesville, Hapeville, Marietta, Newnan, and Norcross in the metro area. Not all buses stop at all the suburban stations.

Tickets may be purchased by phone with a credit card; however, you must allow two weeks to receive them by mail. To travel on shorter notice, you must make your reservations at a Greyhound terminal. For the nearest location, check the business pages of the phone book.

History

This was, indeed, a curious spot to build a town. Unlike any of the previously established European-style cities in the New World, the wilderness that was to become Atlanta had few redeeming qualities to white settlers—deep in the northwest Georgia woods, more than 1,000 feet above sea level, near no commercially navigable waterway, on land of marginal agricultural value in an area sporadically settled and hunted on by the sometimes-hostile Cherokee and Creek Nations, and on land that a Federal treaty declared permanently "Indian territory." Even to the ancient Native American nations, little seemed attractive about the area surrounding what some called "Hog Ridge"; although Native Americans had lived in and around the future glittering downtown area for some 8,000 years, by the early 19th century, no village stood on this spot.

But in the early 1800s, Georgia, the largest state east of the Mississippi River, badly needed a better transportation corridor between the coastal ports and towns to the interior trade routes along the Ohio and Mississippi Rivers in order to become commercially competitive with other states. In 1826 state surveyors began mapping out possible routes between the state capital of Milledgeville and the river port of Chattanooga, Tennessee. Initially, some thought was given to building a grand canal between the two towns, but the first survey of the rocky, mountainous terrain dashed that idea.

Instead, in 1837 engineers for the Western & Atlantic Railroad surveyed a route from Chattanooga southeast to a hilltop spot 7 miles east of the Chattahoochee River, at a point where three tall granite ridges converged. Here, the new line was to link with the planned extension of the Georgia Railroad from Augusta and Milledgeville, as well as planned extensions of railroads from other parts of the state. In what today would seem an unacceptable damper on free-market competition, that same year the state legislature voted to fund and build the new rail line, in direct competition with other railroad companies also planning to move into the newly opened territory.

The tiny railroad settlement atop the granite ridgeline had a humble beginning. Even its name—Terminus—said this was the end of the line. "The terminus," declared W&A engineer Stephen Long in 1837, "will be a good location for one tavern, a blacksmith shop, a grocery store, and nothing else."

In fact, as unbelievable as it would have seemed at the time, little Terminus (briefly called Marthasville, then Atlanta) was already on its way to becoming the economic and cultural center of the southern United States. Just 20 years after regular train service began, Atlanta was linked by rail to Chattanooga, Tennessee; Augusta, Georgia; Macon, Georgia; Mobile, Alabama; and many points beyond.

Because the tracks made it a crossroads in the quickly booming overland transportation industry, Atlanta evolved from the start as a new kind of town: an inland port. People, goods, money, and news were always moving through. The constant flow of travelers and rough-and-ready railroad men gave the town a bawdy flavor. The first tavern opened in 1835; the first church-and-schoolhouse had to wait until 1845. In the first mayoral election in 1848, the temperance candidate was defeated by a Decatur Street tinsmith and still-maker backed by the Free and Rowdy Party. The name of the town itself is a re-

The Atlanta Terminal Station was built in 1905 and served as the hub of railroad traffic until it closed in 1970. The building was demolished in 1972. The Richard B. Russell Federal Building now stands on the site. PHOTO: COURTESY OF THE TRACY W. O'NEAL PHOTOGRAPHIC COLLECTION, SPECIAL COLLECTIONS DEPT., PULLEN LIBRARY, GEORGIA STATE UNIVERSITY

flection of this heritage—it is the coined feminine version of "Atlantic," to designate the depot of the Western & Atlantic Railroad.

From the very beginning, Atlanta promoted itself as a modern city, different from the tradition-bound South. Atlanta's bustling, forward-looking spirit is well evidenced in the following two items quoted by Norman Shavin and Bruce Galphin in their excellent illustrated history, *Atlanta: Triumph of a People*. An educator who arrived in 1847 found the citizens quite welcoming, noting that they "bow and shake hands with everybody they meet, as there are so many coming in all the time that they cannot remember with whom they are acquainted." And an 1859 city directory boasted, "Our people show their democratic impulses by each allowing his neighbor to attend to his own business, and our ladies are even allowed to attend to their domestic and household affairs without being ruled out of respectable society." Between 1850 and 1860, Atlanta's population swelled from 2,500 to nearly 10,000.

The Civil War

But proud Atlanta's shining rails were about to be twisted into its noose. The U.S. Civil War was the first war in history in which railroads played a major role, and Atlanta beat as the iron heart of the Confederacy, with its factories, supply depots, and interconnecting rail lines pumping soldiers and supplies to battle fronts across the South. In the unsentimental eyes of Union Major General William Tecumseh Sherman, the small city represented just as much a threat to his army as any military force. He held a burning, very personal antipathy toward Georgia, and Atlanta in particular, which meshed well with his ideas about "total war." Literal years of seeing the words "Atlanta Depot" stenciled on the sides of captured supply wagons and containers convinced him that the road to and from Atlanta needed not only to be taken but also laid to waste so that it could never again be used against the Union. An added benefit was that this "scorched earth" policy would horrify and subdue the populace, who might otherwise engage his forces in guerrilla warfare or other harassing actions.

By the late spring of 1864, Atlantans knew Sherman was on the march from the Tennessee border and that he had set his sights on their city, but most were confident that Confederate Lieutenant General Joseph Eggleston Johnston's Army of Tennessee would halt the advance. Besides, most believed that the city, ringed by two and sometimes three rings of fortifications, a total of 10 miles of sharpened stakes (called "abatis"), rifle pits, and forts with several hundred heavy cannon, would never fall. In fact, the fortifications did hold: Not a single Union soldier fought his way across them. (Ironically, a Yankee designed them: Col. Lemuel P. Grant was a brilliant civil engineer who moved South in the railroad-building prewar years. Today Grant Park, home to Zoo Atlanta and the Cyclorama, bears his name.)

By late June, the city's bravado was replaced by dread as the booming battles, now within easy earshot of the city, grew louder every day. After suffering about

14,000 casualties in the three main July battles around the city (Peachtree Creek, East Atlanta, and Ezra Church), Confederate troops were forced to withdraw from offensive actions and take refuge inside the city's fortifications.

On July 20, four 20-pounder Parrott rifles of Union Captain Francis DeGress were set up near today's Piedmont Hospital on Peachtree Road, and soon began firing the first of thousands of artillery shells into the city itself. The first shell exploded at the intersection of Ivy and East Ellis Streets, killing a young girl who had been walking with her parents past Frank P. Rice's lumber dealership on the northwest corner. Shelling continued for several weeks at the rate of one round every 15 minutes, increasing to a much higher rate from time to time as more and more Union batteries came on line, while terrified residents cowered in makeshift bomb shelters and watched their food supplies rapidly dwindle.

Frustrated by his inability to starve or force the Confederate army out of the city's fortifications, Sherman ordered his artillery to increase their rate of fire. On August 1, after a disastrous attempt to defeat the Confederates in an assault west of the city, at Utoy Creek, he sent for large artillery guns and plenty of ammunition. Two 30-pounder Parrott rifles, specifically for building destruction, were brought in from Chattanooga, and eight huge 4.5-inch siege guns were brought in and mounted by August 8. On August 9, Sherman ordered every battery within range to open fire, "and make the inside of Atlanta too hot to be endured." That day alone more than 5,000 shells slammed into the city's heart. Sherman kept the intense bombardment up for more than two weeks, gradually wearing away the strength and endurance of the hollow-eyed soldiers within the city fortifications. During the war years, Atlanta's population had swelled to nearly 30,000, but most civilians left the city for safer points south before the bombardment really increased. At least 500 families stayed for various reasons and suffered along with the soldiers. Twenty of their number were killed by the Union shells, including

Insiders' Tip

Although barely 25 years old and still considered somewhat of a frontier town in recently Indian territory northern Georgia, Atlanta was both the logistics center of the Confederacy and the center of attention for most of the fighting in the Western Theater of the Civil War.

Solomon Luckie, a well-liked freed black barber, killed by a bursting shell next to a lamppost near today's Five Points (the original damaged lamppost still exists, and can be seen in the walkway between Underground Atlanta and the Five Points MARTA station).

Then, suddenly, on August 25, all the guns fell silent. Confederate commander John Bell Hood (who had replaced the beloved Johnston just before the battle of Peachtree Creek) hoped for a moment that Sherman had given up and was withdrawing, but his hopes were dashed when word came of yet another Union attack. Sherman had sent nearly half his total force around the west of Atlanta, to sweep down on the Atlanta & West Point Railroad 9 miles southwest of East Point. Hood could not hope to muster any sort of force to stop them, but pulled nearly his entire army out of Atlanta to try and protect the last remaining railway south of the city, leaving one-third of his badly weakened army, along with "old men and boys" of the Georgia Militia, to hold the city lines.

After unsuccessfully fighting Sherman's huge force over two bloody days at

Headstrong Heroine

It took Margaret Mitchell 10 years to complete Gone With the Wind.

PHOTO: ATLANTA HISTORICAL SOCIETY

She was small, but it's said she enjoyed corn liquor, cigarettes, and a good dirty joke. Peggy Mitchell was a popular features writer when she left the *Atlanta Journal* in 1926 to nurse an injured ankle and make a life with her new husband. In response to his persistent suggestions, she began a novel.

Born in 1900 in a house that had been spared Sherman's torch, Mitchell was fascinated by the Civil War and spent many childhood hours listening to the harrowing tales of its elderly survivors. So vivid were their recollections that Mitchell thought the war had ended just before she was born, and she was utterly astonished at age 10 when some black farm workers broke the news to her that the South had actually lost the war.

Typing at the table she used as a desk, dressed in her husband's baggy clothes, and wearing a writer's green eyeshade, Margaret Mitchell spent the next 10 years writing a novel (originally called *Another Day*, then *Tomorrow Is Another Day*) about a strong-willed Southern girl of Irish descent (originally named Pansy O'Hara) who came of age in the last days before the war, survived the destruction of Atlanta, and grew rich during Reconstruction.

Mitchell began by writing the novel's last chapter. When visitors came calling, she hid the growing stacks of manuscripts under a large towel, for she jealously guarded her privacy and shuddered to think that anyone would find the novel autobiographi-

Jonesboro, the Confederates realized their hopeless plight and abandoned Atlanta for good on the night of September 1. As they withdrew, Hood ordered the destruction of everything of military value that he could not take with him, including 81 freight cars full of ammunition, seven locomotives, and the Atlanta rolling mill—one of only two factories in the South that could turn out badly needed iron rails.

After the mayor's formal surrender on September 2, Atlanta became a Union camp. Sherman ordered the remaining civilians expelled from the city: A total of 1,644 people were forced out to face more hardships farther south. This action, although sound from a purely military point of view, further hardened Southern hatred of the "blue suits." Hood, after exchanging a series of rude notes with Sherman over his treatment of the noncombatants, summed up these feelings well: "We will fight you to the death," he wrote back to Sherman, "better die a thousand deaths than submit to live under you."

Preparing to leave Atlanta in mid-November for an attempt to capture Savannah, Sherman gave orders that anything of "military value" in north Georgia be destroyed by his troops gathering for the

cal. (In fact, the twice-married, headstrong Mitchell had much in common with her plucky heroine.)

Most reluctantly, Mitchell gave the ragtag manuscript to a Macmillian agent scouting the South for new writers in 1935; she then immediately panicked and wired him: "Send the manuscript back. I've changed my mind." But it was too late. The agent, like the millions and millions of readers who followed him, was instantly hooked.

Gone With the Wind sold 50,000 copies on the first day it was offered. In the years since, it has sold more than 28 million copies around the world and remains the best-selling novel of all time. David O. Selznick paid $50,000 for the movie rights; the December 15, 1939, world premiere in Atlanta was a spectacular event reported around the globe; the movie won 10 Academy Awards and, by its 50th anniversary, had grossed more than $840 million.

Mitchell's modern outlook and ideas caused minor scandals more than once, so it's easy to understand the bewilderment she expressed in a 1936 letter. "Being a product of the Jazz Age, being one of those short-haired, short-skirted, hard-boiled women who preachers said would go to hell or be hanged before they were thirty, I am naturally a little embarrassed at finding myself the incarnate spirit of the old South!"

The Margaret Mitchell House shows a rich history of the author of one of the world's most beloved novels. PHOTO: ATLANTA CONVENTION & VISITORS BUREAU

In a letter written the year before *GWTW*'s 1936 publication, Mitchell confided, "In a weak moment, I have written a book. . . ." It was a book that catapulted its author to international celebrity and forever affected the way the world thought of her hometown.

march south. Rome, Acworth, and Marietta were all consigned to the torch, and soon little was visible of the once pretty small towns but heaps of smoldering ruins and lonely chimneys standing like pickets. Atlanta was next. The railroad roundhouse, factories, warehouses, residences, and masonry buildings were soon battered down by demolition gangs to piles of rubble. Under other buildings Union soldiers piled stacks of mattresses, oil-soaked wagon parts, broken fence rails, and just about anything else that would burn. Atop everything they piled artillery shot and shells abandoned by Hood's re-

treating army. In a touch of irony, sentries were then posted to prevent "unauthorized" acts of arson.

Finally ready to move out of Atlanta, Sherman ordered "everything of military value" to be set on fire late on the afternoon of November 15. Within a few minutes, the "authorized" fires had been set, at first confined to factories and warehouses containing Hood's abandoned supplies. An early evening wind soon built up the fires, and spraying sparks and burning cinders in every direction, the fires spread like, well, wildfire. Pleased by the sight of the soon out-of-control fires raging through the city, Sherman was moved to remark only that he supposed the flames could be visible from Griffin, about 45 miles to the south.

As a sort of explanation to his staff, who were starting to view the wanton destruction with unease, Sherman remarked, "This city has done more and contributed more to carry on and sustain the war than any other, save perhaps Richmond. We have been fighting Atlanta all the time, in the past; have been capturing guns, wagons, etc., etc., marked Atlanta and made here, all the time; and now since they have been doing so much to destroy us and our Government we have to destroy them, at least enough to prevent any more of that."

As the huge fire built and built, block after block literally exploded into flame, the thick smoke choking the Union soldiers who clapped and danced with glee among the ruins, barely waiting until the flames died down to start their looting and drunken revelry once again. What initially escaped the "authorized" fires did not escape these undisciplined wretches away from their officers, who helped spread the flames by burning homes and businesses to cover up their crimes. In the midst of the chaotic riot, the 33rd Massachusetts Regimental Band stood, calmly and righteously playing "John Brown's Soul Goes Marching On." Union Major George Ward Nichols, Sherman's aide-de-

camp, remarked without a hint of sarcasm that he had "never heard that noble anthem when it was so grand, so solemn, so inspiring."

Other Union soldiers and officers viewed the destruction differently, remarking that the burning and looting of private property was not necessary and a "disgraceful piece of business." Another summed up the view more widely held by their Confederate opponents: "We hardly deserve success."

As the flames died down overnight, dawn on November 16 revealed that more than 4,100 of the 4,500 buildings in town, including every single business, had been leveled by the flames and rioting Union troops. Sherman mounted his horse, Sam, and slowly led his 60,598 men out of the ruined city, bound for Savannah and the Atlantic Ocean. One month shy of the 17th anniversary of its incorporation as a city, Atlanta lay in ruins.

(For more on the history of Atlanta during this brutal war, see our sister publication, *Insiders' Guide to Civil War Sites in the Southern States*.)

Rising from the Ashes

"Throughout the South for fifty years there would be bitter-eyed women who looked backward, to dead times, to dead men, evoking memories that hurt and

Completed in 1889, the dome of the Capitol is topped with 23-karat gold mined from Dahlonega, Georgia, the site of the nation's first gold rush. PHOTO: ATLANTA CONVENTION & VISITORS BUREAU

were futile, bearing poverty with bitter pride because they had those memories. But Scarlett was never to look back."

—Chapter 25, *Gone With the Wind*

The numbers tell the tragic tale: The Civil War claimed more than 618,000 American lives, more than the combined U.S. losses of every other American war (except World War II). That bloody spring and summer of 1864, 4,423 Union troops and 3,044 Confederates were killed in combat action in the Atlanta Campaign, with another 41,774 being wounded and 17,335 captured or missing on both sides. Several thousand more on both sides died of disease, hunger, and wounds during and after the grand campaign.

After Confederate General Robert E. Lee's surrender on April 9, 1865, and Confederate General Joseph E. Johnston's surrender of the pitiful remnants of the western armies that defended Georgia on April 26, a pall of misery and destitution hung heavy over once-haughty Dixie. But Atlanta, like the spitfire heroine who would symbolize the city in Margaret Mitchell's novel 70 years later, got on with life. The South was split into five military governor-

ships and, as the headquarters of the third Military District under U.S. General John Pope, Atlanta was again at the center of things. Federal troops continued to occupy the city for the better part of 10 years.

The railroads had been wrecked in the war, as Union soldiers ripped up the rails, roasted them over fires, and twisted them into what were called "Sherman's neckties." But with help from the Army, newly liberated black workers, and Northern investors, the four rail lines were restored in just two years, and a new line was working its way to Charlotte, North Carolina, by 1869.

Life was tough in the harsh winter of 1864–65, and a smallpox epidemic swept through in 1866. Even so, the town was struggling its way back to civilization. Theatrical performances resumed in 1865, and by 1866 the reborn city boasted two opera houses. That October, a 75-member touring company presented Italian grand opera on three consecutive nights, although the steep ticket price ($2) kept many Atlantans away.

In 1868, the Georgia capital was relocated to Atlanta from Milledgeville, a decision that was ratified in a popular referendum in 1877. By 1867, 250 stores were open in the city. Atlanta was home to 21,000 people in 1870 and to 37,000 in 1880.

The signs of progress were everywhere. In 1871 the first horse-drawn streetcar began to service a 2-mile route. In the 1870s the city inaugurated free mail delivery and a downtown garbage collection service.

In 1886 Atlanta produced what remains its most famous export. John Pemberton, a Marietta Street pharmacist, blended a "brain tonic" with a secret recipe of extracts from the coca plant and kola nuts. When a customer happened to order his Coca-Cola syrup with soda instead of plain water, the world's favorite soft drink was born. Dr. Pemberton sold ownership of his product for $2,300 to entrepreneur Asa Candler in 1887. Available only in Atlanta and only at soda fountains at first, Coca-Cola soon spread across the South and the nation. By 1899, the company was shipping 300,000 gallons of syrup a year and beginning to sell the premixed drink in bottles.

In 1890 the city had 65,000 residents, only 12 percent of whom had called the "first" Atlanta home. In the South, only Richmond, Virginia; Nashville, Tennessee; and New Orleans, Louisiana were larger than Atlanta. By 1894, electricity, not mules, powered the streetcars.

Foreshadowing the importance of the modern-day convention business, Atlanta hosted large expositions in 1881, 1887, and 1895, attracting international attention and investment. General Sherman himself came to the 1881 exposition; President Grover Cleveland attended the 1887 fair. The Liberty Bell was displayed at the 1895 Cotton States and International Exposition, which attracted nearly a million visitors in its three-month run and boldly included pavilions celebrating the progress and accomplishments of blacks and women. The latter two fairs were held on the site of the present Piedmont Park, which was purchased by the city for $93,000.

The Dawning of a New Century

As the 20th century dawned, Atlanta's population stood at 90,000; by 1910, it had jumped to 155,000.

Atlanta's African-American population grew rapidly during the war years as slaves were ordered in to aid the Confederacy, and many of these new citizens returned to make their homes in the city after the war. By 1870, the black community was five times larger than it had been in 1860. By 1890, African Americans made up 43 percent of the population and 50 percent of the workforce.

Northern missionaries and other reformers started Freedmen's Schools to educate ex-slaves and their children. (One such school operated in a boxcar divided into classrooms.) This early movement planted the seeds that made Atlanta a center of black higher education, and today the Atlanta University Center is the largest consortium of historically African-American colleges in the nation.

Even in the days of enforced racial separation, Atlanta prided itself on being a town with the good sense to put business before prejudice—although it was not always successful. On September 22, 1906, a white mob, enraged by inflammatory newspaper reports of numerous "outrages" against white women, attacked and murdered blacks and burned black homes. Order was not fully restored until September 27, and the rioting left a dozen blacks and several whites dead. The white rampage, reported throughout the nation and in Europe, badly damaged Atlanta's emerging reputation.

In the wake of the riot, much of Atlanta's African-American business community withdrew to Auburn Avenue (then called Wheat Street). Auburn became Atlanta's other main street, offering a full range of retail, service, and entertainment concerns as well as religious and social organizations. Among its most successful businesses was Atlanta Life Insurance Co., founded by Alonzo Herndon, an ex-slave and sharecropper who built a lucrative barber business and became Atlanta's first African-American millionaire. In 1956, *Fortune* magazine called Auburn "the richest Negro street in the world."

Civil Rights

It was only natural that Atlanta, long a center of black culture and education, would become a center of civil rights activities in the tumultuous 1960s. And although integration was certainly a contentious issue, forward-thinking black and white leaders helped Atlanta avoid the eruptions of violence that tore apart so many U.S. cities in those years. It was tough, but Atlanta lived up to Mayor William Hartsfield's boast in a 1959 *Newsweek* article: "Atlanta is a city too busy to hate."

At the center of the civil rights movement throughout its most dramatic years was Dr. Martin Luther King Jr. He was born in a modest frame house on Auburn Avenue on January 15, 1929. A gifted student, he was admitted to Morehouse College at age 15 and earned his doctorate from Boston University in 1955. After leading the successful drive to desegregate buses in Montgomery, Alabama, King returned to Atlanta in 1960 as president and cofounder of the Southern Christian Leadership Conference and co-pastor (with his father) of Ebenezer Baptist Church.

In October of 1960, King and 51 others were arrested when they staged a sit-in to protest segregation at Rich's department store; in all, some 180 people went to jail. Most refused to post bail in order to attract attention to their demands. King's arrest was especially problematic because he was on probation for driving without a Georgia license (his license was from Alabama). His probation was revoked, and he was sentenced to six months in the state penitentiary. Presidential candidate John F. Kennedy quietly intervened personally to secure King's early release.

In Atlanta, as in most Southern communities, the desegregation of public schools was hotly debated. But here inte-

Alonzo Herndon founded the Atlanta Life Insurance Co. and became Atlanta's first African-American millionaire. PHOTO: THE HERNDON HOME

gration proceeded far more smoothly than in many cities. On August 30, 1961, nine black students made history by enrolling in formerly all-white high schools. That afternoon, President Kennedy publicly congratulated the city, urging other communities "to look closely at what Atlanta has done and to meet their responsibility, as the officials of Atlanta and Georgia have done, with courage, tolerance and, above all, respect for the law."

To the chagrin of many conservatives, King was awarded the Nobel Prize for Peace in 1964. Although still a very controversial figure in his hometown, King was honored with a banquet staged by city leaders, Coca-Cola magnate Robert W. Woodruff among them.

On April 4, 1968, an assassin's bullet stilled King's voice for peace and progress. Gripped by grief and rage, more than 100 U.S. cities exploded in violence, but Atlanta, again, was spared. The eyes of the world focused on the city on April 9, when hundreds of thousands watched King's cortege make its way slowly from Ebenezer Baptist Church to Morehouse College,

Civil rights leader Martin Luther King Jr. was one of Morehouse College's most outstanding alumni.
PHOTO: MOREHOUSE COLLEGE

where president emeritus Dr. Benjamin E. Mays said, "To be honored by being requested to give the eulogy at the funeral of Dr. Martin Luther King is like asking one to eulogize his deceased son, so close and so precious was he to me."

Today King's body rests in an elevated marble tomb at the Martin Luther King Jr. Center for Nonviolent Social Change on Auburn Avenue, near his boyhood home and beside his church. The Center lies within the boundaries of the 42-acre Martin Luther King Jr. National Historic Site and welcomes about a million visitors each year, making it one of the city's leading tourist attractions.

After King's death, Atlanta continued to make important strides toward social justice. In 1974, 35-year-old Maynard Jackson became the youngest mayor in Atlanta's history and the first African American to head a major Southern city. Jackson's aunt, Metropolitan Opera soprano Mattiwilda Dobbs, performed at his inauguration; she had refused to sing in Atlanta when audiences here were segregated.

The atmosphere fostered by the coalition of civil rights leaders and white liberals made the city a progressive oasis in conservative Georgia. Even as some affluent whites fled the city for the suburbs in the 1960s and '70s, many more people took their places. Flower children, gays and lesbians, peace activists, and a variety of intellectuals and nonconformists made their homes here, eager to live in a harmonious and evolving integrated urban environment.

For years, the city's politics remained decidedly left-leaning. In the '70s Atlanta was a center of antiwar activity: Presidential candidate Senator George McGovern once led a peace march down Auburn Avenue with Mayor Sam Massell. In the '80s Atlanta was deeply involved in the fight to free South Africa. Former political prisoner Nelson Mandela was wildly received by an enormous throng at Georgia Tech's Bobby Dodd Stadium when he came here to thank the city in 1990. In the 1990s His Holiness Tenzin Gaytso, the 14th Dalai Lama and exiled leader of Tibet, began regular visits to Atlanta, culminating in the establishment of both a Tibetan Buddhist center and an associated Department of Buddhist Studies at Emory University. And each June, the mayor proclaims Lesbian and Gay Pride Week in recognition of that community's contributions to the city's life.

One high-profile and unusually divisive issue of the past few years is the matter of the Georgia state flag. The Georgia Legislature modified the flag in 1956, in what some sources indicate was a defiant anti-integration gesture, to include the Confederate battle emblem, the well-known "Southern Cross" (other sources indicate this was done as part of the 100th anniversary commemorations of the Civil War). After a movement to remove it initially failed in the state legislature, Atlanta City Council acted on its own, banishing the banner from City Hall and replacing it (on February 4, 1993) with the pre-1956 flag, which contains a lesser-known Confederate symbol, the "Stars and Bars" (part of the 1st Confederate National Flag). In January 2001, with little public notice and under threats of economic boycotts like South Carolina had suffered, Georgia Governor Roy Barnes introduced legislation to change the state flag, which was quickly passed with little debate by both houses of the state legislature, and just as quickly signed into law by the governor.

While the 2000 presidential elections provided high drama and controversy to the nation, the 2002 Georgia gubernatorial elections proved even more shocking to the Peach State. Although vastly outnumbered in the fund-raising department by incumbent Governor Barnes, and given little initial chance of even appearing in double digits in the final vote tallies, Sonny Perdue of the tiny middle-Georgia town of Bonaire was elected as Georgia's first Republican governor since Reconstruction. An unlikely coalition of classroom teachers, old-Georgia-flag supporters, and "transplanted" Northern Republicans is widely credited with bringing this sea change to Georgia politics, which also saw Republicans gain unprecedented majorities in the Georgia legislature and occupy both U.S. Senate seats.

Ushering in the Jet Age

If Atlanta was born in 1837 on the day the Western & Atlantic surveyors drove in the "zero milepost" that marked the end of the rail line, modern Atlanta was born in 1925 on the day the city took a five-year, rent-free lease on an abandoned auto race-track in Hapeville, 10 miles south of town, promising to develop the overgrown 287-acre site as an airfield.

Interest in flying built slowly at first. Atlanta was already at the center of a web of tracks and roads; aviation was more of an expensive curiosity than a major factor

in transportation. But when young William Hartsfield looked at planes, he saw the future. First as an alderman, then as Atlanta's mayor for 22 years, Hartsfield pushed for improvements in aviation. By the early 1930s, Atlanta had the second-largest number of air routes in the country.

From the beginning, the demand for aviation services far outstripped Candler Field's capacity. More land was acquired, runways added, and better facilities built, but the booming aviation business quickly outgrew each improvement. In 1955, two million passengers passed through the airport, making it the busiest in the nation. A $21 million, ultramodern facility (the largest single terminal building in the country) opened in 1961. It, too, was quickly too small. "Whether you're bound for heaven or hell," said the old joke, "you'll have to change planes in Atlanta."

In January 1977, work began on the world's largest terminal building at the airport (now renamed Hartsfield Atlanta International Airport to honor the mayor whose vision had readied Atlanta for the jet age). The project cost a half-billion dollars and took more than three years to complete. Throughout construction, normal operations continued. The new Hartsfield, built around a space-age, automated people-moving system 40 feet underground, opened to much fanfare on September 21, 1980. Hartsfield is home to Delta Air Lines, one of the world's leading carriers. Delta, in conjunction with its wholly owned subsidiary ASA, offers more than 900 domestic and international flights a day out of the airport. In 1999 the airline carried more than 106 million passengers, making it the most-traveled airline in the world. Two and a half million people fly out of Atlanta on Delta each month.

Even huge Hartsfield had its limitations, and in September 1994, the city unveiled the new Concourse E for international travel. It is, predictably, the largest concourse in the nation. A dramatic new central atrium connecting the north and south terminals opened in late 1995, just one of some 60 airport improvement projects that made Hartsfield a more welcoming first stop for Atlanta's Olympic visitors in 1996.

Accommodating Atlantans and the World

Throughout recent decades, Atlanta has continued to acquire the high-visibility accessories of a world-class city and to host events of international interest.

The city built an arts center with the largest regional theater in the Southeast and a symphony hall; a 4,591-seat civic center that hosted the Metropolitan Opera; a 16,000-seat coliseum; a baseball/football stadium; a 2.5-million-square-foot convention center; and the world's largest cable-supported domed stadium. Atlantans even pulled together in 1976 to prevent the destruction of the lavish, 4,678-seat Fox Theatre, built in 1929, and now one of the nation's few surviving grand movie palaces.

In 1966 Atlanta became the first city ever to acquire professional baseball (the Braves) and football (the Falcons) teams in the same year. Professional basketball (the Hawks) followed in 1968, and the city's first professional hockey team in 1972 (that team, the Flames, left for Calgary in 1980, and a new team, the Thrashers, began play in 1999). Atlanta's Omni com-

plex was the site of the 1988 National Democratic Convention, which was watched worldwide. The city's new Georgia Dome hosted Super Bowl XXVIII in 1994 and XXXIV in 2000, attracting sports fans and media from around the world.

The unbelievable happened in 1990, when Atlanta shocked the world by overcoming stiff competition and winning the 1996 Olympics, the 100th anniversary of the modern Olympic Games. At first, all seemed to be theory and planning. But in 1994 the Olympics began to change Atlanta's silhouette.

Atlantans watched the Olympic Village rise on the west side of the Downtown Connector, and we saw the mammoth Olympic stadium take shape right beside Atlanta–Fulton County Stadium, then the home of the Braves. The number of international visitors, which was always significant, seemed to skyrocket as people from around the world showed up for an advance look at the Olympic city.

Preparing to welcome the world was quite a tall order, but Atlanta had plenty of practice. The still-rebuilding city hosted a major exposition just 17 years after it was burned to the ground. Atlantans and Georgians from across the state responded to the challenges of the Olympics with energy and enthusiasm. Though it only lasted for two weeks in that summer of 1996, the Olympics remain a milestone event for many who eagerly share their remembrances of the excitement and pride that spilled into every street. The lasting legacy of the Games can be found in various locations around town: where kids still splash in the fountains at Centennial Park; where the Braves play at Turner Field, the former Olympic stadium; where outdoor sculptures, murals, and other artworks adorn parks and street corners.

Now that you understand a bit about Atlanta's past, it's time to begin exploring the modern city. So drop this book in your bag, grab your sunglasses and/or your umbrella (more about the weather later), and let's have some fun in Atlanta!

International Atlanta

For the past two decades, Atlanta has been billing itself as an International City, yet until a few years ago one would have been hard-pressed to find anything but English-speaking shops anywhere in the city. Today, Atlanta is international, with entire sections of town that can be claimed as Korean, Chinese, or Hispanic. In fact, we've become so diverse that in Duluth an ordinance was passed requiring signage in English as well as the clientele's language so that police officers and the fire department would be able to figure out just where they were supposed to show up when there was a problem. The area's immigrant population has rapidly grown to the point that areas such as Buford Highway and Sandy Springs are now seeing their second or third "wave" of nationalities setting up shop (literally).

Our city's excellent location as a transportation hub, its role as the economic capital of the South, and its welcoming climate have made it a magnet for tourists and new residents alike, not only from the United States but also from all over the globe. As people from other nations have taken advantage of Atlanta's welcome, the city's demographic makeup has become increasingly international.

The Centennial Olympics in 1996 no doubt encouraged folks from near and far to take up residence in our city and to bring their businesses with them—but we have no firm statistics on that as of yet. What we do know is that since the 1970s Atlanta has experienced a 500-plus percent increase in its foreign-born population, representing about 80 countries and speaking more than 100 different languages. According to the 2000 census statistics, there are now well over 420,000 foreign-born residents in metro Atlanta, about 10.3 percent of the population. The Asian population is growing the fastest, and according to 1997 calculations from the Georgia State University Center for Applied Research in Anthropology, we have approximately 193,200 people of Asian descent, who, along with the Hispanic population, live mostly in DeKalb County. In DeKalb's Cross Keys High School, more than 35 separate, distinct languages and major dialects are spoken as the students' primary language. Gwinnett County is the second most populated county for foreign-born residents. In Gwinnett's Norcross Elementary School, for example, children in the English as a Second Language classes speak 33 different native tongues.

As the number of international Atlantans has grown, so has the marketplace for international products and services. The number and variety of businesses and social organizations each community supports is empirical evidence of its own particular tastes as well as a graphic demonstration of its buying power.

This chapter has been compiled with three groups of readers in mind: international visitors to our city, new Atlantans who have moved here from other countries, and everyone who enjoys the excitement of learning about other cultures without having to cross borders to do it. You'll find international shopping opportunities in Atlanta, currency exchange information, and a sampling of some of the city's many multicultural social and educational groups. Atlanta area consulates of foreign governments are listed for the benefit of visitors who need to speak with a diplomatic representative of their home nation during their visit.

You can find international dining in the various ethnic categories of our Restaurants chapter. There are about 10 foreign language papers published in our city, some of which are noted in our Media section. Many of these publications are available at the shops that attract a foreign-born clientele. Newspapers from all over the globe are distributed at some area newsstands.

Currency Exchange

If you're staying at a major hotel, ask the concierge to direct you to the nearest supplier of currency exchange services. Many banks offering same-day, on-site currency exchange are in the downtown area. Some branches that don't offer full-service currency exchange do sell dollars on demand. Call the numbers shown below for each bank's policies.

Thomas Cook Currency Services Inc. has three locations inside Hartsfield Airport, all on the international Concourse E. Call toll-free, (800) 287-7362, for specific information.

American Express Travel Service Buckhead office, 3384 Peachtree Road; (800) 525-7623.

International Exchange Corp., 133 Carnegie Way, Suite 210, downtown; (404) 521-2600.

Ruesch International, 191 Peachtree Street, downtown; (404) 222-9300.

Bank of America offers on-site currency exchange at the Bank of America Plaza, 600 Peachtree Street; (404) 607-4850.

SouthTrust Bank sells dollars at all of its approximately 100 Atlanta area offices. Customers selling dollars may pick up their foreign currency the next day.

SunTrust Bank offers on-site currency exchange at 10 offices, including its Five Points location at One Park Place.

Insiders' Tip

The majority of newly arrived immigrants, and the shops and services that support them, tend to be clustered around the Buford Highway corridor in Doraville and Chamblee, and the South Cobb Drive corridor in Smyrna.

Wachovia offers on-site currency exchange at its Five Points location, 2 Peachtree Street, and some branch offices.

Consulates

Quite a few nations have consulates in Atlanta. Check the phone book for listings.

International Malls

Until fairly recently, Atlanta did not have geographically compact districts populated largely by a single immigrant community. Now, however, you can drive to specific parts of town and find apartment housing with resident managers who speak your language, as well as locate shops that sell just the herbs, vegetables, or fabrics popular in a specific country.

For example, Buford Highway, beginning at the crossroads of North Druid Hills Road, is populated by people from Central and South America. From the Clairmont Road crossing on toward Interstate 285, the population changes to Asian peoples, first Vietnamese, then Korean and Chinese. Outside the Perimeter highway, the culture becomes primarily Hispanic again as you enter Gwinnett County and Norcross. You'll see billboards and shop signage in three or more languages at some locations. Mexican restaurants, Vietnamese videos, Chinese herbs, Spanish greeting cards, and Asian foods of every variety bombard the senses.

The area around South Cobb Drive and Windy Hill Road in the Smyrna part of Cobb County, as well as locations in Gainesville and other areas, have seen a recent influx of Hispanic residents. Business signs in Spanish proclaim Mexican, Guatemalan, and Peruvian restaurants, and other businesses announce, "Se habla Español." A more recent development is a concentration of Iranian immigrants around the Roswell Road/I-285 area, and the Toco Hills area, long an Orthodox Jewish community, has begun attracting Jewish immigrants from the former Soviet republics.

Asian Square
5150 Buford Highway
no phone

You'll find 99 Ranch market (a full-size Asian supermarket), a bakery, a jewelry store, and a Vietnamese video store in this square.

Korea Town Mall
5302 Buford Highway
no phone

Korea Town Mall is home to a Korean video shop, gift shops, a sushi bar, and a Chinese restaurant.

Northwoods Plaza
Buford Highway and Shallowford Road
no phone

There are many international tenants at this strip mall including an herb store, an Asian fashion shop, and an Oriental food market.

Plaza Fiesta
4166 Buford Highway, just beyond Clairmont Road
no phone

Formerly the Buford-Clairmont Mall, Outlet Square, and Oriental Mall, this mall was purchased and renovated as a Latin-themed entertainment and retail center in 2000. Hair and nail salons, a furniture shop, and legal and medical services are among the attractions. The mall is anchored by Marshall's and Burlington Coat Factory stores. Among the stores is the Atlanta Farmers' Market, a store as large as a Kroger or Publix. Japanese dried mushrooms, Vietnamese fish paste, Chinese noodles, fresh veggies, raw fish, flip-flop slippers, pots and pans, ginseng—the Atlanta Farmers' Market has it. The market is well staffed by folks who speak all manner of Asian dialects as well as English.

Pinetree Plaza
5269 Buford Highway
no phone

Another center with multinational shopping, Pinetree Plaza includes many Asian restaurants and a furniture store. Around the back is unassuming Kim's Pharmacy and Herb Store, which serves as the office

from which Kim, a California-licensed acupuncturist, conducts his practice.

Little Saigon
4646 Buford Highway
no phone

Vietnamese restaurants, a nail supply boutique, a fashion store, and other shops catering to the Vietnamese community can be found here.

Roland Center
3640-54 Shallowford Road
no phone

Just north of its intersection with Buford Highway, Roland Center has several Latin American businesses including a bakery, grocery, and music shop that offers CDs, tapes, videos, and greeting cards in Spanish.

Centro Norcross
Buford Highway, Norcross
no phone

Anchored by the Guadalajara grocery store, this newer shopping center features a number of smaller businesses as well.

Plaza Latina
Buford Highway, Norcross
no phone

Across the street from Centro Norcross, another grocery store and collection of small businesses cater to Spanish-speaking customers.

DeKalb Farmers' Market
3000 East Ponce de Leon Avenue, Decatur
(404) 377-6400

DeKalb Farmers' Market, the oldest of the truly international food markets, attracts busloads of folks from Alabama, Ten-

Insiders' Tip
Atlanta has the third-highest per-capita Hispanic population among major cities in the United States.

More than 200 countries sell Coca-Cola. PHOTO: THE WORLD OF COCA-COLA ATLANTA

nessee—even Florida. All mingle with the locals searching for exotic spices, canned goods, fresh fish, breads, and pastries made on the premises, as well as regional and imported vegetables and fruit. Employees come from every corner of the globe and wear badges listing the languages they speak.

Harry's Farmers' Markets
2025 Satellite Point, Duluth
(770) 416–6900
1180 Upper Hembree Road, Roswell
(770) 664–6300
70 Powers Ferry Road, Marietta
(770) 578–4400

Harry's Farmers' Markets are a gourmet's dream-come-true, filled with delicacies from around the world. From the commonplace to the exotic, including fish, cheese, wine, flowers, coffee, and gourmet meals to go, at Harry's you can eat well and grow large. Harry's has recently been purchased by Whole Foods Markets, a national "natural foods" chain, which has

promised to keep the well-loved supermarkets more or less intact but has closed the Harry's in a Hurry take-out shops.

Educational, Cultural, and Business Organizations

Alliance Française d'Atlanta
1360 Peachtree Street NE, Suite 850
(404) 875–1211
www.afatl.com

Founded in Paris in 1883, Alliance Française has more than 1,200 chapters in 120 nations. The Atlanta chapter, one of 150 in the United States, was founded in 1912 to encourage the study of the French language and culture and to promote friendly relations between French-speaking people and Americans.

In addition to a full range of French language courses, the Alliance has a library of 3,500 volumes and sponsors many special activities, which include art exhibits, recitals, annual trips to French-speaking countries, and a big bash to celebrate Bastille Day, July 14.

Atlanta Hispanic Chamber of Commerce
1961 North Druid Hills Road NE, Suite 201B
(404) 929–9998

The Chamber of Commerce sponsors annual awards honoring Hispanic business-people making a mark in Atlanta. With Hispanic buying power in Georgia of approximately $2.7 billion in '97 (the last full year accurate figures are available for), it's not difficult to understand why this group has approximately 400 members.

Atlanta International Museum
285 Peachtree Center Avenue
(404) 688–2467

The small but eclectic museum's mission is to advance global understanding by celebrating and experiencing the many cultures of the world through exhibitions of international art and design. Recent exhibitions have included Scottish tartans, Guatemalan art, Japanese tsuzure-ori, and African textiles.

Atlanta International School
2890 North Fulton Drive
(404) 841–3896
www.aischool.org

Atlanta International School is an independent school for American and international students in kindergarten through 12th grade. Primary school students participate in a dual language program, taking all subjects in English and another language—French, German, or Spanish. Secondary students follow a curriculum leading to an International Baccalaureate diploma. More than half of the 800 students are international, representing 57 countries, and the faculty represents 27 nationalities. The school is accredited in the United States and recognized by educational authorities in France and Germany.

American-Israel Chamber of Commerce
1150 Lakehearn Drive
(404) 843–9426

Like most other chambers of commerce, this one is dedicated primarily to enhancing business. In this case the Chamber facilitates the development of business between the southeastern United States and Israel. Many members, however, join so that they might network among themselves. There is a social as well as educational element to all Chamber of Commerce gatherings since most include a speaker and refreshments. The American-Israel Chamber also sponsors trade trips to Israel.

Atlanta Virtuosi Foundation, Inc.
P.O. Box 77047, Atlanta 30357
(770) 938–8611

The objective of this group is to preserve the musical traditions of the Hispanic world. See our Festivals and Events chapter for details on presentations and festivals sponsored by the Foundation, including the Annual Hispanic Festival of the Arts.

British American Business Group
1199 Euclid Avenue
(404) 681–2224
www.babg.mindspring.com

British American Business Group strives to open lines of communication (business and social) between British companies doing business in Georgia and U.S. companies transacting business in Great Britain. The Canadian American Society and the Australian American Chamber of Commerce are also handled out of these offices. These groups serve as affinity gatherings for folks who just want to have fun with like-minded individuals. Social get-togethers from formal balls to pub crawls are scheduled throughout the year for each group.

Daughters of the British Empire
www.accessatlanta.com/community/
groups/habershamdbe/

This nonprofit, nonpolitical group is open to women of British or Commonwealth birth or ancestry, or women married to men of British or Commonwealth birth. Five chapters in Georgia (two in Atlanta, plus Cobb, Peachtree City, and Macon) hold social events and fund-raisers for the

Southern District Home, which is in Texas and serves elderly men and women of all nationalities. The spouse of the British counsel general is honorary state president of the society.

Georgia Council for International Visitors
3340 Peachtree Road NE
(404) 832–5560

The Georgia Council for International Visitors arranges professional and cultural exchanges among international visitors and U.S. citizens. The group's services include arranging host families for international visitors, conducting an eight-week discussion group on world affairs, and holding monthly meetings of the International Businesswomen's Network.

German American Chamber of Commerce
225 Peachtree Street NE, Suite 506
(404) 586–6800

The exclusive purpose of this Chamber is to facilitate business between the United States and Germany. The Chamber has 450 members who attend luncheons and galas, and make alliances through the Chamber with delegations from the German business sector.

Goethe-Institut Atlanta
Colony Square, Plaza Level
1197 Peachtree Street NE
(404) 892–2388
www.goethe.de/uk/atl/enindex.htm

The Atlanta institute is one of 11 U.S. locations of the Munich-based Goethe-Institut that was created in 1951 to promote the German language and intercultural exchanges. It is supported by the German government.

Goethe-Institut Atlanta offers German language courses at levels from beginning through advanced. Its library, containing more than 10,000 volumes, is free and open to the public. The Institut's programs include art exhibits, films, lectures, and performances. Many special events are free, and visitors enjoy free parking in the Colony Square garage. The Institut also organizes language courses in Germany. Call the Institut for a calendar of events and more information.

Hibernian Benevolent Society
P.O. Box 52641, Atlanta 30355
(404) 505–1208
www.atlantaweb.net/hibernian

This Society organizes the annual St. Patrick's Day parade in Buckhead, the Samhain Festival, concerts, and parties. It meets monthly at various locations. In addition, it is one of the supporting organizations of the Irish Information Center of Atlanta, a nonprofit cooperative effort of numerous Irish organizations to keep the area's Irish connected and informed. The center's phone number is (770) 594–5110.

Irish Social and Information Club
(404) 705–8008

This group helps newcomers from Ireland settle into life in Atlanta. It holds monthly meetings at various locations and proudly notes that "social" comes before "information" in its name. Call for information.

Japan-America Society of Georgia
233 Peachtree Street
Harris Tower, Suite 2222
(404) 524–7399
www.us-japan.org

Insiders' Tip

Atlanta hosts a series of festivals devoted to the international community, from the late winter African-American History Month celebrations to the springtime Atlanta Celtic Festival to the late summer JapanFest and Atlanta Greek Festival to the fall Scottish Highland Games and the Latin American Film Festival.

In 1980 a group of business and academic leaders formed the Japan-America Society of Georgia to increase knowledge among Georgians about Japanese culture; today it has more than 1,000 members. The society sponsors many programs throughout the year to enhance Georgians' understanding of Japan's customs and people and to provide Japanese visitors with an opportunity to make friends with Georgians. JapanFest, held each autumn, is a series of entertainment and educational events. Classes in Japanese arts, such as flower arranging and lantern making, are scheduled throughout the year. In 1990 the society hosted a dinner for Toshiki Kaifu on the occasion of the first-ever visit to the South by a Japanese prime minister.

Japanese Chamber of Commerce of Georgia
245 Peachtree Center Avenue
2201 Marquis Tower
(404) 522–0122

With more than 200 corporate members, the Japanese Chamber of Commerce of Georgia encourages business relations between the Peach State and Japan. In addition, it helps coordinate Japanese-themed events such as the JapanFest. (See our Festivals and Events chapter.)

League of United Latin American Citizens
Concilio 950 de Atlanta, P.O. Box 12104
Atlanta 30355
(770) 924–3440

If you're looking for information about social services and existing laws concerning the Hispanic community, this would be a good place to start.

Southern Center for International Studies
320 West Paces Ferry Road NW
(404) 261–5763
www.southerncenter.org

The Southern Center for International Studies is a nonprofit educational institution dedicated to increasing awareness and understanding of other countries, international issues, and the global environment. It holds conferences, develops educational materials, and provides re-

sources and contacts. It is housed in the historic Goodrum House, across West Paces Ferry Road from the Georgia Governor's Mansion.

Foreign Language/Music Radio Programs

Radio Free Georgia
WRFG 89.3 FM
(404) 523–3471
www.wrfg.org

WRFG is Atlanta's only community-operated station. It has extensive international programming. Call the station to have a one-page program guide faxed to you. Here are a few of the highlights, all of which are subject to change without notice. Many of the DJs work gratis—if they leave, so goes the program.

World Party (music and talk from Africa, North America, and the Caribbean), noon to 4:00 P.M. Monday through Friday

Pacifica News, 4:30 to 5:00 P.M. Monday through Friday

African Experience, noon to 3:00 P.M. Saturday

Rockers International, 3:00 to 6:00 P.M. Saturday

Serenata Latina, 6:00 to 9:00 P.M. Saturday

Music from India, 11:00 A.M. to 1:00 P.M. Sunday

The Celtic Show, 5:00 to 7:00 P.M. Sunday

The following radio stations also are primarily non-English music, news, or talk:

WPOL-AM (610) Spanish
WPBC-AM (1310) Korean
WXEM-AM (1460) Spanish
WAZX-AM (1550) and WAZX-FM (101.9) Spanish
WAOS-AM (1600) Spanish

In addition, Comcast and other metro cable TV systems carry Telemundo and a few other Spanish-language programming stations.

The Atlanta Hilton Hotel at dusk. PHOTO: ATLANTA CONVENTION & VISITORS BUREAU

Accommodations

Our goal is to present a good cross section of the various types of hospitality properties available around Atlanta. Due to space limitations, we cannot list every Atlanta location for each national chain. If you prefer to lodge with a particular chain, but don't see a hotel listed that's convenient for you, ask the company's central 800-number operator about other Atlanta locations. Unlike other chapters in this guide, we're breaking this chapter into more specific geographic locations for your convenience.

For more accommodations options, be sure to see our Bed-and-Breakfasts chapter.

Price Code

Each hotel's listing includes a symbol indicating a price range for a one-night stay, midweek, double occupancy, excluding tax. All hotels accept major credit cards unless otherwise noted.

$	Less than $75
$$	$76 to $125
$$$	$126 to $175
$$$$	$176 and more

Rates are often higher during major conventions or other peak travel times. On weekends and whenever business travel slows down, even the best hotels may cut their rates dramatically. Off-peak specials can easily take the rate into the next lower price category.

In the city of Atlanta and in Fulton County, hotels charge a 7 percent room tax in addition to the usual 6 percent sales tax.

Downtown

Interstates 85, 75, and 20 all come together where you see the gold dome of the capitol building. From here north to Fifth and Peachtree Streets and fanning out east to Boulevard Drive and west to Northside Drive is referred to as Downtown Atlanta.

Atlanta Downtown Travelodge $$
311 Courtland Street NE
(404) 659–4545, (800) 578–7878

Two blocks off Peachtree Street, this family-owned and -operated 71-room hotel is near the Marriott Marquis and Atlanta Hilton. Its amenities include a free continental breakfast and daily newspaper; cable TV with HBO; in-room coffeemaker; free covered parking; and a heated outdoor pool. The hotel is just off the Downtown Connector at the Courtland Street exit and within walking distance of Macy's.

Atlanta Hilton and Towers $$$–$$$$
255 Courtland Street NE
(404) 659–2000, (800) HILTONS

The 30-story downtown Hilton has 1,224 rooms (including 40 suites), a health club with an outdoor pool, and four outdoor tennis courts. The top three guest floors comprise the private Hilton Towers, whose lounge offers complimentary continental breakfast in the morning and hot hors d'oeuvres in the evening. Atop the hotel are the nightclub Another World and the renowned fine dining restaurant Nikolai's Roof (see our Restaurants chapter); downstairs is the South Pacific cuisine of Trader Vic's.

Atlanta Marriott Marquis $$$–$$$$
265 Peachtree Center Avenue NE
(404) 521–0000, (800) 228–9290

This is the hotel we take our houseguests to see. Just park the car in the circular entry (ask permission of the staff before you leave the vehicle: Tell them you want to go and gawk), take the escalator up one level and just look up and gasp. Suspended from the ceiling is a Japanese-kite–style work of art that swoops downward and seems to float for miles inside the 500-foot-high open atrium. Throughout the hotel are 25,000 plants, which lend a softening touch to this otherwise high-tech environment. The John Portman–designed, 50-story Marquis offers 32 elevators, two of which travel at 1,000 feet per minute, and a few of them are glass enclosed for those of us who enjoy what feels like a near death experience to some. Instead of being aligned, the floors are offset, producing an effect rather like a fan unfolding. Each floor has windows in the corridors offering great views of the city.

The 1,674-room Marquis is Atlanta's largest hotel and has received AAA's Four-Diamond Award. It has 150,000 square feet of function space, five restaurants, and 10 bars. There is also a health club (complimentary for guests) with an indoor/outdoor heated swimming pool. The hotel is connected directly to MARTA via Peachtree Center.

Atlanta Renaissance Hotel Downtown $$$
590 West Peachtree Street NW
(404) 881–6000, (800) 468–3571

The 25-story Renaissance is just east of the I–75/85 connector in the northern part of the Downtown district; it's actually closer to Midtown. The hotel has 504 rooms, two restaurants, and an outdoor pool. Guests on the Renaissance Club floors receive deluxe accommodations and amenities, including a complimentary continental breakfast. The North Avenue MARTA station is just up the street.

Courtyard Downtown Atlanta $$–$$$
175 Piedmont Avenue NE
(404) 659–2727, (800) 831–0224

On Piedmont Avenue just off the Downtown Connector (the merged I–75/85), this Courtyard has 211 rooms and suites, an outdoor pool, and a fitness center. The hotel offers limited convention and banquet services for up to 25 people. This is an enclosed building primarily attracting more of a business clientele than its sister hotel, the Marriott Fairfield. It has more upscale furnishings, a coffeemaker, an iron, and voice mail in each room.

Days Inn Atlanta/Downtown $$–$$$
300 Spring Street NW
(404) 523–1144

Across from the Apparel, Inforum, and Merchandise marts, this 263-room hotel offers remote-control cable TV with HBO and an outdoor pool. Kids 17 and younger stay free.

Fairfield Downtown Atlanta $$
175 Piedmont Avenue NE
(404) 659–7777, (800) 228–2800

Run by the same folks as the Courtyard Downtown Atlanta (mentioned previously), the Fairfield shares the same address, parking lot, outdoor pool, and fitness center with its sister facility. An exterior corridor hotel, the hotel has 242 rooms and suites and banquet services for 35.

Hampton Inn Atlanta $–$$
759 Washington Street
(404) 658–1961, (800) HAMPTON

You can't get much closer to big-league action than this 87-room hotel just up the street from Turner Field, the home of the Braves. The hotel has an outdoor pool and a weight room and is convenient to

Insiders' Tip

Whenever you check in, even with a previously made reservation, it is worth inquiring about the room rate. Frequently, the desk clerk will quote the "rack rate," which is the maximum normal rate, but will sometimes offer a reduced rate upon a polite, "Is this the best rate you could offer me?"

Downtown, the Georgia Capitol, City Hall, Zoo Atlanta, and the Georgia State MARTA station. It is just off I-20. Guests enjoy complimentary continental breakfasts and free local phone calls.

Holiday Inn Downtown Atlanta $$$
101 International Boulevard NE
(404) 524-5555, (800) 535-0707

This 260-room property is convenient to the Apparel, Merchandise, and Inforum marts, and it's adjacent to Centennial Olympic Park. On-site parking, a restaurant, a lounge, and an outdoor pool are among the hotel's amenities.

Hyatt Regency Atlanta $$$-$$$$
265 Peachtree Street NE
(404) 577-1234, (800) 233-1234

If you had moved to Atlanta in the '60s, the bold blue dome of the Hyatt Regency would have been the most dominant structure of Atlanta's skyline. It symbolized the brash city's enchantment with the future. Even now, though it's overshadowed by taller buildings, the John Portman–designed Hyatt Regency and its glowing UFO-shaped top remain among the city's best-known landmarks (though it is getting harder and harder to spot!).

The 23-story open atrium, a stunning architectural first when the hotel opened in 1967, is still beautiful today with its space-age glass elevators gracefully zipping up and down, a concept that has been copied throughout the world. In the Avanzare restaurant you can savor Italian cuisine while you gaze at exotic fish in the 1,800-gallon saltwater aquarium. Beneath the blue dome is the revolving Polaris restaurant and cocktail lounge. Nearby buildings on three sides now limit the view from the Polaris, but it's still a great meeting place and a lot of fun when you get a glimpse of Stone Mountain as the bar swings past an adjacent structure. The hotel has 1,264 guest rooms and 285,000 square feet of function space; it's served by the Peachtree Center MARTA station.

In an adjoining building a 30,000-square-foot ballroom, a 40,000-square-foot exhibit hall, and a 19,750-square-foot conference center help make up the complex.

Omni Hotel at CNN Center $$$$
100 CNN Center
(404) 659-0000, (800) THE OMNI

The Omni Hotel is inside CNN Center and adjacent to Georgia World Congress Center, the Georgia Dome, Philips Arena, and MARTA, and within walking distance of the headquarters of the *Atlanta Journal-Constitution* newspaper (which does offer tours). It has 465 deluxe rooms and suites and 40,000 square feet of meeting space. Within CNN Center are restaurants, shops, a six-screen movie theater, and the always-bustling CNN newsrooms. A $70 million expansion is currently under way, which will add more than 600 guest rooms to the property. It is scheduled for completion in 2003.

Paschal's Motor Hotel $
830 Martin Luther King Jr. Drive SW
(404) 577-3150

Five minutes west of downtown near the Georgia Dome and Atlanta University Center, Paschal's is an important part of Atlanta's history. What started as a modest restaurant opened by brothers James and Robert Paschal eventually became a large restaurant and a 120-room hotel (see our Restaurants chapter). Today it caters mainly to Clark Atlanta University students who rent on a monthly basis. Only two floors are available to guests other than the students. Paschal's is a nerve center of Atlanta's African-American community; it's said that much political history has taken place over the restaurant's famous fried chicken. Many R&B legends have played its Le Carousel Lounge.

The Ritz-Carlton Atlanta $$$$
181 Peachtree Street NE
(404) 659-0400, (800) 241-3333

Luxury is always the order of the day at the highly rated Ritz. Oil paintings and Persian rugs adorn the lobby; each of the 447 rooms and suites has a bay window. This elegant hotel and its mate, the Ritz-Carlton Buckhead, are favorites of visiting celebrities. Tea is served each afternoon in The Lobby Lounge and The Bar; The Restaurant serves award-winning French cuisine.

Sheraton Atlanta Hotel $$$–$$$$
165 Courtland Street
(404) 659–6500, (800) 335–3535

One block from Peachtree Center, the 765-room Sheraton, formerly a Radisson hotel, features an indoor pool, a business center, and a fully equipped health club. The hotel has 60,000 square feet of meeting space and offers two-level hospitality suites for entertaining.

The Suite Hotel at Underground $$$
54 Peachtree Street NE
(404) 223–5555, (877) 477–5549

On the Peachtree Street level at the west end of Underground Atlanta, this is Downtown's only all-suite hotel. The building dates from 1916. Each one of the 157 suites includes a marble bath, two cable TVs with movies, and three telephones; some suites feature whirlpool tubs. You can't beat the location for convenience: It's adjacent to all the shopping and fun at Underground, directly across Peachtree Street from the Five Points MARTA station, and close to the Capitol and state, county, and city office buildings.

The Westin Peachtree Plaza $$$$
210 Peachtree Street NW
(404) 659–1400, (800) 228–3000

The amazing John Portman–designed Peachtree Plaza opened in 1976 and for years was the tallest hotel in the world (it's still the tallest hotel in the United States). Within the 73-story glass cylinder are 1,068 rooms, including six bilevel supersuites suitable for entertaining up to 150 guests. The hotel includes three restaurants and an indoor/outdoor pool with health club facilities.

Even if you don't stay here, you owe yourself a drink in the rotating Sun Dial Lounge (see our Restaurants and Nightlife chapters). The ride up—nonstop to the 71st floor inside a glass elevator on the outside of the building—is the closest most people ever come to being fired from a cannon. The drinks are pricey, but the view is priceless. There's a $7.50 charge per person to visit the lounge/observation tower. The Peachtree Plaza is served by the Peachtree Center MARTA station.

Midtown

When the landscape changes from mainly tall office buildings to apartments and lovely, renovated homes, you'll know you are in Midtown. Unofficially it begins around Fifth and Peachtree Streets and continues north past the High Museum to Peachtree Road, meeting West Peachtree Street at a fork just opposite The Temple. In the east, Midtown crosses Piedmont Road and continues over until Ponce de Leon Avenue. It's bounded on the west by I–85.

Atlanta Marriott Suites Midtown $$$$
35 14th Street NW
(404) 876–8888, (800) 228–9290

Each of the 254 suites in this 18-story Marriott has a living room, a king-size bed, a marble bath with separate tub and shower, two remote-controlled TVs, two dual-line telephones, a refrigerator, and a wet bar. Complimentary coffee is served each morning. The health club has a whirlpool and an indoor/outdoor pool. The hotel is convenient to Colony Square, Woodruff Arts Center, One Atlantic Center, the AT&T building, and numerous restaurants and nightclubs.

Cheshire Motor Inn $
Cheshire Bridge Road
(404) 872–9628, (800) 827–9628

At the edge of Midtown, the Cheshire Motor Inn is inexpensive and no frills but right in the heart of things if you have to go downtown, uptown, or out of town and are on a tight budget. Located just off I–85 (and almost at the junction of GA 400), Cheshire Motor Inn has seen the neighborhood through all its ups and downs. At the moment, Cheshire Bridge Road is both funky and nice: funky because numerous strip clubs and gay bars are found scattered amongst some of Atlanta's nicest and most popular restaurants, including Nino's (see our Restaurants chapter). Cheshire Bridge also has more than its fair share of Thai restaurants. At this inn, you can drive your car right to your room and if you pick one toward the back end of the complex, when you go out your door you'll have a view of towering pines, kudzu, and the handsomely landscaped backyards of a few snazzy Morningside homes.

Courtyard by Marriott Midtown $$$–$$$$
1132 Techwood Drive NW
(404) 607–1112, (800) 321–2211

The Midtown Courtyard is off 14th Street on the Georgia Tech side of the Downtown Connector. The hotel has an outdoor pool and cable TV with HBO; it also offers a complimentary shuttle service to the Midtown MARTA station, Georgia Tech, and the downtown stores.

Days Inn-Midtown Peachtree Street $–$$
683 Peachtree Street NE
(404) 874–9200, (800) 329–7466

Frankly, my dear, this 12-story, 138-room Days Inn is right beside the Georgian Terrace, where the stars of *Gone With the Wind* stayed during its gala 1939 world premiere. It was built in 1925, and its location—directly across Peachtree from the Fox—is especially convenient for those in town to attend performances at the great theater. Numerous restaurants and bars are close by. A complimentary continental breakfast is offered; guest parking is $6 per day with unlimited in/out privileges for guests who give a deposit and receive a parking card.

Four Seasons $$$$
75 14th Street NE
(404) 881–9898, (800) 952–0702

Formerly the Continental Grand, this Four Seasons hotel has retained all that was grand: In the three-story lobby, light from the 10-foot-high Baccarat chandelier plays across the rose-colored Spanish marble walls around the broad grand staircase. A lounge on the mezzanine serves cocktails and afternoon high tea. Park 75 is a sit-down, white-tablecloth restaurant that serves breakfast, lunch, and dinner from early morning until 11:00 P.M. every day. The menu is "international with a Southern flair." The Ballroom showcases a skyline view from its 6,000-square-foot open terrace. The health club boasts the latest exercise equipment, and its gor-

Insiders' Tip

Look for deeply discounted hotel rates on weekends and holidays at major hotels, but not on July Fourth, when Atlanta is booked up for the Peachtree Road Race (see our Spectator Sports chapter).

geous indoor lap pool suggests a Roman bath.

The hotel occupies the first 20 floors of The Grand, a striking, 51-story skyscraper designed by the Atlanta firm Rabun Hatch & Associates. Offices and luxury condos are above the hotel.

The Granada Suite Hotel $$$
1302 West Peachtree Street
(404) 876–6100, (800) 548–5631

Built in 1924, the Granada has a charming Spanish Colonial style not often seen in Atlanta. Originally designed as a garden apartment building, it underwent an award-winning renovation in 1986. Suites feature a full-size kitchen with a wet bar, refrigerator, microwave, and coffeemaker. Enjoy a daily complimentary continental breakfast and complimentary cocktails on weekday evenings. An evening courtesy shuttle ferries guests to Midtown and downtown restaurants and clubs; the Arts Center MARTA station is right across the street.

The Highland Inn $$
644 North Highland Avenue
(404) 874–5756

Tucked away in the heart of the Virginia-Highland nightlife and shopping district, this three-story, 105-room inn has the flavor of a European hotel. Each room is furnished differently, with a variety of paintings and accents. Guests are invited to help themselves to a continental breakfast of pastries and croissants, served each morning in the lobby. Rooms include cable TV, air-conditioning units, radiators, and private bathrooms.

Ramada Inn and Conference Center $$-$$$
418 Armour Drive
(404) 873–4661, (800) 282–8222

Formerly the Lanier Plaza Hotel and a Holiday Inn, this hotel is just 5 miles from the hustle and bustle of downtown. More like a rural hacienda than a major metropolitan hotel, there are more than 34,000 square feet of meeting and banquet spaces as well as 346 rooms spread out around a large patio pool area with adjacent reflecting pool, fountain, and lush garden. Fifteen suites have fireplaces, whirlpools, and wet bars. The 120-seat restaurant and the lounge, a 40-seat facility, handle a mostly business crowd who arrive by airport shuttle or car. Parking is abundant right on the grounds.

Regency Suites Hotel $$-$$$
975 West Peachtree Street
at 10th Street
(404) 876–5003, (800) 642–3629

Each of the Regency's 96 suites includes a microwave-equipped kitchen, cable TV with HBO, and a living room with a queen-size sleeper sofa. In addition to a free continental breakfast daily, the hotel serves a complimentary "lite fare" dinner Monday through Thursday evenings. The

Insiders' Tip
The new breed of "extended stay" hotels very often have single-night rooms available, especially on weekends, and offer upscale amenities at bargain basement rates.

location is superb: Downtown and Buckhead are just minutes away, and the Midtown MARTA station is right next door.

Residence Inn by Marriott-Midtown $$$
1041 West Peachtree Street NW
(404) 872–8885, (800) 331–3131

Here's a convenient location: on West Peachtree (one way, northbound) between the Downtown Connector and the Midtown MARTA station. West Peachtree and the parallel Spring Street (one way, southbound) are nearly always quick routes between downtown and Midtown. Each of the 66 suites has a fully equipped kitchen and cable TV with HBO. A complimentary continental breakfast is served daily.

The hotel has a terrific landmark: It's right behind the giant broadcast tower that beams out the signal for WTBS Channel 17, the original cable SuperStation.

Sheraton Colony Square $$$-$$$$
188 14th Street NE
(404) 892–6000, (800) 422–7895

The 461-room Sheraton is part of Colony Square, which opened in 1969 as the South's first multiuse complex, which also features offices, luxury residences, and 160,000 square feet of retail space and restaurants. Piedmont Park and the Woodruff Arts Center are just one block away; there are numerous good restaurants within a couple of blocks.

Wyndham Midtown $$$
125 10th Street NE
(404) 873–4800, (800) 996–3426

Renovations in 1997 have freshened this centrally located, 11-story hotel. Being on the busy corner of Peachtree and 10th in the heart of Midtown, you'll have an easy walk to the Fox Theatre, Woodruff Arts Center, Piedmont Park, and numerous Midtown restaurants and clubs. The 191-room Wyndham's 7,000-square-foot Midtown Athletic Club features an indoor lap pool. Hotel amenities include in-room coffeemakers and cable TV. The deluxe band buses frequently parked outside attest to the well-located Wyndham's popularity with touring rock and country music stars. (The hotel is across 10th

Street from the Margaret Mitchell Museum, which is housed in the apartment building where Mitchell wrote *Gone With the Wind*. See our Attractions chapter.) A van is available to take groups to local restaurants and shops. The Terra Nova Cal-Ital Bar & Grill offers a blend of northern Californian and Italian cuisines for breakfast, lunch, and supper. The Terra Nova Lounge is a casual place to relax with friends, offering an extensive wine selection.

Buckhead

Beginning at about Pharr and Peachtree Roads and continuing north for a few miles, Buckhead, the poshest section of Atlanta, fans out east until Piedmont Road and west to Northside Drive. Here you'll find the Governor's Mansion and million-dollar homes as well as restaurants, galleries, and the finest shopping centers.

Courtyard Marriott Buckhead $$$–$$$$
3332 Peachtree Road
(404) 869–0818, (800) 321–2211

Within waving distance of the Grand Hyatt Atlanta and Wyndham Garden Hotel, competition must be stiff at this busy spot just off Piedmont Road at Tower Place. This Courtyard Marriott has real street appeal with a nicely landscaped corner and a charming bronze sculpture of three frolicking kids and their dog trying to fly kites. The marble lobby is also inviting with a centrally located fireplace that is an ideal meeting place in the winter. A full wall of glass overlooks a small but green sunning garden just off the indoor pool and exercise room. Nine floors with 181 rooms—of which one on each floor has a Jacuzzi in the living area—include coffeemaker, iron, hair dryers available upon request, and cable TV with HBO. A shuttle will deliver you to any destination within a 1-mile radius of the hotel (meaning you can get to malls and restaurants without having to do the short walk yourself, a blessing during Atlanta's withering heat in the summer and frequent downpours in the winter).

Doubletree Hotel Atlanta Buckhead $$$$
3342 Peachtree Road NE
(404) 231–1234

Just beyond the Grand Hyatt and facing the Courtyard Marriott and Tower Place is the Doubletree, formerly the Wyndham Garden Hotel, with 221 rooms on five floors. Formerly called the Tower Place hotel, its dark, masculine, library-style paneling throughout the lobby and lounge are a holdover from the early days. A restaurant on the first floor is where you can have all your meals if you opt not to partake of the fabulous restaurants at Lenox Square or Phipps Plaza nearby. Anthony's is also an easy walk down Piedmont Road, as is Bone's (see our Restaurants chapter). And Soto's for sushi is just across Piedmont Road. Amenities include coffeemakers with complimentary coffee, hair dryers, and remote-controlled cable TV. A real plus is complimentary privileges at Sports Life Fitness Center right there at Tower Walk. The hotel has 7,290 square feet of meeting space.

Embassy Suites Atlanta/Buckhead $$$
3285 Peachtree Road NE
(404) 261–7733, (800) EMBASSY

On Peachtree Road in Buckhead, each of the Embassy hotel's suites has two remote-control TVs, two telephone lines with voice mail, a refrigerator, a microwave, and a coffeemaker. There are indoor and outdoor pools, whirlpool and sauna facilities. There is also free transportation within a mile radius, which includes Phipps Plaza, Lenox Square, Lenox MARTA Station, and many restaurants and bars. Arriving guests may telephone from Lenox and Buckhead MARTA stations for free pickup. Secured parking for hotel guests is available.

Grand Hyatt Atlanta $$$$
3300 Peachtree Road NE
(404) 365–8100, (800) 233–1234

Atlanta's luxury hotels compete fiercely for the many prestigious charity balls that fill the social calendar during the year. This hotel opened in 1990 as the Nikko and immediately attracted high-profile affairs. The dramatic 440-room hotel's lavish lobby overlooks a three-story waterfall topped by a garden. You can stroll the Japanese garden via the second floor, where the Serenity Garden is true to its name. A pebble path leads you past native azaleas and other flora and gently flowing fountains. Along the way there are plank benches for sitting a spell and contemplating the day. The garden terminates at an American-style bar surrounding a very large swimming pool and sunning deck. The Lobby Lounge serves cocktails in a cozy clublike atmosphere, and the Cassis Restaurant offers bistro-style fare for breakfast and lunch. Guests on the top five floors have access to a private lounge with a view of the city. Excellent service is a hallmark of this hotel.

Hampton Inn/Atlanta Buckhead $$
3398 Piedmont Road NE
(404) 233–5656, (800) HAMPTON

Here's a moderately priced hotel in the heart of Buckhead. The 154-room Hampton is centrally located between Buckhead's major dining/entertainment area and megamalls Lenox Square and Phipps Plaza, near the Grand Hyatt and the Tower Place office complex. A free continental breakfast is served daily; there's no charge for local calls; and the hotel has an outdoor pool.

Holiday Inn at Lenox $$–$$$
3377 Peachtree Road NE
(404) 264–1111, (800) 526–0247

It's a shopper's dream come true: The 11-floor, 297-room Holiday Inn at Lenox is beside Lenox Square and just south of Phipps Plaza. Rooms include cable TV with HBO, voice mail, modem hookups, and coffeemakers. There's an outdoor pool, and the Lenox MARTA station is a short walk away.

J.W. Marriott Hotel at Lenox $$$$
3300 Lenox Road NE
(404) 262–3344, (800) 228–9290

This mirrored building was built literally in the back parking lot of Lenox Square and is directly across from the Lenox MARTA station entrance. There are 371 guest rooms, including four suites and six executive parlors equipped with Murphy beds that, when raised, allow for a business meeting space. Special features include a health club with an indoor pool. All rooms are equipped with cable TV (with movies), dedicated modem jacks, two telephones, robes, hair dryers, and designer toiletries. An enclosed walkway, lined with the work of local and regional artists, leads to the 1.5-million-square-foot Lenox Square.

The New Sheraton Garden Buckhead $$$–$$$$
3405 Lenox Road NE
(404) 261–9250, (800) 241–8260

Lenox Square, Phipps Plaza, and the Lenox MARTA station are just steps away from the hotel, where the 360 rooms and suites feature cable TV, voice mail, and computer ports. Club level guests get deluxe accommodations and complimentary continental breakfasts.

Residence Inn by Marriott Buckhead $$$
2960 Piedmont Road NE
(404) 239–0677, (800) 331–3131

Just south of the intersection of Piedmont and Pharr Roads and landscaped with pretty crape myrtle trees in fuchsia and white, this Residence Inn has a great location—close to the Buckhead Diner and the Buckhead Life Group's other restaurants, including Pricci (see our Restaurants chapter). Amenities appeal especially to long-term travelers: fully equipped kitchens, complimentary breakfast and hospitality hours, newspapers, and health club privileges. There's also an outdoor pool. Most suites have curbside parking and a private entrance.

The Ritz-Carlton Buckhead $$$$
3434 Peachtree Road NE
(404) 237–2700, (800) 241–3333

Directly across from Lenox Square and Phipps Plaza stands the flagship hotel in the Ritz-Carlton chain. Lavishly appointed with art and antiques, the 553-room Ritz is a favorite of celebrities (everyone from touring rock superstars to visiting royalty stays here). The Dining Room is one of the city's best-known fine dining restaurants (see our Restaurants chapter). The fitness center has an indoor pool. Guests on the Club level enjoy greater privacy, an exclusive lounge, and five complimentary meal presentations daily. On weekends, guests dance to a three-piece band with a singer.

Summerfield Suites
Hotel Atlanta Buckhead $$$–$$$$
505 Pharr Road
(404) 262–7880, (800) 833–4353

Suites at this hotel include two or three color TVs and a VCR; the larger suites have three beds and two baths. There's a complimentary grocery shopping service Monday through Friday. The hotel hosts a complimentary beer and wine happy hour Monday through Thursday and offers a continental breakfast every morning. On weekdays, the hotel's shuttle provides free transportation within a 3-mile radius, which covers all of Buckhead. The exercise facility has a heated pool and whirlpool.

Swissôtel Atlanta $$$–$$$$
3391 Peachtree Road NE
(404) 365–0065, (800) 253–1397

The Swissôtel is patterned after the elegant fashion of modern Europe: sleek and smooth with curving lines and sweeping

The posh surroundings in the Ritz-Carlton Lobby Lounge offer patrons the elegant atmosphere typical of Buckhead area accommodations.

PHOTO: THE RITZ-CARLTON, BUCKHEAD

expanses of glass. It was designed by the Atlanta firm Rabun Hatch & Associates. The interior art is spectacular and belies the rather uninteresting exterior. The hotel is the site of numerous charity balls during the year. Each of the 365 guest rooms in the 22-floor property features three phones and a modem hookup, voice mail, cable TV with HBO, bathrobes, and a hair dryer. The hotel's health club has an indoor pool. A special benefit is a complimentary shuttle service to destinations within 3 miles of the hotel, which includes all of Buckhead. Lenox Square is next door; the Lenox MARTA station is only a half-mile from the hotel. Celebrity visitors to the Swissôtel have included Whitney Houston and The Judds.

Northeast Expressway/ Emory

On both sides of I-85 are former service roads that were used during the construction of the expressway. These roads are now lined with warehouses, discount shops, hotels, and motels attracting people on the move.

Emory University has spawned its own host of motels and hotels around and about the campus for visiting parents and business folk. Take I-85 east at Clairmont Road and proceed to North Decatur Road, where you'll turn right. You can't miss the campus and surrounding accommodations.

Atlanta Marriott Century Center $$$
2000 Century Center Boulevard NE
(404) 325-0000, (800) 325-3535
Alongside I-85, 8 miles northeast of downtown Atlanta, Century Center is a major corporate development that includes the Marriott hotel. Its 287 rooms surround a 15-story atrium. Guest rooms include in-room movies and a dual-line phone system. With easy access to both the Northeast Expressway and the Perimeter, the hotel is well situated for those doing business on the north side and in the counties northeast of Atlanta.

Emory Conference Center Hotel $$-$$$
1615 Clifton Road NE
(404) 712-6000, (800) 933-6679
On five floors available for groups or individuals, this hotel has 198 rooms with amenities, including exercise facilities with an indoor pool, sauna, spa with a massage therapist available by appointment, iron and board in every room, and coffeemaker. There's a lobby lounge with pool tables and a large-screen TV, and a dining room with full kitchen service providing food service during off hours. A tennis court and a basketball court are on the premises. A nature trail for less strenuous exercise is also part of the grounds.

Nearby is Fernbank Museum (see our Attractions chapter), Emory Hospital and University, and Centers for Disease Control and Prevention (see our Health Care chapter), and it's an easy cab ride to Virginia-Highland and all the nightlife and restaurants that have made the neighborhood a hub for in-town folks.

Emory Inn $$
1641 Clifton Road NE
(404) 712-6700, (800) 933-6679
Emory Inn is near the center of the Emory University and Hospital area, directly across the street from the Centers for Disease Control and Prevention. The inn has 105 guest rooms, a lounge, and cafe; a pool and a hydrotherapy pool are outside. The inn also manages the nearby D. Abbott Turner Center, an architecturally award-winning, 7,000-square-foot facility that can accommodate groups of up to 250 people. Amenities are identical to those listed for the Emory Conference Center Hotel (detailed previously), which this group also manages.

Hampton Inn North Druid Hills $$
1975 North Druid Hills Road NE
(404) 320-6600, (800) HAMPTON
With 111 rooms, this Hampton Inn is conveniently situated between the Emory area and Buckhead at exit 31 off I-85. There's a complimentary continental breakfast daily, and the hotel has a pool and an exercise room. The immediate area offers a range of moderately priced dining choices.

Holiday Inn Select Decatur $$
130 Clairmont Avenue
(404) 371-0204, (800) 225-6079
In downtown Decatur, this 185-room hotel pampers its guests with an amenities package that includes in-room hair dryers, irons and ironing boards, and coffeemakers, plus free local phone calls, editions of *USA Today,* and transportation within a 5-mile radius. On the Executive Level, enjoy complimentary continental breakfast and the Sunday-through-Thursday nightly cocktail reception. The nearby Decatur MARTA station makes getting around the metro area a snap.

Holiday Inn Select Perimeter Dunwoody $$$
4386 Chamblee Dunwoody Road
(770) 457–6363, (800) HOLIDAY

This hotel is southwest of the intersection of Chamblee Dunwoody Road and I-285 (exit 22), convenient to the Perimeter Mall area. Each of the 250 guest rooms has two telephones and cable TV with HBO. The fitness center has an outdoor pool. The hotel has a New Orleans look with wrought iron detailing.

Radisson Northlake $$
4156 LaVista Road
(770) 938–1026

Just inside the Perimeter in the busy Northlake area, this Radisson's amenities include cable TV with movies, an exercise facility, and an outdoor pool with a hot tub on deck. In the hotel's restaurant, you may order from the menu or choose from the breakfast or lunch buffet. For large functions, the ballroom seats 350; it has its own entrance lobby and a deck overlooking the pool and patio.

Northwest Expressway

Up and down the corridors surrounding I-75 are hotels and motels for businesspeople visiting or traveling through Georgia.

Courtyard by Marriott Cumberland Center $$
3000 Cumberland Circle
(770) 952–2555, (800) 321–2211

This 182-room hotel across from Cumberland Mall has a full-service health club with an indoor pool, sauna, and spa. Covered parking and in-room coffee are complimentary; rooms include cable TV with HBO.

Crowne Plaza Powers Ferry $$
6345 Powers Ferry Road NW
(770) 955–1700

The Crowne Plaza has 299 sleeping rooms and four parlor suites. All rooms have an AM/FM clock radio. At the fitness center you'll find an indoor/outdoor heated pool. A courtesy van provides free transportation within a 3-mile radius. The hotel staff

speak several languages, including French, Spanish, Portuguese, and German.

Embassy Suites Galleria $$
2815 Akers Mill Road
(770) 984–9300, (800) EMBASSY

Walking to Cumberland Mall, the Galleria, and the Cobb Convention Center is just a stroll, really, through the various parking lots around these shopping and meeting facilities. With the pedestrian walkway over Cobb Parkway now complete, it's a breeze to get to the only Sears inside the Perimeter in this part of town. With 261 rooms on nine stories, this Embassy Suites has an interesting lobby with palm trees surrounding a pyramid restaurant. Although there is no exercise room in the building, a shuttle good for a 3-mile radius will drive to a nearby health club that offers guest privileges. Two-room suites, full American breakfast in the lobby, and free daily cocktail receptions are part of the amenities.

Hampton Inn Atlanta Cumberland $$
2775 Cumberland Parkway
(770) 333–6006, (800) HAMPTON

One block from Cumberland Mall, Cobb Galleria Centre, and the Galleria Specialty Mall, this 128-room inn offers guests free continental breakfasts, free local calls, and cable TV with HBO.

Homewood Suites Atlanta-Cumberland $$
3200 Cobb Parkway SW
(770) 988–9449, (800) CALL HOME

Each of the Homewood's 124 luxury suites designed for extended stay include two color TVs, a VCR, and a kitchen with a refrigerator, stove, microwave, and coffeemaker; 28 suites even have fireplaces. Guests receive a free *USA Today* and continental breakfast served in the lobby, plus there's a complimentary evening social hour. Free transportation is provided within a 5-mile radius.

Renaissance Waverly $$$
2450 Galleria Parkway
(770) 953–4500, (800) HOTELS1

Connected to the $50 million Cobb Galleria Centre trade show complex, this luxury hotel has 521 rooms arranged around a sunlit, 14-story atrium. Guest rooms have two telephones and cable TV. Coffee and a copy of *USA Today* are delivered free of charge with a guest's wake-up call. The Club Floor offers complimentary continental breakfast and evening hors d'oeuvres and nonalcoholic beverages, plus deluxe accommodations and amenities. Through the Galleria and across the street is the 150-store Cumberland Mall. The hotel provides free transportation within a 1-mile radius.

Sheraton Galleria $$$
2844 Cobb Parkway SE
(770) 955–3900

The 17-story, all-suite Sheraton is next to the 1.2-million-square-foot Cumberland Mall and across the street from Cobb Galleria Centre and the Galleria Specialty Mall. Each suite includes two phones with voice mail, two remote-control TVs, a VCR (movies may be rented), a refrigerator with an honor bar, a microwave, and a coffeemaker with free coffee and tea. The fitness center has indoor and outdoor pools, and a courtesy van provides free transportation within a 3-mile radius. The business center is available around the clock.

Wyndham Garden Hotel-Vinings $$$
2857 Paces Ferry Road
(770) 432–5555, (800) 996–3426

The Vinings Wyndham is inside I-285 south of its intersection with U.S. Highway 41. Each of the 159 guest rooms includes remote-control cable TV, a hair dryer, and a coffeemaker. There is an adjacent athletic center with a heated outdoor pool and two lighted tennis courts that hotel guests may use. At the center of the property, you'll find a landscaped, tree-shaded garden. The Garden Cafe serves breakfast, lunch, and dinner daily. Cumberland Mall and Cobb Galleria Centre are five minutes away; downtown Atlanta is 15 minutes southeast.

Airport

Atlanta Airport Hilton and Towers $$–$$$
1031 Virginia Avenue
(404) 767–9000, (800) HILTONS

North of Hartsfield Airport, this 503-room hotel has in-room coffeemakers and a sports bar with a 100-inch TV. Monitors in the lobby display updated flight information for all the major airlines. Children, regardless of age, stay for free in their parents' room.

Courtyard by Marriott Atlanta Airport North $$$
3399 International Boulevard, Hapeville
(404) 559–1043, (800) 321–2211

The world headquarters of Delta Air Lines is a quarter-mile from this Courtyard, which operates a complimentary airport shuttle. The hotel has an exercise room and an outdoor pool; guest rooms include coffee and tea service and remote-control cable TV with HBO.

Courtyard by Marriott Atlanta Airport South $$
2050 Sullivan Road, College Park
(770) 997–2220, (800) 321–2211

This Courtyard is inside the Perimeter just south of Hartsfield Airport. It has an indoor pool and operates a free airport shuttle service for guests. You'll find HBO, CNN, and movies in each room, accessible through the remote control at your bedside. There are computer and fax hookups in each room. Weekday copies of *USA Today* are delivered to your door. All rooms feature coffee and tea service.

Embassy Suites Atlanta Airport $$–$$$
4700 Southport Road at Embassy Drive
(404) 767–1988, (800) EMBASSY

This 234-suite hotel has coffeemakers, hair dryers, irons and boards, microwaves, and refrigerators in its two-room suites. Like all of the other Embassy Suites, there are two TVs with cable and HBO in each room. Kids younger than 18 stay free in their parents' room. A complimentary full breakfast is cooked to order daily, and evening hors d'oeuvres with alcoholic and nonalcoholic drinks can be found at happy hour every night.

Hampton Inn Atlanta Airport $$
3450 Bobby Brown Parkway, East Point
(404) 767–9300, (800) HAMPTON

This hotel is a new eight-story property just 2 miles from the airport. All rooms feature a microwave and refrigerator, coffeemaker, and 27-inch TV. There is a free continental breakfast each morning, and coffe and fresh-baked cookies are served in the lobby in the evenings.

Holiday Inn Atlanta Airport North $$$
1380 Virginia Avenue
(404) 762–8411

Hartsfield Airport is just a mile away from this 500-room Holiday Inn, and there's a complimentary, 24-hour airport shuttle service for guests; you can also use the shuttle to access the Airport MARTA station for quick transportation into town. Fitness buffs will enjoy the outdoor pool, exercise room, and lighted tennis courts. The hotel has a coffee shop, restaurant, and lounge.

Radisson Airport $$
5010 Old National Highway
(404) 761–4000, (800) 334–3364

This 232-room hotel is just outside the Perimeter and south of Hartsfield Airport. Amenities include airport pickup and complimentary morning coffee. Two hospitality suites are ideal for entertaining; the conference center has nine function rooms and a ballroom for 350. The hotel has an indoor/outdoor heated pool and a health club.

Renaissance Atlanta Hotel-Concourse $$$
One Hartsfield Centre Parkway
(404) 209–9999, (800) HOTELS1

Just seven minutes from the airport, Renaissance Atlanta Hotel has 387 rooms and 17 suites. Call from the airport and receive direct pickup services when you arrive. When departing, the free shuttle takes you to MARTA from the hotel so you may catch the train direct to the airport. Each room has a coffeemaker, cable TV, and a minibar. The hotel's health club has a swimming pool, sauna, and whirlpool open to all guests. There's a restaurant serving breakfast, lunch, and dinner, a bar, and a lobby gift shop.

Beyond Atlanta

Barrow County

Château Élan $$$$
100 Rue Charlemagne, Braselton
(678) 425–0900, (800) 233–WINE

Set on 3,100 acres 45 minutes northeast

Insiders' Tip

The "continental breakfast" frequently seen offered by chain motels means primarily a light meal of sweet rolls, muffins, fruit, juices, and coffee. A few chains now offer "cooked-to-order breakfast," which is more along the line of a typical American breakfast you would find in a regular restaurant.

of Atlanta off I-85, this unusual resort mixes business with pleasure. The complex includes a French-inspired chateau; a 25,000-square-foot conference center; 306 rooms; 170 acres that hold 63 holes of golf; a par 3 walking course; a Stan Smith–designed, seven-court tennis center; an equestrian show center; an art gallery; a European-style health spa; a wine market; horseback and nature trails; and more than 200 acres of vineyards producing a variety of fine wines.

Each of the resort's deluxe rooms and suites includes an oversize bath with separate garden tub and shower, three dual-line phones, a personal safe, and a minibar. Guests staying at the spa have their pick of 14 individually appointed rooms, from Victorian wicker to Georgia Peach. Golf, tennis, and luxurious spa packages are offered. The ground's seven restaurants offer a range from fine dining to pub food in the Irish tavern that was hauled piece by piece across the Atlantic. Since it opened in 1984, the Château Élan winery has received numerous awards for excellence. Today, it produces 15 varieties of wine; free tours with wine tastings take place every day except Christmas.

Clayton County

Holiday Inn Atlanta South $$
6288 Old Dixie Highway, Jonesboro
(770) 968–4300

Seven miles south of Hartsfield Airport, this 180-room Holiday Inn offers free parking, an outdoor pool and sundeck, cable TV, pay-per-view movies, desks with data ports, and a self-service laundry. The restaurant serves three meals daily; the bar re-creates the feel of an old library, complete with books. Clayton State College, with its world-class recital facility Spivey Hall, is just 3 miles away.

Cobb County

Atlanta Marriott Northwest $$$
200 Interstate North Parkway
(770) 952–7900, (800) 228–9290

Each room includes cable TV with HBO, two direct-dial phones with voice mail,

high-speed Internet access, and an iron and ironing board. The fitness center includes three lighted tennis courts, an indoor/outdoor pool, and a whirlpool. This 16-floor hotel has three concierge levels. Airport shuttles take guests nonstop to the airport.

Drury Inn and Suites $$
1170 Powers Ferry Plaza, Marietta
(770) 612–0900

This seven-story inn has 143 rooms, an exercise center with a whirlpool, an indoor/outdoor pool, and a complimentary breakfast. Deluxe rooms with king-size beds come with refrigerators stocked with snacks. Children under 18 stay free with parents; small pets less than 20 pounds are welcome.

Fairfield Inn $$
2191 Northwest Parkway, Marietta
(770) 952–9863

Just minutes from Dobbins Air Reserve Base, White Water park, and American Adventures amusement park, this 130-room hotel has an outdoor heated pool and a complimentary breakfast. Children under 18 stay free with parents.

Hampton Inn Six Flags $$
1100 North Blairs Bridge Road, Austell
(770) 941–1499, (800) HAMPTON

The 74-room Hampton Inn has a pool and cable TV service. It's only 3 miles from all the screams and excitement of Six Flags Over Georgia, and about 15 minutes from downtown Atlanta on I-20.

Hawthorn Suites Hotel Atlanta-Northwest $$–$$$
1500 Parkwood Circle
(770) 952–9595, (800) 338–7812

The 280-unit, all-suite Hawthorn is nestled on 13 landscaped acres northeast of the I-75/I-285 interchange. A complimentary breakfast buffet is served daily, and the outdoor picnic areas feature gas grills. Each one- or two-bedroom suite includes cable TVs, a fully equipped kitchen with microwave, plus a balcony or patio. The recreational amenities include an outdoor pool with waterfalls and a whirlpool, two lighted tennis courts, and a basketball court.

Hyatt Regency Suites Perimeter Northwest $$$
2999 Windy Hill Road, Marietta
(770) 956–1234

All of the 200 rooms in this seven-story hotel are suites, with hair dryers, coffeemakers, irons and ironing boards, and three televisions. A heated outdoor pool and a fitness center with a whirlpool are on the grounds, located about 10 minutes from Dobbins Air Reserve Base, the Galleria Specialty Mall, and Cumberland Mall. Children under 18 stay free with parents.

Marietta Conference Center and Resort $$$
500 Powder Springs Street, Marietta
(770) 427–2500, (888) 685–2500

Sitting on one of the highest spots in the city of Marietta, this hotel, resort, and conference center offers spectacular views of the county's countryside. Located just a few blocks from the town square, the center sits on 132 acres with 199 rooms, all with desks, computers with Internet access, two phones with data lines and voice mail, minibars, hair dryers, coffeemakers, terry cloth robes, and irons and ironing boards. There's a 20,000-square-foot meeting area as well as a 6,500-square-foot ballroom, an outdoor pool with hot tub, a health club, two lighted tennis courts, and a golf course.

At the time of the Civil War, the center's grounds were home to the Georgia Military Institute. Union forces burned the school but left behind the headmaster's home, Brumby Hall. The modest cottage, decorated in period furnishings, and its extensive formal gardens are popular for outdoor events and weddings.

The center has a pub with billiard tables, darts, and televisions. The elegant Hamilton's restaurant has a main room overlooking the golf course, as well as an intimate private dining room (see our Restaurants chapter).

Northwest Atlanta Hilton $$–$$$
2055 South Park Place, Marietta
(770) 953–9300, (800) 234–9304

Insiders' Tip

Room prices for area motels and hotels fall dramatically the farther you travel in any direction from downtown, so if you have traveled here by car, it is worth the extra travel time to check out the offerings a few exits up the highway.

Near the Windy Hill exit off I-75 in Marietta, the Hilton has 222 deluxe guest rooms, an indoor/outdoor pool, and a fitness room. You'll receive a complimentary paper daily. A van provides free transportation to attractions within a 5-mile radius, which include the Galleria Centre, Cumberland Mall, and the wet, wild thrills of White Water amusement park. There is no charge for children, regardless of age, when they occupy the same room as their parents.

Wingate Inn $$
1250 Franklin Road, Marietta
(770) 989–0071

This new facility close to I-75 has 80 rooms, an indoor pool, and a fitness center with whirlpool, and serves a free continental breakfast. Each unit features a coffeemaker, refrigerator, two-line phones, and data ports. Children under 18 stay free.

DeKalb County

Crowne Plaza Ravinia $$$
4355 Ashford-Dunwoody Road
(770) 395–7700, (800) 227–6963

In a parklike, wooded, 10-acre setting near Perimeter Mall, the Crowne Plaza Ravinia has a two-story greenhouse lobby. Its 15 floors include 495 rooms, 29 deluxe suites, and a club level with a private lounge, where guests enjoy a complimentary breakfast buffet and evening cocktail hour. The fitness center has an indoor pool, a lighted tennis court, a sauna, and a whirlpool. Off the lobby is the Market, a cafe court where guests can pick up yogurt, pizza, or French pastries.

Embassy Suites Perimeter Center $$$
1030 Crowne Pointe Parkway
(770) 394–5454, (800) EMBASSY

Each of the 241 suites includes a living room with a queen-size sofa bed, a separate bedroom, plus two televisions, a coffeemaker, microwave, wet bar, and refrigerator. There's an indoor pool, and guests are invited for a free, cooked-to-order breakfast every morning as well as a two-hour reception nightly. A shuttle will drop you off at Perimeter Mall or the corporate offices within a 3-mile radius.

Hampton Inn Stone Mountain $$
1737 Mountain Industrial Boulevard
Stone Mountain
(770) 934–0004, (800) HAMPTON

The 129-room Hampton Inn is 20 minutes east of downtown and just 3 miles from all the fun at Georgia's Stone Mountain Park. Amenities include an exercise room and a pool, free continental breakfast, and free local calls, as well as cable TV and microwaves.

Marriott Perimeter Center $$$$
246 Perimeter Center Parkway NE
(770) 394–6500, (800) 228–9290

The 402-room Marriott is just outside I-285 at exit 21 about halfway between I-75 and I-85 at the heart of the booming Perimeter Center area. It offers an indoor/outdoor pool, lighted tennis courts, an exercise center with a spa, a lounge, and a full-service restaurant that provides room service. Guest rooms feature two phones and cable TV. Concierge-level guests receive a complimentary newspaper, a continental breakfast, and hors d'oeuvres. Right across the street is the 1.2-million-square-foot Perimeter Mall and the Dunwoody MARTA station; the surrounding area is a booming retail mecca, featuring everything from exclu-

sive specialty shops to the large electronics discounter Best Buy.

W Hotel Atlanta $$$$
111 Perimeter Center West
(770) 396–6800, (800) 683–6100

Opened in 1999 as the second W in the United States, this luxury hotel with a restaurant and lounge has a parklike setting near Perimeter Mall. The 252 rooms have balconies and cable TV; 22 suites have fully equipped kitchens. The fitness center includes an exercise room and an outdoor pool.

Fulton County

Courtyard by Marriott Roswell $$–$$$
1500 Market Boulevard, Roswell
(770) 992–7200, (800) 321–2211

This north metro hotel is 3 miles from historic Roswell and close by the Chattahoochee Nature Center. The 154 rooms include coffee and tea service and cable TV with HBO. There's an outdoor pool, an indoor whirlpool, and a minigym. Ask about special rates for extended stays.

Doubletree Guest Suites $$$
6120 Peachtree Dunwoody Road
(770) 668–0808, (800) 222–TREE

Two blocks from Perimeter Mall, this 224-suite hotel features an indoor/outdoor pool, fully equipped health club, restaurant, and room service. Each suite has two cable TVs, a coffeemaker, wet bar, refrigerator, and a patio or balcony. A complimentary business center is available 24 hours a day. All suites have high-speed Internet access.

Hilton Garden Inn $$
4025 Windward Plaza, Alpharetta
(770) 360–7766

This six-story, 164-room inn is close to GA 400 and the homes, restaurants, and businesses of the Windward area. Each room features a desk area, two phones, voice mail, data port, microwave, refrigerator, coffeemaker, iron and ironing board, and hair dryer. The property includes a 24-hour business center with computer rentals, indoor pool, fitness center, coin laundry, and a restaurant that is open 24 hours. Children under 18 stay free with parents.

Holiday Inn Atlanta Roswell $$$$
1075 Holcomb Bridge Road
(770) 992–9600, (800) HOLIDAY

Billed as Roswell's only full-service hotel, this 172-room hotel is 3 miles from North Point Mall and Chattahoochee River Park. Amenities include remote satellite TV with Showtime and free morning coffee every day. Airport shuttle and secretarial services are available. The hotel also has a restaurant, bar, and banquet and conference facilities for up to 400 people.

Masters Economy Inn Six Flags $
4120 Fulton Industrial Boulevard
(404) 696–4690, (800) 633–3434

This 167-room motel is 7 miles west of downtown and just 3 miles from Six Flags Over Georgia. Local calls are free; rooms include cable TV with HBO. There's an outdoor pool.

SpringHill Suites by Marriott $$
12730 Deerfield Parkway, Alpharetta
(770) 751–6900

This three-story hotel has 82 suites, with voice mail, data ports, two-line phones, wet bar, and hair dryer. Wake up to a continental breakfast or relax in the outdoor pool and spa. An exercise center, a gift shop, and newsstand are also on the grounds.

Summerfield Suites Hotel $$$
760 Mt. Vernon Highway
(404) 250–0110, (800) 833–4353

The Summerfield is in the Perimeter Mall area; the 122 one- and two-bedroom suites have full kitchens, videocassette players, and voice mail. A complimentary breakfast buffet is served each morning; a beer and wine social is offered Monday through Thursday evenings. Barbecue grills, an exercise room, a pool, and a whirlpool are available for guests.

Westin Atlanta North $$$–$$$$
7 Concourse Parkway
(770) 395–3900, (800) WESTIN–1

At the Concourse, a wooded 64-acre corporate center near Perimeter Mall, the 370-room Westin rises 20 stories above a lake. Sixteen suites are offered, with CD players, desks with data ports, coffeemakers, irons and ironing boards, and hair dryers. There are also 26 meeting rooms, a tiered conference room, and a business center. Guests pay $10 per day to use the adjacent 85,000-square-foot Concourse Athletic Club, which has seven clay tennis courts, indoor and outdoor 25-meter pools, a full-size gym, a cushioned indoor running track, and private tanning. The on-site restaurant serves breakfast, lunch, and dinner. Children 17 and under stay free with parents.

Wingate Inn $$
1005 Kingswood Place, Alpharetta
(770) 649–0955

Close to GA 400, this 94-room inn features a business center and fitness center with spa. Rooms have coffeemakers, hair dryers, and data ports. Kids under 18 stay free with parents. Complimentary wine and beer reception Monday through Wednesday.

Wyndham Garden Hotel Perimeter Center $$$
800 Hammond Drive NE
(404) 252–3344, (800) WYNDHAM

Five minutes from Perimeter Mall, the 104-room, 34-suite Wyndham features a landscaped garden, an indoor/outdoor pool, and a fully equipped exercise room with whirlpool. Rooms include cable TV, two telephones, and coffeemakers. The hotel operates a complimentary shuttle to local offices and attractions.

Gwinnett County

Courtyard by Marriott $$–$$$
3550 Venture Parkway, Duluth
(770) 476–4666, (800) 321–2211

The shopping excitement of the 1.2-million-square-foot Gwinnett Place Mall is just a quarter-mile from this 146-room Courtyard, which is 18 miles from downtown and 30 miles from Hartsfield Airport. Along with standard rooms, there are 12 suites, an outdoor pool, a spa, evening room service, meeting rooms, a laundry, in-room coffee and tea service, and cable TV with HBO.

Microtel Inn & Suites $
215 Collins Industrial Way, Lawrenceville
(770) 237–5992

Close to Lake Lanier and several area golf courses, this inn serves a complimentary continental breakfast daily. Amenities include an outdoor pool, exercise room, and business center. Rooms are furnished with coffeemakers, data ports, microwaves, refrigerators, and hair dryers; executive suites feature spa tubs and queen-size beds. Children under 16 stay free.

StudioPLUS $$
7065 Jimmy Carter Boulevard, Norcross
(770) 582–9984

This extended-stay hotel features spacious studio suites with queen-size beds, fully equipped kitchens, cable TV, weekly housekeeping, and personal phone lines. Mail, faxes, and packages are delivered right to your room. A fitness center, laundry room, and outdoor pool are on the property. Extended-stay rates are also available.

Hall County

Comfort Inn $$
I–985 at Mundy Mill Road, Gainesville
(770) 287–1000, (800) 221–2222

This 72-room hotel is 5 miles south of Gainesville and 4.5 miles from all the action at the Road Atlanta racetrack. There are five king suites, five whirlpool suites, and an outdoor pool. A deluxe complimentary continental breakfast is served each morning.

Renaissance PineIsle Resort $$$–$$$$
9000 Holiday Road, Buford
(770) 945–8921, (800) HOTELS–1

Nestled amid a 1,200-acre pine forest on the edge of Lake Lanier, each of the Renaissance's 250 rooms includes cable TV, two robes, a stocked refreshment center, and a safe. There's a hot tub on an enclosed patio outside each of the 28 spa rooms. Complimentary coffee and a newspaper are delivered with each guest's wake-up call. Guests can golf on the par 72 course, play tennis on one of the four outdoor lighted courts or three enclosed courts, ride horses, swim in the indoor/outdoor pool, bike and boat, or relax in the three-story elevated outdoor hot tub. On Friday nights during the summer, the hotel serves a Lobster Boil, featuring lobsters, fresh crab, and shrimp in its restaurant overlooking the lake.

Bed-and-Breakfasts

Atlantans, best noted for their devotion to Southern hospitality, are also known for the pride they take in their homes. The combination of the two is best discovered in the area's bed-and-breakfasts, where owners throw open their doors and treat guests like members of the family.

In historic homes, Victorian cottages, and cozy bungalows, Atlanta's many bed-and-breakfast inns offer visitors a range of options, from homelike comfort to elegant pampering. The variety of bed-and-breakfast accommodations has grown, particularly in the years leading up to the arrival of the Olympic Games in 1996.

There are several general guidelines shared by the majority of Atlanta's bed-and-breakfast establishments. Of course, there are exceptions to every rule. We have tried to indicate where an inn may be different, but it's always a good idea to have the innkeeper answer any specific questions you may have about children, pets, smoking, and payment. On the whole, smoking is not allowed anywhere inside the building, but often guests may smoke outside in a designated area. There's usually no accommodation for pets or, in some cases, children. Other innkeepers only permit children older than 12.

While old houses and cottages provide quaint guest rooms, they usually do not have wheelchair-accessible facilities. Some innkeepers do not accept credit cards on site but will allow reservations to be charged through a central reservation service. The metro area has a free reservation service to help visitors find an inn that best suits their style. Bed & Breakfast Atlanta, (404) 875-0525 or (800) 967-3224, operates Monday through Friday, 9:00 A.M. to 5:00 P.M. Inn rates are the same whether booked directly or through the innkeeper. Major credit cards can be used to book a room, even if the individual innkeepers do not accept them.

Price Code

Each inn's listing includes a symbol indicating a price range for a one-night, double occupancy stay (excluding tax) in the middle of the week.

$	$50 to $100
$$	$101 to $150
$$$	$151 and more

Note: Pricing information was provided by the inns and is presented as a guide to help you approximate costs. Rates may be higher during major conventions or other peak travel times, but generally, innkeepers say their prices are the same each evening.

Atlanta

Ansley Inn $$–$$$
253 15th Street
(404) 872-9000, (800) 446-5416
www.ansleyinn.com

This Midtown inn, within walking distance of Symphony Hall and the High Museum of Art, features 22 guest rooms equipped with cable TVs, coffeemakers, and private baths with spa tubs. Guests enjoy a daily full breakfast buffet. Extended rates are available, and discounts are extended to seniors and AAA Club members.

Bentley's Bed and Breakfast $$-$$$
6860 Peachtree-Dunwoody Road
(770) 396-1742
www.bentleysbandb.com

Magnolias, oaks, and dogwoods surround this 1930s house that has been innkeeper Sally Bentley's home for two decades. Inside, the warm hardwood floors, fireplaces, and porches invite guests to linger. There are six guest rooms, each with a private bath. Breakfast includes an array of choices each day, served on antique silver, china, and crystal.

Beverly Hills Inn $$-$$$
65 Sheridan Drive NE
(404) 233-8520
www.beverlyhillsinn.com

Just three minutes from the Atlanta History Center and five minutes from Lenox Square and Phipps Plaza, this 1929, four-level inn is operated like an intimate European hotel. It was originally built as a chic apartment house, which explains why each of the 18 guest rooms has a kitchen. Other room amenities include a balcony; a private, tiled bath; cable TV and data ports; and an ironing board and iron. The inn's common areas show off the original hardwood floors, decorated with Oriental rugs. The library has a bottle of sherry for guests to share as well as a fax and modem hookup. The conservatory on the lower level opens to a cool patio where a complimentary breakfast is served daily. Arriving guests receive a welcoming bottle of wine and a hearty handshake from innkeeper Mit Amin. Check out his London cab parked at the curb.

Buckhead Bed & Breakfast Inn $$
70 Lenox Pointe
(404) 261-8284

This elegant Buckhead inn provides romantic getaway weekends to the locals, as well as gracious accommodations to travelers. There are 19 rooms, many with their motifs in their titles (the Holly Room, the Oak Room). Each has a private bath, four-poster bed, writing desk, armoire, and computer modem lines. Conference facilities can accommodate 50 people. Innkeeper

Jerry Cates and his staff serve a light complimentary breakfast of pastries, fruit salads, and beverages.

Fallin Gate $-$$
381 Cherokee Avenue
(404) 522-7371

Built in 1895, this late Victorian cottage in Grant Park is named for its original owner. Behind the white picket fence are two guest rooms: one with a queen-size bed, armoire, and fireplace; another with a brass double bed, carved mantel over the fireplace, and an oak dresser. Full breakfasts may include such treats as pear crepes, baked eggs, and fresh breads and biscuits. Guests not from the South are required by owner Sandra Bemis to at least try the grits. (Don't worry—they come with cheese and other flavorings for novices.)

The Gaslight Inn $$$
1001 St. Charles Avenue NE
(404) 875-1001
www.gaslightinn.com

This 1913 Virginia-Highland inn was completely renovated by owner Jim Moss in 1990. The white and blue house is decorated with period furnishings; an old-time gaslight beside the front walk is a welcoming beacon. Three guest rooms are decorated with features such as stained-glass windows, four-poster beds, and fireplaces; one has a private entrance to a small garden. There are also two suites: The English suite has a fireplace, steam shower, whirlpool tub, and deck overlooking a walled garden; the St. Charles suite has a private balcony, fireplace, wet bar, and whirlpool tub. Behind the main house is the Ivy Cottage, a tiny house whose entire second floor is a mini-apartment, with a fully equipped kitchen, living area, and bedroom. All rooms have a private bath and TV and come with an elaborate continental breakfast of cereals, juices, fruit salads, and homemade bagels, muffins, and croissants. The grounds, complete with fishpond, are particularly colorful in spring, when more than 2,000 bulbs burst into bloom.

Greycourt Bed and Breakfast $–$$
47 Delta Place
(404) 523-4239

This two-story Victorian was built in Inman Park in 1904 for a saloon keeper. Today, innkeepers John and Kris Dwyer maintain it. The ground-floor suite includes the home's original library, a private phone, and a stocked kitchen. Two additional bedrooms are on the second floor. The entire home is decorated in Victorian antiques, but you may find it hard to leave the luxurious front porch, where antique wicker chairs and rockers beckon. A continental breakfast is served during the week, including breads, English muffins, bagels, fruit, pancakes, egg dishes, and yogurt. On weekends, the Dwyers go all out, offering blueberry pancakes, egg dishes, or any items requested by guests of the inn.

Heartfield Manor Bed and Breakfast $$
182 Elizabeth Street
(404) 523-8633

Since the 1980s, this renovated apartment house in Inman Park has served as a bed-and-breakfast. Built in 1903, the Craftsman-style house now has three guest rooms, all with private baths that overlook a small neighborhood park. The decor is English cottage, with beamed ceilings, wood fireplaces, and period antiques. The rear deck doubles as a playscape for kids, who will find plenty of toys, courtesy of owner Sandra Heartfield's grandchildren. Croissants, muffins, and fresh fruits await hungry guests in the morning.

King-Keith House Bed & Breakfast $–$$
889 Edgewood Avenue NE
(404) 688-7330, (800) 728-3879
www.kingkeith.com

An 1890 Queen Anne–style home in a National Register of Historic Places neighborhood, this inn is one of the oldest homes in Inman Park and is named for its original owner, hardware magnate George King. It features a wraparound porch with an attached gazebo and delicate lace-work arches. The Inman Park/Reynoldstown MARTA station is 2 blocks away, and it's a pleasant walk down the tree-shaded streets of Inman Park to the shops, restaurants, and clubs of Little Five Points.

Five guest rooms have private baths and are furnished in period antiques. Guests have access to a private, upstairs porch. The house has 12-foot ceilings, carved fireplaces, and a baby grand piano. Innkeepers Windell and Jan Keith serve a full breakfast every day that always includes different breads, cereals, and fruits with either eggs, French toast, or quiche.

Shellmont Bed & Breakfast $$
821 Piedmont Avenue NE
(404) 872-9290

Built in 1891 and designed by noted architect Walter T. Downing, the Shellmont is listed on the National Register of Historic Places and is a designated Atlanta city landmark. The architect broke with tradition and took his inspiration in Renaissance and Classical forms, rather than in the prevailing Queen Anne style. Stained-glass windows, original stenciling, and three fishponds in the gardens are some of the features. It's in the wonderfully wooded Midtown neighborhood and is close to Piedmont Park and the Fox Theatre. All rooms have queen-size beds, private baths, TVs, and data port phones. Lodging is offered in five rooms in the main house; each is decorated in different styles of the Victorian period. One has a carved Eastlake bed with matching dresser and armoire and walls that are decorated with reproductions of the original wallpaper border. Another room boasts a collection of Victorian oak pieces, including a settee and chair. Innkeepers Debbie and Ed McCord welcome children 12 and younger to stay in the carriage house, complete with living room, bath, and equipped kitchen. A full breakfast is served every day; look for Belgian waffles and whipped cream, fresh and dried fruits, and three kinds of cereals to jump-start your morning.

Springvale-East Bed & Breakfast $–$$
960 Edgewood Avenue NE
(404) 523-5804

Across the street from the historic Edgewood Trolley Barn in Inman Park, Springvale-East has two main-floor sleeping

The King-Keith House is among Inman Park's best Victorian houses. PHOTO: KING-KEITH HOUSE BED & BREAKFAST

rooms, each with a double bed and shared bath. Up the spiral stairs is a self-contained, second-floor unit with a queen-size bed in a large living/sleeping area, a kitchen, a dining area, a laundry room, and a bath with a shower. Off-street parking is available. Innkeeper Bob Eberwein says most of his guests don't want more than coffee in the morning, but he willingly whips up whatever they do get a hankering for—be it eggs or cereal.

Sugar Magnolia $$–$$$
804 Edgewood Avenue NE
(404) 222–0226

This charming Queen Anne Victorian home in Inman Park was built in 1892. It has a three-story turret, a grand staircase, and six fireplaces. Innkeepers Debi Starnes and Jim Emshoff serve a continental breakfast of fresh fruits, muffins, cereals, and juices in the dining room. There are three guest rooms in the main house; there's also an efficiency apartment in a cottage. Each room has period furnishings, TV, and a private bath. The guest rooms don't share adjoining walls, so it's nice and quiet.

Virginia Highland Inn $$–$$$
630 Orme Circle NE
(404) 892–2735
www.virginiahighlandbb.com

This 1920s bungalow has two suites, Albert and Victoria, with their own private entrances, sitting porches, TVs, desks, and baths. Recently restored, the house is furnished with 20th-century antiques. The spacious cottage garden provides the seasonal bouquets throughout the house. There's also a pond and an outside cat who tries to charm guests into letting him in. Innkeeper Adele Northrup serves a full breakfast in either the sunny kitchen or near the fireplace in the formal dining room.

Beyond Atlanta

Abbett Inn $$
1746 Virginia Avenue, College Park
(404) 767-3708

This quaint Queen Anne house, dating from the 1880s, is set on a wooded lot just minutes from the MARTA line. It boasts six rooms, four with private baths, and one suite. There's an equipped and snack-stocked kitchen, laundry, fax, and Internet line for guests to use. Breakfast is continental, with fresh breads, fruit, cereals, and beverages. Innkeepers Donald Taylor-Farmer and John Hoard provide complimentary shuttle service to the nearby airport and train.

Abigail's Victorian $
542 Main Street, Palmetto
(770) 463-9329

Innkeepers Gail and A.W. Amanns turned this 1885 Victorian in the small town of Palmetto into an antique oasis. The large house, with a wraparound porch and large rear deck, boasts antique pieces in most rooms. There are three guest rooms, with queen or double beds; one has a private bath. A full breakfast is served daily.

Blue and Gray Bed and Breakfast $
2511 Kingswood Drive, Marietta
(770) 425-0392

This bed-and-breakfast is in the home of John and Connie Kone. The owners welcome guests into their residence's two rooms: One has a double bed; the other has a double and a twin. Both have televisions and VCRs, and guests are invited to peruse the owners' extensive video collection. A full breakfast may include quiche, fresh fruit, orange juice, and cinnamon or sausage rolls. In warm weather, guests may enjoy their meals on the back porch overlooking woods and a horse pasture.

Old Garden Inn $
51 Temple Avenue, Newnan
(770) 304-0594, (800) 731-5011

A turn-of-the-century Greek Revival house, this bed-and-breakfast boasts 132 beveled window panes in the entrance hall, a wide front porch, and guest rooms with robes, hair dryers, and refrigerators. Breakfast may include such delights as banana dumplings with raspberry sauce. The inn is within walking distance of Newnan's shopping and business district, as well as its historic neighborhoods.

River Birch $
6051 Burnt Hickory Trail, Powder Springs
(770) 949-1767

Nestled on five acres with towering southern oak trees, River Birch has three suites with king or queen beds and private baths. A glassed-in porch overlooks the gardens (that supply the inn with fresh blueberries). There's also a workout room and spa. Breakfast includes traditional Southern fare, with fresh muffins, fruit, and biscuits with sausage gravy.

Serenbe Bed and Breakfast $$-$$$
10950 Hutcheson Ferry Road
Palmetto
(770) 463-2610
www.serenbe.com

"Elegance and wilderness" is the theme of this turn-of-the-century farm that is now home to a luxurious bed-and-breakfast. The property of innkeepers Steve and Marie Nygren includes 350 acres of rolling countryside south of the city and more than 100 farm animals. A stocked lake provides fishing and canoeing opportunities. There's a pool and hot tub and several flower and vegetable gardens

> ## Insiders' Tip
> The metro area has a free reservation service to help visitors find an inn that best suits their style. Bed & Breakfast Atlanta, (404) 875-0525 or (800) 967-3224, specializes in 80 inns, private homes, and guest cottages.

to enjoy. Hayrides and marshmallow roasts will enthrall the youngsters. The inn has a three-bedroom, four-bath guesthouse and a two-bedroom cottage. Both are decorated with regional folk art and antiques and have fireplaces. There's also a conference facility that can handle meetings for up to 35 people.

Breakfast is a major affair that frequently features Southern favorites such as grits soufflé with collards, scrambled eggs, homemade muffins, Canadian bacon, and French toast with sautéed pears picked fresh from the owners' orchard.

60 Polk Street $$
60 Polk Street, Marietta
(770) 419–1688, (800) 845–7266
www.sixtypolkstreet.com

Just a short walk away from the historic Marietta square, this restored, two-story Victorian is decorated with period antiques and lighting. Innkeepers Joe and Glenda Mertes manage four guest rooms, each with a private bath. Guests are invited to browse the books in the library, linger on the rocking chairs on the front porch, or relax on the rear screened porch. A full Southern-style breakfast is included.

Village Inn Bed and Breakfast $$–$$$
992 Ridge Avenue, Stone Mountain
(770) 469–3459
www.villageinnbb.com

In the heart of historic Stone Mountain Village, the inn's 1850s Federal farmhouse is one of the oldest houses in the area. During the Civil War, it functioned as a Confederate hospital. The three-story inn has six rooms, all with private baths. Five have two-person whirlpool tubs and antique country furnishings. The full breakfast usually includes an egg dish, grits or hash browns, and a selection of breads.

Whitlock Inn $$–$$$
57 Whitlock Avenue, Marietta
(770) 428–1495
www.whitlockinn.com

Whitlock Inn, built in the 1900s, sits in a National Historic Register district, a block from the Marietta courthouse square and across the street from the First Methodist Church, whose bells still mark the evensong with hymns. There are five guest rooms, each with private baths, cable TVs, and phones. A rooftop garden and rocking chair porches offer quiet retreats. There's also a ballroom that seats 100 for special events or conferences. A continental breakfast includes fruits, muffins, breads, and beverages; afternoon snacks are served in the parlor by innkeeper Alexis Edwards.

Restaurants

Eating out and eating well are one and the same in metro Atlanta, which has more than 8,000 restaurants, according to the Georgia Hospitality and Travel Association! Quite something when you consider that the entire state of Georgia has approximately 18,500 restaurants in all.

But it's not so surprising when you consider that the Atlanta restaurant industry has several built-in advantages. The city's advanced transportation network and numerous farmers' markets make fresh food accessible and affordable. And Atlanta is a magnet to people from many backgrounds, so ethnic cooking is readily accessible. Economic diversity also exerts a demand for good food at practically every price level. Consequently, in Atlanta one may dine in sumptuous luxury at the Ritz-Carlton Buckhead or, just a few miles away, have possibly the world's best onion rings brought right to your car at the North Avenue Varsity Drive-In.

Such a vibrant marketplace naturally promotes change: For every Atlanta restaurant that succeeds, there are many more that don't. With so much competition for the public's dining dollar, customers and critics alike do not tolerate bad food or bad service for very long. Restaurants that don't make the grade are usually out of business within a year. In nearly every case, we've restricted our restaurant recommendations to places that have been open at least one year; some have been in business for decades.

With so many restaurants to choose from, you could eat at a different one every day for almost 22 years! Clearly, our task—choosing a tiny fraction of those available to tell you about—is not easy. We've tried to let neither haute cuisine nor hot dog stands hog too much space; there is, as we've said, excellent food at nearly every price in Atlanta. Whether you're looking for an outdoor patio to lunch al fresco on a lovely spring day, a place to grab a veggie burger, or somewhere to celebrate a special occasion, you'll find it among our selections.

National restaurant chains have locations everywhere you look in the metro area. Because you already know about most of them, and due to space limitations, we generally don't include chains in our chapter. If you're craving a particular chain's food, the Yellow Pages in the telephone book is the place to look. You will find a few chain restaurants in this guide that either originated here, such as Mick's, or can only be found in a few other cities, such as the Hard Rock Cafe and the Zesto Drive-Ins.

We've divided this chapter into two major parts: Atlanta and Beyond Atlanta. Restaurants in the Atlanta section are within the I-285 Perimeter. Those in the Beyond Atlanta section are outside the Perimeter. So, take your time, browse through this chapter, and visit some of our favorite dining spots. Bon appetit!

Price Code

The price key symbol in each listing gives the range for the cost of dinner for two, excluding cocktails, beer or wine, appetizer, dessert, tax, and tip. Your bill at a given restaurant may be higher or lower, depending on what you order and fluctuating restaurant prices. These symbols provide only a general guide.

$	Less than $15
$$	$15 to $30
$$$	$31 to $50
$$$$	$51 and more

Most Atlanta restaurants take all major credit cards; we will let you know those that do not accept credit cards.

Real Southern food is neither low-fat nor "light" in flavor, texture, or its appetite-satisfying capacities; Southerners generally take the attitude that food is more than just a way to avoid starvation—it is an essential part of their culture and social life. Real Southern cooks would no more pay attention to the cholesterol-enhancing factors of a given ingredient than they would even consider sending someone away from their kitchens still hungry.

Atlanta

Basic American

Agnes & Muriel's $$
1514 Monroe Drive
(404) 885-1000

This old Craftsman cottage in Midtown is a cross between a diner and a Southern-style tearoom, packed most evenings with folks hankering for food that Mom used to make. (In fact, this eatery is named for the owners' moms.) Huge portions of comfort food—meat loaf, potpie, pork chops, and scrumptious desserts—are served up in cozy, sunlit rooms, along with lots of nostalgia and '50s kitsch. Service is continuous from 11:00 A.M. to 11:00 P.M. during the week and from 10:00 A.M. to 11:00 P.M. on weekends.

American Roadhouse $$
842 North Highland Avenue NE
(404) 872-2822

Serving breakfast all day and blue plate specials, American Roadhouse is popular with neighbors in Virginia-Highland. Main dishes include meat loaf, huge juicy burgers, and pasta; the vegetables are fresh. The Roadhouse has beer and wine and free parking; it's open from 7:00 A.M. to 10:00 P.M. nightly and until midnight on weekends.

Atkins Park $$
794 North Highland Avenue NE
(404) 876-7249

With a liquor license first issued in 1927, Atkins Park has the distinction of being the oldest bar in Atlanta. It harkens back to the age of dark, wood-paneled, beery neighborhood bars. A perennial favorite in Virginia-Highland, Atkins Park offers a changing menu, including Cajun favorites, basic pub food, and deli sandwiches, as well as seafood and pasta. Atkins Park is open nightly until 3:00 A.M. and serves brunch on Saturday and Sunday until 3:00 P.M. When available, there is free parking in the rear.

Blue Ribbon Grill $$$
4006 LaVista Road, Tucker
(770) 491-1570

The fare at Blue Ribbon ranges from meat loaf and other Southern favorites to hand-cut steaks, prime rib, chicken potpie, and fresh fish. There's a full bar, and the restaurant seats about 156 diners. Large parties may call ahead for reservations or even fax in their order if they prefer. The restaurant is open for lunch on weekdays, for brunch on Saturday, and for dinner Monday through Saturday.

Buckhead Bread Company & Corner Café $$
3070 Piedmont Road
(404) 240-1978
www.buckheadrestaurants.com

This European-influenced, bright and airy uptown breakfast and lunch spot boasts some of the city's best breads, pastries, and muffins. Executive chef Jeff Gomez describes his offerings as "Southern American," though they better reflect his training at Atlanta's heavily French-influenced Culinary Institute and his experience at the upscale Buckhead Diner and Nava. Menu items include grilled country French ham and Gruyère on French bread, roasted rosemary lamb on tomato and onion focaccia, shrimp and pasta salads, chicken quesadillas served with baby farm lettuce and avocado-tomato vinaigrette salads, and sides such as new potato salads, freshly made creamy cole slaw, and white balsamic pasta salads.

Buckhead Bread offers a pleasant terrace dining area in good weather and is open Monday through Friday from 6:30 A.M. to 5:00 P.M. and on weekends from 8:00 A.M. to 5:00 P.M. As per usual for this central-Buckhead location, the expected attire is "dressy casual," no reservations are accepted, and parking can be an issue (several pay lots are relatively close by, but street parking is not a good idea during the business day).

Cabbagetown Grill $$
727 Wylie Street
(404) 525–8818
Tucked into one of the city's funkiest neighborhoods, the Grill is a favorite spot of locals as well as tourists stopping by Oakland Cemetery and Zoo Atlanta. Veggie plates, grilled chicken sandwiches, and oversize salads, as well as basic American entrees, fill the menu. There's a spacious outdoor patio and a full bar with an excellent selection of draft beers, including an old-time and rarely found favorite, Pabst Blue Ribbon. Service is continuous from 11:00 A.M. during the week, and from 2:00 P.M. on the weekends.

Cheesecake Factory $$
3024 Peachtree Road NW
(404) 816–2555
Yes, you'll find plenty of cheesecake (some 50 varieties!) in this large Buckhead eatery, but there's also much more to enjoy. The casually elegant decor attracts families and singles alike for an eclectic American menu featuring pasta, steaks, seafood, and salads, all in enormous portions that beg to be taken home! There is

also a full bar (offering some really strangely flavored martinis) and one of the best outdoor patios in town, overlooking Peachtree. The Factory is open from 11:30 A.M. to 11:30 P.M. daily and to 12:30 A.M. on weekends. You'll find the valet parking particularly useful in this busy Buckhead neighborhood.

Downwind Restaurant and Lounge $$
DeKalb-Peachtree Airport, 2000 Airport Road
(770) 452–0973
You can get a close-up view of the air traffic at DeKalb-Peachtree Airport (Georgia's second-busiest) while you dine at the Downwind. PDK (as it's called in aviation lingo) is a general aviation airport heavily used by private pilots, and it's fun to hang out on the big deck and watch the planes, close enough to smell the kerosene fumes (which is both appetizing and intoxicating to aviation buffs!). There's a full bar, and lunch and dinner specials daily. Steak, seafood, and pasta are all featured. Downwind is open for lunch and for dinner until 11:00 P.M.

Einstein's $$
1077 Juniper Street NE
(404) 876–7925
You don't have to be a genius to see that Einstein's has caught on in a big way since opening in 1992. It has since consumed almost an entire block on Juniper Street, which is walking distance to the Woodruff Art Center and Piedmont Park. Popular munchables include Einstein's Reuben sandwich, the hummus dip appetizer, and a variety of pastas. Dine indoors or on one of the two outside patios, where gas heat lamps chase away the chill in cooler months. The restaurant serves lunch and dinner daily; it's open late and is a fun place to grab a drink and a snack after the theater.

Good News Café $
1271 Glenwood Avenue
(404) 635–1611
This most casual of Southern-style eateries in the emerging East Atlanta neighborhood offers up well-presented, very reasonably priced barbecued ribs, blackened

catfish, grilled chicken, fresh vegetables, and all the other treats you can expect in the better Southern meats-and-threes. The "Good News" moniker is in reference to the restaurant's single gimmick, naming all the dishes after media sources and movies. For example, the "Jaws" is a blackened catfish, romaine, Parmesan, and tomato wrap with a ranch dressing–based sauce, while the "St. Louis Dispatch" is a traditional bacon, lettuce, and tomato sandwich.

Good News is the local version of James Crocker and David Corley's restaurant by the same name in Ellijay, and has recently emerged as one of the best spots to get the wonderful North Georgia–style breakfasts in the city. One notable house special is the aptly named Ellijay, two thick slices of apple-bread French toast along with two eggs and a choice of bacon, sausage links, or patties. Good News is open Tuesday through Friday 7:30 A.M. to 3:00 P.M., Saturday 8:00 A.M. to 4:00 P.M., and Sunday 9:00 A.M. to 4:00 P.M. Free parking on the street. Cash and credit cards are okay, but no checks are accepted.

Manuel's Tavern $
602 North Highland Avenue NE
(404) 525–3447
4877 Memorial Drive, Stone Mountain
(404) 296–6919

Manuel's Tavern has been an in-town gathering place since 1956, when Manuel Maloof founded the North Highland Avenue spot. Maloof was politically active his entire life (at one time he was CEO of DeKalb County), and today the walls of his tavern are covered with beer signs and pictures of sports heroes, Democratic Party leaders, and icons who frequent the place. Through the years, the Atlanta Press Club has held meetings and debates here, and the *New York Times* has described it as "Atlanta's quintessential neighborhood bar." Regulars roam from the main room to the "ballroom" (really the dining room), from bar to booth to table, catching up on all the latest while enjoying Manuel's wings, sandwiches, burgers, and salads. Most Atlanta cops, firefighters, and paramedics consider this "the" place to conduct "choir practice," so expect to see quite a few uniforms at any given time. It can get hectic

Two Atlanta icons—Manuel's Tavern in Virginia-Highlands and Coca-Cola. PHOTO: JOHN MCKAY

on a busy night, but the atmosphere is friendly and inviting. Both locations are open daily for lunch and dinner.

Max Lager's $$$
320 Peachtree Street
(404) 525–4400
www.maxlagers.com

Pull up a polished table in this downtown brewpub—set up like an artist's loft—and order a sampler of the ales and lagers made on the premises. Team them with a beefy burger, wood-fired pizza, or a meaty steak. Along with the hearty entrees, there's a lineup of standard pub munchies, from chicken strips to spicy nachos to wings. Lunch and dinner are served daily.

Mick's $$
229 Peachtree Street
(404) 688–6425
557 Peachtree Street
(404) 875–6425
2110 Peachtree Road
(404) 351–6425
Lenox Square, 3393 Peachtree Road NE
(404) 262–6425
4540 Ashford Dunwoody Road
(770) 394–6425
116 East Ponce de Leon Avenue, Decatur
(404) 373–7797
Underground Atlanta
75 Upper Alabama Street
(404) 525–2825
Cumberland Mall, 1320 Cumberland Parkway
(770) 431–7190

The first address is the original Mick's. It was started by two young men who have since retired after selling their string of popular eateries to a conglomerate. The second location is at the entrance to the Bennett Street antiques and arts shopping district (see The Arts and Shopping chapters) and has a lovely outdoor patio on Peachtree Road. All Mick's are upbeat, welcoming restaurants noted for their tasty food and large portions. The big burgers are a favorite; other popular items include chicken with penne pasta, fried chicken salad, fried green tomatoes, corn, and tomato linguine. For dessert, try the

signature Oreo cheesecake or fresh cobbler of the day. The wide-ranging menu and good value make Mick's a hit with families and couples alike. All locations have a full bar. For additional suburban locations, check the Yellow Pages.

R. Thomas Deluxe Grill $$
1812 Peachtree Road NW
(404) 872–2942

R. Thomas' year-round outdoor patio has, without a doubt, one of the most eclectic outdoor statuary and ornament collections of any Atlanta restaurant. But those attracted to the yard art and big covered patio end up staying for the eats, which include big burgers (both meaty and meatless), penne pasta, vegetarian tacos, and plump wings. Beer and wine are served, and parking is free. A number of exotic birds reside in cages against the Grill's exterior wall, even during the winter, when a heat lamp keeps them talking. R. Thomas is open 24 hours a day, seven days a week.

Taco Mac $$
1006 North Highland Avenue NE
(404) 873–6529
375 Pharr Road NE
(404) 239–0650
5830 Roswell Road NW
(404) 257–0735
www.taco-mac.com

Taco Mac has been a laid-back Atlanta party spot since 1979, when it first opened on North Highland Avenue. The fare is American bar food with a Mexican twang: Favorites include chicken salad, chicken wings, burritos, tacos, and salads. Each location is a little different, but each is noted for its truly extensive selection of beers; some offer more than 100 different beers. Most locations have a patio for warm-weather fun outdoors. There are numerous suburban locations as well. Lunch and dinner are served daily.

Vinocity Wine Bar $$
36 13th Street
(404) 870–8886

Located in the old Atlanta Theosophical Society building in Midtown, newly opened Vinocity offers both one of the area's best wine selections and an upscale version of American-style wrapped sandwiches and salads. Unlike the other small bistros that have opened in this transition area, Vinocity leans much more toward being a dining destination than a place to pop in for before-theater snacks.

Chef Brian Barfield stacks the plates with a mixture of garnishes and sauces to showcase his artful use of seemingly conflicting elements; prosciutto-wrapped bitter greens towering over grape tomatoes, candied nuts, and small fruits is one of his signature dishes. Highly recommended (when available) is his pine nut–crusted swordfish steaks, massively cut yet with a melt-in-your-mouth texture, and his risotto with asparagus, mushrooms, and cheese. Vinocity's wine selection has a unique offering, thanks to its Cruvient wine preservation system; even its finest vintages can be enjoyed by the glass rather than only by the bottle. The usual French and Italian finer selections are offered, of course, but the real fun is in the extensive list of very small-production Americans in Riedel glasses.

Vinocity is open 5:30 to 11:00 P.M. Monday through Saturday, parking is available only in adjacent paid lots, reservations are recommended, and perhaps most important, this is by no means a child-friendly restaurant.

Vortex Bar & Grill $$
438 Moreland Avenue
(404) 688–1828
878 Peachtree Street
(404) 875–1667

For burgers, beer, and an outrageous ambience, nothing beats the Vortex. The Peachtree location in Midtown is new and decorated with "flea market" stuff. Having moved from a former site on West Peachtree Street, the new space is 4,500 square feet, which means never having to hear, "there's a wait." At the Vortex on Moreland Avenue in Little Five Points, you can't miss the shocking skull entrance. Though the decor is way out, the food is fairly traditional. Aside from 15 varieties of hamburgers and a gigantic beefy hot dog, bar food such as nachos and chicken wings and strips are good bets. Lunch and dinner are served daily until 1:45 A.M.

Fine Dining

Bacchanalia $$$$
1198 Howell Mill Road
(404) 365–0410

This former Buckhead restaurant took a bold step and relocated to a renovated factory closer to downtown, in a neighborhood that is in transition, but most delicately can be described as "interesting." But the crowds who love the eatery's delectable, fixed-price, four-course dinners of California nouvelle cuisine are still putting their names on the reservation list. Along with an extensive wine list, you'll find plenty of seafood selections and updated American classics. Dinner is served Tuesday through Saturday (the restaurant is closed Sunday and Monday), and there's plenty of on-site parking.

Blue Ridge Grill $$$
1261 West Paces Ferry Road NW
(404) 233–5030

With large booths, a welcoming porch, beamed ceilings, and a large stone fireplace, this restaurant's decor evokes the charm of a lodge in the southern Appalachian Mountains. Its new Southern cuisine fare includes dishes such as swordfish, horseradish-crusted grouper, barbecued pork chops, and Georgia game mixed grill. All vegetables are organically grown, and for lunch, don't miss the fried dill pickles. Relax at the full bar. Blue Ridge Grill is open for lunch and dinner.

Buckhead Diner $$$
3073 Piedmont Road NE
(404) 262–3336

Definitely not what the word "diner" suggests, this eatery is more like a plush dining car from the Orient Express with an eclectic modern American cuisine. Part of the noted Buckhead Life Restaurant Group chain including Pricci and Pano's & Paul's, Buckhead Diner provides excellence from the first morsel to the last. You might want to start with the salt and pepper calamari, go on to a specialty, such as the veal and wild mushroom meat loaf or the grilled smoked pork chop, and finish up with the white chocolate banana cream pie. A diner with valet parking? You bet! And if you want a close-up look at the kitchen in action, ask for a seat in the "theater district"—a counter with stools overlooking the line. The diner is open daily for lunch and dinner.

Canoe $$$
4199 Paces Ferry Road SE
(770) 432–2663

On the banks of the Chattahoochee River in northwest Atlanta, Canoe is housed in a barrel-vaulted brick building once known as Robinson's Tropical Gardens. It's said many a young romance bloomed at this riverfront restaurant and nightspot in the golden post-WWII years. Today, wedding parties have been known to arrive in canoes for a luscious reception.

In accordance with its goal of offering delicious, healthy food for today's diner, Canoe's fare includes grilled farm-raised chicken with wild mushroom potato puree with port wine and cranberries; goat cheese and potato tortellini with artichokes, autumn greens, pine nuts, and white truffle oil; and a wild mushroom soup with polenta croutons. There's also an assortment of beef and seafood. You can call ahead for reservations, or take advantage of any waiting time to stroll riverside. Valet parking is available. Dinner is served nightly.

City Grill $$$$
50 Hurt Plaza
(404) 524–2489

This downtown restaurant, in a former Federal Reserve Bank built in 1913, may well be one of the city's most elegant dining rooms. Its decor conveys an appropriate sense of affluence: soaring windows, graceful columns, and a double curving marble staircase. The cuisine is American regional with a Southern flair: Specialties include Southern-fried quail, barbecued shrimp, crab cakes, and an especially good lobster-corn chowder. The atmosphere is fine dining on the relaxed side. Call for reservations. City Grill is closed on Sunday; it's a favorite power-lunch spot during the week and a special-occasion spot for dinner Monday through Saturday.

Dailey's Restaurant and Bar $$$
17 International Boulevard NW
(404) 681–3303

Dailey's opened in 1981 and immediately became a favorite spot for power lunches among the downtown executive set. It's a shadowy, noisy, and altogether pleasant downtown eatery serving creative American fare. The big sellers are the wild-mushroom–encrusted sea bass, strip steak, and rice-paper salmon; for lunch, it's the pecan chicken salad. Before deciding on the famous french-fried ice cream, take a tour of the calorie-laden dessert bar. Dinner is served nightly; lunch is served daily, except Sunday.

The Food Studio $$$
887 West Marietta Street, Suite K102
(404) 815–6677
www.thefoodstudio.com

Tucked into the King Plow Arts Center, a renovated agricultural forge, this New American cuisine two-tier eatery is enormously popular with the in-town crowd. There's a chic bar, an open kitchen, and dressed-up industrial accents, including a beehive fireplace. Start with the foie gras, the cheese plates, then try the ahi tuna or the risotto. A courtyard provides an entrance and a fun spot to enjoy a glass from the Studio's extensive wine list. Dinner is served daily from 5:30 P.M.

Horseradish Grill $$$
4320 Powers Ferry Road NW
(404) 255-7277
www.horseradishgrill.com

This trendy, casual restaurant just south of Chastain Park opened in 1994. Its cuisine is in-season Southern fare, and all grilled items are cooked over a hickory fire. Specialty dishes include a peanut-and-cracker-encrusted Georgia mountain trout, veal chops with wild mushrooms and sweet-potato dumpling, strip steaks, and shrimp grits. During the summer months, diners are apt to find daily vegetable specials plucked to order from the wonderful garden behind the restaurant. The full bar has a dazzling array of spirits; enjoy a single-malt scotch on the flagstone patio. The Horseradish Grill is open daily for lunch (except Saturday) and dinner; there's valet parking.

Palm Restaurant $$$$
3391 Peachtree Road, in the Swissôtel
Atlanta
(404) 814-1955

Sketches of the regulars decorate the walls of this upscale eatery, where giant lobsters and even bigger steaks crowd the a la carte menu. Along with the three-pound crustaceans and assorted prime beef cuts, there are crab cakes, salmon, chicken, veal, pasta, and a full bar. Lunch and dinner are served daily.

Pano's & Paul's $$$$
1232 West Paces Ferry Road NW
(404) 261-3662

Since 1979, Pano's & Paul's has been "the place" of old Buckhead, serving modern American/continental cuisine in a luxurious environment of chandeliers and tuxedoed waiters. Well-heeled locals frequent the place for its superb aged meats and the signature batter-fried lobster tails with Chinese honey mustard dressing.

Pano's & Paul's was the first of the notable restaurants now known as the Buckhead Life Restaurant Group, and is famous for the fantastic breads it makes for all its places. The restaurant has a full bar, requires reservations, and recommends jackets for gentlemen. A recent renovation has given the shopping center site the look of an Art Deco supper club. Pano's & Paul's serves dinner only Monday through Saturday.

Seeger's $$$$
111 West Paces Ferry Road
(404) 846-9779

Chef Guenter Seeger's masterwork restaurant is Bacchanalia's primary competition for the ranking of Atlanta's best dining experience. Located in a lovely Craftsman-style bungalow just off the main business district of Buckhead, Seeger's menu changes daily but circles around that large category of "contemporary-continental cuisine," with small portions of perfectly presented and well-designed entrees, prix fixe menus, and rarified wines. Seeger himself is the recipient of both the Beard Award and a Mobil 5-Star ranking, and it shows in literally everything he does here. The meals are not just plates of foods—the whole experience is orchestrated to showcase the Asian-influenced cuisine in its visual appeal (which is quite spectacular), taste, and textures.

Seeger's wine list is of the caliber expected in this category, with an unusually high number of by-the-glass selections and a breathtaking $40 corkage fee. Sommelier Mark Mendoza has a genius for suggesting perfect mid-range reds and has a cellar full of wonderful Rhônes and Germans, with a special emphasis on Burgundies. The five-course prix fixe menu is $69, the eight-course grand tasting menu is $85, both not including wines, and several menu options are available at extra cost—the $84 caviar supplement for one example.

Seeger's is open from 5:30 to 10:00 P.M. Monday through Saturday, parking is available in their own lot, and reservations are suggested.

Steak Houses

Bone's $$$$
3130 Piedmont Road NE
(404) 237-2663

In business since 1979, Bone's serves steak and seafood in a fine dining atmosphere that's clubby yet lively. The all a la carte menu favorites include live Maine lobster (flown in daily), rib eye steaks, and lamb chops. Bone's has a full bar, is cigar friendly with an extensive wine list, and offers valet parking. The restaurant recommends reservations and that gentlemen wear a coat and tie. Bone's is open weekdays for lunch and every night for dinner.

Chops $$$$
70 West Paces Ferry Road NW
(404) 262-2675

Chops steak house, open since 1989, is considered to be the Tiffany's of Atlanta steak houses. The atmosphere is plush and chic, suggesting a 1930s-era men's club with dark wood, Art Deco light fixtures, and oversize chairs. The menu includes steaks, lamb chops, fish, and lobsters. The wine list is a connoisseur's dream, with more than 400 in literally all price ranges. Reservations are strongly recommended; there's valet parking. Chops is open every night for dinner and for lunch on weekdays. The Lobster Bar on the lower level, (404) 231-7128, offers lobsters from one to eight pounds, steaks, and a raw bar.

Highland Tap $$$
1026 North Highland Avenue NE
(404) 875-3673

This popular in-town steak house and bar is in a granite-walled cellar below the intersection of North Highland and Virginia Avenues. In a masculine room reminiscent of the 1940s, the restaurant's menu includes steaks, lamb chops, and duck. Martini aficionados should try the Tap's four-ounce "world-class martini." The restaurant is open every day for lunch and dinner, except there's no lunch on Monday. Brunch is served on weekends.

Morton's of Chicago $$$$
303 Peachtree Street
(404) 577-4366
3379 Peachtree Road NE
(404) 816-6535

Morton's masculine, clubby decor suggests a Chicago speakeasy. You'll enjoy porterhouse, prime rib, or live Maine lobster. Morton's is open nightly for dinner. Reservations are recommended, as are jackets for the gentlemen. There's valet parking.

Pilgreen's Restaurant and Lounge $$$
1081 Lee Street SW
(404) 758-4669
6335 Jonesboro Road, Morrow
(770) 961-1666

Pilgreen's steak house is an Atlanta tradition, operated by the family that established it in 1932. The atmosphere is casual and friendly, and many customers are regulars. Specialties of the house include filets, T-bones, and the steak for two. Each location has a full bar. The original Lee Street restaurant has free secured parking; it's closed on Sunday and after 3:00 P.M. on Monday. Lunch and dinner are served the rest of the week. The Morrow location is open for lunch and dinner Sunday through Friday and for dinner only on Saturday.

Sun Dial Restaurant and Lounge $$$$
Westin Peachtree Plaza Hotel
210 Peachtree Street NW
(404) 589-7506

Seventy-two stories above the city, Sun Dial is a room with a dazzling view; and, since the whole place rotates, you'll get to see it all while dining on luscious cuts of beef as well as chicken, swordfish, and salmon. The Sun Dial is open every day for lunch and dinner, including all holidays; reservations are accepted. Even if you only stop by for a cocktail in the upper-level lounge, the Sun Dial (especially the non-stop ride up in the glass-enclosed elevator outside the building!) is always a thrill. There's a $7.50-per-person charge to visit the lounge/observation level.

Tasty, Quick, and Cheap

EATS $
600 Ponce de Leon Avenue NE
(404) 888-9149

EATS is a favorite with college kids and other Generation Xers who groove on the casual atmosphere, eclectic music, and terrific, inexpensive food. There are separate counters and sometimes long lines: One serves pasta (the big seller is cheese tortellini with marinara sauce), and another serves jerk chicken and vegetables. EATS is open daily for lunch and dinner. Beer and wine are sold here. No credit cards are accepted.

Java Jive $$
790 Ponce de Leon Avenue
(404) 876-6161

Remember that old Formica kitchen table you had as a kid? It's joined its siblings at this funky Midtown restaurant where the hearty breakfasts and lunches are just like Mom used to serve. The pecan waffles with whipped cream are decadent. Service starts early, at 8:00 A.M. during the week, and 9:00 A.M. on weekends. The restaurant is closed on Monday.

The Varsity $
61 North Avenue NW
(404) 881-1706
1085 Lindbergh Drive NE
(404) 261-8843
6045 Dawson Boulevard NW, Norcross
(770) 840-8519
2790 Town Center Drive, Kennesaw
(770) 795-0802

At the corner of Spring Street, the original Varsity is just across the North Avenue bridge from Georgia Tech. It opened in 1928 and claims the distinction of being the world's largest drive-in: Every day, this single restaurant serves up to 2 miles of hot dogs, a ton of onion rings, and 5,000 pies. The city put The Varsity at North Avenue on its registry of historic buildings, which will keep it from changing forever after. Friendly carhops ask "What'll ya have?" then bring your food to your car, or you can eat inside and watch TV in one of the several large dining rooms. The serving counters inside are a beehive of activity: The slogan here is "Have your money in your hand and your order in your mind." The Varsity does not serve alcohol, and no credit cards are accepted.

Woody's Famous Philadelphia Cheesesteaks $
981 Monroe Drive NE
(404) 876-1939

Woody's, just across from Grady High School on a spit of land between Monroe Drive and Virginia Avenue, has been providing students and Insiders with good cheesesteaks and submarine sandwiches since 1975. This tiny restaurant is nothing fancy, and its operating hours are only 11:00 A.M. until 5:00 P.M., Tuesday through Saturday. Check out the extensive variety of Breyer's ice creams. No alcohol is served, and credit cards aren't accepted.

Zesto Drive-In $
377 Moreland Avenue
(404) 523-1973
1181 East Confederate Avenue
(404) 622-4254
151 Forest Parkway, Forest Park
(404) 366-0564
544 Ponce de Leon Avenue NE
(404) 607-1118

Since 1949, Atlanta has been stopping by Zesto's. The Illinois-based soft-ice-cream chain was once in 46 states. Today, few

> ## Insiders' Tip
> The Varsity was one of the first "drive-in" restaurants in the nation and still holds the distinction of being the largest in the world. Most native Atlantans consider their onion rings to be one of the major food groups essential to a balanced diet.

restaurants remain, but, with four locations, Atlanta is still a hotbed of them. Try a Chubby Decker hamburger and a side order of fried okra (if you're in the right Zesto's—each one's menu is quirkily different from the others) and top it off with a Nut Brown Crown. The satiny soft ice cream is the real thing. The Ponce de Leon restaurant, a chrome-colored classic diner, is the best-looking Zesto's.

Caribbean/African

Bridgetown Grill $$
2997 Cumberland Circle
(770) 438–6888
3316 Piedmont Road, Buckhead
(404) 266–1500

Bridgetown Grill serves what some people call fusion; others call it Jamaican. Whatever you call it, the food is simply delicious. Dig into the jerk chicken, guava-barbecued ribs, conch fritters, and Jamaican burritos, two spicy chicken burritos topped with Habanero cheese sauce, guacamole, and salsa served with black beans and rice and plantains. Service is friendly in this casual, relaxed setting. Brightly painted walls, banners, and artwork create an upbeat atmosphere. You can get lunch and dinner seven days a week. All locations have full-service bars.

The Casbah $$$
465 North Highland Avenue
(404) 524–5777

Step into this Moroccan tent where belly dancers and tarot readers entertain between a la carte courses of shish kebab, couscous, and other spicy fare. Cushioned benches surround the low tables, where there's no silverware unless you ask. Dinner begins at 6:00 P.M. Tuesday through Sunday.

Imperial Fez $$$$
2285 Peachtree Road NE
(404) 351–0870

Leave your worries (and your shoes) at the door and be swept into the sultan's palace for an evening of tinkling bells, pulsating drums, and lovely ladies swaying in the old-fashioned (Eastern) way. This promises to be an exotic experience with sinuous veiled dancers and tantalizing aromas and flavors. Be prepared to sit on cushions (if you have a bad back, request extra cushions or be sure to pick a spot against a bolster). Feast on authentic Moroccan cuisine with no MSG, curry, or lard in the dishes. It's not unusual for a guest (male more often than female) to spontaneously stand and dance with a performer, which adds to the evening's fun. There are special prices for children 12 and younger; otherwise, everyone else at a table must order his or her own entree; no separate checks. A fixed price of $45 per person gets you a six-course meal with selections of soup, five different salads, appetizers, a choice of entrees including lamb, Cornish hen with apricots, seafood and vegetarian specialties, and dessert of fresh fruits and pastries. Bring extra dollars to place in the dancers' garb when they dance at your table. Reservations are recommended.

Chinese

Chin Chin $$
3887 Peachtree Road NE
(404) 816–2229
699 Ponce de Leon Avenue
(404) 881–1511
1100 Hammond Drive
(770) 913–0266
7820 Holcomb Bridge Road, Norcross
(770) 840–9898

Enjoy mouthwatering Chinese cuisine in these pleasant surroundings. Crowd-pleasing entrees include tangerine steak, golden crispy prawns, shredded pork in garlic sauce, and sautéed vegetables. Open every day for lunch and dinner, Chin Chin offers a full bar and free delivery within a 3-mile radius. Chin Chin's chef's specials and a few other entrees will take you higher than the range we cited above, but you can grab a good bargain with the lunch special. On Sunday, it opens at 3:00 P.M.

Chopstix $$$
4279 Roswell Road NE
(404) 255–4868
www.oceanpalacerestaurant.com

Don't let the name fool you. This is not standard Chinese food fare, nor are the prices. At Chopstix you eat gourmet Chinese food worthy of the prices by candlelight and soft piano music, on fine china, from linen-covered tables. Most of the clientele are loyal followers who have discovered this excellent restaurant almost hidden in Chastain Square.

Hot and cold appetizers include stir-fried alligator and mango roasted duck salad. The extensive menu includes many shrimp and scallop dishes as well as seafood, shellfish, pork, chicken, and beef entrees. Princess prawn, ginger duck in a crispy rice-bowl, and Satay seafood hot pot with eggplant, shrimp, scallops, and lobster are among the favorites. Dress casually and relax with cocktails, beer, or wine in the piano bar. Reservations are recommended. Chopstix serves lunch on weekdays and dinner every night.

Grand China $$
2975 Peachtree Road NE
(404) 231–8690

Order from a sizable menu for reliable food in this longtime Buckhead fixture. Szechuan, Cantonese, and Taiwanese entrees join those originating in Singapore. The bar, with its lattice motif bamboo shades, offers a pleasant setting. Try the General Tsao chicken, small chunks of boneless chicken breast lightly fried, then covered with a hot-sour sauce and sesame seeds. Noodle dishes, both hot and cold, are favorites. An outdoor section is open in good weather. Grand China is open every day for lunch and dinner. No reservations are needed.

Hsu's at Peachtree Center $$$
192 Peachtree Center Avenue
(404) 659–2788
www.hsus.com

For fine dining in downtown Atlanta, visit this charming and picturesque restaurant. The food is new Cantonese cuisine in Hong Kong style and has won many fans among residents and visitors. Try the shrimp with fresh mango, grilled stuffed scallops, or Peking duck served in two courses: crispy skin in a Chinese pan-cake and grilled duck meat with honey ginger sauce; and the spicy noodle soup. Hsu's offers a full-service bar as well as wines by the glass or bottle.

Lee's Golden Buddha $$
3861 Roswell Road
(404) 261–3777
1905 Clairmont Road, Decatur
(404) 633–5252
4300 Buford Drive, Buford
(770) 945–1224
www.leesgoldenbuddha.com

Lee's is a small Atlanta-based chain of traditional Chinese restaurants and, unusual for this area's fickle dining public, has been in business since 1975. Lee's features a pleasant, inviting dining atmosphere that is well suited for family-style dining (it is very child friendly), and for special events, several private dining rooms are available. The menu of authentic Mandarin and Szechuan cuisine offers an extensive array of selections, including Peking duck, Peking ribs, sesame chicken, golden Buddha chicken, beef soong, and princess chicken.

All three locations of Lee's offer free delivery (within a limited area; call for information), and all are open Monday through Thursday 11:30 A.M. to 10:00 P.M., Friday 11:30 A.M. to 11:00 P.M., Saturday noon to 11:00 P.M., and Sunday noon to 10:00 P.M.

Little Szechuan $
Northwoods Plaza, 5091-C Buford Highway
(770) 451–0192

Another of the good Asian restaurants clustered in strip centers on Buford Highway, Little Szechuan concentrates on food, not atmosphere. Mandarin Chinese cuisine with Szechuan spices dominates the menu. Creative and well-seasoned, the dishes here include stir-fried Szechuan string beans, shredded pork with garlic sauce, chicken in sherry with garlic sauce, steamed fish with black beans, and spicy garlic shrimp. Look for sizable portions and fast service. You can buy beer and wine, and there's lots of free parking outside. Little Szechuan serves lunch and dinner every day except Tuesday. The restaurant accepts reservations for parties of six or more and has a big party room for parties of up to 50.

The Orient at Vinings $$$
4199 Paces Ferry Road
(770) 438–8866

Cantonese cuisine with modern touches is the specialty here in a relaxed contemporary setting that includes a refurbished railroad car next to the still busy tracks. Specialties include firecracker pork, rainbow shrimp, and Szechuan cuttlefish. Ask about the weekly lunch special. Friendly service is a mainstay of this popular restaurant. The Orient is open for dinner every night and for lunch Monday through Friday, as well as brunch on Sunday. Reservations are suggested.

P. F. Chang's $$
500 Ashwood Parkway, Dunwoody
(770) 352–0500
7925 North Point Parkway, Alpharetta
(770) 992–3070
Mall of Georgia, 3333 Buford Drive, Buford
(678) 546–9005
www.pfchangs.com

P. F. Chang's is a modified, suburbanized version of the traditional Chinese experience; for one, you find open kitchens there, which you would *never* find in the seriously authentic restaurants along Buford Highway (not that you really would *want* to, though!). That said, however, Chang's does offer an excellent menu with some truly tasty variations on the normally expected dishes. The chicken in soothing lettuce wraps are some of the best wraps in the city. The diced and spiced chicken is served in a tasty soy-based sauce with clean, fresh lettuce cups. Even better are the wok-braised and meaty northern-style spare ribs, which are seasoned with a dry rub. Chang's orange peel chicken has a combination of mild spices and citrus that marry well.

Chang's menu focuses on chicken, along with two pork choices and a small selection of seafood including scallops and calamari. Open Sunday through Thursday 11:00 A.M. to 11:00 P.M., Friday and Saturday 11:00 A.M. to midnight.

Uncle Tai's, A Chinese Bistro $$
Phipps Plaza, 3500 Peachtree Road
(404) 816–8888

Upscale and sophisticated, this restaurant specializes in authentic Hunan cuisine. Gourmet specialties include jumbo shrimp in chili sauce and sliced lamb with scallions. You may also order salads, soups, and light fare. You can order all dishes hot, medium, or mild. The restaurant's Phipps Plaza setting (across from Lenox Square) makes it a natural for important business gatherings or social events. You can eat in or take out. It's open for lunch and dinner seven days a week.

Continental

103 West $$$
103 West Paces Ferry Road NW
(404) 233–5993

In the heart of Buckhead, 103 West serves continental and French cuisine in an atmosphere of fine dining and interior decor that is heavy and just dripping with faux 17th-century opulence. You can count on enjoying the most delicious breads—they make their own and are famous for them. Popular menu items include grilled cold-water lobster tail in a

Insiders' Tip

The old Southern names for meals—"dinner" for the midday and "supper" for the evening—are not often used anymore, except by older native Southerners, but you may encounter them. If you're in doubt about which meals a restaurant serves, you can clear up the question by asking the hours of service.

Anthony's is housed in an antebellum mansion relocated to Buckhead from south Georgia.

PHOTO: ANTHONY'S RESTAURANT

thin, crisp batter with honey and Chinese mustard sauce, roasted breast of rare duck, and Parmesan-crusted medallions of veal with select vegetables and garganelli pasta in tarragon butter. There's valet parking; 103 West serves dinner only and is closed on Sunday; jackets are requested for the gentlemen. Noontime is reserved for the many associations that hold their monthly luncheons in the sunny downstairs ballroom.

The Abbey $$$$
163 Ponce de Leon Avenue
(404) 876–8532
www.theabbeyrestaurant.com

Looking for a dinner that's almost a religious experience? Try The Abbey, a fine dining restaurant serving contemporary cuisine in a deconsecrated Methodist church that takes up a whole block between Ponce de Leon and North Avenues. Roasted lamb loin with goat cheese, grilled venison loin and pan-seared squab, and glazed breast of duck in a spicy Oriental sauce are popular entrees. The restaurant has been in business since 1968 and has been at this location since 1978; it draws tourists as well as locals out

celebrating that special occasion. It's open daily for dinner only; there's valet parking; reservations are suggested.

Anthony's $$$$
3109 Piedmont Road NE
(404) 262–7379
www.anthonysfinedining.com

It's easy to miss Anthony's signage on Piedmont because the restaurant itself is hidden way back in the woods on one of the largest undeveloped pieces of land on this otherwise busy road. In a beautiful 1797 plantation home with seven working fireplaces, Anthony's house was originally built in Washington, Georgia, where it was spared by General Sherman, supposedly because the family had an infant. An Atlanta restaurant landmark since 1967, Anthony's offers fine dining in a unique atmosphere. Each room is decorated with antique paintings, chandeliers, chairs, and tables. The second-floor sun porch is a popular spot for anniversaries, birthdays, and other special occasions that require intimate dining. Popular entrees include Veal Anthony (milk-fed veal loin topped with asparagus, crabmeat, and hollandaise sauce). Another favorite is the oakwood-grilled grouper and roasted rack of lamb. Anthony's is open seven nights a week for dinner; reservations are suggested. There's valet parking.

Babette's Cafe $$$
573 North Highland Avenue
(404) 523–9121

On the outskirts of Little Five Points, Babette's presents European provincial fare that includes a fried oyster appetizer on dill biscuits with cucumber sauce, artichoke and olive ravioli, mussels with strawberries and serrano peppers, and the seasonal French stew cassoulet. There's a full bar; dinner is served nightly Tuesday through Sunday; brunch is served on Sunday. There's usually a wait at this intimate spot, enormously popular with locals.

The Dining Room $$$$
The Ritz-Carlton Buckhead
3434 Peachtree Road NE
(404) 237–2700

Frequently named one of the finest restaurants in Atlanta, The Dining Room is a dimly lit, intimate, wood-paneled room, elegantly appointed with art and antiques. The menu is a prix fixe dinner nightly except Sunday, with or without special wines from the master sommelier. We highly recommend you take the sommelier's suggestions and experience the meal the way the chef intended. You may also order a la carte. Under the direction of Frenchman Joel Antunes, the menu has become continental with a vivid touch of the Orient—not surprising since the young chef perfected his craft in Bangkok, Thailand, at the Oriental Hotel, a posh resort. Dishes change nightly. Appetizers might include foie gras and artichoke terrine, rare tuna with tarragon and chervil served with julienned beets, or shelled mussels with hot pepper and cumin seasoned tomatoes. Entrees for the evening might feature medallions of lamb in a brown sauce with sweet and sour eggplant confit and fava beans and chickpeas; veal with artichoke risotto, cherry tomatoes tarted up with lemon grass and chanterelles; or smoked salmon with parsley sauce. Best of all are the desserts, which come to the table looking more like sculptures than edible pastry, fruits, mousse, and chocolates. The Dining Room strongly encourages reservations, provides valet parking, and asks that gentlemen wear jackets.

Eno $$$
800 Peachtree Street
(404) 685–3191

With its glass doors opening to Peachtree Street and a pretty sidewalk of tables and chairs, this corner restaurant and wine bar reminds guests of a French cafe. The menu sports heavy European and Mediterranean influences, with entrees such as cumin and mint lamb sausage, or Provençal seafood stew. But the real stars at Eno ("wine") are the vintages. More than 150 bottles are offered by the glass, along with small sample plates of food. There's also a private dining room and an ongoing series of wine tastings and dinners. Lunch is served during the week; dinner begins at 5:00 P.M. every day except Sunday.

The Mansion $$
179 Ponce de Leon Avenue NE
(404) 876–0727

A grand 1885 home on a hill is the setting for The Mansion, a continental restaurant that opened in 1976. The estate,

Eno, a European-Mediterranean–influenced food and wine experience, is located in Midtown Atlanta. PHOTO: ENO

which occupies an entire block, was the home of Edward Peters, whose father, Richard, was the original developer of Atlanta's Midtown neighborhood. In surroundings rich with period furnishings and antiques, The Mansion serves lunch and dinner daily and brunch on Sunday. You may wish to start with an appetizer, such as steamed lobster with wilted spinach and lobster bisque, then choose from entrees such as beef Wellington, potato-crusted snapper with roasted peppers and dual pepper sauce, or pan-seared breast of chicken with saffron rice. The Mansion's elegant walled pool area is a popular spot for weddings. Dress is smart; reservations are accepted.

Nikolai's Roof $$$$
The Atlanta Hilton and Towers
255 Courtland Street NE
(404) 221–6362

When nothing less than total extravagance will do, there's Nikolai's Roof. (Don't be fooled by the Russian connection: The czar was a devotee of French food not unlike the lavish assortment on the prix fixe menu.) The service is as close to royalty as a diner can get, particularly when the waiters present silver-domed plates with a flourish.

Advance reservations are nearly always necessary at this famous fine dining restaurant atop the Atlanta Hilton. The menu changes with the availability of game and other specialty items. There's an impressive wine list and a number of flavored Russian vodkas. Coat and tie are requested for the gentlemen. Nikolai's, which provides stupendous views of Atlanta north of Downtown, has been dazzling diners since 1976.

Park 75 $$$$
75 14th Street, in the Four Seasons Hotel
(404) 253–3840

The plush second-floor dining room of the Four Seasons is under the capable hands of executive chef Kevin Hickey, who turns out exceptional seasonal American cuisine. Two four-course tasting menus are offered at dinner (one is vegetarian). There's also a

The view of Downtown and Midtown is magnificent from Nikolai's Roof atop the Atlanta Hilton.
PHOTO: ATLANTA HILTON

full bar, a strong wine list, and a waitstaff that's one of the city's best. Park 75 serves breakfast, lunch, and dinner, Monday through Saturday as well as daily afternoon tea and Sunday brunch.

Cross-Cultural Favorites

Cafe Tu Tu Tango $$
220 Pharr Road
(404) 841–6222
www.cafetututango.com

This Buckhead restaurant evokes the air of an artist's loft with creative use of light and color and a profusion of regional artwork. The setting includes a roving musician and a painter at work before an easel. Called multiethnic in influence, the tapas-style menu consists of appetizer-size entrees intended for sharing. The choices are invariably delicious and highly original. Barcelona stir-fry, Cajun chicken egg rolls, seared tuna sashimi—see what we mean by multiethnic? The cafe's full-service bar is a popular meeting spot. The restaurant is open every day for lunch and dinner and until the wee hours on the weekend.

Dante's Down the Hatch $$$
3380 Peachtree Road NE
(404) 266–1600

How about a place that looks like a big ship tied to a wharf where you can hear live jazz, watch alligators swim past the bar, and eat all your courses from a fondue pot? That's Dante's. The original

Dante's was one of the best-known spots in the first Underground Atlanta. It closed downtown for a while and opened uptown in Buckhead. The design of both restaurants was similar to a sailing ship at dock, and there's live jazz on the ship seven nights a week. The fare is fondue from meat to fruits, and your server will be happy to instruct you in the basics. The full bar boasts more than 300 wines. Dante's serves dinner nightly; reservations are recommended. See our Nightlife chapter for more details about Dante's.

English/Irish

Fado Irish Pub $
3035 Peachtree Road
(404) 841–0066

They decorated this multiroom Irish pub with newspapers, signs, and advertisements just like you'd see across the pond. But in the heart of Buckhead's nightlife district, it offers a bit of the old sod, with taps of Guinness, entrees of cottage pie, and weekend breakfasts loaded with black pudding, toasted soda bread, and grilled tomatoes. Late-night brings live Irish music and much socializing in the two bar areas, but there's usually a quiet booth by the fireplace or on the rear patio. Weekend mornings start off with soccer games on the satellite TV. There's also a gift shop with an assortment of Irish items. Fado opens for lunch daily, and service continues throughout the day into the wee hours. (Note: Since half of

Fado is a bar, children are allowed in before 8:00 P.M. on weekdays only.)

Rose and Crown $$
288 East Paces Ferry Road
(404) 233–8168

Fish 'n' chips, shepherd's pie, and great British ales are part of the ambience at this English pub. Weekend mornings include big breakfasts. In between pints—Harp, Boddington, and Guinness are all on tap—try your hand at billiards or darts. The big outdoor patio draws a crowd to the heart of Buckhead whenever the weather is warm. Service begins at 11:30 A.M. and goes into the early morning hours.

Owners of the Rose and Crown also operate Fox and Hounds, 1193 Collier Road, and the Prince of Wales, 1144 Piedmont Avenue.

French

Anis $$
2974 Grandview Avenue NE
(404) 233–9889

You know the food will be good when a French restaurant has a large French clientele. Anis has built a good reputation quickly since opening in 1994 and is quite popular. The fare is French Provincial, and many of the waitstaff speak French. Located in a brick house on a once-quiet Buckhead street that now boasts a number of restaurants, Anis has a large patio that is great for outdoor dining. It can get crowded, but the staff knows its business, and everyone is taken care of. Prices are reasonable. Beer and wine are available. There's live entertainment on Thursday night. Anis is open Monday through Saturday for lunch and dinner. The restaurant opens at 6:00 P.M. on Sunday for dinner. Parking on this formerly residential street, now restaurant row, is always challenging. There is underground parking available across the street at Colony Square and open air lots throughout the 14th and Peachtree Streets area.

Au Rendez Vous $
1328 Windsor Parkway
(404) 303–1968

This well-hidden gem is the perfect spot for serious working-class French—delicious and filling food minus the attitude plus decent prices, in other words. Chef Jean-Claude Changivy presents the sort of menu found in many overcrowded back-street Parisian restaurants, including *two* beef stews (done in red or white wine reductions), soups that are packed with odd bits of fresh herbs and vegetables, small side salads in bowls, and freshly steamed vegetables as complements.

We especially liked the fresh fennel soup, the coq sauté aux champignons, and the "to die for" chocolate and banana crepes. The downside is that this small BYOB (no pouring license yet) in the Brookhaven neighborhood has been discovered by Atlanta's foodie crowd, and waiting times for tables at lunch can be excessive. Open from 11:00 A.M. to 2:00 P.M. Tuesday though Friday, 5:00 to 9:30 P.M. Tuesday through Sunday. Brunch is served from 11:00 A.M. to 2:00 P.M. on weekends.

Brasserie Le Coze $$$
Lenox Square
3393 Peachtree Road NE
(404) 266–1440

Designed as a reproduction of a turn-of-the-century Parisian brasserie with dark wood paneling and brass, this highly praised restaurant serves French and other cuisines. Signature dishes include mussels with white wine and shallots; seared salmon with lentils, pearl onions, and lardons; or roast skate wings served with spinach potato in a brown butter caper sauce. Le Coze has its own pastry chef. There's a full bar; an outdoor patio is open in warm weather. Lunch and dinner are served Monday through Saturday; reservations are accepted.

Le Saint Amour $$$$
1620 Piedmont Avenue
(404) 881–0300

In 1997 a plain Midtown bungalow was transformed into a French country home that houses Le Saint Amour. This cozy, intimate restaurant, run by two French women, serves authentic delights from

Coquilles St. Jacques with warm foie gras to eight-ounce filets with béarnaise or bordelaise sauce. An assortment of casseroles, from lamb and veal stews to confit of duck, are also on the menu, along with a cheese course and desserts of soufflés and sabayons. The flagstone patio is a sunny spot for lunch Monday through Friday. Dinner is served nightly.

Petite Auberge $$
Toco Hills Shopping Center
2935 North Druid Hills Road NE
(404) 634–6268
www.petiteauberge.com

This French continental restaurant opened in 1974 and can easily be missed in the family-oriented mall in which it has been located from the beginning. Standout entrees include sea bass, bouillabaisse maison, filet mignon, and beef Wellington. It's open Monday through Saturday for dinner and on weekdays only for lunch. Dinner reservations are accepted.

South of France $$
Cheshire Square
2345 Cheshire Bridge Road
(404) 325–6963

South of France has been serving simple French cuisine in an intimate atmosphere since 1977. Specialties include quail with port wine, roast duckling with a brandied peach sauce, and braised rabbit in red wine sauce. South of France serves dinner Monday through Saturday and lunch on weekdays. There's a full bar, and the restaurant accepts reservations. SoF is probably the most perfect romantic restaurant in all of Atlanta!

Greek/Mediterranean

Basil's Mediterranean Cafe $$
2985 Grandview Avenue NE
(404) 233–9755

In the heart of Buckhead, Basil's outdoor patio is a big hit. Favorites of patrons here include vegetable pasta, grilled salmon on ratatouille with pesto, and traditional shish kebabs. After dinner, unwind with a delightful coffee drink from the full bar.

Appetizers are terrific, including a Mideastern dish comprised of tabbouleh, hummus, and baba ghanoush. Basil's serves lunch and dinner daily except Sunday; reservations are accepted.

Oasis Cafe $$
Sage Hill Shopping Center
1799 Briarcliff Road
(404) 876–0003

This family-owned restaurant makes everything up fresh. Its Middle Eastern specialties include kebabs, stuffed grape leaves, and mjadra (made with lentils, rice, onions, tomato, yogurt, and cucumber). All entrees include soup and a salad; there are lunch and dinner specials daily. Beer and wine are served. Friday and Saturday night a violin and guitarist play classical music. The Oasis is closed on Sunday.

Shipfeifer on Peachtree $$
1814 Peachtree Road
(404) 875–1106

Specializing in Mediterranean and vegetarian food since 1974 (when it was the only place in Atlanta where you could buy a gyro), this cozy place is popular with patrons from nearby office buildings and residents of the in-town area. You could eat for less than the price range shown by choosing from the menu's sandwich and sandwich wrap sections. The menu aims to please many tastes with a variety of dishes. Try the filling moussaka, a casserole of ground beef blended with herbs, spices, and eggplant, topped with feta cheese and a creamy Béchamel sauce. A puff pastry filled with mushrooms, calamata olives, artichokes, peppers, onions, tomatoes, and cheese will satisfy a craving for vegetables. Children's meals are offered. Baklava, the famous Greek honey-nut pastry, is the star dessert. For a beverage, you may choose from domestic or imported beers and specialty coffees. Free parking is provided behind the restaurant, which is open for lunch and dinner seven days a week. Half the menu is geared toward the vegetarian palate.

Living High on the Hog

Barbecue as a Southern tradition began well before the states even had names. North American Indians showed European explorers how to dry meat and fish on a framework of green saplings spread over a slowly smoldering fire. The explorers called this *barbacoa,* a term still used in Spanish. In the early 1700s, when North Carolina was a colony, barbecuing was part of the celebration for the end of the tobacco harvest. When French settlers applied the technology, they preferred to slowly roast whole animals on an open fire, and this cooking method was known as *Barbe a queue.*

With this kind of ancient—by American standards—history, it is not surprising that passions run deep about barbecue. In the South, where everyone has an opinion about how a hog should be prepared, which cuts of meat to use, what variety of animal should be chosen, whether it should be pulled, sliced, or chopped, and even how to spell the word (barbecue or barbeque), folks get pretty hot under the collar about what makes a particular recipe the best.

In Kentucky, according to author Calvin Trillin, mutton rather than pig is the barbecue meat of preference while in Oklahoma and Texas brisket and sausage get the thumbs up. But the most controversial issue by far involves the sauce. "And that is a river of debate that burns smoky brown or clear red, depending on your geographic preference," states barbecue maven and Atlanta writer Jim Auchmutey, waxing poetically about his favorite topic. In most Southern states, including Texas, the preference is for a thick, sweet, tomato-based sauce. But in the lowlands of South Carolina, barbecue sauces are prepared with a cider vinegar and black-pepper base that proves to be a complex taste combination some folks either love or hate.

Pig Pickin', where an entire hog is cooked, is the popular method of barbecuing. Die-hards use a homemade rig consisting of an old water tank or a pit in the ground

Indian

Calcutta $$
1138 Euclid Avenue
(404) 681–1838
Set in the Little Five Points district, Calcutta is known for high-quality dishes and low prices. Chicken tandoori is a favorite with many diners here. Lunch and dinner are served seven days a week. Wine and Indian beers are available.

Haveli Indian Cuisine $$
225 Spring Street NE
(404) 522–4545
2650 Cobb Parkway, Smyrna
(770) 955–4525

Haveli's menu includes seafood, vegetarian dishes, goat, lamb, and chicken, with tandoori and curry specialties. Open for dinner seven nights a week, Haveli serves lunch every day except on Sunday and features an all-you-can-eat lunch buffet.

Himalayas Indian Restaurant $$
5520 Peachtree Industrial Boulevard
Chamblee
(770) 458–6557
Located in an older, very large strip mall, Himalayas offers large portions of well-prepared traditional and tandoori-style dinners. A nice touch is the listed reminder that the food will be cooked to your spice/heat level (as it actually is in almost any Indian restaurant), from mild enough

upon which the meat is slow-cooked on a bed of wood. When the meat is ready, the crowds, hungry from their hours-long wait, pick the meat from the bone with their fingers.

In Atlanta you can find the best of both sauce styles—the tangy South Carolina barbecue as well as the more popular tomato-based sauce. Both are slavered on pork or beef that is pulled, chopped, or sliced, and tiny cups of extra sauce may be placed on your plate for dipping.

A profile of the barbecue tradition in the South exists in Bennett Brown III and his Atlanta catering company, LowCountry Barbeque. Started in 1986, the company specializes in Pig Pickin' parties, and Brown has introduced many bigwigs, including cookbook writer and TV star Julia Child, to the joys of the whole hog.

Brown's childhood memories include long nights of watching his dad and cronies dig a pit and stay up through the night and into the following day keeping wood stoked under a slow-cooking hog for the next evening's party. The men would tell stories, drink beer, and enjoy each other's company. At 11 years old, Brown was permitted to fix a pig in a pit by himself. It was a rite of passage, and so meaningful, he made a career out of barbecuing.

Great barbecue is available to all of us in Atlanta at downright country prices, and we don't have to stay up all night roasting a pig for it either. Dozens of restaurants specialize in nothing but barbecue. It's easy to sample the local fare and join in the debate about where you get the best. And while you're at it, don't forget to order Brunswick stew, another Southern tradition. It'll be right there on the menu; it might even come with your platter of pulled pork, bun, and pickles. What's Brunswick stew? It's a concoction of veggies and bits and pieces of meat. According to Christianne Lauterbach, food critic for *Atlanta Magazine,* the best stew should be "thick enough to spread on crackers, sweet with the goodness of pork and golden corn, and most generous in its meat-to-vegetable ratio."

Hungry? Well, come and get it.

for Grandma to searing-the-eyebrows hot. The usual array of curries, vegetarian dishes, and assorted meat dishes are offered, along with exceptional nan (bread) varieties. The only downside, admittedly somewhat minor, is the taciturn waitstaff and their somewhat overstated cultural paternal attitude toward female customers. Himalayas is open for lunch and supper daily.

Indian Delights $
1707 Church Street, Decatur
(404) 296-2965

High on food quality, this cafeteria-style restaurant features dishes from the southern part of India. The spotlight is on creatively seasoned grains and vegetables at inexpensive prices. Masala dosa, a large crepe filled with curried potatoes, is a favorite. Spicy soups, homemade noodles, and hot sauces will bring you back for more. Indian Delights doesn't serve alcohol. The restaurant is open for lunch and dinner every day but Monday; no credit cards accepted.

Raja Indian Restaurant $$
2955 Peachtree Road NE
(404) 237-2661

This small restaurant has developed a following of residents by serving an assortment of fine entrees. Offerings include tandoori specials, vegetarian dishes, hot curries, and samosas. Rice entrees include the tasty shrimp biryani, pilau rice cooked with shrimp, raisins, nuts, and peas. For your beverage, choose from American and Indian beers, plus Indian herbal teas. It's open for lunch and dinner seven nights a week.

Italian and Pizza

Baraonda Caffè Italiano $$
710 Peachtree Street
(404) 879–9962

The Naples origin of Baraonda's owners is reflected in its warm wooden furnishings, rustic decor, and intimate feeling, but most especially in its wood-fired pizzas, the heart of its menu. Other Italian traditionals are available—antipasti, calzones, panini, pasta dishes, and salads—but Baraonda's pizzas are in a whole other category than the usual American-style, heavy, cheese-laden standard. The intensely hot pizza oven produces a quickly cooked, very light and flavorful crispy crust, and it does not dry out the toppings in the process.

Our favorites are the pesto pizze bianche, a white pizza with pesto, olives, mozzarella, and cherry tomatoes, and the prosciutto pizze, a red pizza with tomatoes, Parma ham, mozzarella, arugula, and Parmiggiano. We also recommend (when available) the cozze in bianco antipasti, mussels in white wine with fresh tomatoes and crushed red peppers. Baraonda is open for lunch Monday through Friday from 11:30 A.M. to 2:30 P.M., for supper Monday through Thursday from 5:00 to 10:30 P.M. and Friday and Saturday from 5:00 P.M. to midnight, and Sunday from 11:30 A.M. to 9:00 P.M. Parking is available in nearby lots, with some limited streetside parking, and reservations are not accepted.

California Pizza Kitchen $$
Lenox Square, 3393 Peachtree Road NE
(404) 262–9221
4600 Ashford Dunwoody Road NE
(770) 393–0390
6301 North Point Parkway, Alpharetta
(770) 664–8246

You can feast on imaginative pizzas, pastas, and salads for both lunch and dinner in this casual contemporary atmosphere. Entrees from the impressive menu include a mind-boggling array of pizzas with nearly 30 gourmet toppings including barbecued chicken, Peking duck, and Southwestern burrito. Other entrees include chicken tequila pasta, pasta primavera, and focaccia-bread sandwiches. Hours and alcohol availability vary by location.

Fellini's Pizza $
2809 Peachtree Road NE
(404) 266–0082
1991 Howell Mill Road NW
(404) 352–0799
923 Ponce de Leon Avenue NE
(404) 873–3088
4429 Roswell Road NE
(404) 303–8248
422 Seminole Avenue NE
(404) 525–2530
1634 McLendon Avenue NE
(404) 687–9190

Wacky decor, spacious outdoor seating, and classic-style pizza in a casual, high-energy setting—that's Fellini's in all six locations. Don't expect finesse (or manners), just good eats. Made with the freshest ingredients, the pizzas are regular or Sicilian. Besides the traditional toppings, try the white pizza, which is especially good here. Plump calzones stuffed with sausage and cheese will fill you with satisfaction, as will the salads. The large vegetarian pizza is excellent. Fellini's serves beer and wine and is open seven days a week for lunch and dinner. Fellini's does not take credit cards.

Fratelli di Napoli $$$
2101-B Tula Street
(404) 351–1533
928 Canton Street, Roswell
(770) 642–9917

Head up the stairs to the second level of this warehouse-turned-eatery for an Italian extravaganza of food. Heaping platters of steaks, chops, chicken, pasta, and seafood are Fratelli's signature—at both locations. Kid-size portions, a full bar, and monthly wine tastings are part of the attraction. Dinner is served nightly.

La Grotta Buckhead $$$$
2637 Peachtree Road NE
(404) 231–1368
Ravinia Center
4355 Ashford Dunwoody Road
(770) 395–9925

Fine Italian cuisine here includes pasta dishes and favorites such as roasted quail stuffed with Italian sausage, grilled polenta, and balsamic vinegar sauce, and fillet of swordfish on a bed of spinach and Roma tomato with red pepper, and fresh thyme coulis. Dinner is served Monday through Saturday at the Peachtree Road location, and reservations are recommended. The Ravinia location is open for lunch and dinner and is more airy and modern than the Buckhead restaurant, with a wonderful view of the hotel's gardens from huge glass windows. Favorite menu items include grilled veal chop with herbs, shallots, and finocchio sautéed in butter, and beef tenderloin grilled with Barolo mustard with mushrooms, spinach, and roasted garlic mashed potatoes.

Maggiano's Little Italy $$$
4400 Ashford Dunwoody Road, Dunwoody
(770) 804–3313
3368 Peachtree Road
(404) 816–9650

There's no escaping this New York–style Italian eatery without a doggie bag—or two. The pastas, salads, steaks, chops, and seafood are big enough to serve two people—a suggestion frequently made by the waitstaff. Particular favorites are the homemade gnocchi, mushroom ravioli, and any of the several veal dishes. Private

dining rooms, a large bar, and a bakery are part of the premises. Valet parking is available. Service is continuous daily from 11:30 A.M., with a "happy hour" buffet offered Monday, Wednesday, and Friday 5:00 to 7:00 P.M.

Nino's $$$
1931 Cheshire Bridge Road NE
(404) 874–6505

This cozy, dim Italian restaurant is more authentic than most you'll find in the city. Even the waiters speak the language. Nino's serves both northern and southern cuisine quite simply without dressing up the plates, or the prices for that matter. House specialties include a number of pasta dishes as well as a variety of veal, beef, chicken, and seafood entrees. Nino's offers a full bar and serves dinner Monday through Sunday. Reservations are accepted and even recommended, especially for weekend dining.

Pricci $$$$
500 Pharr Road NE
(404) 237–2941

Even amidst the Buckhead district's estimated 200-plus restaurants, Pricci's glamorous setting makes it stand out in the midst of Atlanta's most concentrated area of restaurants, bars, and nightclubs. Delicacies await you in a chic interior where upscale informality reigns. Among the house specialties are regional dishes, homemade pastas, and pizzas from wood-burning ovens. But pizza is not what this Italian restaurant is really about. A favorite with diners is the cold-water lobster tails sautéed with garlic, lemon, and pinot grigio with black-and-white linguine marinara. Or try the baby lamb shank in Barolo wine sauce with pastina, braised vegetables, and roasted garlic. A full-service bar and extensive wine list will meet high expectations. Pricci's recommends reservations. Lunch is served Monday through Saturday, and dinner is served every night.

Rocky's Brick Oven Pizzeria $$
1770 Peachtree Street NW
(404) 870-7625

This source of delectable pizzas, pasta, and other authentic treats is a popular gathering place. In this homey, bustling restaurant, mouthwatering pizzas can be mixed and matched from an extensive selection of ingredients. Indulge in the Rudolph Valentino pizza, complete with a sweet-onion sauce and rosemary-seasoned roasted new potatoes on thin crust, or pick a robust thick-bottomed pie. The restaurant, named for the owner's dad, serves pizza baked in hickory- and oakwood-burning ovens made in Milan. Pricing is slightly different for either Neapolitan (thin) or Sicilian (thick) crusts. Pasta dishes are slightly more expensive. Rocky's serves beer and wine; dinner is served seven nights a week. Rocky's also serves lunch on weekdays.

Sotto Sotto $$–$$$
313 North Highland Avenue
(404) 523-6678

At Sotto Sotto, located in the reemerging Inman Park neighborhood, executive chef Riccardo Ullio stresses food quality rather than quantity. The seasonal menu reflects a traditional Italian emphasis on fresh ingredients and made-from-scratch sensibilities, and this shows in the wonderful flavors and food textures. Sotto Sotto's two signature dishes are its antipasto misto, an assortment of meats and cheeses with olives, mushrooms, and estate-bottled olive oils; and the tortelli di Michelangelo, a veal, chicken, and pork ravioli dish purportedly based on a recipe found in the artist's notebooks. We also liked the cappellacci di zucca, butternut squash cooked with brown butter and

sage, and the risotto ai frutti di mare, traditionally prepared carnaroli rice with mixed fresh seafood.

Sotto Sotto is open Monday through Thursday from 5:30 to 11:00 P.M.; Friday and Saturday from 5:30 P.M. to midnight. Parking is readily available, and reservations are highly recommended.

Veni Vidi Vici $$$$
41 14th Street NE
(404) 875-8424

If authentic northern Italian cuisine in a cosmopolitan, elegant atmosphere suits you, this is your kind of restaurant. Smack in the middle of the Midtown scene, Veni Vidi Vici rarely disappoints. Peruse the extensive hot and cold antipasti piccoli, which are small appetizers well designed to pique, not squash, your appetite. Among the restaurant's specialties are braised rabbit, suckling pig, pounded veal chop, and spinach and egg lasagna with veal and sausage. Visit the bocce ball court next to the patio. Lunch is served on weekdays, and dinner is served every night. There's a full-service bar on the premises. Reservations are recommended.

Japanese

Hashiguchi Jr. $$$
3400 Wooddale Drive NE
(404) 841-9229
3000 Windy Hill Road, Marietta
(770) 955-2337

In the Around Lenox Shopping Center near Lenox Square, this Japanese restaurant is a popular spot with sushi fanatics. Good service is yours at the full sushi counter. The spicy tuna roll will awaken your taste buds, as will the clams steamed over sake. Check out the traditional tempura dishes, one of which features bass. Tofu, crisply fried and dressed with shredded ginger, shows culinary imagination. For beverages, try Japanese beer or sake, and finish your meal with a dish of green tea ice cream. Closed on Monday, Hashiguchi serves lunch with sushi specials and dinner Tuesday through Sunday. Reservations are accepted.

Ru San's $$

1529 Piedmont Avenue NE
(404) 875–7042
2315 Windy Hill Road, Marietta
(770) 933–8315
3365 Piedmont Road
(404) 239–9557

California-style sushi and Japanese fusion entrees fill the menu of this restaurant, which opened in 1993. Ru San's on Piedmont Avenue is frequented mostly by the collegiate set, who enjoy the fast pace, lively atmosphere, and laid-back presentation (think "Iron Chef"). Ru San's is open for dinner every night and for lunch every day but Sunday. Sushi, tempura, and yakitori bargains are wildly popular. The sushi slices are enormous compared to other restaurants that feature this kind of food. Beer and wine are available. The Marietta location has tepan tables (food is cooked at the table), and reservations are taken at that location only. The Ru San's at Piedmont Road boasts a 100-foot-long sushi bar and a quick-serve take-out counter.

Korean

Asiana Garden $$

5150 Buford Highway, No. A-220, Doraville
(770) 452–1677

This restaurant is a combination of Korean and Japanese cuisine served to a mostly Asian clientele. The Korean-style barbecue is a favorite, as are Japanese dishes, which include shrimp and vegetable tempura, unaki-don (traditional broiled eel with special eel sauce), and a variety of noodle and soup dishes. Seafood, pork, poultry, and beef entrees in generous portions are described in English on your menu. Miso soup comes free with your sushi order, and if you purchase noodle soup, six or more little bowls of interesting food to add to the soup come to your table. These include tiny fish, kim chee cabbage, green veggies, and other goodies. Asiana is open for lunch Monday through Friday and for dinner seven nights a week.

Mirror of Korea $$

1047 Ponce de Leon Avenue NE
(404) 874–6243

Two miles from downtown, this restaurant offers authentic Korean cuisine. You'll find Korean specialties such as kim chee, spicy marinated cabbage; bool go ghi, a barbecue beef dish; and gahl bee, a beef short rib entree. Mirror of Korea also serves sushi, Chinese dishes, and vegetarian items. The restaurant serves beer and wine and opens for lunch and dinner Monday through Saturday.

Latin

Caramba Cafe $$

1409-D North Highland Avenue
(404) 874–1343

The food at this family-owned Mexican restaurant is prepared using vegetable oil. In addition to burritos, tacos, quesadillas, and chalupas, the menu features a number of meat-free and cheese-free dishes. The margaritas are crowd-pleasers, and so is the homemade flan. Dinner is served nightly; parties of six or more may call for reservations.

Coco Loco $$

2625 Piedmont Road NE
(404) 364–0212

This small restaurant in a shopping center has been preparing delicious Cuban and Caribbean dishes, such as jerk chicken, fried plantains, conch fritters, paella, arroz con pollo, and Cuban sandwiches, since 1988. There's a full bar, and live entertainment is featured on Saturday night. Coco Loco, where the attitude is fun and tropical, is open for lunch and dinner every day.

Don Juan's $$$

1927 Piedmont Circle NE
(404) 874–4285

Prints of Goya and Velazquez decorate this Spanish continental restaurant, opened in 1977. Specialties of the house include tapas, paella, veal, a variety of fresh fish, and black bean soup. Dinner is served Monday through Saturday; parking is free. Don Juan's has a full bar.

El Azteca $$
3424 Piedmont Road NE
(404) 266–3787
939 Ponce de Leon Avenue
(404) 881–6040
5800 Buford Highway, Doraville
(770) 452–7192
9925 Haynes Bridge Road, Alpharetta
(770) 569–5234

As you roam around Atlanta, you're often not far from a friendly, colorful El Azteca restaurant. The local chain has been serving spicy, reasonably priced Mexican food since 1981. All locations have a full bar with great margaritas and an outside patio. The menu offers inexpensive lunch specials, an array of combination plates, and specialty entrees such as beef and chicken fajitas and quesadillas. Lunch and dinner are served daily. Check the Yellow Pages for other suburban locations.

El Toro $$
5899 Roswell Road NE
(404) 257–9951
1775 Lawrenceville Highway, Decatur
(404) 294–8478
4300 Buford Highway
(404) 636–7090
2973-B Cobb Parkway
(770) 980–1386
5288 Buford Highway
(770) 455–6884

El Toro prepares all your deliciously flavored Mexican favorites served quickly. Choose from an almost endless variety of combination platters and specialties. All locations have a full bar and are open daily for lunch and dinner. Check the Yellow Pages for suburban locations.

La Bamba Restaurante Mexicano $$
1139 West Peachtree Street NE
(404) 892–8888

In a brightly painted house in the shadow of the IBM building at West Peachtree and 14th Streets, La Bamba serves up big portions of traditional Mexican favorites, such as fajitas, quesadillas, pepper steak, and more. Margaritas are a specialty, and

the best place to enjoy them (weather permitting) is the large outdoor deck. La Bamba is open daily for lunch and dinner. Parties of six or more may call for reservations. Parking is free.

La Fonda Latina $$
1150 Euclid Avenue
(404) 577–8317
2813 Peachtree Road NE
(404) 816–8311
4427 Roswell Road NE
(404) 303–8201
639 McClendon Avenue
(404) 378–5200

The ambience here is in the style of a Mexican cantina, with floral murals, fountains, perky music, and friendly service. The location at Euclid Avenue is the place to go in Little Five Points for spicy Latin-influenced food, including the highly recommended paella served in a sizzling iron skillet, either as a vegetarian dish or loaded with chicken, seafood, and sausage. The quesadillas come with big portions of black beans and yellow rice. Beer, wine, and a delicious homemade sangria are poured at La Fonda. It's open daily for lunch and dinner.

Mambo Restaurante Cubano $$$
1402 North Highland Avenue NE
(404) 876–2626

Mambo, which features a 9-foot-tall mural of a stylized Carmen Miranda, serves Cuban cuisine nightly for dinner. Crowd-pleasers include paella, Chino-Latino (a Cuban-Chinese fish dish), and ropa vieja (a dish of shredded beef, garlic, tomatoes, and peppers). A "must try" is the shrimp veradura. Beer and wine are served; lively Latin music is featured on CDs; reservations are accepted. If you have to wait to be seated, visit the art galleries and shops next door (see The Arts and Shopping chapters).

Mexico City Gourmet $$
2134 North Decatur Road NE
(404) 634–1128
5500 Chamblee Dunwoody Road, Dunwoody
(770) 396–1111

Upscale but friendly, this restaurant delivers what its name suggests: imaginatively prepared Mexican food. Fish dishes and other specials are offered with favorites such as shrimp fajitas and chile rellenos. Both locations have a full bar; try the Perfect Margarita, made with Grand Marnier instead of triple sec. Mexico City Gourmet is open daily for lunch and dinner.

Oh Maria! $$
3167-G Peachtree Road
(404) 261–2032

Not your typical chips-guac-Margarita Slushy sort of place, Oh Maria! specializes in variations of traditional Mexican dishes complemented with fresh vegetables. We liked the enchiladas verdes, rolled tortillas with shredded chicken breast cooked in a spicy tomatillo salsa, with rice and beans, and the pescado Veracruz, red snapper stuffed with Mexican truffles, salsa poblano, rice, and vegetables.

Corking fee is $25, and parking is not an issue (unusual for this area of Midtown). Oh Maria! is open Monday through Thursday for lunch 11:30 A.M. to 2:30 P.M. and for supper 5:30 to 11:00 P.M., Friday 5:30 P.M. to 1:00 A.M., Saturday 11:30 A.M. to 1:00 A.M., and Sunday 11:30 A.M. to midnight.

Rio Bravo Cantina $$
3172 Roswell Road NW
(404) 262–7431
5565 New Northside Drive NW
(770) 952–3241
440 Ernest W. Barrett Parkway NW
Kennesaw
(770) 429–0602

Rio Bravo started serving its Tex-Mex fare in Buckhead in 1984 and since has expanded to the suburbs, Tennessee, Florida, and Alabama. Crowd-pleasers include the fajitas, quesadillas, and cheese dip. There's a large patio that fills up on the weekends and evenings. Rio Bravo is open every day for lunch and dinner. All locations have a full bar. Check the Yellow Pages for several suburban locations.

Sundown Cafe $$$
2165 Cheshire Bridge Road NE
(404) 321–1118

Creative Mexican and Southwestern food is the attraction at Sundown. The menu changes frequently to showcase various appetizers and entrees. Eddie's pork, grilled and served with jalapeño gravy, is popular. Try the spicy Mexican turnip greens. There's a full bar. Lunch is served weekdays; dinner is served Monday through Saturday. Patio dining is available here, too.

Tortillas $
774 Ponce de Leon Avenue NE
(404) 892–0193

This fun, lively California-style burrito place is big with students and anyone who likes inexpensive spicy food. These fat burritos are bursting with beans and rice, and the sauces are bright and bold. From the second-floor outdoor porch you can soak up the ever-changing scene on Ponce while downing cold brews and guacamole. Tortillas is open daily for lunch and dinner; no credit cards accepted.

Seafood

Atlanta Fish Market $$$
265 Pharr Road NE
(404) 262–3165

A huge fish sculpture looms over this popular Buckhead restaurant, which is part of the Buckhead Life Restaurant Group. Unveiled in November 1995, "the great fish," a 50-ton solid copper and steel artwork, is either an eyesore or a great Atlanta landmark depending on whom you ask. The sculpture stands on its tail and curves upward, dwarfing the building. Inside, a pleasing combination of casual atmosphere and superior food sets the tone of this restaurant, a 13,000-square-foot complex that includes a lounge, second-floor private dining room, and boutique-style food shop. The menu changes daily based on the availability of fresh seafood in season. Local favorites include stone crab claws and raw oysters. You can order the catch of the day charbroiled or steamed Hong Kong style with fresh ginger and scallions in a light sherry soy sauce. Reservations are suggested for dinner seven nights a week. Lunch is served every day

This 50-ton fish sculpture at the Atlanta Fish Market is an unmistakable landmark in Buckhead. PHOTO: JOHN MCKAY

except Sunday. The Fish Market offers cocktails, beer, and wine. The Pano's Food Shop is the on-site take-out shop.

Joe's Crab Shack $–$$
1590 Pleasant Hill Road, Duluth
(770) 381–6333
2501 Cobb Place Boulevard, Kennesaw
(770) 429–7703
1965 Mt. Zion Road, Morrow
(770) 472–0024

Joe's Crab Shack is part of a large, nationwide chain of seafood-oriented restaurants, yet manages to feel more like a beach-town original. Most important, and rarest of all, the food here is some of the best Gulf-coastal style available anywhere in Atlanta for this price range. As the name implies, Joe's leans very heavily toward shellfish, both raw and very well prepared in a wide range of styles, including blackened, grilled, pan sautéed, and encrusted with a number of available finishings. Other fish dishes such as mountain trout, salmon, and tuna are also available in an equal number of different styles, and a number of deep-fried items that appeal to the Southern palate are offered.

When you first walk in, two things strike you immediately. First, the decor can best be described as looking like a Parrothead's garage exploded inside, and second, there is a high degree of emphasis on the number and variety of bar and frozen alcoholic beverages available. Despite this seeming "meat market" attitude, these are most decidedly family restaurants, where everyone is encouraged to have a good time and even join in on the scheduled spontaneous dancing of the happy natives. All the Joe's in the Atlanta area are very, very popular, and waits on weekends can easily range over an hour. Joe's is open daily for lunch and supper.

McKinnon's Louisiane Restaurant and Seafood Grill $$$
3209 Maple Drive NE
(404) 237–1313
www.mckinnons.com

For more than 20 years, McKinnon's has provided superior Cajun seafood to appreciative diners in two settings: the upscale main dining room and the more casual Grill Room. There's nothing ordinary about the offerings, such as crawfish tails salad. Blackened amberjack, crunchy on the outside, moist and tender on the inside, is a favorite. Crab cakes, oysters, and crawfish étouffée are others. Guests can sing along at the piano on Friday and Saturday. At the intersection of Maple Drive and Peachtree Road, the restaurant accepts reservations for dinner every night except Sunday.

Ray's on the River $$$
6700 Powers Ferry Road, Marietta
(770) 955–1187
www.raysontheriver.com

Ray's has drawn a lively crowd to its huge, many-roomed setting on the banks of the

Chattahoochee River since 1984. Seafood flown in daily and fresh pasta are favorites here. Grilled, blackened, broiled, sautéed, baked, or fried—have your choice of how your entree is prepared. Among the popular choices are oysters on the half shell and blackened fish Alexander, which is topped with Mornay sauce, shrimp, and scallops. Other entrees include prime rib, chicken, large salads, homemade soups, and desserts. A full-service bar, extensive wine list, and live jazz create an enjoyable atmosphere. A call for priority seating will move you to the head of the line if you arrive at your appointed time. Ray's serves lunch and dinner seven days a week, plus one of the city's most bountiful Sunday brunch buffets. On Tuesday through Saturday evenings, Ray's features jazz musicians.

Southern Food and Barbecue

Barbecue Kitchen $$
1437 Virginia Avenue, College Park
(404) 766-9906

If you love Southern food and lots of it, you'll flip at the Barbecue Kitchen. The main dishes include country ham, fried chicken, and the restaurant's own pork barbecue, which is smoked right out back. Your dinner comes with three vegetables, such as mashed potatoes, collards, and fried okra, and you can get a free reorder of each—but since you can order the same vegetables or three different ones, you're really getting a meat and six. All this place lacks is someone to help happy diners waddle back to their cars. This totally nonsmoking restaurant is open daily

from 7:30 A.M. to 10:00 P.M. No alcohol is served, and no credit cards are accepted.

The Beautiful Restaurant $$
2260 Cascade Road SW
(404) 752-5931
397 Auburn Avenue NE
(404) 223-0080

Fresh vegetables, baked chicken, beef ribs, banana pudding, and corn bread are all popular with diners at The Beautiful soul food restaurants. The Cascade Road location is open 24 hours Thursday, Friday, and Saturday, and 7:00 A.M. until midnight the rest of the week; the Auburn Avenue restaurant, which is across from Ebenezer Baptist Church, operates from 7:00 A.M. till 8:30 P.M. seven days a week. No alcohol is served, and credit cards are not accepted.

The Colonnade $$$
1879 Cheshire Bridge Road NE
(404) 874-5642

This large Southern restaurant has been an Atlanta tradition since 1927 and is a favorite with the older set as well as young people and families. Turkey and dressing, fried chicken, and more than 30 vegetables top the list of offerings. After church on Sunday, things really get crowded here. The Colonnade is open daily for lunch and dinner and has a full bar. Credit cards are not accepted.

Dusty's Barbecue $$
1815 Briarcliff Road NE
(404) 320-6264

There's always country music playing in the background at Dusty's, a tiny place on a triangle of land near Sage Hill Shopping

Center and just down the block from the Emory University campus. Dusty's is decorated entirely in a "pig" motif. The barbecue (pork, beef, or chicken) is the main attraction, but the potato salad, fried okra, and hush puppies are good too, and the sweet tea is excellent. Beer and wine are available. Dusty's opened in 1981 and serves lunch and dinner daily.

Evans Fine Foods $
2125 North Decatur Road NE
(404) 634–6294

Evans has been fixing Southern food since 1946. Specialties include smothered breast of chicken, country-fried steak, rib eyes, and blueberry and blackberry cobbler. About 15 vegetables are offered daily. Evans is closed on Sunday and open other days from 5:30 A.M. to 9:00 P.M. No alcohol is served. No credit cards are accepted.

Fat Matt's Rib Shack $$
1811 Piedmont Avenue NE
(404) 607–1622

It really does look like a shack. Fat Matt's exterior was created by Atlanta airbrush legend sign painter "J.J. of L.A.," whose murals of food embellish numerous stores and restaurants in the city. Matt's fixes ribs (which we simply drool over), chopped pork barbecue, and barbecued chicken, plus side dishes such as rum-baked beans. It's open every day for lunch and dinner, and there's live blues every night. You can pig out until 11:30 P.M. weeknights and until 12:30 A.M. on weekends. Beer is sold here, but no credit cards are accepted.

Flying Pig $$
856 Virginia Avenue, Hapeville
(404) 559–1000

The management of this spot, which originally opened in the 1950s, has quickly won the respect of barbecue lovers—even if it is a bit hard to find, close to the airport. Beef, pork, and ribs are pit-cooked on site; smoked chicken wings are also a crowd-pleaser. All the food is prepared in the kitchen right in front of the customers. There's an outside deck for warm-weather dining. The Pig is closed on Saturday and Sunday. No alcohol is served. Credit cards are not accepted.

Mary Mac's Tea Room $$
224 Ponce de Leon Avenue NE
(404) 876–1800

The absolute "Grande Dame" of Atlanta restaurants, Mary Mac's has been in business for 50-plus years at this location, and the restaurant remains a famous landmark of traditional Southern food. It also maintains a few Southern traditions, such as writing out your own order with pads and pencils on each table. Favorites at the Tea Room include baked chicken and dressing, fried chicken, sweet-potato soufflé, fresh-baked yeast rolls, and the rich "pot liquor" broth. Mary Mac's serves lunch and dinner daily and breakfast on Saturday and Sunday. There's a full bar, but smoking is not allowed, and credit cards are not accepted.

Paschal's Restaurant $$
830 Martin Luther King Drive SW
(404) 577–3150

Much history in the civil rights movement is said to have taken place over Paschal's soul food (catfish, pork chops, short ribs, steaks, collard greens, macaroni and cheese, and yams), and the restaurant remains a landmark in the African-American community. Brothers James and Robert Paschal founded the restaurant in a smaller building across the street in 1947; it was so successful that they eventually built the current restaurant and a 150-room motor hotel that is now used for student housing. There's a full bar; Paschal's is open daily for breakfast, lunch, and dinner. There's free parking in the lot behind the motor hotel.

Pittypat's Porch $$$$
25 International Boulevard
(404) 525–8228

Think Tara, Southern belles, tables groaning with wonderful food, and magnolia trees blowing in the breeze. Or, at least the Technicolor version of this mythical scene. Pittypat's offers traditional Southern cooking (pork fat rules!) for tourists and transplants (the rest of us get it at

Mama's house), and the house decorations feature an unusual and quite interesting coating of assorted newspaper clippings covering the walls. Open for supper daily.

Silver Grill $$
900 Monroe Drive NE
(404) 876–8145

Now being run by the third generation of its founding family, the Silver Grill has been cooking Southern food at this location since 1945. Fried chicken, country-fried steak, and grilled chicken breast are longtime menu standouts; about 10 vegetables are generally offered each day. The Grill is open weekdays for lunch and dinner; no alcohol is served. No credit cards accepted.

Son's Place $
100 Hurt Street
(404) 581–0530

Son's Place traces its lineage back to Burton's Grill, a soul food landmark in Atlanta, where the late Deacon Burton, regal in his tall chef's hat, presided over a small army of women (all of whom he called "mama") who cooked up the best skillet-fried chicken in town. The vegetables, such as mashed potatoes, collard greens, and creamed corn, are deliciously flavored and thoroughly cooked in the traditional Southern fashion. Son's is a favorite with everyone from media people to civil rights leaders. It's right beside the Inman Park/Reynoldstown MARTA station; breakfast and lunch, but no alcohol, are served Monday through Friday. This is the real thing, folks—don't pass up an opportunity to eat here! No credit cards accepted.

South City Kitchen $$$
1144 Crescent Avenue NE
(404) 873–7358
www.southcity.com

In an old Midtown house, South City cooks up a new Southern cuisine that would no doubt baffle the Southern cooks of a century ago, but the place is going gangbusters. The innovative menu includes a grilled center-cut pork chop on stir-fried mustard greens, sautéed shrimp and scallops over stone-ground grits with garlic gravy, roasted cinnamon chicken over corn bread stuffing and a sour mash jus. South City is open daily for lunch and dinner.

Cajun

Fuzzy's
2015 North Druid Hills Road
(404) 321–6166

Atlantan Joe Dale made a name for himself as one of the city's leading Cajun cooks. For years he operated his own restaurant; now, his crawfish étouffée and Cajun chicken sandwiches are on the menu at Fuzzy's, where '70s music and live blues bands keep guests entertained. Lunch and dinner are served daily, and everything is available to go.

Huey's $$
1816 Peachtree Street
(404) 873–2037

Relax on the covered sidewalk patio or peruse the collection of Mardi Gras memorabilia in the dining room of this always busy Cajun eatery. Weekend mornings are bustling with diners crowding in for the hot, sugary beignets and rich brunch dishes such as eggs sardou. Lunch is

> ## Insiders' Tip
> If you'd rather do it yourself, the chefs at the Kroger School of Cooking are ready to show you how at 12460 Crabapple Road in Alpharetta. They offer a variety of courses designed to let you try it at home. For the latest programs, call (770) 740-2068.

served during the week; dinner is offered Monday through Saturday. There's plenty of free parking behind the restaurant.

Thai

Bangkok Thai $$
1492 Piedmont Road NE
(404) 874-2514

Bangkok, which opened in 1977, claims to be the oldest Thai restaurant in Atlanta. In the Ansley Square Shopping Center, just south of the intersection of Piedmont Road and Monroe Drive in Midtown, Bangkok serves an adventurous and delicious version of Thai cuisine. If you like it hot, start with the spicy, aromatic tom yum (lemon grass) soup, then go for the spicy catfish with red curry sauce or the chicken or shrimp stir-fry with green beans, carrots, and bamboo shoots in red chili sauce. Afterward, cool off with the exquisite homemade coconut ice cream. Bangkok has beer and wine; it's open weekdays for lunch and nightly for dinner.

King & I $$
1510-F Piedmont Avenue NE
(404) 892-7743
4058 Peachtree Road NE
(404) 262-7985

Delicious Thai food served by a friendly staff is the attraction at King & I, which joined the Atlanta restaurant scene in the early '80s. Recommended dishes include the spring roll appetizer, pad Thai noodles, and shrimp with hot garlic sauce. King & I serves large portions at reasonable prices. Beer and wine are available; the restaurant serves lunch on weekdays and dinner nightly.

Pad Thai $$$
1021 Virginia Avenue
(404) 892-2070

Owned by the same folks as the King & I, Pad Thai is the more elegant of the two, although you don't have to be any more dressed for the occasion. This charming restaurant in the heart of the Virginia-Highland community is known for seafood dishes with squid, eggplant, and hoisin sauce and basil rolls. If you are looking for a tête-à-tête to go with your Thai eggplant, choose Pad Thai for lunch or dinner.

Surin of Thailand $$
810 North Highland Avenue NE
(404) 892-7789
www.surinofthailand.com

Since opening in 1991, Surin continues to draw faithful followers with delicacies served in a delightful setting. Gleaming wooden floors, dark blue tablecloths, and Thai banners create a charming backdrop. Traditional dishes include chicken coconut soup and Thai noodles pan-fried with shrimp and egg and garnished with peanuts and bean sprouts. Or try Koa-Mok-Kai, a luncheon special of marinated chicken and rice. The array of appetizers tempts you to make a meal of them. Try the tender poached basil rolls filled with shrimp, shredded pork, basil lettuce, and bean sprouts, or the Surin baskets, six edible baskets filled with a mixture of spiced chicken, shrimp, and corn. Surin offers a full bar and parking behind the restaurant. Surin serves lunch and dinner seven days a week and doesn't take reservations.

Zab-E-Lee $$
Service Merchandise Plaza
4837 Old National Highway, College Park
(404) 768-2705

This relaxed, no-frills storefront place serves flavorful meat salads, curries, pad Thai, and other delicious dishes. Restaurant critics rave about the food at Zab-E-Lee, which takes no reservations. Beer and wine are available.

Vegetarian

Cafe Sunflower $$
2140 Peachtree Road
(404) 352-8859
5975 Roswell Road
(404) 256-1675
www.cafesunflower.com

This upscale vegetarian restaurant offers an array of healthy dishes so tasty you won't miss the meat. Check out the West African stew and macro-stir-fries. Lunch and dinner are served Monday through Saturday.

Flying Biscuit $$
1655 McLendon Avenue NE
(404) 687–8888
1001 Piedmont Avenue
(404) 874–8887
www.flyingbiscuit.com

Known to many as an all-day breakfast cafe, the Biscuit displays its unique personality at lunch and dinner as well. For breakfast, try Egg-ceptional Eggs, served yolk-up on black-bean cakes with a fresh tomatillo salsa. For a side order, how about fresh turkey sausage with sage and creamy rosemary potatoes? Or dig into fluffy stacks of organic oatmeal pancakes topped with warm maple syrup. Lunch and dinner choices include hearty burgers (grain, vegetable, or turkey) and moist turkey meat loaf dressed with horseradish sauce. Service is friendly, and you can graze for little or spend more to feast. Closed on Monday, the Flying Biscuit does not accept reservations, and there's almost always a wait. Both locations open at 7:00 A.M.

Vietnamese

Dong Khanh Restaurant $$
4646 Buford Highway NE
(770) 457–4840

Open seven days a week for lunch and dinner, Dong Khanh offers many Vietnamese and Chinese specials at reasonable prices. Spicy chicken, sautéed chili and lemon root, salted fish hot pot, fried pig intestine, and frog legs sautéed with curry sauce are just a few of the varied dishes on this restaurant's extensive menu. Dong Khanh serves beer.

Vietnamese Cuisine $$
3375 Buford Highway NE
(404) 321–1840

Bring your appetite to this storefront eatery that promises gourmet Vietnamese food and lots of choices. Popular dishes include stir-fried chicken with lemon grass, pepper rolls, and a soup that mixes vegetables, shrimp, and pork. The restaurant of-fers beer and wine and serves lunch and dinner seven days a week. Some entrees will take you into a higher price category. Vietnamese Cuisine, in the Northeast Plaza, has plenty of free parking.

Beyond Atlanta

American

American Pie $$
5840 Roswell Road NW
(404) 255–7571
www.american-pie.com

American Pie is the restaurant that thinks it's on Ocean Boulevard in Myrtle Beach instead of on Roswell Road in Sandy Springs (just outside the Perimeter). The swinging atmosphere is that of a beach club bar and grill, and the gaudy decor carries the theme through. You want TV? The Pie has about 50 TVs. You want refreshment? The Pie has five full bars. You want food? Try the grilled chicken supreme sandwich with barbecue sauce. You want big events? The Pie frequently stages big radio station promotions and other happenings to amuse its guests, who tend to be sports-loving singles out for fun. It's open Sunday from noon to 4:00 P.M. and Monday through Saturday from 11:00 A.M. to 4:00 A.M., but closes at 3:00 A.M. Saturday night.

Good Ol' Days $
5841 Roswell Road
(404) 257–9183

The unique thing about Good Ol' Days is that the menu's sandwiches are prepared and served out of flower pots (don't ask why, just enjoy). Chicken wings are another specialty. This Sandy Springs location has a full bar; it's open daily for dinner and weekends for lunch. There is an outdoor patio and big-screen TV. You can dance the night away seven days a week— Good Ol' Days is open until 4:00 A.M.

Green Manor $$$
6400 Westbrook Street, Union City
(770) 964–4343

Built in 1910, this two-story brick manor

house has a wide, wraparound porch, rocking chairs, a full bar, a picturesque gazebo, and a ghost, said to appear in the upstairs windows. Taste some of the menu's elegant dishes on the sampler platter with petite filet, chicken, and jumbo shrimp. Fresh vegetables and corn bread salad are specialties. Miss Emma's banana pudding and peach cobbler are some of the homemade desserts. Lunch features a Southern country buffet with fried okra and crispy green tomatoes. Linen-covered tables are spread throughout the home's high-ceilinged parlor, dining room, and sun porch. Lunch is served Monday through Friday and Sunday; dinner is served Friday.

Greenwoods on Green Street $$
1087 Green Street, Roswell
(770) 992-5383

Oversized portions of American favorites, from fried chicken to potpie, are on the simple menu at Greenwoods, based in a renovated cottage behind Roswell's historic district. If there's too much food to finish, take it home along with one of the restaurant's famous pies, sold whole to go. There's no alcohol. Personal checks are accepted, but credit cards are not. Open Wednesday through Saturday 5:00 to 10:00 P.M., Sunday 11:30 A.M. to 2:30 P.M. and 5:00 to 9:00 P.M.

Magnolia Restaurant and Tea Room $$$
5459 East Mountain Street, Stone Mountain
(770) 498-6304
www.magnoliarestaurant.com

This 1854 gingerbread house sits on more than two acres in the heart of Stone Mountain Village. The classic Southern setting provides a relaxed atmosphere in which to enjoy the Magnolia's American and French cuisine. Specialties include chicken salad stuffed into a heart-shaped puff pastry, banana cheesecake with pralines, and daily seafood specials. The Sunday buffet is loaded with everything from eggs Benedict to carved roast beef. Lunch is served Thursday through Sunday. Reservations are encouraged. Beer and wine are served. Credit cards are not accepted.

Mittie's Tea Room $$
925 Canton Street, Roswell
(770) 594-8822

This old store in Roswell's historic district has been a tearoom since 1987. A mix of antique tables and buffets are decorated with teapots, cups, and an assortment of tea paraphernalia. Lunch is light, with a variety of salads, quiches, soups, and a selection of wines and beers. And yes, tea-lovers, tea is served daily—and correctly, in a china pot. Mittie's Tea Room is open seven days a week from 11:00 A.M. to 4:00 P.M.

Norcross Station Cafe $$
40 South Peachtree Street, Norcross
(770) 409-9889

Like a little shaking and rattling with your burger or barbecued chicken? The trains that rumble by Norcross Station, in the town's restored depot, frequently send vibrations through the floorboards and table legs right to the silverware. It's part of the charm of this restaurant, where lunch and dinner are served every day but Sunday. Pull up a chair inside the rustic, high-ceilinged main room, or enjoy the enclosed and heated year-round outdoor deck overlooking the town's restored business district. Soups, salads, quiches, and sandwiches are big for lunch; dinner features chef's specials as well as Creole and Cajun dishes, steaks, ribs, and pastas.

Public House Restaurant and Bar $$–$$$
605 South Atlanta Street, Roswell
(770) 992-4646

One of the very few buildings in this area of metro Atlanta to escape Sherman's pyromania, this 1854-era building on Roswell's historic square is both a beloved landmark and newly reopened dining alternative to the infestation of chains in the region.

Chef Jeff Hornsby provides heartier specialties such as his turn on french onion soup, massively large lump crab cakes, ahi tuna, and tea-smoked salmon fillet, served in a bare-brick, somewhat loud but well-appointed dining room. Live "cabaret-style" entertainment is provided on Friday and Saturday evenings, from 7:15 P.M. to closing, when only limited reservations are accepted, and full reservations are accepted for all other lunch and supper times.

A full bar is available; smoking is allowed in an adjacent lounge area, which is supplied with its own cigar humidor; and due to the age of the building and its historic status, handicapped access is limited (and nonexistent in the bathrooms). Dress is upscale casual. The Public House is open for lunch Monday through Friday from 11:30 A.M. to 2:30 P.M., and Saturday and Sunday from 11:30 A.M. to 3:00 P.M. Supper is served Monday through Thursday from 5:30 to 10:00 P.M., Friday and Saturday 5:30 to 11:00 P.M., and Sunday 5:30 to 9:00 P.M. It is closed only on Thanksgiving Day and Christmas Day.

Shillings on the Square $$$
19 North Park Square, Marietta
(770) 428-9520
www.shillingsonthesquare.com

This casual restaurant and bar has anchored a corner of the Marietta square for more than 20 years. Its neighborhood pub style is a favorite of locals looking for oversized sandwiches and finger foods late into the night or during a short lunch break. The kitchen opens at 10:30 A.M. and serves until midnight during the week; 2:00 A.M. on weekends.

For those with more elegant tastes, Upstairs at Shillings is an 80-seat fine dining room, with white tablecloths, candles, and soft piano tunes putting diners in a relaxed mood. Entrees of steaks, seafood, veal, lamb, and chicken are offered. Dinner is served from 5:30 to 10:00 P.M. on weekdays, midnight on weekends. Sunday brunch is served from 10:30 A.M. to 2:00 P.M.

Showcase Eatery $$$
5549 Old National Highway
(404) 669-0504

This upscale spot serves handmade food with a special touch. Try the grilled California chicken on a bed of spinach and fettuccine or the trout. African and African-American art on the walls warms up the ambience. The Showcase Eatery is open for lunch Tuesday through Friday and dinner Tuesday through Sunday. Reservations are suggested for large parties.

Steak Houses

Killer Creek Chophouse $$$
1700 Mansell Road, Alpharetta
(770) 649-0064

Yes, the steaks here are killers, but that's not where the name comes from. In fact, the enormous glass windows of this sleek restaurant overlook Foe Killer Creek. But even the pretty view from the patio won't distract you from the luscious London broil, wood-fired rack of lamb, and roasted bass. Dinner is served from 5:00 P.M. during the week, and from 4:00 P.M. on the weekends. Sundays are family dinner nights, with several classic favorites (meat loaf, fried shrimp) served with a selection of vegetables family style.

LongHorn Steakhouse $$$
6390 Roswell Road NW
(404) 843-1215
900 Mansell Road, Roswell
(770) 642-8588
2700 Town Center Drive, Kennesaw
(770) 421-1101
7882 Tara Boulevard, Jonesboro
(770) 477-5365
2120 Killian Hill Road, Snellville
(770) 972-4188
www.longhornsteakhouse.com

Established in Buckhead in 1981, Longhorn now has 37 restaurants in Georgia and another 140 in other states and Puerto Rico. The steaks, such as the seven- or nine-ounce filet and the 20-ounce porterhouse, are cut fresh daily by hand; the salmon is farm-raised in Canada. The atmosphere is steak house–Western. The service is friendly, and the bar is well stocked. Steaks are reasonably priced. Most locations are open daily for lunch and dinner. Call as you're heading out to get your name on the waiting list. Check the Yellow Pages for more locations.

McKendrick's Steak House $$$
4505 Ashford Dunwoody Road
(770) 512-8888

Be hungry when you head to this '40s-style bistro where USDA prime Midwestern beef, tempura lobster, and one-pound cold-water lobster tails are the specialties.

Beer, wine, and alcohol are served. McKendrick's offers lunch Monday through Friday and dinner nightly.

Ruth's Chris Steakhouse $$$
5788 Roswell Road
(404) 255-0035
950 East Paces Ferry Road NE
(404) 365-0660
276 Marietta Street NW
(404) 223-6500

Offering fine dining in a clubby, casual atmosphere, this split-level building has four fireplaces and an overall attitude of contemporary luxury. Popular menu items include the stuffed mushroom appetizer, filet, lobster, bread pudding with whiskey sauce, and chocolate mousse cheesecake. Dinner is served nightly at both locations. The Buckhead restaurant at East Paces Ferry Road also serves lunch on weekdays.

Stoney River Legendary Steaks $$$
5800 States Bridge Road, Duluth
(770) 476-0102
10524 Alpharetta Highway, Roswell
(678) 461-7900

Don't let the name fool you: There's much more to this eatery and bar than just steak. Although certified Angus beef is a specialty, the menu includes coastal shrimp, salmon, trout, baby-back ribs, bourbon chicken, and pasta. The atmosphere is rustic country, with lots of cedar, stacked stone, hardwood floors, and an open-hearth fireplace. Dinner is served seven days a week; brunch is added on Sunday. Stoney River is one of the area's most popular places to eat but does not take reservations: Don't be surprised if there's a two-hour wait on the weekends.

Cajun

Pappadeaux Seafood Kitchen $$$
2830 Windy Hill Road, Marietta
(770) 984-8899
5635 Jimmy Carter Boulevard, Norcross
(770) 849-0600
10795 Davis Drive, Alpharetta
(770) 992-5566

This Cajun seafood house always draws a crowd; even at lunch, the wait can be more than 45 minutes! But it's worth it: The portions are large, the selection vast, and the tastes delectable. The wait passes quickly at the enormous bar. In addition to Cajun favorites, there are grilled, broiled, and baked items, soups, and salads. The setting is casual and noisy (no one will notice the kids' chatter in the large dining room). Lunch is served Monday through Friday; dinner begins at 3:00 P.M. on weekends. Pappadeaux does not take reservations.

Razzoo's Cajun Café $–$$
5970 North Point Parkway, Alpharetta
(770) 777-1810

"Les bon temps les roillets" in Alpharetta! This sorely needed spot just across the street from North Point Mall serves up slightly (with heavy emphasis on "slightly") cooled-down Cajun specialties from the western parts of Louisiana (though they punch up the New Orleans connection, NOLA is really in Creole territory, which has a very different cuisine). It is one of the very few spots to get a real po'-boy sandwich in the metro area, with the just-right crusty French bread overstuffed with shrimps, oysters, or chicken (!), though we got a blank stare when we asked for an "original" po'-boy, which is stuffed with french fries instead of meat. Also highly recommended is the creamy jalapeño chicken, battered chicken strips over rice with a jalapeño sauce and broccoli; and the shrimp en brochette, six large butterfly shrimps stuffed with jalapeño slices and cheese, wrapped in bacon and broiled, served over dirty rice, and topped with lemon-garlic butter.

The dining area is faux-rustic and somewhat loud, but with a great selection of Cajun and Zydeco music usually blasting away to enhance the burning sensation in your mouth. Seriously casual dress is the rule here, a huge free parking lot is right outside the door, and a full bar is offered. Razzoo's is open Monday through Thursday from 11:00 A.M. to 11:00 P.M. and Friday and Saturday from 11:00 A.M. to midnight.

Continental and Fine Dining

Asher $$$$
1085 Canton Street, Roswell
(770) 650–9838

Chef Andy Badgett's jewel of a restaurant has become both the latest "in" dining spot in upscale north Atlanta and a serious award-winning gastronomic experience for equally serious foodies. Asher offers a four-course prix fixe menu for $49, with appropriate wine pairings for each course for an additional $39. A matched cheese course is available for an unbelievably low (for this scale of restaurant) extra cost of $6. Two nightly seatings can accommodate 55 diners each, so reservations are, for all practical purposes, mandatory. The three dining rooms are tight but comfortable in the small Victorian house setting, with a semi-open kitchen visible through a large stained-glass window.

Menu choices change frequently, reflecting both the seasons and what the chefs find in the local markets, but on our last visit we enjoyed the Alaskan king crab with avocado mousseline and cumin and fleur de sel crisps; the prosciutto-wrapped rabbit loin with escarole, shallots, and Tuscan white bean soup; a "blanquette de veau" with cipollini onions, mushrooms, and white truffle sauce; a cheese course consisting of roaring forties "Danish style" blue cheese with fig jam; a "pre-dessert" of pink grapefruit sorbet with citrus tuile; and a dessert of comice pear "façon pithivier" with rum raisin ice cream (hungry yet?). Occasional and equally highly recommended "wine dinners" center around specific vintners and cost $135 all-inclusive.

We were surprised (and delighted) to find out the source of Asher's name, which is taken from the Old Testament book of Genesis in the Bible. Jacob is blessing his twelve sons, and the blessing for his eighth son is, "Asher's food will be rich. He will provide delicacies fit for a king" (Genesis 49:20). Indeed it does! Asher is open Tuesday through Saturday for dinner. Parking is available in the rear (valet) or in nearby street lots, and very upscale casual dress is noted.

dick and harry's $$$
1570 Holcomb Bridge Road, Roswell
(770) 641–8757
www.dickandharrys.com

Stepping inside the contemporary design of this eatery, it's easy to think you're really in New York or Chicago instead of Roswell. The 20-foot ceilings, hardwood floors, and wood columns add to the sophisticated look. Though the menu's heavy on fresh fish and seafood (wood-grilled barbecue salmon and luscious 100-percent crab cakes), the kitchen also does a good job on oversized salads, pastas, and chicken. Check out the full sheet of daily specials, from appetizers to desserts, before ordering. There's no printed children's menu, but if you ask, the staff gladly serves chicken fingers and pastas to the tykes. Lunch and dinner are served Monday through Friday, dinner only on Saturday.

1848 House $$$$
780 South Cobb Drive, Marietta
(770) 428–1848

The setting for this restaurant and bar is an authentic 1848 Greek Revival plantation home on 13 acres of land. Six of the 10 dining rooms feature fireplaces. The fare is contemporary Southern and American; specialties are the Charleston she-crab soup, pan-roasted quail, roast saddle of venison, and grilled salmon with spaghetti squash, bacon, and lemon sauce. During the Civil War, the house was used as a Union hospital, which is why it wasn't reduced to rubble (wait until after dessert to ask which room was used for surgery). The owners recently restored the original stone kitchen behind the house; the rustic room with a huge fireplace and beamed ceiling seats 16 and can be reserved for a fee. The house is listed on the National Register of Historic Places. Dinner is served Tuesday through Sunday; a jazz brunch is presented Sunday; reservations are accepted.

Hamilton's $$$$
500 Powder Springs Street, Marietta
(770) 427-2500

This restaurant in the Marietta Conference Center and Resort has beautiful views of Cobb County's Kennesaw Mountain. In warmer weather, dine on the outdoor terrace. The food is great, too: Lunch includes an all-you-can-eat buffet with an extensive salad bar, several grilled and baked entrees, soups, and a luscious dessert bar. Breakfast and dinner are also served daily.

Hi Life Kitchen & Cocktails $$$
3380 Holcomb Bridge Road, Norcross
(770) 409-0101

"Reinvented American cuisine" is how the owners of this Gwinnett eatery describe their fusion of specialties: stuffed shrimp with vegetable spring rolls and trout with stir-fry vegetables. A private dining room is available. Reservations are accepted for lunch and dinner, served continuously from 11:00 A.M. every day but Saturday, when the kitchen opens at 4:00 P.M.

Holyfield's New South Grill $$$$
6075 Roswell Road, Sandy Springs
(404) 531-0300

Owner and champion boxer Evander Holyfield makes regular appearances at his northside restaurant, where the clientele comes from across the city to enjoy chef John Akhile's take on Southern classics. The seafood strudel, cranberry-crusted turkey breast, and desserts are standouts. The chic, contemporary setting includes a cozy area of armchairs beside a fireplace, a long bar, and a private room with an enormous plate glass window that gives diners an unobstructed view of the kitchen at work. Holyfield's is open for lunch and dinner.

Joey D's $$$
1015 Crown Pointe Parkway, Dunwoody
(770) 512-7063

American cuisine takes center stage at this upscale casual restaurant. Recommended items include New Orleans spicy shrimp, grilled seafood, steaks, and chops. Joey D's opened in 1990 and has a full bar and free parking. Reservations are accepted. Joey D's serves lunch and dinner daily.

Kurt's $$$
4225 River Green Parkway, Duluth
(770) 623-4128, (770) 623-9413

There's a distinctly German twist to this longtime suburban restaurant, where the menu includes everything from oysters and crab to Wiener schnitzel, sauerbraten, and rack of lamb. There are also filet and pork tenderloins. The atmosphere is elegant; service is offered with a flourish. Roving chefs perform flaming feats tableside, and there's a full bar. Reservations are a must for dinner, served Monday through Saturday. The back porch/patio area is called Vreny's Biergarten, an authentic German hideaway. Select from a long list of beers to wash down the potato soup served in a beer stein.

L'Assiette $$
5805 State Bridge Road, Duluth
(770) 418-2353

Owned by two Frenchmen, this intimate restaurant is a bistro boasting classic cuisine from their homeland. The menu changes seasonally, so expect to find coq au vin or cassoulet when the weather calls for it. A children's menu and a good variety of wines by the glass are available. L'Assiette is open for lunch and dinner Monday through Saturday.

Lickskillet Farm Restaurant $$$$
1380 Old Roswell Road, Roswell
(770) 475-6484

Lickskillet Farm really was a farm at one time. The house dates to 1846, and today, diners are seated in various rooms, from the parlor with a fireplace to the sun porch. Tables on the rear deck overlook the pond and the kitchen's herb garden. Fine dining in a casual setting is the offering here: The American continental gourmet menu features Cornish hen, rack of lamb, filet mignon, veal, and seafood pasta. Dinner is served nightly; lunch is served Tuesday through Friday; brunch is served Sunday. Reservations are recommended.

Little Gardens $$$
3571 Lawrenceville Highway, Lawrenceville
(770) 923–3434
www.littlegardens.com

Set amid acres of beautiful gardens, this romantic restaurant is housed in an antebellum mansion. It's not unusual to see a wedding party in the gazebo, or to hear that the couple at the upstairs windowside table has just gotten engaged. Even if it's not a special occasion, the rack of lamb, beef Wellington, and array of fine seafood dishes will make it seem like one. Reservations are suggested for lunch Monday through Friday, and dinner Monday through Saturday.

Pastis $$$
936 Canton Street, Roswell
(770) 640–3870

This two-level eatery in the Roswell historic district features a comfortable bar, several dining areas, and a second-story porch overlooking the street. The specialties from Provence include eggplant caviar and roasted peppers, mussels mariniere, and sea bass. Save room for the luscious desserts! Pastis serves lunch and dinner, Tuesday through Saturday.

Sia's $$$$
10305 Medlock Bridge Road, Duluth
(770) 497–9727
www.siasrestaurant.com

One of the northside's best new restaurants, Sia's is named for owner Sia Moshk, a graduate of the Buckhead Life Restaurant Group and a definite presence in his dining room, where guests are frequently greeted by name at tables gently lit by beaded candles. Chef Scott Serpas turns out fusion specialties from ginger-seared salmon to cranberry-crusted lamb chops for lunch and dinner. A full-service bar, patio, and private dining room with fireplace are part of the space. Both chef and owner are active in a range of community affairs; look for special one-of-a-kind fund-raising dinners that frequently showcase the talents of Atlanta's best cooks.

Van Gogh's Restaurant $$$$
70 West Crossville Road, Roswell
(770) 993–1156

Van Gogh's is like a bit of Buckhead out in Roswell: fabulous food, impeccable service, and a long wait on line. The five dining rooms are adorned with original art, which is for sale; and there's a fireplace and a lovely antique bar. The ethnic-influenced American fare includes fresh lump meat crab cakes, grilled portobello mushrooms, fresh pastas, and veal chops. Reservations are recommended. Lunch and dinner are served daily; dinner only is served on Sunday.

Vinny's on Windward $$$–$$$$
5355 Windward Parkway
Alpharetta
(770) 772–4644

Set in a low-slung, cabin-type building that opens up to a gorgeous dining hall with soaring ceilings, exposed brickwork, marble accents, and modern art, Vinny's is a new but already popular Italian restaurant that stands head and shoulders above the other, equally new offerings in this booming suburban (and heavily corporate) community. Executive chef Brian Kibler's menu features dishes made with high-quality, very fresh ingredients. We especially liked the butternut squash soup with spiced date mascarpone and the tomato-ciabatta bread soup with Parmigiano Reggiano (we do love a good soup!), as well as the Georges Bank haddock with sweet corn fritters, tomato, arugula, and snap peas.

Vinny's is open Monday through Thursday from 11:00 A.M. to 10:30 P.M., Friday and Saturday from 11:00 A.M. to 11:00 P.M., and Sunday from 5:00 to 10:30 P.M. Dress is business casual (you see a lot of conservative suits) and a full bar is available. The one serious downfall is the mandatory valet parking. To avoid this unnecessary overcharge, you can park in the nearby Wal-Mart or Home Depot parking lots and stroll across the street.

Chinese

China Inn **$$**
2500 Dallas Highway, Marietta
(770) 590–8861

Hidden next to the Publix grocery store, the China Inn offers a full menu of traditional Chinese plates. An attention-getter is the shrimp sizzling plate, which the waiter brings to your table fajita-style—emptying the plate onto a sizzling platter. Open Sunday through Thursday from 11:00 A.M. to 10:00 P.M. and Friday and Saturday 11:00 A.M. to 11:00 P.M.

Mandarin House **$$**
6263 Roswell Road NE
(404) 255–5707
1500 Pleasant Hill Road, Duluth
(770) 925–1050
1750 Marietta Highway, Canton
(770) 479–7621

Opened in 1977, Mandarin House is Atlanta's longest-operating Chinese restaurant. Its extensive menu includes princess chicken; chicken and Chinese greens in an optional hot bean sauce; Szechuan-style kung pau beef, which mixes beef, peanuts, and Chinese greens in a hot pepper sauce; and moo shu pork, a dish featuring pork and Chinese pancakes. Lunch and dinner are served daily.

Indian

Dawat Indian Cafe **$$**
4025-K Satellite Boulevard, Duluth
(770) 623–6133

Tiny but tidy, Dawat Indian Cafe offers a sumptuous vegetarian lunch buffet with curries, soup, rice pilau, and much more. Entrees include chicken tikka masala, a dish involving chicken, tomatoes, and cream, and lamb vindaloo, a spicy lamb dish. Dawat offers plenty of convenient parking and serves lunch daily, featuring a buffet on Saturday and Sunday, and dinner nightly.

Italian and Pizza

Brooklyn Cafe **$$$**
220 Sandy Springs Circle NW
(404) 843–8377
www.brooklyncafe.com

A mural of the Brooklyn Bridge, floral-patterned tablecloths, an old-fashioned dark wood bar, and attentive, friendly service contribute to the cozy, relaxed atmosphere of the Brooklyn Cafe. Founded by two Yankee transplants, the friendly Italian eatery offers "New York without the attitude" and an innovative menu with fresh takes on pasta, seafood, chicken, and veal. Popular dishes include fried calamari with fra diavolo sauce; roast chicken with Italian sausage, roasted potatoes, black olives, and pepperoncini; and veal sorrentino with roasted bell peppers, salami, and provolone cheese in a marsala wine sauce. The restaurant features an extensive beer and wine list and daily dessert specials. Brooklyn Cafe serves lunch Monday through Friday. Dinner begins at 5:30 P.M. and goes until 10:30 P.M. on weeknights, 11:30 P.M. on weekends. The cafe doesn't take reservations, but if you call ahead and come at the time recommended, you'll step to the head of the line for a table.

Insiders' Tip

The Atlanta-based diner chain Waffle House has every necessary element of the beloved small-town Southern dining experience: friendly waitresses with warm words to go with your hot eggs; fresh, hot coffee in "bottomless" mugs; "reserved" stools and tables for the local regulars; a jukebox; and most important, hash browns served scattered, smothered, and covered (fried potatoes cooked with onions and cheese)!

di Paolo Cucina $$
8560 Holcomb Bridge Road, Alpharetta
(770) 587–1051

The brother-and-sister team that owns this intimate Italian spot keeps the menu fresh with seasonal changes. Some classics show up by popular demand year-round: lasagne alla bolognese, rigatoni with Italian sausage and artichokes, and a variety of seafood. Homemade desserts and a selection of Italian and Californian wines and beer are on the menu. Dinner is served daily from 5:30 P.M., and reservations are accepted.

Dominick's $$
95 South Peachtree Street, Norcross
(770) 449–1611

In a historic building in old downtown Norcross, this family-style Italian restaurant serves its dishes on large platters meant to be shared. (The menu also lists prices for half-platters for those with skimpier appetites.) With both hearty, traditional Italian fare and lighter, health-conscious items, Dominick's menu includes pasta, chicken, veal, and seafood dishes. Popular house specialties such as eggplant parmigiana and lasagna bolognese delight diners and keep them coming back to this friendly, welcoming place. Lunch is served on weekdays; dinner is served nightly.

Ippolito's Family Style Italian Restaurant $$
1525 Holcomb Bridge Road, Roswell
(770) 998–5683
Abernathy Square, 6623 Roswell Road
(404) 256–3546
11585 Jones Bridge Road, Alpharetta
(770) 663–0050
425 Ernest Barrett Parkway
(770) 514–8500

This friendly, mom-and-pop Italian restaurant is a favorite with locals. Ippolito's menu includes mussels marinara, pizzas, hoagies, calzones, salads, pasta, chicken, veal, and seafood. The yeasty garlic rolls are served piping hot and swimming in butter. Dress is casual, and kids are welcome. Ippolito's serves lunch on weekdays and dinner seven nights a week. And you can count on Ol' Blue Eyes or Dino for the background music.

Mi Spia $$$
4505 Ashford Dunwoody Road
(770) 393–1333
www.mispia.com

The sophisticated Mi Spia offers Italian food with a contemporary flair. This neighborhood bar and grill features a garden patio and a lively cocktail hour. Wood-trimmed French doors overlook a courtyard and enliven the airy dining room. The contemporary Italian menu, including oak-grilled veal chops, seafood, chicken, homemade breads, and desserts, keeps the customers coming back. Mi Spia opens for dinner every night and serves lunch on weekdays. Smoking is allowed in the bar area only. Reservations are accepted.

New York Pizza Exchange $$
2810 Paces Ferry Road NE, Vinings
(770) 434–9355

This upscale pizza house features pies, pasta dishes, calzones, strombolis, and killer desserts such as Death by Chocolate cheesecake and raspberry white chocolate cheesecake. House specialties include the Spinach 'n' Stix appetizer, a fresh spinach and vegetable dip topped with mozzarella cheese; you dip Italian breadsticks into the luscious mixture. New York Pizza also serves salads, subs, beer, and wine. The restaurant is open for lunch and dinner daily.

Villa Christina $$$
4000 Summit Boulevard
(404) 303–0133
www.villachristina.com

You don't expect to find such an elegant, upscale eatery as the Villa tucked into a business campus (getting there is tricky, too—call ahead for directions). But the view from the dining room is pastoral, taking in the surrounding gardens and stream. The restaurant also hosts wine dinners throughout the year. Lunch and dinner are served Monday through Saturday.

Japanese

Hachi Hachi $$
10875 Jones Bridge Road
(678) 297–5588

An unusually good full-service Japanese

restaurant in a neighborhood setting straight out of *American Beauty,* Hachi Hachi offers the expected Benihana's-style cooking theater in their hibachi section, as well as standard restaurant seating for more interesting fare and a well-stocked full bar and an excellent (and quite large) sushi bar. The food—mostly variations on standard and traditional dishes—is very well prepared and interestingly presented, and some of the sushi box and platter creations are absolute works of art. Open Monday through Saturday for lunch and supper.

Haru Ichiban $$–$$$
3646 Satellite Boulevard, Duluth
(770) 622–4060

Hands down, this is our favorite Japanese restaurant in the metro area. Owner/sushi chef Yukio Watanabe, who claims to have opened Georgia's first sushi bar (in 1980 on Buford Highway), offers both expected traditional and seasonal specialties, albeit at a quality and artistic level head and shoulders above others, along with some very interesting East-West fusion experiments. Among these experiments are Italian cold cuts and cheese rolls along with the California rolls and yellowfin from the sushi bar. Open daily for lunch and supper.

Mt. Fuji Japanese Steak House and Sushi Bar $$$
180 Cobb Parkway, Marietta
(770) 428–0955

Watching your food being sliced, diced, sautéed, and flambéed right before your eyes is half the fun of eating at this cozy restaurant, hidden in a corner of the Marietta Trade shopping center. You'll be seated in a group around a large stainless-steel cooktop, where a chef will prepare the food to your exact specifications. And the chefs put on a show while doing it—flipping shrimp tails into their tall hats, tossing knives into the air, and juggling soy sauce bottles behind their backs. Start with a sampling of sushi at the bar in the restaurant's lobby, but save room for dinner. There's usually more food than you can finish. Dinner is served nightly.

Shiki Japanese Restaurant $$$
1492 Pleasant Hill Road, Duluth
(770) 279–0097

Shiki has a traditional dining room where, among many other entrees, you can order impeccably fresh fish presented artfully. At the sushi bar at the rear of the main room, a chef prepares a wide variety of tempting treats. On the hibachi side of the restaurant, you'll find quality steaks and seafood cooked on tableside grills. No matter which section you choose, you'll find exquisite presentation and thoughtful and gracious service. Shiki is open seven days a week and serves beer and wine. The restaurant recommends reservations.

Latin

Azteca Grill $$
1140 Mt. Zion Road, Morrow
(770) 968–0908

Spicy specialties at this Mexican and Southwestern restaurant include poblano corn chowder and a Mexican version of turnip greens. Enjoy your favorite beverages at this grill's full bar and outside dining in warm weather. The food comes continuously from 11:00 A.M. Monday through Saturday and from noon on Sunday.

Cozumel Mexican Restaurant $$
2697 Spring Road, Smyrna
(770) 801–1487

This Mexican eatery northwest of Atlanta offers popular items such as steak ranchero, mixed fajitas, and carne asada. Beer and wine are available. Cozumel is open every day for lunch and dinner.

Jose's Mexican Restaurant $$
722 Whitlock Avenue, Marietta
(770) 499–9455

This family-run neighborhood Mexican restaurant draws a loyal clientele to this hidden jewel in a hard-to-find shopping center. The menu is loaded with delicious combinations of enchiladas, chimichangas, and burritos. The bar mixes a mean margarita, and the beer list includes both Mexican and "gringo" beers. Open for lunch and dinner every day.

Seafood

Chequers Seafood Grill $$$
236 Perimeter Center Parkway
(770) 391–9383
Monarch Plaza, 3424 Peachtree Road
(404) 842–9997

For 15-plus years, this clubby spot has been a favorite for seafood and steak lovers. And the oversized biscuits are pretty incredible, too. Lunch and dinner menus feature an array of fresh fish, as well as filet, crab cakes, soups, and salads. Sunday brunch is an extensive affair, with made-to-order omelets, shrimp, and blintzes. Lunch is served Monday through Friday. Dinner is served nightly.

Embers Seafood Grill $$$
234 Hildebrand Drive NW
(404) 256–0977

Excellent preparation, good service, sizable portions—what more could you ask for? The Embers' decor could be called a dressed-up seafood shack scheme. Good service and well-trained staff will gladly explain the details of entrees. There's a catch of the day as well as grilled Atlantic salmon, swordfish, grouper, and tuna. Scallops, shrimp, lobster, steaks, and chicken round out an extensive menu that includes such favorites as blackened amberjack and the combo kebab combining swordfish, tuna, sea scallops, red onions, and green peppers. A few pasta dishes and entree-size salads, made with fish, are also on the menu. For an appetizer, you might try the smoked barbecued shrimp or the delicious crab cakes. Dinner is served nightly; lunch is offered Monday through Friday.

Slocum's Tavern & Grill $$
6025 Peachtree Parkway, Norcross
(770) 446–7725

Slocum's house specialty is yellowfin tuna marinated in teriyaki sauce, then grilled. There's a casual, neighborhood-pub atmosphere, complete with neon beer signs and TVs tuned to sports in the bar area. Slocum's draws anyone who loves juicy, fresh fish, great steaks, burgers, and chicken wings, among other items. The restaurant serves lunch Monday through Saturday and dinner seven nights a week. Reservations are accepted for parties of six or more.

Squid Roe $$$
2940 Johnson Ferry Road NE, Marietta
(770) 587–3474

This Key West–inspired East Cobb restaurant transports diners back to their favorite beach hangouts with its casual, nautical decor, starting with the sand outside the front door. Specializing in fresh seafood, Squid Roe offers a variety of daily specials as well as its signature she-crab soup and conch fritters. Although it only takes reservations for large parties, you can call ahead to get your name on a waiting list. Lunch is served Monday through Friday. Dinner is served daily.

Southern Food and Barbecue

Blue Willow Inn Restaurant $$
294 North Cherokee Road, Social Circle
(770) 464–2131

On five acres of land, the Blue Willow is housed in a 1907 Greek Revival mansion, where diners linger after dinner in the rocking chairs on the wide porch or in the gift shop. The fare, served buffet style, is authentic Southern cooking, including fried chicken, fried green tomatoes, and bread pudding. There's none of that low-cholesterol, big-city stuff here, thank you. Four to five meats and 10 to 12 vegetables are generally offered. In warm weather, you may choose to dine outside by the pool. Reservations are accepted. Due to local regulations, sweet tea and lemonade are the most potent drinks; however, patrons are welcome to bring their own wine or champagne. Credit cards are not accepted. Social Circle is 45 minutes east of Atlanta; take I-20 to exit 47.

Doug's Place $
696 Georgia Highway 293, Emerson
(770) 382–9063

Doug's Place is a down-home place that's loaded with Southern staples, from country-fried steak and gravy or chicken livers to fried okra, butter beans, and creamed corn. But the regulars go for the catfish. Open for lunch Monday through Friday until 2:00 P.M., and for dinner Wednesday and Friday night from 4:30 to 9:00 P.M. No alcohol is served.

Dreamland Barbecue $
10730 Alpharetta Highway, Roswell
(678) 352-7999

The first branch of the famed Tuscaloosa, Alabama, institution, Dreamland is a mecca for fans of Georgia/Alabama style 'que, characterized by pulled pork covered liberally with a spicy, vinegary tomato-based sauce. The slow-cooked meat (chicken is also available) is done with loving care and is wonderful for eating without any sauce at all. Go very hungry, or be prepared to sack home several lunches, as the portions are huge. One "sign" that you are dining in an establishment of unusual refinement and breeding: the 10-foot-long, neon-lit advisement hanging over the lobby, NO FARTING. Open daily for lunch and supper.

Puckett's Restaurant $
4840 South Lee Street, Buford
(770) 945-6031

Puckett's fixes breakfast, lunch, and dinner on weekdays only, from 7:00 A.M. to 7:00 P.M. A typical day begins at 4:30 A.M., when the homemade pies are baked. Other specialties include fried chicken and country-fried steak; seven or so vegetables are available. Friendly, down-home Puckett's has been in business since 1953. No alcohol is served, and credit cards are not accepted.

Williamson Brothers Bar-B-Q $$
1425 Roswell Road, Marietta
(770) 971-3201

Williamson Brothers is a Marietta institution. Folks rave about the crusty, meaty ribs. Pork is shredded, not sliced. The sauce, also sold separately, is Alabama-style. Reservations accepted. Open every day for lunch and dinner.

Thai

Royal Thai Cuisine $$
6365-A Spalding Drive, Norcross
(770) 449-7796

Take your seat in the cozy upholstered booths surrounded by wood paneling and deep-green fabric panels, or dine on the outdoor deck of this small place known for good food. House specialties include soft-shelled crab with curry, boneless crispy duck in a basil sauce, and lamb with tea rose dumplings. Royal Thai serves Thai beer. You'll find efficient friendly service at lunch Monday through Friday. Dinner is served nightly.

Vegetarian

Cafe Sunflower $$
5975 Roswell Road NE
(404) 256-1675
2140 Peachtree Road NW
(404) 352-8859

Just a half-mile outside the Perimeter in Hammond Springs Shopping Center, Cafe Sunflower is a comfortable restaurant that specializes in imaginative and well-prepared wholesome food. The cuisine is a combo of Asian, Mediterranean, and Southwestern influences. Try the fresh vegetables over fluffy brown rice or the wild mushroom fettuccine. No alcohol is served, nor is smoking allowed. Cafe Sunflower welcomes reservations for lunch during the week and on Saturdays. Dinner reservations can be made seven days a week.

Unicorn Place Vegetarian Cuisine $$
220 Sandy Springs Circle NW
(404) 252-1165

Fresh and healthy food is the treat here, with lots of vegetables and salads to satisfy your hunger. An extensive menu of more than 40 items includes such novelties as veggie hot dogs and vegetarian sweet-and-sour pork. Unicorn serves lunch Monday through Saturday and dinner nightly.

Nightlife

"I love the nightlife!
I've got to boogie!"
—Atlanta's own Alicia Bridges

When the sun goes down, Atlanta gets a new attitude. Night brings an end to the day's problems, replacing them with more pleasant concerns. For a few happy hours, "Where are we going?" "Who's meeting us there?" and "What's everyone doing later?" become the most important issues.

Nightlife has always been a part of Atlanta. The first tavern, after all, opened 10 years before the first church. And Moses Formwalt, a tinsmith and still-maker backed by the Free and Rowdy Party, defeated the Morals Party's temperance candidate in the first mayoral election in 1848.

In the late 1960s and '70s, Atlanta's nightlife exploded. At legendary (now closed) nightclubs such as Richard's, the Electric Ballroom, the Agora Ballroom, Finnochio, the Great Southeast Music Hall, the 688 Club, and Rumors, Atlanta audiences rocked out up close to stars such as the Allman Brothers, the Police, the Clash, Bonnie Raitt, and the B-52's, as well as legendary local bands like the Dead Kennedys, Love Tractor, R.E.M., and Col. Bruce Hampton and the Aquarium Rescue Unit. Locals and tourists alike flocked to the original Underground Atlanta, a shadowy, boozy adult playground that was quite different from the present-day shopping and entertainment complex. Those were wild days in Atlanta: Midtown was a hippie zone, Piedmont Park was the site of frequent anti-war protests and drug raids, and X-rated bookstores and cinemas were as commonplace as today's coffeehouses.

Today there's still something for everyone in Atlanta's nightlife lineup. You can relax with friends at an unpretentious neighborhood pub; sip pricey martinis at the latest see-and-be-seen trendy bar; gossip and giggle at a drag show; whoop and holler like a cowboy at an urban roadhouse; dance from dusk to dawn in a packed discotheque; groove to the latest, loudest live rock; mellow out to acoustic, folk, or jazz performances; laugh yourself to tears at a comedy hotspot; or, if you prefer, sip cocktails while totally nude female or male dancers entertain.

The ever-changing nature of life in Atlanta is nowhere more evident than in the city's nightlife. Clubs, bars, and coffeehouses open, close, remodel, and disappear with amazing speed. We could tell you about the pricey seafood restaurant that's now a live music club showcasing the latest bands or the leather bar that became an upscale steak house, but take our word for it: Everything about Atlanta nightlife is subject to change, so call first or check the local press for up-to-date info.

Theme nights are a continuing trend in Atlanta nightspots. A club may have live rock bands one night, a gay dance party the next, and attract a largely African-American singles crowd yet another evening. Even though a club's name remains the same, its nightly ambience, music, and entertainment may change with the wind.

Don't assume, just because you've been to a club before, that its entertainment and door policies will be the same when you return. It's always a good idea to call first if you're not sure. Many of the larger clubs now have sophisticated answering systems you can access with a touch-tone phone or sites on the Internet that give travel directions and information about entertainment, nightly specials, and cover charges.

A little about the history of prohibition in Atlanta is in order here. Imposed once by a county referendum, then later by the state and the federal governments, laws about drinking were not popular and were widely disregarded.

Atlanta first went dry on July 1, 1886, after a Fulton County referendum. But on November 26, 1887, the law was repealed—again, by referendum—and 40 liquor stores were operating in 1888.

A state prohibition law took effect in 1908, shutting down more than 100 Atlanta saloons and liquor stores and one brewery, but a loophole allowing alcohol sales in private clubs led to the proliferation of "locker clubs," typically upstairs in office buildings, which called themselves private clubs but were basically bars. Legally, at least, Atlanta had been dry for a dozen years when prohibition became law nationally.

Following the 1933 repeal of prohibition, Georgia Governor E. D. Rivers signed legislation in 1938 allowing local option alcohol sales. Fulton County went wet by a margin of better than three to one. A dozen liquor stores opened on April 25, 1938, and the *Atlanta Constitution* reported: "With their tongues 'hanging out,' hundreds of Atlantans flocked to the legal liquor stores to make purchases of state-stamped legal whiskey, many of them buying legal liquor for the first time in their lives." For more historical information about prohibition, or Atlanta history in general, Franklin Garrett's book *Atlanta and Environs* is the place to look.

These days, the sale of alcohol in supermarkets and liquor stores ends before midnight on Saturday night and does not resume until Monday morning.

Several local periodicals, which are detailed in our Media chapter, offer up-to-the-minute coverage for Atlanta's night crawlers: These are the best ways to find out what's happening on any given night or weekend in Atlanta. Look to the Weekend Preview section in Friday's *Atlanta Journal-Constitution* or the weekly *Creative Loafing* for an entertainment calendar with extensive information on the nightly action at dozens of clubs; the *University Reporter* for hot spots for college students and 20-somethings; and for information on some of the 30 bars and clubs that cater to gays and lesbians, pick up a copy of *Southern Voice*.

Things to Keep in Your Mind and in Your Wallet

Bars in Atlanta may stay open as late as 4:00 A.M., though not all do. On Saturday nights, all bars are required to close an hour earlier, at 3:00 A.M., but a handful of clubs have special licenses that allow them to stay open and serve liquor around the clock. They are noted below.

A pair of fatal stabbings outside one Buckhead club after the 2000 Super Bowl brought about a call for changes in the popular club district. The Atlanta City Council has considered moving up closing times to 2:00 A.M. in response to numerous complaints about noise and after-hours crime, but as of this writing, there has not been any action taken to change the hours.

Acceptance of credit cards varies. Some places that don't accept plastic at the door will let you pay your tab with a card. Others don't accept credit cards but have an ATM on the premises. If your plan is "party now, pay later," call the club first and make sure your card will be accepted.

All persons entering a bar are required to have a picture ID. This is not about how old you look, and it's not about attendants who want to hassle you. It's about keeping within the law, and most clubs will refuse admittance to anyone, regardless of age, who does not have a picture ID. Avoid aggravation by making sure every person in your group has one.

Information on cover charges is given as a guide only and may not reflect the actual cost to enter a club on a given night; for example, many clubs hike the door charge on big nights such as New Year's Eve and Halloween or when there's special entertainment.

The drinking age for liquor, beer, and wine in Georgia is 21. "18 to party, 21 to drink" is the rule at some clubs, which usually issue a special bracelet authorizing your purchase of alcohol. Some clubs cater to a swank older crowd and have a higher minimum age (such as 23) for admittance. Call ahead to avoid disappointment. If you'll be partying in Downtown, please note: Many Downtown streets are designated no parking, and the police issue parking tickets at night. Avoid tickets, and keep your car safe by parking in an attended pay lot.

Finally, Georgia's drunk driving laws are very strict and getting stricter all the time. Any driver who registers a blood-alcohol level of 0.08 or higher is considered legally drunk. Any driver younger than 21 who registers any measurable blood-alcohol level is considered intoxicated (the actual statute states "at or above .02," but this is the accuracy limit of most testing devices). The police use random roadblocks to apprehend drunk drivers; these are often on two-lane (as opposed to wider) streets in areas with a heavy concentration of nightclubs. Rather than taking a chance on getting busted or endangering yourself or others, take a cab, use a sober designated driver, or ride MARTA. Unlike other major cities such as New York, Atlanta does not have cabs that cruise the streets looking for fares. However, you may find cabs around areas where there are many clubs. You can always ask club personnel to call a cab for you a few minutes before you're ready to leave.

To help you plan your nocturnal prowlings in Atlanta, this chapter describes some of the offerings in the major Atlanta entertainment districts: Buckhead, Downtown, and Midtown/Little Five Points/Virginia-Highland. All bars listed within a geographic section may not necessarily be within walking distance—this is especially true in Buckhead. Bars of note outside these five zones are covered next, along with comedy clubs and sports bars.

Bars, Clubs, and Lounges

Buckhead

Buckhead is the nexus of Atlanta nightlife and dining, boasting more than 200 restaurants and clubs.

The Buckhead district is spread out, and many establishments just outside the area locals call Buckhead may use the name in describing where they are. The intersection of Peachtree Road and Pharr Road is near its center, with acres of party places nearby, but you can find a quiet or rowdy place to spend the evening anywhere from Midtown on the south to Sandy Springs on the north. If you want to spend an evening in one district with lots of entertainment options, come on up to Buckhead.

Asti's Terrace Lounge
3199 Paces Ferry Road NW
(404) 364-9160

The cozy club is connected to Asti's Italian restaurant and offers live jazz and Latin music for dancing.

Bar
250 East Paces Ferry Road NE
(404) 841-0033

"No theme, no attitude, just Bar" is the slogan at this bar without a story where patrons enjoy chugging "bobsled shooters," which are poured through an ice sculpture. Bar is open Wednesday through Saturday nights, and there's a small cover after 10:00 P.M. on weekends. Thursdays are college nights.

The Bar at the Palm
3391 Peachtree Road NE, in the Swissôtel Atlanta
(404) 814-1955

After enjoying the pricey steak dinners at the lobby restaurant of the upscale Swissôtel, slip into the adjacent bar for a quiet drink in a decidedly unsnooty location. The general manager has been known to boast, "I just run a saloon."

The Bar at the Ritz-Carlton Buckhead
3434 Peachtree Road NE
(404) 237-2700

The Ritz, is, well, the ritz. It's plush, quiet, and elegant with cloth napkins, impeccable service, and a cool jazz trio.

Beluga
3115 Piedmont Road NE
(404) 869–1090

Take it easy with easy listening at this cozy, upscale nightspot. There's nightly entertainment Monday through Saturday, with alternating jazz and contemporary/pop/show tunes. Shows start at 10:30 P.M. It was rated "Best Piano Bar" in 2000.

The Brandyhouse
4365 Roswell Road NE
(404) 252–7784

This English-style restaurant and pub plays pop and rock from local and national bands on a sound system that's a cut above many local live music venues.

The Chili Pepper
208 Pharr Road NE
(404) 812–9266

The Chili Pepper offers lots of dancing on three levels and a rooftop terrace in the heart of all the Buckhead club action. Neon-lit bars, cartoon-decorated walls, velvet sofas, and more fill this eclectic club where a DJ spins discs. Sorry, no food is served. After 10:30 P.M., you'll pay a moderate cover charge.

CJ's Landing
270 Buckhead Avenue NE
(404) 237–7657

Bar food and brews as well as dance music from the '70s and '80s are the attractions. That and the 100-year-old oak tree that grows through the roof on the covered deck. Open from 8:00 P.M. to 2:00 A.M. Tuesday through Thursday and Sunday, 7:00 P.M. to 3:00 or 4:00 A.M. Friday and Saturday.

Dance City Ballroom
2581 Piedmont Road NE
Lindbergh Plaza, Suite B-930
(404) 266–0166

Enjoy ballroom dancing in a smoke-free and alcohol-free environment. The Ballroom hosts public dances at 9:00 P.M. Wednesday and Saturday for a small cover. Lessons are also available.

Dante's Down the Hatch
3380 Peachtree Road NE
(404) 266–1600
www.dantesdownthehatch.com

An Atlanta institution run by noted restaurateur and car collector Dante Stephenson. The decor resembles a pirate ship docked in a European port, complete with moats and some imported crocodiles. The Paul Mitchell Trio, the classy house band, performs jazz and pop standards six nights a week on the Ship. Other jazz and acoustic acts appear on the Wharf.

Have a Nice Day! Cafe
3095 Peachtree Road NE
(404) 261–8898

Just like its name implies, this casual place to meet is right out of the '70s. Open Wednesday through Saturday; the music starts at 8:00 P.M. Bellbottoms and unbuttoned shirts with lots of gold chains seem to be the uniform of choice here.

Johnny's Hideaway
3771 Roswell Road
(404) 233–8026

This self-described "nightclub for big kids" showcases music from the '40s to the '80s. Dress is business casual, and the crowd tends to be 35 and older. Johnny's is open every night. It's all request Monday and rock 'n' roll Wednesday.

Liquid Assets
293 Pharr Road NE
(404) 262–0604

A friendly, diverse 30-and-up crowd that likes to dress up. This trilevel dance club offers live jazz and recorded R&B music.

Lulu's Bait Shack
3057 Peachtree Road NE (enter from Bolling Way)
(404) 262–5220

Lulu's Bait Shack is famous for its fishbowl-size super-drinks; alligator tail, catfish, and chicken are on the menu. Dance the night away to recorded music from 10:00 P.M. to 4:00 A.M.

The city lights up at night and offers neighborhood pubs, trendy bars, and dance clubs.

PHOTO: THE WORLD OF COCA-COLA

Sambuca Jazz Cafe
3102 Peachtree Road NE
(404) 237–5299

It's part of a Texas-based chain, but it's still one of the favorites for those looking for an upscale jazz supper club. Swing's also the thing here Mondays and when swings acts are in town. No cover.

Sanctuary
3209 Paces Ferry Place
(404) 262–1377
www.sanctuarynightclub.com

This is one of the oldest—and still the hottest—Latin nightclubs in the metro area. The 1,000-square-foot dance floor opens at 9:00 P.M. on Friday, featuring free salsa dance lessons the first hour each night. It opens at 10:00 P.M. on Saturday. Moderate cover.

Tongue & Groove
3055 Peachtree Road NE
(404) 261–2325

When Tongue & Groove opened in Buckhead in 1994, it promised to "turn down the music and turn up the taste, letting people and their personalities take center stage in a stunningly designed space filled with subtle beauty." It remains an eclectic drinking, dancing, velvet-ropes kind of place. The club's interior is contemporary yet romantic and features custom furnishings and flattering lighting. Sushi and light fare are available. Expensive cigars and jumbo martinis are the rage at Tongue & Groove, which has a dance floor in the back room. Dress is upscale. Moderate cover after 10:00 P.M.

The World Bar
3071 Peachtree Road NE
(404) 266–0627

The World Bar has urban music, a dance floor, and pool tables. The self-proclaimed "largest club in Buckhead" is open Friday and Saturday nights. There's a moderate cover, but all drinks are $3.

Downtown

As more and more people move into the increasing number of lofts, condos, and apartments Downtown, the nightlife will surely follow. More shops, bars, and restaurants are opening to make Downtown more than just a 9-to-5 environment. And the growing Georgia State University campus lends a younger touch to the population.

Once the focus of Downtown, Underground Atlanta has seen many bars and restaurants come and go. Most of its bars and sit-down restaurants are arranged around the large open courtyard, Kenny's Alley.

The Cotton Club
152 Luckie Street NW
(404) 688–1193

The Cotton Club is a large performance club that showcases local and national pop and rock bands; the cover charge is small to moderate. It is located in the basement at The Tabernacle, a former church that has been converted into one of the city's premier music venues. (See Venues in the Arts section.) Tickets run in the $8 to $10 range, with the club open on Friday and Saturday nights and other nights when acts are in town.

Fandangles
165 Courtland Street NE
Sheraton Atlanta Hotel
(404) 659–6500

The ultramodern lounge features Europop music, a bold color scheme, and private sitting rooms.

Hard Rock Café
215 Peachtree Street NE
(404) 420–5842

You know the chain and love its rock music-themed decor. It's always crowded with visitors to Atlanta.

Hyatt Regency Atlanta
265 Peachtree Street
(404) 577–1234

The revolving Polaris atop this first of John Portman's hotels looks like a flying saucer with shocking-blue glass from the outside. The Polaris room serves drinks and dinner. The Hyatt once towered over downtown; now taller buildings on three sides limit its view. But when your table slides by the northern windows, you'll enjoy a thrilling view of Midtown and north Atlanta.

Karma
79-A Poplar Street
(404) 577–6967

The red canopy on the street gives this nightspot a very New York feel. It's one of the places where the beautiful people hang. It's open Wednesday through Saturday 10:00 A.M. to 4:00 A.M.

Mumbo Jumbo
89 Park Place NE
(404) 523–0330

The long bar stretches along the left wall when you walk in. Sexy, clubby feel where everyone from bankers to hip-hoppers hang out starting at lunch and into the night.

Ritz-Carlton Atlanta
181 Peachtree Street NE
(404) 659–0400

Like its corporate partner in Buckhead, the Ritz-Carlton is elegance personified. It's a posh place to enjoy a quiet drink and the jazz combo.

Riviera Club
1055 Peachtree Street NE
(404) 607–8050
www.therivieraclub.com

Special licensing (members only get around closing regulations) allows this dance club to stay open 24 hours, seven days a week. You'll pay a moderate cover charge to enjoy disco in the evenings; four bars and a $250,000 sound and lighting system keep the upscale 25–40-year-old patrons dancing to high-energy techno and contemporary music. Memberships are available at the door.

The Tap Room
231 Peachtree Street NE
(404) 577–7860

The martinis are the thing. The bartender just pulls a lever to mix the perfect drink. In the big martini tap, a spring-activated gush of air injects the fluid through a frozen tube to a glass waiting inches away. It's something you have to see to believe, like a grown-up version of the old 7-11 Slurpee machine.

The Westin Peachtree Plaza
Peachtree Street at International Boulevard
(404) 659–1400

The Sun Dial Lounge atop the Westin Peachtree Plaza, another of the many John Portman–designed structures in Atlanta, is the ultimate roof room. Dusk is an especially lovely time to visit, when thousands of lights glitter to life. If the air is clear during daylight hours, you can see all the way to Stone Mountain. There is a $7.50 per-person charge to visit the lounge; no charge if you're having lunch or dinner. Hop on one of the outside, glassed-in elevators for a two-minute ride to the top of the hotel. By the time you get there, you'll need a drink!

Midtown/Little Five Points/Virginia-Highland

Much of Midtown's nightlife is on or near Peachtree Street between 10th and 14th Streets. Once known as The Strip, this was Atlanta's hippie mecca in the 1970s. It has prospered as a lively nightclub and theater zone since the '80s. The fun area is more eclectic and hip than Buckhead to the north. But like Buckhead, you still can expect to see the beautiful people, stylish lounges, and strict door policies.

Then there's Little Five Points, about 2 miles east of Downtown. Its major intersection is the convergence of Moreland, Euclid, and McLendon Avenues. Little Five Points is Atlanta's most integrated multicultural district, and the emphasis here is on the avant garde. The district's stores are filled with the most cutting-edge clubwear, and in its public areas you'll see lots of leather, body piercings, tattoos, and exotic hair styles. When the weather's nice, Little Five is one of the best places in Atlanta to relax and soak up the scene.

The pleasant neighborhood around the intersection of Virginia and North Highland Avenues is the closest Atlanta gets to a New York City strolling strip where interesting, well-designed shops beckon with window decor, sounds, and aromas.

Midtown

Backstreet
845 Peachtree Street
(404) 873–1986
www.backstreetatlanta.com

For a quarter-century, Backstreet has been Atlanta's leading gay bar, but now it's mostly mixed gay and straight. Open 24 hours a day through special licensing that requires membership. No big deal—you can become a member at the door. This huge palace is a three-level entertainment complex with a 2,500-square-foot, high-energy disco dance floor and a separate room for live shows. Some of Atlanta's best-known female impersonators perform upstairs; the weekend shows go until dawn. Although Backstreet is way-gay, fun-loving straights have a blast here as well, particularly if they're into dancing. Photo IDs are required no matter if you are 21 or 91.

Churchill Grounds
660 Peachtree Street NE
(404) 876–3030
www.churchillgrounds.com

Next to the Fox Theatre, this intimate and classy club attracts some of the city's best jazz acts. It was voted "Best Jazz Club" in 2002.

Insiders' Tip

The MARTA station at the Georgia Dome serves three very popular (and crowded) large-capacity venues: the Georgia Dome itself, Philips Arena, and the Georgia World Congress Center, as well as CNN Center and Centennial Park. When events collide at these venues, the station can quickly become overwhelmed, and it is well worth the 3-block walk east down Marietta Street to avoid the crowd and access the trains at the MARTA Five Points Station.

Deux Plex
1789 Cheshire Bridge Road NE
(404) 733-5900

One of the newest restaurants/dance clubs (hence the "deux") in Atlanta, Deux Plex draws a diverse "in" crowd. It's not your normal nightclub, with a schedule loaded with Latin nights, runway fashion shows, art openings, AIDS benefits, chef's samplings, and liquor tastings. The top floor is an enormous French bistro, and the dance club is on the bottom. The bistro is open from 6:30 to 11:30 P.M. Tuesday though Sunday, but the club grooves from 9:00 P.M. to 4:00 A.M. Friday and 10:00 P.M. to 3:00 A.M. Saturday.

Encore Bistro and Club
1374 West Peachtree Street NW
(404) 885-1105

Like the name implies, the music is oldies, big bands, and disco—along with contemporary music—back for an encore. A different theme Tuesdays through Saturdays, 6:00 P.M. to 2:00 A.M. Upscale dining, 6:00 to 11:00 P.M.

Fat Matt's Rib Shack
1811 Piedmont Road NE
(404) 607-1622

If you want barbecue—and if you come to the South, you do want barbecue—Fat Matt's is the place to get it along with a generous side order of music. Local blues bands rock the rafters of this faux roadhouse.

Hoedown's
931 Monroe Drive
(404) 876-0001

In the Midtown Promenade shopping center off Monroe Drive at Virginia Avenue, mostly gay and lesbian clientele pack the place, and there's a buffet on Sundays. Free dance lessons (Can you guess what style? Country, of course!) are offered on Sunday, Tuesday, and Thursday.

Kaya
1068 Peachtree Street NE
(404) 874-4460

This spacious dance club has an entertainment lineup as diverse as its clientele—from Latin music to drag shows to live bands. Kaya is open Tuesday through Friday from 11:30 A.M. to 4:00 A.M., Saturday from 10:00 P.M. to 3:00 A.M., and Sunday from 3:00 P.M. to midnight.

Leopard Lounge
84 12th Street NE
(404) 875-7562
www.leopardlounge.com

"From the outside, the lounge looks like the kind of jazz joint jet-setters flocked to in old movies. The atmosphere is pure cocktail culture with 'Cats' or 'Dolls' on the rest room doors," wrote the *Atlanta Journal-Constitution*.

Martini Club
1140 Crescent Avenue
(404) 873-0794

Open from 5:00 P.M. till 2:00 A.M. nightly, the Martini Club features 101 varieties of martinis, including a Georgia Peach martini. Relax in the 1930s-style bar with chaise lounges. You can also buy and smoke cigars here. Live piano music is featured nightly, and there's a jazz trio on weekends.

Masquerade
695 North Avenue NE
(404) 577–8178
www.masq.com

Masquerade is the kind of place your mama must have warned you about; there are a lot more body piercings and tattoos per person than on the average business-person. But those into the gothic, punk, and alternative rock scenes will have a blast here. But that's not all there is. In an antique factory that once turned out excelsior (wood shavings used as packing straw), Masquerade's monstrous space is divided into three theme areas: Hell, the throbbing downstairs dance room with a DJ; Heaven, the big upstairs concert hall; and Purgatory, a more low-key bar that's—you guessed it—between the two. Masquerade showcases lots of local talent and books national acts for major concerts. It's open Wednesday through Sunday; the cover charge is moderate but varies significantly depending on who's playing.

MJQ Concourse
736 Ponce de Leon Avenue NE
(404) 870–0575

The hip, hot, and urban DJ bar features funk, techno, jazz, and experimental music that sometimes defies categorization. The new subterranean digs and new stage and sound system make it suitable for live music. But the focus for now is recorded and spun by nationally known DJs. Especially popular are the Brit Pop Wednesdays and the monthly no-static hip-hop parties.

Northside Tavern
1058 Howell Mill Road NW
(404) 874–8745
www.northsidetavern.com

Truly off the beaten track, you'll find the Northside Tavern for music and dancing after you've had a great meal or seen some swell theater at King Plow. But know that you will definitely be overdressed because this is a casual place. The place offers a very diverse group of folks on any particular night. If you enjoy blues, this is the place to be.

The Otherside
1924 Piedmont Avenue
(404) 875–5238

Primarily a lesbian bar with live music and a small cover on the weekends, The Otherside draws a gay and straight crowd as

Ticketmaster

One surefire way to get tickets to just about anything—sporting events, concerts, theater—is through Ticketmaster. You have to pay a service fee that you could avoid by getting tickets at the door, but it is convenient, especially if you are from out of town. To order tickets, call (404) 249–6400 in Atlanta; long distance, dial (800) 326–4000. Tickets are also sold at Ticketmaster's retail locations in Georgia and on-line at www.ticketmaster.com. You can use a credit card on the phone or on-line. Some venues don't accept plastic, but all Ticketmaster retail centers require cash payment. Ticketmaster adds a service charge for both phone and in-person orders.

And be prepared to wait a long time on hold or in line for the tickets in greatest demand.

well. The bar made national headlines in 1997 when a bomber (police believe it is the same person who set the bombs at an abortion clinic and at Centennial Olympic Park in 1996) placed two explosive devices at this site. Fortunately, no one was killed when they detonated.

Smith's Olde Bar
1578 Piedmont Avenue NE
(404) 875–1522

Smith's, near Ansley Mall, features local and national rock, jazz, folk, and alternative bands for the post-college crowd. It opens daily for lunch and stays open until 4:00 A.M. weekdays and 3:00 A.M. on Saturday. The cover charge in the upstairs showroom varies from small to moderate, depending on who's playing.

Little Five Points

Euclid Avenue Yacht Club
1136 Euclid Avenue NE
(404) 688–2582

The Yacht Club is a neighborhood bar with a limited menu. Grab a front booth to take in the passing scene on the street in this Little Five Points neighborhood joint where pink hair and pierced bodies are more common than apple pie. The mahogany-paneled bar is decorated in a yacht-club theme with stuffed fish, an actual canoe, and maritime photos from all over the world on the walls.

Star Community Bar
437 Moreland Avenue NE
(404) 681–9018

Star Community Bar, identified as "Atlanta's best honky-tonk," is open nightly with college, garage, and rockabilly bands several nights a week; occasionally there's a show by a national act on the college circuit. The cover charge is small to moderate, depending on who's playing. The Star has an all-Elvis jukebox and an Elvis shrine housed in a former bank vault. In the basement is the Little Vinyl Lounge subterranean deco bar with a jukebox featuring 5,000 choices.

Virginia-Highland

Blind Willie's
828 North Highland Avenue NE
(404) 873–2583

A neon alligator in the window welcomes you to Blind Willie's, another landmark Atlanta blues joint. Mose Allison and Jr.

Little Five Points is a great spot to soak up the Atlanta scene. PHOTO: JOHN MCKAY

Wells have played here, and there's live entertainment every night. There's a full bar with bar food; a moderate cover is charged nightly. Music starts at 10:00 P.M.

Dark Horse Tavern
816 North Highland Avenue NE
(404) 873–3607
www.darkhorseatlanta.com

The trendy Dark Horse Tavern has a rock performance space in the basement where local and national college bands play. If there is a cover for the showroom, it's usually small. The street-level room has a large bar and windows from which to observe the street life.

George's
1041 North Highland Avenue NE
(404) 892–3648

At the heart of Virginia-Highland, George's is a favorite hangout for neighborhood residents. Grab a burger and a beer and sit at an outside table any night except Sunday.

Highland Tap
1026 North Highland Avenue NE
(404) 875–3673

The Tap is cozy, smoky, and dark. Its jumbo four-ounce martini is big with those who like their cocktails high and dry.

Limerick Junction
822 North Highland Avenue
(404) 874–7147

Celebrate Celtic culture at this Irish pub. There's a sing-along or live contemporary Irish or folk music. There's a small cover on Friday and Saturday nights.

Outside In-town Atlanta

There's a big divide in metro Atlanta: those inside the Perimeter (our "beltway" highway) and those outside. "Insiders" think of themselves as just that—urbane, sophisticated, the "in" crowd. Inside the Perimeter, you'll find most of the trendy clubs and top-rated restaurants.

But for those who brave the commute outside the Perimeter, or those who live inside the Perimeter but beyond the Buckhead or Midtown communities, there is life—and nightlife, too.

Grant Park and East Atlanta are up-and-coming neighborhoods with vibrant clubs and bars. And out where the suburbanites live—in Sandy Springs, north Fulton, Cobb, and Gwinnett Counties—people find cozy, comfortable, even cutting-edge, entertainment.

Grant Park/East Atlanta
E.A.R.L.
488 Flat Shoals Avenue SE
(404) 522–3950

Rock and jazz are among the everyday music offerings at this restaurant/bar/live music venue. Open daily; hours vary. Brunch on Sunday.

Echo Lounge
551 Flat Shoals Avenue SE
(404) 681–3600
www.echostatic.com/echolounge

The doors open at 9:00 P.M. for this 18-and-up club that features heavy rock, punk, and ska sounds, along with an occasional '80s night.

Lenny's Bar
307 Memorial Drive SE
(404) 377–7721

Lenny's is a fun little honky-tonk near Grant Park. It has a full bar and is open Monday through Saturday. There's usually a live band of the alternative music genre on Wednesday, Friday, and Saturday. There's a small cover on entertainment nights for the local and national bands. Closed Sunday.

Dunwoody/Roswell/Sandy Springs/North Fulton County
Arturo's Piano Bar
5486 Chamblee Dunwoody Road
Dunwoody
(770) 396–0335

Enjoy a drink (or two!) and a variety of tunes in the upscale piano bar attached to a casual trattoria.

Cafe 290
290 Hildebrand Drive NE
Sandy Springs
(404) 256–3942

Cafe 290, just north of I–285, is open nightly with live jazz or blues. A separate section houses a sports bar. A full menu is available. There's no cover if you dine in; otherwise, on weekends you'll pay a cover.

Rendezvous
4711 Ashford Dunwoody Road, Dunwoody
(770) 901–9995

A DJ spins popular dance music as the high-tech lighting and sound system accompany a video program. Open Monday through Saturday, usually starting at 4:00 P.M. and going as late—or is it early—as 4:00 A.M., all for a moderate cover.

Galleria/Cobb County

Cowboy's Dance Hall
1750 North Roberts Road
Kennesaw
(770) 426–5006
www.cowboysdancehall.com

Cowboy's—a 4,800-square-foot country club with a 4,000-square-foot dance floor—holds about 3,700 people and is open Wednesday through Sunday, with Wednesday ladies' night and Sunday no-alcohol family night. Most nights there's a small cover, which varies with the entertainment. If you don't know your line dance from a two-step, lessons are offered Saturday, Sunday, and Monday (when the club is open just for lessons).

Darwin's
1598 Roswell Road, Marietta
(770) 578–6872

This Marietta bar caters to the educated blues enthusiast with local and regional acts.

Dave and Buster's
2215 D&B Drive, Marietta
(770) 951–5554

This incredible amusement park for adults defies easy classification. Dave and Buster's is a 53,000-square-foot world of fun with billiard tables, shuffleboard courts, video games, and virtual reality simulators, a "for-fun" casino, a restaurant, full-service bars, and a mystery dinner theater where the audience helps solve the crime. Dave & Buster's is open every day from before noon until midnight or later. Accompanied children are welcome but must remain with their parents at all times. Because Dave & Buster's serves alcohol, after 10:00 P.M. anyone younger than 21 must leave the premises. There is another Dave & Buster's in Gwinnett County.

The Hanger
117 North Park Square, Marietta
(770) 424–9711

The sign outside sometimes doesn't keep up with the name changes, but inside is a dance club with a space-age/sci-fi decor to be enjoyed for those 18 and older. Need a break from dancing? Play pool or games in the Apollo Room. There is a small cover charge, but discounts are offered for those with college IDs. Doors open at 9:00 P.M., but call to make sure the music will be to your liking. The club is housed in the historic Strand Theater on the Square in Marietta.

Decatur/DeKalb County

City Lights Dance Club
4001 Presidential Parkway
(770) 451–5461
www.citylightsdanceclub.com

This smoke-free and alcohol-free club has ballroom, swing, and Latin music from 8:00 P.M. to midnight Friday and Saturday. Moderate cover.

Eddie's Attic
515 McDonough Street, Decatur
(404) 377–4976
www.eddiesattic.com

Eddie's Attic is a comfy Decatur club noted as a proving ground for local acoustic acts. The Indigo Girls, for example, had an opening party here in '97. There's no cover charge on the patio, which is open year-round. A cover charge starts small and goes up for big-name acts for the music hall.

Mama's Country Showcase
3952 Covington Highway, Decatur
(404) 288–6262
www.mamascountryshowcase.com

Country music is featured at Mama's, where a 3,000-square-foot dance floor holds about 2,000 boot-scooters. The format is high-energy "young" country with music suited to line dancing. As the evening goes on, the DJ widens the dance music repertoire to include music that gets rockin'. If you're brave, you can hop on Tornado the mechanical bull. Mama's is open Friday and Saturday from 8:00 P.M. to 4:00 A.M. Cover charge varies with age.

Gwinnett County

Dave and Buster's
4000 Venture Drive, Duluth
(770) 497–1152

Like its Cobb County counterpart, this amusement park for adults has billiard tables, shuffleboard courts, video games, and virtual reality simulators, a "for-fun" casino, a restaurant, full-service bars, and a mystery dinner theater where the audience helps solve the crime. Dave and Buster's is open every day from before noon until midnight or later. Accompanied children are welcome but must remain with their parents at all times. Because Dave and Buster's serves alcohol, after 10:00 P.M. anyone younger than 21 must leave the premises.

Flying Machine
510 Briscoe Boulevard, Lawrenceville
(770) 962–2262

Combine airplanes and country music, and you have Flying Machine. The aeronautically themed restaurant has a runway view of Gwinnett County's airport and regular menu of local country and western performers. It's open from 7:00 to 10:30 P.M.

Comedy

Punch Line
280 Hildebrand Drive NE
(404) 252–5233

A list of comedians who have played the Punch Line reads like *TV Guide:* Jerry Seinfeld, Ellen Degeneres, Tim Allen, and Brett Butler have all made audiences laugh, laugh, laugh here where they frequently try out their new material. Pam Stone of the TV series *Coach* got her start here as a waitress. The club is open Tuesday through Sunday; the cover charge varies depending upon who's performing. For weekends and special engagements, purchase tickets in advance. Seats go fast.

Uptown Comedy Corner
2140 Peachtree Road NW
(404) 350–6990

Uptown Comedy Corner showcases popular urban comedians and draws a primarily African-American, upscale crowd. The club holds about 300 people. There are three shows Friday and Saturday and one show on Tuesday, Wednesday, and Thursday. The cover charge is moderate during the week and higher for shows on Friday and Saturday.

Sports Bars

Metro Atlanta is full of transplants, and they like to follow their sports teams from around the country. Thanks to satellites and fan clubs, they can hang out with like-minded fans, cheering on teams from the Miami Hurricanes to the Seattle Seahawks or Boston Red Sox to the Los Angeles Lakers. Among the most popular locales are sports bars, from neighborhood pubs to the massive national chains.

If you watched any of ESPN's pregame coverage of the 2000 Super Bowl, you saw the latest addition to Atlanta's already crowded sports bar scene, ESPN Zone in Buckhead.

Each fall, college and pro football enthusiasts gather in fan clubs for nearly every major college and pro team. Listed below is just a sampling of the many sports bars in town. Check the sports section of the *Atlanta Journal-Constitution* for the meeting time and place for the many fan clubs. You can bet they've already found a good place to have a beer and watch the game.

Caddy's Sports Bar
1381 Iris Drive, Salem Gate Shopping Center at I–20 and GA 138, Conyers
(770) 860–8660
There are drink specials here every time the Braves score. You're bound to get a view on at least one of the 25 televisions, including four big screens (one of them a projector).

ESPN Zone
3030 Peachtree Road
(404) 682–3776
The 33,000-square-foot megasports complex opened Super Bowl week to special cablecasts and parties for the country's sports elite. By the Super Sunday, it was open to the rest of us. To make sure fans never miss a moment of the action, there are 210 television screens—some of which are even in the rest rooms.

Famous Pub and Sports Palace
2947 North Druid Hills Road, Toco Hills Shopping Center
(404) 633–3555
The Famous Pub is like *Cheers* on steroids. It has six big screens with surround sound, a four-page menu, and a regular Saturday gathering of Tennessee Volunteers.

Frankie's Food, Sports, and Spirits
5600 Roswell Road, Prado Shopping Center
(404) 843–9444
Commercial breaks are dance breaks at this videodrome. There are almost as many TVs (175) as there are inside seats, and 50 monitors outside on the heated patio. Even the rest rooms are plugged in.

Rafters Neighborhood Bar & Grille
10955 Jones Bridge Road, north Fulton County
(770) 664–4242
13695 GA 9, north Fulton County
(678) 366–0007
Mike Kenn, the former Atlanta Falcons star and now chairman of the Fulton County Commission, is the owner of Rafters' two locations. Each Rafters features more than 50 TV sets.

Y-Knot Sports Bar
216 North Lake Drive, Peachtree City
(770) 487–9111
Three levels of viewing areas and three large screens (including one measuring 10 by 10 feet) mean it's hard to miss a play at this complex.

Shopping

A transportation hub from its beginning, Atlanta naturally became a retail center as well. Just two years after the Civil War, more than 250 stores were wheeling and dealing in Atlanta. (Remember all the money Scarlett O'Hara and her second husband, Frank Kennedy, made with their store and lumberyard during Reconstruction?) Atlanta is nothing if not a booming retail market with amazing extremes. Here you can shop Saks, Tiffany & Co., Gucci, Cartier, and Neiman Marcus in megamalls that have become tourist attractions in themselves, while just a few rail stops away, you can shop the thrift stores to find designer jeans for less than $10. Every weekend with halfway decent weather, you'll find street after street of yard sales. Telephone poles are plastered with signs advertising upcoming yard sales, and the "Yard Sales" section in *Creative Loafing* and the "Garage Sales" section in the *Atlanta Journal-Constitution* offer the organized shopper who doesn't want to waste time aimlessly roaming the blocks a plan of attack.

Here's a glimpse of some of Atlanta's best-known retail centers and some lesser-known ones, too. We start at the city's malls and continue to outlets, shopping districts, antiques, thrift stores, consignment shops, farmers' markets, bookstores, music stores, and New Age shopping venues. Look to our International Atlanta chapter for some intriguing shopping destinations that reflect our city's cultural diversity.

Malls

Atlanta

CNN Center
Marietta Street at Techwood Drive NW
(404) 827–2491
CNN Center includes the Omni Hotel and the studios and world headquarters of the Cable News Network. It offers a variety of restaurants and Atlanta-themed gift stores, such as the Atlanta Shop, the Braves Clubhouse Store (a great place to buy tickets as well as souvenirs), and the Turner Store.

You can take a 45-minute tour of the CNN headquarters. (See our Attractions chapter for more information on these tours.)

Cumberland Mall
Cobb Parkway NW, south of I–285/75 in Cobb County
(770) 435–2206
The 1.2-million-square-foot Cumberland Mall opened in the early 1970s and was renovated in 1989; its anchors are Rich's-Macy's, Sears, and JCPenney. Other stores include Ann Taylor, Bachrach, the Bombay Company, Abercrombie & Fitch, and Gap Kids. The food court offers an array of choices, including Mick's, a restaurant that originated in Atlanta and has become a national chain (see our Restaurants chapter).

Guest Services at Cumberland Mall provides shoppers with details of ongoing

Insiders' Tip

Federated Department Stores announced in January 2003 that it would combine its two Atlanta department store chains, forming Rich's-Macy's, and will bring in Bloomingdale's to Lenox Square and Perimeter Malls late in 2003.

store and mall events, easy access to strollers and wheelchairs, and gift certificates redeemable in all mall stores. A complimentary personal shopper service is available on request.

Galleria Specialty Mall
One Galleria Parkway NW, Cobb County
(770) 955–9100

The Cobb Galleria Centre complex includes a 108,000-square-foot exhibition hall, the Renaissance Waverly Hotel, and the Galleria Specialty Mall. The Galleria Specialty Mall offers a number of boutiques owned and operated by local entrepreneurs, featuring men's, women's, and children's apparel, gifts, jewelry, and sports merchandise, including Peter Glenn for specialty sports such as in-line skating and skiing and H. Stockton for men's fashion. In addition, the mall has a variety of restaurants including Jocks & Jills sports bar, Ruby Tuesday, and Winfield's. Service establishments include hairstylists, a newsstand, American Express Travel, and a photography studio. Want to be entertained? The mall has an eight-screen theater and Cyberstation, a family entertainment center with state-of-the-art video games.

Galleria Specialty Mall is at the intersection of I-75, I-285, and Cobb Parkway.

Greenbriar Mall
2841 Greenbriar Parkway SW
(404) 344–6611

The second of Atlanta's original malls, Greenbriar opened in August 1965. Its 678,000 square feet include Rich's-Macy's, Circuit City, Cub Foods, Burlington Coat Factory, and the Magic Johnson Theatres with 12 screens and stadium seating. Greenbriar features a large selection of stores carrying Afrocentric fashions and accessories for the home. If you're lost or confused, take heart: Greenbriar's Customer Service Booth can help you get oriented. You'll also find information about how to purchase a Greenbriar Mall Certificate, redeemable at any of the mall's retail merchants.

Follow I-285 to Lakewood Freeway; take exit 4A off the freeway to get to the mall.

Lenox Square
3393 Peachtree Road NE
(404) 233–6767

Atlanta's first large suburban shopping mall opened in 1959 with 52 stores and 665,000 square feet. Buckhead was still on the fringes of Atlanta, and Atlantans were stunned at the $32 million cost of the new shopping center. The shopping center was enclosed and expanded in 1972 and expanded again in 1987; its food court grew in 1993.

Today, Lenox is the largest mall inside I-285, and the second largest in the entire metro Atlanta area. It has 250 stores, attracts an amazing 14 million visitors annually, and its rate of sales per square foot is among the highest of all U.S. shopping centers. A $60 million expansion completed in 1995 increased its size to 1.5 million square feet.

Rich's-Macy's, Neiman Marcus, and (soon!) Bloomingdale's anchor the 61-acre mall; other shops include Louis Vuitton, Cartier, Warner Bros., Disney, and the Metropolitan Museum of Art Shop. There is also an expanded FAO Schwartz concept store that's triple the size of its original Lenox location. Other merchants include Betsy Johnson, Bare Escentuals, and The Franklin Mint Gallery. If you have questions, Lenox's concierges will be glad to help.

Lenox has acres of free parking (a true rarity in Buckhead!) and sections where valet parking is available for a modest fee (about $3), or you can take the train to the Lenox MARTA station. Opposite the station is the J.W. Marriott Hotel; adjacent to it, the Lenox Building has an enclosed passageway. Called Art Walk, it is decorated with intriguing art shows. The Art Walk leads directly to the mall.

Insiders' Tip
The first modern shopping mall in the southeastern United States, Lenox Square, opened in 1959.

The Mall at Peachtree Center
Peachtree Street NE at International Boulevard
(404) 524-3787

This is the first retail complex in Downtown and a component of the huge Peachtree Center development designed by famed Atlanta architect John Portman. Pedestrian bridges connect the Mall to many Downtown buildings, including the Marriott Marquis and Hyatt Regency. More than 75 mall businesses offer a variety of shopping and services.

Dine at fine restaurants such as Azio and Benihana's, or grab a quick bite at a selection of food-court eateries. Shop for apparel and accessories at a variety of stores such as Brooks Brothers and Gallery Shoes. Buy sports merchandise at Stadium Stuff or collectibles at Atlanta International Museum Gift Shop.

Personal and travel service companies abound at this mall. Executive Shoe Shine, UPS Air Center, and La Grande convenience store are among the variety of places dedicated to making your life simpler.

Architectural Book Center, owned by the American Institute of Architects (AIA), is a museum shop frequented by conventioneers and other city visitors. Peachtree Center is served by the Peachtree Center MARTA station.

North DeKalb Mall
Lawrenceville Highway at North Druid Hills Road
(404) 320-7960

One of Atlanta's first malls (it opened in 1965), North DeKalb Mall, known for a short time as Market Square, was renovated in 1986. Its 650,657 square feet include Rich's-Macy's and Stein Mart. The mall features a food court, a movie theater, and a variety of retailers selling everything from sporting goods to jewelry.

To get to the mall from I-285, take the Lawrenceville Highway exit.

Northlake Mall
4800 Briarcliff Road
(770) 938-3564

Northlake has 125 specialty stores, along with Sears, Rich's-Macy's, JCPenney, and Parisian (an upscale Alabama-based department store). At nearby Northlake Tower Festival, 3983 LaVista Road, you'll find numerous "big box" superstores, such as PetSmart and Toys "R" Us. Take I-285 and exit at LaVista Road.

Phipps Plaza
3500 Peachtree Road NE
(404) 262-0992

Diagonally across Peachtree from Lenox Square, Phipps Plaza is devoted strictly to upscale stores. When it opened in 1969, Phipps was the first two-story mall in the Southeast. A $140 million renovation in 1992 added a three-level wing and Parisian, which joined existing anchors Lord & Taylor and Saks Fifth Avenue. Other shops of note include the amazingly modernistic 24,000-square-foot Nike Town, Abercrombie & Fitch, and Lassiter's Bath & Boudoir. It also includes the only Atlanta locations of Tiffany & Co., Ross-Simons, Gucci, Gianni Versace, A/X Armani Exchange, and Kenneth Cole. The mall also has a 14-screen movie theater, a food court, and five white-tablecloth restaurants.

Underground Atlanta
Peachtree at Alabama Streets SW
(404) 523-2311
www.underatl.com

Underground Atlanta evolved as a curious by-product of the city's growth. By 1890, more than 100 trains a day were passing through the downtown depot. Temporary iron bridges were built across the tracks to alleviate traffic congestion; then, in the 1920s, a permanent concrete viaduct was added, and the street was elevated. Businesses on old Alabama Street relocated upward to new Alabama Street, and the old storefronts sat abandoned below the street until they were rediscovered by a Georgia Tech graduate who developed the area as a retail and entertainment center in 1969.

Throughout most of the 1970s, Underground boomed as a rowdy party spot that was a favorite of locals and tourists. But after it lost about half its space to MARTA construction and the perception of crime became a problem, the old Underground closed in 1981.

One entrance to Underground Atlanta is on Peachtree Street. PHOTO: JOHN MCKAY

Redeveloped as a public/private venture, the new Underground opened in 1989 and is almost three times the size of its predecessor. During the Centennial Olympics the Underground was a big success with locals and visitors who enjoyed the shops and vendor carts that lined both subterranean Lower Alabama Street and the aboveground, pedestrian-only Upper Alabama Street. Since then, Underground has, pardon the pun, been on shaky ground, struggling to attract new vendors and restaurants. But considering its history, Underground will most likely see another renaissance. This next renaissance may already be under way, with several new restaurants and shops to be opened late in 2003 and early 2004.

The food court has a good mix of ethnic and fast food. The open-air Kenny's Alley is a courtyard of bars and restaurants.

The entrance to the Underground parking decks is on M. L. King Jr. Drive (one-way, westbound); there are other decks in the area as well. Or take MARTA to the Five Points station and enter through the pedestrian tunnel under Peachtree; it's on your right just before you exit the station.

Vinings Jubilee
4200 Paces Ferry Road NW, Cobb County
(770) 438–8080

In historic Vinings Village, browse in a Victorian shopping center. More than 20 specialty boutiques, antiques shops, and eateries offer nourishment, apparel, decorative home accessories, and antiques. Stores include Talbots, The Sandpiper, and Pappagallo. If all that shopping leaves you famished, drop by the Atlanta Bread Company for a light lunch. If you need a quick jolt of caffeine, grab an espresso at Starbuck's or Caribou Coffee.

Beyond Atlanta

Arbor Place
6700 Douglas Boulevard, Douglasville
(770) 947–4244

One of the metro area's newest malls, and the first in Douglas County, this 1.4-

million-square-foot center features three anchors—Dillard's, Parisian, and Sears. Another 117 stores are on the premises. Along with a food court, there's a soft play area for kids and environmental wall depicting the area's wetlands.

The Avenue East Cobb
4475 Roswell Road, Marietta

This new "retro mall" takes shoppers back to the days of their youth, when the stores were clustered around the parking lot and sidewalks. It's a bit dressier than those malls of yesteryear, but the concept's the same. Pull right up in front of Williams Sonoma, Seattle's Best Coffee, or Victoria's Secret. The 236,000-square-foot project includes landscaped walking paths with benches well away from the traffic.

Discovery Mills
5900 Sugarloaf Parkway, Lawrenceville
(678) 847–5201

Discovery Mills is Atlanta's newest mall, marketed as a kind of outlet center–traditional mall fusion. It is 25 miles northeast of downtown Atlanta, at the junction of I-85, Georgia State Road 120, and Sugarloaf Parkway, located in the very heart of one of the fastest-growing suburban areas in the southeastern United States. The major "anchor" stores are not the usual Atlanta mall inhabitants, either: Bass Pro Shops Outdoor World, Books-A-Million, Burlington Coat Factory, Last Call from Neiman Marcus, and Off 5th–Saks Fifth Avenue Outlet. The 200 other stores include Bath & Body Works, Bose, Charlotte Russe, Eddie Bauer Outlet, joan vass usa Outlet, Jones New York Country Store, Kenneth Cole New York Outlet, Mikasa Factory Store, Strasburg Children, and WestPoint Stevens.

Gwinnett Place
2100 Pleasant Hill Road, Duluth
(770) 476–5160

This 1.2-million-square-foot mall opened in 1984 and expanded in 1993. It has 220 shops and department stores, including Rich's-Macy's, Parisian, and Sears. The surrounding streets are a favorite stop for car buyers: Most of the major car makers have dealerships in this area, mostly clustered around Satellite Boulevard behind the mall.

The Mall of Georgia
3333 Buford Drive, Buford
(678) 482–8788

Opened in 1999, the metro area's super-mall stretches out over 1.7 million square feet. Inside, the wings are decorated in the style of various state regions, i.e., the Magnolia lowlands and the north Georgia mountains. In between are JCPenney, Rich's-Macy's, Lord & Taylor, Nordstroms, and Dillard's. A movie and IMAX theater, an outdoor performing stage, and several smaller shops are lined along a Main Street setting on the edge of the property. Several upscale restaurants and a fast-food court provide a range of nourishment for hungry shoppers.

All the signs of a major regional center developing are here, and progress has been slow but steady over the past few years, which should provide many more outlying shopping centers and restaurants before too much longer.

North Point Mall
1000 North Point Circle, Alpharetta
(770) 740–9273

Opened in 1993, the 1.4-million-square-foot North Point features JCPenney, Lord & Taylor, Dillard's, Parisian, Rich's-Macy's, and Sears. Nearly 200 specialty retailers, including The Body Shop, Ann Taylor, The Pet Stop, The Discovery Channel Store, and Littlewear, USA, offer a variety of goods to the mall's affluent clientele. North Point has a full-service customer service facility with an intercom/phone system attached to all freestanding mall directories, fax and photocopy services, and stroller and wheelchair availability. R.J. Reynolds Tobacco Co. has a smoking lounge inside this mall that is similar to one at the Northgate Mall in Chattanooga. This is the only place in the mall where you can smoke.

The food court has 15 restaurants and an outdoor patio. In a huge glass atrium beside the food court, a 30-foot-high carousel accommodates 38 riders; rides cost $1 per person.

Perimeter Mall
4400 Ashford Dunwoody Road NE
(770) 394-4270

Perimeter Mall opened in 1971, was expanded in 1982, and was renovated in 1993. Sitting just north of I–285, the 1.2-million-square-foot mall is the nerve center of the hyperdeveloped, always-busy northeast Perimeter sector in DeKalb County. Its anchors include Rich's-Macy's, and the newest anchor is Atlanta's first Nordstroms, which has a cafe that serves Starbuck's coffee with free refills and a 125,000-pair-strong shoe department. Perimeter Mall's Shopper Service Center offers strollers and wheelchairs; fax and photocopy services; emergency supplies such as aspirin, diapers, and bandages; and gift wrapping and shipping. Greeters stationed at the three main mall entrances can help you find what you're looking for.

Just across Hammond Drive is Perimeter Expo, which includes Home Depot's upscale Expo Design Center; Best Buy, a large discounter of electronics, appliances, and CDs; and Marshall's, a clothing discounter. Across Ashford Dunwoody Road is Park Place, an upscale, open-air specialty center featuring two hair salons, men's and women's apparel shops including H. Stockton and Talbots, and restaurants such as Cafe Intermezzo, Mi Spia, and Mick's (see our Restaurants chapter).

To get to the mall on I–285, take exit 21. From GA 400, take exit 5.

Insiders' Tip
Shopping for lots of items or heavy clothes? Take along wheeled luggage or a grocery cart and lug your purchases from department to department without straining your back or elbows by carrying armloads of merchandise.

Shannon Southpark Mall
I–85 at Union City
(770) 964-2200

Shannon opened in 1980 and expanded in 1986. More than 770,651 square feet house 110 stores including anchors Rich's-Macy's and Sears. The mall has a customer service center and offers numerous health and personal services such as shoe repair, hair cutting, a vision center, and a dental practice. Shannon Southpark also has a food court and various specialty shops selling home furnishings, athletic equipment, jewelry, books, electronics, gifts, and apparel.

Southlake Mall
I–75 at Highway 54, Morrow
(770) 961-1050

On 88 acres south of town, the 1-million-square-foot Southlake Mall in Clayton County includes JCPenney, Rich's-Macy's, Sears, and some 120 shops. Southlake, which opened in 1976, annually welcomes more than 11 million shoppers. This mall is convenient to Hartsfield International Airport.

Town Center at Cobb
I–75 at Barrett Parkway, Kennesaw
(770) 424-9486

Opened in 1986 and expanded in 1992, this 1.2-million-square-foot mall in Cobb County has 200 stores including Rich's-Macy's, JCPenney, Parisian, and Sears. At the Town Center Courtesy Center, the staff can help you with gift ideas, point you toward the right store, or sell you a mall gift certificate.

Bargain and Outlet Shopping

Atlanta

Metro Atlanta is hog-heaven for bargain hunters, offering malls, thrift stores, and outlet centers with pricing and quality that beats any other place in the country. Dedicated shoppers can find deals on everything from earrings to armoires, designer duds to floor lamps. In this section we've listed a few individual stores and outlet centers where savings are a staple.

Amsterdam Walk
500 Amsterdam Avenue NE

Monroe Drive intersects with Amsterdam Avenue about .5 mile north of the corner of Monroe and Virginia Avenue. Turn left; at the end of this dead-end street you'll find Amsterdam Walk (formerly Midtown Outlets), an eclectic mix of off-price and specialty shops where you can find bargains galore. Stores include Cook's Warehouse, Shoemakers' Warehouse, Intaglia Home Collection, Gado Gado, and Oriental Designer Rugs.

Hill Street Warehouse
2050 Hills Avenue NE
(404) 352–5001

This 50,000-square-foot warehouse holds a variety of home decorative accessories including antiques, Italian ceramics, and terra cotta. Some merchandise is priced 70 percent below retail.

To get to the Warehouse, take I-75, exit at Howell Mill, and go left on Collier Road.

Beyond Atlanta

North Georgia Premium Outlets
Highway 400 North at Dawsonville
(706) 216–3609

About 30 minutes north of Atlanta (and even less than that from the target-customer bases of east Cobb and north Fulton), this very unusual outlet center is aimed squarely at the upscale crowd, with the South's first Saks Fifth Avenue outlet store, Off 5th, and a number of outlets for "name" labels, such as Anne Klein, Brooks Brothers, Donna Karan, Jones New York, Jos A. Bank, North Face, and Polo Ralph Lauren. The 140 stores include other seldom-seen outlets, including Johnston & Murphy Shoes, Lego, Bostonian Clarks, Etienne Aigner, Crate & Barrel, and Fossil.

Prime Outlets at Calhoun
455 Bellwood Road, Calhoun
(706) 602–1300

This center is closer to Chattanooga than Atlanta, but its more than 60 shops include outlets for Old Navy, Nike, Tommy Hilfiger, Jones New York, Springmaid/Wamsutta, and Mikasa. To get to Prime Outlets, take I-75 north and go east on Georgia Highway 53, take a right on Outlet Center Drive, then follow the signs.

Tanger Factory Outlet Center
I–85 at U.S. Highway 441, Commerce
(706) 335–4537

About an hour north of Atlanta, this center has 45 shops and promises savings of up to 65 percent off retail. Among others, you'll find Geoffrey Beene, Bass, Liz Claiborne, and Reebok. Cross to the south side of I-85 and you'll find another Tanger's outlet center. This one is anchored by Vanity Fair and other shops including Adidas, Nautica, and Rue 21.

Tanger Factory Outlet Center
I–75 to Locust Grove
(770) 957–0238

Approximately 30 miles south of Atlanta and 50 miles north of Macon, this center features 36 designer and brand-name manufacturers' outlet stores. Toy Liquidators, Perfumania, Cape Isle Knitters, Leslie Fay, and Russell/Jerzees are just a few of the popular outlets you'll find here.

Shopping Districts

Atlanta

Buckhead
Roswell, Peachtree, and Piedmont Roads

Buckhead retailing is dominated by the huge malls Lenox Square and Phipps Plaza, but there are also plenty of small shops with unusual merchandise. The district covers a big area, some say all the way to Piedmont Road as well as up and down Peachtree Road.

Architectural Accents, 2711 Piedmont Road NE, is full of fireplace surrounds, old tiles, antique frames, and more antique locks, handles, and window hardware than you can imagine. Seeing Is Believing, 3167 Peachtree Road NE, carries the most unusual eyewear. Staff at the Beverly Bremer Silver Shop, 3164 Peachtree Road NE, can find replacements for damaged or missing pieces to complete heirloom silverware. Beverly Hall Furniture Galleries, 2789 Piedmont Road NE, has handsome, new traditional pieces and carries contemporary items made by traditional manufacturers.

Chattahoochee Avenue Warehouse Shopping District
Take I–75 to Howell Mill, turn west, then right onto Chattahoochee Avenue

Bargains abound in the Chattahoochee Avenue warehouse shopping district. A no-returns policy at any of these places means careful shopping is a must. And because these are warehouse showrooms, use the bathroom before you leave home. Also, it would be best to leave the kids with the nanny because this is strictly an adults-only kind of area, and usually massively crowded. Most warehouses are open Friday, Saturday, and Sunday only. Call to check days and hours of operation.

Most men don't live in town long before hearing about the K&G Men's outlet, 1750 Ellsworth Industrial Drive. From ties and shirts to suits and tuxedos, this massive warehouse offers an enormous selection of men's clothes and accessories at substantial savings. While the guys are browsing, their girlfriends and spouses head two blocks away to the AJS Shoe Warehouse, 1788 Ellsworth Industrial Drive, where they can find real deals on women's shoes, handbags, and accessories in a barn of a place. Ballard's Backroom, 1670 DeFoor Avenue NW, features unique, decorative household items at true discounts. Freedman Men's Shoe Outlet, 1240-A Old Chattahoochee Avenue NW, has been known in Atlanta for years as a retailer of name-brand, quality men's shoes.

Little Five Points
Moreland, Euclid, and McLendon Avenues

This area is rather like Atlanta's answer to New York's East Village: Hip, funky, and artistic shops with names such as Throb and Boomerang provide lingerie, hosiery, latex, leather, and other hip-hop, shiny clubwear. The district's many old storefronts make it a favorite location site for movies and TV: Most memorably, this was where Morgan Freeman drove Jessica Tandy to the grocery store in *Driving Miss Daisy*. The part of the Piggly-Wiggly supermarket was portrayed by Sevananda Natural Foods, 467 Moreland Avenue.

Check the Junkman's Daughter, 464 Moreland Avenue NE, for new and used clubwear and novelties. Kolo, 1144 Euclid Avenue NE, and Urban Tribe across the street, provide body-piercing services. Stefan, 1160 Euclid Avenue, sells used clothes with panache. Crystal Blue, 1168 Euclid Avenue, has incense, mood tapes, and wonderful wooden pill boxes.

Need a pit stop or a beer in between shopping? La Fonda Latina and the Vortex are great for that. (See our Restaurants chapter.) Little Five Points is served by the Inman Park/Reynoldstown MARTA station. Be sure to exit on the north side of the tracks, especially at night. From the station walk north on Hurt Street, then right on Euclid (about six blocks); or take the 48 Lenox bus.

Insiders' Tip

Many of the smaller towns and cities within an hour or two of Atlanta have revitalized their downtown squares by turning them into antiques and boutique centers, all aimed at luring shoppers away from the crowded in-town shopping districts.

Virginia Avenue at North Highland Avenue

You'll see plenty of street life in the Highland Area all the way from the Poncey-Highlands (which extends from North Avenue up to and somewhat beyond St. Charles Place) through to North Highland Avenue and Lanier Boulevard. Beyond that, it's all residential until you come to Sage Hill Shopping Center.

Affairs, 1401 North Highland Avenue NE, has small furniture, home accessories, and lots of interesting knickknacks to investigate. At Back to Square One, 1054 North Highland Avenue NE, you'll find handmade crafts by regional artists for the home and garden, including planters, garden sculptures, birdhouses, and primitive antiques (contemporary, American-made furniture with peeling paint). Even if you're not in the market for nails and bolts, stop by Highland Hardware, 1045 North Highland, and browse their selection of plants, garden, and gift items, as well as their exquisite collection of fine woodworking tools on the second floor.

The Common Pond, 996 Virginia Avenue NE, has environmentally friendly gifts for people and their pets. Women's clothes, jewelry, and gift items are very reasonably priced at Mooncake, 1019 Virginia Avenue NE. 20th Century Antiques, 1044 North Highland Avenue NE, which is really two stores in one, has everything from jewelry to cutlery, hand-painted end tables to chimes in one shop and mostly furniture, from '50s dinettes to '30s dressing tables, in the other. Silver jewelry and funky art, including hand-painted shower curtains, are sold at Jules Jewels, 1037 North Highland NE.

Antiques, Decorator Items, and Flea Markets

In addition to dozens of yard and estate sales nearly every weekend, Atlanta has several antiques shopping districts and large flea markets. Prices at these estab-

Virginia Highlands offers lots of opportunities for shopping and snacking. PHOTO: JOHN MCKAY

lishments range from rock-bottom to sky-high. In many antiques shops the price tag is just a starting point for negotiations; if you like to bargain hard, you may save big bucks.

Remember to use your common sense at the flea markets: We hope you're not too shocked to learn that those red vinyl bags on sale for $10 are not real Chanel—even though they are crudely stitched with the famous double-C logo.

Atlanta

Bennett Street
3 blocks north of Piedmont Hospital on the west side of Peachtree Road

Little Bennett Street is home to a large selection of antiques and decorative art dealers. These are not junk shops; most of the merchandise here is of the "better" category, and the prices reflect this. If you're looking for fine antiques, you'll find them here. Near the end of Bennett Street is the TULA complex of showrooms and galleries (see TULA's listing under "Galleries" in The Arts chapter).

Chamblee Antiques Row
3519 Broad Street, Chamblee
(770) 455–4751

More than 200 antiques dealers offer a cornucopia of antiques and collectibles in this architecturally interesting shopping district. Many shops operate out of old homes, churches, and stores, some dating from the mid-1800s. Antiques Row is within walking distance of the Chamblee MARTA station; you can also get there on the No. 25 Tilly Mill bus. Driving, turn off Peachtree Industrial Boulevard onto Broad Street; follow to the intersection of Broad Street and Peachtree Road. (We told you all the Peachtrees could get confusing!)

Cheshire Bridge Road NE
Between Piedmont and LaVista Roads

On Cheshire Bridge Road between Piedmont and LaVista, numerous antiques dealers are scattered among the restaurants, bars, and "lingerie modeling" businesses. The larger antiques shops rent out spaces to dealers, who always seem to be moving in or out. Competition for customers (and dealers) is keen. Expect to save at least 10 percent off the asking price unless an item is already marked down.

Georgia Lighting
530 14th Street NW
(404) 875–4754

Georgia Lighting's main store has a huge lighting showroom with an extensive collection of lighting products from all over the world, including landscape lighting and track lighting. A tent sale once a year always offers great bargains.

Great Gatsby's Auction Gallery
5070 Peachtree Industrial Boulevard
Chamblee
(770) 457–1903

This 100,000-square-foot "wholesale to the public" market is one of Atlanta's most fun stores. You can spend hours ogling everything including exquisite antiques, kitschy advertising memorabilia, and huge architectural fragments. Gatsby's supplies hotels worldwide with unusual furnishings; one of John Lennon's guitars was once sold here at auction. Gatsby's is 2 miles inside I-285 on Peachtree Industrial Boulevard.

Lakewood Antiques Market
2000 Lakewood Avenue SE
(404) 622-4488

When Robert Redford needed props for his 1930s movie *The Legend of Bagger Vance* (shot in Savannah), this is where he went. The popular market is held on the second weekend of each month and features thousands of unusual antiques and collectibles. Parking is free; admission is $3 for adults and free for children 12 and younger. The market is held Friday, Saturday, and Sunday, but there's a special early buyers' day on Thursday, when admission is $5. Take I-75/85 south from downtown; exit at Lakewood Freeway East and follow the signs.

Miami Circle NE

This short street is full of antique and decorator merchandise, and though it's primarily frequented by the city's interior designers, many of the stores are open to the public. As you drive north on Piedmont Road, Miami Circle is on your right; it's north of the Lindbergh MARTA station and just past the Cub Foods shopping center. Shops of note include Bobby Dobb Antiques, The Gables Antiques, and Antonio Raimo Galleries, where rare and unusual books and prints are for sale.

The Wrecking Bar
292 Moreland Avenue NE
(404) 525-0468

On Moreland just south of the Little Five Points intersection in a huge mansion is the Wrecking Bar, selling architectural art and antiques, from hardware and chandeliers to large mantels and statuary. The store occupies an 1895 mansion listed on the National Register of Historic Places.

Beyond Atlanta

A Flea An'Tique
4300 Georgia Highway 20, Buford
(770) 932-6833

This upscale flea market, which bills itself as "North Atlanta's Best Kept Secret," features a variety of finds such as antiques, collectibles, and quality used furniture. Going north on I-85, take exit 45; if you're on I-985, take exit 1. The market is behind Ace Hardware inside Buford Mall.

The Cotton House
21 Milton Avenue, Alpharetta
(770) 475-3100

In business for more than 40 years, this store has a large collection of furniture, gifts, home accessories, and collectibles. It offers a variety of well-known name brands at competitive prices.

Crabapple Corners
790 Mayfield Road, Alpharetta
(770) 475-4545

This old country store at the crossroads of the Crabapple community north of Alpharetta is packed with early American furniture, pictures, rugs, and collectibles. Stroll to the back room and accept the owner's gracious offer of a cold Coke in an original hourglass bottle.

Lamps N Things
1205 Johnson Ferry Road NE, Marietta
(770) 971-0874

In the Woodlawn Square Shopping Center, this 3,800-square-foot store offers thousands of lamp shades, lamps, mirrors, art, antiques, and other home accessories. The store's personnel also custom-make shades and lamps for individuals and decorators and repair lamps.

Picket Fences
One South Main Street, Alpharetta
(770) 475-5758

This shop sells hand-painted furniture, home accessories, and collectibles by Goebel, Spode, and Beatrix Potter. It carries gourmet foods, such as syrups, jams, and jellies, as well as a line of Georgia products, including trivets, refrigerator magnets, Christmas ornaments, and other items made of Buckley's Georgia clay.

Pride of Dixie Antique Market
1700 Jeurgens Court, Norcross
(770) 279-9853

Held monthly on the fourth weekend,

this market hosts some 800 booths. It's held in the North Atlanta Trade Center in Norcross. Take I–85 to exit 38; east on Indian Trail; right on Oakbrook Parkway; right on Jeurgens Court. Admission is $4; look for a $1-off coupon in the weekend section of the *Atlanta Journal-Constitution* on Sunday prior to the these weekends. Parking is free.

Scott Antique Market
3650 Jonesboro Road, in the Atlanta Expo Center, Jonesboro
(404) 361–2000

Open the second weekend of each month from 8:00 A.M. to 5:00 P.M., this market offers everything from American antiques to English porcelain displayed by 1,500 dealers from across the country. Call for specific shows. To get there, take I–285 to exit 40 (Jonesboro Road). Atlanta Expo Center is right off the exit. The Atlanta Expo Center actually straddles I–285, with one building inside the highway and the other across the road.

Sharon's House of Lamps & Shades
5544 Peachtree Industrial Boulevard
Chamblee
(770) 457–1522

This enormous showroom offers an extensive collection of lighting options, with more than 6,000 table lamps, wall lamps, and floor lamps, and 10,000 shades from well-known manufacturers.

Thrift Stores

Confirmed thrift store shoppers know that little islands of great value can some-

times be found amid the oceans of junk in Atlanta's thrift stores. If you're of an adventurous mind, you might discover an elegant outfit, or at least maybe your next Halloween getup.

We've described some of the major thrifts; most of them have several locations, so see the Yellow Pages for the location nearest you.

Goodwill Industries of Atlanta
2201 Glenwood Avenue SE
(404) 486–4800

Goodwill Stores offer affordable prices on a variety of quality furniture, clothing, and household items. Each store has a donation center, and other donation centers are scattered throughout the metro area. Check the Yellow Pages for Goodwill Industries' nine other locations.

Salvation Army
740 Marietta Street NW
(404) 522–9783

The Salvation Army picks up more than 50 truckloads of donated furniture, clothing, and household items every week. These donations provide merchandise for the Army's thrift stores, proceeds from which help support the Adult Rehabilitation Center. There are four other locations in the area.

St. Vincent de Paul
5748 Buford Highway
(770) 457–9648

This store (plus five others) stocks just about everything: clothing, household items, furniture, appliances, books, records, tapes, jewelry, and miscellaneous items. Ninety percent of the proceeds go to this charity, which provides, among other things, emergency rent checks to working folks in a bind.

Thrift House of the Cathedral of St. Philip
Lindbergh Plaza Shopping Center
2581 Piedmont Road
(404) 233–8652

Books, clothes, shoes, draperies, housewares, knickknacks, and more are bargain priced at this thrift. The compact store is chock-full of good deals on all kinds of

Insiders' Tip
Many thrift stores only take cash, so hit the ATM or your piggy bank before you hit the stores.

items, from silver trays to wicker baskets; you'll also find the occasional piece of furniture. The store is on the plaza's upper level, #A-700.

Value Village
1320 Moreland Avenue
(770) 840–7283

Bargain hunters can find name-brand clothes, some with price tags still attached, among the used items at this, the largest thrift store operation in the metro area. Donations to the Kidney Foundation stock the shop, which in addition to clothing include furniture, accessories, and items for children. On Memorial Day and the Fourth of July, everything goes for half the ticket price. Value Village has five other locations.

Vintage

Vintage wear is a step up from thrift-store quality and price. Some clothing that starts out in thrift stores winds up cleaned, pressed, and marked up in the vintage shops. Still, because the thrifts can be downright grungy, many people who can afford to prefer to shop the vintage stores, which are generally cleaner, take credit cards, and have dressing rooms.

You can find great bargains at the many consignment shops throughout the metro area. These establishments are clothing recyclers; many carry current fashions and designer labels. Some also deal in vintage clothing. In this section we've listed a sampling of the consignment and vintage shops for men's and women's apparel.

Junkman's Daughter
464 Moreland Avenue
(404) 577–3188

In Little Five Points, you can't miss this place with its fantastic, space-age mural frontage in brilliant sky blue. Shop here along with pink-haired teens and hip grandmas for vintage and new clothing, housewares, tobacco, costumes, and all sorts of accessories. You can rent outfits for Halloween, too. Think of Junkman's

Daughter as an off-the-wall Target. There is another branch of this store, Junkman's Brother, in Athens, near the UGA campus.

Stefan's
1160 Euclid Avenue NE
(404) 688–4929

Also in Little Five Points, Stefan's stocks a high-quality selection of vintage duds for men and women. The merchandise includes hats, scarves, jewelry, and other old-time accessories.

Consignment Shops

ChickiBea
2130 North Decatur Plaza
(404) 634–6995

One of the first consignment shops in Atlanta, ChickiBea celebrated its 30th year in business in 2001. This is an upscale resale boutique for couture and designer women's clothes.

Consignshop
Toco Hills Shopping Center
2899-A North Druid Hills Road NE
(404) 633–6257

Consignshop offers something for both genders, featuring quality consignment clothing for men and women. It even has maternity and plus sizes.

Fantastic Finds
220 Sandy Springs Circle NW, Suite 189
(404) 303–1313

Shop here for high-quality, previously owned women's clothing. The shop is independently owned.

Hand-Me-Ups
4448 Marietta Street, Powder Springs
(770) 439–8200

Located on the main street of historic Powder Springs, Hand-Me-Ups offers a range of women's and children's clothing at bargain prices.

Nan's Upscale Resale
529 10th Street NW
(404) 876–1554

Both Goodwill In-
dustries and the
Salvation Army
maintain several
thrift stores in
and around Atlanta,
all of which are
excellent sources of
secondhand goods at
fire-sale prices.

Nestled behind Camille's restaurant in Virginia-Highland, this shop sells quality consignment apparel for men. It's closed on Sunday and Monday.

Play It Again
273 Buckhead Avenue
(404) 261-2135

Play It Again is one of the first consign-ment shops in Atlanta. It offers second-hand women's apparel in the heart of the city. Call and find out what day Play It Again will look at your goodies if you want to trade up.

Psycho Sisters
1052 St. Charles Avenue
(404) 892-7340
428 Moreland Avenue
(404) 523-0100
8610 Roswell Road NW, Dunwoody
(770) 993-3727
1355 Roswell Road, Marietta
(770) 565-6310

Promising "cool clothes at cheap prices for cool people," these wacky siblings buy/sell/trade/consign a variety of garb. The name can be found on eight other loca-tions, some of which are franchise opera-tions. The locations noted above are owned by the two sisters who started it all.

Costumes

Whether you're impersonating a pope or a pirate, a belle or a baboon, you'll find just the right disguise at an Atlanta costume shop. These stores are busiest in October; don't wait until the day before Halloween to make your selection.

Atlanta

Atlanta Costume
2089 Monroe Drive NE
(404) 874-7511

Need a Santa suit? Costumes for a play or promotion? Hats, wigs, makeup? This large costumer can help. Atlanta Costume also offers stage lighting supplies, mas-cots (big heads and bodies), and custom designing. The shop has extended hours in October.

Costumes Etc.
318 Pharr Road NE
(404) 239-9422

Costumes Etc. offers theatrical costumes, party disguises, and much more. It builds mascots at the store, offers custom de-sign, and provides specialty costumes for photo and video shoots. Need puppets? Costumes Etc. has got them!

Beyond Atlanta

Eddie's Trick & Novelty
3675 Satellite Boulevard, Duluth
(770) 814-9700
70 South Park Square, Marietta
(770) 428-4314

This store has a large selection of masks and costumes for theater, clowns, and masquerade. Check out the big supply of costumes for adults and children. Eddie's has everything from the Easter Bunny to Uncle Sam, the Old South to the Roaring '20s. Eddie's offers mascots, accessories, makeup, and magic supplies as well.

Farmers' Markets

Atlanta

DeKalb Farmers' Market
3000 East Ponce de Leon Avenue, Decatur
(404) 377-6400

DeKalb Farmers' Market, the oldest of the truly international food markets, attracts busloads of folks from Alabama, Tennessee, and even Florida. All mingle with the locals searching for exotic spices, canned goods, fresh fish, and breads and pastries made on the premises as well as regional and imported vegetables and fruit. Employees come from every corner of the globe and wear badges listing the languages they speak. Register at the customer service desk to have your checks accepted at checkout or use the on-site teller machine to get cash.

Take a lunch (or dinner) break at the Market's cafeteria (same food both times of day): You pay by the ounce at bargain rates and can fill a plate with many of the foods found in the employees' native lands for just a few dollars. Bottled beverages like Jamaican Ginger Beer and Mango Nectar are available.

International Farmers' Market
5193 Peachtree Industrial Boulevard
Chamblee
(770) 455–1777

International Farmers' Market offers fresh fruits and vegetables, seafood, meats and cheeses, and baked goods. Spices are sold in bulk. Beer and wine are available.

Morningside Farmers' Market
1325 North Highland Avenue NE
no phone

This outdoor market in the parking lot in front of Eclectic Electric (see "Galleries" in The Arts chapter) is open only on Saturday mornings in spring and summer (it closes at 1:00 P.M.), but it's the place to go in town when you want organic fruits and vegetables. The scene also includes local chefs demonstrating favorite seasonal dishes, neighborhood celebs, and a mingle-and-gab mood. Edible wildflowers, soybeans in the pod, and other more recognizable foods are also for sale. You can shop from 8:00 A.M. until noon, but arrive early for a chance at a parking space in this tight, urban residential neighborhood.

Beyond Atlanta

Atlanta Farmers' Market
4166 Buford Highway, Doraville
(404) 325–3999

This market claims to be "the biggest international grocer in Georgia" and stocks a variety of fresh produce, meats, and fish. You'll find exotic items from all over, gourmet coffee, and traditional grocery-store fare. It is located at the Plaza Fiesta Mall (formerly known as the Buford-Clairmont Mall).

Atlanta State Farmers' Market
16 Forest Parkway, Forest Park
(404) 675–1782

A 146-acre, open-air retail and wholesale market, Atlanta State Farmers' Market claims the distinction of being the largest in the Southeast and one of the largest in the world. It's open to the public round-the-clock every day except Christmas. More than 7,000 people visit the market each day. Inside the fenced compound, you drive your car around to visit vendors of everything from fresh produce to homemade preserves to Christmas trees during the holidays. From I–75, take exit 78.

Harry's Farmers' Markets
1180 Upper Hembree Road, Alpharetta
(770) 664–6300
2025 Satellite Parkway, Duluth
(770) 416–6900
70 Powers Ferry Road, Marietta
(770) 578–4400

Harry's Farmers' Markets is a more upscale version of DeKalb Farmers' Market (which is owned by Harry's brother). All of these farmers' markets are chock-full of delicacies from around the world as well as the staples of life. The markets have it all, from the commonplace to the exotic, including fish, cheese, wine, flowers, coffee, and vegetables. Whole Foods Markets, a national natural foods chain, recently purchased the small Harry's chain, but except for introducing the Whole Foods brand, little has changed in these beloved super-farmers' markets.

Books and Periodicals

Barnes & Noble
2900 Peachtree Road NW
(404) 261–7747
7660 North Point Parkway, Suite 200
Alpharetta
(770) 993–8340
120 Perimeter Centre West, Dunwoody
(770) 396–1200
2205 Pleasant Hill Road, Duluth
(770) 495-7200
50 Ernest Barrett Parkway, Kennesaw
(770) 422–2261

At Barnes & Noble you'll find books, magazines, CDs, and hot coffee in a roomy store that's easy to shop. Barnes & Noble stages about 30 events each month, including book signings, historical roundtables and local history discussions, and live musical performances. The store stocks more than 150,000 titles in every category and can special order from a database of more than 160,000 publishers. The Peachtree location decor is wood-paneled and elegant.

Barnes & Noble also owns Doubleday Book Shop and B. Dalton Bookseller. Doubleday has locations at Phipps Plaza and Underground Atlanta; B. Daltons are scattered throughout the metro area.

Borders Books & Music
3637 Peachtree Road NE
(404) 237–0707

Across the street from Phipps Plaza, the Peachtree Borders book shop is a bright and cheery place of roughly 35,000 square feet with more than 83,000 titles and one of the best area selections of newspapers and magazines. Borders features an espresso bar/cafe and book signings with celebrity authors as well as local writers. The store carries an extensive collection of foreign language publications and lots of out-of-town newspapers. There are numerous other Borders stores in the metro Atlanta area.

Chapter 11, The Discount Bookstore
Ansley Mall, 1544 Piedmont Road NE
(404) 872–7986
Peachtree Battle Shopping Center
2345 Peachtree Road
(404) 237-7199

This Atlanta chain evolved from one store and has grown dramatically in the last few years to include 13 locations. All of the books sold are discounted by at least—you guessed it—11 percent. The Peachtree Battle store is in the old Oxford Bookstore (a late lamented and dearly beloved local independent bookstore) location, which was gutted and redesigned to make room for more books and a brighter atmosphere. Chapter 11 sponsors many author book signings; be sure to ask which author is coming up on the calendar the next time you stop by one of the stores. (Check the Yellow Pages for other locations.)

Final Touch Gallery & Books
133 East Court Square, Decatur
(404) 378–5300

The owners of this quaint shop started off just selling books but found they had to expand the inventory to stay in business. Fortunately, they kept the mix interesting, adding unusual items of furniture and gifts along with plenty of books. The

Insiders' Tip

Several shopping centers clustered along Buford Highway near I-285 are aimed at that location's booming Asian population and have some of Atlanta's best Vietnamese, Korean, and Malaysian restaurants, as well as a number of very good markets with imported foods and clothing.

store is particularly noted for its fabulous book signings, which are more like parties with catered food, wine, and flowers. Check out the extensive selection of cookbooks.

Tall Tales
2105 LaVista Road NE
(404) 636-2498
Tall Tales is a full-service independent bookstore that has extensive children's and fiction sections and a base of loyal customers. That's because service is the specialty here: Special-order books can often be delivered the very next day. The store will also search for out-of-print books. The highly literate staff will gladly help you make your selections.

Special-Interest Book Shops

Atlanta

Architectural Book Center
Peachtree Center Mall, 231 Peachtree Street
(404) 222-9920
This bookstore shares a suite with AIA (American Institute of Architects, Georgia chapter). It sells retail books about architecture as well as gift items including statuary, frames, cards, and puzzles oftentimes but not always related to architecture.

Brushstrokes
1510 Piedmont Avenue NE
(404) 876-6567
In the Ansley Square Shopping Center just south of the intersection of Piedmont and Monroe, Brushstrokes is a popular stop for gay and lesbian magazines and gifts.

Cathedral of St. Philip
2744 Peachtree Road NW
(404) 365-1000
Religious books and gifts are for sale at the bookstore in the Episcopal cathedral.

Charis Books & More
1189 Euclid Avenue
(404) 524-0304
This is a pleasant store in Little Five Points selling feminist books, gay and lesbian literature, music, and children's books. It sponsors weekly community-oriented programs that often involve readings and book signings by noted authors.

The Civilized Traveller
Phipps Plaza, 3500 Peachtree Road NE
(404) 264-1252
This store offers a big selection of travel books and tour guides, plus luggage, binoculars, and other travel accessories.

Cokesbury Books and Church Supplies
2495 Lawrenceville Highway, Decatur
(404) 320-1034
Cokesbury sells religious books and other materials. It's affiliated with the United Methodist Church.

Eastern National Park & Monument
Association Book Store
Inside the Cyclorama
800 Cherokee Avenue SE
(404) 622-6264
This is a small shop with a fine collection of well-selected and -presented Civil War books and maps. Eastern National now runs most of the National Parks bookstores in the South, including other fine locations at the Chickamauga Battlefield and Fort Sumter National Monument.

Georgia Book Store Inc.
124 Edgewood Avenue NE
(404) 659-0959
Georgia Book Store Inc. gets a lot of walk-in traffic. On the corner of Edgewood Avenue and Courtland Street, across from Georgia State University, this bookstore is only a few blocks from some major Downtown hotels and the Martin Luther King Jr. National Historic Site. Although it's primarily a textbook store, carrying books offered for GSU courses as well as test-prep materials, Georgia Book Store also has sports-related items and local

and regional souvenirs. The store still has some Olympic memorabilia for sale. Georgia Book Store has been in business since 1957. The original owner pioneered the idea of buying college students' books back when the courses were over; that's a staple of the business now.

Outwrite
991 Piedmont Road
(404) 607–0082

Outwrite is at the corner of 10th Street and Piedmont Road in Midtown. Outwrite sells coffee-table books, as well as gay and lesbian books, magazines, and cards.

Science Fiction & Mystery
Cheshire Pointe Shopping Center, 2000-F
Cheshire Bridge Road
(404) 634–3226

If you just have to find out whodunit—or you think you already know—sleuth on over to the Science Fiction & Mystery book shop. It also carries fantasy books. Owner Mark Stevens briefly considered closing the shop in early 2001, but after a local outcry, decided to look for a better location for the beloved but seriously underpatronized shop.

Shrine of the Black Madonna
Ralph David Abernathy Boulevard SW
(404) 752–6125

In West End, you'll find an excellent source of African-American books for both adults and children at the Shrine of the Black Madonna. The shrine also sponsors book signings.

Beyond Atlanta

Fayette Book Shop
692 Glynn Street, Fayetteville
(770) 461–5907

Tucked away in the back of an older shopping center, this independently owned bookstore has been providing great reading material and personalized customer service to readers on the south side of Atlanta for around 20 years.

There's also an extensive collection of teacher's materials books, bulletin boards, and stickers as well as best-sellers, children's books, and biographies.

Greater Atlanta Christian Bookstore
1575 Indian Trail-Lilburn Road
Norcross
(770) 243–2000

This store has a big selection of Christian books, music, gifts, and cards. It's on the campus of the Greater Atlanta Christian School.

Iwase
6251 Peachtree Industrial Boulevard
Doraville
(404) 531–4100

Iwase features thousands of Japanese-language books, periodicals, and the ever-popular Japanese comic books. Some of the staff speak English.

Music

Earwax Records
1052 Peachtree Street NE
(404) 875–5600

Earwax specializes in hip-hop, house, and R&B with a little bit of reggae and jazz thrown in for good measure.

E D's Gourmet Records
1875 Piedmont Road NE
(404) 876–1557

E D's is a favorite stop for club DJs. E D's sells both vinyl and CDs.

Full Moon Records
1653 McLendon Avenue NE
(404) 377–1919

A mile east of Little Five Points in Candler Park, Full Moon Records buys, sells, and trades records, tapes, and CDs. Full Moon has a big selection of $1 records.

Tower Records
3232 Peachtree Road NW
(404) 264–1217
Next door to Lenox Square, Tower Records is a music superstore with a large separate classical room, thousands of books, magazines, and sing-along tapes for karaoke. Pick up the slick, informative free magazines *Pulse!* and *Classical Pulse!*

Vibes
145-B Sycamore Street, Decatur
(404) 373–5099
Great prices, great service, and the phattest selection of old and new sounds on CD, cassette, and 12-inch wax are what you'll find in this music store in downtown Decatur. Don't see what you want? Ask! The staff will special order it for you at no extra charge.

Wax N Facts
432 Moreland Avenue NE
(404) 525–2275
Wax N Facts sells new and used records, CDs, tapes, and band T-shirts. A bit of trivia: Back in the '70s, the owner's independent record label released the first single by the B-52s.

Wherehouse Music
2099 Peachtree Road
(404) 605–7131
Formerly Blockbuster Music, this is the dominant music chain in Atlanta, with more than 60 metro locations. The largest store (address listed previously) is just opposite the entrance to Bennett Street.

Note: In February 2003 Wherehouse announced it was filing for Chapter 11 bankruptcy and closing "some" stores nationally. Only one location, in Atlanta at Merchant's Walk, has a closing sign as of this writing, however.

Wuxtry
2096 North Decatur Road
(404) 329–0020

Located a hop, skip, and a jump from Emory University on the corner of Clairmont and North Decatur Roads, Wuxtry carries T-shirts for the college crowd and new and used records, tapes, and CDs.

New Age Shops

We're using New Age as an umbrella term to denote shops catering to patrons interested in personal growth and awareness, metaphysical issues, holistic health, and related concerns. The following stores handle a variety of merchandise, including herbs, aromatherapy products, metaphysical books and tapes, incense, candles, oils, crystals, and tarot cards.

Atlanta

Crystal Blue
1168 Euclid Avenue NE
(404) 522–4605
Crystal Blue in the Little Five Points shopping district carries a variety of products including minerals, crystals, wind chimes, figurines, crystal balls, incense, candles, tapes, and books.

Insiders' Tip
The best bargains in yard sales can be found on Saturday mornings in the more upscale neighborhoods in east Cobb, north Fulton, and Gwinnett Counties, and are frequently only advertised by one or two signs nailed up at the entrances to subdivisions.

Sphinx
1510 Piedmont Avenue NE
(404) 875-BOOK

The Sphinx, in the Ansley Square Shopping Center, is just south of the intersection of Piedmont Avenue and Monroe Drive. Shop here for merchandise that includes metaphysical books, incense, statues, and music.

Unity Bookstore
4146 Chamblee Dunwoody Road NE
(770) 457-9888

This bookstore offers metaphysical books, music, greeting cards, candles, angels, gift items, and recovery and 12-step materials. It's in the Atlanta Unity Church.

Beyond Atlanta

Krysalis
2785 Buford Highway, Duluth
(770) 418-0903

Krysalis offers a selection of metaphysical books, gifts, medallions, jewelry, crystals, candles, and incense. You can also find self-help, self-discovery, and 12-step program materials including books, cassettes, games, and T-shirts.

Phoenix and Dragon
5531 Roswell Road, Sandy Springs
(404) 255-5207

This New Age bookstore promises "Miracles and Merriment!" It offers a wide selection of books on metaphysics, spirituality, holistic health, planetary healing, recovery, and self-help as well as music, art, crystals, gemstones, scents, and candles.

Synchronicity Metaphysical Dynasty
1028 Alpharetta Street, Roswell
(770) 640-8184

Synchronicity accepts art consignments from talented local artists. Metaphysical goodies on sale include books, magazines, jewelry, candles, incense, crystals, music, and Native American items. Synchronicity offers psychic readings every Saturday.

Attractions

Are you a history buff? An adventure junkie? A news hound? An animal lover? An armchair scientist? Whatever your interest, Atlanta has an attraction for you! In fact, there's so much to see and do in this city, your problem will be finding time to fit it all in.

It's been more than 160 years since Atlanta was first chartered as a city, but those years have been action-packed. Though still young compared to many other U.S. cities, Atlanta has seen a lot of history.

Though we Atlantans are always excited about the new and improved, we're also very curious about those places that speak to us about where our city and its people came from. All around the modern metropolis you'll find vivid reminders of other eras with their own triumphs, tragedies, heroes, and villains. We've listed a number of places where bright glimpses of yesterday can still be seen today.

But proud as we are of our history, we live in the present and look toward the future. And while we're looking, we take time out for fun. This chapter highlights a variety of popular attractions that draw visitors year after year. You'll find more inviting destinations in The Arts, Parks and Recreation, and Day Trips and Weekend Getaways chapters. Don't forget: Always call first to verify hours, dates of operation, and admission prices. Funsters on a budget, please note our Fun Freebies section at the end of the chapter. Have a great time!

Atlanta

The APEX Museum
135 Auburn Avenue NE
(404) 521–APEX (2739)
The APEX (African-American Panoramic Experience) Museum is housed in a small building beside the Auburn Avenue Research Library on African-American Culture and History and across the street from the headquarters of the Atlanta Life Insurance Co. Eventually, plans call for the museum to have its own specially designed 97,000-square-foot facility on this site; its different sections will spotlight African-American achievement in various areas of endeavor, such as politics, entertainment, and sports.

The present facility includes a replica of an Atlanta streetcar where visitors sit to watch a film, with narration by Julian Bond and a dramatic reading by Cicely Tyson that tells of Auburn Avenue's rich history as a center of black commerce and culture. Exhibits of African and slavery-era artifacts occupy the museum's main room

along with a replica of Yates & Milton, a black-owned drugstore that originated on Auburn and eventually had four Atlanta locations. Among other items, the gift shop offers a reasonably priced and fascinating pictorial history book, *Sweet Auburn: Street of Pride,* published by the museum. Admission is $4 for adults and $3 for students and seniors. The museum is open 10:00 A.M. to 5:00 P.M. Tuesday through Saturday and 1:00 to 5:00 P.M. Sunday during summer months.

Atlanta Botanical Garden
1345 Piedmont Avenue NE
Piedmont Park at the Prado
(404) 876–5859
www.atlantabotanicalgarden.org
Three miles from Downtown stands a living museum to nature and gardening that is more passion than pastime for a great many Atlantans. Perched on 30 acres overlooking Midtown's Piedmont Park, the Atlanta Botanical Garden (ABG) features 15 acres of outdoor display gardens and the 15-acre Storza Woods, one

of the few remaining urban forests in Atlanta.

More than 3,000 ornamental plants flourish in the display gardens. Special sections devoted to roses, herbs, irises, and summer bulbs will delight you as you stroll through the innovatively landscaped grounds. Meditate a moment in the peaceful Japanese Garden, or delight your olfactory sense in the Fragrance Garden. Stroll along sidewalks under vine-covered arbors, or relax near one of the cooling fountains. The ABG is full of pleasant, shaded seating areas, including the Alston Overlook, a covered structure nestled among the trees. Sculpture placed throughout the grounds enhances the natural beauty of the plants and flowers.

The Dorothy Chapman Fuqua Conservatory is a $5.5 million glass house that is home to an assortment of endangered and valuable plants. The Tropical Room's steamy, leafy environment makes you feel like you've left Atlanta for the Amazon. The Desert Room transports you through an arid spectacle of lush succulents. Adventurous types will love the special plants section with scary, dangling ant plants and a display of carnivores including the Venus's-flytrap. A sign dares you to stick a finger into one of the plants' hungry leaves. But you won't be invited to fondle the 12 varieties of poison dart frogs from Central and South America that live in three large terrariums filled with rainforest plants.

Dorothy and J. B. Fuqua traveled for two years to study 15 conservatories around the world before building the setting for this worldwide collection. Tiny, colorful birds flit among the trees and dart beneath a waterfall. The visual feast ranges from blooming orchids and unusual bromeliads to sprawling cacti and coffee plants. You can catch a spectacular view of part of the Atlanta skyline as you approach the conservatory from the ABG display gardens.

The ABG offers classes, lectures, symposia, and demonstrations for ABG members and nonmembers. For information on ABG classes and tours, call the Education Department at (404) 876–5859, extension 226.

New in town and seeking fellow rose garden enthusiasts? ABG will refer you to an appropriate group. Many garden clubs and specialty societies meet regularly at

The Dorothy Chapman Fuqua Conservatory houses endangered and valuable plants at the Atlanta Botanical Garden. PHOTO: L. A. MIDDLESTEADT, ABG

ABG, with exhibits and competitions scheduled year-round. The annual Southeast Flower Show presents an entire range of garden-related events such as artistic design displays, children's activities, and more to benefit ABG (see our Festivals and Events chapter).

If you have questions about a particular plant or gardening method, call the Plant Hotline. A volunteer horticulturist or master gardener will be on hand, or return your call. The Sheffield Botanical Library stocks some 2,000 books and 80 periodicals for on-site library research only.

The ABG's Museum Shop is filled with unexpected finds for the gardeners on your gift list. Or what the heck, buy something for yourself! From April through October, you can lunch on sandwiches, salads, and desserts on Lanier Terrace, overlooking the Rose Garden.

The Atlanta Botanical Garden is in the northwest corner of Piedmont Park. The entrance is on Piedmont Road between 14th Street and Monroe Drive, across from the intersection of Piedmont Avenue and The Prado. The garden allows child strollers everywhere but in the Conservatory. Limited parking is available. For public transportation, take MARTA to the Arts Center Station, where you may transfer to the No. 36 North Decatur bus. On Sunday take the No. 31 Lindbergh bus from MARTA's Lindbergh or Five Points station.

Atlanta Botanical Garden is open Tuesday through Sunday from 9:00 A.M. to 5:00 P.M., October through March; from April through September, the Garden stays open from 9:00 A.M. to 7:00 P.M. We recommend you allow at least an hour to tour the garden. The Fuqua Conservatory and the Museum Shop open at 10:00 A.M. The garden is closed every Monday and on Thanksgiving, Christmas, and New Year's Day.

Admission costs $10 for adults, $7 for seniors older than 65, and $5 for children ages 6 to 12 and students with ID. Children younger than 3 and Atlanta Botanical Garden members get in free. Groups of 15 or more enjoy special admission rates if they schedule their visit in advance. After 3:00 P.M. every Thursday, everybody gets in free.

Atlanta Cyclorama and Civil War Museum
800 Cherokee Avenue SE
(404) 624–1071

At the Atlanta Cyclorama, the scene never changes: It is forever the blistering afternoon of July 22, 1864, and out by the Georgia Railroad line 2 miles east of Five Points, thousands of men are locked in a desperate battle that will lead to the fall of Atlanta and the Confederacy's defeat.

Housed in a massive, custom-built structure in Grant Park, the Cyclorama is an amazingly vivid re-creation of the Battle of Atlanta (sometimes and more accurately called the "Battle of East Atlanta"). Taller than a five-story building and 358 feet in circumference, the 9,334-pound oil painting on canvas is thought to be the world's largest and has quite an interesting history.

Huge, round panorama paintings, most often depicting battle scenes, were once a popular form of entertainment. In 1885 the Milwaukee-based American Panorama Studio brought a team of expert European panorama artists to Atlanta. From a 40-foot observation tower constructed near the present-day intersection of DeKalb and Moreland Avenues (in present-day Little Five Points), the artists surveyed the battlefield, which had changed little in the two decades since the war. During their months of research in Atlanta, the artists sought the war recollections of numerous veterans and citizens.

The artists worked for 22 months in the studio to complete the painting, which was first exhibited in Minneapolis in 1887 and then brought to Atlanta in 1892 and exhibited in a drum-shaped wooden building on Edgewood Avenue. Patronage waned by the following year, and the painting was sold at a sheriff's auction for $1,100. It was eventually donated to the City of Atlanta in 1898 and displayed in a wooden building in Grant Park. Fear of fire led to the construction of an artificial stone structure, which was designed in the neoclassical style by John Francis Downing and dedicated in 1921. A huge central column was both the viewing platform and the roof's support. During the Depression, noted Atlanta historian and artist Wilbur Kurtz directed a restora-

The Atlanta Cyclorama. PHOTO: JOHN MCKAY

tion of the painting, and Work Projects Administration artists crafted the many foreground figures of soldiers, horses, and wagons that make the Cyclorama a three-dimensional experience.

By 1979 the deteriorating Cyclorama was attracting more rats than tourists and badly needed extensive repairs. Noted conservator Gustav A. Berger's restoration team undertook the task. But the artists needed access to the fragile painting's back as well as its front, and it could not be removed from its specially designed building. Ingeniously, they removed a section of the structure's wall and hung the painting from an overhead track; this allowed them to rotate various sections into the work area as needed.

The project was not only tedious but also downright dangerous, because the canvas had been coated with lead, arsenic, and other toxins to repel insects. The diorama figures were restored under the direction of Joseph Hurt, a descendant of Troup Hurt, whose large brick house dominates the painting. The rather odd-looking modern space-frame system that spans the

building's roof was necessitated when the load-bearing central column was replaced with a better viewing area. The $11 million restoration was completed in 1982.

Your visit to the Cyclorama begins with a 14-minute film narrated by James Earl Jones that features hundreds of costumed Civil War reenactors. The film recounts Confederate generals Johnston and Hood's increasingly desperate efforts to protect Atlanta from Sherman's advancing troops. The guide then directs everyone upstairs to the Cyclorama. There, surrounded by the battle scene, the audience sits on a tiered viewing platform that slowly revolves as various parts of the painting come alive with computerized narration and light and sound effects.

For the most dramatic experience, skip the Cyclorama's front rows and head up to the back section. These high seats afford a wider view of the entire battle scene and better capture the original panoramic effect. It's fun to bring a pair of binoculars to spot small details in the painting and see where the artists attached the figures to the canvas.

During the gala events surrounding the 1939 world premiere of *Gone With the Wind* in Atlanta, Mayor William B. Hartsfield took the movie's stars to see the Cyclorama. Clark Gable is said to have remarked, "The only thing missing to make the Cyclorama perfect is Rhett Butler." In short order, the face of one figure—a fallen Union soldier in the foreground—was changed to a likeness of the famous actor.

Unlike most battlefield paintings, the Cyclorama does not represent a "frozen moment" in time, but instead displays actions during about a three-hour span of time during the battle. The level of detail is amazing; not only are major units, commanders, and actions portrayed exactly as they occurred, but also some very minor and obscure actions are rendered accurately. Take a careful look at the railway cut, next to the redbrick two-story building. In the treeline to the left, a Confederate unit can be seen assaulting over the low hilltop. This is the 1st Regiment of the Georgia State Line, an unusual (and very obscure) "state army" on loan to Confederate Lieutenant General John Bell Hood's Army of Tennessee, as they were on their way to capturing a Union artillery battery, at about 4:00 P.M.

The Cyclorama's museum has numerous informative displays about the Civil War and the painting itself. A half-hour video explains the tremendous restoration project. The museum also houses the locomotive Texas that was used in the Great Locomotive Chase (see the listing for Southern Museum of Civil War and Locomotive History under Cobb County in this chapter). The gift shop has an extensive collection of Civil War books as well as souvenirs. It's worth mentioning that the Cyclorama does not espouse the Confederate point of view: It was restored during the tenure of Atlanta's first African-American mayor, Maynard Jackson, and its prevailing mood is accuracy of events, not pro-Confederate.

The Atlanta Cyclorama is open daily from 9:20 A.M. to 4:30 P.M. from Labor Day through May 31 and until 5:30 P.M. during the summer. It's closed Thanksgiving, Christmas, New Year's, and Martin Luther

King Jr.'s birthday. Presentations begin every 30 minutes throughout the day. Admission is $6 for adults, $5 for seniors 60 and older, $4 for children 6 to 12, and free for children younger than 6.

Atlanta History Center
130 West Paces Ferry Road NW
(404) 814-4000

Why was Atlanta of such strategic value in the Civil War? What was it like to live on a rural farm in the antebellum South or in an opulent Atlanta mansion in the 1930s? And what was a shotgun house, anyway? You'll find the answers to these and many more questions at the Atlanta Historical Society's Atlanta History Center.

The society was formed in 1926; in 1966 it acquired the Edward Inman family's grand 25-acre estate, including the elegant Swan House mansion and most of the original furnishings. Many improvements were made over the years, culminating with the 1993 opening of the 83,000-square-foot Atlanta History Museum. The history center is fun as well as educational. Here are a few of its highlights.

Start off at the permanent museum exhibit "Metropolitan Frontiers," a walk-through display where you can learn about the Native Americans who once called this region home, the arrival of the railroads, Atlanta's destruction and renaissance, and the modern city's achieve-

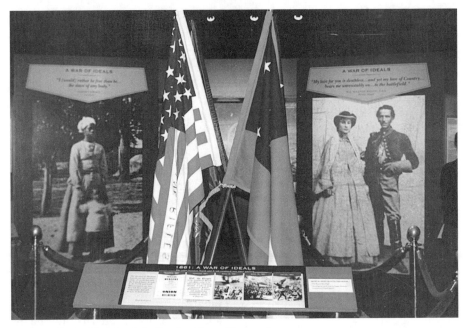

Civil War display "Turning Point" at the Atlanta History Center. PHOTO: JOHN MCKAY

ment of international status.

Behind the museum is the Tullie Smith Farm, an 1845 house that was moved to the center from its original site on an 800-acre tract near the present-day North Druid Hills Road and I-85. A costumed guide takes guests through the house and describes the farm family's daily routine. Outside are a separate kitchen, a blacksmith shop, and other outbuildings. Sturdy and unpretentious, this house is said to be a better example of a typical plantation home than the palatial, white-columned estates usually associated with the South.

Farther south is the Swan House, the 1928 mansion built by cotton broker and real estate magnate Edward Inman. Lavishly designed in a classic style, this grand home is one of the best-known examples of the work of famous Atlanta-based architect Philip Trammell Shutze. A guide shows visitors through the classically influenced yet personal home, whose futuristic residents insisted on having the recently invented shower instead of old-fashioned tubs in three of the four bathrooms. The Atlanta History Center's distinctive star emblem duplicates the pattern on the floor of the Swan House's foyer. A cascading fountain stretches from the home's front down across the terraced lawn facing the original entrance on Andrews Drive.

The center also includes a Victorian playhouse and 32 acres of botanically labeled gardens. The 3.5-million-item McElreath Hall research facility and archives is free and open to the public Tuesday through Saturday, 10:00 A.M. to 5:00 P.M. Also on the grounds is the Swan Coach House Restaurant, 3130 Slaton Drive NW, where delectables from chicken salad croissants to crab cakes are served Monday through Saturday in the mansion's former coach house. While there, check out the attached gift shop and art gallery, where jewelry, infant clothing, and specialty items produced by local artisans are featured at remarkably reasonable prices. You may shop or dine at the restaurant (on divine crab cakes or the classic chicken salad) without purchasing a ticket to the History Center.

Periodically, the Atlanta History Center mounts ambitious exhibitions in the galleries of the History Museum, but there are permanent displays worth noting. As well as being an outstanding general history museum, it is the crown jewel of Civil War museums in the South, and perhaps the nation. Centered around the large Beverly M. DuBose general artifact and the huge Thomas Swift Dickey ordnance collections (we bet that you didn't know anyone actually collected old shells!), both donated permanently to the center, changing exhibits keep the displays fresh and invite even the casually interested visitor back time and again.

The current "permanent" Civil War display, "Turning Point," leads you through the changing stages of the war, with artifacts carefully chosen and displayed as appropriate and accurate for each year. Multimedia use is extensive, with four films, several sound displays, and many small scenes and dioramas. The sole remaining Union supply wagon is an unusual and unique display. As one curator mentioned, everyone wanted to save the unusual or unique things, but they have a hard time finding the mundane.

The Atlanta History Center hosts annual Civil War "encampments," which provide a better-than-average display of the camp and battle life of the common soldier, grouped around the circa 1845 Tullie Smith Farm. Recent encampments have featured rifle and artillery demonstrations, cavalry and infantry maneuvers, and even mail call and food ration distributions. A special treat in the summer 2000 encampment was an appearance by the 8th Regimental Band, a very high-quality gathering of musicians playing period music on period instruments.

"Shaping Traditions: Folk Arts in a Changing South" opened in May 1996. Crafts, textiles, pottery, music, and more are examined as the means whereby communities build bridges between the past and present. Included in the 5,000-square-foot display are interactive videos and audio presentations of music and stories. There's also a permanent display of golf memorabilia belonging to golf great Bobby Jones, including one of the only green winner's jackets awarded at the Masters golf tournament that is housed outside of Augusta, Georgia.

Thirsty sight-seers will find refreshment in the museum's Coca-Cola Cafe, a re-creation of a '50s diner, where the menu includes a sweet Coca-Cola cake. The cafe is open from 10:00 A.M. to 4:00 P.M.

The center's regular hours are Monday through Saturday 10:00 A.M. to 5:30 P.M., and Sunday noon to 5:30 P.M. Admission is $12 for adults, $10 for students older than 18 and seniors, $7 for youths 3 to 17, and free for kids under 3. For frequent visitors and Atlanta residents, it is well worth considering a museum membership. There is a large variety of membership "levels" available, one pretty much for any budget, including a very nice $25 yearly membership level for teachers.

Atlanta Preservation Center
Walking Tours
537 Peachtree Street
(404) 876-2041

Progress has its price, and much of the architecture that once symbolized Atlanta has, for various reasons, disappeared. Even so, the visitor to the modern city can still encounter remarkably preserved places that afford insight into how Atlantans once lived. The Atlanta Preservation Center's walking tours through Atlanta's historic districts are a great way to experience different parts of the city's heritage.

APC's tour of the Fox Theatre, offered four times weekly throughout the year, is especially popular, since it's the only way to see the grand movie palace's interior without buying a ticket to a show. The Fox tour is given Monday, Wednesday, and Thursday at 10:00 A.M. and Saturday at 10:00 and 11:00 A.M.; meet at the 660 Peachtree Street entrance.

APC's other tours, which are all conducted outdoors, are given from March through November. All tours (except the Fox Theatre) are canceled in the event of rain; no tours are given on legal holidays. Admission for each tour is $10 for adults, $5 for students and persons 65 and older. Reservations are necessary only for groups of 10 or more. On-board guides for bus tours are also available. Here's what's featured on the outdoor tours:

The Sweet Auburn/MLK District tour takes visitors through this center of African-American Atlanta's early commerce and social life. At the heart of the community is the Martin Luther King Jr. National Historic District, featuring Dr. King's birth home, church, and tomb. The tour is given on Saturdays at 10:00 A.M.; meet in front of the APEX Museum, 135 Auburn Avenue, near Courtland Street.

The Historic Downtown tour spotlights the architecture at the core of Atlanta's first high-rise district and includes six historic building interiors. The tour is given Friday at noon, Saturday at 10:00 A.M., and 2:00 P.M. Sunday; meet at the Candler Building, 127 Peachtree Street.

What is Underground Atlanta, and how did it get down there? You can get the whole story on the Historic Underground/Birth of Atlanta tour that also features the Georgia State Capitol, several other government buildings, and three prominent churches founded before the Civil War. The tour is given by request on Saturday or Sunday.

The Walking Miss Daisy's Druid Hills tour will take you through the elegant 1893 neighborhood laid out by Frederick Law Olmsted and featured in the Oscar-winning movie for best picture, *Driving Miss Daisy*. Here, along winding, tree-lined streets, are exquisite mansions designed by renowned Atlanta-based architects Neel Reid, W. T. Downing, and Philip Shutze. For maximum impact, take this tour in the springtime when Druid Hills is splendidly arrayed with blooming dogwoods and azaleas. The tour is given Saturdays

and Wednesdays at 10:00 A.M.; meet in front of St. John's Lutheran Church, 1410 Ponce de Leon Avenue, at the corner of Oakdale Road.

On the Ansley Park tour, you can enjoy the lovely lawns and elegant homes of another of Atlanta's original suburbs designed with automobile (not trolley car) commuters in mind. Ansley Park has many fine homes by such architects as Downing, Reid, and Shutze and was the site of the Georgia Governor's Mansion for more than 40 years. The tour is given Sunday at 2:00 P.M. and Thursday at noon; meet in front of the First Church of Christ Scientist at the corner of Peachtree Road and 15th Street.

The Inman Park tour has visitors strolling through Atlanta's first planned suburb, which was developed by Joel Hurt in the 1880s. Not coincidentally, Hurt ran Atlanta's first electric streetcar line to his new suburb 2 miles east of Downtown, which was then part of a separate town called Edgewood. Hurt's own home is still standing, as are the homes of Coca-Cola magnates Asa Candler and Ernest Woodruff. After many years of decline, Inman Park began to rouse itself in the late 1960s and is now a nationally recognized symbol of neighborhood preservation and revitalization. The tour is given Thursday and Sunday at 2:00 P.M.; meet at the King-Keith House Bed & Breakfast, 889 Edgewood Avenue.

Carter Presidential Center
1 Copenhill Avenue NE
(404) 331–0296

The Carter Presidential Center occupies a hilltop known as Copenhill. From the Augustus Hurt house that stood here, U.S. General William Tecumseh Sherman watched the raging Battle of Atlanta in 1864.

This privately financed $25 million center was completed in 1986 after two years' construction. The Jimmy Carter Library and Museum are the center's public portions. This 70,000-square-foot building contains some 27 million pages of original documents from the Carter White House, along with 1.5 million photographs and other materials.

Insiders' Tip

The Carter Presidential Center stands on the site used by General Sherman as his headquarters during the 1864 Battle of Atlanta.

Take a stroll through the gardens at the Carter Presidential Library. PHOTO: ATLANTA CONVENTION & VISITORS BUREAU

The museum features a 30-minute film on the presidency in general and on Carter's four-year term, a collection of miniature gowns that are replicas of those worn by first ladies of the past, and interactive displays focusing on the accomplishments (human rights) and the challenges (the Iran hostage crisis) of the Carter years. You can also visit a reproduction of the Oval Office and see some of the gifts presented to President and Mrs. Carter by other heads of state. Those with a special interest in Carter, his years in the White House, and presidential trivia will thoroughly enjoy the museum. The gift shop sells Carter campaign memorabilia as well as Atlanta souvenirs and reproductions of various presidential china patterns.

The museum is open Monday through Saturday from 9:00 A.M. to 4:45 P.M. and Sunday from noon to 4:45 P.M. Admission is $7 for adults and $5 for senior citizens 55 and older; children 16 and younger are admitted free. The Carter Presidential Center can be accessed via the Freedom Parkway or North Highland Avenue; there's plenty of free parking.

No admission is necessary to dine in the cafe (which has a lovely outdoor patio), visit the public rest rooms, or stroll the landscaped grounds. The center's four interconnected buildings frame an elaborate Japanese garden and a pond; this area boasts a splendid view of the Downtown skyline.

Centennial Olympic Park
Marietta Street and Techwood Drive
(404) 222-7275

For a few days during the summer of 1996, the focus of the world shifted from the Olympic Games to the fatal bombing at one of the city's newest attractions: Centennial Olympic Park. Although the association with that tragic event is sure to be on visitors' minds as they stroll past the victims' memorial, the park remains a delightful open space in the heart of Downtown. The hot summer days still draw crowds who come to frolic in the Fountain of Rings that shoots streams of water into the air from ground level. At night the tall towers that line the park's walkways are dotted with lights. A major draw for many out-of-towners and locals alike is discovering the exact location of the Olympic brick they bought with their name on it. An information center with brick locators, cafe, and shopping spots are also part of the park.

CNN Center
1 CNN Center, Marietta Street at Techwood Drive NW
(404) 827–2201

You'll find lots to see and do at CNN Center, headquarters of Ted Turner's mighty communications empire. Get a behind-the-scenes look at news in the making through the popular Cable News Network Studio Tour. You'll spend about 45 minutes touring three studios: CNN, Headline News, and CNN International. Studio tours run from 9:00 A.M. to 6:00 P.M. daily. Call (404) 827–2300 for advance reservations. For tours that haven't sold out, walk-up tickets go on sale on a first-come, first-served basis at 8:30 A.M. every day. Tours cost $8 for adults, $6 for seniors 65 and older, and $5 for children under 12. For groups of 20 or more, admission is $7. Public tours usually have 35 people. Those with deeper pockets might want to check out the VIP Tour, an up-close-and-personal excursion that costs $25. VIPs tour the studios in groups of eight or less and enjoy extended access to the newsroom floor. This tour also offers a small gift package, including pen, key chain, and mug, and a snack at the commissary.

Other fun things at CNN include such Atlanta-themed shops as the Braves Clubhouse Store, the Atlanta Shop, and the Turner Store. You can snack in the food court, dine in full-service restaurants, or take in a movie at the Cinema Six. You can even spend the night at the Omni Hotel.

CNN Center, across the street from Centennial Park, is within walking distance of the Georgia Dome and the Georgia World Congress Center. It's just a stroll away from Underground Atlanta. You can get there on MARTA. CNN is also listed in our Shopping and Media chapters.

Coca-Cola Excursion
Various sites around Atlanta
no phone

Make no mistake: When you're in Atlanta, you're in Coca-Cola country. The world's most popular soft drink was invented here, and it was all the rage in Atlanta before it was available anywhere else. Over the years the company's leaders, especially founder Asa G. Candler and longtime president Robert West Woodruff, poured money into worthy Atlanta institutions (most notably Emory University), often through generous but anonymous gifts.

Coca-Cola was invented by Dr. John S. Pemberton in his home, which stood at 107 Marietta Street. It was first served to a thirsty world in May 1886 at Jacobs' Pharmacy, 2 Marietta Street. The recipe for Coke's top-secret essence, code-named "Merchandise 7X," is kept under lock and key in a vault in the SunTrust Bank building, Park Place at Auburn Avenue. The nearby 17-story Candler Building, Peachtree Street at Dobbs Avenue, was once home to Coke's executive offices. An architectural marvel when new, the Candler Building has been grandly restored.

Coca-Cola's world headquarters building towers over Midtown at 1 Coca-Cola Plaza on the corner of North Avenue and Luckie Street. Just down the street is The Varsity, North Avenue at Spring Street, the world's largest drive-in and predictably the world's largest retail user of Coca-Cola syrup. May Heaven protect you should you ask for that "other" cola drink here.

Inman Park, Atlanta's first suburb, was home to Coke's founder, Asa Candler, from 1903 to 1916. His redbrick mansion, now a private residence, stands on the corner of Euclid Avenue and Elizabeth Street and was named Callan Castle after the

Insiders' Tip
The escalator in the CNN Center is the longest free-standing escalator in the world, rising 160 feet or approximately 8 stories in height.

family's ancestral home in Ireland. Near the Virginia-Highland area, Candler's eldest son, Howard, built the magnificent Gothic-Tudor mansion Callanwolde at 980 Briarcliff Road; today it's a fine arts center maintained by DeKalb County (see our related entry in The Arts chapter). Asa Griggs Candler Jr.'s home at 1260 Briarcliff Road is now part of the Georgia Mental Health Institute. Lullwater House, 1463 Clifton Road NE, built in 1925 for Candler's son, Walter Turner Candler, has been the residence of Emory University's presidents since 1963. St. John's Melkite Catholic Church, 1428 Ponce de Leon Avenue NE, is another former home of Asa Candler.

Atlanta's loyalty to the Coca-Cola tradition is steadfast. Remember the backlash against that all-but-forgotten marketing disaster, "New Coke"? When company executives rolled out the "new, improved taste" in a flashy downtown celebration at Woodruff Park on April 23, 1985, the crowd included lifelong Atlanta Coke consumers who—in front of the world's media—poured bottles of the new, sweeter drink onto the street. Less than three months later, with Coke drinkers around the country still clamoring for their old favorite, the corporation acquiesced and returned the original formula to the market as "Coca-Cola Classic." By 1994 the overall soft drink market share of New Coke (renamed Coke II) had fallen to 0.1 percent.

If you'll settle for nothing less than being fully awash in a river of Coca-Cola history, images, and lore, go directly to the World of Coca-Cola (see separate item in this chapter). And while you're in Atlanta, don't forget: Things go better with the pause that refreshes! It's the real thing! Refreshing! Delicious!

Fernbank Museum of Natural History
767 Clifton Road NE
(404) 378–0127

The very popular Fernbank Museum is the largest natural history museum in the Southeast. Since it opened in 1992, more than 2.5 million visitors have flocked to Fernbank.

Permanent exhibits include "A Walk Through Time in Georgia," 17 galleries that explore landform regions of Georgia and the chronological development of life on Earth. Highlights include the *Origin of the Universe,* a high-definition video that projects the drama of Earth's formation. Dinosaur Hall features seven life-size dinosaurs and three massive murals of the Cretaceous, Jurassic, and Triassic eras. The Okefenokee Swamp Gallery surrounds the visitor with the sights, sounds, and exotic beauty of the swamp.

Fernbank boasts Georgia's first IMAX Theater, with a five-story screen to accommodate the largest film format in the world. IMAX's special curved screen and powerful digitally recorded sound system draw you right into the action.

Other permanent exhibits include the "McClatchey Gallery, Cultures of the World," which houses a significant jewelry collection donated by Mrs. Dorothy McClatchey, a prominent resident of Atlanta. "The World of Shells" features shells from around the globe and a Caribbean coral reef saltwater aquarium.

"Spectrum of the Senses" presents 65 interactive exhibits that help visitors understand the scientific principles of light and sound. This gallery brims over with computers, colored lights, video projectors, and lasers. For everyone from brainy science nerds to the scientifically impaired, this popular gallery features activities that can be experienced at several intellectual levels. Some are simple; others are high-tech.

The museum is open Monday through Saturday 10:00 A.M. to 5:00 P.M., Sunday noon to 5:00 P.M. Friday evenings (except in May and December) are reserved for Martinis and IMAX, where a full bar serves refreshments before special showings of the films at 7:00 P.M.

Admission costs $12 for adults, $11 for students and seniors older than 62, and $10 for children 3 to 12. Fernbank members and children younger than 3 get in free. IMAX Theater admission only is $10 for adults, $9 for students and seniors, and $8 for children 3 to 12. Combination IMAX and museum tickets cost $17 for adults, $15 for students and seniors, and $13 for children 3 to 12.

Fernbank Science Center
156 Heaton Park Drive NE
(678) 874-7102

Fernbank Science Center is an intriguing attraction about a mile from the Fernbank Museum of Natural History. Home to one of the nation's largest planetariums, the Science Center also boasts an exhibit hall featuring an authentic moon rock, an original Apollo space capsule, and much more.

If you're into stargazing, you've come to the right place. On clear Thursday and Friday nights, the Science Center's observatory lets you step up to its big telescope and view whatever celestial body—Venus, Mercury, the moon—is looking good that night. Questions about the heavens? Ask the astronomer on duty.

Nature lovers can explore the 1.5 miles of trails through the 65-acre Fernbank Forest. A relaxing respite from the hubbub of city life, this virgin forest is one of the largest remaining in any metropolitan area in the Southeast.

Staffers and visiting scientists conduct active research projects at the Science Center. Currently scientists are using a 132-foot-high meteorological tower to study low-level ozone and the effects of vegetation on mediating weather.

The center is open Monday 8:30 A.M. to 5:00 P.M., Tuesday through Friday 8:30 A.M. to 10:00 P.M., Saturday 10:00 A.M. to 5:00 P.M., and Sunday 1:00 to 5:00 P.M. The Science Center is owned and funded by the DeKalb County school system. That means it's closed on school system administrative holidays. Call to make sure you haven't hit one.

General admission is free. Planetarium shows cost $4 for adults, $3 for students and children. Children under 5 are admitted but only at the parent's discretion; this is *not* a museum very young children would enjoy! Special children's programs cost $2 per person. To reach the Science Center from Ponce de Leon Avenue, turn on Artwood Road then follow the signs directing you to the Center on Heaton Park Drive.

Fox Theatre
660 Peachtree Street NE
(404) 881-2100
www.foxtheatre.org

To visit the Fox Theatre is to be swept into another world. In an age of minimalist architecture and 12-plex movies in minimalls, the Fox is the real deal: no mere theater but a complete environment, lush and ornate almost beyond belief. This

Sing along with the Mighty Moeller organ at the Fox Theatre. PHOTO: MICHAEL PORTMAN/THE FOX THEATRE

dazzling movie palace is so closely associated with Atlanta today that it's inconceivable it was almost torn down in 1975.

Planning for the structure began in 1916. It was to be the headquarters for the Yaarab Temple of the Ancient Arabic Order of the Nobles of the Mystic Shrine (the Shriners). In 1929, as it neared completion, financial difficulties forced the Shriners into a deal with movie magnate William Fox, and the temple's plans were altered to include a spectacular movie theater and exterior street-level retail space.

Oozing with Middle Eastern opulence, the Fox opened on Christmas Day 1929. One awed newspaper reporter wrote that the building possessed "an almost disturbing grandeur beyond imagination." But after a mere 125 weeks featuring talking pictures, the Fox, squeezed by the Great Depression, closed. After having been built at a cost of more than $2.75 million, it was sold at auction for $75,000. The theater reopened in 1935.

Then in 1947, when the Fox gained immeasurable prestige, it became the venue for the touring Metropolitan Opera's Atlanta performances. Beneath the great theater's twinkling starry ceiling, thousands thrilled to such vocal greats as Ezio Pinza, Robert Merrill, Richard Tucker, Renata Tebaldi, Roberta Peters, Anna Moffo, Teresa Stratas, Montserrat Caballe, and others. The Met's stars often got lost inside the Fox's cavernous backstage areas until someone came up with an ingenious solution: the names of the New York streets around the Metropolitan Opera House were chalked on the Fox's walls to help the singers find their way.

The Met's annual springtime visits to the Fox were a high point in Atlanta's social year. Tickets were much-sought-after treasures, and music lovers from around the South poured in for the weeklong round of parties, performances, and midnight suppers. Peachtree was closed to allow patrons easy access to the Georgian Terrace Hotel (and its bar) across the street from the theater.

A 1948 weather-related calamity made headlines around the world when it almost caused what would have been only the second canceled performance in the

Insiders' Tip

The Fox Theatre was built during the era of racial segregation, which is why the upper balcony section has its own rest rooms and a separate outside stairwell entrance (no longer used for entry, but a great way to escape the crowd when leaving!).

long history of the Met's spring tour. Torrential rains washed out the tracks between Richmond and Atlanta, delaying for hours the arrival of the train carrying the company's costumes. At last the decision was made to perform *Carmen* in street clothes. The performance began at 10:00 P.M.; the costumes arrived after the first act; and the curtain did not come down until 1:00 A.M. The Met last performed at the Fox in 1968.

By 1975, unable to fill its nearly 5,000 seats as a first-run movie house, the Fox closed again; this time things looked grim indeed. Plans were to raze the theater to make way for the skyscraper headquarters of Southern Bell. Distraught by the looming loss of this architectural jewel, thousands of Atlantans joined in the work of Atlanta Landmarks Inc., a nonprofit organization. The necessary $1.8 million was raised six months in advance of the deadline, and the Fox was saved and reopened in time to celebrate its 50th birthday. Since then, the group has spent more than $6 million to fix the Fox.

Today the Fox is a favorite venue for concerts and touring Broadway shows; a summer film series still affords the unequaled experience of seeing a movie in a "real" movie theater.

The Fox is too amazing to describe briefly, but here are a few highlights and tips:

Backstage at the Fox

Since it opened in 1929, the Fox Theatre has hosted some remarkable performances under the twinkling starlike lights in its blue sky ceiling. Among the most famous were the traveling shows of the touring Metropolitan Opera that brought some of the great divas to the Atlanta stage.

Today, the Fox plays a variety of roles: movie house, concert hall, first-run theater, and a place for magician David Copperfield to disappear. Through the years it has survived problems of low attendance, bankruptcy, and near-destruction by fire; it continues to be one of the city's premier performing venues.

But some of the best acts the Fox has seen didn't take place on stage in front of the audience. Stories of the antics and quirks of guest actors, singers, and artists are handed down from crew to crew each year. Here are just a few of the backstage shows the public didn't see:

• In 1982, *The King and I*'s Yul Brynner insisted on remodeling the main dressing room in a dark chocolate color scheme, which provoked severe candy attacks among crew members who visited his room.

• Stephanie Mills, of *The Wiz,* had her dressing room repainted a shocking shade of pink.

• Kenny Rogers insisted that his wardrobe be crisply pressed and laid out. He even asked the stage manager to iron his socks!

• Bob Hope was known to ask a stagehand to hold a Styrofoam cup to catch his putts during backstage golf practice.

You can't work with complicated, full-scale productions in a theater the size of the Fox without a few glitches now and then. And there have been some memorable ones:

• During a performance of *Sleeping Beauty* presented by the Atlanta Ballet, the lighting crew was furiously keeping up with the lighting cues. When the floodlights accidently came on too early, they exposed Prince and Beauty casually waiting at the rear of the stage, their arms folded. The two scrambled to the front of the stage, and Beauty leapt into bed. The performance was forever remembered as Leaping Beauty.

• Singer Johnny Mathis got his microphone cord stuck in the crack between the elevator lifts on stage. While still singing, he tried to push it down

The Fox Theatre was intended to be the headquarters for the Shriners. PHOTO: MICHAEL PORTMAN/THE FOX THEATRE

into the crack to release it, but the cord kept getting shorter and shorter. Finally, Mathis finished on his knees as stagehands appeared with a replacement microphone.

• The Rolling Stones literally rolled in just minutes before a 1981 concert. Their flight from a sight-seeing trip to Savannah was fogged in for so long, it looked as if the show wouldn't go on. Their plane finally was able to land in Macon, and the band was hurriedly driven to Atlanta, while the audience waited almost two hours after the opening act.

• There have only been four times in the Fox's recent history when the show was completely interrupted. *The Nutcracker's* Mouse King fell into the orchestra pit onto the horn and cello players. The giant turntable that rotated the stage got stuck during a 1989 performance of *Les Miz*. The fog machine malfunctioned during a 1990 run of *Starlight Express,* leaving an oil slick just as the skaters hit the stage. The performers fell in a heap, and the show was stopped to mop up the mess. The computerized soundtrack used during Lily Tomlin's performance was out of sync and had to be reprogrammed.

With six motorized elevator lifts, the 140-foot-wide stage remains one of the largest ever built. Another elevator raises and lowers the 3,622-pipe, four-keyboard Mighty Moeller organ, which is played for a sing-along before each movie during the summer film series, just as it was in the 1930s.

The ceiling of the 64,000-square-foot auditorium suggests night under a Bedouin chieftain's tent beneath a clear desert sky. The tent is not canvas, as might be expected, but a reinforced plaster canopy that helps draw sound up to the rear of the balcony. The 96 stars twinkling in the blue sky are 11-watt bulbs fixed above 2-inch crystals. Clouds, rain, and other special effects are produced by projector. The premovie sing-along usually includes "Sunrise, Sunset," during which the theater's sky brightens from darkness to day before slipping back to dusk.

The entire second level of the Fox (the loge, first, and second dress circles and gallery) and the front of the orchestra section enjoy views of the sky. To the rear of row M in the orchestra section, the balcony overhang hides the sky. Especially for movies, the front rows of the loge are the best in the house.

Don't miss the marble and velvet rest rooms and lounges! Even these areas are fabulous in the Fox.

Several full bars serve cocktails and other beverages during all events, including movies, and you're welcome to enjoy drinks and snacks inside the auditorium during most performances. Smoking is permitted only in the exterior entrance arcade and on the smoking porch facing Ponce de Leon Avenue.

For information on touring the Fox, see our entry on the Atlanta Preservation Center's walking tours.

Georgia Department of Archives and History
5800 Jonesboro Road, Morrow
(404) 651–6474

Although not set up as a tourist attraction, the Georgia Department of Archives and History is an invaluable resource for serious scholars and those researching genealogy. The department was created in 1918. From 1931 to 1965, the state's archives were maintained in Rhodes Hall (see separate listing later in this chapter).

The Ben West Fortson Jr. State Archives and Records Building between the Capitol and Turner Field was often mistaken for a prison, but the tall, windowless structure provided a secure, controlled environment for some 85,000 cubic feet of official records and more than 65,000 reels of records on microfilm. Among these governmental and nongovernmental documents are family letters and papers, business account books, organizational and church records, and photographs.

The new facility opened on the campus of Clayton State College in June 2003 and will be open to the public Tuesday through Saturday, 8:30 A.M. to 5:00 P.M. Visitors must show identification and complete an application for a research card to gain access to the Search Room. To protect the fragile records and documents that date back to the Revolutionary War, the department has strict rules regulating what materials may be brought inside. For more information, call the department's reference line, (404) 651–6474.

Georgia Governor's Mansion
391 West Paces Ferry Road NE
(404) 261–1776

The Georgia Governor's Mansion was dedicated in 1968. Like the state's first Governor's Mansion, built in Milledgeville in 1838, the modern mansion is in the Greek Revival style; it was designed by Georgia architect A. Thomas Bradbury. The 24,000-square-foot house is the property of Georgia's citizens and, by law, remains the same even when its primary resident changes.

Neoclassical paintings and furnishings from the 19th century complement the mansion's design. On the main floor are a library with many books by Georgia authors and the state drawing and dining rooms. The second floor is the first family's private home and includes the large Presidential Suite for visiting dignitaries. The lower floor of the mansion boasts a ballroom that seats 150 for dinner.

The Governor's Mansion is open to the public each week on Tuesday, Wednesday, and Thursday from 10:00 to 11:30 A.M. The tour is self-guided, but hostesses in each room explain items of significance. The tour is free, but reservations are required for groups of 15 or more. Drive up to the main gate; there's parking on the 18-acre grounds. While you're at the mansion, you may wish to visit the Atlanta History Center, just down the road and mentioned previously in this chapter.

Georgia's Historical Markers
Various locations around Atlanta and Georgia
Georgia Parks and Historic Sites Division
(404) 656–7092

As you explore Atlanta and Georgia, you can gain a wealth of background from the state's historical markers. You can't miss them: The olive-green, cast-aluminum signs are 42 by 38 inches and are emblazoned with the state seal. Statewide, there are some 2,000 markers, about 700 of which concern the Civil War. The metro Atlanta area has about 600 historical markers.

The program was launched in 1951 and strongly emphasized Civil War history in the buildup to the 100th anniversary of the conflict. Artist and historian Wilbur Kurtz, who was a consultant on the movies *Gone With the Wind* and *Song of the South,* wrote the text for the markers between Tennessee and Atlanta. Another prominent historian, Col. Allen P. Julian, described Sherman's March to the Sea on the markers south of Atlanta to Savannah.

Historical markers are scattered across metro Atlanta. You can see some along DeKalb Avenue about 2 miles east of Five Points, the area that was at the center of the Battle of Atlanta. There are several markers around the Inman Park/Reynoldstown MARTA station; the fighting at this location is depicted in the Atlanta Cyclorama. There are also several in the Buckhead area near Peachtree Creek.

Georgia State Capitol
Intersection of Capitol Avenue,
M.L. King Jr. Drive, Washington Avenue, and
Mitchell Street
(404) 656–2844

The Georgia Legislature first met in Atlanta in 1868, but the $1 million needed for construction of the capitol was not provided until 1883. Work got under way in October of 1884; when it was completed, the state treasury had spent all but $118.43. The building was dedicated on July 4, 1889.

The Chicago architectural firm of Edbrooke and Burnham designed the capitol, which was built of Indiana oolitic limestone by Miles and Horne of Toledo,

Ohio. Georgia marble, judged impractically expensive for the exterior, was used for the floors, walls, and steps. The open rotunda peaks at a height of more than 237 feet. The building's classical design pays homage to the U.S. Capitol in Washington, as if to avow post–Civil War Georgia's fealty to the Union.

Outside, atop the dome, stands a 15-foot-tall, 2,000-pound, Greek-inspired statue of a female figure holding a torch in one hand and a sword in the other: It commemorates Georgia's war dead.

During a 1956 renovation program, 43 ounces of native gold, donated by the people of Dahlonega and Lumpkin County, site of America's first major gold rush in 1828, were applied to the dome's exterior. Another application of gold in 1981 restored the dome's brilliance. The capitol was named a National Historic Landmark in 1977.

Another extensive renovation was completed in 2001, with the interior walls repainted and retrimmed to their original appearance. Both legislative chambers were remodeled to the original look as well, including reopening the outside windows that had been boarded over since the 1970s.

Inside and out, the capitol's memorials and mementos tell Georgia's diverse history. Statues of famous segregationists share the grounds with the touching modern sculpture *Expelled Because of Their Color*, commissioned in 1976 by the General Assembly's black legislative caucus. It is "dedicated to the memory of the 33 black state legislators who were elected, yet expelled from the Georgia House because of their color in 1868" and is on the northeast side of the grounds.

The Georgia State Museum of Science and Industry on the first and fourth floors showcases Georgia's wildlife and minerals; other features include Native American artifacts and battle flags flown by Georgia regiments in various wars.

The capitol is open daily, 8:00 A.M. to 5:00 P.M. Free guided tours are offered year-round, Monday through Friday, four times a day. The tour times change when the legislature is in session. The tour desk is on the main floor in the West Wing just

Statue of Georgia Governor Joseph Brown at the state capitol building, Atlanta. PHOTO: JOHN MCKAY

outside the governor's office. The capitol is also open on weekends, but no tours are given. Call for more information or to arrange a group tour or tour for hearing- or sight-impaired persons.

The Herndon Home
587 University Place NW
(404) 581–9813

This 1910 Beaux Arts Classical mansion near Atlanta University is as amazing as the African-American family that built it. Alonzo Herndon began life as a slave in Social Circle, Georgia. As a young man possessing only one year of formal education, he learned the barbering trade and moved to Atlanta. Here Herndon's hard

The Herndon Home is open to the public Tuesday through Saturday from 10:00 A.M. to 4:00 P.M. Guided tours begin on the hour. Admission is free, but donations are gratefully accepted.

Margaret Mitchell House and Museum
990 Peachtree Street
(404) 249–7012

Gone With the Wind was not the first novel about the Civil War, and few serious scholars place it at the pinnacle of Southern literature. But along the road to becoming the most popular novel of all time, Margaret Mitchell's compelling masterpiece created an indelible mark on history. As a book and as a movie, *Gone With the Wind* continues to influence the way Southerners, Northerners, and people around the world view Atlanta, the South, and the Civil War.

On May 16, 1997, after 10 years of renovations that were interrupted by two fires, the Margaret Mitchell House opened as the city's tribute to its most famous author. It was listed on the National Register of Historic Places the year before it opened. From 1925 to 1932, Mitchell and her husband, John Marsh, rented a modest apartment on the first floor of the building on the southwest corner of Peachtree and 10th Streets. It was here, typing at a table she used as a desk, that Mitchell created her unforgettable characters. Mitchell herself had hated the apartment, and remarked frequently in later years about how much she had despised living there. In accordance with her wishes, no attempt was made to preserve the structure immediately after both the book and movie's premiere or after her own death in 1947. Abandoned for years and occupying coveted Peachtree Street real estate, the apartment house was slated for destruction in 1988 when a board of distinguished Atlantans rallied to preserve it.

Tourism officials report they annually receive more than a million inquiries about the novelist and her novel, and visitors were invariably astonished at the city's apparent lack of regard for the book's birthplace. In September 1994, while its roof was covered with a concep-

work was richly rewarded. His barber shop eventually employed some 40 men, and he founded the Atlanta Life Insurance Co. and became one of the city's wealthiest African Americans.

On a tall hill overlooking the city, Herndon and his wife, the former Adrienne McNeil, built their dream home, designing it themselves without an architect. Constructed entirely by black craftsmen at a cost of $10,000, the mansion was completed in 1910 after two and a half years of work and included such ultramodern conveniences as electricity, central plumbing, and steam heat. Tragically, the ailing Mrs. Herndon died just one week after moving into the home. The Herndons' only son, Norris, lived in the house until his death in 1977; since then, the Herndon Foundation has owned and operated the home.

The Herndon Home is opulent and magnificent with nine fireplaces, a lavish mahogany dining room, and a recurring lion's-head motif. Other aspects, though, are charmingly personal. In the living room is a mural that tells the story of the elder Herndon's rise from slavery to riches. The flat roof was Adrienne's idea. A drama teacher and Shakespearean actress, she envisioned it as the ideal place for outdoor dramatic performances.

tual art piece of thousands of inflated rubber gloves containing written messages urging world peace, the house was badly damaged in a mysterious fire. Another fire broke out during renovations, but no deliberate cause was found for either blaze. The long road to save the building Mitchell despairingly called "The Dump" seemed to have reached a brick wall.

But, as Scarlett taught us, "tomorrow is another day." Help arrived in the form of a $5 million donation from Daimler-Benz, the Germany-based maker of Mercedes Benz cars. In his announcement, chairman Edzard Reuter explained the South's growing importance to his company: "About 6,000 Americans will be part of the Daimler-Benz family by 1997 in just that one region of the United States. That, in itself, is reason enough for our social and cultural involvement in Atlanta, the growing business capital of the South."

In the project, Mitchell's apartment was restored and decorated with period furniture. Her original Remington portable typewriter is on loan from the Fulton County Public Library, as is her Pulitzer Prize. The remainder of the 10-unit building was gutted, remodeled, and modernized for use as meeting and exhibit space. A separate visitor center includes retail space, a video of Mitchell's story, and photo galleries. There are two landscaped gardens designed to accommodate events, and a well-stocked gift shop.

In 1999, the Gone With the Wind Museum opened behind the house. The one-level hall is packed with memorabilia and collectibles from the film itself: Scarlett's famous corset, outfits, and the life-size oil painting of actress Vivian Leigh as the heroine. A black-and-white newsreel captured the events surrounding the movie premiere. Original scripts and photographs from the set are included.

Ironically, this section of Peachtree Street figured tragically in the final chapter of Mitchell's life. Three blocks north of her old apartment on August 11, 1949, Mitchell and Marsh (on their way to see the British art film *A Canterbury Tale*) were walking across Peachtree at the unmarked

Clark Gable and other cast members of Gone With the Wind *appeared at the 1939 premiere of the movie in Atlanta. Memorabilia from the film is housed in the Gone With the Wind Museum at the Margaret Mitchell House.* PHOTO: COURTESY OF THE TRACY W. O'NEAL PHOTOGRAPHIC COLLECTION, SPECIAL COLLECTIONS DEPT., PULLEN LIBRARY, GEORGIA STATE UNIVERSITY

13th Street crossing when a speeding car appeared. Mitchell panicked, screamed, and bolted back across Peachtree toward her parked car. As he swerved left to miss the couple, the driver struck the retreating Mitchell directly; Marsh was unharmed.

Mitchell died on August 16 at Grady Memorial Hospital. Her funeral service was held at H.M. Patterson & Son's Spring Hill funeral home, Spring at 10th Streets. The cortege followed the same route as the December 15, 1939, parade when 300,000 people packed Atlanta's streets to celebrate the world premiere of *Gone With the Wind* and get a glimpse of its stars. Mitchell and Marsh, who died in 1952, are buried at Oakland Cemetery.

The house is open daily from 9:30 A.M. to 5:00 P.M. The last tour starts at 4:00 P.M.; allow 40 minutes. Admission is $12 for adults, $9 for seniors, $5 for youth ages 7 to 17, and free for children 6 and younger. The museum shop is open an hour after the last tour. Group tours and special events rentals are available.

Martin Luther King Jr. Center for Nonviolent Social Change
449 Auburn Avenue NE
(404) 526-8900

The King Center is Atlanta's preeminent tourist attraction. All day, every day, visitors make their way past the eternal flame in the center's plaza and toward the tiered reflecting pool, in the center of which stands Dr. King's elevated marble tomb. West of the tomb is Ebenezer Baptist Church, where Dr. King was co-pastor. East of the tomb is the King Center's main facility (see the Martin Luther King Jr. National Historic Site later in this chapter). Across the Boulevard is King's restored birth home, 526 Auburn Avenue.

King was assassinated on April 4, 1968, while in Memphis, Tennessee, lending his support to striking sanitation workers. Upon learning of the sudden tragedy, Atlanta Mayor Ivan Allen Jr. immediately began to prepare the city for the funeral that would become one of the largest events in its history. When Dr. King won the Nobel Peace Prize in 1964, Robert Woodruff led the movement to honor him with a gala banquet. In the hours after the tragedy, the Coca-Cola president called the mayor and insisted that no expense be spared in preparing the city to accommodate thousands of mourners and the international media. Woodruff himself guaranteed payment of any cost overruns.

During the grief-stricken days that followed the assassination, rioting in 126 U.S. cities claimed some 46 lives, but Atlanta remained calm. Mayor Allen and Police Chief Herbert Jenkins walked the streets of the city's black neighborhoods, expressing their sympathy and support. Hundreds of volunteers at the Southern Christian Leadership Conference offices worked around the clock to assist the thousands of mourners streaming into the city.

Central Presbyterian Church downtown announced it was opening its doors to black visitors; hundreds of other white churches followed suit.

On April 9, more than 100,000 people crowded around Ebenezer Baptist Church for the funeral. Hundreds of dignitaries and celebrities attended, including Jacqueline and Bobby Kennedy, Wilt Chamber-

Dr. Martin Luther King Jr.'s tomb and memorial site is one of Atlanta's most visited sites.

PHOTO: ATLANTA CONVENTION & VISITORS BUREAU

lain, James Brown, Nelson Rockefeller, Richard Nixon, Harry Belafonte, and Vice President Hubert Humphrey. Georgia's Governor Lester Maddox, a pick-handle-waving segregationist who had complained about plans to fly flags at half-mast in the city, remained in his office under the protection of state troopers.

Some 200,000 mourners followed the humble mule-drawn wagon that carried Dr. King's body along Auburn Avenue and back to his alma mater, Morehouse College, where he had lain in state. There he was eulogized by Dr. Benjamin E. Mays, president emeritus of Morehouse.

Mrs. Coretta Scott King and seven-year-old son Dexter went to Memphis only four days after the murder to march with the striking sanitation workers. Within three months, the King Memorial Center had opened. The family has worked to keep Dr. King's dream alive. Following extensive lobbying and much controversy, Dr. King's birthday became a national holiday in 1986.

Many people today do not readily recall that Ebenezer Baptist Church was the scene of another unexpected tragedy in the life of the King family. During worship services on June 30, 1974, as she played "The Lord's Prayer" on the church organ, the 69-year-old Alberta King (affectionately known as "Mama King"), mother of Martin Luther King Jr., was shot dead by a young black man. Church deacon Edward Boykin was also slain, and another man was wounded. The gunman, Marcus Chennault of Dayton, Ohio, was a cult member who had come to Atlanta hoping to kill the Rev. Martin Luther King Sr. (known as "Daddy King"); Chennault believed black Christian ministers were deceiving African Americans. Chennault was convicted of the murders; his death sentence was later commuted to life in prison. Following a stroke, Chennault died in August 1995. He was 44.

The King Center's exhibition hall contains a permanent display of photographs and memorabilia of Dr. King's public and private life. Freedom Hall is a space for meetings and other gatherings. The center's library and archives house the world's largest collection of primary information

on the civil rights movement. There is no charge to visit Freedom Hall. It's open daily from 9:00 A.M. to 5:00 P.M.; during the summer, hours are extended to 6:00 P.M. See the following entry for parking information.

The Martin Luther King Jr. National Historic Site
450 Auburn Avenue NE
(404) 331–5190

The 42-acre Martin Luther King Jr. National Historic Site encompasses the King Center and the King birth home on Auburn Avenue. The visitor center has exhibits about Dr. King and Atlanta as well as information on other national parks in our area and the entire Southeast. Parking has always been lacking in the perpetually busy King district, but the center includes a large parking lot just north of Irwin Street that is 1 block north of Auburn Avenue.

The National Park Service conducts guided tours of the King birth home daily every hour from 10:00 A.M. to 5:00 P.M. The tour is free, but visitors must obtain a ticket at the National Park Service office. The site is closed on Christmas and New Year's Days. Call (404) 331–6922 for information.

Oakland Cemetery
248 Oakland Avenue
(404) 688–2107

Almost in the shadows of Downtown's skyscrapers lies one of Atlanta's most serene places: shaded, hilly Oakland Cemetery. In 1850 city leaders purchased 6 acres of land east of the city limits for a municipal burial ground. This was in keeping with the rural cemetery movement of the time that held a single large graveyard established on a city's outskirts was preferable to a plethora of church or private burial grounds scattered throughout the town.

Very nearly every person who died in Atlanta between 1850 and 1884 (when Westview Cemetery opened) was buried at Oakland, whose brick walls eventually came to enfold 88 acres. Majestic oaks and some of the oldest magnolias in Atlanta line its narrow lanes. Here are the unmarked graves of black and white paupers; here also are the stunning monuments and private mausoleums of the city's wealthiest families. In the years before Atlanta established public parks, families picnicked and relaxed here on weekend afternoons. Oakland's central road was once known as Old Hunter Street. Hunter Street is now Martin Luther King Jr. Drive, which begins at Oakland's front gate.

As you enter Oakland, the cemetery's oldest section lies just to your right and left. Above the door to his mausoleum, a life-size statue of businessman Jasper Newton Smith sits in a chair facing downtown. Even in death, Smith is without a tie; he hated ties and refused to wear one. Also in this section is the grave of Martha Lumpkin Compton, daughter of Gov. Wilson Lumpkin, in whose honor pre-Atlanta was briefly called Marthasville. Along the Memorial Drive wall lies the grave of golfing legend Bobby Jones. Here you may see the occasional golf tee and ball left by a fellow duffer in lieu of flowers.

In the two Jewish sections, most graves are closely spaced, and many monuments have Hebrew inscriptions. Rich's department store founders Emanuel and Morris Rich are buried here. Following Jewish tradition, some visitors bring small stones as tokens of respect and place them on the headstones.

"CSA" (Confederate States Army) is inscribed on the headstones of the 3,723 soldiers who lie buried in the Confederate section, which includes the remains of 20 Yankees who died in area hospitals. Of special interest in this section is the Monument to the Confederate Dead—an obelisk of Stone Mountain granite, it was once the tallest structure in Atlanta. Also, the Confederate Lion, an image of a mortally wounded lion, was carved from a single block of Georgia marble and is dedicated to the memory of the unknown Confederate dead. In the northeast corner of the cemetery along the railroad tracks are the graves of paupers and the marked and unmarked graves of thousands of people, both enslaved and free. The black section contains only one mausoleum—that of real estate broker Antoine Graves.

Margaret Mitchell's grave is Oakland's most frequently visited site, but it's not easy to find, since the famous author requested a plain headstone. To locate Mitchell's plot, go to the west side of the large white tower building (the cemetery office) at the center of Oakland and face the western wall (along Oakland Avenue). Nearby you'll see the large obelisk of another Mitchell family near the end of a lane. Follow this lane about halfway to the cemetery's western wall. Mitchell's plot will be on your left, marked by four cone-shaped shrubs. The headstone reads "Mitchell" on the eastern side and "Marsh" on the western side. The inscription above the author's grave reads simply "Margaret Mitchell Marsh."

Over the years, the elements have taken their toll on Oakland, which is listed on the National Register of Historic Places. But happily the city of Atlanta and the dedicated volunteers of the Historic Oakland Foundation are restoring this Victorian treasure plot by plot. In the "Adopt-a-Plot" program, individuals assume responsibility for abandoned gravesites, clearing away weeds and planting greenery and flowers that were typical of the era of burial.

A helpful $1 brochure from the cemetery office will assist you in locating graves and sections of interest. From March through November, a guide leads a tour of Oakland at 10:00 A.M. and 2:00 P.M. on Saturday and at 2:00 P.M. on Sunday. The tour is $5 for adults, $3 for seniors and students and children. You are permitted to drive around Oakland, but proceed slowly and only on the asphalt-paved roads. Stone rubbings are prohibited; photography and sketching are encouraged. From the King Memorial MARTA station, walk south on Grant Street; go left on Martin Luther King Jr. Drive, which leads directly to the main gate.

Rhodes Hall
Georgia Trust for Historic Preservation
1516 Peachtree Street NW
(404) 885–7800

Lavish Victorian-era mansions once lined parts of Peachtree Street, but very few remain today. One that has survived is Rhodes Hall, built in 1902–1904 by furniture tycoon Amos G. Rhodes. He asked architect Willis Denny to design the home in the style of the Rhineland castles Rhodes had seen in Europe. The result is a most unusual, eclectic, Romanesque mansion.

The house's most imposing feature, however, is not European at all, but distinctly Southern. As a boy growing up in Kentucky during the Civil War, Rhodes often saw both Yankee and Confederate troops. For his mansion, he commissioned a series of elaborate painted and stained-glass windows as a memorial to the Confederacy. In nine panels the windows show Jefferson Davis's inauguration, the firing on Fort Sumter, Stonewall Jackson at Manassas, and Robert E. Lee at Appomattox. The windows curve around the massive carved mahogany staircase between the first and second floors.

Mr. Rhodes died in 1928; the following year, his family deeded the home to the State of Georgia. It was listed on the National Register of Historic Places in 1974. The Georgia Departments of Archives and History were housed in the mansion from 1931 to 1965. The original 150-acre estate has been reduced to a single acre. Since 1983 the mansion has been the headquarters for the Georgia Trust for Historic Preservation; it's also available as a rental reception facility. Rhodes Hall is open to the public Monday through Friday from 11:00 A.M. to 4:00 P.M., Sunday noon to 3:00 P.M. Admission is $5 per person.

SciTrek
395 Piedmont Avenue NE
(404) 522–5500

SciTrek, Atlanta's science and technology museum, is a hands-on interactive museum that allows visitors to explore science, math, and technology in fun and interesting ways that relate these disciplines to everyday life. Lift a racecar engine with one hand, whisper to a friend on the other side of the room, or freeze your shadow on the wall. All this and more awaits you at SciTrek, a place that's entertaining and informative for both adults and kids.

Permanent displays at SciTrek include a 40-foot-tall lighted replica of the Eiffel Tower made of Erector set pieces that officially joined SciTrek's permanent exhibit collection on Bastille Day (July 14), 1993. The SciTrek Amateur Radio Station (STARS) lets users reach radio communicators worldwide. STARS is staffed by volunteer ham radio operators who help visitors use the station. SciTrek features an Information Petting Zoo, a series of exhibit stations that allow visitors to get hands-on experience with new multimedia, computer, and Internet technologies. A section of Simple Machines is full of levers and pulleys as well as the people-by-the-pound scale.

Other permanent exhibit stations include Electric Magnetic Junction, which lets you close a circuit with your own body, take a ride in an electric taxi, and witness a 1,500-volt electrical discharge; Mind's Eye, a perception and illusion exhibit that lets you explore the range and limits of human senses; and the Color Factory, where you can play with electrons and photons to produce an array of hues and split a beam of white light into a rainbow of colors.

Kidspace is a special play area where 2- to 7-year-olds can make music, face paint, or build a foam house while learning scientific principles through play.

SciTrek is open Monday through Saturday 10:00 A.M. to 5:00 P.M., and Sunday noon to 5:00 P.M. Admission costs $9.50 for adults, $7.50 for kids 3 to 17, and $6 for students with ID, senior citizens, and military personnel. Children younger than 3 and teachers with ID are admitted free. If you're coming with a group of 12 or more, make reservations two weeks in advance; special group rates apply.

Southern Christian Leadership
Conference National Office
334 Auburn Avenue NE
(404) 522–1420
Founded in 1965 by Dr. Martin Luther King Jr. and others, the SCLC continues to fight for civil rights under the leadership of current president Martin Luther King III. The group's Auburn Avenue national headquarters is a working office (not a tourist attraction), but visitors are welcome to stop in, examine the historic photos from the civil rights movement, and take photos of their own. The office is open from 9:00 A.M. to 5:00 P.M. Monday through Friday.

Insiders' Tip

The oldest buildings in downtown Atlanta are the Georgia Railroad Freight Depot at the eastern end of Underground Atlanta, built in 1869, and the Shrine of the Immaculate Conception at the corner of Martin Luther King Jr. Drive and Central Avenue, built in 1873.

Underground Atlanta
Peachtree at Alabama Streets SW
(404) 523–2311
Want to hear a Dixieland band, buy a flag, quiz a fortune-teller, feast your eyes on fossils, or watch candy makers in action? All that and more awaits you at Underground Atlanta! In the heart of Downtown, covering six city blocks, Underground is a must-see. The historic birthplace of Downtown Atlanta, Underground resulted from our city's growth.

By the turn of the century, Railroad Gulch, a tangle of rail lines running through the center of town, had become a major hazard, tying up traffic at busy intersections and endangering pedestrians' lives. Bridges over the tracks provided a temporary solution, but by the 1920s it was clear that Atlanta had to separate itself from its railroad tracks.

A viaduct project completed in 1929 placed most of Atlanta's original town-center streets underground. Businesses moved aboveground, many using their original first floors and basements as warehouses. Gradually, those lower floors were abandoned, and Old Atlanta decayed.

In 1969 the carefully restored Victorian-era buildings of old Atlanta once again bustled with activity. Underground Atlanta opened as an entertainment complex that would emphasize the area's historical aspects while providing a much-needed downtown party zone. A rousing success at first, that Underground Atlanta gradually succumbed to an economic recession, closing in the early '80s. In the true phoenix-rising spirit of Atlanta, community leaders vowed to rebuild.

The current complex, which opened in 1989, lets you touch Atlanta's history while enjoying its present. With retail and specialty shops, a food court, restaurants, a museum, colorful pushcart vendors, nightclubs, live concerts, street performers, galleries, murals, and sculpture, Underground Atlanta offers an eclectic cornucopia of fun and excitement.

Underground Atlanta is easily accessible from I-75, I-85, and I-20. If you're riding MARTA, get off at the Five Points station, which has a pedestrian tunnel to the complex. Two parking decks adjacent to the project provide 1,250 parking spaces. The complex is open Monday through Saturday from 10:00 A.M. to 9:30 P.M. and Sunday from noon to 6:00 P.M. Hours may be extended in the summer. Restaurants and clubs stay open until midnight and beyond. See our Shopping and Nightlife chapters for more on Underground Atlanta.

Westview Cemetery
1680 Westview Drive SW
(404) 755–6611

In 1884 a private corporation purchased the land for Westview Cemetery. This enormous graveyard comprises some 600 acres, of which 300 are yet to be developed. Within Westview's walls are 22 miles of paved roads. During the Civil War, the city's western siege line passed through Westview's rolling hills; a fragment of Confederate breastwork remains.

Although other mausoleums have grown larger through additions, Westview Abbey is the largest mausoleum ever built from a single set of plans: It has spaces for 11,444 entombments. Its exotic design suggests a medieval Italian monastery, and it is finished in 35 varieties of marble. Twenty-seven stained-glass panels depict the life of Christ. The hushed and shadowy chapel, with its marble floors and stained-glass windows, is especially opulent.

Well-known persons buried at Westview include journalists Joel Chandler Harris, Henry Grady, and Ralph McGill; Coca-Cola's leaders Asa G. Candler and Robert West Woodruff; and Atlanta mayors I. N. Ragsdale and William B. Hartsfield. A free map of the cemetery is available in the office near the main gate.

To reach Westview from downtown, take I-20 West to Ashby Street, turn left, then turn right at the second light onto Ralph David Abernathy Boulevard. Stay on Abernathy when it bears right and follow it a little more than .75 mile; you'll see Westview's entrance to your left. An alternate route is to take Westview Drive from the Atlanta University Center area directly to the cemetery's front gate.

World of Coca-Cola Atlanta
55 Martin Luther King Jr. Drive SW
(404) 676–5151

Atlanta citizens have been swilling Coca-Cola since Dr. Pemberton first concocted the marvelous elixir in 1886. Legions of us went into mourning during the regrettable New Coke debacle of 1985. Since we're so loyal to Coke, it's fitting that our city boasts a museum dedicated to the world's favorite soft drink.

The World of Coca-Cola tells the story of Coke's past, present, and future. You can view the largest collection of Coca-Cola memorabilia ever assembled, a nostalgic array of items dating from Coke's inception. A kinetic sculpture presents a whimsical facsimile of the early bottling process. Interactive video stations tell Coca-Cola history in five-year vignettes, and a film highlights Coke's international character, emphasizing that people the world over agree: Coke is the real thing.

The pavilion houses a replica of a 1930s soda fountain, where an old-fashioned soda jerk demonstrates how Coke was prepared way back when. Time marches on, as the ultramodern futuristic fountain shows. Here, sprays of Coke products shoot across the room into paper cups. It's really cool!

In the International Video Lounge, sample an array of international sodas the Coca-Cola company distributes—from the delicate apricot taste of Japan's Vegita Beta to the tangy Beverly from Italy. Watch international TV while you sip. Other fun features of the World of Coca-Cola include vintage TV ads, radio jingles, old vending machines, and an array of Coke bottles from around the world.

At the end of your tour (for which you should allot at least an hour and a half), you exit through a shop jam-packed with Coca-Cola merchandise. Bring home an authentic Coca-Cola souvenir for a friend or family member. Choose from hats, T-shirts, sweatshirts, Coke trays, glasses, pencils, and dancing Coke cans, to name a few.

The World of Coca-Cola averages a million visitors each year. Next to Underground Atlanta, it's hard to miss. A big red Coca-Cola globe dangles 18 feet above the entrance. When you call the previously

At the end of a self-guided tour, World of Coca-Cola visitors can enjoy a refreshing glass of Coca-Cola from a futuristic soda fountain. PHOTO: ATLANTA CONVENTION & VISITORS BUREAU

listed number, a recorded message gives detailed directions, whether you're traveling by car or on MARTA.

The Coca-Cola pavilion is open for self-guided tours every day of the week. Monday through Saturday, the World of Coca-Cola opens at 9:00 A.M. with last admission at 5:00 P.M. Sunday hours run from noon to 6:00 P.M. The pavilion closes Fourth of July, Thanksgiving, Christmas Eve, Christmas Day, New Year's Day, the second Sunday in January (for maintenance), and Easter.

Admission is $6 for adults, $4 for seniors 55 and older, and $3 for children 6 to 11. Kids younger than 5 enter free with an adult. If you just want to shop, tell them at the information desk and they'll let you enter the store without a ticket.

Wren's Nest
1050 Ralph David Abernathy Boulevard SW
(404) 753-7735

Joel Chandler Harris was a teenager during the Civil War. At the Turnwold plantation near Harris's hometown of Eatonton, Georgia, about 70 miles east of Atlanta off I–20 (see our Getaways chapter), the young Harris learned the printing trade and spent many hours listening wide-eyed to an elderly slave, George Terrell, who amused the boy with folk tales and fables of African origin.

Harris' printing background led him into journalism. After a stint at the *Macon Telegraph,* he went to work at the *Atlanta Constitution,* where, in 1877, he was asked to write a story in dialect. (Such pieces were popular features and continued to appear in some Southern newspapers as late as the 1960s.) He called upon memories of his happy boyhood hours with Terrell and penned a story in which kindly Uncle Remus fascinates a young boy with a fable about plucky Br'er Rabbit. Harris's work instantly resonated with both black and white readers, many of whom recalled similar tales from their own childhoods.

Not content to rely on his memory alone, Harris meticulously researched the folk tales, eventually collecting more than 200 of them. Although the dialect in the stories understandably makes some readers uncomfortable, many scholars credit Harris, a charter member of the American Folklore Society, with preserving a fragile literary heritage that otherwise might have been lost.

In 1881 Harris and family rented a five-room West End farmhouse that had been built shortly after the Civil War. He bought the house in 1883 and added several rooms. One day, when Harris discovered that tiny wrens had built a nest in his mailbox, the house got its nickname. The shy and gentle Harris wrote many of his stories in his "summer living room" (the broad front porch), and folks enjoyed riding by to glimpse the famous author at work. Harris died in 1908; the Uncle Remus Memorial Association operated the house from 1913 to 1984.

In 1984 the Joel Chandler Harris Association took over and began painstakingly restoring the house to its original condition. Today the Wren's Nest is again as it was when Harris lived there. On display are original and foreign editions of his works and some of the many gifts he was sent by admiring readers, including a stuffed great horned owl from President Theodore Roosevelt, whose mother was from Roswell, Georgia, and who entertained Harris at a White House dinner.

The Wren's Nest is open Tuesday through Saturday from 10:00 A.M. to 2:30 P.M. Tours last about an hour. Groups of 25 or more may make tour appointments. Admission is $7 for adults, $6 for seniors and teens, and $4 for children under 12. Storytelling is often an added attraction and is included in the admission. There's a small shop with lots of Uncle Remus books and gifts.

Zoo Atlanta
Grant Park, 800 Cherokee Avenue SE
(404) 624–5600
www.zooatlanta.org

Zoo Atlanta, in historic Grant Park, is one of the 10 oldest zoos in continuous operation in the United States. Founded in 1889, the zoo eventually fell into a state of disrepair. A multimillion-dollar redevelopment project begun in 1985 has made profound changes, catapulting Zoo Atlanta into *Good Housekeeping* magazine's 1994 list of "Great Zoos" in the nation. The zoo's administration plays a preeminent role in nationwide zoo management and in worldwide efforts on behalf of endangered animals and the environment.

The zoo creates naturalistic environments that mimic the natural habitats of more than 250 species from all over the world. Many threatened and endangered animals call Zoo Atlanta home, including giant pandas, high-climbing orangutans, Sumatran tigers, black rhinos, African elephants, Komodo monitors, big-mouthed African dwarf crocodiles, a Japanese giant salamander, and western lowland gorillas, including Atlanta favorite Kudzoo. Especially important to the zoo are a pair of giant pandas from China, Lun Lun and Yang Yang. In April 2001, a life-size statue was unveiled of the beloved silverback gorilla Willie B., who died in 2000 after more than 40 years at the zoo.

The gorillas hang out in the Ford African Rain Forest, a one-acre habitat that also houses the Monkeys of Makokou exhibit, where drill baboons and mona monkeys forage in tropical foliage and climb a man-made tree. Visitors can view the rain forest from a number of viewing stations, including the Sanaga Overlook, a walk-through aviary full of colorful African birds. Other species cavort in such areas as

Walk through an aviary full of African birds at Zoo Atlanta. PHOTO: J. SEBO/ZOO ATLANTA

Flamingo Plaza, the Orangutans of Ketambe, the Sumatran Tiger Forest, and the five-acre Masai Mara, a savannah/grassland that simulates East African terrain. It's home to lions, rhinos, ostriches, giraffes, zebras, gazelles, impalas, white storks, and crowned cranes. A moat separates Masai Mara's black rhino exhibit from the public, allowing close-up viewing.

To reach Zoo Atlanta from Downtown, take I-20 East to Boulevard and turn right. You'll find Zoo Atlanta 1.5 miles away on the right. Park free at lots on Boulevard and Cherokee Avenue. On MARTA, take the No. 97 Cherokee Avenue bus from the Five Points station. The zoo is open from 9:30 A.M. to 4:30 P.M. Monday through Friday, 9:30 A.M. to 5:30 P.M. Saturday and Sunday, but the last tickets are sold at 4:30 P.M. Hours are extended during the summer and on weekends. The zoo closes on New Year's Day, Thanksgiving, and Christmas. Admission costs $16.50 for adults, $12.50 for senior citizens, and $11.50 for children 3 to 11. Kids younger than 3 and zoo members get in free. Stroller rentals are $5 for a single and $8 for a double plus a $2 refundable deposit. Wheelchairs are available for free.

Be sure to get a copy at the gate of the daily feeding schedule. Feeding times are when you get the best view of the animals. This is especially important in the summertime when the heat keeps the animals sitting far away in the shade. (See the Kidstuff chapter for more activities offered at the zoo.)

Beyond Atlanta

Cobb County

Confederate Cemetery
Corner of North 120 Loop and Cemetery Street, Marietta
no phone
Established in 1863, this cemetery holds the remains of more than 3,000 Confederate soldiers buried in graves arranged by home state. Most of the soldiers fell in the fighting around Kennesaw and Marietta. The cemetery is always open.

Kennesaw Mountain National Battlefield
905 Kennesaw Mountain Drive, Kennesaw
(770) 427-4686
In the spring and summer of 1864, the armies of U.S. Gen. William Sherman and Confederate Gen. Joseph Johnston played a deadly game of cat and mouse across north Georgia. Each time Sherman encountered strong Confederate lines, his troops would swing wide around them in a flanking maneuver, forcing the Confederates to drop back and retrench—a pattern that brought the fighting ever closer to Atlanta.

When the Union troops reached Kennesaw Mountain, they found the Confederates strongly entrenched in superbly prepared fortifications. Tired of his own effective but time-consuming flanking maneuvers, Sherman ordered an assault on these Confederate positions and was bloodily rebuffed after more than a week of skirmishes and pitched battles. He then resumed his flanking strategy, and the Rebels, on July 2, were forced to abandon their fortifications and fall back yet again.

Today the Kennesaw battlefield is preserved as part of a 2,884-acre national park with 16 miles of hiking trails featuring troop movement maps, historical markers, monuments, cannon emplacements, and preserved trenchworks. In the visitor center you'll find a good selection of Civil War books for sale and a slide presentation that explains the Atlanta Campaign and the importance of the area's several battles.

On weekdays you can drive your own car to the top of the mountain. Due to the

Insiders' Tip
Kennesaw was originally called "Big Shanty," in reference to the rather shambled appearance of the place in its early days.

high volume of visitors, the mountain road is closed to private vehicles on weekends for much of the year, but there's a free shuttle bus to the top every 30 minutes beginning at 9:30 A.M. and ending at 6:00 P.M. From the summit on a clear day, you can easily see downtown Atlanta, Decatur, and Stone Mountain. To preserve the fragile mountain ecology, hikers must stay on trails or roadways. The possession or use of metal detectors in any National Parks battlefield is illegal, and has resulted in several criminal charges being brought lately (the market for Civil War–related artifacts is big and wealthy enough to attract this class of criminal activity, which is frankly little short of abject grave robbing). Grills are available in the visitor center to use in the two picnic areas. The park is free and open daily to the public from 7:30 A.M. until dusk.

Marietta History Museum
1 Depot Street, Marietta
(770) 528–0431

Opened in 1996, the city museum is housed in elegant, Civil War–era Kennesaw Hotel. Volunteers renovated the second level for exhibits and displays. A general exhibit of Marietta history features artifacts that were donated by residents, and it changes regularly as new donations arrive. View the displays and visit the small gift shop daily, Monday through Saturday from 11:00 A.M. to 4:00 P.M.; Sunday from 1:00 to 4:00 P.M. Admission is $3 for adults, $2 for seniors and students; children 6 and under are free.

Marietta National Military Cemetery
500 Washington Avenue, Marietta
(770) 428–5631

More than 17,000 veterans, beginning with those from the Civil War, are buried in this 25.3-acre cemetery. Some 10,000 known and 3,000 unknown Civil War soldiers are interred here.

Six Flags Over Georgia
275 Riverside Parkway, Austell
(770) 948–9290
www.sixflags.com

"A World of Fun, Not a World Away!" is a fitting motto for this sprawling, family-oriented theme park 12 miles west of downtown Atlanta. Thrills, chills, and excitement abound in more than 88 acres of attractions divided into eight themed areas that highlight the historical heritage of our region.

But to heck with history—the real fun at Six Flags lies in the delicious terror of some truly spectacular rides. Thrill to the whipsawing motion of monster roller-coasters: the Great American Scream Machine, the Mind Bender, the Dahlonega Mine Train, the Georgia Cyclone, the Ninja, and the venomous Viper, which sends you from 0 to 60 mph in six seconds through a 360-degree elliptical loop, up a 70-degree incline, then does it all again, backwards. Yikes! Perhaps you favor that suspended-in-space feeling. If so, the Looping Starship, the Great Gasp parachute drop, and the Free Fall, which simulates the feeling of falling from a 10-story building, are for you.

If water rides are your thing, you'll find plenty of fun on Ragin' River, where you can splash down contoured water channels in a two-person inflatable boat, and the Log Flume, a cool trip through chutes modeled after a feature of Georgia's early logging camps. Thunder River re-creates the thrill of white-water rafting, and Splashwater Falls sends you racing down a roaring 50-foot waterfall. Be sure to wear something that can drip dry!

But Six Flags isn't just rides; it's show business, too. The Batman Stunt Spectacular takes place in a re-creation of Gotham City and features rockets, explosions, and other daring exploits familiar to fans of the Caped Crusader. Other shows include the Wildwest Comedy Gunfight Show, sing-alongs on the Rabun Gap Stage, and a nostalgia fest at the Remember When Drive-In. See a contemporary country music review at The Crystal Pistol Music Hall, or take in a concert at the Southern Star Amphitheater, which hosts a full season of concerts featuring top performers from country, rock, and contemporary Christian music. There's usually an additional charge for amphitheater concerts.

You'll find plenty of food stands, restaurants, and souvenir shops scattered throughout the park. A games area offers a variety of challenging games of skill.

Take I-20 West to the Six Flags exit. If you're riding MARTA, take the westbound line from the Five Points station and get off at the Hightower station. From there, MARTA bus No. 201 will take you to the park.

Six Flags is open weekends early March through mid-May, except for spring-break week in early April, when the park opens every night to accommodate fun seekers on vacation from school. Daily operations go from mid-May to early September, when the weekend schedule resumes until the end of the month. In October the park adds Friday nights to its schedule for the October Fright Fest. The park opens at 10:00 A.M.; closing times vary.

Admission costs $42 for adults and $26.50 for seniors and children under 48 inches tall.

For information on group rates for 15 or more people, call (770) 739-3430. Admission prices include unlimited use of all rides, shows, and attractions; you pay extra for parking, food, souvenirs, and some games of skill. Parking is $10 per car.

Six Flags White Water Atlanta
250 North Cobb Parkway, Marietta
(770) 424-WAVE

Forty scenic acres of water attractions, adjacent to American Adventures (see our Kidstuff chapter), make for a wild day of fun. You'll find more than 50 rides, from body flumes and a wave pool to a lazy river full of inner tubes that are designed to keep you cool. Relax in the Little Hooch River, or enjoy thrills and spills sluicing down the Bermuda Triangle and Black River Falls. The truly brave will be challenged by Runaway River, which is a fast-moving, enclosed raft ride, and Cliffhanger, a 90-foot water free fall. Tree House Island offers four stories of wet fun for kiddies, including Little Squirt's Island and Captain Kid's Cove.

With five restaurants on the premises, guests aren't allowed to bring their own food into the park, but there are picnic tables just outside the main entrance. No thong or G-string bathing suits or street clothes are allowed either. Shower and locker facilities are available. The park is open from 10:00 A.M. to 8:00 P.M., Memorial Day through the first weekend in September. Hours are shorter on weekends during the early spring and late fall.

Admission is $29.99 for anyone taller than 4 feet; $19.99 for those under 4 feet tall; senior citizens pay $19.99.

Southern Museum of Civil War and Locomotive History
2829 Cherokee Street, Kennesaw
(770) 427-2117

The bizarre Civil War railroad adventure that took place in this tiny town has been the subject of two famous motion pictures: Buster Keaton's *The General* and Walt Disney's *The Great Locomotive Chase*. On April 12, 1862, in the town of Big Shanty, now called Kennesaw, a party of Union spies led by James J. Andrews stole the locomotive General while its conductor and crew were breakfasting nearby. They absconded northward on the Western & Atlantic line with the intention of burning bridges and cutting the rail line to Chattanooga.

Their plan might have succeeded but for the General's conductor, Capt. William Fuller, and his crew, who gave furious chase on foot, on a push car, and on three different locomotives. Finally, running the locomotive Texas in reverse, Fuller and his men caught up to the General above Ringgold, Georgia, before the raiding party could burn the targeted bridges. Of the

---

Insiders' Tip

Atlanta has developed an interesting weather phenomenon related to its rapid urban growth—it has turned into a "heat island," where many thunderstorms simply break apart before entering the city and re-form on the other side of it.

The General, part of the Great Locomotive Chase during the Civil War, is displayed in the Southern Museum of Civil War and Locomotive History. PHOTO: JOHN MCKAY

captured raiders, some escaped to Union lines; others were held as prisoners of war until the following year; seven were executed by hanging at the present intersection of Memorial Drive and Park Avenue in Atlanta; Andrews was hanged at the present intersection of Juniper and Third Streets in Midtown.

In 1972, following a legal battle over its ownership that went all the way to the U.S. Supreme Court, the General steamed into an old cotton gin that had been newly renovated as its permanent home at this museum in the center of town, which briefly closed and underwent both a renovation and name change in 2002–03. The museum tour includes numerous descriptive exhibits and a narrated slide presentation. Frequent living-history and Civil War–era military displays are held on the

grounds outside. It is open Monday through Saturday 9:30 A.M. to 5:00 P.M. and Sunday noon to 5:00 P.M. Admission is $7.50 for adults, $6.50 for seniors and AAA members, $5.50 for kids 6 to 12, and free for children 5 and younger.

The reverse-racing Texas is on permanent display in the lobby of the Atlanta Cyclorama.

DeKalb County

Old Courthouse on the Square
101 East Court Square, Decatur
(404) 373–1088

The city of Decatur is 6 miles east of downtown Atlanta. Founded in 1823, it's more than a decade older than its big, noisy neighbor.

It's said that Decatur was considered

the terminus point for the Western & Atlantic railroad in the 1830s, but local residents objected, fearing the smoke and general confusion. Instead the railroad line ended at what became Five Points, and the rest, as they say, is history. On July 22, 1864, a skirmish at Decatur's cemetery resulted in one of the few Confederate victories in the fighting around Atlanta.

Decatur, so near the center of the Atlanta metropolitan region, has been able to preserve its villagelike atmosphere. The Old Courthouse (so named to distinguish it from the current modern DeKalb County Courthouse) presides over Decatur's central square, site of the first courthouse, a log cabin structure put up in 1823. Surrounding the square are numerous interesting structures from the early 20th century and even some from before the Civil War.

The Old Courthouse is the home of the DeKalb Welcome Center, (404) 373-1088, and the DeKalb Historical Society, (404) 373-1088.

The Society's museum includes portraits of Baron DeKalb (the French mercenary and Revolutionary War hero for whom the county is named), Commodore Stephen Decatur (a naval hero in the War of 1812 for whom the city is named), and Mary Harris Gay (a Decaturite whose wartime diaries were published as *Life in Dixie During the War*). Two-thirds of what is called the Battle of Atlanta was fought in DeKalb County, and the museum has a Civil War collection that includes

> ## Insiders' Tip
> The Old DeKalb County Courthouse on Decatur's square hosts an annual Primitive Baptist Music Festival, popular among fans of the unusual "shaped-note" singing style.

weapons, flags, and medical equipment. The museum is open Monday through Friday from 9:00 A.M. to 4:30 P.M.

Stone Mountain Park
U.S. Highway 78, Stone Mountain Village
(770) 498-5690
www.stonemountainpark.com

The world's largest exposed mass of granite, Stone Mountain, stands 825 feet high, rises 1,683 feet above sea level, and covers 583 acres of rolling plateau. Formed when molten lava began pushing upward through the earth's surface, Stone Mountain took 300 million years to emerge in its present state.

Stone Mountain Park—encompassing 3,200 acres of lakes, woodlands, and attractions—surrounds the mountain and hosts millions of visitors each year. Many pour in to see the world's largest bas-relief carving on the mountain's north face. The 90-foot-high by 190-foot-wide sculpture depicts Confederate war heroes Robert E. Lee, Thomas Jonathan "Stonewall" Jackson, and Jefferson Davis, all on horseback. The project, conceived in 1912, took more than 50 years to complete due to creative differences and technical problems. Originally, the plan called for a continuous line of Confederates on foot and on horseback to "wrap" all the way around the mountain.

In case you ever need them for a trivia game, here are a few colossal facts about the memorial carving:

Its area is three acres, or more than a city block.

At its deepest, the carving sinks 42 feet into the mountain's surface.

Lee's horse Traveler is 147 feet long; a 6-foot man can stand comfortably inside the mouth of Davis's horse Kentucky.

To celebrate the memorial's completion, 20 people ate lunch on Lee's shoulder!

Although no major Civil War battles were fought on the soil of Stone Mountain (a small cavalry action took place in the nearby village during the July battles around Atlanta), Sherman destroyed the Georgia Railroad Line between Stone Mountain and Decatur during his march to the sea. The Union army came within close range when it burned New Gibralter,

Take a ride on the paddle-wheel riverboat, the Scarlett O'Hara, *on Stone Mountain Lake.*

PHOTO: STONE MOUNTAIN PARK

the small town at the base of the mountain. Today the rebuilt town is known as the Village of Stone Mountain.

Spend a day at Stone Mountain Park. Diverse recreational, leisure, historic, and scenic attractions ensure something for everyone. Athletic types will enjoy the 15 miles of scenic sidewalks for walkers and joggers as well as the nature trails set aside for hiking. A 1.3-mile trail leads to the top of the mountain, where you're rewarded with a panoramic view of the Atlanta metro area and a glimpse of the Appalachian Mountains. If you want the view without the work, ride the Mountaintop Skylift to the huge rock's summit.

On the skylift, you'll be whisked up and will pass right by the memorial carving on the quiet ride to the summit. There you'll enjoy a sweeping view that includes Atlanta

and Kennesaw Mountain to the west and the Olympic Velodrome to the south.

Stone Mountain was designated the Olympic Sports Park for the 1996 Olympic Games. The park boasts a 36-hole championship golf course (read more about this in our Parks and Recreation chapter).

The park's Sports Center offers 18 holes of minigolf, eight lighted tennis courts, batting cages, a game room, and bicycle and stroller rental.

Fishing buffs can angle in the park's stocked lake from mid-March through October. The 363-acre Stone Mountain Lake offers swimming and sunning at the beach as well as canoe, rowboat, hydro-bike, pedalboat, and pontoon rentals. Those who prefer being piloted can traverse the lake aboard an authentic paddlewheel riverboat, the *Scarlett O'Hara*. Train aficionados

The Antebellum Plantation at Stone Mountain Park includes restored and authentically decorated buildings. PHOTO: STONE MOUNTAIN PARK

will enjoy the Stone Mountain Scenic Railroad. This attraction gives you a 25-minute ride around the base of the mountain in one of three Civil War–era steam trains.

Fans of Robert James Waller will delight in the century-old covered bridge on the site of Stone Mountain's Grist Mill, a rustic structure moved to the park from its original site in Ellijay, Georgia. For history buffs, Confederate Hall houses a 3-D look at the Civil War in Georgia. The Antebellum Plantation emulates a pre–Civil War agricultural establishment with 19 restored and authentically decorated buildings. The Road to Tara Museum, a name taken from one of the several titles Margaret Mitchell originally considered for her best-seller, is a collection of autographed and foreign editions of *Gone With the Wind*, movie posters, artists' renderings of key scenes, and *Gone With the Wind* dolls. The Auto & Music Museum offers an intriguing array of antique automobiles and eclectic musical memorabilia.

On spring and fall weekends and every night from May to mid-August, Atlantans and visitors enjoy Stone Mountain Park's spectacular Lasershow, a free extravaganza that begins after dark. As the audience relaxes on the park's Memorial Lawn, the mountain's north face lights up with laser-projected stories, special effects, and graphic images. Rousing musical accompaniment adds to the drama (see our Festivals and Events chapter).

Special events scheduled throughout the year include Taste of the South food festival in May and the Scottish Highland Games in the fall (see our Festivals and Events chapter for details and other events at Stone Mountain). Guests can find accommodations at the Stone Mountain Inn or pitch a tent or hook up an RV at the 441-site lakeside campground. The park's Evergreen Conference Center and Resort is a popular destination for meetings and other large indoor events.

Stone Mountain Park is approximately 15 miles east of downtown Atlanta, easily accessible from U.S. Highway 78, also called the Stone Mountain Freeway. The park opens at 6:00 A.M. and closes at midnight every day of the year. Attractions open at 10:00 A.M. and close at 7:00 P.M. during the summer; hours are 10:00 A.M. until 5:00 P.M. September through May. Attractions close on Christmas Day.

A $7 daily parking permit buys admission to the park, and a $30 yearly parking permit is available; daily attraction prices are $23 plus 7 percent tax for adults and $17.00 plus 7 percent tax for children 3 to 11. The multiattraction pass (adults, $42.80; additional passes available as part of several pricing packages) buys admission to the riverboat, the Antebellum Plantation, the Auto & Music Museum, the wildlife trails, the skylift, and the railroad. The multiattraction pass is nonrefundable and good for the entire year. The park also offers group rates.

Fulton County

Archibald Smith Plantation Home
935 Alpharetta Street, Roswell
(770) 641-3978

Built in 1845, this restored plantation includes an elegant home and several outbuildings that provide insight into the daily life of a farm in the days prior to the Civil War. Tours are offered at 11:00 A.M. and 2:00 P.M. Monday through Friday; and at 11:00 A.M., noon, and 1:00 P.M. Sunday. Admission is $6 for adults and $4 for children.

Bulloch Hall
180 Bulloch Avenue, Roswell
(770) 992-1731

One block west of the Roswell town square, Bulloch Hall is a Greek Revival mansion constructed of aged heart pine and completed in 1840. At the home in 1853, Major Bulloch's daughter Mittie married Theodore Roosevelt Sr.; from their marriage came the future President Teddy Roosevelt, who visited his mother's childhood home in 1905. The senior Roosevelt's other son was the father of Eleanor Roosevelt, the wife of FDR. During her husband's therapeutic visits to Warm Springs, Georgia, Mrs. Roosevelt would sometimes drive to Roswell for a visit at the hall.

Bulloch Hall is open to the public daily. Tours are given on the hour from 10:00 A.M. to 3:00 P.M. Monday through Saturday and from 1:00 to 3:00 P.M. on Sunday. It is also home to guilds that keep alive such crafts as quilting and basketry. Periodic activities include the reenactment of Mittie's 1853 wedding, Civil War encampments, and cannon-firing demonstrations. Admission is $6 for adults and $4 for children 6 to 16.

Chattahoochee Nature Center
9135 Willeo Road, Roswell
(770) 992-2055

On 127 acres along the banks of the Chattahoochee River, the Chattahoochee Nature Center is an environmental sanctuary with miles of freshwater ponds, wooded uplands, and river marshes. The center offers a variety of classes and activities for children and adults. During weekly canoe floats in the summer, families can learn basic boating skills while viewing native plants and wildlife. Special Sunday classes during the summer touch on everything from reptiles to how Native Americans used the marsh. You'll learn even more on weekend naturalist-guided walks through woodland or river marsh habitats.

Chattahoochee Nature Center stays open year-round. Enjoy the gardens, pond studies, and nature trails on a nice day any time of year; indoor exhibits entertain and edify when it's too hot or cold to be outdoors. Shopaholics will surely find something enticing at the Nature Store.

Chattahoochee Nature Center is open Monday through Saturday from 9:00 A.M. to 5:00 P.M., and Sunday noon to 5:00 P.M. Adults pay a $3 admission fee; the cost is $1 for kids and seniors.

Gwinnett County

Gwinnett Historic Courthouse
185 Crogan Street, Lawrenceville
(770) 822–5174

Designed by E. G. Lind in 1885, the Gwinnett County Courthouse evolved in an eclectic combination of Romanesque, Second Empire, and WPA styles. It was last an active courthouse in 1988; an extensive renovation and restoration program was completed in 1992.

The courthouse stands on a full block at the center of the Lawrenceville town square and around it are monuments, picnic tables, and a gazebo. In their upstairs headquarters, members of the Gwinnett County History Center will gladly give you information on other county attractions and historic sites. Society members staff the office from 9:30 A.M. to 1:00 P.M. Monday through Friday.

Visitors are welcome to explore the courthouse on a self-guided tour Tuesday through Friday from 10:00 A.M. to 4:00 P.M. There is no admission charge. The courthouse is available as a rental facility for public and private gatherings both large and small.

Lake Lanier Islands
7000 Holiday Road, Buford
(770) 932–7200
www.lakelanierislands.com

Grown-ups and kids alike will have a great time at this beach and water park, with Wild Waves, Georgia's largest wave pool,

and spine-tingling water slides, including the Intimidator, the Triple Threat, and the Twister. SplashDown and Racing Waters are twin-flume speed slides guaranteed to thrill, and Blackout sends riders down 160 feet of water in total darkness. Chattahoochee Rapids let you innertube through more than 725 feet of winding, shooting rapids. Smaller kids will enjoy Wiggle Waves, a kiddie wave pool featuring 6- to 12-inch waves, two 8-foot slides, and colorful fountains of water bubbles.

You can rent a paddleboat, sailboat, or canoe. Take a swim off the 1.5-mile sandy beach, or play 18 holes of miniature golf. Lake Lanier Islands Stables offer trail rides, pony rides, and lessons. Or rent a bike and explore more than 1,200 acres of beautiful woodlands.

At South Beach, try out SurfWave (a simulated body-boarding experience), a rock-climbing wall, and video games. South Beach also has a DJ or some form of live entertainment on weekends; North Beach has a DJ from 11:00 A.M. to 4:00 P.M. all week. Wave-runners are available to those 18 or older for $10 an hour, $5 an hour for each extra rider.

Lake Lanier Islands is also a great place for a birthday party. A complete package includes lunch, ice cream, cake, and tickets to the beach and water park.

Admission is $25.99 for adults, $16.99 for senior citizens and children under 42 inches, and free for children 2 or younger. Season passes are also available. There's a $7 fee for each car entering the grounds. The park is open daily from 10:00 A.M. to 6:00 P.M. Memorial Day through Labor Day; Saturdays until 7:00 P.M.

Southeastern Railway Museum
3595 Peachtree Road, Duluth
(770) 476–2013

This popular 30-acre outdoor museum has been open since 1970; it moved to its present location in 1999. Train buffs will revel in the displays of more than 80 pieces of retired rolling stock including vintage steam locomotives and historic wooden cars. Tour the 1911 Pullman used by President Harding. You can even take a train ride in a restored caboose that traverses the museum's half-mile loop track.

The museum is open every Saturday from 10:00 A.M. to 4:00 P.M. and the third Sunday of every month from noon to 5:00 P.M. From April through November it is also open Thursday and Friday 10:00 A.M. to 5:00 P.M. Admission costs $7 for adults, $5 for senior citizens, and $4 for children. Your admission price pays for train rides.

Fun Freebies

Atlanta International Museum of Art and Design
Peachtree Center, Marquis Two
285 Peachtree Center Avenue
(404) 688–2467

This museum celebrates the craftsmanship of the world's cultures through ethnographic, folk art, and design exhibits. See The Arts chapter for more details.

The *Atlanta Journal-Constitution*
72 Marietta Street
(404) 526–5151

Tours of the newspaper building are conducted on weekdays, but in the summer of 2003 they were being revamped. Call the newspaper for more details and reservations.

Callanwolde Fine Arts Center
980 Briarcliff Road
(404) 872–5338

Originally the home of Howard Candler, the eldest son of Coca-Cola's founder, Callanwolde now is a fine arts center. A nonprofit foundation directs a variety of arts programs, including dance, drama, painting, photography, pottery, textiles, writing, and more. In 1996, just prior to the Olympics, the center was renovated to house the Italian Delegation. New plantings and a restructuring of the greenhouse area were just a few of the changes made. See The Arts chapter for a complete description of the center's offerings.

Crawford W. Long Museum
550 Peachtree Street NE
(404) 686–4411

In the Davis Fischer Building of Crawford Long Hospital, a few blocks south of the Fox Theatre on Peachtree Street, this medical museum honors Atlanta legend Dr. Crawford W. Long, who died in 1878. Reputedly the first physician to use anesthesia during surgery, Long was one of the many forward-thinking Atlantans of his time. Tour the fine array of medical tools and accessories from the days of horse-and-buggy doctoring (back when doctors still made house calls!).

The museum is open during hospital visiting hours. There is no direct line to the museum; for more information, call the hospital at the above number.

High Museum of Art
Folk Art and Photography Galleries
30 John Wesley Dobbs Avenue NE
(404) 577–6940

This multilevel Downtown branch of the High Museum showcases photography and folk art. It's open Monday through Saturday from 9:00 A.M. to 5:00 P.M.; on the first Thursday of each month it's open until 8:00 P.M. See The Arts chapter for a complete description.

Johnny Mercer Exhibit
103 Decatur Street SE
(404) 651–2477

Find this exhibit in Special Collections on the eighth floor of Georgia State University's Pullen Library South. Music lovers will enjoy seeing displays of awards, manuscripts, photos, and letters from the life of this composer of enduring music. Savannah-born Mercer wrote such standards as "Blues in the Night," "Jeepers Creepers," and "Come Rain or Come Shine." Tour the Johnny Mercer Exhibit Monday through Friday, 8:30 A.M. to 5:00 P.M., except on university holidays.

Margaret Mitchell Exhibit
Central Library
One Margaret Mitchell Square
(404) 730–1700

This permanent display on the main floor of the library features reproductions of the author's pages from the *Gone With the*

Wind manuscript, a movie script, the coat Mitchell wore while volunteering with the Red Cross, her library card, and other rare memorabilia. View this exhibit during regular Central Library hours: Monday through Thursday 9:00 A.M. to 9:00 P.M., Friday and Saturday 9:00 A.M. to 6:00 P.M., and Sunday 2:00 to 6:00 P.M.

Telephone Museum
675 West Peachtree Street NE
(404) 223–3661

This unusual attraction presents the social and political history of the communications systems we depend on so heavily. In the plaza level of the Southern Bell Center, it's open Monday through Friday from 11:00 A.M. to 1:00 P.M.

Kidstuff

Be sure not to tell the kids our little secret: Adults can have just as much fun as their children in the loud, scary, splashy fun places listed in this chapter. Sports arcades, water parks, museums, art activities, wildlife shelters, and more beckon youngsters to play, learn, and explore. While many of the highlights touched upon here require an admission fee, don't forget that many of Atlanta's attractions are free and fun for folks of all ages.

Many of the activities we list here are staged at venues already mentioned in the more-extensive Attractions chapter. Here are some special highlights the kiddies will enjoy.

Amusements

Amusement Parks

American Adventures
250 North Cobb Parkway, Marietta
(770) 948–9290
www.whitewaterpark.com

American Adventures, next to Six Flags White Water in Marietta (See Attractions chapter), is an eclectic amusement park with appeal to funsters of all ages. You can play outdoor miniature golf, speed around a racetrack, test your mettle in the arcade, ride the Super Slide, or frolic in foam balls. When you're finished with that, there's still the carousel and a train ride. Kids are partial to the Foam Factory, a three-story, interactive arena where 50,000 foam balls are slung around the area.

The park's open Monday through Friday from 4:00 to 8:00 P.M. (longer hours in the summer), 10:00 A.M. to 7:00 P.M. Saturday, and from noon to 7:00 P.M. Sunday. Winter hours vary but generally run from noon to 6:00 P.M. daily. Take exit 113 off I–75 North to reach American Adventures. Be prepared to pay a $2 parking fee. There's no admission charge, but each attraction costs money. You can pay as you go or opt for one of the economy packages. All-day fun passes cost $15 for kids 4 through 17; parent fun passes are $5; toddlers are $5. There's no charge for parents

of children who need assistance on rides and in the play area.

Six Flags Over Georgia
275 Riverside Parkway, Austell
(770) 948–9290
www.sixflags.com

Although this family-oriented theme park is fun for all ages, children will delight in a special section designed just for them. Bugs Bunny World features scaled-down attractions and rides designed for little thrill-seekers, including Convoy Grande, Swing Seville, and The Little Aviator. The What's Up, Rock? show gives kids a chance to take part in the action, while Bugs Bunny's Playfort allows tots to explore soft play components and meet with the Looney Tunes characters. Monster Plantation takes kids on a boat ride through a flooded antebellum plantation, where lovable and not-so-frightening monsters come to life through computer electronics and animation technology. Small ones are thrilled to see Santa Maria, a fun-filled adventure on pirate ships that fly through the air, and laugh at the antics of the Bullfrog Review, three wacky animated amphibians. The Riverview Carousel features 69 hand-carved wooden horses. The Carrot Club offers buffet-style family fare, a specially designed game room, Bugs Bunny cartoons, and special appearances by the Looney Tunes clan.

Check our Attractions chapter for complete hours and admission charges.

Water Parks and Beaches

**The Beach at Clayton County
International Park
2300 Highway 138 SE, Jonesboro
(770) 473–5425
www.thebeachccip.com**

Clayton County operates this 200-acre family water and recreation park that hosted the beach volleyball competition during the 1996 Olympic Games. Frolic on the white sandy beach circling an eight-acre spring-fed lake, or enjoy minigolf, two water slides, paddleboats, a 13-acre fishing lake, and a kiddie pool with a small water slide. The park also features beach volleyball courts, softball fields, picnic tables, and pavilions for parties, family reunions, and other functions. No alcohol, pets, or glass are permitted.

Admission is $9 for adults, and $7 for seniors and kids ages 3 to 12. The beach is open on weekends in May and September from 10:00 A.M. to 6:00 P.M.; during the summer, the hours are extended—10:00 A.M. to 6:00 P.M. Wednesday, Thursday, and Friday and 10:00 A.M. to 8:00 P.M. Saturday and Sunday. Inclement weather may force the beach to close, so it's best to call ahead.

**Centennial Olympic Park
Marietta Street at International Boulevard
(404) 223–7275
www.centennialpark.com**

This park is described more fully in our Attractions chapter, but there are special places and things to do with children.

To start with, the Rings the Thing. The Olympic Rings fountain squirts water all year long, but the street-level water attraction becomes a water park when the weather is warm. Children of all ages can run among the pulsating and varying water rhythms. There also is a children's garden and playground.

One weekend a month and on holidays in spring and summer, the park comes alive with themed activities for the whole family, including displays, an artists market, performances, and children's art

activities. Best of all, the activities and performances are free.

**Lake Lanier Islands
7000 Holiday Road, Lake Lanier Islands
Buford
(770) 932–7200
www.lakelanierislands.com**

Kids will love Lake Lanier Islands' beach and water park, with Wild Waves, Georgia's largest wave pool, and water slides including the Intimidator, the Triple Threat, and the Twister. They must be more than 42 inches tall to ride most slides and be 48 inches to ride the Surf Wave and FunDunker. Smaller kids will enjoy Wiggle Waves and Kiddie Lagoon.

For a family excursion, rent a paddleboat, sailboat, or canoe; take a swim off the 1.5-mile sandy beach; or play 18 holes of miniature golf. Lake Lanier Islands Stables offer trail rides, pony rides, and lessons.

Lake Lanier Islands' birthday club will host your child's birthday party, offering a complete package including lunch, ice cream and cake, tickets, and admission to the beach and water park.

Beach and water park admission is $25.99 for adults; senior citizens and children under 42 inches tall get in for $16.99; children 2 or younger are admitted free. Season passes are also available. The Islands charge a $7 fee for each car entering the grounds. The beach and water park are open daily from 10:00 A.M. to 6:00 P.M. and 10:00 A.M. to 7:00 P.M. on Saturday, from Memorial Day through Labor Day.

Insiders' Tip

Amusement parks aren't the only place to catch a ride on a carousel. You'll find the horses raring to go on a 30-foot-high merry-go-round inside the North Point Mall. Rides are $1 apiece.

Six Flags White Water Atlanta
250 North Cobb Parkway
Marietta
(770) 424-WAVE
www.whitewaterpark.com

Forty scenic acres of water attractions, adjacent to American Adventures, make for a wild day of fun. You'll find more than 40 rides—body flumes, a wave pool, a lazy river, and more—from the relaxing to the shriek provoking. Laze in the Little Hooch River, or enjoy thrills and spills sluicing down the Bermuda Triangle and Black River Falls. Tree House Island offers four stories of fun-filled activities, and Little Squirt's Island and Captain Kid's Cove let younger kids play safely with their peers.

With five restaurants on the premises, guests aren't allowed to bring their own food, but there are plenty of picnic tables just outside the main entrance. No thong or G-string bathing suits or street clothes are allowed either. Shower and locker facilities are available. The park is open from 10:00 A.M. to 8:00 P.M., Memorial Day through the first weekend in September; hours are shorter on early spring and late fall weekends.

Admission is $19.99 for kids 3 years to 4 feet tall; guests taller than 4 feet pay $29.99, and over age 55 is $19.99. Season passes are $52.49 per person. Parking is $5. Discount coupons are available around the city.

Sun Valley Beach
5350 Holloman Road, Powder Springs
(770) 943-5900
www.sunvalleybeach.com

Fourteen miles west of Atlanta, Sun Valley has one of the Southeast's largest swimming pools, 1.5 acres, surrounded by a white sandy beach. The pool has 12 water slides, a Tarzan swing, a cascading umbrella, and a log roll. Play volleyball on the beach, or enjoy softball, basketball, and tennis on the fields and courts provided. Try your hand at minigolf, pitch some horseshoes, or play on the playgrounds and in the game room. Racers will enjoy the fast-paced go-cart track. Picnic spots and concession stands dot the 40-acre site, which is open weekends in May and daily from 10:00 A.M. to 8:00 P.M., Memorial Day through Labor Day. Weekday admission is $12 for adults, $10 for children. On weekends and holidays, adults pay $15, kids $13. Senior citizens pay $8 at all times. Seasonal memberships and summer day camp with extended care are also available.

Arts

Classes, Workshops, and Activities

Abernathy Arts Center
254 Johnson Ferry Road, Sandy Springs
(404) 303-6172

This arts center, a program of the Fulton County Arts Council, offers year-round classes and workshops for kids as well as adults. Youth classes, which are taught in six- to 12-week sessions, cover such topics as oil painting, drawing, wheel pottery, and multimedia. One- and two-day workshops include a holiday-themed program, in which children learn to make a manger scene or menorah, and a printing and stamping workshop that teaches kids how to create designs to print on paper for gift wrap and greeting cards. Similar programs are offered at Arts Council centers in College Park, 4645 Butner Road, (770) 306-3087, and Duluth, 9800 Medlock Bridge Road, (770) 442-0190. Children's workshops run about $33. (Adult sessions range from $80 to $126; seniors receive a 15 percent discount.)

ART Station
5384 Manor Drive, Stone Mountain
(770) 469-1105
www.artstation.org

ART Station, a contemporary arts center in the heart of Stone Mountain Village, is a place where art is an activity rather than a spectator sport. The facility includes classrooms, a dance studio, two private music rehearsal rooms, and a pottery studio. The station introduces children to the creative process through classes taught by professional artists. Art camps for youngsters ages 5 to 13 are available all year long, meeting on Saturdays in fall, winter, and spring. Fees are $115 ($105 for members). In addition, the station holds drama and pottery and sponsors the ongoing Ambassador Dance Team, with age groups from 5 to over 13. Open Tuesday through Saturday, 10:00 A.M. to 5:00 P.M.

High Museum of Art
1280 Peachtree Street NE
(404) 733–4501
www.high.org

The High Museum sponsors family weekend workshops in which kids 6 to 12 and their parents can learn more about art and the creative process. On two Saturdays a month, workshops are held from 10:00 A.M. to noon and 1:00 to 3:00 P.M. and include a gallery tour. Reservations are required for these two sessions. The Sunday Studio is a drop-in program that welcomes kids 6 though 12 between 1:00

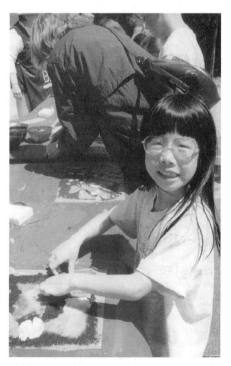

Children can make masterpieces from paper at the Robert C. Williams American Museum of Papermaking. PHOTO: ROBERT C. WILLIAMS AMERICAN MUSEUM OF PAPERMAKING

and 4:00 P.M. for a variety of hands-on art activities.

Art camp is also scheduled over the summer; call for prices for this program. All family programs are free with museum admission: $6 for adults, $4 for students with ID, and $2 for kids 6 to 17. Youngsters 6 and younger are free.

(See The Arts chapter for more information about the High.)

Robert C. Williams American Museum of Papermaking
500 10th Street NW
(404) 894–6663
www.ipst.edu/amp

In addition to its national touring exhibition on papermaking, the American Museum of Papermaking in Midtown also has hands-on workshops for kids and grown-ups, who can have all kinds of wet and wild fun actually making paper and artistic creations. Besides, the museum exhibits the art and industry of papermaking, as well as recycling. Prices are $12 to $35 for the half- or full-day workshops, but members get a discount, and so do children (sometimes). Special workshops are held three times a year—Valentine's Day, summer, and the winter holiday season. Others are held in connection with visiting artists and often use off-the-wall materials like old blue jeans or shredded money to make paper. Open Monday through Friday, 9:00 A.M. to 5:00 P.M.

Spruill Center for the Arts
5339 Chamblee Dunwoody Road, Dunwoody
(770) 394–3447
www.spruillarts.org

The Spruill Center sponsors a summer series of morning performances for children that include storytelling and craft projects at its art gallery, 4681 Ashford Dunwoody Road. Story sessions are free; craft classes run about $8 per child.

Summer camps focusing on the performing and visual arts are held on the Center grounds each week from 9:00 A.M. to 2:00 P.M. Call for fees.

Theater

Center for Puppetry Arts
1404 Spring Street NW
(404) 873-3391
www.puppet.org

The Center for Puppetry Arts hosts a family series of performances presenting original adaptations of classic stories and new works in a variety of puppetry styles. These performances run September through May, Tuesday through Saturday; call or check the Web site for hours. (See The Arts chapter for more information.)

The center also holds Create-A-Puppet workshops for children ages 4 and older; adults are welcome to tag along. Puppet designs are based on themes of the shows being presented in the theater. Puppet workshops run September through May; call or check the Web site for days and hours.

Admission to the center costs $12, which includes a performance, workshop, and admission to the museum. You can also buy individual tickets for a workshop or museum admission.

To see what goes on backstage, ask for a behind-the-scenes tour: $7 for adults, $6 for children, students, and seniors; $4 with another activity.

Children can get hands-on experience in puppet making at the Center for Puppetry Arts workshop. PHOTO: CENTER FOR PUPPETRY ARTS

Little General Playhouse
2060 Lower Roswell Road, Suite 300
Marietta
(770) 565-3995
www.littlegeneralplayhouse.com

This kids' arts center puts on about 12 children's plays during the year that feature local child actors in favorites such as *The Sound of Music, Alice in Wonderland,* and *Cinderella.* At Halloween the playhouse hosts *The House of Little Horrors,* a stage show that includes an audience walk through a haunted house. Kids as young as 3 are welcome to join in the harmless fun and to have their faces painted or work on spooky arts and crafts projects. Tickets for all shows are $8. Children younger than 3 are free with a paid adult; grandparents are $5 with a paid child.

Art and drama classes are offered after school from 4:00 to 7:00 P.M. After-school pickup is available. Registration is by the month; fees start at $40 a week for a once-a-week class. The playhouse also holds an art and drama summer day camp from 9:00 A.M. to 3:00 P.M. for children younger than 12. Prices are $155 for one week.

Museums

Fernbank Museum of Natural History
767 Clifton Road NE
(404) 929-6300
www.fernbank.edu

Fernbank, described more fully in our Attractions chapter, has many exhibits to fascinate both adults and children. Specifically for the small fry, Fernbank provides two bright, colorful environments in which kids can develop their natural curiosity. The Fantasy Forest, for kids 3 to 5, and the Coca-Cola Georgia Adventure, for the 6-to-10 set, teach youngsters about their natural environment through carefully designed quick experiments. Fantasy Forest gives children a chance to try on a bee glove and pick up "pollen balls" to "pollinate" large, brightly colored flowers. Georgia Adventure includes a colorful shrimp boat and simulations of the Chattahoochee River and the Okefenokee Swamp, where children can play and pretend to fish. Admittance to both is included in a museum ticket. Note: Sometimes during the school year, the Forest and the Adventure exhibits are reserved for class trips, so it's best to call ahead to make sure they're open to the public. Also at the museum is the 315-seat, five-story IMAX theater, which brings thrilling adventure and science films right in your face.

The museum is open Monday through Saturday, 10:00 A.M. to 5:00 P.M., and Sunday, noon to 5:00 P.M. Admission is $12 for adults, $11 for students and seniors older than 62, and $10 for children 3 to 12. IMAX is an additional $10 for adults, $9 for students, and $8 for children 3 to 12. Combination museum/ IMAX tickets are available for $17 for adults, $15 for students, and $13 for children ages 3 to 12.

Fernbank Science Center
156 Heaton Park Drive NE
(678) 874–7100, (678) 874–7102
www.fernbank.edu

Each weekend, the center offers special planetarium shows with terminology and photos geared toward kids. Times are Saturday and Sunday at 1:30 P.M. Admission is $2 for all ages.

The center is open Monday, 8:30 A.M. to 5:00 P.M.; Tuesday through Friday, 8:30 A.M. to 10:00 P.M.; Saturday, 10:00 A.M. to 5:00 P.M.; and Sunday, 1:00 to 5:00 P.M. (See our Attractions chapter for information about the center.)

Imagine It! The Children's Museum of Atlanta
275 Centennial Olympic Park Drive
(404) 659–5437
imagineit-cma.org

After years of operating as a "museum without walls" in Atlanta area schools, Imagine It! opened in March 2003, in a 16,000-square-foot interactive exhibition hall, created with the intention to "create environments and activities where young children experience the power of imagination and the pure delight of learning with each other and with grown-ups."

The museum is divided into seven major areas: Fundamentally Food celebrates food in both form and aspect of life. Let Your Creativity Flow lets children express themselves through movement, manipulation, and sound (think *loud!*). Tools for Solutions encourages children to engage in creative problem-solving to presented situations, working both individually and cooperatively. Leaping into Learning is designed for toddlers and preschoolers, who find a friendly forest and myriad opportunities for discovery and make-believe. The Family Resource Center offers parents information about raising healthy kids and nursing mothers a private place to feed their infants. There is also a Town Square, which serves as an extended lobby, and the Morph Gallery, which is a changing exhibit gallery intended to host traveling exhibits from around the country.

Although a physically stimulating and quite beautiful facility, the museum and exhibits are a tad on the "looks nice but what is it?" side, and the fact that none of the exhibits have any instructions, directions, or clues to the children about how to handle them tends to make one wonder how it will all come across. According to preopening "play testing," however, this turned out not to be a problem in the slightest. One review summed it up best: "Plan to spend hours here, Mom and Dad, the kids are going to go buck wild and not want to leave."

The museum is open 10:00 A.M. to 5:00 P.M. daily; tickets are $11 for everyone over age 3, $5.50 each for preregistered groups of 10 or more; and several birthday party packages are available ranging from $250 to $525.

SciTrek: The Science and Technology Museum of Atlanta
395 Piedmont Avenue
(404) 522–5500
www.scitrek.org

Fun for all ages, SciTrek has some special exhibits just for kids. KidSpace is a special area exclusively for kids 2 to 7 and their parents or adult companions. Children can see themselves on TV, paint their faces, learn to turn a water wheel, create a dam, and build a kid-size house.

New for 2003 is the addition of the first Challenger Learning Center in Georgia, a space shuttle simulation to encourage interest in space travel. By sad coincidence, this center's opening weekend occurred on the day the space shuttle *Columbia* was lost.

The Holiday Express is an annual holiday exhibit that rolls in around Thanksgiving and stays until the New Year. The festive model railroad display features a collection of turn-of-the-century toy trains that run through miniature landscapes, animals, and people on 400 feet of track.

SciTrek Summer Day Camps program offers one-week summer sessions designed for children 4 through 13. Kids learn about a broad range of topics including light, color, chemistry, electricity, sound, outer space, earth science, biology, rocket science, architecture, ecology, and more. Sessions include hands-on science, creative play, and fun explorations. A spe-

The Mission Control Center at SciTrek's Challenger Center. PHOTO: JOHN MCKAY

cial summer program in conjunction with Lockheed Martin Aerospace Corp. and Peach State STARBASE (a Department of Defense program for at-risk youth) is new for 2003. Full-day sessions are $45, and weeklong session prices are $190 for members, $220 for nonmembers.

SciTrek is open Monday through Saturday from 10:00 A.M. to 5:00 P.M., Sunday, noon to 5:00 P.M. General admission is $9.50 for adults, $7.50 for children 3 to 12, and $6 for college students, seniors, and military personnel.

Southeastern Railway Museum
3595 Peachtree Road, Duluth
(770) 476–2013
www.srmduluth.org

All kids think trains are cool, and the place to give them their fill is the Southeastern Railway Museum. These trains are no toys; the 30-acre outdoor museum has full-size steam and diesel locomotives, Pullman cars, coaches, an Army cooking car, and even an old Jim Crow car to show what life was like when the railroads were segregated.

The Pullman car is the one that took President Warren G. Harding to his ill-fated West Coast trip and brought back his coffin after he died in San Francisco.

The Southeastern Railway Museum is open April through December Thursday, Friday, and Saturday from 10:00 A.M. to 5:00 P.M., plus noon to 5:00 P.M. the third Sunday of each month. January through March, it is open Saturday only from 10:00 A.M. to 4:00 P.M. Admission is $7 for adults, $5 for seniors, and $4 for children age 2 to 12.

The Wren's Nest
1050 Ralph David Abernathy Boulevard SW
(404) 753–7735

Joel Chandler Harris, author of the Uncle Remus tales, lived in this Victorian home. In keeping with his tradition of telling folk tales, the home hosts a Saturday storytelling at 1:00 P.M. Story hours may vary depending on attendance; call to verify times. Storytimes are covered by the admission charge. Local storytellers are featured. There's also a museum shop with lots of Uncle Remus books and gifts.

Visitors are welcome at the storytelling programs at the Wren's Nest, home of the author of the Uncle Remus tales. PHOTO: ATLANTA CONVENTION & VISITORS BUREAU

The Wren's Nest is open Tuesday through Saturday from 10:00 A.M. to 2:30 P.M. and is closed Sunday. Admission is $7 for adults, $6 for seniors and teens, and $4 for children 4 to 12.

Our World

Atlanta Botanical Garden
1345 Piedmont Avenue NE
Piedmont Park at the Prado
(404) 876–5859
www.atlantabotanicalgarden.org

The $3 million Children's Healthcare of Atlanta Children's Garden opened in September 1999, with a health and wellness theme and a freestanding Woodland Treehouse. Besides learning how plants help people grow, the small-scale interactive garden also is fun.

The Atlanta Botanical Garden offers day camps in the spring, summer, and fall; drop-in kids' classes for children and their families; a preschoolers' activity program called Young Sprouts; and Saturday morning amphitheater programs. A children's calendar of events is available on-line.

The garden is open Tuesday through Sunday, 9:00 A.M. to 5:00 P.M., October through March; from April to September, the hours are extended to 7:00 P.M. General admission is $10 for adults, $7 for seniors, and $5 for children 3 through 12 and students. Children younger than 3 are admitted free. There's no extra charge for the Children's Garden. For more information see our Attractions chapter.

Chattahoochee Nature Center
9135 Willeo Road, Roswell
(770) 992–2055
www.vickery.net/cnc

More than 55,000 schoolchildren visit this center annually. Kidstuff at the Chattahoochee Nature Center includes the chance to view small woodland creatures in the center's wildlife rehabilitation program. Night Owls overnight sleep-ins featuring wildlife workshops, live animal demonstrations, and night hikes occur most Friday and Saturday nights from October through May. You must reserve a spot at least one month in advance.

The center also hosts birthday parties, which include nature walks and other activities, for kids ages 4 and older. Summer afternoon children's programs, on themes such as "Don't Bug Me" and "Wet and Slimy," continue the learning begun by the center's after-school programs during the school year. Monthly Young Naturalist's meetings benefit children aged 4 to 11. Those kids can also enjoy non-scary Halloween hikes in October, featuring an educational walk through the woods. Other outings include guided evening canoe floats.

A summer day-camp program, Camp Kingfisher, increases awareness and appreciation of nature and includes traditional outdoor recreation. Weekly sessions run from June through August. Kids from 5 to 12 are eligible for this popular camp. For more about Chattahoochee Nature Center, see our Attractions chapter.

The center is open Monday through Saturday, 9:00 A.M. to 5:00 P.M., and Sunday, noon to 5:00 P.M. Admission is $3 for adults, $2 for children and seniors.

Davidson-Arabia Mountain Nature Preserve
3787 Klondike Road, Lithonia
(770) 484–3060
www.arabiaalliance.org

This nature preserve is open to the public every day from 7:00 A.M. until dark. Admission is free. Featuring 535 acres of natural area, a gigantic rock outcropping (similar to Stone Mountain), an abandoned rock quarry, and a lake, the preserve offers a variety of hiking and fishing opportunities. School and private groups can tour the area by appointment and learn about the endangered plant species that thrive there. Kids can also explore the life cycles of amphibians by observing the resident salamander population. A house on the grounds has been converted to a nature center for live animals.

Dunwoody Nature Center
5343 Roberts Drive, Dunwoody
(770) 394–3322
www.dunwoodynature.org

Dunwoody Nature Center, in Dunwoody Park, was founded to develop, improve, and preserve Dunwoody Park as a wildlife habitat and outdoor learning center. The park includes hardwood and pine forests, a meadowland, a creek, and wetlands. A 1.3-mile discovery path runs through the grounds.

The nature center is open Monday through Friday from 9:00 A.M. to 5:00 P.M. Dunwoody Park is open seven days a week, from sunup to sundown. Admission to both the center and the park is free.

The center offers outdoor discovery classes in weeklong sessions for kids ages 4 to 10; prices range from $125 to $145, depending on the program, and registration is required. There are also field trips for grades kindergarten through eight. Spring Break Camp is held when the schools are out in the spring; the cost is $95. Holiday Earth Camp, held in December, teaches campers about worldwide holiday celebrations and allows them to observe nature in winter. The center also schedules special nature festivals, workshops, and a Halloween celebration, Bats and Bones. These family programs generally cost about $6 for adults and $4 for children.

Families can join the center for $40; individuals can join for $25, seniors for $15. Members enjoy discounted rates on classes and programs.

Noah's Ark Rehabilitation Center Inc.
712 Locust Grove Road, Locust Grove
(770) 957-0888
www.noahs-ark.org

This outdoor wildlife rehabilitation center has all kinds of exotic animals: cougars, tigers, bears, wolves, monkeys, baboons, iguanas, and jungle birds. The Ark also accepts injured, orphaned, and unwanted wildlife. Among the farm animals it has taken in are a pasture full of horses as well as cows, sheep, goats, and pigs.

The Ark is open noon to 3:00 P.M. Tuesday through Saturday for self-guided tours. Guided tours are only by appointment. No tours are conducted when it rains or if the Ark is hosting a special event; it's best to call ahead to make sure they are open.

Noah's Ark is a nonprofit organization supported entirely by donations. Admission is free, but donations are appreciated. The Ark is about 40 miles south of downtown Atlanta.

Outdoor Activity Center
1442 Richland Road SW
(404) 752-5385

Three miles southwest of downtown Atlanta, the Outdoor Activity Center is a 26-acre nature preserve with a hardwood urban forest, an interpretive center, a treehouse classroom, 650-gallon freshwater aquarium, picnic tables, and Naturescape, an ecological playscape. The center hosts tours and programs for grades kindergarten through 12, covering such topics as Tree Treasures, Urban Wildlife, Reptile Riches, Animals in Winter, and Footprints of the Past, a program celebrating American Indian culture. The center is open Monday through Friday, 9:00 A.M. to 4:00 P.M. Tours are $4 per person.

W. H. Reynolds Memorial Nature Preserve
5665 Reynolds Road, Morrow
(770) 603-4188

About 4 miles of walking paths, ponds, springs, a wheelchair-accessible native plants trail, a compost demonstration site, and a heritage garden are among the many pleasures this preserve has to offer.

Children get a close-up view of the black rhinos at the Masai Mara exhibit of Zoo Atlanta.

PHOTO: J. SEBO/ZOO ATLANTA

An indoor nature center teaches kids about various flora and fauna. The nature center is open Monday through Friday from 8:30 A.M. to 5:30 P.M. The grounds open daily from 8:30 A.M. to dusk. Admission is free.

Yellow River Game Ranch
4525 Highway 78, Lilburn
(770) 972–6643
www.yellowrivergameranch.com

Six hundred animals and birds representing more than 25 indigenous Georgia species live here, including prairie dogs, goats, buffalo, white-tailed deer, and Georgia black bears. General Beauregard Lee, the internationally renowned groundhog, resides in his own antebellum plantation house. Three Georgia governors have proclaimed General Lee the Official Weather Prognosticator for the state, and he's been recognized by the National Weather Service. He's the one who either sees or doesn't see his shadow on Groundhog Day, letting us know how much longer winter may last. General Lee has his own mailbox, and each child who writes to him gets a personal answer.

The game ranch sponsors a Sheep Shearing Saturday each year in mid-May. A professional shearer teaches kids about the shearing process, and a hand spinner spins the wool. Kids can take a sample of fleece to their schools' show-and-tell.

Every day is different at Yellow River Game Ranch, with various species having babies at different times of year. Kids can walk down a mile-long marked trail and pet the animals who come up to nuzzle. The ranch allows kids to feed the animals with food purchased at the ranch.

Yellow River opens every day 9:30 A.M. to 6:00 P.M. Adults pay $7 admission; kids 3 to 11 are $6. One child younger than 3 gets in free with a paying adult.

Zoo Atlanta
Grant Park, 800 Cherokee Avenue SE
(404) 624–5600
www.zooatlanta.org

Described more fully in our Attractions chapter, Zoo Atlanta offers a wide variety of kids' attractions and activities after you've seen the pandas. The Children's Healthcare of Atlanta Ark Playground is open daily throughout the year, weather permitting. This smart playground features rocking elephants, turtles, bears, rabbits, and lambs, as well as a telegraph station, climbing nets, steering wheels, and compasses. The playground encourages kids to use their imaginations and helps educate parents about playground safety.

The Norfolk Southern Zoo Express is a handcrafted replica of an 1863 locomotive. The natural-gas-burning train features wide, comfortable seats and covered passenger coaches. Passengers wait in the Victorian-style train station for their turn on the train, which costs $1.50 per person and runs several times a day. Kids younger than 2 ride free.

Breakfast with a Keeper, scheduled on certain Saturdays throughout the summer, gives children 8 and older a chance to find out what it's like to care for zoo animals. Nightcrawlers Family Overnight, scheduled throughout the year, allows parents and kids 6 and older to enjoy a night hike, animal commissary tour, and creature encounters. In October the zoo hosts a Halloween event that includes a costume contest, trick-or-treat stations, face painting, and more for little ghouls and goblins.

Zoo Atlanta's Summer Safari Day Camp opens doors to a world of animals, conservation, and environmental discovery for students as young as 4 years old up through seventh graders. Sessions last a week, and campers can enjoy special events, arts and crafts, games, and discovery activities. The zoo offers full-day and morning programs as well as extended care from 7:30 A.M. to 6:00 P.M., $20 for half-day students, $25 for full-day students. Camp costs range from $95 to $215.

Recreation

Dixieland Fun Park
1675 Georgia Highway 85 North
Fayetteville
(770) 460–5862
www.dixielandfunpark.com
Dixieland Fun Park features go-cart tracks, bumper boats, miniature golf, batting cages, and an outdoor sky coaster.

The Pavilion has a video arcade, laser tag, and a playmaze for little ones.

The park opens weekends August 13 through May 27 from 4:00 to 11:00 P.M. Friday, 11:00 A.M. to 11:00 P.M. Saturday, and 1:00 to 9:00 P.M. Sunday. The rest of the year, the park is open every day: noon to 11:00 P.M. Monday through Thursday, noon to midnight Friday, 11:00 A.M. to midnight Saturday, and 1:00 to 11:00 P.M. Sunday.

Tickets for rides are $4 each but may be bought in bulk: 10 tickets are $35 and 50 tickets are $150. It's $5 for laser tag. A full day in the playmaze, for children 9 and younger, costs $5 for the first child and $3 for additional siblings.

Ice Forum
2300 Satellite Boulevard, Duluth
(770) 813–1010
Town Center, 3061 Busbee Parkway
Kennesaw
(770) 218–1010
Southlake, 7130 Mt. Zion Boulevard
Jonesboro
(770) 477–5112
www.iceforum.com
These enormous ice rinks offer skating sessions of various lengths every day of the week. A special treat is the chance to see professional hockey players in practice at the Duluth facility, as this is the home of the Atlanta Thrashers! The cost ranges from $5 to $7 per person, depending on how long you skate. Skate rentals are $3.

Malibu Grand Prix
5400 Brook Hollow Parkway, Norcross
(770) 416–7630
www.malibugrandprix.com
You can either speed up or slow down at Malibu Grand Prix, a sports and video arcade for the whole family. Bumper boats, batting cages, a video arcade, go-carts, and Grand Prix race cars entertain the action-oriented. More laid-back family members can meander through a miniature golf course or settle back to watch races on a big-screen TV. Birthday parties and overnight lock-ins are popular here.

Malibu is open Monday through Thursday, noon to 10:00 P.M.; Friday and Saturday, noon to midnight; and Sunday,

1:00 to 10:00 P.M. A round of miniature golf costs $6 per adult and $5 for kids younger than 12. Most of the attractions, such as bumper boats and go-carts, are $5 for each five-minute session. Arcade tokens are 25 cents each.

Mountasia Family Fun Center
175 Ernest Barrett Parkway, Marietta
(770) 422–7227
www.mountasia.com

Mountasia fun center stays open year-round, offering miniature golf, go-carts, bumper boats, and video game rooms. For 18 holes of golf, adults pay $5.25, while kids pay $4.95. Arcade games generally use from one to three 25-cent tokens. It's open Monday through Thursday from noon to 9:00 P.M., Friday and Saturday from 11:00 A.M. to 11:00 P.M., and Sunday from 11:00 A.M. to 9:00 P.M.

Peachtree Golf Center
2833 Peachtree Industrial Boulevard
(770) 497–9265

This family entertainment center features lighted golf stations, minigolf courses, driving ranges, and softball and baseball batting cages. It's open from 8:00 A.M. to 11:00 P.M. every day. Miniature golf costs $4.25 for 18 holes, $6 for 36 holes for kids younger than 19 and senior citizens. Adults pay $5.25 for 18 holes and $7 for 36 holes. Batting tokens are $20 for 18, $5 for 4, or $1.50 each (25 pitches per token).

Q-Zar
3750 Venture Drive, Duluth
(770) 497–1313

This high-tech spot seems like a video game come to life. Q-Zar's darkened mazes pit teams against each other in a combative game of hide-and-seek laser tag. Teams zap opponents with safe laser beams until one side emerges victorious.

Admission costs $7.50 per person per game. Groups of 20 or more get $1.50 per person off admission. Hours are Monday through Thursday, 4:00 to 8:00 P.M.; Friday, 1:00 P.M. to midnight; Saturday, 10:00 A.M. to midnight; and Sunday, 1:00 to 8:00 P.M. An unusual offering is free Bible study classes on Saturday from 6:00 to 8:00 P.M.

Hours are extended during the summer months, but call before you go—private parties may book the entire place.

Stone Mountain Park
U.S. Highway 78, Stone Mountain Village
(770) 498–5600
www.stonemountainpark.org

Stone Mountain offers a diverse array of entertainment for the whole family. Special kidstuff includes a petting zoo, minigolf, water slides at the beach, a playground, softball and baseball batting cages, and a train ride around the base of the mountain. During the Christmas holidays, the youngsters will get a kick out of singing carols on the train as it winds its way around several wintry scenes of the North Pole.

The park opens at 6:00 A.M. and closes at midnight every day of the year, except Christmas. Attractions open at 10:00 A.M. and close at 7:00 P.M. during the summer and at 5:00 P.M. September through May.

A $7 parking permit buys admission to the park; admission prices to the attractions are $23 plus 7 percent tax for adults and $17 plus 7 percent tax for children 3 to 11. (See our Attractions chapter.)

Shopping

FAO Schwarz
Lenox Square, 3393 Peachtree Road NE
(404) 814–1675
www.faoschwarz.com

There are many fine toy stores and kids' specialty shops in the Atlanta area, but this one merits a mention simply because FAO Schwarz, which opened at Lenox Square in

Insiders' Tip

Q-Zar is a high-tech gaming facility that offers an unusual extra attraction: Christian Bible studies on Saturday evenings.

November 1995, is a mini-version of the store's famous Fifth Avenue location in New York. Features include a rain forest inhabited by a talking dinosaur, toucans, roaring lions, and a bicycling Curious George; a book department kids enter by walking through a giant book monster's legs; and the World of Barbie boutique. Other Lenox Square stores of special interest to kids include Warner Bros. Studio Store and The Disney Store.

The store is open during regular mall hours: Monday through Saturday from 10:00 A.M. to 9:00 P.M., Sunday from noon to 6:00 P.M. Hours are extended during the Christmas holiday season.

Another store is in the Mall of Georgia in Gwinnett County.

Hobbit Hall
120 Bulloch Avenue, Roswell
(770) 587-0907, (800) 468-0480
www.hobbithall.com

This bookstore in Roswell's historic district has a goldfish pond in front and a fenced garden and children's playhouse in back. Hobbit Hall carries approximately 25,000 titles and 100,000 volumes of quality children's books plus educational toys, games, puzzles, and activity kits. Hobbit Hall events include interactive preschool story times on Monday and Tuesday at 10:00 A.M. School-age kids are invited to special events (tea and cookies, beanie baby swaps) on Saturday at 10:00 A.M. Well-known children's authors and illustrators regularly visit the store and participate in Hobbit Hall's Meet the Authors/Illustrators in the Schools program. The cozy Victorian setting is also a favorite for birthday parties. All activities are free. Hobbit Hall is open Monday through Friday from 10:00 A.M. to 5:00 P.M., Saturday from 10:00 A.M. to 5:30 P.M., and Sunday for special events only.

Festivals and Events

Atlantans love any excuse to throw a party. On most weekends throughout the year, there are festivals and special events going on somewhere in the metro area.

Some of these affairs are cozy block parties where nearly everyone knows everyone else. Many of the city's rejuvenated in-town neighborhoods hold festivals and tours of homes, inviting folks from all over to share in the community's life. Religious groups and international clubs parade their cultures and customs for others to experience and enjoy. And periodically there are truly massive events—drawing 100,000 and more—that organizers work throughout the year to stage.

In a city where nearly everyone came from somewhere else, these events may also help newcomers find their way by bringing people of similar interests or backgrounds together. And they can remind us all just how kaleidoscopically varied are the people making their lives here.

Many festivals are held in parks. For specific information on Atlanta's parks, see our Parks and Recreation chapter. Here's a quick location guide to parks that serve as venues to many events throughout the year:

Piedmont Park is in Midtown; it's bordered primarily by 10th Street, Monroe Drive, and Piedmont Avenue.

Grant Park is in southeast Atlanta; its main entrances are on Cherokee Avenue and on Boulevard. Zoo Atlanta and the Cyclorama occupy the southern portion; festivals take place in the park's northern area.

Chastain Park is in northwest Atlanta; take Roswell Road north through Buckhead; turn left on West Wieuca Road and follow the signs.

To reach Georgia's Stone Mountain Park, take U.S. 78 (Ponce de Leon Avenue–Scott Boulevard–Lawrenceville Highway–Stone Mountain Parkway) east of Atlanta to the Stone Mountain Park exit. A per-vehicle admission is always charged here: It's $7 per car. An annual pass is $30.

In this chapter, we'll tell you about some of the annual events that make life in Atlanta exciting.

January

King Week and the Martin Luther King Jr. National Holiday
Martin Luther King Jr. Center for Nonviolent Social Change
449 Auburn Avenue NE (and other locations)
(404) 526–8900

Dr. Martin Luther King Jr. was born in Atlanta on January 15, 1929. A national holiday was declared in his honor in 1986. Long before that, we Atlantans had been staging an annual celebration to laud our Nobel laureate. King Week, held the week preceding the Martin Luther King Jr. National Holiday, includes many free performances, concerts, special religious services, and educational presentations. Check with the Center for specific times and places of events.

Cathedral Antiques Show
Cathedral of St. Philip
2744 Peachtree Road
(404) 365–1000

One of the premier antiques shows in the Southeast is held near the end of the month at this Buckhead cathedral. The show opens with a tour of several exclusive Buckhead homes and condominiums; tickets are usually around $25. A Gala Preview Party ($50) gives guests a sneak peek at the antiques collected from around the country that are for sale. Daily admission tickets are $10. The event usually features a lecture with a noted historian or antiquities expert. Proceeds from the four-day event always benefit a worthy cause.

February

African-American History Month
Various locations

Atlanta, the center of the civil rights movement for years, marks African-American History Month with numerous educational and entertainment events. The commemoration lasts the entire month. Big Bethel AME Church, 220 Auburn Avenue near the King Center, hosts an assortment of musical performances, lectures, and programs that explore the African-American experience. The Atlanta-Fulton Public Library System sponsors special lectures on African-American authors. The Fernbank Science Center takes a look at the skies over the Dark Continent with its program, African Astronomy. Check with individual locations for specific dates and times.

Groundhog Day
Yellow River Game Ranch
4525 Highway 78, Lilburn
(770) 972–6643

There's always a small crowd gathered in the chilly predawn air on February 2 to watch General Beauregard Lee emerge from his groundhog abode. But will he see his shadow? Find out in person for a $7 adult admission; $6 for kids 3 to 11.

Insiders' Tip

The Southeastern Flower Show, held in February, is considered the kickoff event for Atlanta's long gardening season.

Southeastern Flower Show
Atlanta Exposition Center
3650 Jonesboro Road
(404) 366–0833

This show, held over a weekend late in the month, benefits the Atlanta Botanical Garden. It features a wide range of garden-related events including displays, demonstrations, workshops, and children's activities. Adults pay $20 on the days of the show or $30 for an advance two-day ticket.

The Best of Atlanta Party
Cobb Galleria Center, 2 Galleria Parkway
(404) 872–3100

Atlanta Magazine sponsors this annual showcase of readers' selections for the city's best restaurants. More than 60 chefs show off their award-winning dishes while jazz musicians entertain and local celebrities pass out door prizes. Tickets are $60; proceeds benefit Camp Twin Lakes for children with special needs.

March

Atlanta Fair
Turner Field
755 Hank Aaron Drive
(770) 740–1962

This affordable annual fair is an old-fashioned fun time, with a midway, rides, food, and children's activities. Tickets are $5 for adults, $1 for children.

Atlanta Passion Play
Atlanta Civic Center
395 Piedmont Avenue
(770) 234–8400

Since 1976, the First Baptist Church of Atlanta has annually presented this pageant portraying Christ's life, death, and resurrection. Its reputation is so widespread, it now draws people from around the country. Each year's production varies slightly with different focuses on the story line and different music. The elaborately staged and costumed play is the work of more than 500 people, including a chorus and full orchestra. Due to the three-hour length, the sacred nature of the performance, and the graphic portrayal of Christ's death, children younger than 6 are not admitted. The play is performed the final three weekends of Lent, not including Easter weekend. Tickets range from $8 to $18.

Conyers Cherry Blossom Festival
International Horse Park
1996 Centennial Olympic Parkway, Conyers
(770) 918–2169

In 1980 Hitachi Maxell's president donated 500 cherry trees to the city of Conyers, 30 minutes east of Atlanta on I-20, home to Maxell Corp. of America. The Conyers Cherry Blossom Festival has greeted spring here since 1982. The monthlong calendar of events includes art exhibits, a road race, other sporting tournaments, a beauty pageant, music, and more. Most of the events are free, but there is a $5 parking fee. The Festival Day is usually held on the third or fourth Saturday at the Georgia International Horse Park on the edge of town.

St. Patrick's Day
Buckhead and Downtown

Atlanta goes green with St. Patrick's Day celebrations. Sponsored by the Hibernian Society, the Atlanta St. Patrick's Day Parade is the highlight, having been held for almost 115 years. But the day usually begins with an early morning mass at the Cathedral of Christ the King in Buckhead, where proper dress and propriety are required. But the revelers let their hair down soon afterward, starting at 11:30 A.M. with the parade through Downtown. Across the city, Irish hangouts are packed with partygoers: check out the green beer and Irish stew at Fado's and McDuff's Irish Pub in Buckhead; Limerick Junction in Virginia-Highland; Danny O'Shea's in Marietta; and McColgan's in Alpharetta. Depending on what day the feast falls, the celebration may extend for a day or two before and after the 17th. Look for an array of concerts, readings, and lectures at various locations around town. Theatre Gael, the Celtic-inspired dramatic group, and the W. B. Yeats Foundation at Emory University usually feature special programs. The city of Decatur, a few miles

east of downtown Atlanta, holds its own parade near the day of green as well.

April

Atlanta Dogwood Festival
Piedmont Park
10th Street and Piedmont Avenue
(404) 329–0501
www.dogwood.org

For a few precious weeks each spring, Atlanta is bathed in a brilliant floral finery. The Dogwood Festival pays homage to the city's legendary botanical beauty; its highlights include a colorful hot-air balloon race, concerts, children's parades, and the dog Frisbee championships. Most events are free. Note: Atlanta's dogwoods and azaleas bloom on a schedule all their own, and their peak does not always coincide with this festival that is held on a weekend in mid-April.

Bear on the Square Mountain Festival
Downtown Dahlonega
(800) 231–5543
www.dahlonega.org

One of the first in a series of festivals in the nearby north Georgia mountain communities, this one is devoted to a celebration of bluegrass and "old-time" music (it used to be called "hillbilly" music, and was featured in the movie *O Brother Where Art Thou?*). Typical for Dahlonega festivals, the square is filled up with booths selling anything from the finest of fine art to the lowest of folk art crafts, with stages scattered about hosting clog dancers, storytellers, jam sessions, and of course, some of the best Appalachian music makers in the area. Most activities are free, including parking. Concert tickets are $5, and the festival is always scheduled for the third weekend in April.

Druid Hills Home and Garden Tour
Various Druid Hills homes
(404) 524–TOUR
www.druidhillstour.org

With an overall landscape plan by the world-renowned Olmsted firm and stunning homes designed by famous architects such as Neil Reid and Walter T. Downing, the elegant Druid Hills neighborhood is listed on the National Register of Historic Places. This weekend event in late April affords you a rare opportunity to tour selected homes and gardens in the $300,000 to million-dollar range. Tickets are available for the entire tour or for individual homes, and are $17 in advance and $20 on the tour day.

Easter Sunrise Services
Stone Mountain Park
U.S. Highway 78
Stone Mountain Village
(770) 498–5702

In the predawn darkness on Easter Sunday morning, the faithful gather atop Stone Mountain to await the sunrise on the holiest day of the Christian year. As morning breaks, local ministers lead an ecumenical worship service. This inspiring celebration is a long-standing Atlanta tradition. The weather is often windy and cold, so you might need to bring a blanket. The service is free, but you'll pay $7 per car to be admitted into the park.

Inman Park Spring Festival
Edgewood and Euclid Avenues and other
Inman Park Streets
(770) 242–4895
www.inmanpark.org

Two miles east of Five Points, Inman Park was developed in the 1880s as Atlanta's

first suburb, and along its broad, tree-lined streets are imposing Victorian mansions and charming bungalows. Coca-Cola founder Asa Candler lived here in the early 1900s; Mayor Bill Campbell lives here today. Inman Park declined precipitously after World War II until it was little better than a slum. Then, in the late 1960s forward-looking citizens rediscovered the area, renovating once-grand homes and reclaiming the area as one of Atlanta's premier addresses. You'll find a parade, a tour of homes, antiques, food, crafts, music, and more at this two-day street party held the last weekend of the month. The festival is free; home tour tickets are $15 per person and are good for the entire weekend. This is the oldest of Atlanta's many neighborhood festivals.

Georgia Renaissance Festival
I–85 at exit 61, Fairburn
(770) 964–8575
www.garenfest.com

Forsooth, this rollicking re-creation of the English Renaissance features more than 100 performances daily on 10 stages scattered across the 93-acre festival grounds. Strolling musicians, minstrels, magicians, and other costumed characters are all part of the fun, along with knights in armor jousting on horseback. The festival is open seven consecutive weekends (Saturday and Sunday only) beginning in late April and lasting through the end of May or early June. Admission is $15 for adults, $7 for seniors and kids ages 6 to 12. There is no admission charge for children younger than 6.

Sheep to Shawl Day
Atlanta History Center
130 West Paces Ferry Road
(404) 814–4004
www.atlantahistorycenter.com

For city dwellers who don't get down to the farm too often, here's a day to experience nature—particularly sheep. Held the first Saturday of the month, the event features demonstrations in the art of sheep shearing, followed by the entire process required to turn it into something wearable. Spectators observe the fresh wool

Shop in medieval castles, Tudor homes, and enchanted cottages for arts and crafts created by village artisans at the Georgia Renaissance Festival. PHOTO: GEORGIA RENAISSANCE FESTIVAL

through the washing, spinning, dyeing, and weaving cycles. The completed process produces a new shawl. Displays are ongoing throughout the day. The center is open from 10:00 A.M. to 5:30 P.M. the day of the event. Admission is $12 for adults, $10 for those over age 65, $7 for kids ages 3 to 17, and free to children under 3.

Spring Folklife Festival
Atlanta History Center
130 West Paces Ferry Road
(404) 814–4000
www.atlantahistorycenter.com

Celebrate Atlanta's rural heritage at this annual festival at the Tullie Smith Farm on the grounds of the History Center. Costumed craftspeople play traditional music, serve apple cider, and demonstrate a range of long-lost arts, from dipping candles, weaving baskets, and quilting to open-hearth cooking and making pomander balls. Visitors can try their hands at butter churning and weaving. Admission is $11 for adults, $9 for those over

age 65, $4 for kids 6 to 17, and free to children 5 and younger.

WalkAmerica
Various metro Atlanta streets
(404) 352–WALK, (404) 350–9800

Benefiting the March of Dimes, this walkathon annually attracts some 20,000 participants who sign up pledge donors and walk one of eight routes throughout the metro area. The minimum donation is usually $30. The proceeds help fight birth defects and infant mortality. The event is held on a Saturday in late April.

May

Atlanta Celtic Festival
Oglethorpe University
4484 Peachtree Road
(404) 572–8045
www.atlantacelticfestival.org

Don your kilts, laddies, and head for this two-day event, held the third weekend of the month, that celebrates the history and cultural heritage of Ireland, Scotland, and Wales. International, national, and local musicians, dancers, and speakers are on hand, along with Celtic crafts, foods, and merchandise. There are free lessons in Scottish country dancing, children's games, and sheepdog demonstrations. Members of Atlanta's Theatre Gael perform short works and entertain with storytelling. Hours are 10:00 A.M. to 11:00 P.M. Saturday and 11:00 A.M. to 6:00 P.M. Sunday. Admission is $10 for adults, $5 for seniors, students, and children 6 to 12.

Atlanta Jazz Festival
Piedmont Park
Piedmont Avenue and 14th Street
(404) 817-6851

Sponsored by the City of Atlanta, this showcase of local and national jazz talent, which began in 1977, is one of the largest of its kind in the city. All events on the Saturday, Sunday, and Monday of Memorial Day weekend are free and run from 1:00 to 10:00 P.M. Prior to the event, various jazz artists give free, brown-bag lunchtime concerts in Woodruff Park, at Marietta and Peachtree Streets downtown.

Decatur Arts Festival
Decatur
(404) 371-9583

The city of Decatur, 6 miles east of Downtown, hosts this popular free festival that attracts about 40,000 people each year. The event kicks off on Memorial Day weekend with an Art Walk that winds through the city's art galleries and stores. Among the other activities on tap are art exhibits, a children's festival, storytellers, jugglers, magicians, pony rides, international music and dance, a garden tour, and literary events.

Lasershow
Stone Mountain Park
U.S. Highway 78
Stone Mountain Village
(770) 498-5702
www.stonemountainpark.com

Seven nights a week from early May into August, the sky over Stone Mountain explodes with a rainbow of laser light. To stirring musical accompaniment, lasers are projected on the mountain's north face, which becomes a natural million-square-foot screen. Bring a blanket and relax under the stars. The show is free with admission to the park—$7 per car.

Marietta Bluegrass Festival
Jim Miller Park
2245 Callaway Road, Marietta
(770) 528-8875

Door prizes, 20 bands, and a foot-stompin' good time are on tap at this two-day festival of bluegrass music sponsored by the Georgia Bluegrass Association. Tickets to the Friday evening performances are $9; admission to the Saturday lineup starting in the early afternoon is $12. The fun happens on the third weekend of the month, then again on the second weekend of November.

Music Midtown Festival
Atlanta Civic Center
395 Piedmont Avenue
(404) 233-8889
www.musicmidtown.com

First held in 1994, this three-day outdoor festival on the month's first weekend scored an immediate hit. Some of the best-known performers take to the six stages, including Bob Dylan, Santana, ZZTop, Cake, Silverchair, and the Steve Miller Band. Tickets for the entire weekend (usually the first one in May) are $45.

National Historic Preservation Month
Various locations
(404) 876-2041

More than 20 Atlanta area historic sites and homes take part in marking their heritage and encourage visitors to learn more about them. Also, for one week in the middle of the month, the Atlanta Preservation Center offers its walking tours of historic Atlanta districts free of charge. The APC's tours are fun and highly informative; take advantage of this annual opportunity to enjoy them and save some money. (See our Attractions chapter for details on the tours offered.)

Springfest
Stone Mountain Park
U.S. Highway 78
Stone Mountain Village
(770) 498–5702

Cooks from around the South compete in a barbecue cook-off for thousands of dollars in cash and prizes. In addition to live music, the weekend in early May includes a huge garage sale that's a junk lover's dream come true. A registration fee is required for sellers. The event is free, but you'll pay $7 per car to get into the park. Bring your appetite! There's no charge for samples.

Taste of the South
Stone Mountain Park
U.S. Highway 78
Stone Mountain Village
(770) 498–5702

If you've always been curious about okra (boiled or fried), grits (cheese or regular), and greens (collard or turnip), here's your chance to taste what you've been missing. Each Southern state shows off its best offerings in food, entertainment, travel, and more over Memorial Day weekend. Admission to the park requires a $7 parking permit. The event itself is free, but be sure to bring a few bucks if you plan on doing a little taste-testing.

June

Georgia Shakespeare Festival
Conant Performing Arts Center
Oglethorpe University, 4484 Peachtree Road
(404) 264–0020
www.gashakespeare.org

Shakespeare has come to Oglethorpe University every summer for more than a decade. The festival usually includes three plays by the Bard as well as some lighter fare by his contemporaries. The season opens in mid-June, with productions going on through October. About 90 minutes before each evening's performance or Sunday matinee, showgoers are invited to picnic on the lawn around the Center. Even if you're not a fan of Shakespeare, it's worth the price of admission to sit in the fabulous Conant Center. With only 509

seats, the feeling is intimate. And during the pleasant spring and fall weather, the walls of the Center are raised to the open air. But don't worry—it's also completely air-conditioned to handle hot, muggy July nights. Tickets for the festival shows range from $23 to $32, and discounts are offered to seniors, students, and groups.

Virginia-Highland Summerfest
John Howell Park, Virginia Avenue
(404) 222–8244

Founded in 1916 and originally known as North Boulevard Park, the Virginia-Highland neighborhood annually throws this popular, free party featuring an artists' market, bands, food from area restaurants, and lots of fun for the kids. It's held the first full weekend in June at Virginia Avenue at Ponce de Leon Place.

July

Fantastic Fourth Celebration
Stone Mountain Park
U.S. Highway 78
Stone Mountain Village
(770) 498–5633
www.stonemountainpark.com

The park throws a three-day birthday party for America beginning on the Fourth, with major concerts and other entertainment, plus nightly fireworks in addition to the Lasershow. Bring a blanket, picnic food, swim clothes, running shoes, bug spray, and suntan lotion in case you want to spend the entire day and take advantage of all the offerings. The celebration is free with admission to the park, which is $7 per car, per day.

Peachtree Road Race
Peachtree Road from Lenox Square to
Piedmont Park
(404) 262–RACE
www.atlantatrackclub.org

You don't have to be in the horde of runners to enjoy this Fourth of July event, which is free to watch. Peachtree is lined with revelers cheering on the participants. There are entry fees for runners, but the forms are snapped up within hours of distribution. It's run by the Atlanta Track Club, 3097 East Shadowlawn Avenue NE, (404) 231-9064.

Independence Day
Various locations

There's almost too much fun to be had around Atlanta on the Fourth. The action gets under way at the crack of dawn as 200,000 spectators line Peachtree Street to watch 50,000 runners compete in the annual Peachtree Road Race (see Spectator Sports). Midday there's WSB-TV's Salute 2 America parade with bands, balloons, and celebrities; it's the largest Independence Day parade in the nation. The parade starts at 1:00 P.M. at Centennial Olympic Park, where there are plenty of pre- and post-parade activities for the whole family, then continues on Marietta Street and up West Peachtree Street. All in all the parade lasts about 90 minutes.

Marietta's historic town square welcomes visitors with Fourth in the Park. The Freedom Parade begins at 10:00 A.M. at the Roswell Street Baptist Church and ends at Cherokee Street and the North Loop. And in historic Roswell Square, you'll enjoy carnival games, musical and theater performances, arts and crafts, food, and evening fireworks. It's all free. For information, call (770) 528-0615.

Decatur throws a free party in the town square with bands and fireworks. It's sponsored by the Decatur Downtown Develop Authority. For details, call (404) 371-8386.

After dark, Atlanta skies explode in pyrotechnic glory. The Southeast's largest display is at Lenox Square, 3393 Peachtree Road, (404) 233-6767; it's always free. Live bands start playing at 6:00 P.M., and the fireworks begin at 9:00 P.M. Also enjoy a children's entertainment area and food and drink concessions. People park in the Square's enormous lot or across the street at the Phipps Plaza lot. You'll have to get there early if you hope to find a space.

Braves fans get a dandy display at Turner Field, 755 Hank Aaron Drive, following the ball game; call (404) 522-7630 (see Spectator Sports for more information).

Patrons at Lake Lanier Islands beach and water park can enjoy a variety of musical performances, capped by fireworks over the lake. Admission to the park is $25.99 per adult and $16.99 for seniors and children. After 5:00 P.M. it's half-price. For more information call (770) 932-7200.

National Black Arts Festival
Studioplex, 659 Auburn Avenue, Suite 254
(404) 730-7315
www.nbaf.org

The National Black Arts Festival is presented biannually in early July. Events are held at various venues throughout the city. The celebration spotlights the work of artists of African descent in eight disciplines: music, dance, theater, film, folk art, visual arts, performance art, and literature. Works by artists from the United States, Africa, the Caribbean, Europe, and South America are featured, as is an artists market. Events range in price from $5 and up. Call for information or a catalog of merchandise, which includes posters, caps, mugs, and more.

August

Atlanta Virtuosi's Hispanic Festival of the Arts
Embry Hills United Methodist Church
Chamblee
(770) 938-8611
The Atlanta Virtuosi sponsors this festival of the arts from Hispanic-speaking people of Colombia, Peru, Dominican Republic, Brazil, Panama, and many other nations. Lectures, displays of fine arts, storytelling, dance performances, photography exhibits, concerts, and food complete the event. Admission is $15 for adults, $10 for students and seniors, and free for children younger than 12.

Hotlanta River Expo
Chattahoochee River and various venues
(404) 874-3976
www.hotlanta.org
Thousands of gay men from around the nation arrive for this weekend in mid-August for intense partying and entertainment. It's an especially festive event that raises money for charities. Individual event admission fees start at $20 or you can buy a weekend pass.

September

U.S. 10K Classic and Family Sports Festival
The Cobb Galleria Centre
I-285 and Cobb Parkway
(770) 432-0100
While the sportspeople in your family bike, skate, or run in this annual Labor Day event that begins at Cumberland Mall and ends at White Water park, the rest of the family can party at the Galleria. Pony rides, exhibits, and other activities keep the youngsters busy from 10:00 A.M. until 5:00 P.M., and they're free. The racers pay a $20 registration fee and get to compete with about 10,000 others including wheelchair racers and walkers. There are

$75,000 in prizes, which brings out the Olympians as well as other hopefuls. The 1998 festival adds a cycling competition and a longer route around Dobbins Air Reserve Base.

Montreaux Atlanta International Music Festival
Piedmont Park, 1085 Piedmont Avenue
(404) 817-6820
Jazz, gospel, and reggae acts perform at this free outdoor festival sponsored by the City of Atlanta. The event kicks off the week prior to Labor Day with local groups performing afternoon concerts in downtown Atlanta at either Woodruff Park or Centennial Park. The three days of Montreaux concerts are held at Piedmont Park in Midtown and feature jazz, reggae, blues, rock, and country music. Admission is free.

Yellow Daisy Festival
Stone Mountain Park
U.S. Highway 78
Stone Mountain Village
(770) 498-5633
www.stonemountainpark.com
For 35 years in early September, Stone Mountain Park has staged this celebration of the Confederate Yellow Daisy, fields of which adorn the mountainside

Insiders' Tip

Don't even think about driving your car down to Lenox Square or Piedmont Park to watch the Peachtree Road Race, as the more than 10,000 runners and 50,000-plus spectators crowd every inch of both venues. Take MARTA instead!

and bloom about this time. Arts and crafts booths line the wooded paved trails in the Special Events Meadow and Woodlands. Expect to see more than 400 vendors, live entertainment, a flower show, lots of food, and more. The sale begins Saturday at 10:00 A.M. and closes at 6:00 P.M. People show up to buy even earlier. The event is free with admission to the park—$7 per car, per day.

Civil War Encampment
Atlanta History Center
130 West Paces Ferry Road
(404) 814–4000
www.atlantahistorycenter.com

History comes alive; it's the summer of 1864 and Atlanta is in imminent danger of falling to the Federal troops of Gen. William Tecumseh Sherman. The scene is re-created in mid-September with Confederate camps of soldiers, artillery, drills, cavalry, music, and storytelling. Fees are $11 for adults, $4 for ages 6 through 17, and free for children 5 and under. Also throughout the summer, Civil War (or, to use the Southern term, "Late Unpleasantness") reenactors hold camps and drills at numerous sites in the metro area. Among them is Kennesaw Mountain National Battlefield Park in Marietta (see our Parks and Recreation chapter).

JapanFest
Stone Mountain Park
U.S. Highway 78
Stone Mountain Village
(404) 524–7399, (770) 498–5633
www.stonemountainpark.com

In mid-September this daylong celebration of Japanese culture offers a wide variety of demonstrations as well as performing arts workshops and exhibitions. It's sponsored by the Japanese Chamber of Commerce of Georgia, Japan American Society of Georgia, and the consulate general of Japan in Georgia. The event is an additional fee beyond admission to the park—$7 per car, per day.

Street of Dreams
Locations vary annually
(770) 614–7841

A popular September event, the Street of Dreams is always held at a new subdivision. A half-dozen expensive model homes are decorated by local designers and then opened for viewing. Each home is like a magazine page in 3D from the finest decor magazines where the au courant fabrics, colors, and gizmos can be examined in depth. The homes are open for viewing every day except Mondays throughout the entire month. Tickets cost $8.50 for adults, $7.50 for children 4 through 12. Proceeds go to Habitat for Humanity and other charities.

Ansley Park Home Tour
Various homes
(404) 872–TOUR

On a weekend in late September, owners of some of Atlanta's most distinctive older homes open their doors to visitors so that their neighborhood association can earn funds. Tickets are $18 in advance or $23 on tour days to view all the homes. With your ticket you receive a walking map listing the homes you can see during the weekend. Visit one or many to get ideas on home renovation and decorating or to sneak a peek at how the other half lives.

Atlanta Greek Festival
Greek Orthodox Cathedral of the Annunciation
2500 Clairmont Road
(404) 633–5870

This annual fall tribute to Greek culture attracts more than 50,000 people over four days in late September. There's Greek music, dancing, wine, and Opa! what food: souvlaki, moussaka, gyros, and honey-dripping baklava are made by members of the church. Admission is $5 for adults and $1 for children younger than 12.

The *Atlanta Journal-Constitution* Barbecue Fest
Gwinnett County Fairgrounds
2405 Sugarloaf Parkway, Lawrenceville
(770) 963–6522

On a weekend in late September, Atlanta's major daily hosts this annual event that features blues bands and barbecue. Participants get to vote on their favorite 'cue, stroll around and watch cooking demonstrations, enjoy children's activities, and more. Children younger than 12 are free; everyone else pays $2 plus the cost of the food.

Grant Park Tour of Homes
Various homes
(404) 522–7131
www.grantpark.org

Grant Park is named for Col. Lemuel P. Grant, the transplanted Yankee civil engineer who designed the elaborate fortifications around Atlanta during the Civil War and who later donated 100 acres of wooded, hilly land near his home for a city park with no racial restrictions. The neighborhood around the park has many historic Victorian homes, both massive and modest. The 30th annual tour was held in 2003; tickets were $15. No advance purchase is necessary. Tickets are distributed on the day of the tour in late September.

Sweet Auburn Heritage Festival
Auburn Avenue
(404) 525–0205

For nearly a century Auburn Avenue has been the backbone of black Atlanta. It picked up the "sweet" label at a time when it was functioning as the city's "other" main street, offering a full array of commercial, religious, and entertainment institutions. Dr. Martin Luther King Jr.'s birth home, church, and tomb are part of a National Historic Site on Auburn. The famous Royal Peacock Lounge once showcased soul music stars such as James Brown and Stevie Wonder; it continues to operate today. This festival in late September celebrates the street's rich heritage with three days of music, food, fun, and shopping. No admission charged.

Candler Park & Lake Claire Music & Arts Festival
Candler Park Drive at McLendon Avenue
(404) 370–1003

The pleasant, laid-back neighborhoods of Candler Park and Lake Claire come together at their shared business district for

a free street party with refreshments and bands. The mid-month weekend also includes the Lake Claire Tour of Funky Homes, an up-close look at a dozen bungalows and cottages for about $12.

October

Chili Cook-Off
Stone Mountain Park
U.S. Highway 78
Stone Mountain Village
(770) 498–5633
www.stonemountainpark.com

On a Saturday in early October, Stone Mountain Park catches fire as some 200 teams participate in creative chili cooking. There's live entertainment and cold beer to help you cool off afterward. Park admission of $7 per car, per day. Tickets are $8 at the gate.

Fright Fest
Six Flags Over Georgia
275 Riverside Parkway, Austell
(770) 948–9290

There's more than scary thrill rides at Six Flags Over Georgia theme park. The normally normal park becomes really scary when ghosts and goblins become part of the Halloween celebration; $42 for adults, $26.50 for children under 48 inches tall, and $10 for parking.

Tour of Southern Ghosts
Stone Mountain Park
U.S. Highway 78
Stone Mountain Village
(770) 498–5633
www.stonemountainpark.com

In mid-October something terrifying is happening out at the old plantation house. For more than two weeks, ghosts, monsters, and "haunts" take over the mansion at Stone Mountain. Storytellers spin webs of horror during evening candlelight tours of the antebellum plantation. Tours begin at 7:00 P.M.; the last tickets are sold at 9:00 P.M. You'll pay $8 per adult and $5 per child (if you dare) in addition to the park's daily fee—$7 per car.

Oktoberfest
Helen
(706) 878–2181, (800) 858–8027

Oompah pa! Hidden in the mountains just 70 miles northeast from Atlanta is an Alpine village look-alike. During September and October, Helen stages an Oktoberfest replete with lederhosen-clad bands, dancing ladies in dirndl skirts, and beer,

beer, beer. Bands perform on their Festhalle. But if you prefer shopping to sitting, Alpine Helen, decorated like a Bavarian village, has lots of interesting shops along its cobblestone alleys that sell imported woolens and trinkets. Restaurants abound. Admission to the festival is $7 on weekdays, $9 on Saturdays, $3 for children 6 through 12, or free for those younger than 5. To get there from Atlanta, proceed north on I–85 to I–985; follow U.S. 129 to Cleveland, Georgia, until GA 75, which takes you directly to Helen. (See our Day Trips and Weekend Getaways chapter for more information about Helen.)

Scottish Highland Games and Gathering of the Clans
Stone Mountain Park
U.S. Highway 78
Stone Mountain Village
(770) 498–5633, (770) 521–0228
www.smhg.org

It's time to pull the old kilt out of mothballs and tune up the pipes for this annual celebration of Scottish heritage. Also known as "Scots on the Rock," this event is always held on the third weekend of the

The Atlanta Pipe Band at the Highland Games. PHOTO: JOHN MCKAY

month. Kilted Scots engage in athletic events, plus there are parades and pageantry galore with bagpiping, drumming, and several different types of Highland and country dancing. Daily admission is $15 or $17 for adults and $5 for kids. There are also pipe and drum bands and brass bands, Highland dancers, and country dancers. Plenty of vendors are always present to fit you out in the latest (18th century, that is!) in Highland wear, as well as those carrying a wide selection of books, jewelry, music CDs, and authentic British food.

All admission fees and ticket prices are in addition to the usual park admission of $7 per day, per car.

Latin American Film Festival
Rich Auditorium of Woodruff Art Center
1280 Peachtree Road
(404) 733–4570
www.latinfilm.org

Sponsored by the Latin American Art Circle of the High Museum of Art, this film festival is held at the end of October and extends through the beginning of November. Atlanta premieres of recent feature films from Latin America bring in film lovers and the cognoscenti. General admission is $5. Students and seniors pay $4.50, and museum members receive another discount. Frequently, talent from the films are present, and free receptions accompany the movies.

Puppetry Arts Festival
Center for Puppetry Arts
1404 Spring Street
(404) 873–3391

The world-renowned Center for Puppetry Arts stages its annual extravaganza in October with performances by nationally and internationally known artists as well as local puppeteers. Children's puppet-making workshops and strolling performers are also part of the festivities.

Sunday in the Park
Oakland Cemetery, Historic Oakland
Foundation
248 Oakland Avenue SE
(404) 688–2107
www.oaklandcemetery.com

Historic Oakland Foundation hosts its major event of the year, Sunday in the Park, each fall. More than 1,500 people attend this annual event, which features free tours, a Victorian hat contest, Teddy Bear Tea and face painting for children, music, a photography contest, and decorated mausolea.

November

Lighting of Rich's-Macy's Great Tree
Lenox Square, Peachtree Road
(770) 913–5551

Rich's, Atlanta's home-grown department store, started this holiday tradition in 1948 downtown. But in 2000, the celebration moved to Buckhead and the flagship store at Lenox Square. At 7:00 P.M. on Thanksgiving night, thousands of Atlantans gather to sing carols with mass choirs and await the lighting of the Great Tree, an enormous evergreen decorated with basketball-size ornaments. Even the scroogiest Scrooge is hard-pressed to produce a "Bah, humbug!" when (during the highest note of "Oh, Holy Night") the switch is thrown, and the huge tree explodes with light. To share the fun from the privacy of your own home, tune in to the live broadcast on WSB-TV Channel 2.

A Southern Christmas
Stone Mountain Park
U.S. Highway 78
Stone Mountain Village
(770) 498–5633
www.stonemountainpark.com

From mid-November through the week after Christmas, the party is on at Stone

Mountain. Running on Friday nights through December 15 and nightly thereafter (except for Christmas Eve and Christmas Day), there are horse-drawn carriage rides, a decorated plantation home, Christmas music, and a holiday laser show. The guest of honor, of course, is jolly ol' St. Nick, accompanied by his merry elves. More than two million lights are strung throughout the park, and you can go on a driving tour to see all the designs. Admission is $7 per car, per day.

December

The Atlanta Ballet—*The Nutcracker*
The Fox Theatre
660 Peachtree Street NE
(404) 873-5811

The Atlanta Ballet's annual production of *The Nutcracker,* staged from early December through Christmas, has been a holiday tradition for more than 30 years. In 1994, for the first time in 10 years, the production returned to the Fox Theatre, which was the Atlanta Ballet's home for many years. (The ballet company and the movie palace share a common birth year: 1929.) The production features an orchestra, a full company of dancers, and more than 200 children. Ticket prices range from $20 to $50. Senior and children discounts are available. Tickets go on sale in the beginning of October.

Atlanta Botanical Garden Country Christmas
1345 Piedmont Avenue NE
(404) 876-5859

Since 1979, the Atlanta Botanical Garden

has presented this one-day event, which attracts more than 2,000 visitors, as its gift to the city. The event is held the first Sunday afternoon in December. The garden and conservatory are bedecked in high holiday style, and there's fun for the whole family, with face painting, dancing, other entertainment, and storytelling. Vendors sell a variety of foods, plus fresh greenery, and Santa himself pops in. There's very little parking on-site, so a free shuttle bus brings visitors from a nearby parking garage; call for the location of the garage. Admission is free.

Atlanta History Center Candlelight Tours
130 West Paces Ferry Road NW
(404) 814-4000
www.atlantahistorycenter.com

In early December, hundreds of candles illuminate acres of gardens and nature trails at the History Center in the heart of Buckhead. Traditional music and a bonfire enliven the Tullie Smith farmhouse; the grand 1928 Swan House mansion shimmers in holiday finery to the accompaniment of jazz music. Many of the center's paths are unpaved and not suitable for wheelchairs, but center personnel will gladly make arrangements for physically challenged persons. Phone ahead for assistance. Admission is $10 for adults, $4 for children 6 to 16.

Christmas at Callanwolde
980 Briarcliff Road NE
(404) 872-5338
www.callanwolde.org

The first two weeks of December, you'll find Callanwolde bedecked in holiday finery. This elaborate, 27,000-square-foot mansion was once home to the eldest son of Coca-Cola's founder; now it's operated as a fine arts center. Some 20,000 people tour the lavishly decorated home during this two-week event. A special attraction is holiday music played on the gigantic 3,752-pipe, 20,000-pound Aeolian organ, the largest of its kind still in playable condition, around which the house was built. Admission is $12 for adults and $6 for children 4 through 12.

Children's Healthcare of Atlanta Christmas Parade
Downtown Atlanta streets
(404) 325–6635
Children's Healthcare of Atlanta sponsors this annual Christmas parade through downtown Atlanta. The parade begins at 10:30 A.M. at Marietta Street and International Boulevard and continues up Peachtree Street, where it concludes at the intersection of West Peachtree and Peachtree Streets at about 12:30 P.M. Held the first Saturday morning in December, the parade features giant balloons, celebrities, bands, floats, and Santa Claus. WSB-TV 2 telecasts the parade live; WFOX 97.1 FM broadcasts it on the radio.

Festival of Trees, Festival of Lights
Georgia World Congress Center
285 International Boulevard
(404) 325–NOEL
For nine days in early December, the Georgia World Congress Center (GWCC) sparkles with more than 200 trees and holiday vignettes created by noted interior designers as a fund-raiser for Children's Healthcare of Atlanta. The kiddies can get their kicks on an antique carousel and a choo-choo train. Arts activities, shops, and entertainment complete the picture. Admission is $10 for adults, $5 for children 2 through 12 and for seniors. In 1997 a Festival of Lights became part of this event. For the month of December and into the first week of January just across the boulevard from GWCC, Centennial Olympic Park is ablaze with holiday decorations including mega-light

structures such as a 50-foot "giving" tree. Each night, school and church choirs perform. Viewing the park lights and listening to the choirs are free.

Christmas lights
Various locations
Load up the car with Grandma and the kids and see the holidays shine at several locations. Bring along some snacks and something to drink, because you will be in a parade of cars "ooing" and "ahhing" at the festive displays. Displays that charge an admission fee include Callaway Gardens in Pine Mountain, southwest of Atlanta; Georgia International Horse Park in Conyers; Lake Lanier Islands in Buford; and Château Élan in Braselton. Free car tours go through the north Georgia mountain town of Helen and the Life University campus in Marietta.

Peach Bowl Parade
Downtown Atlanta streets
(404) 586–8500
The Peach Bowl is played in the Georgia Dome around New Year's Eve each year. A big downtown parade preceding the game honors the collegiate contenders. Usually 20 to 30 high school marching bands from across the United States perform. Interspersed among floats and baton groups and old-fashioned cars are clowns and other street entertainment. The parade begins at North Avenue and West Peachtree Street, continues up Peachtree Street, and terminates at Centennial Park. For more information about the football game, see our Spectator Sports chapter.

Atlanta Rings in the New Year
Underground Atlanta
50 Upper Alabama Street
(404) 523–2311
A huge throng gathers every New Year's Eve to ring out the old and ring in the new on the plaza at Underground. Never to be outdone by the Big Apple, Atlanta drops its own enormous piece of electrified fruit (a big peach, of course!) down a tower to mark the beginning of the New Year. It's fun and free, but not for the claustrophobic.

The Arts

From the early days, Atlantans have had a taste for big-city entertainment. These days, it is no longer necessary to leave town to have the best cultural experiences. Within the last decade there has been tremendous growth in the Atlanta gallery and theater scene. In fact, an increasing number of Atlanta productions have made it successfully to off-Broadway and Broadway stages, and many of Atlanta's visual artists make fine livings right here, thank you very much.

With our ever-increasing population and our position as a rail hub, Atlanta has always been a natural stop for touring theater and opera companies, orchestras, and lecturers. Our cultural interests were evident even during the tough years of Reconstruction when the arts were becoming big business: Two new opera houses opened in 1866, less than two years after Atlanta was put to the torch.

In 1882 Oscar Wilde, the Irish poet and apostle of Aestheticism, stopped in Atlanta near the end of a very successful U.S. lecture tour. (The long-haired, then 27-year-old was so well known here that a local man, Smith Clayton, had made a name for himself impersonating Wilde in a comedy act called "Wild Oscar.") During that visit to Atlanta, Wilde urged the audience to support the arts and encourage young artists.

As years passed and the city grew, Atlantans, wearied of importing their art from elsewhere, decided to heed Wilde's urgings and formed the city's first performance companies. The Atlanta Ballet danced its inaugural season in 1929; the Atlanta Symphony Orchestra first tuned up in 1945. In the 1970s and '80s, entrepreneurial directors and their supporters boldly launched theater groups in storefronts and attics. Some of these modest efforts survived to become leading Atlanta companies with widespread reputations for innovative theater.

Today, Atlanta's position as the cultural capital of the South affords patrons an array of arts options. The presence of both traditional and experimental arts organizations means that neither the classics nor avant-garde works are neglected: A typical year's offerings include traditional Shakespeare, symphony, and grand opera as well as adult-oriented puppet theater, postmodern psychological drama, and alternative productions of well-known works.

You can find varied offerings in the visual arts, too. Besides such well-known venues as the architecturally renowned High Museum of Art, Emory University's Michael C. Carlos Museum, and the High Museum of Art's Folk Art and Photography Galleries, the city has myriad private and public galleries that show a variety of artists and styles. Traditional, primitive, and modern painting, sculpture, studio crafts, drawing, photography, and site-specific pieces are part of the smorgasbord of artistic offerings on view at any given time in our city's vibrant gallery scene. We've listed a sampling of the many fine galleries in Atlanta. The *Atlanta Journal-Constitution* has a more complete listing of galleries and exhibits in its Saturday "Living & Leisure" section. Also check *Creative Loafing*'s "Happenings" section under "Visual Arts."

We've organized this chapter into the following categories: Performing Arts, including Music, Dance, and Theater, in Atlanta and Beyond Atlanta; and Visual Arts, including Museums, Arts Centers, and Galleries, in Atlanta and Beyond Atlanta.

Call for performance dates and ticket information. Keep in mind that you save money by purchasing series or subscription tickets. We'll let you know when a group's performance venue is different than the address given after its name.

Performing Arts

Atlanta

Music and Dance

Atlanta Ballet
1400 West Peachtree Street NE
(404) 873–5811
www.atlantaballet.com

The Atlanta Ballet has been a part of the city's life since dance visionary Dorothy Moses Alexander founded it in 1929. It's the oldest continually operating dance company in America and the official State Ballet Company of Georgia. Artistic director John McFall is in his eighth season with the Atlanta Ballet, and Dan Allcott is music director.

The centerpiece of the company's production is *The Nutcracker*, the traditional dazzling, snowy production of Tchaikovsky's masterpiece staged by McFall.

Aside from his activities with the Ballet, McFall leads the Atlanta Ballet Centre for Dance Education, established in August 1996, which operates out of the Ballet's Midtown studios and satellite facility at 4279 Roswell Road in Buckhead. The Ballet Centre offers, among other things, classes in flamenco and yoga as well as instruction for children in a preprofessional program of ballet, tap, jazz, or creative movement techniques.

The Atlanta Opera

728 West Peachtree Street
(404) 355–3311
www.atlantaopera.org

Opera has long held an important place in Atlanta's cultural life. From 1910 to 1987, the city was a regular stop on the Metropolitan Opera's tour, and Atlantans were treated to such legendary vocal talents as Enrico Caruso, Geraldine Farrar, Olive Fremstad, and Birgit Nilsson. When the Met gave up touring for financial reasons in 1987, Atlanta was said to be the only city on the tour still meeting its financial obligation to the company.

Atlanta was the birthplace of the great diva Mattiwilda Dobbs. When she made her operatic debut in 1950 at age 25 at La

Insiders' Tip
Every Wednesday, *Creative Loafing,* Atlanta's best-known free paper, includes an "Arts" section that lists current and upcoming events in theater, dance, classical music, and visual arts.

Scala in Milan, Italy, the soprano was the first African American to perform in that famous opera house. Dobbs, who graduated from Spelman College, went on to sing with the Metropolitan Opera. When her nephew, Maynard Jackson, was elected Atlanta's first black mayor, Dobbs returned to Atlanta to sing at his inauguration.

Several local companies produced a variety of operas through the years; then, in 1985, the Atlanta Opera was formed. The company produces fully staged operas with an excellent chorus of local singers and principal singers from around the nation and the world. Numerous veterans of the Metropolitan Opera have appeared in recent years, including Martile Rowland, Jan Grissom, Tatiana Troyanos, Hao Jiang Tian, and Timothy Noble. The Atlanta Opera received such widespread acclaim and exceptional attendance that it added a production as well as a subscription series and a matinee series to the '97–'98 season. Ironically, though the loss of the touring Met company was thought to be a blow to the city's opera lovers, it was this cultural hole that allowed this small, struggling company to thrive.

All performances are given in the original language with English supertitles projected above the stage. Performances are held at the fabulous Fox Theatre.

The company's Atlanta Opera Studio is an educational outreach program that brings fully staged and costumed operas into schools across Georgia. To charge season or individual tickets, call the Atlanta Opera at the number listed above or call (800) 35-OPERA. Individual ticket prices range from $24 to $140.

Atlanta Symphony Orchestra
Symphony Hall, Woodruff Arts Center
1280 Peachtree Street NE
(404) 733-5000
www.atlantasymphony.org

Since its first concerts in 1945, the Atlanta Symphony Orchestra (ASO) grew from an inspired group of high school music students into a major orchestra with an international reputation. Since the 1976 release of its first commercial recording, the ASO's work has earned 14 Grammy Awards. The orchestra's renown grew steadily under the leadership of Robert Shaw, who passed the baton to Yoel Levi in 1988 after 21 years as music director. In 2000 Robert Spano, music director of the Brooklyn Philharmonic, was named to replace Levi, and Donald Runnicles, music director of the San Francisco Opera, was named principal guest conductor.

The ASO has commissioned and premiered works by Aaron Copland, Leonard Bernstein, Philip Glass, and Gian Carlo Menotti. In 1994 the Pointer Sisters headlined the ASO's Gospel Christmas concerts, which were taped and broadcast nationally on PBS.

The regular ASO season runs from September to May. The festive summer series, inaugurated in 1972, takes place under the stars in the 6,000-seat amphitheater at Chastain Park in Buckhead. This very popular series, attracting more than 150,000 patrons, has grown to include 30 concerts headlined by famous pop and country stars. All shows feature reserved tables for picnicking in style. In 2003 the Atlanta Symphony celebrated its 30th season at Chastain.

Also during the summer, watch for the orchestra's free concerts in Piedmont and other city parks. Here you'll find tens of thousands of Atlantans lounging on blankets amid flickering candles, transported by the magic of music as the heat of the day breaks and the evening cool sweeps through the park.

A variety of full- and partial-season subscription packages is offered; call the Season Ticket Office, (404) 733-4800. For tickets to orchestra concerts, call (404) 733-5000 or visit the High Museum Shop in Perimeter Mall, 4400 Ashford Dunwoody Road NE (a service charge applies). Ticket prices for individual concerts range from $15 to $90 but are reduced for family concerts and youth orchestra concerts. Public sneak preview rehearsals are held before the opening of six regular season concerts. These previews are given in Symphony Hall on the Thursday morning before the program's Thursday night premiere.

Capitol City Opera Company
1266 West Paces Ferry Road
(770) 592-4197

This local company produces traditional and modern operas at various performance venues during the year. The troupe also performs at the Michael C. Carlos Museum and in 200 schools.

Music at Emory
Glenn Memorial Auditorium
1652 North Decatur Road
Emory Performing Arts Studio
1804 North Decatur Road
(404) 727-5050
www.emory.edu/ARTS/

Emory's Flora Glenn Candler International Artists series and Music a la Carte bring Atlanta audiences international stars. Past performers have included the Academy of St. Martin in the Fields and "The Three Concertmasters," a program with three renowned violinists: Cecilia Arzewski of the Atlanta Symphony Orchestra, Martin Chalifour of the Los Angeles Symphony, and William Preucil of the Cleveland Orchestra.

Theater

7 Stages
1105 Euclid Avenue NE
(404) 523-7647
www.7stages.org

From its humble beginnings in a storefront in 1979, 7 Stages has grown into a major company operating two theaters in a former Little Five Points movie house. Risk-taking is a hallmark: An anti-Klan musical staged here in 1986 provoked the first Ku Klux Klan rally in the city in 30 years. Typical productions include experimental plays, dramas by local writers, international works, and alternative stagings of classics. The complex has a 200-seat main stage and a 90-seat black box space (entrance in the rear). A past season featured Brecht's *In the Jungle of Cities, The Burning Lake* by Celeste Miller, *The Bald Soprano* by Ionesco, The Freddie Hendricks Youth Ensemble of Atlanta in *PSALM 13,* and *Dream Boy,* adapted and directed by Eric Rosen. Ticket prices begin at $10.

The Academy Theatre
501 Means Street NW
(404) 525–4111

The Academy produces all-original works and performs before school and community groups as well as at the playhouse. Through the spring, new plays are showcased through staged readings in the New Plays series.

Offerings in the Academy's Theatre for Youth program include *Mixin' at the Mall,* a company-developed vehicle that explores conflict resolution and violence for grades six through eight, and *It's Mine, I Had It First,* an introduction to theater for children in preschool through second grade.

Actor's Express
King Plow Arts Center
887 West Marietta Street NW, Suite J-107
(404) 607–7467

Founded in 1988 in a church basement, Actor's Express has grown into one of Atlanta's most respected theater companies, led by artistic director Ware Harmon. The group got its big break in 1991 when it produced the world premiere of *The Harvey Milk Show,* a musical based on the life of the assassinated San Francisco gay rights leader. It played to sold-out audiences and was later produced in other cities. In 1997 Actor's Express stepped on some toes when it modified *Oklahoma.* The publishers and copyright holders of the Rodgers & Hammerstein work objected to the changes to the original *Okla-* *homa* script, so the director and cast had to make last-minute changes back to the original script or close the show.

A typical season includes classics, comedies, and tough psychological dramas.

Agatha's—A Taste of Mystery
693 Peachtree Street NE
(404) 875–1610

Here's where you go when you can't decide whether to have dinner or solve a murder. Agatha's is a mystery dinner theater where the audience is part of the show. When guests arrive, each is given a small assignment, such as making up goofy song lyrics or delivering a short line upon request. The plays are all originals with absurd names such as *An Affair to Dismember* and *Cat on a Hot Tin Streetcar.*

But while you're being entertained, you're also being wined and dined in high style: The evening includes a five-course meal, wine, and beverages. (Cocktails, tax, and tip are extra.) Admission is $45 per person Monday through Thursday and $55 per person on Friday, Saturday, Sunday, and holidays. Monday through Saturday seatings are at 7:30 P.M.; on Sundays the fun starts at 7:00 P.M. Agatha's is across from the Fox Theatre; call for reservations.

Alliance Theatre Company
Woodruff Arts Center
1280 Peachtree Street NE
(404) 733–5000
www.alliancetheatre.org

The Alliance's status as a company of national importance was only enhanced when the Alfred Uhry (an Atlantan by birth) play *Last Night at Ballyhoo* won a Tony in 1996. Like his *Driving Miss Daisy, Last Night* premiered in Atlanta at this Broadway-type theater in the heart of Midtown. More recently, Elton John's *Elaborate Lives,* a retelling of the classic story of Aida, was premiered at the Alliance before it was retitled and taken to Broadway.

The theater was also one of only three U.S. theaters chosen by playwright Tony Kushner to mount productions of his

Tony Award– and Pulitzer Prize–winning play *Angels in America: Millennium Approaches*.

The Alliance Theatre Company is a nonprofit, professional company that produces mainstage, studio, and children's productions. The company has historically been a vanguard for theatrical productions with world premieres including Tennessee Williams' *Tiger Tale* and Ed Gracyk's *Come Back to the Five and Dime, Jimmy Dean, Jimmy Dean.*

Seasons typically include contemporary plays, classic dramas, and musicals. Past productions included *A Question of Mercy* by David Rabe, *The Colored Museum* by George C. Wolfe, *Medea* by Euripides, Richard Kalinoski's *Beast on the Moon,* and Jon Marans' *Old Wicked Songs.*

In addition, Alliance Theatre artists bring performing art into metro Atlanta's schools throughout the year.

Season ticket holders save 45 percent off the single-ticket price. A generous ticket exchange program exists that also means you might be able to pick up a last minute exchanged ticket. There isn't a bad seat in the house, so take whatever is available. Call (404) 733–4600 for details.

Atlanta Broadway Series
659 Peachtree Street NE, Suite 900
(404) 873–4300
(800) 278–4447 (subscribers' hotline)

The Fox Theatre is the setting for the American Express Atlanta Broadway Series, which presents national touring companies in top-notch productions of Broadway hits. Recent shows included *Riverdance, Les Misérables,* and David Copperfield's *Grand Illusion* at the Atlanta Civic Center.

Tickets go on sale at the theater's box office six to eight weeks before a show opens. To charge by phone, call Ticketmaster, (404) 817–8700; a convenience charge applies.

Barking Dog Theatre
175 14th Street NE
(404) 885–1621

Barking Dog Theatre was started by two 20-something Atlanta actors as a community of apprentices who speak about life

The Fox Theatre brings some of the world's greatest concerts, musical performances, and plays to Atlanta. The ceiling gives the audience a simulated view of the night sky, complete with moving clouds and twinkling stars. PHOTO: ATLANTA CONVENTION & VISITORS BUREAU

with a collective voice that is raw, energetic, and loud. The company presents an eclectic range of works each season. One of these was *Frankie and Johnny at the Claire de Lune.*

First staged in Atlanta in 1989 by Horizon Theatre, *Frankie and Johnny* was a shocker, since Horizon staged it with two actors getting out of bed with full frontal nudity for a brief segment at curtain rise. At the time, the city solicitor's office was run by a radical conservative who was responsible for having figurative paintings of undressed female models removed from public spaces as well as railing about other "public decency" issues. We often wondered how Horizon not only made it through that show's run without being raided but mounted the production a second time in 1990.

Center for Puppetry Arts
1404 Spring Street NW
(404) 873-3391
www.puppet.org

Founded in 1978, this unusual theater and museum annually attracts more than 350,000 visitors. Housing three separate theaters and a museum featuring authentic Muppet characters plus puppets from around the world, the center is the largest facility of its kind in North America. Programs include family-oriented shows and puppet-making workshops and classes. (Read more about these programs in our Kidstuff chapter.)

The center also has two adult-oriented series: the New Direction Series, which features innovative shows by the center's company as well as national and international artists, and the Xperimental Puppetry Theater, an annual showcase for works in progress for adult audiences.

Call the above number for reservations or check the Web site for details on admission, reservations, and hours.

Georgia Shakespeare Festival
Oglethorpe University
4484 Peachtree Road NE
(404) 264-0020
www.gashakespeare.org

This festival has seen its annual atten-
dance more than double since its inaugural season in 1985. Performances are held on the campus of Oglethorpe University, whose Gothic architecture affords a fine setting for productions of Shakespeare. Originally staged in a tent, the festival now has its own $5.7 million theater. The feel of the open-air tent has been retained through the use of roll-up walls for when the evenings are pleasant. But for those typical Georgia nights rich with humidity and occasional thunderstorms, the walls will stay in place and air-conditioning will keep actors and audience blissfully comfortable.

An evening at the festival begins at 6:30 P.M. when the grounds open for picnicking. At 7:00 P.M., there's cabaret-style entertainment. Performances begin at 8:00 P.M.

Horizon Theatre Company
1083 Austin Avenue NE
(404) 584-7450
www.horizontheatre.com

Lisa and Jeff Adler have operated Horizon since 1983 out of an intimate, 185-seat theater in a rehabilitated school building at the intersection of Euclid and Austin Avenues in Little Five Points. The professional, nonprofit company's productions range from satire to drama with a special emphasis on new plays and playwrights. In addition to four mainstage productions annually, Horizon develops new writers through its New Horizons readings and cultivates new theater-lovers through its Teen Ensemble and Senior Citizens Ensemble acting and playwriting programs.

Past productions included *Abducting Hillary* by Dario Fo, Nicky Silver's *The Food Chain,* David Hare's *Racing Demon,* and *The Screened-in Porch* by Marian X.

Jewish Theatre of the South
5342 Tilly Mill Road, Dunwoody
(770) 395-2654

Jewish Theatre of the South presented its first musical in 1998 with *Hello Muddah! Hello Faddah!* The Allan Sherman Musical as well as its first production of an American Jewish theater classic, Elmer Rice's

From Great Tragedy, Great Hope

Atlanta's vibrant and thriving arts scene is a living and fitting memorial to the victims of one of the saddest events in the city's history. As part of a European tour organized by the Atlanta Art Association, 106 Atlantans boarded a chartered Air France 707 on June 3, 1962, at Orly airport in Paris. But as it taxied down the runway, the jet was unable to reach takeoff speed. The pilot tried unsuccessfully to abort, and the plane ran off the runway and exploded into flames. All 130 people on board, except three flight attendants in the tail section, were killed.

In that awful moment, Atlanta lost many of its most ardent patrons of the arts. The arts movement in the city might have died with them but for the determination of Atlantans to continue the mission for which the 106 had lost their lives. In their memory, $13 million was raised through private donations to build the Atlanta Memorial Arts Center, 1280 Peachtree Street NE, which opened in 1968.

The 10-acre arts complex was renamed the Robert W. Woodruff Arts Center in 1985 after its benefactor of the same name, an heir to the Coca-Cola fortune, but the structure that houses Symphony Hall, the Alliance Theatre, and the Atlanta College of Art retains the name Memorial Arts Building.

The Richard Meier–designed High Museum of Art opened next door in 1983 featuring a blazing white marble facade. After a quarter-century as the physical and symbolic center of the Atlanta arts scene, the much-used Memorial Arts Building needed refurbishing. A $15 million renovation program was undertaken in mid-1994 and was completed in time for the '96 Olympics. During that time, the Memorial Arts Building reception area between Symphony Hall and the Alliance Theatre was dramatically redesigned and today features two stairways that flow like outstretched arms into the lobby where, at intermission, you can buy enormous raisin or chocolate chip cookies, alcohol, coffees, or juice that must be consumed prior to returning to your seat. Displays of student artwork frequently are showcased on moveable exhibit units in this area. The building's facade was also modernized and is now more in sync, design-wise, with the look of the Meier structure next door.

On the lawn between the Memorial Arts Building and the High Museum stand two bronze sculptures; one is a striking, cigar-smoking Woodruff, the other is a casting of Rodin's L'Ombre (The Shade). It was donated by the French government in memory of the 106 Atlantans who died at Orly; their names are inscribed on black marble markers encircling the statue.

The American Institute of Architects named the High Museum of Art one of the top 10 works of American architecture of the 1980s.

PHOTO: THE HIGH MUSEUM OF ART

Counselor-at-Law. In the past, the Jewish community had attempted to create an audience for theater through the now defunct Habima, which began in the '70s under the direction of attorney/actor Howard Stopeck, but the Jewish Community Center auditorium was more like a high school stage than a professional theater. Now the theater is housed in the Morris & Rae Frank Theatre in Zaban Park.

Jomandi Productions
1444 Mayson Street NE
(404) 876–6346
www.jomandi.com

Founded in 1978, Jomandi is Georgia's oldest and largest African-American professional theater company. Jomandi has received numerous grants from prominent national arts organizations and tours more extensively than any other professional company in the Southeast. More than half its mainstage productions have been premieres; the remainder have been stage adaptations of works by established black writers. Performances are given at 14th Street Playhouse, 14th at Juniper Streets.

The Shakespeare Tavern
499 Peachtree Street NE
(404) 874–5299
www.shakespearetavern.com

Four blocks south of the Fox Theatre, this company produces the plays of Shakespeare and other classical authors. Although the setting is casual (chairs and tables for 175 people are arranged tavern-style), the productions are traditional—no need to worry that you'll find King Lear pushing a shopping cart through a post-nuclear slum. The company produces the tragedies as well as the comedies and tries hard to incorporate some of the lesser-known works.

Dine from a British pub-style menu provided by Chef for a Night catering before performances. You can buy beer, wine, coffee, tea, and soft drinks before performances and at intermission. Ticket prices range from $10 to $19.50.

Theater Emory
Mary Gray Munroe Theater
Dobbs University Center
600 Ashbury Circle
(404) 727–5050

Theater Emory has constructed a full-scale replica of an Elizabethan playhouse. Called "The Black Rose," both actors and studio audiences experience what it might have been like to go to a theater during the Elizabethan era.

Theater of the Stars
P.O. Box 11748, Atlanta 30355
(404) 252–8960

Since 1952, Theater of the Stars has brought national touring companies' shows to Atlanta. The regular season runs from June to August, and performances are given at The Fox Theatre, 660 Peachtree Street. Past presentations have included *Stomp, A Chorus Line, Les Misérables, The Music Man, Phantom of the Opera,* and *The King and I* with Hayley Mills. Having seen these same productions on Broadway, we can attest to the fact that the touring company shows are staged as glamorously and performed as diligently at ticket prices well below Big Apple fare.

Theatre Gael
14th Street Playhouse
173 14th Street
(404) 876–1138
www.theatregael.com

Theatre Gael explores Celtic culture through the plays, poetry, and music of Ireland, Scotland, and Wales. Theatre Gael has staged *Farewell the Fair Country* by Atlantan John Stephens.

Theatrical Outfit
Rialto Center for the Performing Arts
80 Forsyth Street
(404) 651–4727
www.theatricaloutfit.org

Theatrical Outfit was founded in 1976 in a space above an old laundromat in Virginia-Highland. In 1985 the company scored a big hit with a lavish production of *The Rocky Horror Picture Show* that featured soon-to-be-famous, cross-dressing Atlantan RuPaul. Now the company stages four productions a year at the 14th Street Playhouse. The Outfit's annually updated *Appalachian Christmas*, a play written by local writer Tom Key, has become an Atlanta holiday tradition.

Beyond Atlanta

Music and Theater

Spivey Hall
Clayton State College and University
5900 North Lee Street, Morrow
(770) 961–3683
www.spiveyhall.org

Fifteen miles south of Atlanta (off I-75), Clayton State College is home to what many view as the finest performance venue in the entire metro area. Since it opened in 1991, the $4.5 million Spivey Hall has won raves from critics and performers alike. Overlooking a 12-acre lake, the 398-seat hall's centerpiece is its 79-rank, 4,413-pipe Ruffatti organ.

Spivey Hall presents some 175 concerts annually, covering a broad range of musical traditions. Subscription packages let patrons choose to attend all the concerts of a certain type, such as piano, organ, or jazz, or custom-design their series with six or more concerts. In addition to guest-artist concerts, Clayton State College music students and faculty perform in the hall.

Theatre in the Square
11 Whitlock Avenue, Marietta
(770) 422–8369
www.theatreinthesquare.com

This professional company, whose 225-seat facility is housed in a former cotton warehouse, attracts the second-largest audience of any Atlanta area theater (the Alliance Theatre takes the top spot). The company found itself at the center of an international controversy in 1995 when local politicians, outraged at a risqué comedy staged here, *Lips Together, Teeth Apart*, passed Cobb County's infamous and divisive resolution condemning "the gay lifestyle." The ensuing uproar caused the Atlanta Committee for the Olympic Games to move the preliminary Olympic volleyball events Cobb County had been scheduled to host.

The theater's traditional holiday offering is *1940s Radio Hour*.

Visual Arts

Atlanta

Museums

Atlanta International Museum of Art and Design
Peachtree Center, Marquis Two
285 Peachtree Center Avenue NE
(404) 688–2467

Established in 1989, this museum celebrates the craftsmanship of the world's cultures through ethnographic, folk art, and design exhibits. It is a nonprofit educational organization supported by public and private funds. Admission is free; the museum is open Tuesday through Saturday, 11:00 A.M. to 5:00 P.M.

Clark Atlanta University Art Galleries
Trevor Arnett Hall, Clark Atlanta University
223 James P. Brawley Drive SW
(404) 880–6644

Open from 11:00 A.M. to 4:00 P.M. Tuesday through Friday and noon to 4:00 P.M. Saturday, this college art gallery has an extensive collection of African-American work. Included in the collection are examples from 20th-century masters Charles White, Jacob Lawrence, Elizabeth Catlett, Henry Ossawa Tanner, and Romare Bearden. The galleries are on the second floor. Admission is free.

The Hammonds House Galleries and Resource Center of African-American Art
503 Peeples Street SW
(404) 752–8730
www.hammondshouse.org

Housed in one of the oldest homes in historic West End, Hammonds House is the only Georgia museum dedicated to African-American fine art. What is believed to have been the first kindergarten in Atlanta once operated in one wing of this pre–Civil War home. Today the building houses a collection of more than 250 works of art, mainly by African Americans. National and local artists are represented in the collection that also includes African and Haitian works. In addition to exhibitions, Hammonds House offers lectures, classes, and a resource center for scholars (by appointment).

Admission is a $2 donation for adults and a $1 donation for children and seniors; the facility is closed to the public on Mondays. Hours are 10:00 A.M. to 6:00 P.M. Tuesday through Friday and 1:00 to 5:00 P.M. Saturday and Sunday. Hammonds House has free parking.

High Museum of Art
Woodruff Arts Center
1280 Peachtree Street NE
(404) 733–HIGH
www.high.org

When the High Museum of Art opened in its new building in October 1983, the *New York Times* called it "among the best museum structures any city has built in at least a generation." Richard Meier designed the gleaming white museum with its curved glass wall overlooking Peachtree Street. Its effect is at once both classical and ultramodern, rather like a wedding cake for the Jetsons. The $20 million High has won numerous design awards; in 1991 the American Institute of Architects named it one of the top 10 works of American architecture of the 1980s.

Inside the huge, skylit central atrium, sloping, half-circular ramps conform to the front wall's curve and climb to the top floor. You may wish to start at the top: It's fun to take the elevator all the way up, then walk through the galleries and down the ramps at your own pace. The mu-

seum's 10,000-piece permanent collection includes contemporary and classical paintings and sculpture by European and American artists plus African art, photography, and folk art. Throughout the year, selections from the permanent collection share the space with major traveling exhibitions. The museum gift shop sells exhibition catalogs, posters, and gifts.

The Visual Arts Learning Space on the main floor offers See for Yourself, an interactive computer program designed to introduce visitors to the art disciplines including color, line, composition, and light. The walls of the space are lined with art from the museum's collection, and computers, strategically spaced, have a program that illustrates an artistic element. The goal is for participants to gain comprehension of art concepts through the computer as well as the viewing of actual artifacts.

Past exhibits have included Picasso: Masterworks from the Museum of Modern Art, French Impressionists, the works of Norman Rockwell, and a well-regarded exhibit of photographs from the collection of Atlanta resident Elton John.

The High Museum is open Tuesday through Sunday 10:00 A.M. to 5:00 P.M. It's closed on Mondays and holidays. Weekday admission is $13 for adults, $10 for students with ID and persons older than 64, and $8 for youth 6 to 17. Weekend admission is $15 for adults, $12 for students and seniors. Admission is free for museum members and children younger than 6. Occasionally a special exhibition may have a surcharge but will be free to all on Thursday afternoons from 1:00 to 5:00 P.M. Special admission prices and extended hours prevail during some exhibitions.

The 135,000-square-foot High Museum of Art is part of the Robert West Woodruff Arts Center and is served by the Arts Center MARTA station. Paid parking is available in the Arts Center garage; there is limited on-street parking behind the Arts Center. You may also park on some streets in the Ansley Park neighborhood across Peachtree Street, but be sure to obey all posted regulations and cross busy Peachtree only at the pedestrian crosswalks. The least expensive and hassle-free

Fräbel Glass: An Atlanta Tradition

Without a doubt, the artist whose work is most recognized and exported from Atlanta—through gifts to dignitaries—is the glass torchwork of Hans-Godo Fräbel, a native-born German who arrived in Atlanta in 1966. Queen Elizabeth II, Margaret Thatcher, Jimmy Carter, Julia Child, Anwar Sadat, even Billy Payne (who made the Centennial Olympic Games a reality for Atlanta) have received Fräbel crystal sculptures as gifts from the City of Atlanta, the State of Georgia, or corporate entities who want something special as a commemoration of an event. In fact, you can pretty much count on sitting through a Fräbel-glass gift-giving speech whenever someone important leaves a post, visits the city, or has achieved some importance in Atlanta.

Fräbel (pronounced like table) first learned his craft at the Jena Glaswerke in Mainz, West Germany. After immigrating to Atlanta, Fräbel worked initially at Georgia Tech in the scientific glass lab and later continued his studies of glass as an art form at Georgia State and Emory Universities.

The Fräbel Studio was founded in 1968. In the European tradition, the master artist passes his talent on to apprentices who may work for years before they are considered accomplished enough to produce signature pieces.

What makes a Fräbel sculpture so popular is the fact that it is, after all, glass. Fragile, delicate glass. Secondly, his imagery is easily comprehended and offends no one: magnolia blooms, a peach (Georgia is known as the Peach State), flamingos, and dogwood blossoms are all popular motifs.

The Fräbel Studios design for any profession or sentiment (you can view President Jimmy Carter's glass donkey at the Carter Center), and not just for the rich and famous. Everyone is welcome to stop by the Buckhead gallery for a look-see and consultation. A self-guided tour of Fräbel's Buckhead atelier reveals a working studio and museum where one can experience this unique art form Fräbel calls "sculptural flamework." Seated at stations in the hot glass area, apprentices and masters work

The City of Atlanta has purchased Fräbel Studio glass gifts for visiting emperors, princesses, and prime ministers. PHOTO: FRÄBEL STUDIO

the boron glass with gas-fed torches until the glass tubing has reached a temperature high enough to be fashioned into shapes and pieces. They are then joined together into elaborate branches of trees, arms, and legs of dancers or even the semblance of reeds blowing in the wind. The next stop is the annealing ovens, where the sculptures must slowly cool until the inside and outside of the glass is all one temperature. It is here that poorly crafted pieces will explode if bubbles of air have been trapped in the glass. After six to eight hours the pieces are ready for further surface treatments. Some will be sandblasted to render areas opaque. Many pieces are then exhibited in silhouette against dark velvet in lighted cubicles in the gallery area, which is part of the tour.

Fräbel Studio apprentices spend three months learning the craft and as many as five years as journeymen doing production work in the studio. They may also produce original designs for Mr. Fräbel's consideration. Once the journeymen have achieved a certain level of originality and competence of the art, they may be considered masters themselves. If you wonder how you can tell if a work is that of the master himself or of others from the studio, just look at the bottom of a sculpture: If it is signed "FS," it is probably a production piece. Those artworks that come directly from the hands of Mr. Fräbel are signed "GF." Each of the pieces has a completion date scratched into the surface of the glass.

You don't have to plan to purchase a Fräbel piece to visit the Fräbel Studio and Gallery at 695 Antone Street NW, just off Northside Drive in Buckhead. Tour hours are from 9:00 A.M. to 6:00 P.M., Monday through Friday, and from 9:00 A.M. to 3:00 P.M. on Saturday. Call for the tour (there's a six-person limit) at (404) 351–9794.

transportation option is to take MARTA, exit at the Arts station, and simply walk across Lombardy Way to the museum. This is also the best way to get to the Atlanta Symphony, the Atlanta College of Art, and the Atlanta Theatre.

The High Cafe with Alon's basement-level eatery is open at various hours throughout the museum's hours of operation. Alon's began in Virginia-Highlands, and opened a branch across from the Fox Theatre. Alon's was asked to create a space at the museum. Visitors now get to take a break in this windowed facility munching on Alon's signature sandwiches (delicious crusty bread), soups, croissants, and muffins that look good and taste better.

High Museum of Art
Folk Art and Photography Galleries
30 John Wesley Dobbs Avenue NE
(404) 577–6940

On the ground floor of the Georgia-Pacific Center at the corner of Peachtree Street and John Wesley Dobbs Avenue, just north of Woodruff Park, the multi-

level downtown branch of the High showcases photography and folk art. Open Monday through Saturday, 10:00 A.M. to 5:00 P.M., admission is always free, and this space usually exhibits part of a collection being shown at the other facility, making it perhaps Atlanta's best and least-known arts bargain! It's open until 8:00 P.M. the first Thursday of the month. Take MARTA to the Peachtree Center station; follow the signs to the station's south exit at Ellis Street; the 51-story Georgia-Pacific Center is across Peachtree Street; the museum's main entrance is on the Dobbs Avenue side; you may also enter through the building's lobby.

Michael C. Carlos Museum
Emory University
571 South Kilgo Street NE
(404) 727–4282

Internationally acclaimed architect Michael Graves designed this 45,000-square-foot building on the quadrangle at the heart of Emory University. Finished in rose and white marble, the museum's striking design suggests a temple. Dramatic twin staircases on the building's front rise to the third level, which is adorned by three levels of columns.

The design's interpretation of ancient and classical elements is strikingly appropriate to the museum's 12,000-piece collection that, although varied, is strongest in its selection of objects from antiquity. Art and objects of daily life from ancient Egypt, Greece, Rome, Africa, and the Americas are displayed inside galleries whose proportions and features honor timeless design ideals.

Free parking is allowed on campus except where restricted or reserved; there's a small lot right behind the museum; paid parking is available in the Boisfeuillet Jones Building lot nearby. If you visit the Carlos on a weekend, you should have no trouble parking. On MARTA, take the No. 6 Emory bus (from Lindbergh or Edgewood/Candler Park stations) or the No. 36 North Decatur (from Arts Center or Avondale stations) and get off at the university's white front gate; follow the signs to the museum.

The museum is open seven days a week: Monday to Saturday 10:00 A.M. to 5:00 P.M. (except Friday until 9:00 P.M.); Sunday noon to 5:00 P.M.; it's closed on major holidays. Admission is by donation—$3 is suggested.

Robert C. Williams American Museum of Papermaking
Institute of Paper Science and Technology
500 10th Street NW
(404) 894-7840
www.ipst.edu/amp

On the outer limits of the Georgia Tech campus, this tiny museum is located on the main floor of the Institute of Paper Science and Technology. Each show lasts three months and features artifacts having to do with papermaking by hand or machine from B.C. to present times. Changing exhibitions bring in paper artists so that the entire spectrum of the paper arts from history to art to science is covered.

Hours are 9:00 A.M. to 5:00 P.M. Monday through Friday. Admission is free. The museum also holds papermaking and paper art workshops for children and adults. (For more information, see our Kidstuff chapter.)

William Breman Jewish Heritage Museum
1440 Spring Street NW
(404) 873-1661
www.thebreman.org

The Southeast's largest Jewish museum, dedicated to collecting, preserving, studying, and interpreting the history and culture of the Atlanta Jewish community, opened in June 1996. Rotating exhibits and educational programming and two core museums as well as archives and libraries distinguish the William Breman Jewish Heritage Museum.

Housed in the Atlanta Jewish Federation, the museum undertaking was made possible by a contribution from William Breman and the Atlanta Jewish Federation. A new building on Spring Street (the land itself a gift of the Selig family) was constructed just two blocks south of I-75 in Midtown adjacent to the Center for Puppetry Arts.

The first core gallery documents the Holocaust years, and the second profiles the Jews of Atlanta from 1845 to the present.

The museum also houses the Ida Pearle and Joseph Cuba Community Archives and Genealogy Center, where individual and family papers, business and organizational records, oral histories, and visual arts reveal Atlanta's Jewish history. A library with resource materials for genealogical research and archival materials including Holocaust-related books, videos, and more is available for scholars and students, and a Discovery Center with hands-on activities related to the museum's exhibitions keeps children involved.

The Lillian and A. J. Weinberg Center for Holocaust Education at the museum sponsors summer courses for teachers, exhibitions, school programs, teacher guides, and general public programs designed to heighten Holocaust awareness.

Security is tight at the William Breman Jewish Heritage Museum. Parking is free. Hours are Monday through Thursday 10:00 A.M. to 5:00 P.M., Friday 10:00 A.M. to 3:00 P.M., and Sunday 1:00 to 5:00 P.M. Admission is $6 for adults, $4 for students and seniors 62 and older. Children younger than 6 are admitted gratis if accompanied by an adult. Group rates are available.

Arts Centers and Venues

Atlanta Civic Center
395 Piedmont Avenue
(404) 658–7159
www.atlantaciviccenter.com

The center's big stage has hosted visiting Broadway spectacles such as *Miss Saigon* and *The King and I* as part of the Atlanta Broadway Series. Concerts from *Riverdance* to rock 'n' roll have filled the 4,600-seat venue, one of the city's most spacious.

Atlanta Contemporary Art Center
535 Means Street NW
(404) 688–1970
www.thecontemporary.org

Formerly known as the Nexus Contemporary Art Center, it has been a vibrant force on the Atlanta art scene since it was founded as a co-op storefront gallery in 1973. Later it occupied a former elementary school; then, in 1989, it purchased a historic warehouse complex west of Five Points. The 40,000-square-foot center houses an art book press, studios, a large gallery that presents six major exhibitions annually, and an 1,800-square-foot Performance Cafe.

Admission is free to members. General admission is $5; students and seniors pay $3. The gallery is open Tuesday through Saturday 11:00 A.M. to 5:00 P.M.

Callanwolde Fine Arts Center
980 Briarcliff Road NE
(404) 872–5338
www.callanwolde.org

Today operated as a fine arts center in a combined public/private effort, Callanwolde was originally the home of Howard Candler, the eldest son of Coca-Cola's founder. The dramatic Gothic-Tudor style mansion was designed by Henry Hornbostel, designer of Emory University, and completed in 1920. The 27,000-square-foot mansion's plan stresses openness: Almost all rooms adjoin great halls on each

floor, and the entire building is centered around a large enclosed courtyard.

In addition to details such as walnut paneling, stained glass, and delicate ceiling and fireplace reliefs, the house has an amazing feature: a 3,752-pipe, 20,000-pound Aeolian organ, the largest of its kind still in playable condition, that is audible in every room. In 1920, the new organ cost $48,200.

Callanwolde is in the elegant Druid Hills section (of *Driving Miss Daisy* fame), laid out by famed landscape architect Frederick Law Olmsted, designer of New York's Central Park. The original 27-acre estate has been reduced to 12 acres. With assistance from the federal Housing and Urban Development department and DeKalb County, a neighborhood association purchased the property in 1972 for $360,000 then turned it over to the county to maintain as an arts center.

A nonprofit foundation directs the arts programs, which include classes, performances, and exhibitions. Dance, drama, painting, photography, pottery, textiles, writing, and more are all part of Callanwolde's art offerings.

Christmas at Callanwolde is the center's most popular event: Each year during the first two weeks of December more than 20,000 visitors tour the lavishly decorated mansion and enjoy holiday music on the grand organ. (See December in our Festivals and Events chapter.)

Except for special events, admission to Callanwolde and its formal garden is free. It's open from 9:00 A.M. to 10:00 P.M. weekdays and 9:00 A.M. to 4:00 P.M. Saturday, and is closed on Sunday. The art shop is open Monday through Saturday, 11:00 A.M. to 3:30 P.M., and has ever-changing art on the walls by local artisans. The conservatory has varied hours; call (404) 872-5730 for information.

Chastain Park Amphitheater
4469 Stella Drive
(404) 733–4900
www.chastainpark.org

The Atlanta Symphony Orchestra is the most frequent part of this open-air Atlanta summer tradition, but it's not the only one. Concertgoers pack elegant picnics and settle into one of 6,000 seats to hear internationally known performing artists under the stars. One word of caution, though; "Chastain" is a slang word around town that means to go somewhere to see and be seen, where the music is most decidedly secondary.

Coca-Cola Roxy
3110 Roswell Road
(404) 233–ROXY

This intimate theater in the heart of Buckhead hosts an eclectic series of events, from rock and blues concerts to plays and even boxing matches.

Georgia Tech's Robert Ferst Center for the Arts
349 Ferst Drive NW
(404) 894–9600
www.ferstcenter.gatech.edu

On the campus of Georgia Tech, this center houses galleries, a student-run theater, and the 1,200-seat Robert Ferst Theatre, named for a benefactor who gave more than 50 years of his time, talents, and financial support to his alma mater. Between September and April, the Ferst Theatre hosts an eclectic arts series that typically includes leading artists in international and classical music, dance, and opera. Series tickets are available.

Georgia Tech's student group DramaTech presents three major productions annually plus several one-acts in the Dean James East Dull Theatre. Call (404) 894-2745 for ticket information.

Also performing at the Robert Ferst Center for the Arts at Georgia Tech is the Savoyards Musical Theatre Company. Established in 1980, the Savoyards perform Gilbert and Sullivan as well as other light opera favorites. Call (770) 565-9651 for tickets and information.

The Richards Gallery and the Westbrook Gallery, both housed at the Ferst Center, are side-by-side rooms and can be viewed easily together. The art shows are held in conjunction with performances at the center, and hours change accordingly.

Glenn Memorial Auditorium
1652 North Decatur Road, Decatur
(404) 727–5050

Music lovers pack the pews of this former church on the campus of Emory University for choral, chamber, and small-group performances throughout the year.

HiFi Buys Amphitheatre (formerly Lakewood Amphitheatre)
2002 Lakewood Way
(404) 627–9704

Located in the old Lakewood Fairgrounds on the city's southside, this venue is one of the area's premier outdoor concert sites. Musical stars of rock, country, and blues have packed the property during the warmer months.

Besides music, the fairgrounds host a monthly antiques fair.

Ichiyo Art Center
432 East Paces Ferry Road NE
(404) 233–1846, (800) 535–2263

This arts center focuses on Asian art with special emphasis on Japanese art and culture. The center offers classes for adults and children in various subjects including Chinese brush painting, Japanese cooking, origami (the Japanese art of folded paper shapes), and ikebana (Japanese floral art). Ichiyo mounts exhibits of contemporary Japanese prints and other visual arts and offers a selection of Japanese papers, calligraphy supplies, gifts, and home accessories including Noguchi lamps. Ichiyo has a mail-order catalog for paper, rubber stamps, and ikebana supplies. The center is open Monday through Saturday 10:00 A.M. to 6:00 P.M.

King Plow Arts Center
887 West Marietta Street NW
(404) 885–9933

In an amazing transformation, an antiquated, 165,000-square-foot plow factory near the waterworks in northwest Atlanta became an exciting arts center. King Plow Arts Center, whose first phase opened in 1991, now houses more than 50 tenants. These include galleries representing both fine and commercial art, artists' residential and working space, architectural and graphic design firms, the Actor's Express theater, and the Food Studio, a visually striking restaurant. King Plow's galleries host a variety of shows each year.

Throughout the center, the original brick walls are exposed and dotted here and there with old brick molds and other industrial elements that blend well with the thoughtful renovations. Call for a current listing of art shows.

Use the free valet parking since many of the lot spaces are reserved for tenants.

The Rialto Center for the Performing Arts
80 Forsyth Street
(404) 651–4727
www.rialtocenter.org

New in 1996, this state-of-the-art hall is Atlanta's newest auditorium for the performing arts. It is housed in downtown Atlanta on the site of the old Rialto, a premier movie palace complete with escalator. A declining Downtown economy in the '80s closed the old theater's doors. Georgia State University, in 1991, purchased the site, ultimately transforming it into a professionally managed performing arts complex with 900 seats. Programming includes music, dance, theater, and film to celebrate the cultural diversity and artistic excellence available in Atlanta. The Rialto season caters as much to the blue jeans crowd as to the black-tie set. A sample of the 2003–04 season's offerings includes concerts by Sonny Rollins and Dianne Reeves; "Klezmer Nutcracker" by the Shirim Klezmer Orchestra; and *Waiting for Godot.*

Robert West Woodruff Arts Center
1280 Peachtree Street NE
(404) 733–4200

This multibuilding complex houses some of the city's premier arts institutions. Home to the High Museum, the Atlanta Symphony Orchestra, the Alliance Theatre Company, and the Atlanta College of Art, the center occupies one large city block in the heart of midtown Atlanta. We detail the first three components of the center in other sections of this chapter. The Atlanta College of Art, founded in 1928, is one of the Southeast's outstanding independent art colleges. In addition to its four-year programs, the college offers community education classes. The college has its own gallery that hosts exhibitions of contemporary art and design.

The Tabernacle
152 Luckie Street
(404) 659–9022

The transformation of this abandoned Downtown Baptist church began during the 1996 Olympics when it was converted into the House of Blues concert hall, one of the hottest spots to see and be seen that summer. In 1998, after several attempts to reopen as a House of Blues, the building was reopened as a concert hall that holds 2,500. The cellar of the building is home to the Cotton Club, a nightclub that features up-and-coming musical acts. (See our Nightlife chapter.)

TULA Arts Center
75 Bennett Street NW
(404) 351–3551

TULA is at the end of the Bennett Street antiques shopping district (left off Peachtree Road just north of Piedmont Hospital). A privately developed, multiuse arts center, it houses more than 45 galleries, artists' studios, and arts-related businesses. TULA is home to IMAGE Film/Video Center, (404) 352–4225, which promotes the cinematic arts and exhibits lots of offbeat and experimental movies. Galleries at TULA include Kiang Gallery, (404) 351–5477; Lowe Gallery, (404) 352–8114; and Opus One Gallery, (404) 352–9727. Hours for the complex are 10:00 A.M. to 6:00 P.M. Monday through Saturday and noon to 6:00 P.M. Sunday.

Galleries

Aliya/Ardavin Gallery
1402 North Highland Avenue NE
(404) 892–2835
www.aliyagallery.com

Conveniently located near Mambo, one of the most popular bistros in Atlanta (see our Restaurants chapter), Aliya/Ardavin is open late to accommodate the long waits the restaurant frequently demands. Works from Canadian artists, ceramics, and glass art are featured.

Anthony Ardavin Gallery
309 East Paces Ferry Road NW, Suite 110
(404) 233–9686
www.anthonyardavingallery.com

A casting of Rodin's statue, The Shade, *was given to the Woodruff Arts Center by the French government in memory of the Orly plane crash* victims. PHOTO: WOODRUFF ARTS CENTER

This gallery specializes in young Georgia artists working in a variety of media and styles including narrative and abstract painting. Pablo Cano and Robert Sentz are two of the many artists Ardavin represents.

Bender Fine Arts
309 East Paces Ferry Road NE, Suite 140
(404) 842–1913

This gallery devotes itself to national and international artists who make strong visual impact through either scale, color, or unusual imagery. It's located in the Aaron Building, which faces North Fulton Drive.

City Gallery East
675 Ponce de Leon Avenue NE
(404) 817–7956

Operated by the city's Bureau of Cultural Affairs, the 6,000-square-foot City Gallery

East is on the first floor of the City Hall East government building. Built by Sears, Roebuck & Co., the massive redbrick structure opened in 1926 and was the retailer's Southeast catalog order center for decades. Directly across the street, the Atlanta Crackers baseball team used to play in a now-demolished stadium. (This was back in the days before major league ball came to town.) The gallery presents five major exhibitions each year spotlighting contemporary visual art. Atlanta artists are a special focus, but the gallery does not exclude the works of other U.S. and international artists.

Connell Gallery
333 Buckhead Avenue NE
(404) 261–1712

Specializing in contemporary crafts, the Connell Gallery showcases craft media art incorporating fiber, wood, jewelry, furniture, and ceramics. The gallery features well-known contemporary craft artists from all over the country.

Eclectic Electric
1393 North Highland Avenue NE
(404) 875–2840

This fun gallery features artists who work with light. With everything from sculptural lamps to bicycles-as-chandeliers, Eclectic Electric provides an illuminating (pardon the pun) artistic experience.

Fairlie Poplar Artworks
117 Luckie Street NW
(404) 221–0311

One of the first galleries in the up-and-coming Downtown Fairlie-Poplar District, this urban arts and crafts studio is more than a gallery. Besides a collection of artworks from local residents, some of whom live upstairs from the gallery, it also holds art classes for adults and children and sells artists' supplies.

Fay Gold Gallery
247 Buckhead Avenue NE
(404) 233–3843
www.faygoldgallery.com

Fay Gold taught art privately prior to opening her gallery in 1980. She changed the gallery scene in Atlanta almost single-handedly by bringing in New York artists and others who could command top dollar for their goods. Now located in a 7,000-square-foot space designed by her architect son in the heart of Buckhead, she continues to house solo exhibitions and group shows of some of the biggest names in the art world—Dale Chihuly, Tony Hernandez, John Okulick, Robert Mapplethorpe, and Horst P. Horst, to name just a few. Periodically, the work of local artists is also exhibited.

Galerie Timothy Tew
309 East Paces Ferry Road NE
(404) 869–0511
www.timothytew.com

Galerie Timothy Tew is now on East Paces Ferry, where so many other galleries are located. Artists represented include Haidee Becker, Jonathan Sobol, and Adrian Ryan.

Jackson Fine Art
3115 East Shadowlawn Avenue NE
(404) 233–3739

Specializing in 20th-century and contemporary photography, Jackson's client list includes the Metropolitan Museum of Art, the High Museum of Art, the Los Angeles County Museum of Art, Coca-Cola, Delta Airlines, and the Woodruff Foundation. The gallery's inventory includes works by Ansel Adams, Walker Evans, Edward Steichen, and Eudora Welty.

Lagerquist Gallery
3235 Paces Ferry Place NW
(404) 261–8273

Kind of hidden in a lovely, quiet pocket of exclusive shops, Lagerquist Gallery was established in 1970 and represents Henry Barnes, Beatriz Candioti, Dennis Campay, and Teena Stern, among others.

Lowe Gallery
75 Bennett Street NW, Space A-2 at TULA
(404) 352–8114

The Lowe Gallery showcases artists who play a key role in today's international art marketplace and whose works honor classical traditions while reinterpreting them.

Insiders' Tip
The High Museum of Art is named for Mrs. Joseph M. High, who donated her family's Peachtree Road home in 1926 to provide the museum's first permanent facility.

These include Andrew Saftel, Kathleen Morris, Steven Seinberg, and Udo Nöger.

Marcia Wood Gallery
1198 North Highland Avenue NE
(404) 885–1808

Marcia Wood Gallery showcases contemporary art, especially painting, although it also shows other media using narrative imagery. It represents Michael Pittari, David Baerwalde, Lynda Ray, and William Steiger, among many others.

Modern Primitive Gallery
1393 North Highland Avenue NE
(404) 892–0556
www.modernprimitive.com

Both serious collectors and curious browsers feel right at home at Modern Primitive, which offers folk, self-taught, and local art. Recent shows have been the Quilts of Gee's Bend and Folk Fest 2003.

Rolling Stone Press
Fine Print Gallery, 432 Calhoun Street NW
(404) 873–3322

A lithography atelier and fine print gallery, Rolling Stone Press is located on the border of the Georgia Tech campus. Wayne Kline, director and master printer, works with artists to make original lithographs the traditional way using Bavarian limestone. The gallery usually has four exhibitions per year, one of which is the Printmakers' Renaissance Exhibition. There are also prints on consignment in bins. Call first since Wayne is the only one in attendance.

Sandler Hudson Gallery
1831-A Peachtree Road NE
(404) 350–8480

Sandler Hudson Gallery exhibits provocative imagery in a variety of media including painting, drawing, photography, sculpture, and jewelry. Its primary focus is established contemporary artists from the Southeast.

The Signature Shop & Gallery
3267 Roswell Road
(404) 237–4426

The Signature Shop & Gallery was the creation of Blanche Reeves, who was the first in Atlanta to give fine crafts (weavings, pottery, furniture, and jewelry) a showcase. Because the Signature Shop educated patrons to the art of glass, galleries such as the Vesperman were more accepted into the local art scene. Many local artists got their starts in this modest space more than 35 years ago.

Solomon Projects
1037 Monroe Drive NE
(404) 875–7100

Nancy Solomon's gallery focuses on international contemporary art. Solomon, an art history graduate of Barnard College, grew up in France and Switzerland and has worked in galleries in London, Paris, and New York. The gallery emphasizes conceptual painting, sculpture, video installation, and experimental art.

Trinity Arts Group
315 East Paces Ferry Road NE
(404) 237–0370

Trinity Arts Group carries a range of works from blue-chip investment art-works on paper by such luminaries as Picasso, Chagall, Rembrandt, and Toulouse-Lautrec to contemporary painting, sculpture, and mixed-media pieces.

Vesperman Glass Gallery
309 East Paces Ferry Road
(404) 350–9698

Artists themselves, the Vesperman family opened this gallery to feature glass art exclusively. You can also buy exquisite glass bracelets, earrings, and pins at reasonable prices.

Beyond Atlanta

Museums
Marietta/Cobb Museum of Art
30 Atlanta Street, Marietta
(770) 424–8142

This museum is housed in a 1909 Greek Revival–style post office building just off the square in Marietta. Typical offerings include mainstream exhibitions of American and European art from the 19th and 20th centuries and highlights from the museum's own collection of American art.

Admission is $2 for adults and $1 for seniors and students; the museum is open Tuesday through Saturday, 11:00 A.M. to 5:00 P.M.

Arts Centers
Hambidge Center
Betty's Creek Road, Dillard
(706) 746–5718
www.hambidge.org

Experience the beauty of the Blue Ridge Mountains in north Georgia as you wend your way to Hambidge Center for the annual Jugtown Pottery Show in June and/or the Southern Folk Expressions exhibit in July. Throughout the year nature walks or any number of other delightful exhibitions of local arts and crafts are staged in Georgia's only residential center for creative arts. Founded by Mary Crovatt Hambidge in 1934, the center offers artists' studios situated within the 600 acres of meadows, streams, and woodlands. Approximately 90 fellowships are awarded each year and at any time up to eight artists staying as long as two months will be in attendance at the center. Artists pay $125 per week for a private cottage with kitchen and five vegetarian meals per week.

Hambidge Center is located about 3 miles off GA 441. Admission is free to the gallery, which is open year-round. Hours are 10:00 A.M. to 4:00 P.M. Monday through Saturday.

Hudgens Center for the Arts
6400 Sugarloaf Parkway, Duluth
(770) 623–6002
www.artsgwinnett.org

The Gwinnett Council for the Arts is a nonprofit organization that owns and operates the Jacqueline Casey Hudgens Center for the Arts through contributions from private patrons, corporations, and foundations. Art exhibitions are presented in four areas, and the permanent collection holds works by Picasso and Kandinsky, among others.

Admission is $3 for adults and $2 for students and seniors. Members and children younger than 6 are admitted for free.

Galleries

Heaven Blue Rose
934 Canton Street, Roswell
(770) 642–7380

Heaven Blue Rose, a contemporary cooperative gallery, takes its name from a group Marc Chagall belonged to in 1907. Run by five visual artists, the gallery features contemporary works in diverse media and subject areas. Since the gallery is artist-run, customers can meet at least one of the artists whenever they come in to shop.

Raiford Gallery
1169 Canton Street, Roswell
(770) 645–2050

Judy Raiford, herself a jeweler, has for years offered her home just prior to Christmas to other artists wishing to reach the affluent residents of Roswell seeking unique holiday gifts. With the opening of a formal gallery, these very same artisans and others now have a much needed location in Roswell from which to vend on a daily basis. The Raiford Gallery, a two-story studio north of the city's historic square, was built out of timber frame and is quite unusual. In 9,000 square feet the gallery has room for delicate custom silver necklaces as well as enormous wood carvings, and the range in styles and media reflects the scale of the new exhibition space.

Studio 211
770 County Line–Auburn Road, Winder
(770) 867–4736
www.studiointhewood.com

This gallery offers art, custom framing, and art lessons. The art on display includes works by owners Jann Boxx and Kathy Walters as well as other regional and international artists. To reach Studio 211, take exit 48 off I-85 North, then go south on GA 211.

V. Reed Gallery
4475 Roswell Road, Suite 1000, Marietta
(770) 971–2733

V. Reed Gallery showcases colorful, whimsical works by more than 400 artists. The gallery features an eclectic selection of hand-blown glass, metal and painted furniture, sculpture, ceramics, fine art, handcrafted jewelry, and book art. V. Reed represents more than 200 local artists.

Parks and Recreation

One of the first things visitors and residents alike notice when they fly into Atlanta is that we live in a forest. Trees are everywhere, a characteristic that distinguishes us from most urban areas. Local governments are so protective of our tree canopy that local ordinances require a permit to cut down a tree, and trees that are removed must be replaced.

Trees Atlanta, a nonprofit volunteer advocacy organization, is dedicated to tree conservation and planting. Since it began in 1984, Trees Atlanta has planted more than 15,000 trees along Atlanta's streets and highways. The city has a tree replacement program, providing red maples, redbuds, dogwoods, and crape myrtles to be planted along the right-of-way on city streets. The city plants these trees on request on a first-come, first-served basis. For more information, call the city forester's office, (404) 817-6754.

With our beautiful landscape of rolling hills and abundant greenery beckoning, it's a shame to stay indoors—and few Atlantans do. If you're into boardsailing, bicycling, tennis, soccer, or even paintball, you'll find places to play and people to share your enthusiasm. We've presented a sampling of the leagues, clubs, networks, and facilities available for various sports and hobbies. Not everybody loves being outside and—let's face it—sometimes it does rain, so we've included some indoor sports as well.

For more information on sports clubs and events, pick up a copy of *Sports & Fitness*, a free monthly magazine available at General Nutrition Center stores, various sports shoe stores, fitness centers, and bookstores. In addition to informative articles, the magazine runs an extensive listing of sports events and organizations and has an event hotline, (404) 843-2257. Another good source of information about sports groups and events is the *Atlanta Journal-Constitution*'s "Atlanta at Play" section. It includes listings of clubs, events, and lessons and appears on the first Thursday of the month. Also, the free weekly newspaper, *Creative Loafing*, lists sports events in the "Happenings" section under "Sports and Recreation."

Information about parks in the city of Atlanta can be obtained by calling the Bureau of Parks, 675 Ponce de Leon Avenue, at (404) 817-7644. City parks are open from sunrise to sunset. In addition, all the metro counties and smaller cities operate popular parks. Three of the biggest area parks are operated by the state and federal governments: Stone Mountain in DeKalb County, the Chattahoochee River National Recreation Area in Fulton and Cobb Counties, and Kennesaw Mountain National Battlefield Park. For information, see our chapter on Attractions. Nearby or within an easy drive are numerous state parks, many of them in the lush north Georgia mountains, and the Chattahoochee National Forest. Out a ways, the U.S. Army Corps of Engineers oversees two of the most popular lakes in the Southeast: Lake Sidney Lanier in Hall, Forsyth, and Dawson Counties, and Lake Allatoona in Cobb, Cherokee, and Bartow Counties.

You can hardly throw a stick in this town and not have it land in a park. In this chapter we mention some of the area's most popular parks that offer great spots to spread out a blanket and read or have a picnic. Some have walking and running trails or bike paths. But keep your eyes open; appealing green spaces pop up everywhere.

A word of warning to those from colder climes: Atlanta can get very hot, and besides lots of friendly residents, our city plays host to hordes of hungry bugs. Wise outdoor revelers will use sunscreen and insect repellent to ensure comfortable, itch- and pain-free good times in Atlanta's great outdoors.

Parks and Other Green Spaces

Agnes Scott College Tree Tour
141 East College Avenue, Decatur
(404) 471-6285
www.agnesscott.edu

This college, founded in 1859, has a lovely campus with many trees more than a century old. The college offers a booklet for self-guided tours of its unique tree heritage that includes protected old trees as well as new plantings. Southern magnolias, an incense cedar, sawtooth oaks, and a white ash predating the Civil War are among the trees on this tour. With seven days' notice, the college provides guided tree tours for groups of 10 to 30 people.

Chastain Memorial Park
140 West Wieuca Road
(404) 851-1273

About 8 miles north of downtown, the irregularly shaped Chastain is bounded by three main roads: West Wieuca Road, Powers Ferry Road, and Lake Forrest Drive. For more than 40 years, this multipurpose park has provided respite from city life.

Chastain has a 3.5-mile jogging trail, a gym, and athletic fields for softball, soccer, football, and baseball. The park also boasts picnic and playground areas plus a swimming pool. Chastain Arts Center and Gallery holds exhibits and classes regularly. The tennis facilities are the site of Atlanta Lawn Tennis Association tournaments, and the public golf course remains a popular draw.

The amphitheater seats more than 6,000 patrons. Here Atlantans revel in various entertainments, including symphony concerts, theater productions, and performances by popular musical acts. On most balmy summer evenings, Atlantans pack an elegant picnic dinner and head for Chastain to enjoy an evening under the stars.

You'll find parking lots near the ball fields and the amphitheater. Some street parking is permitted along West Wieuca Road. Or you can leave your car and take the No. 38 Chastain Park bus from the Lindbergh MARTA station.

Chattahoochee Nature Center
9135 Willeo Road, Roswell
(770) 992-2055
www.chattnaturecenter.com

We've described this center in our Attractions and Kidstuff chapters. We mention it again here because the center has two trails that allow hikers to explore different environments. The woodland trail meanders through the forest near the river, which abounds with oak, hickory, and evergreen trees and supports such wildlife as hawks, jays, woodpeckers, and raccoons. The wetlands trail has a boardwalk that winds through Redwing Marsh, a habitat for beavers, muskrats, ducks, geese, red-winged blackbirds, and kingfishers. Hike the trails Monday through Saturday, 9:00 A.M. to 5:00 P.M., and Sunday, noon to 5:00 P.M. Admission is $3 for adults, $1 for children and seniors.

Chattahoochee River National Recreation Area
1978 Island Ford Parkway, Dunwoody
(770) 399-8070
www.nps.gov/chat

This recreation area offers more than 50 miles of trails divided into 16 land units that stretch along 48 miles of the Chattahoochee River's shoreline from Cobb Parkway on the west side of town to Buford Dam on Lake Lanier in the east. All the units offer scenic views of the river and surrounding forests; many also offer

> ## Insiders' Tip
> Chastain Park hosts both Atlanta Symphony Orchestra concerts and performances by well-known performers in a pleasant, outdoor venue perfect for relaxing in on warm summer nights.

fishing and rafting opportunities. In local lingo, rafting or canoeing down the Chattahoochee is known as "shooting the 'Hooch." The area has a 3.1-mile fitness trail beginning at the Cochran Shoals unit off I-285 at Powers Ferry Road, complete with exercise stations. This trail is suitable for walking, jogging, and biking. The trails vary in levels of difficulty; the park staff will advise you on which ones suit your needs and abilities. At Sope Creek off Paper Mill Road in East Cobb and Vickery Creek in Roswell, you can explore the ruins of old mills. Throughout the recreation area, you will observe an array of plant life and wildlife and maybe even get in some people-watching at the more popular units. Parking permits at the various recreation sites are $2 per car. The park is open daily, dawn to dusk.

Grant Park
840 Cherokee Avenue SE
(404) 624-0697

Historic Grant Park is about 2 miles southeast of downtown. Take I-20, get off at the Boulevard exit, go south to Sydney Street, west to Cherokee Avenue, then south to the park entrance.

Loaded with history, Grant Park was once home to Creek Indians. Part of the outer defense belt of fortifications guarding Atlanta from the besieging Union army ran through this area (and a small artillery redoubt still remains—the only visible portion of the maze of defenses that made Atlanta the "most heavily defended city in the world" at the time).

The park was named for Lemuel Grant, a 19th-century philanthropist and former Confederate engineer who designed Atlanta's defenses against Union troops. Colonel Grant donated land for the park from his sizable estate. (All that remains today are the ruins of his house in the adjacent neighborhood.)

Grant Park's athletic fields and pavilions make it a popular relaxation spot. Various amateur leagues for football, softball, and other sports use the park's athletic facilities. Perhaps its prime attractions are Zoo Atlanta and Cyclorama (see our Attractions chapter). Nearby you'll find Oakland Cemetery, a burial ground of famous figures such as Margaret Mitchell, author of *Gone With the Wind,* and golfing great Bobby Jones (read more about Oakland in our Attractions chapter). The area abounds in lovely old Victorian homes reflecting the neighborhood's heyday. Many have been fully restored; some are still in the process of restoration. Every September, the Grant Park Tour of Homes draws crowds to view these reminders of bygone days. Much of the area is on the National Register of Historic Places.

You can take MARTA here from several stations: Five Points, Peachtree Center, and Lindbergh. Then connect with the No. 31 Grant Park/Lindbergh bus to the park.

Insiders' Tip

Grant Park is *not* named for the Union general and later president, as frequently assumed. It is instead named in honor of Lemuel Grant, a Confederate military engineer who donated his own land for this park and who had earlier designed the defenses of Atlanta against the invading Yankee hordes. Coincidentally, the single remaining piece of his powerful defense rings can be found in his namesake park, in the form of a single artillery redoubt that has been turned into a children's playground.

A 12-pounder Napoleon Howitzer in front of Big Kennesaw Mountain. PHOTO: JOHN MCKAY

Kennesaw Mountain National Battlefield Park
905 Kennesaw Mountain Drive, Marietta
(770) 427-4686
www.nps.gov/kemo/

Sixteen miles of hiking trails take you through the 2,884-acre park in which a critical Civil War battle was fought 139 years ago. See Confederate cannon, a monument to slain Union soldiers, preserved trenchworks, and troop movement maps. If you don't care to study war, take in the beautiful mountain scenery instead. The newly built visitor center has maps for self-guided walks, and houses an excellent small museum, video presentation, and bookstore. The park is free and open daily from 8:30 A.M. to 5:00 P.M. See more about Kennesaw Mountain National Battlefield Park in our Attractions chapter.

Laurel Park
151 Manning Road, Marietta
(770) 794-5634

This public park on the west side of Marietta is popular with kids, who love to feed the ducks on the park's small lake. A 1-mile paved jogging trail winds alongside the water and through the woods, with exercise stations along the way. There are also 13 tennis courts; two covered picnic areas; basketball, volleyball, and shuffleboard courts; and a playground. The park is open daily from 6:00 A.M. to 11:00 P.M. To reserve a court or picnic pavilion, call the park office at the previously listed number.

Panola Mountain State Conservation Park
2600 GA 155, Stockbridge
(770) 389-7275

Picture Stone Mountain without the development, but with 600 acres of a preserved natural environment surrounding a 100-acre granite outcropping. The park has 6 miles of trails. You can hike the mountain trails only on scheduled hikes led by park guides, but you can take self-guided hikes on the Watershed and Rock Outcrop trails (combined length, 2 miles) adjacent to the park's Interpretive Center. Panola Mountain State Conservation Park opens at 8:00 A.M. and closes at dark daily. The nature center is open from 9:00

A.M. until 5:00 P.M. Tuesday through Friday, noon to 5:00 P.M. Saturday and Sunday. Parking is $2 per car every day except Wednesday (when it's free).

PATH Foundation
1601 West Peachtree Street NE
(404) 875–PATH (7284)
www.pathfoundation.org

Since 1991 the PATH Foundation has been building a network of greenway trails throughout the city for safe walking, bicycling, and skating. This nonprofit organization relies on support from volunteers, businesses, and government agencies. Construction has been completed on more than 60 miles of greenway trails.

PATH trails are designed not only for riding, rolling, and walking enthusiasts to use in their leisure time but also to provide quick and easy walks or bike rides to MARTA stations for commuters. Trails intersect with rail stations at West Lake, Ashby, and Vine City in the west, and East Lake, Decatur, and Avondale in the east.

The City of Atlanta, the National Parks Service, the Chattahoochee River Keeper, DeKalb County, Cobb County, and Fulton County are participating members of the PATH team. PATH membership entitles you to a quarterly newsletter, an invitation to all PATH activities, and an opportunity to participate in trail building.

Piedmont Park
Piedmont Avenue and 14th Street NE
(404) 892–0117
www.piedmontpark.org

Atlanta's largest park and home of the Atlanta Botanical Garden, Piedmont Park is the site of numerous fairs, festivals, Atlanta Symphony Orchestra concerts, and much more.

In this 185-acre setting, you'll find a paved jogging trail plus other trails for walking, cycling, and skating. Football and baseball games are commonplace, and softball leagues use the park's athletic fields for spring and summer competitions. Even the massive Peachtree Road Race, held each July Fourth, ends in Piedmont Park near the 10th Street entrance.

Piedmont's current happenings in no way outshine its colorful history. The land on which Piedmont Park stands was orig-

The Atlanta Botanical Garden is in the northwest corner of Piedmont Park. PHOTO: THOMAS NESS, ABG

inally part of the Gentlemen's Driving Club (later the Piedmont Driving Club), a group whose members were the force behind Atlanta's progressive development at the end of the 1800s.

In 1895 the Cotton States and International Exposition took place in Piedmont Park. The Olmsted Brothers firm was hired to design the landscaping for the exposition; much of the park's current design dates from this period. The exposition drew close to a million visitors during its three-month duration. John Philip Sousa's band premiered "King Cotton," a march Sousa wrote especially for the event. Such luminaries as President Grover Cleveland, Booker T. Washington, and William McKinley attended the event.

After the exposition, an 1898 reunion of Confederate veterans camped on the grounds. The park was home to the Atlanta Crackers baseball team until its move, following the 1904 season, to Ponce de Leon Park, which was opposite the present City Hall East. In their day, these players were heroes and won 17 pennants, more than any pro team except the Yankees.

Piedmont Park became a public park in 1904 when the city bought the land. A few years later, the solemn unveiling of the Peace Monument at the 14th Street entrance drew respectful crowds. This work of New York sculptor Allan Newman symbolized the growing spirit of peace and reconciliation between the North and the South. It is said to have been built from funds collected mostly from Northern states.

A citizens' support group called the Piedmont Park Conservancy was formed in 1989 to support and conserve the park's natural assets through citizen volunteer efforts. This nonprofit membership sponsors guided walking tours on weekends by appointment, starting at the 12th Street entrance to the park. The group schedules regular work parties to clean and repair features of the park. In 1996, with some of the $6.5 million already donated, the Conservancy refurbished the "ladies' comfort station" as the park's visitor center. Its showpiece is an 800-square-foot mural on the barrel ceiling, depicting the variety of activities that go on in the park. For more information

Insiders' Tip

The Silver Comet Trail has become wildly popular with the area's runners and bikers, who appreciate the chance to run and ride away from Atlanta's increasingly heavily traveled roads. It will eventually connect with two other trails to provide a seamless off-road route between Alabama's Talladega Mountains near Anniston and Georgia's Stone Mountain Park east of Atlanta.

on the Conservancy, write to P.O. Box 7795, Atlanta, GA 30357, or call (404) 875-7275.

A favorite spot with strollers, the park provides slightly hilly terrain with lots of shade trees where you can stretch out to rest your weary bones. An approximately 4-mile loop trail through the park will give you a chance to take in all the scenery.

Parking around the park is limited, and during some events, it's completely prohibited. Make it easy on yourself and leave your car behind. MARTA's Midtown station is on 10th Street between Peachtree and West Peachtree. The Arts Center station is on 15th Street behind the Arts Center. There's regular bus service along Piedmont Avenue on the No. 36 North Decatur bus that travels from the Arts Center station and the Decatur station.

Silver Comet Trail
Cobb, Paulding, and Polk Counties
(404) 875-7284
Built with the cooperation of the Georgia departments of Natural Resources and

Transportation, PATH Foundation, and Cobb County, the Silver Comet Trail winds 57 miles through three counties on a former railroad bed. Bicyclists, walkers, joggers, dog walkers, and skaters—anyone without motors—enjoy the historical remains of the Silver Comet rail line as it passes through small towns and beside abundant plant life and interesting geological formations. Along the way are bridges, tunnels, forests, and farmlands. Although it is graded, only portions of the trail are paved, with other areas still packed gravel. It is wheelchair accessible.

Stone Mountain Park
U.S. Highway 78
Stone Mountain Village
(770) 498–5690, (800) 317–2006
www.stonemountainpark.com

Take a ride on Stone Mountain Park's skylift to get a closer look at Robert E. Lee, Stonewall Jackson, and Jefferson Davis.

About 16 miles east of downtown, Stone Mountain is one of the best-known Atlanta area landmarks. The centerpiece of the park is the gigantic granite outcropping on which the likenesses of Confederate heroes Jefferson Davis, Robert E. Lee, and Stonewall Jackson are carved. Recreational activities include a trail to the top of the mountain, tennis, fishing, a golf course, and a beach. Festivals are scheduled from May through December, with one of the highlights being the Scottish Highland Games, always held the third weekend in October. See listings in our Attractions chapter for information about the park and its many activities.

Sweetwater Creek State Park
Mt. Vernon Road, Lithia Springs
(770) 732–5871

About 18 miles west of downtown, Sweetwater Creek State Park features a trail leading to the ruins of the New Manchester Manufacturing Company. During the Civil War, the New Manchester textile mill supplied goods to the Confederacy. Not surprisingly, the Yankees burned it down and, as happened in Roswell, shipped the mostly women and children mill workers north out of the state. The trail goes through a forest that contains the factory ruins and the ruins of some old homesteads from the abandoned mill village, then proceeds along the banks of Sweetwater Creek to Sweetwater Falls. The half-mile walk to the falls is not an easy trek. You have to climb over boulders and up steep hills. You'll walk about 3 miles if you hike to the ruins, the falls, and back. It costs $2 per car to get into this park, which is open from 7:00 A.M. to 10:00 P.M. daily. The trails close daily at dark.

Sports Clubs

Several clubs in the metro area offer organized league play and special events for members and nonmembers, including newcomers who might want to join. It's a good way to meet people and find congenial groups who share your passion for particular sports.

Atlanta Club Sport
6040 Dawson Boulevard, Suite K, Norcross
(678) 994–0793
www.usclubsport.com

Fifteen hundred members have the chance to play in leagues devoted to ultimate Frisbee, softball, volleyball, golf, soccer, and flag football. The club offers coed and men's leagues and teams at various skill levels for certain sports. Members and nonmembers pay fees to play on teams. Members have the chance to join organized trips sponsored by the club. Annual dues are $40.

Singles Outdoor Adventures Club
2055 Mount Paran Road
(770) 242–2338
www.soa-atl.org

Singles Outdoor Adventures is an informal, nonprofit singles group with a focus on hiking. Activities include backpacking, bicycling, horseback riding, hiking, caving, rafting, and canoeing for people of all skill levels. The annual membership fee of $25 covers summer and winter parties and mailing costs for the monthly calendar of events. Potential members may attend three activities before joining. The group meets once a month; members generally get together for snacks and drinks afterward.

Astronomy

Atlanta Astronomy Club
3595 Canton Road, Suite A9-305, Marietta
(770) 621–2661
www.atlantaastronomy.org

Established in 1947, the Atlanta Astronomy Club is a group of amateur and professional astronomers that meets the third Friday of every month at White Hall on the campus of Emory University, 1380 South Oxford Road NE. In addition to general meetings, the club sponsors at least one bserving session per month at the club's observatory near Villa Rica. The observatory features a 20-inch reflector, the third-largest telescope in Georgia. Members receive the club's monthly publication, "The Focal Point," a journal containing articles by noted astronomers and notices of astronomical activities sponsored by the club and other organizations. All meetings and observing sessions are free and open to the public. Call the hotline number listed above for up-to-the minute information. The hot line answers 24 hours a day.

Automobiles

From classic cars of the 1930s to hot rods of the 1950s, Corvettes, Mustangs, or even Studebakers, there are groups in metro Atlanta that know, and love, their cars.

Besides the regular auto races at Atlanta Motor Speedway, Road Atlanta, and the rural dirt tracks, summer finds car buffs polishing their vehicles for cruise-ins and car shows in parking lots all over the metro area. Others are tuning up their engines for races and road rallies. The best place to find out what's happening or where to go is the calendar in the "Wheels" section of Friday's *Atlanta Journal-Constitution* (www.ajc.com).

Atlanta Motor Speedway
U.S. Highways 19 & 41, near Hampton
(770) 946–4211
www.atlantamotorspeedway.com

Race fans will delight in a visit to this premier facility for motor sports, which is about a 40-minute drive south of downtown Atlanta. Guided tours take you behind the scenes of the raceway, including visits to pit road, the NASCAR garage, and the victory lane where such race-car greats as Bill Elliott, A. J. Foyt, Fireball Roberts, and the late Dale Earnhardt have stood. A video in a luxurious VIP suite explains the speedway's past, present, and future, and fans can visit a statue of Richard Petty in the Richard Petty Garden.

Tours cost $5 for adults; children 7 through 18, $3; and 6 and younger, free. Groups gather on the half-hour from 9:00 A.M. to 4:30 P.M. Monday through Saturday, 1:00 to 4:30 P.M. Sunday. Groups of 15 or more need to make advance reservations. The gift shop is packed with Atlanta Motor Speedway apparel and Winston Cup racing souvenirs.

For serious drivers, the Richard Petty Driving Experience (www.racingschools.com) holds periodic courses at AMS, in addition to other major racetracks around the country. Participants get instruction and experience driving real NASCAR cars. Prices range from $450 for the rookie experience to $15,000 for the advanced course. Call (877) 463–7223 for the schedule and to enroll.

Road Atlanta Panoz Racing School
5300 Winder Highway, Braselton
(888) 282–GTRA
www.panozracingschool.com
Road race enthusiasts can take their turns around the famous Road Atlanta track, experiencing the thrills of GT racing. The Panoz Racing School, which uses the Panoz race cars built nearby, offers basic to advanced classes and hot laps, beginning at $75 for three laps and climbing to $16,000 for multiday classes.

Billiards

Fans of this sport don't have to go to dark, smoky dives to enjoy a game. Several upscale billiards establishments in the Atlanta area offer pleasant surroundings and professional equipment.

Buckhead Billiards
200 Pharr Road
(404) 237–3705
This billiards club has been voted "Number One Place to Play Pool in Atlanta" several times by *Creative Loafing*'s annual Readers' Poll. With 10 billiards tables, a full bar, and eight big-screen TVs, Buckhead Billiards draws a mixed crowd, from young people to business types. Hours vary slightly each day, but generally the place is open from 4:00 P.M. until 2:00 or 3:00 A.M. during the week, 1:00 P.M. to 3:00 A.M. Saturday, and 1:00 P.M. to 1:00 A.M. Sunday. Weekday daytime rates are $5.40 an hour; after 8:00 P.M., it's $7.20 an hour. On weekends, it's $9.60 an hour to play; after 8:00 P.M., you must be 21 or older to get in.

Dave and Buster's
2215 D&B Drive, Marietta
(770) 951–5554
4000 Venture Drive, Duluth
(770) 497–1152
www.daveandbusters.com
This multimedia entertainment complex has 15 full-length billiards tables and one official snooker table crafted in Italian slate, mahogany, and mother of pearl inlay, arranged around the square bar and dining room. Dave & Buster's is open daily at 11:30 A.M. Closing times vary per day. On Friday and Saturday, there's a $3 per person cover charge after 10:00 P.M. (See our Nightlife chapter for more information.)

Player's Billiards
2000 Powers Ferry Road, Marietta
(770) 859–9353
Thirty professional-size billiards tables surround a full-service bar in this billiards establishment. Player's has smoking and nonsmoking sections and a full line of cues and sticks. Play is $8.80 per hour at all times. Player's is open Monday through Thursday from 11:00 A.M. to 2:00 A.M.; Friday and Saturday, 11:00 A.M. to 3:00 A.M.; and Sunday, noon to 2:00 A.M.

Bi-planing

Classic Bi-Plane Rides Inc.
DeKalb-Peachtree Airport
2000 Airport Road, Chamblee
(770) 458–3633
www.biplanesoveratlanta.com
Bill Allison, owner of Classic Bi-Plane Rides Inc., will be glad to take you on a tour of Stone Mountain, Downtown, or the DeKalb-Peachtree Airport, where the firm is based. He offers flights year-round, usually on a same-day or next-day basis. The two planes he uses date from 1943. Flights range from $115 to $475, depending on destination and length. Classic Bi-Plane offers a fun and old-fashioned way to tour the city.

Boardsailing

Atlanta Boardsailing Club
2120 Berryhill Circle, Smyrna
(404) 237–1431
www.windsurfatlanta.org
The Atlanta Boardsailing Club meets the second Tuesday of each month in Buckhead. Meetings are a good source of information about instruction in this sport and where to find the best new and used equipment. The public is welcome at meetings.

Bowling

Brunswick Lanes
3835 Lawrenceville Highway, Lawrenceville
(770) 925–2000
2750 Austell Road, Marietta
(770) 435–2120
2749 Delk Road, Marietta
(770) 988–8813
6345 Spalding Drive, Norcross
(770) 840–8200
785 Old Roswell Road, Roswell
(770) 998–9437
The Atlanta-area Brunswick Lanes are most crowded in the evenings (when leagues bowl) and on rainy days (when everyone wants to get out of the house). To check on lane availability and make reservations, which are highly recommended on weekends but not necessary, call the alley of your choice before you head out. Before 6:00 P.M., you pay $2.69 per game. After 6:00 P.M., the price goes up to $4.09. Shoe rental costs $3.69 or $4.69. Call ahead to confirm hours at the specific location near you.

Express Bowling Lanes
1936 Piedmont Circle NE
(404) 874–5703
This bowling alley closes early only on Christmas Eve; the rest of the year, it's open 24 hours. Groups of 15 or more may call to make a reservation. From 9:00 A.M. to 6:00 P.M. games cost $1.95 per person. After 6:00 P.M., you'll pay $3.75 per game per person. On Friday, Saturday, and Sunday after 6:00 P.M., games are $3.50. Rent shoes for $2.50. You don't bowl but you crave the spotlight? No problem! Head for Express Lane's Sugar Daddy's lounge, where the laser karaoke machine may make you a star.

Parks and Recreation Departments

Surely some of the metro area's greatest assets are the services offered by our fine parks and recreation departments. All four counties in the following listing present programs at various skill levels for youth, adults, seniors, and the physically challenged. Complete written information, well designed for easy reading, is yours with a call to the county of your residence.

What these departments offer would fill a book in itself. Safe to say, virtually no athletic interest is left out. Fitness, music instruction, after-school tutorials, arts and crafts, and so much more are offered free or for small fees.

City of Atlanta Parks & Recreation, 675 Ponce de Leon Avenue NE.
Bureau of Recreation (information on city pools, tennis, junior golf, and other programs); (404) 817–6785.
Bureau of Parks (city park information); (404) 817–6752.
Bureau of Cultural Affairs (information on galleries, amphitheaters, and music festivals); (404) 817–6815.
Cobb County Parks & Recreation, 1792 County Farm Road, Marietta; (770) 528–8800.
DeKalb County Parks & Recreation, 1300 Commerce Drive, Decatur; (404) 371–2631.
Fulton County Parks & Recreation, 1575 Northside Drive NW; (404) 730–6200.
Gwinnett County Parks & Recreation, 75 Langley Drive, Lawrenceville; (770) 822–8840.

Camping

Georgia has 40 state park campgrounds that provide a variety of camping experiences including tent, RV, or trailer camping, walk-in camping, pioneer camping, and group camp facilities. All state campgrounds have modern comfort stations and dump sites, and many have laundries and camping supplies. Tent/RV campsites offer electrical and water hookups, cooking grills, and picnic tables. Many state parks also offer fully equipped cottages and lodges. For more information about camping in the state park system, call Georgia State Parks & Historic Sites, (770) 389-7275 or (800) 864-7275.

You can make reservations for campsites, cottages, and lodges up to 11 months before your date of arrival. We've listed the phone numbers for the state parks described below (Cloudland Canyon, Red Top Mountain, and Victoria Bryant), but you need to make reservations through the central reservation number: Locally, dial (770) 389-7275; from out of town, dial (800) 864-7275. In addition to a few state parks, we've included Stone Mountain Park and Lake Lanier Islands, both of which offer close-in camping facilities.

Cloudland Canyon Park
122 Cloudland Canyon Park Road
Rising Fawn
(706) 657-4050

Off Georgia Highway 136, 25 miles northwest of Lafayette, Cloudland is about a 1.5-hour drive from Atlanta on the western edge of Lookout Mountain. The park has 75 tent and trailer sites, 30 campsites, and 16 cottages. Although there's no lake, the park offers a swimming pool and tennis facilities. Wander the hiking trails and marvel at the scenery of this lovely park in the north Georgia mountains. The first night's deposit holds your reservation. Campsites cost $15 a night for tent sites; $17 for RVs. Cabins have two or three bedrooms and cost $85 or $115 per night. Linens, towels, and kitchen utensils are included in the cost. There's a $2 per car parking fee.

Lake Lanier Islands
6950 Holiday Road, Lake Lanier, Buford
(770) 932-7270
www.lakelanierislands.com

Lake Lanier Islands has more than 300 lakeside campsites available year-round. The campgrounds feature a fishing pier, an outdoor pavilion, laundry facilities, a store for supplies, a dump station, and a boat launch ramp. All RV sites have water and electricity; some have sewer hookups. Primitive sites are $20 per night; sites with water, electricity, and sewer hookups for tents, campers, or RVs are $26. Premier lakefront RV sites are $30 per day.

Red Top Mountain Park
653 Red Top Mountain Road SE, Cartersville
(770) 975-0055

One-and-a-half miles east of I-75 at exit 123, Red Top, on a 1,950-acre peninsula along Lake Allatoona, offers 92 tent and trailer sites for $16 to $20 per night. A 33-room lodge costs $69 per room, double occupancy, during the week, $89 on weekends. There are also 18 fully equipped cottages for $89 a night during the week, $119 on weekends. There is a seven-night minimum stay from Memorial Day through Labor Day. Cottages sleep up to eight people, and while they have no TV or phone, they do have fireplaces, decks, and grills. Adding to the pleasures are 50 picnic sites, fishing, tennis facilities, nature trails, three marinas, boat ramps, and five docks.

Stone Mountain Park Family Campground
U.S. Highway 78
Stone Mountain Village
(770) 498-5710
www.stonemountainpark.com

Just 16 miles east of Atlanta, this park's campground features more than 431 wooded lakeside camping sites as well as a supply store. You can make limited reservations subject to availability. The campground features complete RV hookups as well as rustic tent sites that rent from $23 to $38 per night. You must be 18 years or older to rent a campsite. Besides camping fees, you'll pay $7 per car to enter the park.

Victoria Bryant Park
1105 Bryant Park Road, Royston
(706) 245-6270

This park is 4 miles west of Royston off U.S. Highway 29. It offers 19 RV sites, six tent sites, and one pioneer site for $13 or $15 per night. In addition to being a well-maintained park, Victorian Bryant Park also has a lake for fishing and one fish pond reserved for campers only. You can swim in the pool, and kids can enjoy several playgrounds scattered through the park. You also can play golf or roam the nature and hiking trails.

Canoeing

There are many venues for canoeing adventures close to the city. Stone Mountain Park (listed previously under "Camping") rents canoes to boaters age 16 or older for $5 per hour with a $5 refundable deposit.

Providence Outdoor Recreation Center
13440 Providence Park Drive, Alpharetta
(770) 740-2419

At the Providence Outdoor Recreation Center, qualified instructors will guide you through daylong classes on the basics of canoeing in both moving and flat water. Providence also offers classes in map and compass reading, backpacking, rappelling, and rock climbing. Backpacking excursions take a weekend trip into the north Georgia mountains. Providence supplies the equipment, transportation, and cooking equipment. The center also offers classes in rock climbing. Rock climbing sessions are three days of classes and a full day of climbing at Sand Rock in Alabama. Call for a schedule and fees.

Climbing

Atlanta Climbing Club
(770) 621-5070
www.atlantaclimbingclub.org

If climbing up tall structures turns you on, the folks in the Atlanta Climbing Club are your kind of people. They meet at 7:00 P.M. on the first Tuesday of each month. Call the hot line for directions and more information.

Challenge Rock Climbing School
1085 Capital Club Circle NE
(404) 237-4021

Challenge offers lessons, safety instruction, and equipment as well as monthly free clinics to help you get started in rock climbing. The school teaches individuals, families, and groups. Call for schedule and fees for the one- and two-day sessions.

Cycling

When you're tired of walking, what better way to survey the scene than from the seat of a bike? You'll have lots of company. Cycling grows in popularity each year as Atlantans discover the pleasures and environmental benefits of the sport. Lots of informal groups schedule regular bike rides and welcome newcomers.

North Atlanta Road Club
2800 Canton Road NE, Marietta
(770) 422–5237

Call this club, headquartered in the Free Flite Bicycles Shop, for friendly cycling guidance. With a $30 annual membership, you get a host of goodies: a discount in the Free Flite shop in the northwest metro area of Marietta, a point system for ride participation earning more discounts, newsletters, information about practice rides, and more. The club sponsors a Free Flite ride (with food) on the first and third Saturday morning of each month and weekly practice rides on Tuesday nights. Free Flite sells a full range of bikes as well as parts, clothing, shoes, and triathlon equipment.

Southern Bicycle League
P.O. Box 88550, Atlanta 30356
(678) 418–2330
www.bikesbl.org

This cycling group, which began in 1970, is one of the largest clubs in the country, with a membership of more than 2,000 adults. The league sponsors regularly scheduled bike rides throughout the metro area; nonmembers are welcome. Pick up a copy of the organization's

---

Insiders' Tip
Whether you go whitewater tubing or hiking, your day will be a lot more comfortable if you remember the sunscreen and insect repellent.

---

monthly magazine, *Freewheelin'* ($2), in local bike shops and bookstores. It's full of safety tips, ride calendars, and directions to the best trails.

Southern Off-Road Bicycle Association
P.O. Box 671774, Marietta 30006
(770) 565–1795
www.sorba.org

The Southern Off-Road Bicycle Association sponsors organized rides every weekend during warm weather, roughly late April through summer. The monthly newsletter, *Fat Tire Times,* gives a calendar of these rides. Pick it up free at most metro area bike shops. SORBA is a nonprofit organization dedicated to off-road biking and trail maintenance. There are other chapters of the organization in Athens, Augusta, Ellijay, Gainesville, Macon, Roswell/Alpharetta, and Woodstock.

Field Hockey

Georgia Field Hockey Association
2840 Peachtree Road NE, No. 103
(404) 812–9442, (404) 636–2661
www.gfha.org

Some 175 men and women play field hockey through the association, which has teams for male, female, and children players. The above hotline number will give you current information on leagues and how to join.

Fishing

The placid art of angling requires a license. Nonresidents pay $24 for a license for the whole season. Residents pay $9 for the season. A seven-day license is $7; a one-day license is $3.50. Each of these except the one-day license also requires a $13 trout stamp for fishing in designated trout waters. Georgia fishing licenses are available in many convenient locations such as hardware stores, sports shops, bait and tackle shops, and many discount stores. Popular fishing spots in and near Atlanta include the Chattahoochee River, Lake Lanier, and Lake Allatoona.

The Georgia Wildlife Resources Division are the people who operate public fishing areas around the state. The division can provide you with information about public fishing areas, fishing regulations, and river fishing predictions. In Fulton County they can be reached at (770) 414-3333 or toll-free at (888) 748-6887.

Georgia waters hold a variety of game fish species, including many kinds of trout, bass, bream, catfish, shad, pickerel, and crappie. There is no closed season for fishing in most streams, reservoirs, lakes, and ponds in Georgia except for trout streams, which are generally open from 30 minutes before sunrise to 30 minutes after sunset from the last Saturday in March to the last day in October. Different hours exist for specific managed areas; the Wildlife Resources Division will provide detailed information about this and the special rules on bait and tackle.

Anglers from 16 to 65 years of age must have a Wildlife Managed Area stamp to fish, as well as a trout stamp attached to the Georgia fishing license when fishing in designated trout waters. The exception is the one-day license, which does not require a WMA stamp. Landowners fishing on their own property do not need a trout stamp.

Bass Pro Outdoor World
5900 Sugarloaf Parkway, Lawrenceville
(678) 847-5500
www.basspro-shops.com

This vast store is a one-stop resource for all your fishing, hunting, camping, and other outdoor needs.

Charlie's Tradin' Post
648 McDonough Boulevard SE
(404) 627-4242

Charlie's specializes in all types of fresh- and saltwater fishing equipment, with everything you need for bridge and pier fishing as well.

The Fish Hawk
279 Buckhead Avenue NE
(404) 237-3473
www.thefishhawk.com

At the venerable Fish Hawk, you can get a full line of tackle, gear, and outdoor clothing as well as specialty fly-fishing items. What's more, you'll find advice and another source for fishing licenses. As fishing fanatics know, haunts like this will likely turn up information on where the fish are biting.

Golf

Public Courses

Several municipal golf courses offer convenient locations and excellent playing conditions. Most of these courses feature greens of Bermuda grass on a rolling landscape, with rental clubs available. Many courses require you to drive a cart. Unless otherwise noted, these are 18-hole courses. The following is a representative sampling; for complete lists, call the specific locality's parks and recreation departments listed in the gray box of this chapter.

Fees listed here are subject to change; please call before heading out. For municipally owned courses, residents may be able to play for lower fees. Weekdays on the golf course means Monday through Thursday.

Cobb County

Centennial
5225 Woodstock Road, Acworth
(770) 975-1000
www.larrynelson.com/centennial/index.htm

Larry Nelson, PGA pro, designed this par 72 course. Considered one of the best daily-fee facilities, its winding creeks give golfers a challenge for their fees. These begin at $42 on weekdays, $48 on Friday, and $55 on weekends and holidays. Prices include a cart. Centennial is about a 30-minute drive from Downtown in Cherokee County.

City Club Marietta
510 Powder Springs Street, Marietta
(770) 528-GOLF (4653)

The par 71 golf course owned and run by the city of Marietta is next to the Marietta Resort and Convention Center. Junior and group golf instruction are available,

Golf courses abound in and around Atlanta. PHOTO: CHÂTEAU ÉLAN

and the facility can host corporate events. A driving range, practice greens and bunkers, pro shop, and grill are on the premises.

Weekday fees are $39, with a cart, for residents and nonresidents. Weekends and holidays are $49. Discounts are available for juniors (17 and under) and senior citizens (60 and over).

Cobblestone
4200 Nance Road, Acworth
(770) 917–5151
www.cobblestonegolf.com

This challenging, well-maintained course was designed by Ken Dye. It offers an athletic challenge as well as a tranquil setting of natural beauty. The facility has a golf shop and clubhouse. *Ga Golf News* voted Cobblestone No. 1 among Atlanta public courses for 1994, 1995, and 1997. Monday through Thursday, nine holes are $31, and it is $55 for 18 holes. Friday through Sunday, rates increase to $33.50 and $60. Several discount plans are available. Call for details. Cobblestone is about 25 minutes north of I–285 off I–75 N.

Legacy Golf Links
1825 Windy Hill Road, Smyrna
(770) 434–6331

A combination of beauty and challenge awaits you at this 18-hole course designed by Larry Nelson. Called a challenging executive course, it features sloping doglegs and rolling fairways that conceal fairway bunkers and traps. It has well-maintained Penn Links bent grass greens. A driving and practice range, a clubhouse, and a putting course are on the premises.

Rates range from $26 to $34. The redesign of the driving range was completed in February 2003.

DeKalb County
Candler Park
585 Candler Park Drive NE
(404) 371–1260

This course has nine holes and a par of 32. Fees are $9 for nine holes every day. Candler Park has a putting green, a chipping area, and offers club repair. No carts are available; no tee times are required.

Mystery Valley
6094 Shadowrock Drive, Lithonia
(770) 469–6913
www.mysteryvalley.com

This course has a championship-caliber layout that makes for a challenging round of play. Designed by Dick Wilson, the 18-hole, par 72 course had Bermuda grass fairways and greens until the past few years, when it was refurbished with bent grass. Fees with a cart begin at $28 for weekdays and go up to $35 on weekends for county residents. Mystery Valley is approximately 18 miles from downtown Atlanta.

Fulton County

Alfred Tup Holmes
2300 Wilson Drive SW
(404) 753–6158

This 18-hole course has a par score of 72. Bermuda grass greens cover the slightly hilly terrain with wooded areas nearby. Intermediate golfers find the course a pleasure. Fees for weekday play begin at $20 and rise to $29 on the weekends.

Bobby Jones

384 Woodward Way NE
(404) 355–1009

This is an 18-hole course with a par of 71. The Bermuda grass greens and fairways are popular with intermediate golfers. Weekday rates are $22 to $32 during the week, or $25 to $35 on the weekends. Prices include carts.

North Fulton Golf Course

216 West Wieuca Road NE
(404) 255–0723

The Chastain course was built in the 1940s. Its low, rolling terrain is called a championship course. The stone clubhouse, perhaps in tribute to the country synonymous with golf, is modeled after venerable structures in Scotland. Here you will find a pro shop and snack bar. Weekday fees are $20 to $30, $25 to $35 on weekends. Nonresidents pay $2 extra. Walkers take $10 off fees.

Gwinnett County

Springbrook Golf Course
585 Camp Perrin Road, Lawrenceville
(770) 822–5400

Beautiful Bermuda grass fairways with bent grass greens make this course a pleasure to view as well as to play. The links feature a clubhouse, restaurant, driving range, and putting green. Club and cart rentals are available. Other amenities in this county-operated complex include tennis courts and a pool. Weekday nonresident players pay $36; on weekends, the fee is $42, with a cart. Gwinnett residents pay $6 less.

Privately Owned Courses Open to the Public

Atlanta and the surrounding area are rich with privately owned golf courses. From the championship courses that are regular stops on the PGA, LPGA, and Seniors tours, to top courses designed by big-name pros at upscale golf course subdivisions, there are plenty of holes attracting throngs of golfers virtually all year.

Most private clubs allow members to bring guests, but many private clubs now accept daily-fee players. We can list only a small sampling of the many fine courses in the metro area. To explore new courses, pick up a copy of the locally published *Ga Golf News* (www.gagolfnews.com) or *Fore Georgia* (www.georgiapga.com), available at pro shops.

Château Élan Golf Club

6060 Golf Club Drive, Braselton
(770) 271–6050
www.chateauelan.com

At the Château Élan resort and winery (about an hour from Downtown, off I-85) you'll find two exceptional courses designed by Dennis Griffiths—par 71 and par 72, 18-hole courses. A practice facility simulates the course's challenges and prepares golfers to meet them. Also on the property is a nine-hole, par 3 executive walking course. Rates are $32 to $65 per person Monday through Thursday, $32

Golfers can test their skills on PineIsle Resort course at Lake Lanier. PHOTO: PINEISLE RESORT

to $77 per person Friday through Sunday. The rates include 18 holes of golf, cart rental, and tax. On the par 3 course, fees are $15 for nine holes and $10 for an extra nine. Rates are lower December through March. Adjoining the courses that are open to the public is the noted Legends at Château Élan private club. (See our Accommodations chapter for more information on Château Élan.)

Renaissance PineIsle Resort
9000 Holiday Road
Lake Lanier Islands, Buford
(770) 945–8921

This resort's 18-hole championship course was designed by Gary Player and Ron Kirby & Associates. Eight holes skirt Lake Lanier. *Golfweek* magazine named the course on its list of America's best in 1992 and 1994. Greens fees for 18 holes

are $54 Monday through Thursday and $59 Friday through Sunday.

Stone Mountain Golf Course
U.S. Highway 78
Stone Mountain Village
(770) 465–3278
www.stonemountainpark.com

The public is welcome at Stone Mountain Park's beautiful 36-hole course. Eighteen holes of the course were designed by expert Robert Trent Jones; the other 18, by John La Foy. Nine holes lie beside the park's lake.

There's a pro shop on the premises, with lessons and rental clubs available. The course also features a driving range, practice area, and two large putting greens. Weekends and holidays require about a week's advance reservation. Otherwise, it's first-come, first-served. You'll pay a $7 fee for each car entering the park. Stone Mountain's course is open Monday through Friday from 7:00 A.M. to dark. Eighteen holes cost $45 on weekdays, $48 on the weekends. Prices include a mandatory cart fee. Stone Mountain Golf Course also offers a five-weekend golf school. This includes five rounds of nine holes, one golf lesson per week, and unlimited range balls during the five weeks of the school. For more information, call the course number previously listed or the general information number, (770) 498–5690.

Horseback Riding

Riding enthusiasts of all ages can find plenty of riding academies and stables in the metro area. Lessons, trail rides, boarding, and an assortment of equestrian services are all available. For a list of horseback riding and boarding facilities, call the Georgia Department of Agriculture Equine Division, (404) 656–3713. We've listed two well-recommended facilities.

Lake Lanier Islands Stables
6950 Holiday Road
Lake Lanier Islands, Buford
(770) 932–7233
Enjoy horseback riding on miles of scenic

trails along the shores of Lake Lanier. This stable offers guided walking trail rides, which are great for beginners, as well as pony rides and riding lessons.

Linda's Riding School
3475 Daniels Bridge Road, Conyers
(770) 922–0184
This school and stable offers private and group horseback riding lessons for children and adults, trail riding rentals, and Saturday camp for children and adults as well as special programs, hayrides, company parties, school carnivals, and birthday parties.

Special overnight rides and moonlight rides can be arranged for groups of six or more. Call for rates and arrangements.

Ice Skating

Ice Forum
2300 Satellite Boulevard, Duluth
(770) 813–1010
3061 Busbee Parkway, Kennesaw
(770) 218–1010
These two rinks, one on the northeast and one on the northwest side of town, are open for public skating Monday through Friday, 10:00 A.M. to noon; Monday, Wednesday, and Friday, 4:00 to 6:00 P.M.; Thursday, 8:00 to 9:30 P.M.; Saturday and Sunday, sessions overlap from 1:00 to 3:00, 2:00 to 4:00, and 3:00 to 5:00 P.M. The rink is also open Friday and Saturday, 8:00 to 11:00 P.M., and Sunday from 7:00 to 9:30 P.M. Fees are $6 to $7 per person depending on the length of time the rink is open. Skate rental is $3, if needed. The rinks also provide skating instruction and hockey leagues for all ages.

Martial Arts

Aikido Center of Atlanta
116 Center Street, Avondale Estates
(404) 297–7804, (770) 449–6333
Here you can study the defensive martial art in classes seven days a week. Aikido stresses channeling energy rather than brute strength for the purpose of self-defense. Increased strength and spiritual awareness are among the aims of devotees of aikido. Monthly fees are $70 to $80; new students must commit to three months for $210.

Imperatori Family Karate Center
5290 Roswell Road NE
(404) 252–8200
This large 8,000-square-foot center houses training for men, women, and children, plus a martial arts supplies store. Nationally ranked husband-and-wife team Joey and Sheldon Imperatori teach clients discipline and self-defense techniques while increasing confidence and fitness levels. The center also offers personal trainers and fitness equipment. Costs for each course vary, so call for details.

Paintball

Wildfire Paint Ball Games
3725-C Stone Mountain Highway, Snellville
(770) 982–8180
Wildfire has a 40,000-square-foot warehouse with two indoor playing fields. One is well lighted with barrels and pallets, suitable for competition-style games such as capture the flag. The other 20,000-square-foot room has large boxes arranged in a kind of cityscape, with a Main Street that branches off into side streets and alleyways. Here, players can enjoy elimination games, capture the flag, and other paintball variations.

Wildfire has three outdoor fields: South Fulton, Gwinnett, and one in Madison, about 100 acres with four plywood townscapes, woods with both thick and thin brush, open fields and hills with 80-degree inclines. The outdoor facilities open only on certain weekends, as long as they aren't booked by a private group. The indoor paintball facility opens every day but Monday. Tuesday through Thursday hours are 1:00 to 7:00 P.M.; Friday, 1:00 to 8:00 P.M.; Saturday, noon to 8:00 P.M.; and Sunday, 1:00 to 7:00 P.M. The field opens for play at 4:00 P.M.

Wildfire has a full retail store for supplies and accessories. Indoor players average five to six games per hour; outdoors, a day might be composed of only five to eight games total. All sites charge $14 admission. Gun rental is $11. This includes 50 paint balls plus everything you need to play: mask, vest, and so on. Fees are lower on Fridays. You must be at least 10 years old to play; children younger than 18 need a waiver signed by their parents.

Racquetball

Southern Athletic Club
754 Beaver Ruin Road NW, Lilburn
(770) 923–5400

For a $15 guest fee accompanied by a member, you can play all day on one of seven courts, two of which are challenge courts. Call ahead to reserve a spot. All-inclusive membership fees run about $69 a month and include use of the outdoor pool, a volleyball court, tennis courts, basketball courts, and sundeck. Among the full club amenities are a steam room, a sauna, a whirlpool, lockers, and showers. Full workout equipment includes Body Master, free weights, Stairmasters, stationary bikes, and treadmills.

Southlake Athletic Club
1792 Mt. Zion Road, Morrow
(770) 968–1798

Eight indoor racquetball courts await you for a $15 guest fee. Southlake is a family-oriented facility with child care available. Staff includes a pro racquetball instructor. Members and guests can engage in tournaments and league play. Southlake also offers aerobics, workout equipment, free weights, an indoor track, saunas, and locker rooms. Memberships are available from $45 per month.

Rowing

The Atlanta Rowing Club
8341 Roswell Road
(770) 993–1879
www.atlantarow.org

This club's boathouse is across from the Chattahoochee River Park. The club holds novice clinics monthly from March to October.

Running and Walking

A strong case can be made that Atlanta's most popular recreation is human locomotion. When a city's track club has 10,000 members and when 50,000 participants show up on July Fourth for the world's largest 10K race, you know the place is carrying on a love affair with running and walking (and being seen doing so!).

The city's environment encourages exploration amidst the ivy-covered lawns, the towering tree canopy, and the flower-bedecked walkways. From mall strollers to competitive athletes, Atlanta offers a trail for everyone. And besides, it's a great way to meet people while you become acquainted with the city.

Indoor walking programs, jogging with your dog, runners who prefer track running, walk/runs for kids, speed runners—a program for just about everyone is listed in Atlanta Track Club's *The Wingfoot*. (See the following Atlanta Track Club entry.) Many groups welcome newcomers and sometimes finish off their workout with a meal.

For guidance in walking the city neighborhoods, read a delightfully detailed book called *Atlanta Walks*, by Ren

Insiders' Tip

Atlantans jog, bike, backpack, exercise, and play golf and tennis more than the national average, according to an *Atlanta Journal-Constitution* survey. That's not surprising—considering that our average temperature is 64.2 degrees, most of us can be outdoors almost year-round.

and Helen Davis. Published by Peachtree Publishers, the book sells for $14.95 in local bookstores. It will greatly enhance your walking experience, giving you a thorough grounding in the history and architecture of your favorite routes. You'll also want to try the jogging and walking trails in some of our abundant parks; for more information see the "Parks and Other Green Spaces" section at the beginning of this chapter.

Atlanta Track Club
3097 East Shadowlawn Avenue NE
(404) 231–9064, (404) 262–RACE
www.atlantatrackclub.org

Have questions about running and walking in the metro area? Call the Atlanta Track Club, a top-notch source. To quote directly from the club's monthly magazine, *The Wingfoot,* the club "is a nonprofit, membership organization dedicated to the promotion of health and fitness for youth and adults through programs of amateur road racing, cross country, and track and field in the spirit of fun and competition." Individual memberships are $30.

Organized in 1964, ATC has grown to more than 11,000 members and has become one of the most active clubs of its type in the country. The club promotes some 25 events each year, such as the Thanksgiving morning Atlanta Marathon and Half Marathon.

King of them all is the gigantic Peachtree Road Race, a USA Track and Field–sanctioned event limited to 50,000 runners. Thousands of spectators, armed with water guns and shouting encouragement, create an exhilarating scene along the entire route. Hundreds of volunteers support the race by handling prerace registration, staffing water stations, assisting runners in trouble, and performing dozens of other unseen but necessary tasks behind this major event.

Besides the major races, ATC sponsors low-key biweekly road races and a summer series of informal track and field meets.

Buckhead Road Runners Club
(404) 816–6299

The group meets and runs from the Athlete's Foot at Peachtree Road and Peachtree Battle on Monday evenings and Saturday mornings. It also is a sponsor of the Buckhead Sizzler 10K race.

Walking Club of Georgia
(770) 593–5817
www.walkingclubofgeorgia.com

This club sponsors weekly walks, monthly hikes, judged race walks, and other events in various locations throughout Atlanta. It also publishes a newsletter.

Sailing

Barefoot Sailing Club
(404) 256–6839
www.barefootsailingclub.com

Call the hotline number for updates on monthly meetings and club activities. The club welcomes visitors to its meetings on the fourth Monday of each month in Buckhead. Activities include races for all classes of boats and dinghies, sailing lessons, and social functions.

Lanier Sailing Academy
6920 Holiday Road, Buford
(770) 945–8810
www.laniersail.com

Beginners and more seasoned sailors benefit from instruction here, which encompasses every level from Basic Keelboat to Celestial Navigation. A daylong introduction to sailing course costs about $150 for the class and one-day boat rental. Other classes vary in price depending on number of sessions and where the sessions are held (some take place in the Caribbean). The academy also offers a sailing club, private instruction, charter cruises, and boat rentals.

Windsong Sailing Academy
3966 Secluded Circle, Lilburn
(770) 931–9151
www.windsongsail.com

With facilities on Lake Lanier and Lake Allatoona, Windsong Sailing Academy offers numerous sailing opportunities. Sponsored by the Parks & Recreation services, community adult education programs, marinas, and sailing centers throughout Cobb, DeKalb, and Gwinnett

Counties, Windsong offers affordable courses year-round at a variety of locations. You may take courses in chartering, boat purchase, and navigation, safety, weather, celestial navigation, on-board gourmet cooking, and many other topics. The basic training course costs $149.

Skating

For fast movers who still want to take in the scene, skating provides the solution for many Atlantans and visitors. Catch MARTA to the Midtown area and walk to prime skating territory in Piedmont Park. There are lots of other good skating areas in Atlanta. Skate store personnel can give you tips on fun, safe skating areas, as well as let you know how to join organized skates.

The Golden Glide Roller Skating Rink
2750 Wesley Chapel Road, Decatur
(404) 288–7773

This rink designates specific nights for special age groups, with a basic rate of $1.50 skate rental plus admission price. Tuesdays and Wednesdays are reserved for private parties. On Thursdays from 8:00 P.M. to midnight the rink is reserved for skaters older than 18; admission is $7.

Family Night is Friday from 7:30 to 11:00 P.M.; admission is $5. Family skating is also offered on Saturday afternoons from noon to 6:00 P.M. and Sunday from 3:00 to 7:00 P.M.; there's a $3.50 admission fee. Teen Night is Saturday from 7:30 to 11:30 P.M. with a $5.50 admission fee. On Adults Only Night, Sunday from 8:00 P.M. to midnight, the minimum age is 21; admission is $5.

Sparkles
4054 Jimmy Lee Smith Parkway, Hiram
(770) 943–4446
www.sparklesrollerrinks.com

This roller rink schedules frequent fundraising skates for area schools as well as birthday parties, Christian skates, family nights, adult nights, and ladies' nights. Skating lessons are given on Saturdays at $8 for all ages. Sometimes there are all-night skates, at $12 for the night. Two other Sparkles rinks are in Kennesaw and Riverdale.

Skiing

Atlanta Ski Club
6255 Barfield Road
(404) 303–1460
atlantaskiclub.org

Atlanta Ski Club is one of the largest ski clubs in the world, with approximately 3,000 members. The club sponsors extensive snow skiing programs, year-round adventure trips, and social events. Individual memberships cost $55 to join. Year-round activities include camping, hiking, white-water rafting and canoeing, hot-air ballooning, horseback riding, and windsurfing. The club hosts monthly socials at various restaurants or sports bars around the metro area.

College Park Recreation Department
3636 Main Street, College Park
(404) 669–3767

The College Park Recreation Department offers one annual ski trip to Black Mountain Ski Resort in North Carolina. The excursion is usually planned for February or March.

Skydiving

Atlanta Skydiving Center
Cedartown Airport
500 Airport Road, Cedartown
(770) 684–DIVE
www.skydivecenter.com

Located west of Atlanta, this skydiving outfit will train you and let you jump on your first day. Staffed by many skydiving world-record holders, instructors will take you up in a plane then throw you out (with a parachute, of course.) Experienced jumpers also return regularly to recapture that fabulous free-fall feeling. The cost varies with the type of jump you make. Prices are made available at (770) 684-3483.

Soccer

Soccer fans bow to no one in their enthusiasm, and Atlanta offers both kids and adults ample opportunity to indulge in the sport. Here are some examples of where to find information on league teams and other forms of play.

Georgia State Soccer Association
2323 Perimeter Park Drive
(770) 452–0505
www.GAsoccer.org

Metro Atlanta has a number of soccer leagues and two soccer seasons: fall and spring. The Georgia State Soccer Association is the place to call if you want to find a soccer league in your area for kids or adults. This is the governing body for the sport, and all soccer leagues are their affiliates. This office handles all registration, insurance, and other administrative matters for organized league play. The association also offers coaching and referee courses. The office is open Monday through Friday from 8:00 A.M. to 4:00 P.M. Registration costs vary.

Stone Mountain Youth Soccer Association
(770) 879–1123
www.smysa.org

Boys and girls from 4 to 19 enjoy the sport in this league in spring and fall. Two types of programs are offered, recreational and select, the select being the more competitive. Costs may vary with seasons.

Tophat Soccer Club
1900 Emery Street NW
(404) 351–4466
www.tophatsoccerclub.com

This is an all-girls soccer club of about 700 players in the Buckhead area of Atlanta. It is one of the highest-ranked clubs in the Southeast and is very competitive on state and national levels.

Tucker Youth Soccer Association
2803 Henderson Road, Tucker
(404) 373–1418
www.tysa.com

Approximately 1,100 players make up this club of boys and girls. Both recreational and select programs are available for fall and spring seasons.

Swimming

We may be a distance from the ocean, but there are still beaches. Atlanta Beach was the venue for Olympic beach volleyball, White Water is a fun-splashed amusement park, and crowds flock to the fun and sun at Lake Lanier Islands. (Those places are all in our Attractions chapter.) For residents and visitors alike, there is no lack of area pools. For visitors, most hotels and motels have swimming facilities (see our Accommodations chapter). Residents journey down to their local municipal pool where, for a small fee, they can splash away a summer day. Some pools have seasonal membership cards available.

Atlanta

The City of Atlanta Bureau of Parks maintains 17 outdoor swimming pools and three indoor pools. For a complete listing or the pool nearest you, call the Department of Parks & Recreation, (404) 817-6752. Outdoor pools usually offer lessons in the mornings, then open to the public until 6:00 or 7:00 P.M. After 4:30, fees are $2 for adults and $1 for children 6 through 16. Outdoor pools open in late May or early June and close in mid-August to early September. Major municipal facilities include pools at:

Chastain Memorial Park
235 West Wieuca Road NW
(404) 255–0863

Grant Park, 625 Park Avenue SE
(404) 622–3041

Piedmont Park, 400 Park Drive
(404) 892–0119

Cobb County

The Cobb County Aquatics Center, near the Cobb County Civic Center, (770) 528-8465, houses two heated pools, a diving well, a fitness room, and locker facilities. The center offers instruction, a year-round competitive swim program, public swim times, and a diving program. Two more pools in Cobb County are Sewell Park in east Cobb and Powder Springs in west Cobb. Call (770) 528-8800 for more information.

DeKalb County

The county operates 11 pools open daily during the summer months, closing each year around Labor Day. The pools are staffed by certified lifeguards. Annual passes and family discounts are offered. For information on DeKalb's pools, call (404) 371-2631.

Fulton County

Fulton County operates one pool, the Clarence Duncan Park Natatorium, outside I-285. (Other pools within the boundaries of Fulton County are operated by the City of Atlanta.) The natatorium has open swim hours every day of the week, year-round. The facility offers swim passes in three-month increments and more than a half-dozen different classes, from water safety to arthritis exercise. Hours and classes are subject to change, so call ahead to inquire. The natatorium is at 6000 Rivertown Road, Fairburn; call (770) 306-3137.

Gwinnett County

Gwinnett operates five aquatics centers, four of which are open from Memorial Day weekend to Labor Day weekend. The facility at Mountain Park in Lilburn is open year-round. Each facility offers a variety of swim lessons and classes. Season passes are available. For year-round information on schedules, costs, and hours of operation, call Mountain Park Pool, (770) 564-4650.

Tennis

Tennis is big in the metro area, as you'll see by the many city and county parks with courts. The City of Atlanta alone maintains 50 tennis court locations. And subdivisions from Peachtree City to Alpharetta boast tennis courts for residents. Most of them participate in ALTA. With our temperate weather, the heartiest of aficionados can play pretty much year-round. We'll begin with information on the organization credited with changing the tennis scene in the metro area.

Atlanta

Atlanta Lawn Tennis Association (ALTA)
6849 Peachtree Road NE
(770) 399–5788
www.altatennis.org

A solid boost to the popularity of the sport came in 1971 when ALTA began league play with 1,000 members. Today more than 77,000 individuals pay $15 a year in dues to belong to the organization.

League play is scheduled for women, men, juniors, and wheelchair competitors. ALTA also has a senior league for players older than 45. Leagues are divided according to expertise. Call ALTA's office for more information.

Bitsy Grant Tennis Center
2125 Northside Drive NW
(404) 609-7193

The city's Department of Parks and Recreation also operates the popular Bitsy Grant Tennis Center, named for the local player who became a champion. You can play on 13 outdoor clay courts (six lighted at night) and 10 outdoor hard courts (four lighted). A series of improvements is currently under way. The center also has showers, lockers, and a pro shop. USPTA-certified instructors offer lessons and clinics.

Piedmont Park Tennis Center
Piedmont Park
Piedmont Avenue and 14th Street NE
(404) 853-3461

This tennis center in Piedmont Park has 12 outdoor hard courts lighted for night play. The center includes a pro shop, stringing services, and concessions. Tennis Management, Inc., operates the facility, which also offers tennis lessons and clinics by certified instructors. Piedmont Park Tennis Center is open Monday through Friday from 10:00 A.M. to 9:00 P.M.; Saturday and Sunday, 10:00 A.M. to 6:00 P.M. The fee is $2 per person per hour before 6:00 P.M.; $2.50 per hour with lights.

Beyond Atlanta

Cobb County Parks & Recreation
(770) 528-8800

Cobb County offers several designated tennis centers with league play, partner matching, classes, tournaments, and more. For the location of the center closest to you, call Cobb County Parks & Recreation at the number above. Phone

numbers for the centers are: the Harrison Center, 2650 Shallowford Road, Marietta, (770) 591-3151; Kennworth, 4100 Highway 293, Acworth, (770) 917-5160; Sweetwater, 2447 Clay Road, Austell, (770) 819-3221; Fair Oaks, 1460 Brandon Drive, Marietta, (770) 528-8480; and Terrell Mill, 480 Terrell Mill Road, Marietta, (770) 644-2770.

DeKalb County Parks & Recreation
(404) 371-2631

Residents of DeKalb County, just east of Downtown, enjoy playing on a number of recreational tennis courts in parks throughout the county.

Three of the centers offering tennis facilities in DeKalb are the Sugar Creek Center, 2706 Bouldercrest Road, (404) 243-7149; the Blackburn Center, 3501 Ashford Dunwoody Road, (770) 451-1061; and the DeKalb Center, 1400 McConnell Drive, (404) 325-2520. Call these centers for more information on programs.

Fulton County Parks & Recreation
(404) 730-6200

Fulton County operates several tennis facilities. The North Fulton Tennis Center, 500 Abernathy Road, (404) 303-6182, has 24 lighted courts (20 hard surface and four soft courts). The Tennis Center is complete with a pro shop, showers, lockers, and a full-time teaching staff. Twice, *Tennis Digest* named North Fulton as one of the top-50 public tennis facilities in the United States. Other Fulton County tennis centers include the South Fulton Tennis Center, 5645 Mason Road, College Park, (770) 306-3059, and Burdett Tennis Center, 5975 Old Carriage Road, College Park, (770) 996-3502.

Gwinnett County Parks & Recreation
(770) 822-8840

To the northeast of the city, Gwinnett County residents flock to a beautiful tennis/golf/aquatics complex called Springbrook, 585 Camp Perrin Road, Lawrenceville, (770) 822-5400. The park offers three hard courts. See more about Springbrook golf course in the Golf section of this chapter. Six other Gwinnett

County tennis centers also offer league play, lessons, and tournaments on lighted courts.

Stone Mountain Tennis Center
U.S. Highway 78
Stone Mountain Village
(770) 465–3340
www.stonemountainpark.com

The tennis center at Stone Mountain Park's Sports Complex lets you enjoy the game on 16 lighted courts. Fees are $10 per 1.5 hours. Call for hours, which vary seasonally. And don't forget: you'll also pay $7 per car to enter the park grounds.

Ultimate Frisbee

The Atlanta Flying Disc Club
(404) 351–0914

The Atlanta Flying Disc Club focuses on perfecting the sport of ultimate Frisbee flying discs. The club has a summer league for beginners, but players at all levels find opportunities to play through AFDC. The club holds two annual tournaments. Play adheres to the "spirit of the game" philosophy, in which players respect their opponents more than they try to compete to win. Players call their own fouls—there are no referees or officials— and the emphasis is on having fun more than gaining victory. Contact AFDC in early spring for summer league information and registration forms.

White-water Rafting and Tubing

For thrills that last long after you've soaked your clothing, try your hand at white-water river rafting. Within easy distance of Atlanta, you'll find adventures galore via raft, canoe, and kayak. Closer in, you can also raft and canoe on the Chattahoochee. It's not exactly white water, but it's a fun way to spend the day.

The scenic Chattooga River, 2 to 2.5 hours northeast of the city, was the setting for the movie *Deliverance*. It's one of the last undammed white-water streams in the Southeast. You can choose your level of difficulty on a variety of rapids, but if you dare, you can tackle one of the five rapids that drops more than 70 feet. The challenge varies with the season of the year as water levels change.

You can also find watery adventure on the Ocoee, Nantahala, Nolichucky, and French Broad Rivers. The Chestatee and Etowah Rivers, like the Chattahoochee, are better suited to laid-back tubing and rafting.

Appalachian Outfitters
24 Park Street, Dahlonega
(706) 864–7117
www.canoegeorgia.com

The Appalachian Outfitters near Dahlonega, about 1.5 hours north of Atlanta, offers a couple of hours of lazy tub-

Insiders' Tip

Thirsty from all the exertion? Virgin Pure Spring Water, taken from one of the few artesian springs in the world in Ball Ground, Georgia, is truly natural spring water. Virgin water comes from a protected spring in Cherokee County that has been filtered through a confining layer of marble/dolomite, rising naturally at a constant pressure and temperature, with consistent pH and mineral content. The water is collected in an all-natural marble reservoir and then stored in stainless steel tanks. To find out how to get some, check Virgin Pure Spring Water's Web site, www.purespring.com.

ing, canoeing, and kayaking on the Chestatee and Etowah Rivers. Appalachian Outfitters is open April through September from 9:00 A.M. to 4:00 P.M. on weekends and from 10:00 A.M. to 3:00 P.M. on weekdays.

Atlanta Whitewater Club
(404) 299–3752
www.atlantawhitewater.com

If you want to find like-minded folks to share white-water experiences, call the Atlanta Whitewater Club. This group promotes white-water canoeing, kayaking, rafting, and protecting the river environment. It sponsors trips, clinics, and races for all skill levels. The club meets the first Tuesday of every month; meetings are relaxed, social, and good places to meet paddling buddies.

Nantahala Outdoor Center's Chattooga Outpost
851-A Chattooga Ridge Road
Mountain Rest, S.C.
(800) 232–7238
www.noc.com

Farther north, the Nantahala Outdoor Center's Chattooga Outpost is just across the river from Georgia's northeast corner. Twenty-five-plus years' experience underlies this employee-owned company based in Bryson City, North Carolina. The company also has an Ocoee outpost in Ocoee, Tennessee, which hosted part of the 1996 Olympics white-water competition. If you're writing for information on river trips, direct your letter to NOC's main office, 13077 Highway 19 West, Bryson City, NC 28713.

NOC offers outings on five rivers: the Nantahala, Ocoee, Chattooga, Nolichucky, and French Broad.

Southeastern Expeditions
50 Executive Park Drive South
(404) 329–0433
www.southeasternexpeditions.com

This company has organized white-water outings since 1973. Southeastern's services also include ropes challenges, overnight trips, personalized instruction, and group outings. Call for trip information and directions to the company's Chattooga outpost.

Spectator Sports

Not many cities can claim to have hosted an Olympics, five World Series, and two Super Bowls, but Atlanta has done it all since 1991—and that's just the start.

Major League baseball's 2000 All-Star Game was played in the city, and men's college basketball's Final Four will be here in 2007.

Our Atlanta Braves have had an unparalleled championship run in baseball's National League, the Atlanta Falcons went to the 1999 Super Bowl as champions of the National Football Conference, and the Atlanta Hawks regularly participate in the National Basketball Association playoffs. In 1999–2000, the Atlanta Thrashers joined the National Hockey League.

Add to that our regular menu of professional golf tour events, NASCAR races, top-flight college football and basketball, the Peach Bowl, professional tennis matches, and soccer.

When it comes to pro sports, you gotta have a win now and then to keep ticket sales high. It wasn't until 1995, however, when the Braves bested the Cleveland Indians in the World Series that an Atlanta professional team had a major win. Then in 1998, our Atlanta Falcons confounded the experts by beating "better" teams in the playoffs and earning their first trip to the Super Bowl in 1999. Although they lost the championship to the Denver Broncos, the "Dirty Birds" won the hearts of many transplant citizens who still root for their old home teams.

Things have been looking up.

In 1999 the National Hockey League returned to Atlanta with the expansion Atlanta Thrashers beginning play in the newly built Philips Arena. No, the team is not named for some renegade from World Championship Wrestling—it's named for our state bird, the brown thrasher. Joining the Thrashers in the new venue will be the Atlanta Hawks of the National Basketball Association. While the Hawks have come close a few times, they haven't won a championship since moving to Atlanta from St. Louis in 1968.

Atlanta's long march to a pro sports championship began in 1966 when it became the first city ever to acquire franchises for both professional baseball and football teams in the same year. To meet franchise deadlines, the 58,000-seat Atlanta–Fulton County Stadium was designed and built in less than 12 months. Suddenly, Atlanta was in the big leagues.

For many years, Atlanta was the only city in the South with big-league baseball, football, and basketball teams. Our teams became the "adopted" home team for millions of Southerners, many of whom seldom visit Atlanta and have never attended a game in person. These long-distance fans are fiercely loyal and follow the action as closely as folks in Atlanta.

On the other hand, Atlanta fans can be fickle and take the teams' newfound success for granted. In recent years, playoff games for the Hawks and Braves have not been sell-outs, and just a year after appearing in the Super Bowl, the Falcons had trouble selling out their home games in the Georgia Dome. With so many people coming to Atlanta from elsewhere, they often bring their old loyalties with them. Each weekend in the fall, sports bars throughout the metro area are packed with college and pro football fan clubs cheering on their favorite teams from the Midwest, South, East, or Far West.

But when we win, we know how to party. After the Braves beat the Indians in 1995, thousands filled the streets of Buckhead, where one TV reporter excitedly declared that people were "partying like wild ants." The following Monday, fans packed downtown for the Braves victory parade.

Sports enthusiasm also has a trickle-down effect. There's a scramble every spring for Little League team slots in the rapidly growing suburbs. And local golfers and tennis players jam neighborhood courses and courts to emulate the pros they can see come to town.

Atlanta also has taken its place in the world stage.

The 1996 Olympics, one of the largest staged in its history, was also the second-most-viewed Olympics (Sydney 2000 now holds that crown!), thanks to cable and TV coverage worldwide. For Atlanta, the Olympics was like a three-week street festival highlighted by all the sports you could cram into 24 hours. And we were proud that Atlantans came out looking courteous and caring. Volunteerism was at an all-time high for this Olympics that brought in guests and athletes from close to 200 countries, all requiring assistance from locals who worked almost around the clock doing everything from language translation to carrying water. We were proud that crime was kept to an all-time low, and we handled the Centennial Olympic Park bombing (where more than 100 people were injured and a young mother died) on the 10th day of the event without panic.

The world will not soon forget the image of Muhammad Ali carrying the Olympic torch. But Atlantans also recall torchbearer and Atlantan Olympic swimmer Janet Evans receiving the flame from fellow Atlantan Evander Holyfield. Olympic flag bearers Edwin Moses, Steve Lundquist, Geoff Gaberino, Dave Maggard, Benita Fitzgerald, Katrina Mc-Clain, and Mary T. Meagher-Plant were Atlanta residents.

(Note: Though correct at press time, ticket prices and policies for all sporting events are subject to change. Not all seats are available in all venues; many sections sell out to season ticket holders.)

Baseball

Atlanta Braves
755 Hank Aaron Drive
(404) 522–7630
www.atlantabravesmlb.com

Play ball! Atlanta took its first step toward the World Series and an unprecedented string of divisional championships on April 12, 1966, when major league baseball came to town. The newly relocated Milwaukee Braves brought with them future Hall of Famers Hank Aaron and Phil Niekro. In 1969 the Braves took the National League West title but lost the pennant in three games to the "Miracle" Mets.

In 1973 Hank Aaron, Dave Johnson, and Darrell Evans made the record books by each hitting more than 40 homers. Then came the big moment: On April 8, 1974, millions watched Atlanta–Fulton County Stadium as Aaron smashed his 715th home run, besting Babe Ruth's long-standing record (a moment now immortalized in a large statue outside the stadium).

While the Braves have been in Atlanta only since the mid-1960s, the franchise has a rich history. It started with the Boston Red Stockings in the 1870s and is the longest continually operating professional baseball team. During their history in Boston, the team was also known as the Pilgrims, Doves, Beaneaters, and Bees. In 1914 the "Miracle Braves" were in last place in the National League in July but went on a rampage, winning the pennant by a comfortable margin by September. In 1948 the Braves again won the National League pennant and faced the possibility of an all-Boston World Series as the crosstown Red Sox tied for the American League championship with the Cleveland Indians. However, the Red Sox lost the playoff game and the Braves, too, fell to the Tribe in the World Series.

In 1953 the team was one of the first to move west, heading for Milwaukee. There, the Braves—led by Warren Spahn, Eddie Mathews, and Hank Aaron—beat the New York Yankees in the 1957 World Series but lost a rematch the next year. But dwindling attendance in Milwaukee, just like in Boston, led the team to move again, this time to Atlanta.

Despite the championships and the stars, the stay has not always been easy.

Our brightest star shone early. In 1974 Hank Aaron broke Babe Ruth's career home run record when he launched his 715th home run over the right field wall in Atlanta–Fulton County Stadium. Aaron went on to smash 755 homers for the Braves and Milwaukee Brewers before he retired from playing baseball and returned to an executive job with the Turner organization.

Back in the early 1980s, Braves games sometimes felt more like minor-league contests. Owner Ted Turner tried a number of gimmicks, including ostrich races and managing the team himself. Attendance at games was often below 10,000; fans roamed the stadium freely and sat where they liked. But all that changed in 1982 when the Braves set a new record for the most games won (13) at the beginning of a season. Suddenly the Braves weren't a joke anymore, and Atlantans by the thousands spent their lunch hour standing in line for tickets.

Insiders' Tip

Although the Atlanta-Fulton County Stadium has been demolished and replaced by a parking lot, relics of Hank Aaron's fabulous career in the stadium have been, shall we say, retained. The retaining wall over which Aaron sailed his record-breaking home run still stands, and a spotlight illuminates an outline of the old baseball diamond.

In 1982 and 1983 Dale Murphy won back-to-back National League Most Valuable Player awards, helping the Braves capture the Western Division title in '82 and finish second in '83.

Then came the biggest shock. In 1990 the basement Braves chafed under the worst record in baseball. One year later, the amazing Braves brought the World Series to Atlanta for the first time, becoming the first team in baseball history to go from worst to first in a single season. Records were set for Atlanta wins (94) and for attendance (more than 2.1 million). In the first World Series ever played in the South, the Braves held on until the end, losing to the Minnesota Twins 1-0 in the 10th inning of game seven.

Even though the Braves lost, the city was wild with excitement. Atlanta honored the Braves with a downtown parade that drew 750,000 people—far more fans than turned out in Minneapolis to cheer the victorious Twins.

That began a series of twelve straight divisional championships, interrupted only by the strike year of 1994. First in the West Division, then in the East, the Braves had their share of runaway pennant races and those that went down to the last inning of the last game of the regular season, providing some dramatic moments along the way.

In 1992 the Braves beat the Pittsburgh Pirates in a heart-stopping, seven-game series to win the National League pennant. In the bottom of the ninth of game seven, down one run but with two runners on base, backup catcher Francisco Cabrera hit a double that scored Sid Bream sliding under the catcher's tag at the plate to win the game. The Braves became the first National League team since the 1977-78 Dodgers to win back-to-back pennants. Again, Atlanta hosted the World Series, but again the Braves came up just short, losing to the Toronto Blue Jays in six games.

More records were set in 1993 as the team won 104 games (53 on the road) and drew almost 3.9 million fans to the ballpark. Ten games behind at the All-Star break, the Braves battled back to grab the division title from the San Francisco Giants in the final game of the regular season. Atlantans were again talking World Series, but this time the honor went to the Philadelphia Phillies, who took the pennant in six games but lost the Series to the Toronto Blue Jays.

When the players' strike ended the 1994 season, the Braves were in second place in the National League East, where they had moved in the league's realignment, with a record of 68 wins and 46 losses.

In 1995, their 30th season in Atlanta, the Braves clinched the East Division, then beat the Colorado Rockies three games to one in the playoffs. The Braves swept the Cincinnati Reds for the National League championship. The Atlanta Braves' third World Series appearance got off to a good start when the team beat the American League champion Cleveland Indians in game one (3-2) and game two (4-3) in Atlanta. When the action moved to Cleveland, the Indians bounced back: They took game three (7-6), lost game four to Atlanta (5-2), and won game five (5-4). The Indians kept their dream alive until the end, but the Braves held on to win game six 1-0 and take the series four games to two.

The Braves returned to the World Series in 1996, their last year in Atlanta–Fulton County Stadium. After winning the first two games on the road against the New York Yankees, they blew a 6-0 lead in game four, eventually falling to the American League champions in six games. In 1997 and 1998 the Braves won the East Division handily, but lost first to the wild card Florida Marlins and then to the San Diego Padres in the next two National League championship series.

In 1999 the World Series finally came to Turner Field, but it wasn't easy. First, the Braves had to overcome injuries to three of their key players from the previous year, but they found new stars to go with the old ones to win more than 100 games. Third baseman and fan favorite Chipper Jones put together a career year and was rewarded with the National League's Most Valuable Player award. The Braves and the New York Mets battled down to a three-game series in Atlanta in the last month of the regular season before the Braves prevailed to win the divi-

sion. But the Mets battled back, and the rivalry renewed with intensity in the series to determine the pennant. The Braves broke out to a three games to none lead, but watched as the Mets won two games in a row. The Braves knew they had been in a fight when they wrapped up the pennant in game six in Atlanta. It was more New York in the World Series. A strong Yankee team was defending a world championship and facing the Braves for the title of Team of the Decade. The Yankees showed their power, sweeping the Braves in four games.

The Braves made the playoffs in 2000, 2001, and 2002, but they are still awaiting a return trip to the fall classic.

Turner Field
755 Hank Aaron Drive
(404) 522–7630

New definitely means better in talking about the home of the Atlanta Braves. Many baseball boosters complained bitterly about their old home, Atlanta–Fulton County Stadium, which converted to suit the needs of both baseball and football but put an unnatural distance between fans and the field.

But Turner Field, once the 1996 Olympics and the Paralympics Stadium, underwent sweeping renovations that transformed it to suit the needs of the Braves. Forty-one percent of the Olympic Stadium's 85,000 seats were eliminated, the Olympic track went to Clark Atlanta University, where it still gets a good workout, and leftover construction materials are now supporting the bleachers at a local high school. The remodeled stadium seats 49,831 fans in an environment designed exclusively for baseball.

The wonderful thing, for Atlanta taxpayers anyway, is that Turner Field, as a whopping $242.5 million project, was financed partly by money provided for the 1996 Olympics and partly by the Braves themselves. The team added $35.5 million to the reconstruction budget and got a few perks for doing so: The Braves locker room includes an artificial turf putting green so that ace pitchers, who love to play golf, get in some below-the-knee swings when they are in the mood.

Turner Field can seat close to 50,000 people. PHOTO: TURNER FIELD

Turner Field, named for media mogul and Braves owner Ted Turner, combines revered baseball traditions with the latest in modern amenities. The stadium features steel trusses and an arched masonry facade of red brick with a precast stone base. Elevators, stairs, escalators, and ramps throughout the park provide state-of-the-art vertical circulation among the ballpark's three levels.

The stadium's color scheme features the Braves' team colors of red, white, and blue, along with dark green accents, again evoking the appearance of an older, more traditional ballpark.

The stadium's lower level seats 27,663, including 3,500 in a bleacher section. The second, or club, level holds 5,372 seats, in addition to 58 private suites and three party suites. The club level is an enclosed, climate-controlled concourse with four food courts and a stadium club restaurant and bar. The upper level seats 15,608. The stadium is near Downtown, just south of where I–20 and I–75/I–85 intersect.

Dominating the view above right field is Coca-Cola's Sky Field, towered over by a giant Coke bottle constructed from baseball gear. There, kids can test their speed running the distance from a mockup home plate to first base, while their parents wait for a home run to sail the 500-plus feet into the area. The person who catches it can win $1 million.

The sky explodes with fireworks after each Braves victory, so don't leave early to beat the traffic.

The 755 Club on the club level, a restaurant overlooking left field, is open only during games for lunch and dinner and only to members and guests of the club. It's also available for banquets and functions year round. Call (404) 614–2100 for reservations. Private luxury suites are also available for rental. Call (404) 577–9100 for information.

A Boston firm designed the entertainment complex that is meant to bring in the crowds much earlier than the start of the Braves' game—the goal being to not only get folks to spend money but also to develop a new generation of baseball fans who can play interactive games, visit a museum about baseball, enjoy murals of some of the Braves heroes, and party in the huge plaza at the main gates.

At Turner Field, which is called a "baseball theme park," you get to play as well as watch: There are batting games, electronic kiosks to check out the Braves Internet home page, TVs in the team store that show other major league games in action, and an air-conditioned kids' corner called Tooner Field. You can select from a vast variety of foodstuffs vended by more counters than you'll find at the local mall.

The Braves Museum, which is run by the Atlanta History Center, features memorabilia and interesting tidbits about the team and players as well as the old railroad car used by the Boston and Milwaukee Braves during the '50s. Hank Aaron's bat and ball are there, too. The museum ticket costs $4. It's closed on game days but is open 10:00 A.M. to 2:00 P.M. when the Braves are playing nights or away games. Call (404) 614–2311 for specifics.

A behind-the-scenes tour of Turner Field includes the dugout, broadcast booths, press boxes, and suites, even the Atlanta Braves clubhouse. You can play some of the interactive games that line the breezeways and test your baseball skills. The tour is $8 for adults, $4 for children, and toddlers younger than 3 go free. When the team's in town, tours are given only in the mornings from 9:30 A.M. to noon. You can take a picnic lunch with you, by the way. It's best to call ahead, since hours depend on the team schedule. Dial (404) 614–2311 for specifics.

Turner Field is the Braves' second home in Atlanta.

In 1997 the Braves said good-bye to Atlanta–Fulton County Stadium, their home of 31 years and at one time the pride of Atlanta and the South. It was the site of countless Braves memories, including Hank Aaron's record-breaking 715th home run, the team's first world championship, and three other World Series. It also was home to the National Football League's Atlanta Falcons, hosted a 1965 Beatles concert, and was the site of countless other musical events and tractor pulls.

The stadium was demolished by implosion and fell like dominos on August 2, 1997. A total of about 8,700 much needed parking spaces now occupy the former Atlanta–Fulton County Stadium site adjacent to Turner Field. Part of the old outfield wall is preserved between levels of the parking lot. The location of Aaron's famous home run is marked with a monument, and the old field is outlined in the parking lot pavement.

Turner Field includes Coca-Cola's Sky Field. PHOTO: JOHN MCKAY

Tickets

Patrons may buy tickets at the Braves ticket office outside the main plaza or by mail: Atlanta Braves Mail Order, P.O. Box 4064, Atlanta, GA 30302-4064; include a $6 handling fee. Allow two weeks for delivery, or pick up tickets at Will Call. Tickets are $45 for dugout level; $32 for club level; $27 for field and terrace levels; $18 for field pavilion and terrace pavilion; $12 for upper level; and $5 for upper pavilion. A number of $1 Skyline tickets are sold only on game days, and they usually go quickly.

You may order by phone and charge tickets through the Ticketmaster service. Call (404) 249-6400 in Atlanta; long distance, dial (800) 326-4000. Season and group tickets are available directly from the Braves: Call (404) 577-9100.

If you don't have tickets, you can watch the Braves on SuperStation WTBS and the SportSouth cable network (selected games only). Every game is broadcast over the 150-station Braves Radio Network; Atlanta's flagship station is WSB-AM (750), whose clear-channel signal reaches 38 states at night.

Stadium Rules

Some Atlanta sports and concert venues have more rules than a religious order. In comparison, the Braves' gate policies are positively liberal and getting more so by the moment. Criticism over the cost of concession food may have been responsible for a change in policy on fans bringing in their own chow. When the stadium opened, it was a no-no, but now it's allowed. Upon entry, ticket-takers typically perform a cursory inspection of carry-in items looking for obvious violations of the following rules.

Fans may bring in their own food and beverages in small coolers and plastic containers only if these are small enough to fit easily under the seat or in one's lap.

No alcoholic beverages may be brought into the ballpark.

Glass bottles and cans of any kind (except medicinal aerosol cans) are not allowed.

Foam tomahawks are allowed and sold everywhere; real tomahawks (wooden or metal) are not.

Smoking is not allowed in the stadium except in designated areas on each concourse. (Look for floor markings outlining a yellow box.)

Fans may photograph or videotape the ball game, provided their equipment does not obstruct the view of other fans. However, no film or videotape may be reproduced or broadcast without the Braves' permission.

Banners can only be hung off the upper deck, they must have no commercial references and, of course, they must be in good taste.

Reselling tickets for more than their face value is a violation of Georgia law; both sellers and buyers are subject to prosecution.

If the game is rained out before the end of the fifth inning, your ticket stub is good for a rain check and can be exchanged at the ticket window.

And if you catch a foul ball, go to Guest Relations in the plaza and pick up a "Grandstand Fielder" certificate.

Parking, MARTA, and Getting Around at the Game

Parking is at a premium, and many spaces are reserved for season ticket holders and VIPs. The lots and the main plaza open 3.5

hours prior to game time (the rest of the ballpark opens two hours prior to the first pitch), and the team operates the lots and promises that flaggers will be on-site to provide security throughout the game and handle ins and outs in an orderly fashion. It costs $10 to park at these lots. There are also more than 10,000 private or illegal spaces in lots around the ballpark, but you "pays your money and takes your chances."

Your best bet is to park in one of MARTA's many free lots and take the train to the game ($1.75 for a token). Ninety minutes before each game, you can get a shuttle bus from MARTA's Five Points station on the Forsyth Street side. Ask for a transfer at the MARTA station or else you will have to pay $1.75 for the shuttle itself. Shuttle service begins 90 minutes before each game and continues until the ballpark is empty. The shuttle bus drops you off at the corner of Ralph David Abernathy Drive and Central Avenue and then it's a two-block walk east to Turner Field. The streets are always cordoned off for pedestrians so walking is fun, especially since urban vendors line the streets hawking everything from boiled peanuts to water and kiddie T-shirts to tomahawks.

If you do decide to drive yourself to the stadium, we suggest that you call ahead and find out which gate is the closest to your seat—then try to park somewhere near that gate. Otherwise, be prepared to walk the entire stadium (not so awful considering all the fun things to see and do along the way). Odd aisle numbers are along the first-base line, even ones along the third-base line. Escalators flank the ballpark, and there are ramps and elevators too, but the stairs are easy to navigate and better than waiting for the elevators, which take a lot longer to get to you than they should considering we are only talking about three floors here.

For disabled fans, the Green Lot north of Ralph David Abernathy Drive is a first-come, first-served parking lot for those with state-issued handicapped permits or plates. You can also drop off a disabled person at the stadium's East Gate on Hank Aaron Drive (the old Capitol Avenue). All levels have wheelchair seating

and companion seating on raised areas so you won't have to worry about fans blocking your vision. Courtesy rides, rest rooms, Braille signage, TTY, and TDD services are all available here. There are even phone booths, drinking fountains, and concession counters designed to enable fans who need out-of-the-ordinary services. Nevertheless, if you need more assistance, call (404) 614–1326.

At every game there are more than 100 guest relations personnel to help out. The main Guest Relations window is in the plaza, and there are others on each concourse. First-aid stations are staffed by Emory University Hospital personnel and are located behind home plate on all three concourses.

Football

Atlanta Falcons
4400 Falcon Parkway, Flowery Branch
(770) 965–3115
www.atlantafalcons.com

The high point in the history of the Atlanta Falcons, a team long known for coming up short, came in January 1999, when they won the National Football Conference championship and a trip to their first Super Bowl.

Despite an extraordinary season under Coach Dan Reeves, there were plenty of disbelieving fans. But folks around Geor-

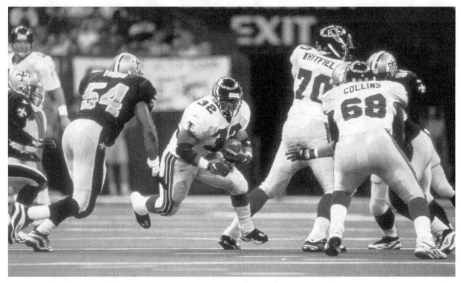

Atlantans have been cheering on the Falcons since 1966. PHOTO: ATLANTA FALCONS

gia started doing the "Dirty Bird," an end zone celebration dance, and the newly christened Dirty Birds displaced the Braves for a time as the city's sports darlings. It didn't matter that the Falcons lost to the Denver Broncos and John Elway in the big game; just getting there was a joy.

Atlanta businessman Rankin Smith was awarded the NFL's 15th franchise in 1965, culminating a long effort to bring big-league sports to Georgia. That fall and winter, fans bought season tickets in record numbers, and the Falcons drafted their first player, Texas All-America linebacker Tommy Nobis.

The fans suffered through a lot of dismal teams and had their hopes shattered in the playoffs when their better teams reached for the top prize. The expansion Falcons played their first game to a sold-out stadium of 54,418 fans in the new Atlanta–Fulton County Stadium on September 11, 1966.

"Falcons" was a popular suggestion for the team name, for reasons best expressed by Griffin, Georgia, schoolteacher Julia Elliot: "The falcon is proud and dignified, with great courage and fight. It never drops its prey. It is deadly and has a great sporting tradition."

Following nine regular season losses and two wins on the road, the Falcons sealed their first home victory on December 11, 1966, beating the St. Louis Cardinals 16-10. Nobis became the first Falcon named to the All-Pro team in 1967. The team's first winning season came in 1971 (7-6-1) under coach Norm Van Brocklin. They made the playoffs three times from 1978 to 1982 with coach Leeman Bennett.

In December 1980 the team earned its first NFC Western Division title. In the playoffs, victory seemed certain as Atlanta led 24-10 going into the fourth quarter—then 60,022 fans (a record) watched in shock as the Cowboys rallied to score 20 points. The final: Dallas 30, Atlanta 27.

The Falcons changed their team colors in 1990, adopting the black uniforms they wear today. In 1991 the Falcons played their last season in Atlanta–Fulton County Stadium and moved to the new Georgia Dome, where they play their games indoors.

The Falcons made the NFL playoffs in both 1991 and 1995, and in 1997 named Dan Reeves, a native Georgian, as head coach. Reeves is the NFL's winningest active coach. Within the decade, the Falcons vaulted to their best season in franchise history. Led by record-breaking running back Jamal Anderson, quarterback Chris Chandler, receiver Terrance Mathis, and defensive back Eugene Robinson, the team posted its best record, 14-2, and defeated the heavily favored Minnesota Vikings in Minnesota for the NFC championship. Perhaps tainted by a cloud of pregame off-the-field problems, the Falcons fell to the Broncos in the Super Bowl in Miami.

In 1991 Falcon Deion Sanders signed to play with the Braves, becoming the first player in 30 years to play two pro sports in the same city. Other notable players to wear Falcons' colors have been quarterback Steve Bartkowski, running back Gerald Riggs, center Jeff Van Note, and receiver Billy "White Shoes" Johnson.

After holding training camps in a variety of locations around the South, the Falcons built a camp northeast of Atlanta off I-85 in Suwanee in April 1978. The Falcons moved to their current year-round training camp in Flowery Branch in 2000, but continue to do most of their preseason summer practice at Furman University in Greenville, South Carolina.

In late 2001, word leaked out that Arthur M. Blank, the cofounder and retired cochairman of Atlanta-based Home Depot, was seeking to purchase the Falcons. This was confirmed by the league and approved by the owners association in February 2002. For the first time in the team's 36-year history, someone from outside the Smith family owned the Falcons.

More recently fans rallied around young quarterback Michael Vick and a playoff-bound 2002 team.

The Georgia Dome
One Georgia Dome Drive
(404) 223–9200
www.gadome.com

The $214 million Georgia Dome is topped by the world's largest cable-supported dome. At its highest point, the roof is 275 feet—or 27 stories—above the playing field. The Teflon-coated Fiberglas roof weighs 68 tons and covers 8.6 acres. When configured as an arena, the Dome's capacity expands to 80,000.

Planning for the Dome began in June 1984. After considerable negotiations, it

was decided in October 1988 that the state would build the Dome with help from the city and county.

In May 1990, the still-unbuilt Dome was selected to host Super Bowl XXVIII in 1994. Construction began the next month. The dome also hosted Super Bowl XXXIV in 2000. In September 1990, Atlanta was awarded the 1996 Olympic Games, and the Dome was proposed as a venue for basketball and gymnastics.

By February 1992, the fabric roof was installed and made watertight. The 71,500 seats were in by June; the Astroturf rolled out in July; in August the Falcons kicked off the action in the brand-new Georgia Dome. Total construction time was 31 months. On August 23, 1992, 66,834 fans watched the Falcons play and win the first football game in the new dome.

Enormous TV monitors hang in each end zone; dozens of smaller monitors are suspended from the ceiling throughout the complex. The four 1,250-ton air conditioners may work too well: Reports are that Dome-goers complain more about being too cold than being too hot. The electricity used to power the Dome could light up a city of 13,000.

The Dome offers 183 executive suites and 5,600 executive club seats that are leased on a 10-year basis. Suite and club-seat members receive Falcons season tickets, one parking pass for every four seats, and access to the private Executive Concourse and the private En-Zone restaurant. Club seats (extra-wide cushioned armchairs with high backs) may be leased by the year; the club section includes waiter service. Executive suites are $20,000 to $120,000 a year and come complete with

The Georgia Dome. PHOTO: ATLANTA CONVENTION & VISITORS BUREAU

custom furnishings (although leasees may bring in a decorator of their choice), cable-ready TVs, a wet bar, and a private rest room. A sliding glass door divides the interior of the suite from the open box, whose seats overlook the field. Suite and club-seat holders get first option to buy tickets to any public dome event.

Tickets

Only season tickets are available for Falcons games, with the exception of a very limited number of individual game tickets that became available in the summertime. Check the Web site for information or call the ticket office at (404) 223–8000.

Falcons games are broadcast over a 27-station radio network. The local flagship is WGST-AM (640).

Note: The Falcons' training camp and team headquarters is at Flowery Branch near Lake Lanier and Gainesville in north Georgia. Preseason training begins about the middle of July and is completed near the end of August. Some training sessions are open to the public without charge.

Dome Amenities

Eight Dome service centers are near the main entrance gates. These provide guests with various services, such as a check stand for items not allowed inside, lost child location, and a designated-driver program. For the hearing impaired, amplification devices are offered with the deposit of a picture ID. (The Dome also features hearing-aid compatible phones with volume control, TDD phones, flashing exit signs, and visual fire alarms.) A variety of food and drink is available at the Dome. There are two food courts on the upper and lower levels. Cocktails are also sold in the Dome, and you're allowed to take drinks to your seats. In fact, every seat comes with its own cup holder.

Dome Rules

Here are some policies to keep in mind when planning your day at the Dome.

Fans are not allowed to bring in the following: food, beverages (including alcoholic beverages), coolers, cans, bottles, and mechanical or compressed-air noisemakers.

Smoking is not allowed, except where designated.

No audio or video recording is allowed at Falcons games.

Fans may use portable TVs and radios (with earphones only) providing they fit on one's lap and do not annoy other guests.

Backpacks, purses, and other such containers larger than 8.5 inches wide, 13 inches long, and 5 inches deep are not permitted inside the stadium. All persons, smaller bags, purses, and containers are subject to search or inspection by security personnel. During major events (such as the Super Bowl) or during heightened security alerts, further inspections and accompanying delays should be expected.

Tickets are required for all children except infants occupying the same seat as their parent.

Parking and MARTA

Mass transit is a key component in the Dome's downtown location. Unlike stadiums built in the middle of acres and acres of parking lots, the Dome is closely surrounded by business and residential areas and the Georgia World Congress Center. There are several thousand parking spaces at the Georgia Dome and the adjacent Georgia World Congress Center, and some of these are reserved for executive members and media. Within walking distance are an additional 17,000 parking spaces in downtown lots, but all these together can only accommodate a fraction of the 71,500 fans at a sold-out Falcons game. Don't get any ideas about parking in the nearby Vine City neighborhood: Only residents with city-issued permits may park on Vine City streets during Dome events.

Parking downtown can be a hassle at best; during Dome events it can be downright impossible. Again, MARTA is the easy answer. The Dome is so huge that it's actually served by two MARTA stations on the east-west line: Vine City on the west side and Dome/Georgia World Congress Center on the east side. Both are on MARTA's east-west line. If you're returning to a station on the north-south line after the game, you can avoid changing trains at Five Points by taking the special express shuttle bus to the Garnett station. These buses board on the Dome's south side.

During Dome events, MARTA runs a shuttle on a downtown loop route; it picks up passengers at downtown parking lots and takes them to the Dome. This shuttle runs every five minutes before and after events and every 25 minutes during events. However, since you'll have to pay the full MARTA fare to ride the shuttle, it's clearly smarter to park for free at a MARTA rail station and take the train to the game.

College Football

Georgia Tech
www.ramblinwreck.com

The four-time national champion Georgia Tech Yellow Jackets carry on one of the longest college football traditions in the nation at Bobby Dodd Stadium/Grant Field near downtown Atlanta. Also known as the Ramblin Wreck, from the school's famous fight song, Tech currently plays in the Atlantic Coast Conference and boasts 15 conference championships since 1916.

While the team battles conference foes such as Florida State and Virginia, the biggest game on Tech's schedule is the season-ending clash with the University of Georgia. The game, chronicled in the book *Good Old-Fashioned Hate,* usually is played around Thanksgiving, alternating between the schools' campuses in Atlanta and Athens.

Among the noted All-Americas to wear Tech's gold and white have been Maxie Baughan, Bobby Davis, Paul Duke, Larry Morris, Rock Perdoni, and Ken Swilling. John Heisman, the coach for whom the famous award is named, was Tech's coach from 1904 to 1919, winning the school's first national championship in 1917. Under coach William Alexander, Tech won the Rose Bowl in 1928 and was co-national champion. Bobby Dodd's teams won the Orange, Sugar, Cotton, and Gator Bowls and shared a national championship in 1952. Tech shared the national title for the third time in 1990 under coach Bobby Ross.

Tickets

Many of the football games are sold out. For information on availability and getting tickets, call the Georgia Tech ticket center toll-free, (888) TECH–TIX, or go on the Tech Web site. Many games are on national or regional television in addition to WGST-AM (640).

University of Georgia
www.georgiadogs.com

About 70 miles away in the small college town of Athens, the Bulldogs of the University of Georgia renew their football legacy in Sanford Stadium on Saturday afternoons in the fall.

UGA was one of the first colleges in the country to take up the new sport of football when the team played Mercer College in January 1892. The next month, a game with Auburn University in Atlanta's Piedmont Park began one of the nation's oldest college football rivalries.

Since then, the Bulldogs have won two national championships, in 1942 and

1980; 10 Southeastern Conference titles; more than 600 games; and made appearances in more different bowls (16) than any team in the country.

Two Bulldogs have won the Heisman Trophy as the country's best player, running backs Frank Sinkwich in 1942 and Herschel Walker in 1982. Other noted players to wear the red and black were Fran Tarkenton, Vernon "Catfish" Smith, Bob McWhorter, Charley Trippi, and Garrison Hearst. Coaches Wally Butts and Vince Dooley also are in the College Football Hall of Fame.

The Southeastern Conference provides a number of long rivalries besides Auburn. Each year, Georgia and Florida battle in the game that accompanies what's known as the "World's Largest Outdoor Cocktail Party" in Jacksonville, Florida, and no Bulldog ever looks past the season-ending clash with Georgia Tech.

The Georgia Bulldogs ended the 2001 season with eight wins and four losses, going on to lose to Boston College in the Music City Bowl. However, their 2002 season went much better with 13 wins and one loss, the best record in the school's history. They defeated Florida State University, 26-13, in the subsequent Sugar Bowl.

Tickets

Many of the games are sold out early. For information on availability and to get tickets, call the University of Georgia Athletic Association ticket office, (706) 542–1231, or toll-free, (877) 542–1231. Besides national and regional television coverage, the Bulldogs games can be heard on WSB-AM (750).

Atlanta University Center

A number of other colleges also play intercollegiate football. While the players often don't have top-dollar athletic scholarships and their teams are not competing for the big-time national championships, the games are exciting, the stadiums more intimate, and the love of the game evident in everyone on the field and in the stands.

Three of the Atlanta University Center schools—Morris Brown, Clark Atlanta, and Morehouse—compete in the NCAA's Division II in the Southern Intercollegiate Athletic Conference (SIAC). Although they are part of the same university system and historically African American in enrollment and philosophy, they are nonetheless rivals. For the 2000 season, however, Morris Brown College moved up to Division I-AA and joined the Southwestern Athletic Conference (SWAC) along with universities such as Grambling, Southern, and Jackson State.

All three teams play their home games in B. T. Harvey Stadium on the AU Center campus. Some of the games are broadcast on WCLK-FM (91.9).

Morris Brown College
643 Martin Luther King Jr. Drive
(404) 220–3628
www.morrisbrown.edu

The Morris Brown fighting Wolverines, clothed in purple, black, and white, recently lost its accreditation, and further participation in sporting events is uncertain at this writing.

Clark Atlanta University
James P. Brawley Drive at Fair Street SW
(404) 880–8123
www.cau.edu

The Panthers, in red, black, and gray, ended their 2002 season with a 1-7 record.

Morehouse College
830 Westview Drive
(404) 215–2669
www.morehouse.edu

The Maroon Tigers, wearing maroon and white uniforms, ended their 2002 season with a 4-4 record.

Bowl Games

Peach Bowl
Georgia Dome, One Georgia Dome Drive
(404) 586–8500
www.peachbowl.com

The Peach Bowl college football game pits rivals from the Southeastern Conference and the Atlantic Coast Conference in a game that has gained prestige since moving indoors to the Georgia Dome. The date varies slightly (between December 30

Insiders' Tip

It is traditional, for some odd reason, for students and alumni to dress up in suits and ties, and the equivalent for ladies, to attend both Georgia and Georgia Tech football home games.

and January 2) to accommodate the TV schedule: It's cablecast on ESPN.

For date and ticket information, call the Peach Bowl information line, (404) 586-8499, or Ticketmaster at (404) 249-6400 or (800) 326-4000; or online at www.ticketmaster.com; a convenience charge applies.

Southeastern Conference Championship Game
Georgia Dome, One Georgia Dome Drive
(404) 223–8427
www.secsports.com

The Georgia Dome also has played host to the football title game in the SEC. Teams from the East and West divisions square off, usually early in December, in a game that frequently has implications for college football's national championship. For date and ticket information, call the Dome ticket office at the number listed above.

Basketball

Atlanta Hawks
One CNN Center at Marietta Street, Suite 405
(404) 249–6400
www.hawks.com

The third jewel in Atlanta's pro sports crown was put into place in 1968 when the St. Louis Hawks basketball team relocated to Atlanta. Before that, the Hawks had been part of three cities' sports scene, first in Tri-Cities (Moline-Rock Island, Illinois–Davenport, Iowa) from 1949–51; Milwaukee, 1951–55; and St. Louis, 1955–68.

It was in St. Louis where the Hawks won their only NBA championship, in 1958, knocking off the Boston Celtics and Bill Russell. Bob Pettit was among the league leaders in scoring and rebounding that year. In 1960 rookie guard Lenny Wilkens joined the Hawks and soon became one of the team's and league's stars. After completing a Hall of Fame career as a player, he became the league's all-time winningest coach, including seven years as coach of the Hawks.

In 1968, with the NBA battling the newly formed American Basketball Association for players and fans' attentions, the Hawks were sold to Atlanta real estate developer Tom Cousins and former Georgia governor Carl Sanders. They moved the franchise south and soon added "Pistol Pete" Maravich to the roster. Atlanta media and sports mogul Ted Turner purchased the team in 1976, squelching rumors that the Hawks might move on.

The Atlanta Hawks battled to first-place Central Division finishes in 1969–70, 1979–80, and 1986–87. In 1993–94 the Hawks tied a franchise record with 57 wins against 25 losses, winning the Central Division and earning the No. 1 seed in the playoff after finishing the season with the best record in the Eastern Conference. After taking the first round three games to two, the Hawks were upset by Indiana in the second round. One of the team's most popular players during this time was University of Georgia standout Dominique Wilkins.

For their first four seasons in Atlanta, the Hawks played in Georgia Tech's Alexander Memorial Coliseum before moving in 1972 to the then-brand-new 16,510-seat Omni Coliseum. In 1997, the Omni was demolished by implosion to make way for Philips Arena, a new entertainment on the site of the old Omni, Downtown between the CNN Center, Georgia World Congress Center, and the Georgia Dome. In their final season at the Omni, Atlanta won a franchise-tying 36 home victories. Splitting home games in the 1997–98 and 1998–99 seasons be-

tween Georgia Tech and the Georgia Dome, the team made it to the playoffs behind center Dikembe Mutombo and guard Steve Smith. In a game against the Chicago Bulls and Michael Jordan, the team set an NBA attendance mark of 62,046 fans to the Dome.

Besides Lenny Wilkens, Atlanta Hawks enshrined in the Basketball Hall of Fame include Walt Bellamy, Connie Hawkins, and Maravich. Retired numbers include those of Pettit (9) and "Sweet Lou" Hudson (23).

Tickets

The Hawks share Philips Arena with the Atlanta Thrashers hockey team. Tickets range from $10 to $450, with virtually all of the higher-priced, closer-in seats sold out before the season starts. Tickets are available at all Ticketmaster retail locations and by phone: Call (404) 249-6400 in Atlanta; (800) 326-4000 long distance; a service charge applies. For season tickets, call the Hawks directly at (404) 827-DUNK.

You can watch the Hawks on Turner South and FoxSportsNet. You can listen to the games on the Atlanta Hawks Radio Network, whose flagship station is WSB-AM (750).

Philips Arena

See the Close-up in this chapter.

College Basketball

Georgia Tech
www.ramblinwreck.com

The Yellow Jackets are often rated among the top teams in the country in men's basketball and play in one of the nation's toughest leagues, the Atlantic Coast Conference.

The Jackets have won five regular season or ACC tournament titles, and made it all the way to the NCAA Final Four in 1990. That year, behind All-Americas Dennis Scott and Kenny Anderson, the team struggled to an 8-6 conference record, good for a third-place tie in the regular season, but won the conference tournament to clinch a bid to the NCAA's Big Dance. As a former member of the South-

Philips Arena

With the word "Atlanta" soaring in 65-foot letters out front, the new Philips Arena opened in 1999 as the home of the Hawks basketball team, and the Thrashers hockey team, and venue for concerts, conventions, and other sporting events.

Its Downtown location is between the CNN Center and the Georgia Dome.

The $213 million structure, for which Philips Electronics purchased the naming rights, replaces the former Omni arena, which was built in 1972 at a cost of $17 million, and demolished in 1997 to make way for the new and larger arena. Philips can seat more than 20,000 for basketball, 18,559 for hockey, and 21,000 for concerts. In addition, there are 1,800 club seats and 91 luxury boxes—all the amenities a tenant could want in an arena.

The ice rink, kept frozen by an underground system of refrigerated tubes, is covered by a protective, insulated layer when the basketball court or concert floor is on top of it. Basketball can add about 1,500 floor-level seats, and another 2,100 seats can be brought in for concerts.

Next to the arena and connecting it to the CNN Center and Omni Hotel is the Hawk Walk, an indoor street of sights, sounds, and shops selling team merchandise, food, and beverages. Inside, but invisible to most fans, is a vast complex of separate locker rooms for home and visiting basketball and hockey teams, weight and training rooms, medical services, offices, media facilities, and an indoor basketball practice court for the Hawks.

In the public areas, Philips Electronics products are everywhere, from the lightbulbs to 500 video monitors in practically every corner. The centerpiece is a 10,000-square-foot fan activity area with 100 52-inch flat-screen television sets that can show individual images or be grouped in various blocks. To manage the noise, the surfaces in the arena area are covered in insulating material. Even the seats have been designed to improve the acoustics. Color-coded fiber-optic lighting even tells passers-by what's going on: blue for the Thrashers, red for the Hawks, and green for non-sporting events.

The arena's first event was an exhibition hockey game between the Thrashers and New York Rangers on September 18, 1999. A grand, gala concert by part-time Atlanta resident Elton John celebrated the arena's grand opening on September 24. It has played host to celebrities such as Cher, the Dixie Chicks, Justin Timberlake and Christina Aguilera, and R.E.M.

"ATLANTA" is spelled out in 65-foot letters on the front of Philips Arena.
PHOTO: EDWARD M. PIO RODA

eastern Conference, the Jackets won that league's crown in 1938.

Other noted Yellow Jacket alumni include Mark Price; Rich Yunkus; Matt Harpring; Travis Best; Stephon Marbury; and Roger Kaiser.

The Lady Jackets are still building their history. Last season was the team's most successful in school history.

The teams play their home games in Alexander Memorial Coliseum.

Tickets

For information on tickets, call the Georgia Tech ticket center toll-free, (888) TECH–TIX. Many of the games are on national or regional television as well as the Jackets flagship radio station, WGST-AM (640).

University of Georgia
www.georgiadogs.com

The Bulldog men's and women's basketball teams each have won Southeastern Conference championships and advanced to the Final Four of their respective NCAA tournaments.

The men's team has a 90-year-plus history playing basketball, but has enjoyed success mostly since 1983, when it made its first appearance in the NCAA tournament and went to the Final Four, including victories over national powerhouses North Carolina and St. John's.

Only one player, All-America Dominique Wilkins, has had his number (21) retired.

The Lady Bulldogs have been one of the nation's most respected women's teams, with three trips to the Final Four in five years and six SEC championships under head coach Andy Landers.

The teams play their home games in Athens' Stegman Coliseum on the UGA campus.

Tickets

For information on tickets, call the University of Georgia Athletic Association ticket office, (706) 542–1231, or toll-free, (877) 542–1231. In addition to national and regional television coverage, games are carried on WSB-AM (750).

Georgia State University

The Panthers have burst into Division I basketball in the past few years, including an appearance in the NCAA men's basketball tournament in 1991. A leap forward was the hiring of the legendary Charles "Lefty" Dreisel as head coach of the men's team in 1997.

The men's and women's teams play in Division I's Trans America Athletic Conference. Home games are played at the Georgia State Sports Arena, on campus at Piedmont and Decatur Streets.

Tickets and information: Call (404) 651-3182.

Smaller Colleges

Many other smaller institutions play men's and women's basketball in the NCAA's small-college divisions. One that has enjoyed a good deal of success recently is Life University in Marietta.

The Running Eagles are the defending NAIA champion. Tickets and information: (770) 426–2765.

Hockey

Atlanta Thrashers
CNN Center
(404) 584–PUCK
www.atlantathrashers.com

One of the newest professional sports teams is the National Hockey League's Atlanta Thrashers. But the team is not the first entry in the NHL. In 1971 Atlanta was awarded an expansion NHL franchise for the Atlanta Flames.

With hockey legend Bernie "Boom Boom" Geoffrion as the team's first coach, they took the ice in 1972. Despite the team's popularity with the fans, new owners moved the Flames to Calgary, Alberta, after the 1979–80 season. For four seasons, the Atlanta Knights played in the International Hockey League, winning the top minor league's championship, the Turner Cup, in 1994.

Thanks in part to the Knights' success, Turner Sports, founded by Ted Turner and now a part of AOL Time-Warner Co., and the NHL awarded an expansion franchise to Atlanta in 1997.

Before the team could take the ice, it needed a coach and players.

Goaltender Damian Rhodes was the first Thrasher, acquired from the Ottawa Senators, followed shortly by forward Andrew Brunette from the Nashville Predators. Defenseman Jamie Pushor was the first player taken in the expansion draft in June 1999, and in the first pick of the 1999 entry draft, the Thrashers selected Patrik Stefan.

The first exhibition game was played September 11, 1999, in Columbus, Georgia, with the Thrashers defeating the Nashville Predators 3-1. In the first regular season game in franchise history, the Thrashers fell to the New Jersey Devils 4-1 before a sellout crowd at Philips Arena on Oct. 2, 1999. Just 12 days later, the team posted its first NHL win, beating the New York Islanders 2-0.

The team's second season was another story, however. As is typical with new expansion teams, the second year of play often does not show a very good record, and the Thrashers were not untypical. After the last game of the 2000–01 season in April, their record was 23-45-12-2. Recent seasons have given fans more reason for optimism.

Home games are played in Philips Arena, and all ticket sales are handled by Ticketmaster.

Turner South is the cable television home of the Thrashers, and WQXI (AM 790) is the flagship radio station.

Golf

The Tour Championship
East Lake Golf Course
2575 Alston Drive
www.eastlakegolfclub.com

East Lake Golf Course, an inner-city Atlanta course rescued by developers and revitalized to be the heart of a thriving community, hosts the Tour Championship in November. Ticket information is to be announced.

The Masters
Augusta National Golf Club, Augusta

Few golfers would argue that The Masters is the quintessential golf tournament of the country. The tournament, started by golf legend and Georgia's own Bobby Jones, is held each year in March or April at Augusta National Golf Club, 150 miles east of Atlanta in Augusta, Georgia. Past champions include legends and future legends of golf: Ben Hogan, Arnold Palmer, Jack Nicklaus, and Tiger Woods. Live TV coverage is on the USA network, with finals live coverage on CBS.

If you don't have tickets already, you can't get them at the door. Augusta National Golf Club has very strict rules and a very long waiting list to get in and to get Masters tickets. In fact, the rights to buy tickets reportedly have been passed down in wills. But if you want to try, contact the club: (706) 667-6000.

BellSouth Classic
TPC at Sugarloaf
2595 Sugarloaf Club Drive, Duluth

Since 1997, this popular PGA Tour tournament has been played in late March or early April at TPC (Tournament Players Club) Sugarloaf in suburban Duluth, Georgia.

The key rounds are typically telecast on network and/or cable TV.

Tickets (for all seven days) are $60 and up and are available from the tournament headquarters, (770) 951-8777, or from Ticketmaster, (404) 249-6400 or (800) 326-4000; a service charge applies. Parking is extra.

Chick-fil-A Charity Championship
Eagle's Landing Country Club
Stockbridge
www.charitychampionship.com

The world's top women golfers compete in the Chick-fil-A Championship, a fixture on the LPGA Tour. It's played in April on the south side of metro Atlanta at Eagle's Landing, one of the area's newer golf courses. Like BellSouth with the men's tour, Chick-fil-A is a local company using sports to help charity.

Ticket information is to be announced.

The BellSouth Classic draws thousands of spectators each May. PHOTO: BELLSOUTH CLASSIC

American Express Championship
Capital City Club
Woodstock
www.worldgolfchampionships.com/r473/
index.html

The Atlanta event of the newly formed World Golf Championships events features players from around the world competing against one another in varied formats (match play, stroke, and team). These championships join the better known and longer established World Tour events (there are five of those, with the European Tour and PGA Tour the best known in these parts) to establish international rankings for elite professional golfers. To qualify for the series, one must be a top player in the Official World Golf Ranking, such as Tiger Woods and David Duval. The World Golf Championships feature some of the largest purses in professional golf. First-prize money is in excess of $1 million.

The American Express Championship is held in September and October and is televised on ESPN and other networks. Information on the myriad of ticket and volunteer opportunities is available on their Web site, www.worldgolfchampionships.com/r473/2003hospitality.html.

Auto Racing

Atlanta Motor Speedway
1500 Highways 19 and 41 South
Hampton
(770) 946-4211
www.atlantarace.com

Atlanta Motor Speedway is an 870-acre racing complex 30 miles south of downtown Atlanta in Hampton, Georgia; it features a 1.522-mile oval and a 2.5-mile road course. The short course is the world's fastest true oval track.

The track hosts NASCAR Winston Cup events in March and November as well as Busch series races and, for the first time, an Indy Racing League event with Indianapolis 500–type cars. Beyond racing, the track hosts club events and auto industry test drives. To book a tour, call (770) 707-7970.

From Atlanta, take I-75 South to U.S. 19/41 South for 15 miles.

Tickets, which run from $10 to $100, are available from the track: To charge by phone, call (770) 946-4211 or by e-mail at amstix@atlantarace.com. Hotel and ticket packages are available from Connections, (800) ATLANTA or (404) 842-0000 or www.atlantaconnections.com. Tickets are also available from Ticketmaster, (404) 249-6400 or (800) 326-4000; a service charge applies. Parking is free. On Winston Cup events, it's wise to plan for heavy traffic both in and out of the track.

Dixie Speedway
150 Dixie Drive
Woodstock
(770) 926–5315
www.dixiespeedway.com

In Woodstock, about 40 miles northwest of Atlanta, there's Saturday night racing weekly from early March through late November at Dixie Speedway. The regular program includes five auto events and one for trucks. Races are sometimes also held on Friday night, and there are special attractions throughout the season, such as monster trucks, demolition derby, and outlaw sprint cars.

The track is a .75-mile clay oval. Admission prices vary depending on whether you choose the pit area, the tailgate section, or the alcohol-free grandstand. Tickets start at $12. Admission for kids 11 and younger is usually free; parking is also free. Tickets are sold at the gate. In September, the track hosts the finals in the Hav-a-Tampa Dirt Racing Series.

Take I-75 North to I-575; exit at Georgia Highway 92 and go west to the speedway.

Road Atlanta
5300 Winder Highway
Braselton
(770) 967-6143, (800) 849–RACE
www.roadatlanta.com

Road Atlanta is a 2.52-mile road racing track about 30 miles northeast of the Perimeter that has attained national stature with its Petit Le Mans race in September. Of local interest is the Panoz racing team, which is headquartered near the track. Both are owned by the Panoz family, which also runs the nearby Château Élan winery and resort.

From March through November, Road Atlanta offers an array of sports car, vintage, motorcycle, motocross, and go-cart races as well as entertainment events. Parking is free and so is infield camping. Adult ticket prices vary with events; kids 12 and younger are always admitted for $5. Infield parking is $5, and infield camping is $25. Ticket prices for events vary. Purchase tickets from the track at (770) 967-6143 or (800) 849-RACE. Tickets also are available from Ticketmaster, (404) 249-6400 or (800) 326-4000; a service charge applies. Or call Road Atlanta, (770) 967-6143. From Atlanta, take I-85 North to exit 49; turn left, and follow the signs.

Running

Peachtree Road Race
3097 East Shadowlawn Avenue
No phone
www.atlantatrackclub.org

Insiders' Tip

During race weekends, Highway 41 (Tara Boulevard) south of Atlanta becomes jammed to a near standstill by thousands of NASCAR fans heading to the Atlanta Motor Speedway. Use I-75 to the east as an alternative route to points farther south.

This annual event is as much a part of an Atlanta Fourth of July as is smuggling fireworks in from South Carolina, Tennessee, and Alabama. The Peachtree is the world's largest 10K road race: Established in 1970, it annually draws 55,000 competitors with a few seeded runners racing for prize money.

The night before the race you'll find athletes and friends carbing up on spaghetti and bread at restaurants throughout the Peachtree corridor. The race starts at Lenox Square at 7:30 A.M. and runs down Peachtree Street, ending in Piedmont Park. Some 200,000 spectators line the route to cheer the huffing and sweating throng. There are plenty of good places to watch the race; many bars and restaurants along the way open early for parties. Or, if you're into watching others suffer, pick a spot along the slope known as "Heartbreak Hill." It begins around Peachtree Battle Shopping Center and crests, conveniently, right in front of Piedmont Hospital.

To request information on how you can run in the Peachtree, write the Atlanta Track Club at the above address prior to March 1 and include a stamped, self-addressed envelope. Then, when you get your entry forms, fill them out immediately and drive right to the post office. The slots are filled on a strictly first-come, first-served basis, and the 50,000 slots fill up almost immediately.

Information, but not registration, is available on-line.

Atlanta Marathon

For runners with more endurance, the Atlanta Marathon is run on Thanksgiving morning. The runners like it then, and if you've ever been in Atlanta in July, you'll know why. And then there's the prospect of a Thanksgiving dinner waiting at home for the exhausted runners.

The course is a big loop, starting downtown near Turner Field, winding up and down hills to near Chamblee in the northeast, and then back, covering a lot of the same territory as the Peachtree. For those not up to a full marathon, there's a half marathon that begins at the same time as the main race but at the halfway point.

Like the Peachtree, there's prize money for the top, seeded finishers, but the race is full of plenty of casual joggers who couldn't get into the Peachtree but still want to test their mettle.

For information, contact the Atlanta Track Club at the address listed under Peachtree Road Race.

Soccer

Atlanta Beat
5901 Peachtree-Dunwoody Road
(404) 269–8353
www.theatlantabeat.com

The Atlanta Beat, the newest pro sports team in Atlanta, is one of eight professional women's soccer teams that make up the Women's United Soccer Association (WUSA). WUSA was originally based around the core of the 1999 U.S. Women's World Cup team, all of whom still play on one of the eight teams, and now features athletes from 14 other countries. The Beat finished the 2002 season—their second full season—in fourth place with a record of 11 wins, nine losses, and one tie. Their season runs from April to August, home games are played at Morris Brown College's Herndon Stadium, and games are televised on the PAX TV network. During the 2002 season these telecasts were from 4:00 to 6:00 P.M. every Saturday, but there is no confirmation at this writing if this schedule will hold for future seasons.

Individual tickets are $10 to $22 for adults, $10 to $16 for children ages 3 to 12. A range of large-group, single-game ticket prices are available, as well as five-game and full-season ticket packages. All tickets and packages are available from the Beat's Web site or from all Ticketmaster outlets.

Atlanta Silverbacks
5960 Crooked Creek Road, Suite 10
Norcross
(770) 248–0492
www.atlantasilverbacks.com

The Silverbacks, named for our famous type of gorilla at Zoo Atlanta, is Atlanta's team in the United Soccer Leagues' A-

League, the nation's highest "minor league" in soccer.

The team was reorganized in 1998 from its predecessor, the Atlanta Ruckus, which debuted in 1995. The city has been home to teams in now-defunct major soccer leagues, with the Atlanta Chiefs the 1968 champion of the old North American Soccer League.

The Silverbacks' season lasts from April to August. The team finished the 2002 season at 15-15-13, good for third place in the Southeast Division. Games are played at DeKalb Memorial Stadium, on Memorial College Drive in Stone Mountain. Tickets are $15 ($10 for children under 12). For information, call (404) 377-5575 or e-mail tickets@atlantasilverbacks.com. Tickets can also be ordered through www.ticketmaster.com.

Equestrian

Atlanta Steeplechase
(404) 237-7436
www.atlantasteeplechase.org

Here's another Atlanta rite of spring: the annual Atlanta Steeplechase. The 'chase is run at Kingston Downs, a 435-acre site on U.S. Highway 411 west of Cartersville. The course accommodates up to 100,000 fans and, in the best Southern tradition, this is as much a cocktail party as it is a race.

Almost more important than the handsome horses are the elaborate hats, outrageous finery, antique cars, and sumptuous buffets. Folks engage in tailgate parties (which is to say, they stand around their cars, trucks, or station wagons) or set up elaborate tents from which they dispense drinks and/or take refuge from the sun or rain, whichever the gods deem appropriate for that year's event. The seven-race steeplechase benefits the Atlanta Speech School, which works with speech-hearing-impaired and learning-disabled students.

Tickets are $25 per person; a parking pass (you'll need one for tailgating) starts at $20. Seating and party packages are higher. Important: Tickets are sold only in advance—not at the gate. Tickets are limited; call well in advance of the big day.

Georgia International Horse Park
1996 Centennial Olympic Parkway
(770) 860–4190

The 1,400-acre Georgia International Horse Park celebrated its grand opening on Labor Day weekend in 1995. During the Olympic Games, the park (about 30 minutes east of Atlanta off I-20) was the venue for equestrian events, mountain bike competitions, and the two final events of the modern pentathlon.

The park includes a 165-acre nature center; an 18-hole Arnold Palmer golf course and driving range; a 200-room hotel; a 205-acre, pedestrian-friendly, traditional neighborhood; a steeplechase course; and a covered arena with seating for 2,000 spectators.

The park's central feature is the open Grand Prix stadium. Permanent seating for 8,000 in an outdoor amphitheater offers excellent sight lines for competitions held on a sand floor. There are also 14 out-

Equestrian events are popular around Atlanta.
PHOTO: GEORGIA DEPARTMENT OF INDUSTRY, TRADE, AND TOURISM

door sand arenas for warm-up and other competitions, a 2,200-seat covered arena for rodeos, dressage, and hunter/jumper shows, and 12 miles of roads and tracks for cross-country events.

The Horse Park's mountain biking trail is the only Olympic course in the world for this sport and features 1,032 feet of elevation change over 8 miles of track. Additionally, the park manages the new Cherokee Run Golf Course designed by Arnold Palmer. This par 72, 7,000-yard course traverses wetlands, granite outcroppings, and rolling hills.

Polo Club of Atlanta
6300 Polo Club Drive, Cumming
(770) 399–0481

The horsy set loves to gather at the Polo Golf and Country Club north of Atlanta. (Take GA 400 north to exit 12; turn left, and follow the signs.) Except for the month of August (when the action is suspended due to the heat), exciting polo matches are held every Sunday from June through October. Gates open at 1:00 P.M., and the action gets under way at 2:00 P.M.; dress is casual. Admission is per person or per vehicle; or, for a little more, your party gets a cabana to relax under (a very good idea on broiling Georgia afternoons). Bring a picnic—everyone does.

Other Events

Georgia Games
(770) 528–3580
www.georgiagames.org

In July 1997 the first annual Georgia Games Championships with 3,000 amateur athletes competing in 18 Olympic-style sports took place. In 1997 more than 14,000 Georgians participated in 38 sports in a four-day event, and the majority of the action took place on venues within which the Centennial Games were held, such as the Georgia Tech Aquatic Center, Georgia Dome, Stone Mountain Tennis Center, Wolf Creek Shooting complex, and others.

The Georgia Games, a legacy of the Centennial Olympic Games, will be an ongoing event for amateur athletes well into the millennium. Originally the vision of Billy Payne, whose dream it was to have the Olympics here in the first place, the Georgia Games gives local athletes a way of achieving recognition and preparing themselves for upcoming Olympics. In all, Georgia Games stages approximately 55 events annually, with more than 10,000 amateur athletes participating in everything from running and biking challenges to tae kwon do, which has been added as an official sport in the Olympic Games.

Day Trips and Weekend Getaways

One of the best aspects of life in Atlanta is the ability to get out of town and into a variety of relaxing locations within a few hours. The city's central location affords easy auto access to the rest of the state's attractions—be they the cool, shady mountains to the north, or the sunny beaches to the east. In between are countless charming small towns where festivals, celebrations, and activities lure weekend guests. Beyond the borders of Georgia lie Chattanooga, Tennessee, Birmingham, Alabama, and Asheville, North Carolina, all distinctive towns with a variety of things to do and see.

Here we just scratch the surface of scenic destinations throughout Georgia. For a broader perspective, contact the Georgia Department of Industry, Trade, and Tourism, (800) VISIT GA. Whenever possible, we've listed street addresses, but some towns are so small that street addresses are sometimes irrelevant or unavailable. If we've left an address out, the restaurant, hotel, or attraction is one you just can't miss once you've gotten into town. We've listed rates for many of the hotels, motels, and bed-and-breakfasts we mention in this chapter. But rates can change; check with the places you want to stay to find out their current prices.

The North Georgia Mountains

When Atlanta temperatures climb to unbearable levels, there's a mass exodus to the calm and cool of the north Georgia mountains. Crystal waterfalls, clear lakes, and small villages offer visitors a chance to savor the fresh air, good food, and a variety of outdoor sports.

Georgia is home to 10 peaks rising 4,000 feet or more. The southernmost portions of the Blue Ridge Mountains extend into north central and northeastern Georgia. Springer Mountain, north of Atlanta in Amicalola Falls State Park, marks the southern end of the 2,150-mile Appalachian Trail that passes through 15 states. In the northwest section of the state near Tennessee, you'll find peaks and valleys covered with evergreens and wildflowers. Don't forget your camera!

Armed with a good map, you'll find many delightful mountain places within a few hours' drive of Atlanta. Charming shops in quaint villages offer handmade quilts, twig baskets, dulcimers, and other traditional items. Carry home jars of mountain honey and apple butter. Browse the many galleries for sculpture, carvings, antiques, handwoven wall hangings, and folk art. The profusion of inns and restaurants in the north Georgia mountains ensures you'll be well fed and close to a bed, or you can camp at one of the many state parks in the area.

A number of the destinations we mention are within easy driving distance of each other. You could start your day shopping in a historic town square, have lunch at a family-style country restaurant, visit a state park in the afternoon, stop by a point of historic interest, and end up at a bed-and-breakfast in a neighboring city.

Amicalola Falls State Park

Amicalola Falls, the highest waterfall east of the Mississippi, takes its name from the

Cherokee word for "tumbling waters." The falls plunge 729 feet in seven cascades. Amicalola Falls State Park has campsites, cottages, scenic trails, a fishing stream, a lodge, and picnic sites. Call the park, (706) 265-8888 or (800) 573-9656, or refer to www.amicalolafalls.com for directions. Or dial the Dawsonville Chamber of Commerce, (706) 265-6278. It takes about 1.5 hours to reach Amicalola Falls from Atlanta, approximately a 65-mile drive. Georgia Highway 183 has signs that will lead you to the park. Amicalola Falls State Park is an easy drive from Dahlonega or Ellijay (see our sections below).

About 15 minutes from Amicalola Falls off Georgia Highway 53 on Amicalola Church Road is the Swan Center Monastery, a spiritual training center for the clergy of the Swanete (Swan-a-te) religion and a rehabilitation center for abused or neglected horses, dogs, cats, and other animals. The Swan Center (www.swancenter.org), on 123 scenic mountain acres, offers the public a place to retreat from the rigors of everyday living. Trail rides, riding lessons for children and adults, dog obedience classes, contemplative walks, and educational workshops and clinics number among the center's many programs. The Swan Center also has a greenhouse and a custom framing shop. Money the center earns from its many outreach programs goes toward the care and feeding of the animals. Call (770) 893-3525 for more information.

Brasstown Bald

Brasstown Bald, a little more than two hours north of Atlanta, is the highest point in Georgia (4,784 feet). Take Georgia Highway 400 to U.S. Highway 19 through Dahlonega, then take Georgia Highway 180 to the mountain. Deep in the heart of the Chattahoochee National Forest, the mountain offers a spectacular view of four states—Tennessee, North Carolina, South Carolina, and Georgia—on clear days. The visitor information center, perched on the top of the mountain, offers interpretive programs, slide presentations, and exhibits that trace the natural and cultural history of the area. (There's a shuttle to get you up the half-mile trail if you're not up for climbing.) You can take in wonderful wildflowers in the spring and bright autumn leaves in the fall. Hike one of the four hiking trails that range from .5 miles to 6 miles long. The Bald also has picnic tables and a log cabin bookstore. You can visit the mountain daily from Memorial Day through October, and on weekends in the early spring and late fall, depending on the weather. To find out more, call the visitor information center June through October, (706) 896-2556.

Brasstown Valley Resort in nearby Young Harris offers hunting lodge–style accommodations and traditional hotel rooms amid spectacular scenery. The resort features a 72-link golf course, tennis courts, an indoor/outdoor pool, a fitness center, interpretive hiking trails, plus trout fishing and bird-watching opportunities. The dining room is open to the public, which piles in for the extensive Sunday brunch buffet. Room rates range from $95 to $250. To find out more, call (800) 201-3205.

Nearby Blairsville hosts the annual Sorghum Festival and Indian Summer in October, a three-weekend event featuring arts and crafts, musical entertainment, clogging, and games. Pick up a supply of sorghum syrup, cooked and jarred right in front of you by local Jaycees. To find out more, call the Blairsville/Union County Chamber of Commerce, (706) 745-5789.

The annual Georgia Mountain Fair, held in August, is a popular event with a long history—it's been the high point of mountain summers since 1950. Just west of Hiawassee on the Georgia Mountain Fairgrounds, the 12-day fair offers music, craft exhibits, and demonstrations. In Pioneer Village, visitors can examine a re-created mountain town and observe the arts of board-splitting, moonshining, quilting, and soapmaking in progress. The fair also hosts a summer-long series of concerts featuring such country music names as Barbara Mandrell, Ronnie Milsap, and Merle Haggard. In October a Fall Celebration takes place on the fairgrounds, featuring fiddling, gospel music, and country music shows. For more information, contact Georgia Mountain Fair, (706) 896–4191.

Three miles west of Hiawassee on U.S. Highway 76 is the rustic Fieldstone Inn and Conference Center on the edge of Lake Chatuge. Many of its 66 rooms overlook the lovely water and marina. A restaurant, outdoor pool, indoor hot tub, and lighted tennis courts complete an inviting package. For information, call (800) 545–3408. Room rates are $109 to $179. You can also find numerous cabins, bed-and-breakfasts, and motels in the Blairsville area.

Other attractions include the Union County Courthouse in Blairsville, a restored 1899 building housing the county's historical society and its museum of local and regional history, (706) 745–5493. Trackrock Campground and Cabins also has a riding academy, which offers horseback riding on scenic mountain trails. The Track Rock Archaeological Area is a 52-acre section with ancient Indian carvings and historical markers to help you find your way. The Wasali-Yi Center, where the Appalachian Trail crosses U.S. Highway 19/129, is an outfitters' facility and rest stop for hikers in the Blood Mountain Archaeological Area, as well as the only spot on the more-than-2,000-mile long wilderness trail where it goes under a roof! The Richard Russell Scenic Highway, Georgia Highway 348, offers 14.1 miles of dramatic mountain views and overlooks; this highway crosses the Appalachian Trail.

Vogel State Park, Woody Gap Recreation Area, DeSoto Falls Scenic Area, and Dukes Creek Falls are among the many outdoor scenic and recreational venues in the region. You can camp at DeSoto Falls Scenic Area and Vogel State Park; Cooper's Creek Scenic and Recreation Area and Lake Nottely are two of the other camping venues in the area. For specifics, call (706) 745–2628.

Clarkesville

Clarkesville and its surrounding area have much to offer visitors. Historic Clarkesville, the Habersham County seat and scene of the annual Mountain Laurel Fes-

Insiders' Tip

The northern Georgia mountainous areas around Brasstown Bald frequently experience ice and snow conditions that close roads and make travel hazardous, even when relatively nearby Atlanta enjoys near-springlike conditions.

tival in May, is a charming little town off U.S. Highway 441. Clarkesville has shopping, bed-and-breakfasts, food, and opportunities for outdoor recreation from golf to camping. The town square, brightened by blooming seasonal flowers, is lined with quaint shops and restaurants. More than 40 structures in town have been listed on the National Register of Historic Places.

Ten miles from the town center on Georgia Highway 197, you'll find Mark of the Potter, a shop offering original, handmade wooden crafts, metal and ceramic jewelry, pottery, hand-blown glass, and weavings, (706) 947–3440. Housed in a converted gristmill by a 14-foot waterfall, the store, which opened in 1969, is the oldest craft shop in Georgia in its original location. Visitors can see mountain trout in their natural habitat from the shop's porch over the Soque (the Cherokee word for "pig") River.

Shopping's not your thing? You just want to relax? Escape to the woods at Clarkesville's Happy Valley Resort, (800) 354–4773, where you can stay in a fully equipped cabin (with a fireplace) for $80 to $100 per night and enjoy hiking trails, gardens, a swimming pool, a fishing pond, a collection of exotic birds, and a variety of farm animals in barns and pastures throughout the grounds. (Note: The resort does not accept children.) You can also rent a cabin at LaPrade's on Lake Burton, (706) 947–3313, a rustic mountain retreat that offers fishing, swimming, hiking, boating, and family-style dining. LaPrade's marina rents fishing boats, lake canoes, pontoon boats, pedal boats, and rowboats. You can also get fishing guide service by appointment. Daily cabin rental rates of $39 to $80 per person include three family-style meals. But you don't have to be a guest to drop in for breakfast, lunch, or dinner.

Sleep in a 100-year-old room at Glen-Ella Springs Country Inn, (877) 456–7527, listed on the National Register of Historic Places. This popular bed-and-breakfast, 8 miles north of Clarkesville in the Chattahoochee National Forest, has 16 guest rooms with private baths. Full breakfasts are included. The inn is on 18 acres that include a meadow, herb, flower, and vegetable gardens, and a swimming pool. Even if you're not a guest, you can enjoy the Glen-Ella's varied cuisine in the dining room, open to the public for dinner. Rooms at Glen-Ella range from $150 to $200. And if you like your weekends to be hair-raising, register for one of the inn's Murder Mystery weekends, where guests can test their detective skills.

You might also want to check out the Burns-Sutton Inn, (706) 754–5565, also on the National Register of Historic Places. Victorian antiques furnish the seven rooms in this 1901 house with wraparound veranda. Room rates are from $75 to $150. Some package deals are offered in conjunction with nearby golf, fishing, and white-water rafting services.

Outdoor enthusiasts can camp at Moccasin Creek State Park, (706) 947–3194, which has 54 wooded sites, supplied with power and water. Some of the spots border the creek or the lake. The campgrounds include showers, rest rooms, a playground, and sports courts. You can also camp at the Terrora Park and Campground adjacent to Tallulah Gorge State Park about 15 miles north of Clarkesville on old U.S. 441 in the town of Tallulah Falls.

Tallulah Gorge State Park, (706) 754–7970, created through a partnership between the Georgia Department of Natural Resources and Georgia Power Com-pany, has a 500-yard walking trail along the rim of Tallulah Gorge. The gorge is 2 miles long and nearly 1,000 feet deep. It's one of the most spectacular gorges in the eastern United States; the breathtaking views make it a favorite stopping point along U.S. 441, the main route between Atlanta and the Great Smoky Mountains. Georgia Heritage Center for the Arts, (706) 754–3276, issues up to 100 permits per day, weather permitting, for hikers, mountain bikers, rock climbers, and rappellers who want to descend to the bottom of the gorge. If you're found on the gorge floor without a permit, you could be fined. The center gives out free permits daily from 8:00 A.M. to 5:00 P.M. No permit is required for the hiking trails, but there is a $2 parking fee. Please note that the four-lane U.S. 441 is a new highway, and the "old" U.S. 441, marked by a small sign and turnoff, follows the very rim of the canyon and passes a variety of 1950s-era tourist attractions.

As we mentioned above, you'll find plenty of spots to camp, picnic, hike, play tennis, fish, and swim (during the summer only) at Terrora Park and Campground, operated by Georgia Power.

Dahlonega

The mountain town of Dahlonega (www.dahlonega.org), site of America's first major gold rush, is about 90 minutes from Atlanta. Head north on GA 400 out of Atlanta to Dahlonega (Dah-LON-a-gah), named after the Cherokee word for "yellow," which has nothing to do with the gold in the area, ironically! (The nearby location of the Cherokee-era village of the same name was referring to the yellowish clay of the Chestatee River.) Turn left off GA 400 at Georgia Highway 60 and go 5 miles on a two-lane road that winds its way to this charming village.

Dahlonega's townspeople celebrate their past; many town buildings are listed on the National Register of Historic Places. More than three dozen gift, jewelry, and specialty shops on the historic town square make for a pleasant afternoon of browsing. Find fine antiques, art, and Appalachian crafts from birdhouses to pottery and painted crocks at a variety of quaint gift stores. The old-fashioned Dahlonega General Store is right off the square. Stroll through Artist Avenue, a gallery showcasing handcrafted items from the north Georgia mountains.

The Downtown Historic District, (706) 864-3711, includes the state-run Gold Museum in the 165-year-old former courthouse. Make sure to look carefully at the original, unrebuilt structure of the courthouse itself; the bricks were tested during renovations in the 1970s and discovered to have trace amounts of gold in them! Walking tours of the area tell the tale of the nation's first gold rush. The discovery of gold near Dahlonega in 1828 encouraged the U.S. government to establish a branch mint here that operated from 1838 to 1861.

Looking southwest from the museum, you can see the steeple of Price Memorial Hall (part of North Georgia College, and built on the site and to the rough design of the original U.S. Mint building) covered in 17 ounces of Dahlonega gold. If you feel gold fever overtaking you, head for Consolidated Gold Mines, (706) 864-8473, inside the town's city limits, and literally under the Wal-Mart store. Consolidated was once the largest gold-mining operation east of the Mississippi. You'll see the mine as it was in the 1800s, go 250 feet straight down into the miners' tunnel systems, and have a chance to pan for gold. Or visit Crisson Gold Mine, (706) 864-6363, for gold panning and gemstone grubbing. Then, rest up from your labors with a trolley tour through historic Dahlonega.

You'll find plenty of places to eat in Dahlonega, from pizza, Chinese, and Mexican to barbecue, ice cream shops, coffeehouses, a natural foods restaurant, several sandwich shops, and an excellent Italian restaurant. Our highest recommendation goes to Rick's, (706) 864-9422, on Park Street South just one block down the hill from the Welcome Center, in the historic Head house. Rick's offers a constantly changing variety of upscale "New American" cuisine, such as lobster-stuffed, panbroiled mountain trout, Caribbean-style oxtail stews, baked grouper covered by a

hazelnuts in brown butter glaze, and crawfish risotto cakes. This is supplemented by a small but very imaginative wine cellar, which fortunately has prices that stay in the sane range.

Dahlonega offers plenty of scenic views, hiking trails, rafting, canoeing, and fishing. If you want to turn your day trip into a weekend getaway, you'll find plenty of places where you can stay overnight: bed-and-breakfasts, cabins, cottages, and motels. The area also offers a number of camping facilities.

Annual events in Dahlonega include the World Championship Gold Panning Competition, held the third weekend in April; the Bear on the Square Mountain Music Festival held the same weekend in April; the Wildflower Festival of the Arts, which takes place on the third weekend in May; and the Bluegrass Festival in June. Dahlonega also hosts Gold Rush Days in October and An Old-Fashioned Christmas and Lighting of the Square in Dahlonega in December. For dates and times, call the Dahlonega-Lumpkin County Welcome Center, (800) 231-5543.

Dalton

Known as Georgia's carpet capital, Dalton (www.daltoncvb.com) and environs also offer a number of historical sites. Eighty-seven miles from Atlanta (take I-75 North and follow the signs), Dalton is one of the gateways to the Chieftain's Trail, designated a state historic trail by the Georgia General Assembly in 1988 as part of the 150th anniversary of the Cherokee Indian Nation's Trail of Tears. The trail traces 150 miles of scenic highways throughout northwest Georgia, telling the story of the Cherokee Indians, whose culture preceded European settlement. You can see homes, villages, and mounds along the trail, as well as museums and ceremonial grounds. Chief Vann House, built in 1904, is a two-story classic brick mansion built by Cherokee Indian Chief James Vann. He contributed to his people's education by inviting Moravian missionaries to teach Cherokee children. Chief Vann House is about 10 miles east of Dalton at the intersection of Georgia Highways 225 and 52A, near the town of Chatsworth. Admission to this historic home costs $3 for adults and $2 for children older than 5. The house is open 9:00 A.M. to 5:00 P.M. Tuesday through Saturday, 2:00 to 5:00 P.M. Sunday. Call (706) 695-2598 for more information.

Dalton, a Confederate hospital and manufacturing town during the Civil War, is part of the Blue and Gray Trail, a series of monuments, plaques, parks, tablets, and markers commemorating points of Civil War historic interest. Blunt House, 506 South Thornton Avenue, is on the National Register of Historic Places. Built in 1848, it was the home of Dalton's first mayor. The house opens by appointment; call (706) 278-0217. The Crown Gardens and Archives, 715 Chattanooga Avenue,

(706) 278-0217, is headquarters of the Whitfield/Murray Historical Society, which maintains a museum in this building that once served as offices for the Crown Cotton Mill. The circa 1890 structure, in a National Register Historic District, is open Tuesday through Friday from 10:00 A.M. to 5:00 P.M. and Saturday, 10:00 A.M. to 1:00 P.M. Admission is a donation. Another National Register historic site, the 1852 Dalton Depot, 110 Depot Street, the only remaining structure from the Civil War era in town, has been transformed into an upscale restaurant/lounge. The lobby contains the original beginning point for surveying the city of Dalton. Dalton Depot's number is (706) 226-3160.

Prater's Mill, a mile east of Georgia Highway 71 on Georgia Highway 2, is 10 miles northeast of Dalton. This historic gristmill was built with slave labor in 1855. The mill itself only opens twice a year, during the semiannual Country Fair in May and October. The grounds of this National Register of Historic Places site are open year-round during daylight hours. Admission is free. Call the Dalton Convention and Visitors Bureau, (706) 272-7676, to find out more.

The Ellis Collection Doll Museum, 810 M. Tibbs Road, (706) 278-9368, welcomes the public to look at a personal collection of more than 1,500 antique and modern dolls. You can view the dolls during store hours Monday through Saturday, 10:00 A.M. to 5:30 P.M.

You can find a number of interesting small shops scattered about in Dalton, as well as more than 100 carpet outlets offering savings from 30 to 70 percent off retail. If you're shopping for more than carpet, try Factory Stores Plaza, on Market Street adjacent to I-75, with 32 factory-direct stores.

Ellijay

Ellijay, approximately 20 miles northwest of Amicalola Falls on GA 52, is about an hour's drive from Atlanta. The city was originally the site of a Cherokee Indian village. Ellijay boasts a number of shops selling mountain crafts, primitive art,

> ## Insiders' Tip
> The high mountain ridge just to the west of Dalton is where the Confederate army first dug in to resist Sherman's invasion of Georgia.

antiques, and more. Rivers Edge Antique Mall, at the intersection of Georgia Highways 515 and 52, features 22 dealers offering a wide selection of antiques and collectibles. Other haunts for avid shoppers include Antiques & More and the Ellijay Antique Mall.

Outdoor enthusiasts will enjoy the many recreational venues in the area. You can canoe, fish, tube, and kayak on the Cartecay River. The Cartecay's class II and III rapids offer thrill-a-minute excitement. Contact Mountaintown Outdoor Expeditions, GA 52 East, (706) 635-2524, to arrange expeditions on the Cartecay. Carters Lake, GA 382, a flood control project of the U.S. Army Corps of Engineers, offers fishing, swimming, camping, and boating. Hikers and mountain bikers will find trails in the nearby Cohutta Wilderness, (706) 635-7400, the Rich Mountain Wilderness, and surrounding National Forest areas in Fannin and Gilmer Counties, (706) 632-3031.

Ellijay is Georgia's apple capital, and throughout the fall, roadside stands abound with mountain apples, homemade apple butter, old-fashioned cider, and other apple products. On the second and third weekends in October, Ellijay hosts the Georgia Apple Festival, an arts and crafts fair that's been attracting people from all over the nation for the past 28 years. Call (706) 635-7400 to find out more.

Cherry Log, just north of Ellijay, also hosts an annual apple festival, the Cherry Log Festival, on weekends in October. From July Fourth until Christmas, apple aficionados can take a self-guided tour through Hillcrest Orchards, (706) 273-3838, where picking your own is a popular sport on the second and third weekend of September. There are also wagon rides, a petting zoo, a cider mill, and a market where you can find homemade jellies and jams, apple bread, apple butter, cider, and other delicious items such as the orchards' own apple cider doughnuts. The kitchen's open so you can watch Hillcrest cooks making pies, doughnuts, and hot caramel or chocolate apples. Hillcrest is popular for school and church field trips. For $3 per person, groups can see an educational video, take a wagon ride, feed the animals

Insiders' Tip

The free weekly *Creative Loafing* frequently covers events and attractions in all these nearby cities and towns.

in the petting zoo with feed provided by Hillcrest, and get an apple, a cup of cider, and a hat. Individuals pay $3 for the wagon ride as well as entrance to the petting zoo. Many families bring their own lunches and dine al fresco in Hillcrest Orchards' picnic grounds.

History fans can explore parts of the Chieftain's Trail (which we mentioned in our section on Dalton) around Ellijay. You may also want to tour such historical sites as the Gilmer County Courthouse, on the square in Ellijay, an 1891 structure listed on the National Register of Historic Places, and the Perry House, 10 Broad Street, home of the Gilmer Arts & Heritage Association. Fort Mountain, about 20 miles from Ellijay, boasts prehistoric rock formations; Fort Mountain State Park, (706) 695-2621, offers camping, fishing, swimming, and hiking trails.

You can camp in and around Ellijay (at Carter's Lake, Fort Mountain State Park, Cohutta Wilderness, and Rich Mountain Wilderness, to name a few) or stay in a motel, lodge, cabin, or cottage. At Whitepath Lodge, (706) 276-7199, guests are ensconced in two-bedroom suites with fully equipped kitchens, laundry facilities, wraparound porches, and panoramic views. The facility also offers tennis and swimming on the grounds; the property is on the 10th tee of the Whitepath Golf Club. Rates are $110 to $200 per night, or $700 to $1,000 a week, year-round.

Gainesville

Gainesville, about an hour's drive northeast of Atlanta (take I-85 to I-985 and follow the signs), boasts the Green Street National Register historic district and a Smithsonian Museum, the Georgia Mountains Museum. Created in 1821, Gainesville became a trading center for the gold mining industry. In the late 1800s, after the railroad came, the town evolved into a prosperous cotton market. Green Street, the town's prime residential district, has a number of Victorian and Neoclassical Revival homes and businesses. To find out about walking and driving tours of the historic half-mile corridor, call the Greater Hall Chamber of Commerce, (770) 532-6206, or the Gainesville Hall County Convention and Visitors Bureau, (770) 536-5209.

The Georgia Mountains Museum, (770) 536-0889, is closed until the winter of 2004 while it moves to a new location. The museum features local history exhibits including the Ed Dodd/Mark Trail Memorabilia Exhibit and the General James A. Longstreet exhibit. Longstreet, a Confederate general, served as one of Robert E. Lee's corps commanders and his de-facto second in command during the Civil War. Longstreet moved to Gainesville in 1875; he was a postmaster and opened a hotel where notables such as Henry Grady, Joel Chandler Harris, and Woodrow Wilson stayed. The museum offers a self-guided tour, and Longstreet himself is buried in the nearby Alta Vista Cemetery. The Georgia Mountains Museum also operates a railroad museum in a renovated baggage car that houses railroad memorabilia and more than 300 cars on an HO gauge layout. The museum is open Tuesday through Friday, 10:00 A.M. to 5:00 P.M. Admission is $2 for adults, $1 for students and seniors. If you'd rather have a piece of history in your home, stop by Antiques and Uniques, 1727 Cleveland Highway, or Stuff, 4760 Dawsonville Highway, another store offering antiques, collectibles, and furniture.

There's more to do in Gainesville than ponder history; the area's rich in recreational venues. The rowing, spring canoe, and kayak events for the 1996 Olympic Games took place in Gainesville's Clarks Bridge Park on Lake Lanier. Nearby Lake Lanier Islands, (770) 932-7200, which we describe in our Kidstuff and Parks and Recreation chapters, offers boating, swimming, sailing, golf, and horseback riding, to name a few activities. Horse fans can find a nice selection of equestrian equipment and apparel at the Horse & Hound Tack Shop, 112 Main Street on the Square. Lanier Point Softball Complex, off Georgia Highway 53, at the end of Lanier Valley Drive, (770) 287-0208, is on the shores of Lake Lanier. The popular complex hosts league play and a number of major tournaments each year. Golfers will like the many challenging courses in the area with lovely scenery.

Every second weekend in October, Gainesville hosts the Mule Camp Market, an arts and crafts festival downtown on the square. Mule Camp features regional folk artists, musicians, cloggers, a children's carnival, and more than 100 vendors selling artworks, pottery, and food. Call the Gainesville Jaycees, (770) 532-7714, for details. Kids and adults can learn about the environment at the Elachee Nature Science Center, 2125 Elachee Drive, (770) 535-1976, a 1,200-acre woodland nature preserve and science museum. The center has interactive exhibits, a natural history discovery center, live animal exhibits, and a native plant garden designed to attract birds, butterflies, and other wildlife. The museum is open from 10:00 A.M. to 5:00 P.M. Monday through Saturday and from noon to 5:00 P.M. Sunday; call for holiday schedules. Nonmember adults pay $5 admission. The center's hiking trails wind through the nature preserve. The trails open from 8:00 A.M. to dusk daily; admission is free.

Places to eat in Gainesville include Rafaello's, (770) 534-8668, 975 Dawsonville Highway, Suite 8. This southern Italian restaurant serves pasta, chicken, veal, and seafood dishes. If you want some down-home cuisine in the Southern "meat and three" style, drop by the L&K Cafe, 839 Jesse Jewel Parkway, (770) 531-0600.

The Renaissance PineIsle Resort, (770) 945-8921, and Emerald Point Resort and Conference Center, (770) 945-8787, are two excellent accommodations nearby.

Helen

Don't be fooled by the Alpine architecture in this charming town, approximately 90 minutes north from Atlanta on Georgia Highway 75. Helen (www.helenga.org) isn't really a Swiss village transported to north Georgia, but it has taken on a new life as a year-round tourist attraction. Helen was a dying lumber mill town in the late '60s when local business leaders approached Clarkesville artist John Kollock for ideas. Having spent time in Bavaria, Kollock designed an Alpine village that melds perfectly with the mountains and river nearby. Funded entirely by local merchants, Helen's Alpine face-lift transformed the town into a Georgia landmark that annually draws hundreds of thousands of visitors from around the world.

The flowering window boxes, rooftop towers with steeples, and beer halls with hearty German fare create a fairytale-like atmosphere. Annual celebrations include Oktoberfest. Shopping ranges from inexpensive souvenirs to costly imported crystal in the 150 import and craft shops. You'll find bargains galore in Alpine Village Outlets' 30 national shops.

But there's lots more to do in Helen besides shop. Parts of the Appalachian Trail cross highways near Helen, and you can find several other trails in the area. Many local stables offer horseback riding: call Sunburst Stables, (706) 947-7433; Chattahoochee Stables, (706) 878-7000; or Cross Creek Stables, (706) 878-3327, to reserve a ride.

You'll find tennis facilities at Unicoi State Park, (706) 878-2201, and White County Recreation Department, (706) 865-2756; golf at Innsbruck Resort, (706) 878-2100, or Skitt Mountain Golf Course, (706) 865-2277. Canoe, raft, or tube on the Chattahoochee River; to organize expeditions, call Cool River Tubing, (706) 878-2665, or Alpine Tubing, (706) 878-8823.

Take a buggy ride around town—call Horne's Buggy Rides, (706) 878-3658. Pan for gold at Duke's Creek Mines, (706) 878-2625.

Nora Mills Granary, on the right going into Helen, (706) 878-2375 (www.

Insiders' Tip

Helen wasn't always a bit of Bavaria plunked into north Georgia; in 1969 it was a sleepy lumber town looking for some way to bring Atlanta tourists north into the hills.

noramill.com), is a working water-powered mill open from 9:00 A.M. to 5:00 P.M. every day but Sunday. Watch them grind the grain they use for a variety of products including whole-grain white and yellow grits, cornmeal, many kinds of flours, pancake mixes, biscuit mixes, bread mixes, and a special concoction called pioneer's porridge.

Accommodations include cabins, cottages, motels, bed-and-breakfast inns, and numerous campsites. The Hofbrauhaus Inn, 1 Main Street, (706) 878-2248, overlooks the Chattahoochee and features a dining room specializing in international cuisine. Georgia Mountain Madness, (706) 878-2851, rents one- and two-bedroom cabins on wooded lots; prices range from $70 to $165. Or try the Innsbruck Resort, (706) 878-3400, on Bahn Road, a family resort offering three- and four-bedroom villas.

Dining is no problem, with numerous restaurants waiting to serve you. At Heidelberg Restaurant & Lounge, in White Horse Square, (706) 878-2986, is Helen's oldest German restaurant featuring a wide variety of home-style German food and a huge selection of imported beer. The Stovall House Country Inn, in nearby Sautee, 1526 Georgia Highway 255 North, (706) 878-3355, offers five guest rooms in a restored 1837 farmhouse that's on the National Register of Historic Places. Feast on creative regional cuisine in the inn's public dining room. Rooms at the Stovall House cost $84 for a double, with breakfast included. Dinners Thursday through Saturday, and Sunday brunch. You may bring your own wine with dinner if you have an extra bottle on hand; Sautee is a dry town. The inn's just a mile from the Sautee-Nacoochee Arts and Community Center, a highly regarded venue for arts and crafts shows and activities. For more information, contact the Greater Helen Area Welcome Center, (706) 878–2181, 726 Brucken Strasse in Helen.

Unicoi State Park, just 2 miles from Helen, offers cottages, campsites, swimming, fishing, boating, plus a year-round schedule of activities including programs on mountain culture and the environment. To find out more about this scenic state park, call (706) 878–2201.

Nearby Anna Ruby Falls, in the heart of the Chattahoochee National Forest, is a spectacular double falls created by the junction of Curtis and York Creeks. Curtis Falls drop 153 feet; York, about 50 feet. A .4-mile paved walking trail leads from the visitor center to the base of the falls. It takes about 30 minutes and walking is easy to moderate. The more challenging 4.6-mile Smith Creek trail leads from the base of Anna Ruby Falls to Unicoi State Park. Cars pay a $5 parking fee; RVs pay $10. To find out more, dial (706) 754–6221.

About 10 miles south of Helen, in the town of Cleveland, visit Babyland General Hospital, (706) 865–2171, the original home of the once-wildly-popular Cabbage Patch Dolls. Housed in a turn-of-the-20th-century medical clinic, the "hospital" is open year-round for families to discover how the cuddly toys are "born." Admission is free; hours are 9:00 A.M. to 5:00 P.M. Monday through Saturday, and 10:00 A.M. to 5:00 P.M. Sunday.

If you're still in the gold-hunting mood, drop by the Gold 'N Gem Grubbin Mine, 75 Gold Nugget Lane, (706) 865–5454. The 100-acre complex includes panning sites for gold and gemstones, a shop that sells costume jewelry, and a miniature golf course.

Eastward, Ho!

Visitors awed by the booming and relatively young metropolis that is Atlanta today often forget that Georgia is a state with a long history that dates back to the colonial era. Long before Atlanta became the leading city, smaller towns were settled and prospered inland from the coast, along the state's western frontier. Some of the oldest and most charming of these towns are connected along U.S. Highway 441, also known as Georgia's Antebellum Trail. This former stagecoach route was clogged with traffic between Athens, home of the University of Georgia, and the big city of Macon and the former state capitol at Milledgeville long before Atlanta became the focus of attention.

Today, you can drive the Trail from start to finish in one leisurely day, including stops at antiques stores and historic sites in Watkinsville, Madison, and Eatonton along the way.

Athens

Athens, population 100,000-plus, is the home of the University of Georgia (UGA), one of the oldest state-chartered universities in the United States, and is also known for spawning rock groups the B-52s and R.E.M. A charming college town rich in history, Athens hosted the 1996 Olympic Games soccer finals, rhythmic gymnastics, and volleyball. From north Atlanta, take I–85 North to Georgia Highway 316 to Athens. From east Atlanta and Gwinnett County, take U.S. Highway 78 East to Athens. It's a trip of approximately 90 minutes. For leisurely touring, avoid football weekends or you'll be surrounded by thousands of barking, howling UGA Bulldogs fans cheering on their team.

Begin your Athens visit at the symmetrical Church-Waddel-Brumby House, 280 East Dougherty Street, (706) 353–1820. Believed to be the city's oldest surviving house, it was built in 1920 for Alonzo Church, who later became president of the university. This fine example of Federal-style architecture is now home to the Athens Welcome Center, (706) 353–1820, which has information on guide services for group tours as well as all attractions.

Established in 1785, the University of Georgia campus, which covers many city blocks, offers various diversions to visitors as well as to its students. You'll see the campus trademark, rounded-globe gaslights trimmed in black wrought iron, shining down on wide streets shaded by towering trees. The Arch, the entrance to the campus on Broad Street at the foot of College Avenue, was built in 1857 to represent the Great Seal of Georgia. The three cast-iron columns signify wisdom, justice, and moderation. The arch was gated when it first went up; it and the surrounding fence were designed to keep wandering livestock off the university campus. The Old North Campus Historic District, which you enter through the arch on Broad Street at the foot of College Avenue, is listed on the National Register of Historic Places and boasts a number of historic buildings, a unique but seldom fired double-barreled cannon from the Civil War era, and the Founder's Memorial Gardens, which surround an 1857 home that's headquarters for the Garden Club of Georgia. The Georgia Museum of Art, designated the State Museum of Art by the General Assembly in 1982, has a permanent collection of more than 7,000 works.

Off campus, follow the scenic tour signs through Athens' historic districts to view a diversity of architectural styles. Take note of the towering Doric columns of the Greek Revival–style Taylor-Grady House, 634 Prince Avenue, built in 1840. Or view the Victorian Gothic grandeur of Emmanuel Episcopal Church, 1899, on the corner of Prince and Pope Streets, built of Georgia granite. Gothic Revival influences can be found in the style of the Sledge-Cobb-Spalding house, 749 Cobb Street, built circa 1860. Even if you're not into architecture, a leisurely drive through Athens' historic districts will impress you with the splendor of the city's historical structures. The city has four local and national historic districts: Boulevard, Cobbham, Bloomfield, and Woodlawn. (You'll find signs throughout these districts, which include numerous streets in various sections of town.) For $3 at the Athens Welcome Center, you can buy a book with a map of these districts and descriptions of the historical sites.

Athens is home to the State Botanical Garden of Georgia. The University of Georgia uses this 313-acre horticultural preserve as a living laboratory for the study and enjoyment of plants and nature. Three miles from the UGA campus at 2450 South Milledge Avenue, (706) 542-1244, the garden features 5 miles of nature trails through diverse ecosystems, 11 specialty gardens, and a three-story conservatory with a permanent display of tropical and semitropical plants. The foyer of the visitor center offers changing exhibitions of original artwork. Admission is free, but the garden accepts donations. The grounds are open daily from 8:00 A.M. to 8:00 P.M.; the visitor center opens from 9:00 A.M. to 4:30 P.M. Monday through Saturday, and from 11:30 A.M. to 4:30 P.M. on Sunday.

Visit Morton Theatre, a living monument to Athens' African-American community, at 195 West Washington Street, (706) 613-3770. Built by African Americans in 1910, the structure is listed on the National Register of Historic Places. Monroe Bowers' 554-seat performing arts center plus the adjoining shops and offices formed the heart of the community's business district. The offices housed professionals such as Dr. Ida Mae Johnson Hiram, the first female African American to be licensed to practice medicine in Georgia. Legendary performers, including Bessie Smith and Cab Calloway, played the Morton. Thanks to efforts of preservationists, the theater is once again thriving.

Athens' music/club scene is a diverse one that ranges from country to new wave, including the legendary 40 Watt Club, 285 West Washington Street, (706) 549-7871,

> ## Insiders' Tip
>
> Athens is the home to the world-renowned rock bands R.E.M. and the B-52s. Both got their start at the 40 Watt Club on West Washington Street.

that launched many local rock bands who went on to national fame. Country fans can find live country and dance music at Bumpers, 1720 Commerce Road, (706) 369-7625.

Diversity rules Athens' food scene too. You'll find fine dining and every ethnic cuisine represented. Feast on inexpensive Mexican dishes at the Mean Bean, 1675 South Lumpkin Street, (706) 549-4868, or sample home-style Southern breakfasts and lunches at Weaver D's Delicious Fine Food, 1016 East Broad Street, (706) 353-7797. Weaver D's motto is the source of the R.E.M. title "Automatic for the People." For some of the best in nouveau American cuisine, check out the Last Resort Grill at 174 West Clayton Street, (706) 549-0810. It is a sort of fine-dining establishment meets art gallery meets serious wine bar, all with a college-town-funkiness veneer.

There are plenty of motels and hotels in Athens. For a change of pace, check into the Nicholson House, 6295 Jefferson Road, (706) 353-2200.

About 10 minutes west of Athens, off Georgia Highway 211 in Statham, you can find an array of antiques and collectibles at the International Antique Gallery & Flea Market, 1946 East Railroad Street. This market, housed in a converted textile mill, offers figurines, glassware, furniture, old vending machines, dolls, and more. Although they're not antiques, the market also sells video games.

Madison

About 65 miles east of Atlanta, Madison (www.madisonga.org) is a showplace of antebellum homes that survived the Civil War. Incorporated in 1809, Madison was a prosperous cotton city and a stop on the stagecoach route from Charleston to New Orleans. Madison politician Joshua Hill was friends with Senator John Sherman, Gen. William Sherman's brother. Hill was opposed to secession and resigned from the Senate when Georgia voted to leave the Union. Hill used his anti-secessionist stance and his influence to save Madison's houses from being burned down when Union soldiers under General Slocum occupied the city.

Madison's Welcome Center, in the Chamber of Commerce building, 115 East Jefferson Street on the picturesque town square, stays open seven days a week. You can find a wealth of information on attractions in the area including an informative book, *As It Was Told to Me,* by Hattie Mina Reid Hicky. This book contains capsule histories of Madison's historic homes as well as recipes, a map, and information on Madison's historic churches and town square. Ms. Hickey's Regal Tours of Madison, Georgia, 651 Dixie Avenue, will arrange tours of the town that allow visitors a peek inside many of Madison's private homes—including her own. Call (706) 342-1612 to make a tour reservation. The Welcome Center offers a walking-tour map and audiocassette for rent as well as information about private home tours, seasonal home tours, cultural events, nearby recreational facilities, and accommodations. Call the Welcome Center at (706) 342-4454.

Madison's town square is loaded with antiques shops, restaurants, and gift shops. Utterly Yours, 182 South Main Street, is a two-story store jam-packed with affordable, unusual gifts for house and garden. Wind chimes, prints, jewelry, silver, lamps, and all manner of whimsical decorative items make this shop a browser's paradise. Find Depression glass, coins, and American furniture from the 1840s to the 1940s at Old Madison Antiques, 184 South Main Street; or drop in at The Creative Mark, 165 South Main Street, a shop featuring pottery, glass, jewelry, paintings, and limited-edition prints by regional artists and craftspeople. Stop for a sandwich and soda at Baldwin Pharmacy, 137 South Main Street, an old-fashioned soda fountain/lunch counter and drugstore that's been on the square since the late 1800s. Or enjoy traditional Southern fare at Ye Olde Colonial Restaurant, 108 East Washington Street, (706) 342-2211, housed in the 1800s Morgan County Bank Building. The main dining room still has the original bank vault, a patterned tile floor, and pressed tin ceiling.

After you've explored the square, take a walking or driving tour through Madison's wide, tree-lined streets. Antebellum and Victorian homes, both opulent and modest, line the roads. Some have been converted to business usage; others are still family-owned. Homes such as the Gingerbread House, 5865 Main Street, a high Victorian; Boxwood, 357 Academy Street, a stately mansion that was the first home in Madison to have a hot-water system; and the Carter-Newton Home, 53 Academy Street, a typical "Gone With the Wind" structure, are just a few of the impressive sights Madison offers.

With more than 32 different sites listed on the National Register of Historic Places, Madison is a history-lover's dream. It has several century-old churches, including St. Paul Methodist, 847 North Fifth Street, the oldest brick Methodist church built by an African-American congregation, and Madison Baptist, 328 South Main Street. Union soldiers stabled their horses in the basement of Madison Baptist during their occupation. A Union soldier stole the silver communion service from Madison Presbyterian Church, 382 South Main Street, but General Slocum ordered him to return it. (Significantly, Slocum did not order the return of the rest of the booty stolen from the town!)

Visit Heritage Hall, 277 South Main Street, a Greek Revival home built in 1811 by Dr. William Johnston, a Madison physician. Headquarters of the Madison County Historical Society, Heritage Hall has period furnishings, rich architectural detail, window etchings, and a ghost silhouette on one of the upstairs hearths. When the girls in Dr. Johnston's family got engaged, they followed the tradition of the day by inscribing some personal message ("I love Will, Stewart, and Jennie") on a window with their diamond rings. The ghost silhouette, which keeps returning after repeated paintings, is said to be the outline of a woman and her baby who died of typhoid fever in one of Heritage Hall's upstairs bedrooms. You can tour Heritage Hall for a $5 donation. It is open Monday through Saturday, 11:00 A.M. to 4:00 P.M., and Sunday, 1:30 to 4:30 P.M. Call (706) 342-9627 to find out more.

The Madison-Morgan Cultural Center, 434 South Main Street, host to a history museum, art galleries, and an auditorium

for plays and concerts, was once the first graded public schoolhouse in Georgia. The center is in a restored Romanesque Revival brick building built in 1895. Historical exhibits include a completely restored turn-of-the-century classroom, portions of a reconstructed log cabin, 19th-century decorative arts, artifacts, and interpretive information about Georgia's Piedmont region. The center's art galleries offer varied exhibits by artists of regional, national, and international renown. The center's apse-shaped playhouse, originally a school auditorium, boasts original woodwork, ceiling, seats, and a chandelier; it's known for its excellent acoustics. The cultural center is open Tuesday through Saturday, 10:00 A.M. to 5:00 P.M., and Sunday, 2:00 to 5:00 P.M. For more information, dial (706) 342-4743.

Morgan County African-American Museum, at 156 Academy Street, highlights African-American heritage and contributions to Southern culture. The museum, in the historic Horace Moore House, has a reference library, period living room, a Morgan County room documenting the county's people and their history, and an African room showcasing African art. The museum is open Tuesday through Friday, 10:00 A.M. to 4:00 P.M.; Saturday, noon to 4:00 P.M. To find out about group tours and annual events, call (706) 342-9191.

Bed-and-breakfasts in Madison include the Brady Inn, 250 North Second Street, (706) 342-4400, and Burnett Place, 317 Old Post Road, (706) 342-4034. The Brady Inn is an 1800s Victorian cottage with pine floors and mantels, functioning fireplaces, and period appointments. The inn has seven rooms with private baths, a suite for larger parties, and a dining room that serves full breakfast, and dinner by reservation. Rooms range from $75 to $85.

Burnett Place is a two-story Federal-style house built around 1830. The current owners spent two years restoring the house and took great pains to retain its original features. A glass panel in an upstairs hall allows guests to view the original construction. Burnett Place has guest rooms with private baths and serves full breakfast, high tea, and wine and cheese. Burnett's rooms cost $85; singles are $75 per night.

To reach Madison from Atlanta, take I-20 East to exit 51. While you're in the area, you might want to stop in nearby Social Circle (exit 47 off I-20 East) and eat at the Blue Willow Inn, 294 North Cherokee Road, (770) 464-2131, which we also mention in our Restaurants chapter. The late *Atlanta Journal-Constitution* columnist and humor writer Lewis Grizzard lavishly praised the food at this authentic Southern restaurant housed in a Greek Revival mansion. In the heart of Social Circle's historic district, the restaurant has beautiful grounds, a wide front porch where guests can relax in rocking chairs, a gift shop, and a fountain. After you've eaten, take a tour and do some tasting at Fox Vineyards & Winery, 225 Georgia Highway 11 South, (770) 787-5402.

Covington, a town near Madison, also warrants a visit. Take the Covington/Oxford exit 45 off I-20 East. Covington, the Newton County seat, is most widely known for its role as Sparta, Mississippi, in the TV series *In the Heat of the Night*. Because this is another antebellum town Sherman didn't fully torch, Covington boasts a historic downtown square, manor homes, cottages, churches, and parks. The city offers tours of its historic homes in the fall and winter. You can also tour nearby Oxford College of Emory University, where the university was born, and where most of the streets dead-end into the charming campus. To find out more, call the Covington/Newton County Convention & Visitors Bureau, (800) 616-8626.

If you're en route to Madison from Athens along U.S. Highway 441, you'll pass through Watkinsville, the tiny seat of Oconee County. Clustered around Main Street are about 40 structures that are part of the town's historic district. Eagle Tavern, (706) 769-5197, is one of the oldest buildings in the county, dating back to the late 1700s when Watkinsville was a frontier town. Today, it is a museum and the Oconee County welcome center. It is open Tuesday through Friday from 9:00 A.M. to 5:00 P.M., and Saturday from 2:00 to 5:00 P.M.

Eatonton

Although author Joel Chandler Harris (1848–1908), creator of the Br'er Rabbit and Uncle Remus tales, is most closely identified with his west Atlanta home, the Wren's Nest (see Attractions), the small town of Eatonton is where he was born and where the children's tales first took shape. About 18 miles east of Madison, Eatonton is the seat of Putnam County. The town is about 70 minutes from Atlanta, along I-20 East and U.S. Highway 441 South. You know you're in the right place when you see the statue of Br'er Rabbit gracing the courthouse lawn.

The Uncle Remus Museum, (706) 485-6856, was fashioned out of two log slave cabins. The rustic building is full of renderings, wood carvings, and paintings of the characters and scenes in the stories. There are also first editions of Harris' work and a collection of period memorabilia. The museum sits in Turner Park, once the grounds of the home place of Joseph Sidney Turner, the inspiration for the stories' "Little Boy" character. Hours are 10:00 A.M. to 5:00 P.M. Monday through Saturday; Sunday from 2:00 to 5:00 P.M. From September to May, the museum is closed on Tuesday. Admission is 50 cents per person.

Eatonton is also the birthplace of Pulitzer Prize–winner Alice Walker, author of *The Color Purple*. Walker grew up here and moved away as a young adult. The Eatonton-Putnam Chamber of Commerce, (706) 485-7701, has a driving map that takes riders past some of Walker's childhood haunts. The town also boasts several streets of antebellum homes, including the Bronson House, the 1822 mansion that houses the local historical society. It is open by appointment; for information, call the Chamber.

Several gracious homes have been converted into bed-and-breakfast inns. Rosewood, (706) 485-9009, is an 1888 cottage where guests can retire to the Color Purple room or the Joel Chandler Harris bath. Make a reservation to enjoy afternoon tea on the porch. Rooms go for $65 to $90 per night. At the Crockett House, (706) 485-2248, guests are invited to roam the gardens on the four-acre grounds or relax on the wraparound porch of the 1895 Victorian home. If you love candlelight and romance, book one of the six rooms that has a claw-foot tub right next to the fireplace. Prices range from $95 to $110, and include a full breakfast. Dinner is served by reservation only, if made 10 days in advance.

U.S. 441 South out of Eatonton leads to Milledgeville, Georgia's antebellum capital. The heart of Baldwin County, Milledgeville was the state capital for more than 60 years before it moved to Atlanta in 1868. The town's historic district includes more than 20 architectural landmarks, such as the Old Governor's Mansion and the Old State Capitol Building, which is now the administration building for Georgia Military College. Believed to be one of the oldest public buildings in the country, the capitol was built in a Gothic style with dramatic arches and gates leading onto the grounds. St. Stephens Episcopal Church, circa 1841,

survived being used as a stable for Union horses during the Civil War. As the home of Georgia College, Milledgeville bustles today with students as well as visitors. The college's library has the Flannery O'Connor Room, where writings of the late Georgia author are collected. For a free brochure highlighting the points of interest, stop by the Milledgeville Convention & Visitors Bureau at 200 West Hancock Street, or call (478) 452-4687 or (800) 653-1804.

Heading South

Two of Georgia's largest cities, Columbus and Macon, sit in the southern regions of the state, surrounded by a scenic countryside of farms, pastures, and rolling hills. Natural beauty abounds in Pine Mountain, where the famous Callaway Gardens draw visitors from around the world. Even President Franklin Roosevelt made this bucolic area his home away from home, building the "Little White House" in Warm Springs, where he enjoyed the healing powers of waters that gave the area its name.

Columbus

About two hours southwest of Atlanta you'll find Columbus (www.columbusga.com), a Chattahoochee-riverbank city planned in the 1800s. Columbus, host of the 1996 Olympic softball competition, offers many attractions, including a restored opera house and a riverwalk along the Chattahoochee where, in good weather, you can rent a bike and traverse the brick walk on wheels. Columbus is home to three museums, two that offer a nice twist with no admission fee. The Woodruff Museum of Civil War Naval History, 202 Fourth Street, (706) 327-9798, is the only museum that focuses on the naval side of the conflict. The museum houses relics of the Confederate navy, including hulls of the ironclad *Jackson* and the gunboat *Chattahoochee*. Admission fees are $4.50 for adults and $3 for children. The National Infantry Museum, on Baltzell Avenue in nearby Fort Benning, (706) 545-2958,

Insiders' Tip

Columbus is the host town of the U.S. Army's Fort Benning, one of the largest infantry training bases in the world, and the home of American paratroopers since 1940.

traces the evolution of the infantry from the 1750s to the present. The Columbus Museum, 1251 Wynnton Road, (706) 649-0713, has 86,000 square feet of exhibit space and classrooms. The museum focuses on regional history and American art and features a hands-on children's gallery called Transformations. Columbus State University is home to the Coca-Cola Space Science Center, (706) 649-1470, where visitors can enjoy laser shows, an observatory, and the interactive Challenger Learning Center. Kids can sit in a mock-up of the space shuttle *Challenger's* cockpit or check out a replica of the *Apollo* capsule, which is on permanent display. The center is open Tuesday through Thursday, 10:00 A.M. to 4:00 P.M.; Friday, 10:00 A.M. to 6:00 P.M.; Saturday, 11:30 A.M. to 6:00 P.M.; and Sunday, 1:30 to 4:00 P.M. Admission is free, but laser show tickets are $4 for everyone.

Much of Columbus' historical architecture is showcased in a revitalized 26-block National Register Historic District, part of the original 1828 plan of the city. The Pemberton House, 11 Seventh Street, is part of Heritage Corner, a collection of five house museums. The cottage, once owned by Dr. John S. Pemberton, the pharmacist who invented Coca-Cola, is a cherished local landmark. (Some Columbus residents insist that the good doctor originated the magic formula in their city instead of in Atlanta.) Call the Historic Columbus Foundation, (706) 322-0756, for information on touring Pemberton House and other museums in this area.

The grandest structure in Columbus seemed doomed until determined citizens took action. The Springer Opera House, which opened in 1871 and played host to such stars as Lillie Langtry and Ethel Barrymore, now shines resplendent and restored with year-round entertainment for the whole family. In 1971 then-governor Jimmy Carter declared the Springer as the State Theatre of Georgia; it has been a National Historic Landmark since 1975.

There are numerous accommodation options in Columbus. One place you might want to check out is Rothschild-Pound House Bed & Breakfast, 201 Seventh Street, (800) 585-4075 or

www.thepoundhouseinn.com. Rothschild-Pound House is an 1870 Victorian structure decorated with antiques and original artwork. Each guest suite has a private bath including a tub and shower, fresh flowers, and a mini-refrigerator stocked with cold drinks. Some suites have working fireplaces. Rates at Rothschild-Pound range from $97 to $195, including full breakfast and evening cocktails and hors d'oeuvres.

Places to eat in Columbus include the Buckhead Grill, 5010 Armour Road, (706) 571-9995. The Grill offers indoor and outdoor dining in a casually upscale atmosphere and serves steaks, pasta dishes, seafood, sandwiches, and salads. Crystal River Seafood, 2606 Manchester Expressway, (706) 324-0055, serves up treasures of the deep-fried, broiled, grilled, or steamed variety. Check out their daily specials. The Olive Branch Cafe, 1032 Broadway, (706) 322-7410, has been lauded by locals as the best fine-dining establishment in town.

To reach Columbus, take I-85 South from Atlanta to La Grange, then take I-185 to Columbus. For more information on the area, call the Columbus Convention and Visitors Bureau at (800) 999-1613.

Macon

Macon, the home of white columns and cherry blossoms, is in the heart of Georgia at the crossroads of two major interstates: I-75 (north-south) and I-16 (east-west). It's an easy trip from Atlanta, approximately 90 miles south on I-75. With the multitude of things to see and do, you may find yourself returning for a second chance to enjoy this hospitable setting.

It's a good thing Macon residents love their history, because they're surrounded by it, from ancient Indian mounds to antebellum mansions. The Macon-Bibb County Convention & Visitors Bureau gives excellent assistance with information on Macon's pleasures. You'll find the CVB in historic Terminal Station at the intersection of Mulberry Street and M. L. King Boulevard, (478) 743-1074 or (800) 768-3401. See also www.maconga.org.

When it comes to historic neighborhoods, Macon is unmatched, with more than 2,000 acres of neighborhoods listed on the National Register of Historic Places. Pick up the Macon CVB brochure that outlines three self-guided walking tours to acquaint you with bygone days of the South.

The See What Sherman Didn't Burn Tour covers several sites of interest, including churches, Tuscan-Victorian homes, and poet Sidney Lanier's Cottage. The White Columns Tour presents magnificently preserved mansions such as the Hay House, an example of Italian Renaissance Revival that had indoor plumbing, an intercom system, an elevator, and 19 Carrara marble mantelpieces—fantastic luxuries when the house was completed in 1861. Other examples include the 1842 Inn, now a bed-and-breakfast with adjoining Victorian cottages, and the Cannonball House, an authentic example of Greek Revival architecture built in 1853 and struck by a Union cannonball, which crashed into the home's parlor and came to rest, intact, in the hall. The Downtown Walking Tour includes homes, churches, government buildings, and the elegantly restored Grand Opera House, built in 1884 and still in use. This opera house once had the biggest stage south of the Mason-Dixon line—large enough for a production of *Ben Hur*.

If you prefer to ride, Sidney's Tours of Historic Macon, (478) 743-1074, leave from the Welcome Center, Terminal Station, at 10:00 A.M. and 2:00 P.M. Monday through Saturday. Sidney's offers costumed tour guides who will escort you by bus through Macon's historic downtown. Practically all of Macon's downtown has been proclaimed a National Historic District, with 48 buildings and homes cited for architectural excellence.

Other Macon landmarks include Wesleyan College, founded in 1836. Wesleyan was the first college in the world chartered to grant degrees to women. Among its well-known graduates is Madame Chiang Kaishek. Brick and marble structures grace the lovely, 240-acre campus at 476 Forsyth Road.

To go farther back in time, visit an ancient Indian community at the Ocmulgee National Monument, 1207 Emery Highway, (478) 752-8257. You may explore a ceremonial earthlodge; its clay floor dates back 1,000 years. A museum, prehistoric trenches, a funeral mound, and several temple mounds provide tantalizing clues to the sequence of cultures that lived on the Macon Plateau. Centuries later, in 1540, Spanish explorer Hernando DeSoto is said to have recorded the first Christian baptism here on the banks of the Ocmulgee River. Admission is free; the site is open from 9:00 A.M. to 5:00 P.M. every day, except Christmas and New Year's Day. The park has a visitor center complete with exhibits, a short film, and other information. From I-75, exit on I-16 East; take either the first or second exit from I-16 and follow U.S. Highway 80 east a mile to the park.

Millions of years ago, the ocean covered what is now Macon. Prehistoric fossils, sand dollars, and shark teeth are frequent finds here. The Museum of Arts and Sciences and the Mark Smith Planetarium, 4182 Forsyth Road, presents nature trails and a 40-million-year-old whale fossil skeleton unearthed near Macon. Hours are 9:00 A.M. to 5:00 P.M., Monday through Thursday and Saturday; 9:00 A.M. to 9:00 P.M. on Friday; and 1:00 to 5:00 P.M. on Sunday. Call (478) 477-3232 for information on the planetarium shows, art galleries, and rotating exhibits.

Macon's African-American history is rich with contributions to the arts, religion, and education. The city's informative brochure, *Macon, Georgia: Black Heritage*, available from the Macon CVB, presents an African-American Heritage Tour and highlights such landmarks as the Harriet Tubman African-American Museum, 340 Walnut Street, (478) 743-8544. Here, past meets present in the works of artists featured in the permanent collections as well as in visiting exhibits. Take note of local artist Wilfred Stroud's seven-panel mural *From Africa to America*, which visually traces a history filled with struggle and accomplishment.

While showing a deep respect for the past, the Macon of today marches to a modern tune. Its leaders guide the city to progress through several ventures. One is the renovation of the Douglass Theatre, where such greats as Cab Calloway, Bessie Smith, Little Richard, and Otis Redding performed. Ground was broken in the summer of 1997 for a Sports Hall of Fame downtown. And the city hosts the Georgia Music Hall of Fame, (478) 750–8555 or (888) 427–6257, a $6 million investment in Georgia's cultural arts that memorializes musical greats from around the state. The hall opened in 1996, next to the historic Terminal Station in downtown Macon on Martin Luther King Jr. Boulevard. The three-story, 38,000-square-foot museum and more than 11,000-square-foot exhibition hall focus on Georgia's rich and diverse musical heritage. The Georgia Music Hall of Fame holds music and memorabilia of Georgia artists such as Lena Horne, Macon's own Otis Redding, the Allman Brothers, and Little Richard, who are featured in a small village created in the exhibit hall. Visitors may enjoy music and memorabilia in a variety of venues including the Rhythm & Blues Revue, the Gospel Chapel, and the 1950s Soda Fountain. The hall is open Monday through Saturday, 9:00 A.M. to 5:00 P.M., and Sunday, 1:00 to 5:00 P.M.

Another special showcase, the Museum of Aviation in Warner Robins, (478) 926–6870, is just 15 miles south of Macon and 7 miles from I-75. The Museum of Aviation presents more than 85 historic aircraft, from the Fairchild UC-119C Flying Boxcar to modern fighters such as the F-15 Eagle. Admission is free, though there's a small charge ($2 per adult, $1 per child younger than 12) for two 30-minute films, *To Fly* and *Flyers,* in a new 250-seat theater with surround sound and a 30-foot-by-40-foot screen. The attached Georgia Aviation Hall of Fame honors notable pilots such as early women aviators, the first African-American military aviator, and the founder of Delta Air Lines. Hours are seven days a week, 9:00 A.M. to 5:00 P.M.

Take a break from Macon's history and unwind in one of the city's many restaurants. From Italian to barbecue, there's an array of dining options. Save room for the classic peach cobbler or mac-aroon pie at Len Bergs Restaurant, (478) 742–9255. At Michael's on Mulberry, (478) 743–3997, there's a quaint outdoor eating area.

In addition to special events scheduled year-round in Macon, a particular highlight occurs each spring. The blooming of Macon's 170,000 flowering Yoshino cherry trees heralds the annual Cherry Blossom Festival. Events, performances, and exhibits topped with Southern hospitality fill the calendar. This event begins on the third weekend of March and lasts one week. The festival even has its own outlet, the Cherry Blossom Festival Gift Shop, 365 Third Street. The shop, open year-round, sells an array of cherry blossom souvenirs and gifts. To find out more about the Cherry Blossom Festival, call the Macon CVB, (478) 743–3401.

The 1842 Inn, 353 College Street, (478) 741–1842 or (800) 336–1842, is an elegant hostelry on a street of beautiful homes. The inn is decorated in antiques that suit the Greek Revival antebellum mansion and an adjoining Victorian house that share a courtyard and garden. This award-winning inn offers in-room full breakfast complete with newspaper and evening hors d'oeuvres in the library, among other amenities. Room rates differ—contact the inn for more information.

Okefenokee Swamp

About 5 hours south from Atlanta, the Okefenokee Swamp (www.okefenokee.fws.gov) teems with abundant plant and animal life. The Okefenokee, a 483,000-acre National Wildlife Refuge and parkland, is 38 miles long and 25 miles wide. The swamp is a vast bog inside a saucer-shaped depression that was once part of the ocean floor.

Okefenokee is white man's version of the Native American words for "land of the trembling earth." Peat deposits in the swamp have spots so unstable that stomping the earth causes nearby bushes and trees to tremble. The swamp contains about 60,000 acres of marshland that harbors herons, egrets, ibises, cranes, and bitterns. Other wildlife in the swamp in-

Take a boat tour through the "land of the trembling earth" at Okefenokee Swamp. PHOTO: THE CREATIVE SOURCE, OKEFENOKEE SWAMP

cludes red-cockaded woodpeckers, American alligators, wood storks, sandhill cranes, deer, bears, and otters.

You can reach the Okefenokee by three entrances, each of which charges admission. The east entrance, near Folkston, gives access to the swamp via the man-made Suwanee Canal. The swamp's most extensive open areas branch off this canal. This entrance has a visitor center, a 4.5-mile wildlife observation drive, 4.5 miles of hiking trails, two observation towers, and a 4,000-foot boardwalk into the swamp. The east entrance is 8 miles southwest of Folkston on Georgia Highway 121/23. Admission is $5 per vehicle. The west entrance lets you enter the park via Stephen C. Foster State Park, where you can camp at designated areas. The park is actually about 18 miles northeast of Fargo; it features cottages, campsites, a camp store, a museum, boating, and boat rentals. Admission is $5 per vehicle. The north entrance to the Okefenokee, near Waycross, (912) 283–0583, takes you in through the Okefenokee Swamp Park, a private, nonprofit attraction operating under a leasing agreement with the U.S. Fish and Wildlife Service. The park, on U.S. Highway 1 South, offers water trails, interpretive exhibits, boat tours, and wilderness walkways. Northside admission is $10, ages 12 to 61, and $9, ages 5 to 11.

Capitalizing on its proximity to the Okefenokee, Waycross has other swamp-related attractions. Obediah's Okefenok, Swamp Road, (912) 287–0090, allows you to view the swamper's life in the mid-1800s through more than 50 exhibits, including a historic log home and living history demonstrations. Hours are 10:00 A.M. to 5:00 P.M. daily. Admission is $4.50 for adults, $3 for children ages 6 to 17, and $3.50 for seniors. The Okefenokee Heritage Center Museum on North Augusta Avenue, (912) 285–4260, has an array of information on the history of the swamp and the early settlers of Waycross. The museum also hosts different art exhibits each month.

Pine Mountain

Pine Mountain (www.pinemountain.org), near Warm Springs, is home to the extraordinary resort complex Callaway Gardens.

Seventy miles south of Atlanta on I–85 and 30 miles north of Columbus on I–185, Callaway Gardens' 14,000 acres of natural beauty include gardens, woodlands, lakes, wildlife, and recreational areas. This floral wonderland was created in 1952 by the husband-and-wife team of Cason Callaway and Virginia Hand Callaway and is a wholesome, family environment for relaxation and inspiration.

Visit Mr. Cason's Vegetable Garden, for years the Southern location of the PBS series *The Victory Garden* and the source of much of the good food served in the resort's restaurants. The Cecil B. Day Butterfly Center, billed as the largest free-flight butterfly conservatory in North America, houses approximately 1,000 free-flight butterflies from three continents. In the John A. Sibley Horticulture Center, a five-acre indoor/outdoor garden, you'll see unusual collections of native and exotic plants and flowers.

Callaway Gardens' most famous flora abound on the Azalea Trail, which has more than 700 varieties of this Southern charmer. Other flower trails include the

---

Insiders' Tip

Since the early 19th century, locals and developers saw the Okefenokee as a "nuisance," and many attempts to drain the swamp were attempted (and failed) over the years. Only with the rise in tourism and a new emphasis on natural resources preservation in the mid-20th century did the swamp gain prestige as a valuable resource in and of itself.

The butterfly conservatory in Callaway Gardens. PHOTO: JOHN MCKAY

Rhododendron and Holly Trails. Take special note of cofounder Virginia Callaway's favorite, the Wildflower Trail. Rest a while in the solitude of the Ida Cason Callaway Memorial Chapel. Dr. Norman Vincent Peale officiated at the chapel's dedication. In the summer, swim at Robin Lake Beach or watch Florida State University's "Flying High" Circus. Meander along the 7.5-mile bike trail through breathtaking scenery. New to Callaway Gardens is the 35,000-square-foot Virginia Hand Callaway Discovery Center. This beautiful lakeside facility showcases the many aspects of Callaway Gardens, with exhibit areas, information kiosks, lecture and museum halls, an education wing, and a theater continuously playing an introductory film, *Time & The Gardens.*

As a guest of Callaway Gardens Resorts, you can take advantage of tennis, fishing, sailing, and golf on the Mountain View course. The resort offers 800 guest rooms and a considerable variety of packages. Prices vary according to length of stay, type of accommodations, meal plans, and activities. For information on all Callaway Gardens attractions, call (800) CALLAWAY.

Visit the Pine Mountain Wild Animal Safari, 1300 Oak Grove Road, (800) 367–2751 (www.animalsafari.com), near Callaway Gardens. Drive your car or ride a safari bus through a 500-acre preserve where llamas, antelopes, camels, and nearly 300 different animal species roam freely. Then visit Old McDonald's Farm with a petting zoo, monkey house, snake house, and alligator pit. Adults pay $13.95; kids 3 to 9 pay $11.95; seniors and students through age 16 pay $12.95. The park is open from 10:00 A.M. to 5:30 P.M. every day except Christmas. Hours extend to 7:30 P.M. in the summer.

A perfect spot for antiques buffs awaits 2 miles north of Callaway Gardens at 230 South Main Street in the Pine Mountain Antique Mall. More than 100 dealer booths and lobby showcases present period furnishings, clocks, books, and jewelry. The Village of Pine Mountain offers a multitude of gift and antiques shops, restaurants, and motels.

Roosevelt Stables, on Georgia Highway 354 in Pine Mountain, (706) 628–7463, offers guided trail rides lasting from one hour up to five days. The stables stay open seven days a week, 9:00 A.M. to 5:00

P.M., year-round. If you call and make an advance reservation, you can ride later than 5:00 P.M.

Besides Callaway Gardens Resorts, Pine Mountain offers a number of accommodations including the Mountain Top Inn (which we describe in our Warm Springs section) and Pine Mountain Club Chalets, a cluster of alpine chalets surrounding a fishing lake, tennis courts, and swimming pool near Callaway Gardens, (800) 535-7622. Room rates are $150 per night. A few minutes from town, Magnolia Hall, (706) 628-4566, is an 1890s Victorian cottage filled with antiques and porch swings. Guest rooms are $105 to $125 and include a full breakfast.

To reach Pine Mountain from Atlanta, take I-85 South to I-185 and continue south to exit 14. Turn left on U.S. Highway 27 and drive 11 miles to Callaway Gardens. For information about all the Pine Mountain attractions, call the Pine Mountain Tourism Association, (800) 441-3502.

Nature lovers will revel in Pine Mountain's 9,000-acre Franklin Delano Roosevelt State Park, approximately 12 miles from the Little White House (see our Warm Springs section) on Georgia Highway 190. This outstanding recreational facility offers camping, rental cabins, and a mountain stone swimming pool. Beautiful woodlands surround lovely lakes for fishing and boating. For more information, call (706) 663-4858. The Pine Mountain Trail, a 23-mile blazed hiking trail, runs from the Callaway Country Store on U.S. 27 to the WJSP-TV tower on GA 85 West. Pick up a trail map at the FDR state park office. The park is open daily from 7:00 A.M. to 10:00 P.M.

Warm Springs

From Atlanta, Warm Springs (www.warmspringsga.com) is about 80 miles south on I-85 and U.S. Alternate 27. Follow the signs to the peaceful place where Franklin Delano Roosevelt built the Little White House, Georgia Highway 85 West, (706) 655-5870. Serene and slow-paced, the setting moves visitors with its low-keyed spirit of tribute. Many of his admin-

istration's policies were formulated there. In the home, it is always April 12, 1945—the day Roosevelt died there.

Roosevelt, who suffered from polio-induced paralysis, had heard of the restorative powers attributed to the natural springs in this resort area. He began visiting Warm Springs in 1924, finding solace not only in the water but also in the countryside's whispering pines and wooded ravines.

It's a short walk from the Little White House to the adjacent and highly personal museum. Stroll along an ornamental walkway flanked with state flags and native stones of the 50 states and the District of Columbia. In the museum you'll find a sense of history in a naturally beautiful environment. Peruse at your own pace Roosevelt's walking cane collection, gifts from heads of state, and exhibits depicting the life of this world leader. Don't miss viewing the historic newsreels, which featured never-seen footage of Roosevelt in leg braces and wheelchairs. The Little White House historic site is open from 9:00 A.M. to 5:00 P.M. daily, with the last tour beginning at 4:00 P.M. It closes on Thanksgiving, Christmas, and New Year's Day.

The nearby Warm Springs Village, which hit hard times after Roosevelt's death, revived in the 1980s with an infusion of craft and antiques shops. A cluster of more than 65 boutiques, restaurants, and accommodations include Spring Street's Bulloch House, (706) 655-9068. Built in 1892, it sits on a hilltop surrounded by birdhouses. Described as "country with class," the restaurant offers home-cooked Southern food with hospitality.

You'll find 14 overnight guest rooms in the Hotel Warm Springs, built in 1907. It's at 17 Broad Street on U.S. Highway 27-Alternate 41, the main thoroughfare of Warm Springs. Revived by owner Geraldine Thompson into a charming bed-and-breakfast, the hotel's history includes glory days when FDR's visits created much excitement. The style of bygone days remains alongside the welcome addition of modern conveniences such as individual heating/cooling units. The rooms feature period antiques as well as furniture made in a New York factory owned by Mrs. Roosevelt, which the owner calls Eleanor furniture. All the rooms have private baths, some with claw-foot tubs. One room has an iron bed more than 100 years old (it belonged to Geraldine's grandmother). Famous guests documented in the hotel's books include the King and Queen of Mexico and the King and Queen of Spain. You'll see a picture of FDR and Bette Davis at breakfast following her stint entertaining the troops at Fort Benning in Columbus. Rooms rent for $45 to $175. For reservations and information, call (800) 366-7616.

Another quality accommodation in the area is the Mountain Top Inn & Resort, on top of Pine Mountain in the 9,000-acre Roosevelt State Park. The inn's location, just a five-minute drive to Warm Springs or Callaway Gardens, is a special advantage. This facility offers house-size log cabins, alpine-style chalets, and world-theme guest rooms, a pool, tennis courts, and hiking trails. Cabins rent for $145 to $185 per day, guest rooms $45 to $85; for information and reservations, call (800) 533-6376.

On the way to Warm Springs, you might want to take a detour at Newnan, about 45 minutes south of Atlanta off I-85. This town, dubbed the City of Homes, has a number of antebellum homes that were preserved due to Newnan's remoteness from the major battlefields and campaign marches during the Civil War. Courthouse Square and the downtown commercial district are on the National Register of Historic Places.

Make an appointment to stroll through the extensive gardens at Catalpa Plantation, 2295 Old Poplar Road, (800) 697-1835. Admission is $5 per person. Or take a driving tour of Newnan; pick up a brochure at the Male Academy Museum, 30 Temple Avenue, (770) 251-0207, which is also the home of the Newnan Historical Society. While you're there, check out the Civil War displays and an 1860s classroom. The museum is open Tuesday, Wednesday, and Thursday from 10:00 A.M. to noon and 1:00 to 3:00 P.M., and 2:00 to 5:00 P.M. Saturday and Sunday. The Newnan–Coweta County Chamber of Commerce, 23 Bullshore Drive, (770) 253-2270, and Coweta County Convention & Visitors Bureau, (770) 254-2629, can give you more information; they, too, have brochures for the driving tour.

But Where's the Beach?

Atlanta, with all its boosterism and bravado, hasn't been able to attract the Atlantic Ocean to its city limits. But beach buffs need not despair. If nothing but the ocean will do, the interstates will get you to the beach in five or six hours.

You may head in either of two directions: due south to the Florida Panhandle and Alabama coast, or southeast to Georgia's Golden Isles. And although it doesn't have a beach of its own, the historic city of Savannah is a must-see destination of the Georgia coastal area. For more information on Savannah, check out the *Insiders' Guide to Savannah*. If Florida is your choice, the drive will take you to the Gulf of Mexico and Panama City's powdery beach. For information, call (800) PC-BEACH. A slightly southwesterly direction from Atlanta takes you to Pensacola, in the northwest corner of Florida's Panhandle. Call the Pensacola Tourist Information Center, (800) 874-1234, for information.

Georgia's beaches offer an unbeatable combination: environmentally unique settings, traditional oceanfront pleasures, and historic sights. You can reach four of the barrier islands protecting Georgia's coast by car: Jekyll Island, Tybee Island, St. Simons Island, and Sea Island. These and a neighboring island, Little St. Simons, are collectively known as Georgia's Golden Isles. Besides the broad beaches, the landscape on these isles features 300-year-old oak trees draped in moss, towering pines, and fragrant magnolias. The area of the barrier islands encompasses 165,000 acres divided between marsh and dry land. Nature's influence is evident in the constantly changing shoreline, reshaped by winds, tides, and the serpentine river channels snaking through the inlets.

To the untrained eye, the barrier islands' marshes look like a sea of dead grass. In reality they are teeming with life, enormously productive, and essential to Georgia's multimillion-dollar seafood industry. Over the course of 25 years, one acre of marsh can produce a half-billion dollars worth of shellfish alone. Wildlife, including alligators, snakes, birds, raccoons, minks, and otters, live, breed, and feed in these ecosystems. On any causeway near the marshland and tidal creeks, you may see the graceful great blue herons or snow-white egrets. Nearly half of the 165,000 acres are protected, with approximately 87,700 acres now developed, a somewhat remarkable ratio compared with other seashore areas.

Cumberland Island

Georgia's southernmost barrier island is a federally protected wilderness and seashore accessible by tour boat only. Cumberland has one small, privately operated inn, the Greyfield Inn, (904) 261-6408. You generally need to book three months in advance for this place, although they do take reservations with as little as 24 hours' notice if they're not fully booked. Rooms run from $395 to $575, double occupancy. Rates include breakfast, lunch, and dinner, a three- to four-hour outing with a naturalist by Jeep, bicycles that can be taken out daily, and round-trip boat fare on the inn's private ferry from Fernandina Beach on Amelia Island, just across the state line in Florida. Although the locals don't brag about it, the Greyfield Inn housed guests for the John Kennedy Jr. nuptials in 1996.

Insiders' Tip

The tall, wispy plants growing on sand dunes at the beach are called sea oats. Picking sea oats is prohibited by law because they are vital in preventing erosion.

(The wedding ceremony took place in a rustic church on the remote north end of the island.)

You can book a table at the Greyfield's dining room if you aren't staying at the inn; you can either come on your own boat or arrange for a special charter off the island after dinner. The dining room serves fresh seafood and produce from the inn's own garden.

Besides the inn, the only place to stay on Cumberland is in wilderness campsites, for which you must make a reservation. Accommodations are available on the mainland in St. Mary's, where the National Parks tour boat docks. Cumberland's appeal is that it's unspoiled. Wild horses and deer roam freely. The marshes are home to ducks and wading birds, while alligators thrive in freshwater lakes. Loggerhead turtles lay eggs by the dunes on Cumberland's pristine beach. You can also spot armadillos, wild turkeys, the occasional bottle-nosed dolphin, and the ruins of two 18th- and 19th-century mansions. To find out more about traveling to Cumberland, call the Cumberland Island National Seashore office at (912) 882-4335 or (888) 817-3421 or see the Web site, www.nps.gov/cuis.

Jekyll Island

In 1886, 100 of America's wealthiest men—including members of the Pulitzer, Rockefeller, Morgan, McCormick, and Gould families—bought Jekyll Island and formed the elite Jekyll Island Club. With their island virtually closed to the outside world, the club members began building vacation "cottages," actually elaborate mansions, in which to spend their winters. They also built an ornate Victorian-style clubhouse and spent the seasons hunting, horseback riding, and playing golf and tennis in their secluded enclave.

At one time, the winter residents of Jekyll were said to control one-sixth of the world's wealth. You can see the telephone where the first interstate calls were made from the president of AT&T to President Woodrow Wilson in Washington, D.C., and to Alexander Graham Bell in New York.

After World War II, skyrocketing taxes and other financial changes made the luxury level on Jekyll impractical, even for barons. In 1947 the State of Georgia bought Jekyll and turned it into a getaway everyone could afford. Most of the 33 old cottages have been restored, and the renovated riverfront clubhouse is now the Jekyll Island Club Hotel, (912) 635-2600. Different rate packages are available. Call for details. The hotel's elegant dining room serves three meals daily. The 240-acre area that the old Jekyll Island Club members inhabited is a National Historic Landmark District. You can tour the area daily; to find out more, call (912) 635-2119.

Nowadays Jekyll attracts families, honeymooners, retirees, conferences, and the entire gamut of pleasure seekers to its 10-mile beach and expansive assortment of fun activities. Jekyll offers accommodations to suit all budgets. Villas by the Sea, (800) 841-6262, is a seaside complex that rents guest rooms and condos. Rates vary from $79 to $269. The Clarion Resort Buccaneer, (912) 635-2261, is an oceanfront property offering rooms facing the beach and rooms facing the island mainland. Summer rates range from $109 to $199, depending on your choice of accommodation, which includes rooms with king-size or double beds and an efficiency unit with two double beds, a kitchen, dining room, sitting area, and patio or balcony.

Cycle along 20 miles of paved trails around the island. You can bring your own bike or rent one at the Mini Golf Course, (912) 635-2648, most hotels, or at the Jekyll Island campground, (912) 635-3021. Arrange fishing trips or sightseeing cruises through Jekyll Harbor Marina, (912) 635-3137. Golfers have four courses to choose from, three 18-hole courses and one nine-hole course that wind through deep woods, around lakes, and along the dunes. For rates and tee times, call Jekyll Island Golf Club, (912) 635-2368.

If you want a bird's-eye view of the coastal life, take part in Jekyll's nature walks offered at 9:30 A.M. on Monday, Tuesday, Wednesday, and Saturday. On Monday, the walk starts at the footbridge

near Clam Creek; Tuesday's walk starts from the South Dunes picnic area, and Wednesday walkers meet at the St. Andrews picnic area. Visitors to the island can get a map at Jekyll's Collection Station (it costs $3 per vehicle to enter the island), which clearly delineates these spots. Nature tours cost $5 for adults, $3 for children, and last a couple of hours. Call the Jekyll Island Historic District office, (912) 635-4092, for more information.

Summer Waves, (912) 635-2074, a family aquatic theme park, opens daily from Memorial Day to Labor Day and on a few select weekends before Memorial Day and after Labor Day. In these 11 acres of planned frivolity, daring adventurers may brave the Hurricane Tornado and Pirate Passage, a five-story enclosed flume ride. Calmer spirits will gravitate toward the Kiddie Pool and the Slow Motion Ocean. Admission is $16.95 for anyone taller than 4 feet, $14.95 for munchkins.

Jekyll is midway between Savannah and Jacksonville, Florida. To get there from Atlanta, take I-75 South, then pick up I-16 near Macon. Follow I-16 South to I-95 (about 80 miles). Take exit 6 off I-95, and turn left onto U.S. Highway 17. Travel 5 miles to Georgia Highway 520, turn left, and follow the Jekyll Island Causeway 6 miles. Contact the Jekyll Island Welcome Center, (877) 453-5955, for help in planning your trip or see www.jekyllisland.com.

Savannah

Between four and five hours southeast of Atlanta, the port city of Savannah (www.savannah-visit.com) is great for a weekend getaway. (Take I-75 South to Macon, then I-16 to Savannah.) On the Savannah River, the city itself doesn't have a beach. Nearby Tybee Island, described below, serves as Savannah's beach. In 1996 Savannah hosted the Summer Olympic yachting events in Wassaw Sound.

Savannah was the first city in the new colony of Georgia founded by English settlers led by Gen. James Edward Oglethorpe in 1733. Oglethorpe's planned grid pattern resulted in a city with two dozen picturesque squares shaded by live oaks and magnolias and blooming with oleander and azaleas. Many of these squares have historical markers and monuments honoring Savannah's rich history. A 2.2-square-mile area of downtown Savannah is one of the largest National Historic Landmark Districts in the United States. Here, you can see more than 1,400 restored 18th- and 19th-century structures. Other points of historical interest include Factor's Walk on Bay Street, the district that housed cotton merchants' offices when Savannah was the center of cotton commerce. Ornate iron bridgeways connect the buildings. The Old City Market, at Jefferson and St. Julian Streets, is a restored historic area featuring food, entertainment, shops, and art galleries. The city's Riverfront Plaza on Old River Street comprises 9 blocks along the Savannah River with fountains and benches. Old cotton warehouses now house shops, restaurants, pubs, and museums. Old Fort Jackson, 1 Fort Jackson Road, (912) 232-3945, 3 miles from downtown, is the oldest standing fort in Georgia. On the south bank of the Savannah River, the fort has the largest cannon in the United States on display. The cannon was used in the War of 1812 and the Civil War. Other displays highlight the history of the city and the coast. The fort is open daily from 9:00 A.M. to 5:00 P.M.; admission is $4 for adults, $3 for students, seniors, and children older than 6.

Just a few miles down Tybee Island Road (also known as U.S. 80) from Fort Jackson is Fort Pulaski, (912) 786-5787, which guarded Savannah from a seaborne

Fountains are popular in Savannah parks. PHOTO: SAVANNAH CONVENTION & VISITORS BUREAU

invasion until bombarded into surrendering early in the Civil War. The old, still battered fort is now restored and operated by the National Park Service, and open for tours. A small museum with a good bookstore contains a bare handful of artifacts and some reasonably well-preserved regimental battle flags, and there are several rather nice "mini-museums" within casements of the fort itself. The fort is open after Memorial Day from 9:00 A.M. to 7:00 P.M. daily. Winter hours are 9:00 A.M. to 5:00 P.M. daily. Admission is $3 (children age 16 and under are free).

Savannah has long been a popular tourist destination, but in the late 1990s its allure got a boost. John Berendt's best-selling book, *Midnight in the Garden of Good and Evil,* has caused even more people to flock to the city to see landmarks and people the author mentioned. Join a tour highlighting Berendt's landmarks.

Fine restaurants, hotels to fit all budgets, and charming bed-and-breakfasts abound in the city. We'll point you toward a few that stand out. The Ballastone Inn and Townhouse, 14 East Oglethorpe Avenue, (800) 822–4553, has been recommended by *Condé Nast Traveler* and the *New York Times.* Built in 1838, the inn has 18 rooms; six more are in a townhouse four blocks away. Call for room rates. The Gastonian, 220 East Gaston Street, (800) 322–6603, is an 1868 award-winning luxury inn. Rooms at this inn range from $180 to $299.

The Pirate's House restaurant, a Savannah landmark at 20 East Broad Street, (912) 233–5757, offers lunch, dinner, and Sunday brunch in an authentic 1733 tavern. Pirates used an underground passage in this establishment to smuggle booty to and from nearby ships. Garibaldi's Cafe, 313 West Congress Street, (912) 232–7118, is a highly praised cafe in the historic district serving nightly seafood specials. It gets crowded; call for reservations. To find out more about all Savannah has to offer, contact the Savannah Convention & Visitors Bureau, (877) SAVANNAH, or pick up a copy of the *Insiders' Guide to Savannah.*

Sea Island

Sea Island (www.seaisland.com) is definitely not for beachgoers on a budget. The Cloister, one of Georgia's most highly rated resorts, is a favorite with the well-heeled. You can also rent private homes on the island, but these highly rated properties run more along the lines of the Jekyll Island Club "cottages"; that is, they're opulent. To give you an idea of how opulent: A two-week stay can run anywhere from $3,500 to $15,000. The Cloister, a truly elegant resort, offers a charming old section as well as new oceanfront rooms and suites that range from $190 and up, depending on the time of year and view. Prices include three full meals. Guests can enjoy seafood in the renovated Beach Club restaurant, play golf or tennis, ride horses, stroll, or swim on the beach, and be pampered at the resort's spa. The Cloisters' executive chef offers a culinary tour, and the grounds supervisor will take guests on a tour of the grounds. For more information about The Cloister, call (800) 732–4752. To rent a cottage through the home rentals, dial (912) 638–5112 or (800) SEA–ISLAND.

St. Simons Island

Rich in history, natural beauty, recreational opportunities, sophisticated shopping, art galleries, and nightlife, St. Simons (www.ssilife.com) is a popular beach destination. The novelist Eugenia Price has helped stimulate interest in the area with her historical novels set on the island. The Sea Island Singers, organized on St. Simons by Mrs. Maxfield Parrish, brought attention to St. Simons and Sea Islands through their performances and recordings. Although most of the original singers have passed away, a new generation carries on the tradition.

Sixteenth-century French explorers encountered the Guale Indians on St. Simons. Spanish Jesuit and then Franciscan missionaries tried to convert the native occupants to no avail. They finally gave up, leaving only their name for the place, "San

Simon," which was later Anglicized to St. Simons. James Edward Oglethorpe, founder of the British colony of Georgia, brought settlers to St. Simons in 1736. They established the town of Frederica and built Fort Frederica, which was destroyed by fire in 1758. Today, the site is a National Monument. National Park Service interpretation helps you gain insight into the settlers' lives as you tour the ruins, (912) 638-3639. Oglethorpe brought John and Charles Wesley with him, and they established Christ Church, on Frederica Road, before returning to England to found the Methodist church. The Bloody Marsh Battle Site on Demere Road is where British troops repelled Spanish invaders in 1742, which marked a turning point in the Spanish invasion of Georgia. Another point of historical interest is the 1872 Lighthouse and Museum of Coastal History, 101 12th Street, (912) 638-4666. Climb the 129 steps to the top of the lighthouse and enjoy a panoramic view.

Besides its historical attractions, St. Simons offers the usual range of island activities: swimming, golfing, fishing, biking, and boating. Several companies offer tours of the area, including a cruise of the coastal waters; contact Golden Isles Touring Company, (912) 638-8092. Take a day trip to Little St. Simons, a privately owned, unspoiled barrier island that, like Cumberland, is accessible only by boat. Little St. Simons offers more than 6 miles of undeveloped beach, swimming, shelling, fishing, canoeing, horseback riding, and bird-watching. The island has one inn, the Lodge on Little St. Simons Island, with 12 rooms that accommodate a maximum of 24 guests. Call (912) 638-7472 to make a reservation. Peak times are October through May; you should call to book a room at least one month in advance. If you want a specific date, call earlier. Rooms rent from $375 in the off-season; rates climb as high as $600 per night in the summer. Prices include three meals and use of all facilities.

Restaurants on St. Simons offer several choices for seafood lovers, including the Georgia Sea Grille, (912) 638-1197. Mullet Bay, 512 Ocean Boulevard, (912) 634-9977, serves lunch and dinner in a re-laxed, Key West–type setting. Several eateries are clustered around the Golden Isles Marina, offering scenic views of the yachts and the water.

You can rent cottages and condos on St. Simons or stay at a variety of hotels and motels. The King and Prince Beach Resort, 201 Arnold Road, (800) 342-0212, is an island standard. Oceanfront rooms range from $189 to $249; two-bedroom villas are $339 per day. The Sea Gate Inn, 1014 Ocean Boulevard, (800) 562-8812, offers oceanfront rooms and suites from $150 to $345. Sports-minded vacationers enjoy the Sea Palms Golf & Tennis Resort, 5445 Frederica Road, (912) 638-3351 or (800) 841-6268, which offers rooms and suites for $119 to $289, with certain golf packages at lower rates. To find out about renting cottages and condos, try Golden Isles Realty, (912) 638-8623, Parker-Kaufman Realtors, (912) 638-3368, or Trupp-Hodnett Enterprises, 520 Ocean Boulevard, (800) 627-6850. To find out more about St. Simons Island, call the St. Simons Island Visitors Center, (912) 638-9014.

Tybee Island

Generations of Savannah families have escaped each summer to Tybee Island (www.tybeeisland.com), where the laid-back atmosphere encourages utter relaxation. Funky beachfront shops and cafes line the wide sandy beach of this closest-to-Atlanta of the barrier islands. Lack of pretension is Tybee's religion, coupled with a certain vagabond flavor that keeps visitors coming back year after year.

Visit the Tybee Island Lighthouse, which dates from 1773 and is one of the first public structures in Georgia. You can take a free guided tour of the lighthouse; for information, call (912) 786-5801. An adjacent museum has exhibits on the island's history.

Locals and tourists favor a bed-and-breakfast inn called Hunter House, 1701 Butler Avenue, (912) 786-7515. Built one block from the ocean in 1910, it's been given a snazzy renovation complete with tastefully decorated dining rooms. Relax with appetizers on the wide front porch before ordering from the full dinner menu. Rooms cost from $75 to $100. Tybee also offers several hotels and motels, beachfront homes, and condos. Call Island Rentals, (912) 786-4217, to see what's available.

Popular restaurants on Tybee include the North Beach Grill, 141-A Meddin Drive, (912) 786-9003, a funky, reggae-filled place where you can eat crab cake sandwiches at an umbrella-covered outdoor table or dine at an inside table or barstool on the screened-in porch. Don't dress up. McElwee's Seafood House, 101 Lovell Avenue, (912) 786-4259, features crab stew, blackened seafood, and steamed oysters on its bill of fare.

To reach Tybee Island, take I-75 South from Atlanta, and follow it to Macon, where you'll take I-16 into Savannah. Take the 37th Street exit off I-16, and turn right onto Abercorn Street. Follow Abercorn to Victory Drive (which turns into GA 80). Turn left onto Victory Drive and follow it for approximately 15 miles straight to the Atlantic and Tybee. To find out more about Tybee Island, call the Tybee Island Welcome Center, (912) 786-5444.

Nearby Major Destinations

One of Atlanta's happy advantages is its proximity and easy access to other major destinations. We'll take a quick look at four: Asheville, Black Mountain, Birmingham, and Chattanooga.

Asheville, North Carolina

Asheville's motto, "The Sky's the Limit," is appropriate given the city's location, high up where the Great Smokies and the Blue Ridge Mountains meet. To enjoy this town of spectacular natural beauty, call the Asheville Travel and Tourism Office, (800) 257-1300, or the Chamber of Commerce, (828) 258-6101, or see the Web site, www.exploreasheville.com. From Atlanta, take I-85 North to I-26, and follow the signs to Asheville.

The Tybee Island Lighthouse dates from 1773.

PHOTO: SAVANNAH CONVENTION & VISITORS BUREAU

Asheville fires the imagination with a wondrous array of attractions and activities. For a complete guide to all that Asheville has to offer, read the *Insiders' Guide to North Carolina's Mountains*. Here, we mention a few attractions to whet your appetite.

First, begin with a few attractions right in the city, such as the home of well-known author Thomas Wolfe. In the shadow of the Radisson Hotel stands the Dixie boardinghouse depicted in his novel *Look Homeward, Angel*. Unfortunately, the house was severely damaged in a fire in July 1998, and tours of the property are limited to the outside while the restoration continues for the next several years. The salvaged furnishings, clothing, and other memorabilia belonging to Wolfe are in an exhibit hall on the grounds. Call (828) 253-8304 for more information.

Asheville's downtown historic district is full of art deco architecture. You'll find crafts and antiques shops, restaurants, and walking tours. Visit the combined Antique Car Museum/North Carolina Homespun Museum, which is open April through December. The museum has no phone, but is adjacent to the Grove Park Inn, (828) 252-2711, another must-see. Erected in 1913 and one of the South's oldest elegant resorts, the inn, in a remarkable feat of engineering, was built of massive granite boulders. Room rates begin at $119. On Macon Avenue off Charlotte Street, just a few blocks from downtown, the inn overlooks Asheville's skyline and the mountains beyond.

Don't miss the Botanical Gardens, (828) 252-5190. This 10-acre area of native plants, open during daylight hours every day, is just off Broadway on Weaver Boulevard. Set aside an afternoon for Pack Place, (828) 257-4500, Asheville's arts and sciences center, 2 South Pack Square downtown. The $14 million complex includes the Asheville Art Museum, the Colburn Gem & Mineral Museum, a 520-seat performing arts theater, and the historically rich African-American cultural center called YMI (Young Men's Institute). Hours are Tuesday through Saturday from 10:00 A.M. to 5:00 P.M., Sunday 1:00 to 5:00 P.M.

The jewel in Asheville's crown has to be the 8,000-acre Biltmore Estate, billed as the largest private home in the United States. Designed by architect Richard Morris Hunt in the style of chateaux in France's Loire Valley, the mansion, completed in 1895, took five years to build. Its original 250 rooms were filled with treasures owner George Vanderbilt collected during his world travels. Works by John Singer Sargent and Pierre Auguste Renoir grace the walls. Wedgewood china, Oriental rugs, and the finest furnishings fill each room.

Guests of the Vanderbilts had a choice of 32 bedrooms. For entertainment, they chose from the billiard room, the winter garden, countless sitting rooms, an indoor pool, a bowling alley, and a gymnasium. Vanderbilt equipped his home with luxuries unbelievable in that era—central heat, indoor bathrooms, mechanical refrigeration, and electric lights and appliances. Currently, 60 rooms are open for your self-guided tour. A 75-acre garden, filled with blooming flowers, offsets the manicured grounds and adjoining forest lands. Vanderbilt commissioned Frederick Law Olmsted, designer of New York's Central Park, to create this living work of art.

Biltmore Estate Winery offers complimentary wine tastings in what were originally the estate's dairy barns. A 3,000-square-foot wine shop displays a wide assortment of gourmet foods, gifts, and a sampling of Biltmore wines. Three restaurants provide dining for visitors who've gotten hungry from all the exploring. Browse through the half-dozen gift shops for candles, Victorian accessories, and unique toys. The winery hours are 11:00 A.M. to 7:00 P.M. Monday through Saturday, noon to 7:00 P.M. Sunday.

Insiders' Tip

In the mountains, you will frequently encounter a local delicacy at roadside stands, boiled peanuts. Every stand seems to have its own subtle difference in making the treat, and true aficionados simply pop the entire shell in their mouths and open the soft shell with their tongues to suck out the mushy nuts inside.

The Biltmore Estate is on U.S. Highway 25 just north of exit 50 or 50B off I–40 in Asheville. The estate is open daily, except Thanksgiving and Christmas, from 8:30 A.M. to 5:00 P.M. Adult tickets cost $36; youngsters from 10 to 15 pay $27; children 9 and younger get in free with a paying parent. From November 12 through the holidays, tickets cost $1 more. For an additional charge, you can take a special behind-the-scenes tour. For more information, call (800) 624–1575, or write Biltmore Estate, One North Pack Square, Asheville, NC 28801, or check the Web site, www.biltmore.com. Allow the better part of a day to see it all.

Black Mountain

Take a short drive (approximately 17 miles from Asheville on I–40) to find Black Mountain, a nostalgic spot with a '50s feel that's a haven for artists. Find unusual pieces and keepsakes in the pottery, antiques, jewelry, and basketry shops in the quaint downtown area. Named for the Black Mountain range north of town, this spot, which was once Cherokee territory and then a railroad town, has a restored train depot, soda fountain drugstores, and beautiful mountain scenery with sprays of waterfalls and countless wildflowers. For information, call the Asheville Travel and Tourism Office, (800) 257–1300.

Birmingham, Alabama

About a three-hour drive from Atlanta on I–20 West, Birmingham, nicknamed the "Magic City," attracts visitors with its friendly atmosphere and many historical, sports, and recreational attractions. The drive takes visitors into the Central Time Zone, so don't forget that the hours for attractions and museums listed here are one hour behind Atlanta.

Named after its counterpart in England, Birmingham was an iron and steel boomtown in the late 19th century. The towering statue of Vulcan, the Roman god of the forge, looms over the city. The tallest cast-iron sculpture in the world, Vulcan has an observation deck that gives a commanding view of Birmingham and

the surrounding area. The statue, at 20th Street South and Valley Avenue, is open for a nominal admission.

Sloss Furnaces National Historic Landmark pays homage to the city's industrial past. The Sloss, shut down in the 1970s, has an industrial museum and serves as a community gathering place for everything from music festivals to artistic metalworking. The Sloss Furnaces, 20 32nd Street, (205) 324–1911, is open Tuesday through Saturday from 10:00 A.M. to 4:00 P.M., Sunday noon to 4:00 P.M. Although proud of its history, Birmingham keeps pace with the times. It's home to the Southern Research Institute, a nationally recognized innovator in the fields of medicine, electronics, metallurgy, engineering, and environmental protection. You can tour the institute, at 2000 Ninth Avenue South, (205) 581–2317, Friday at 2:30 P.M. for free. University Hospital, center of the urban campus of the University of Alabama at Birmingham, is a highly regarded medical care facility. The Birmingham Race Course, 1000 John Rogers Drive, (205) 838–7500, features year-round greyhound racing as well as simulcasts of horse races around the country. In 1996 Birmingham hosted part of the Summer Olympics soccer competition at Legion Field, where the University of Alabama Crimson Tide football team plays three times a year. Every other year, Legion Field hosts the annual Auburn/Alabama game, a fierce collegiate rivalry.

The Birmingham Museum of Art, 2000 Eighth Avenue North, (205) 254–2566, is the largest municipally owned art museum in the Southeast. With a sculpture garden and many examples of American, Renaissance, Oriental, and African art, the museum is a must-see, especially since admission is free. The museum is open Tuesday through Saturday from 10:00 A.M. to 5:00 P.M., Sunday from noon to 5:00 P.M. Other points of interest include the Alabama Jazz Hall of Fame with its memorabilia exhibits in the art deco Carver Theatre, 1140 Fifth Avenue North, (205) 254–2731. Birmingham native Erskine Hawkins wrote "Tuxedo Junction" about a local streetcar crossing, and you'll find an exhibit dedicated to him.

The Hall of Fame is open Tuesday through Saturday, 10:00 A.M. to 5:00 P.M.; Sunday, 1:00 to 5:00 P.M.

The 67-acre Birmingham Botanical Gardens, 2612 Lane Park Road, (205) 414–3900, is open seven days a week, from sunup to sundown, with no admission. Stroll through gardens featuring rhododendrons, camellias, wildflowers, ferns, and delicate bonsai plants. Downtown Birmingham boasts a diversity of architecture as well as civic landmarks, parks, and churches. The Second Avenue district is home to shops, galleries, and offices. The Fourth Avenue district is the historic African-American business area. A statue of Dr. Martin Luther King Jr. stands in Kelly Ingram Park, within view of the 16th Street Baptist Church, site of the infamous bombing that killed four little girls during the days of the civil rights movement. The Birmingham Civil Rights Institute, 520 16th Street North, (205) 328–9696, chronicles some of the events of that tumultuous era. The institute opens Tuesday through Saturday, 10:00 A.M. to 5:00 P.M.; Sunday, 1:00 to 5:00 P.M. Admission is free.

You can find places to stay in Birmingham from economy motels to the historic Tutwiler, Park Place at 21st Street North, (205) 322–2100. The Tutwiler, in downtown Birmingham, is a refurbished old hotel with an excellent reputation. Rooms at the Tutwiler range from $119 to $209. Or try the Mountain Brook Inn, 2800 U.S. Highway 280, (800) 523–7771. This mid-size accommodation is convenient to the shops and restaurants of Mountain Brook Village and Brookwood Mall, the downtown area, and the Birmingham Botanical Gardens. Locals like to gather at the inn's bar. Mountain Brook's room rates start at $89 and go as high as $189 for a suite. The Wynfrey Hotel, 1000 Riverchase Galleria, (205) 987–1600, is a 329-room facility adjoining U.S. Highway 31 and AL Highway 150 at I-459. Room prices range from $199 to $1,000.

Birmingham has a number of popular restaurants, including John's Seafood, 112 21st Street North, (205) 322–6014, for fine dining; and Dreamland, a barbecue place, 1427 14th Avenue South, (205) 933–2133.

Birmingham hosts many annual festivals, including City Stages, a major downtown heritage and music festival held in June. The festival features local and nationally known musicians. For scheduling and information, call (205) 251–1272. The Birmingham International Festival, held each spring, celebrates the culture, arts, and society of a different nation each year. To find out more, call (205) 252–7652. The Greater Birmingham Convention and Visitors Bureau, (800) 458–8085, can send you information to help plan your trip.

Chattanooga, Tennessee

In the mountains, right over the Georgia-Tennessee state line, Chattanooga (www.chattanoogafun.com) is a delightful town just an easy, two-hour drive from Atlanta on I-75 North. Breathtaking scenery, a variety of attractions, a lovely art district, and some excellent factory outlet stores add to Chattanooga's appeal. A convenient downtown shuttle service and helpful, friendly natives are additional positive factors.

The Chattanooga Choo-Choo Holiday Inn features a mall area with formal gardens and picturesque railcars, many of which are elegantly appointed and rented out as guest rooms. (It's $150 a night to sleep in the train cars; $109 in the main hotel.) Dinner in the Diner serves the evening meal in a Victorian-style dining car that harkens back to the golden era of railroad travel. Surrounding the railcars you'll find about a dozen retail shops and the Station House restaurant, where singing servers bring your choice of steaks, ribs, or seafood. Inside the Holiday Inn's main building, which was once Chattanooga's Terminal Station, try Cafe Espresso, a 1930s-style cafe serving gourmet espressos, cappuccino, desserts, and deli selections. The Choo-Choo also boasts the world's largest HO gauge model railroad and offers an antique trolley you can ride around the complex. Call the Choo-Choo Holiday Inn, (800) 872–2529 or www.choochoo.com.

Across from the Choo-Choo in Shuttle Park South, hitch a ride on the electric shuttle that runs roughly every five minutes from 6:00 A.M. to 9:30 P.M. Monday through Friday, from 9:00 A.M. to 9:30 P.M. Saturday, and from 9:00 A.M. until 8:30 P.M. Sunday. The shuttle runs from the Choo-Choo to the Tennessee Aquarium and the Chattanooga Visitors Center, stopping at every block in between to drop you off at a variety of attractions. Get off and shop till you drop at Warehouse Row, 1110 Market Street, a complex of factory shops including Ellen Tracy, Casual Corner, Villery & Boch, and the J. Peterman Company, housed in buildings that were originally railroad warehouses. Let the shuttle drop you off to catch a concert or performance at the Tivoli Theatre, (423) 757-5050.

The Tennessee Aquarium, 1 Broad Street, is one of the largest in the world, featuring more than 6,000 species in a variety of freshwater habitats that include mountain forests, swamps, valleys, and lakes. Surrounded by a park and plaza, the aquarium is a very popular attraction. Visit on weekdays, if possible, to avoid long lines. The aquarium is busiest from spring through Labor Day. If you can visit in the fall or winter, you'll avoid the crowds. The aquarium is open daily except Thanksgiving and Christmas. Tickets go on sale from 10:00 A.M. to 6:00 P.M. The aquarium stays open extended hours from May 1 through Labor Day. Adults pay $14 admission; children 3 through 12 pay $7.50. Kids younger than 3 get in free. Combination tickets that include an IMAX 3-D movie cost $7.75 for adults, $5.25 for ages 3 to 12. Call the Tennessee Aquarium, (800) 262-0695.

Near the Tennessee Aquarium, kids enjoy the Creative Discovery Museum at the corner of Fourth and Chestnut Streets. This hands-on educational facility includes a simulated dinosaur dig, an inventor's workshop, an artist's studio, and a musician's workshop. Creative Discovery is open daily from 10:00 A.M. to 6:00 P.M., May through August. From September through April, the museum is open Tuesday through Saturday, 10:00 A.M. to 5:00 P.M.; Sunday, noon to 5:00 P.M. It closes Thanksgiving and Christmas Day. The last tickets are sold an hour before closing. Admission is $7.95 for adults,

Insiders' Tip

Chattanooga is home to one of the revered snacks/meals of the South: Moon Pies. Try one (or several!) of the chocolate-covered marshmallow cookies with an RC Cola for the real Southern lunchtime experience.

$5.95 for children 2 to 12. For more information, call (423) 756-2738.

Points of interest for history buffs in Chattanooga include the Chattanooga African-American Museum, 730 East Martin Luther King Boulevard, (423) 266-8658, an educational institution that pays homage to African-American contributions to Chattanooga and the nation. Hours are 9:30 A.M. to 5:00 P.M., Monday through Friday; noon to 4:00 P.M. Saturday. Admission is $5 for adults, $3 for students and seniors, and $1.50 for children 6 to 12. The Medal of Honor Museum of Military History, 400 Georgia Avenue, (423) 267-1737, highlights stories of Medal of Honor military history from the Revolutionary War to Desert Storm. The Chickamauga/Chattanooga National Military Park, (706) 866-9241, headquartered in nearby Fort Oglethorpe, Georgia, commemorates the bloody Civil War battle of Chickamauga and the battles for Chattanooga. The park is dedicated to soldiers from both the North and South. The Chickamauga Battlefield park has a visitor center, an audiovisual program, the Fuller Gun Collection, self-guided tours, and hiking trails. At nearby Lookout Mountain, off I-24, the National Park Service maintains Point Park, site of Confederate batteries that were taken without a shot fired in 1863. Other park sites in the area include Missionary Ridge, Orchard Knob, and Signal Point, where the real and very bloody battles for Chattanooga were fought. There is no admission charged at any of these parks. (The famed "Battle Above The Clouds" never really took place—there was a brief but nasty fight on the slopes of Lookout Mountain, but the Confederate general in charge, Braxton Bragg, made a terrible decision and abandoned the well-placed batteries atop the steep mountain without firing a shot at the assaulting Union forces.)

Near the park, the 6th Cavalry Museum, 3370 Fayette Road, (706) 861–2860, is dedicated to showcasing the life of the cavalrymen. The museum sits on a former parade field. While you're in the vicinity, hop over to Cloudland Canyon State Park, (800) 864–7275, where stunning views surround visitors who trek through the canyon, along the trails, and under the waterfalls. Cloudland is also a favorite spot for hang-gliding enthusiasts, as well as those who just enjoy watching the brave souls soar out over the canyon.

Lookout Mountain, near Chattanooga, off I–24, is the site of many popular attractions. The Incline Railway, 827 East Brow Road, Lookout Mountain, Tennessee, is a National Historic Site and National Historic Mechanical Engineering Landmark, featuring trolley-style railcars that take you on a breathtaking ascent up the side of the mountain. With a 72.7 percent grade near the top, the Incline is the steepest passenger railway in the world. At the top, take in the panoramic view on an observation deck high in the clouds. If it's clear, you can see the Great Smoky Mountains in the distance. The Incline Railway runs every day of the year except Christmas, making the trip uphill every 15 minutes. It costs $9 for adults, $4.50 for children. Call (423) 821–4224.

At the top of the Incline Railway, you'll find the popular Lookout Mountain attractions, Rock City and Ruby Falls. Atop Lookout Mountain, Rock City features lush gardens and spectacular rock formations. Fairyland Caverns and Mother Goose Garden delight the small fry, and families and couples enjoy the view of seven states from Lover's Leap. But don't jump! You're still having fun! Grab a bite at one of Rock City's many eateries, then see if you can wiggle your way through the Fat Man's Squeeze, a narrow rock formation. Or go view the white fallow deer at the Deer Park. Rock City Gardens open daily (except Christmas) from 8:30 A.M. to 6:00 P.M. Closing times are later in the summer. Admission is $12.95 for adults, $6.95 for children 3 to 12. For more information, call (800) 854–0675.

Ruby Falls, in Lookout Mountain Caverns, is a 145-foot waterfall more than 1,100 feet deep inside Lookout Mountain. Enter through the Caverns Castle, modeled after 15th-century Irish architecture, and take a one-hour guided tour through the caverns, where you'll see the falls plus fascinating calcite formations. (If you're claustrophobic, you may not thrill at the low rock ceilings and the dimly lit passages.) Catch a great view of Chattanooga and the Tennessee Valley from the top of Lookout Mountain tower, and let kids work off steam in the Fun Forest. Ruby Falls is open from 8:00 A.M. to 9:00 P.M. throughout the year. Tours leave every 15 minutes. Admission is $12.95 for adults, $5.95 for kids 3 to 12. To find out more, dial (423) 821–2544.

Chattanooga's Bluff View Art District is about a 10-minute walk from the Tennessee Aquarium at 1 Broad Street. Anyone at the aquarium or the adjacent Chattanooga Visitors Center can direct you to the district, whose main streets are High Street, Bluff View, and East Second Street. This district offers breathtaking

Insiders' Tip

The "Battle Above the Clouds" on Lookout Mountain never actually occurred— all the fighting was on the sides and at the base of the mountain, well below the fog enveloping the peak.

views of the Tennessee River and the restored pedestrian Walnut Street Bridge, sculpture gardens, a gallery, artists' studios, museums, restaurants, and a delightful bed-and-breakfast called the Bluff View Inn. The Hunter Museum of Art, 10 Bluff View, (423) 267-0968, has an impressive collection of American art including paintings and sculpture. A modern annex adjoins the main building, a lovely old brick mansion restored to its original splendor. Stop by Tuesday through Saturday 9:30 A.M. to 5:00 P.M., Sunday noon to 5:00 P.M. The Houston Museum, 201 High Street, (423) 267-7176, is paradise for fans of the decorative arts. It showcases a collection of decorative glass, antique furniture, and textiles amassed by an eccentric antiques dealer, Anna Safley Houston. Hours are Monday through Saturday 9:30 A.M. to 4:00 P.M., Sunday noon to 4:00 P.M. Admission is $6 for adults and $3.50 for children over 3. River Street Gallery, located at High Street and Bluff View, (423) 265-5033, features an extensive collection of regional and national fine arts and crafts including painting, ceramics, wood carvings, jewelry, and basketry. The River Gallery Sculpture Garden, behind the Bluff View Inn, is a serene place to contemplate artistic shapes.

While you're wandering the district, grab a snack at Rembrandt's, a European-style coffeehouse, or the Back Inn Cafe, an Italian-style bistro. Both are part of the Bluff View Inn, 412 East Second Street, (423) 265-5033. The inn is a charming bed-and-breakfast housed in two beautifully restored buildings filled with antiques. The original building is a 1928 Colonial Revival mansion; this structure has three guest rooms, a sitting room, and the inn's dining room, which is open to the public. The inn's second building, the T. C. Thompson House around the corner, is a sprawling gray frame structure with an old-fashioned front porch, complete with swing. Guests can stay in one of the two suites here, or rent one of the four downstairs rooms. Room rates range from $115 to $270 for a king-size suite. Each room has a private bath, cable TV, phone, and individually controlled heating and air-conditioning.

Popular restaurants outside the Bluff View area include Southside Grill, a downtown neighborhood restaurant at the corner of 14th Street and Cowart, (423) 266-9211. Near the Chattanooga Choo-Choo, the restaurant features an eclectic menu including creative takes on regional foods. The atmosphere is upscale casual; Southside serves lunch and dinner Monday through Saturday and only dinner on Sunday. The Loft, 328 Cherokee Boulevard, (423) 266-3061, is a popular seafood place that also serves beef and chicken dishes. Across from the Tennessee Aquarium, The Loft has been a local favorite for 20 years, serving lunch and dinner daily.

Besides the Bluff View Inn, the many inns in Chattanooga include the Alford House, 5515 Alford Hill Drive, (423) 821-7625.

The Mayor's Mansion, 801 Vine Street, (423) 265-5000, is also in the Fortwood Historic District. This house, listed on the National Register of Historic Places, is an 1889 structure with 16-foot coffered ceilings. Room rates in this small European-style hotel range from $125 to $275, which includes breakfast. Guests and locals can enjoy brunch, lunch, and dinner at Adams Hilborne's Repertoire Restaurant.

Relocation

Welcome South, Brother! As of late 2002, an average of 250 people *per day* were moving into the metro Atlanta area, increasing our already 4 million–plus population by an amazing 3 percent *every year* since the early 1980s!

While many people move or are relocated here for work-related reasons, others move here for the high quality of life that the Capital of the New South has to offer. Atlanta is situated in the high Piedmont region of northwestern Georgia, at an average altitude of about 1,000 feet above sea level, which helps to moderate the typical sweltering Southern summers. At the same time, however, it *is* located in the Deep South, which means the area receives something less than 2 inches of snow, on average, each winter. It is within an easy driving distance of the Appalachian and Great Smoky Mountains to the north, the major caving and river sports areas to the northwest, the Atlantic Ocean to the southeast, and the Gulf of Mexico to the south (the most frequently seen car tags along the "Redneck Riviera" around Panama City Beach, Florida, belong to those from the Atlanta metro area). Within metro Atlanta itself are 57 public golf courses, 54 public parks, four major regional museums, two large lakes, every major (and most minor) professional sports activitiy, and, according to one source, "more shopping center space per capita than any other U.S. city except Chicago."

While other chapters in this book detail services and resources that are useful to both tourists and those relocating, in this chapter we want to highlight the area in terms of the housing market in and around Atlanta. One word of caution, however: Atlanta has a habit of remaking and changing itself, sometimes seemingly overnight, to the point that even lifelong residents of the city (such as your correspondents) have a very hard time keeping up with it all. For example, we now live just outside the small town of Alpharetta, in the northern suburbs of Atlanta, on a street that was constructed less than five years ago, off an exit of Georgia Highway 400 that itself was constructed less than 10 years ago, and in an area that is already overcrowded to the point where major road widening and intersection reconstruction has been under way for the past two years (with seemingly no end in sight yet!). It is best to consider our comments and recommendations as "rule of thumb" suggestions, and visit several areas in person before making any hard and fast decisions to move to one.

Selecting a Neighborhood

If you really want to understand Atlanta, get to know its neighborhoods.

From the mansions of millionaires to the more modest, working-class houses, Atlanta is a city of many different neighborhoods connected by a web of roads and rails. The various distinct communities, each with its own wealth of history and homes, are one of the features that make this city unique.

While the city neighborhoods have been the area's strength for decades, more recent housing history has been made in Atlanta's burgeoning suburbs. The building boom of the last 20 years has made what people once thought of as "Atlanta" an area that now spreads into several adjacent counties and beyond. The metro area has gotten so big that real estate experts have begun to make a distinction between "close-in" suburbs that border Atlanta's Fulton County and "exurbs"—those areas on the outer fringe where the one-way commute downtown may be 75 miles or more.

No matter where they live, Atlantans love to discuss the relative advantages and disadvantages of life in various neighborhoods. You may hear diehard in-towners speak disparagingly of life beyond the I-285 Perimeter. You may also hear suburbanites discussing in-town Atlanta as if it were an outlaw zone or an exotic foreign land. And you'll find many Atlantans playfully but unabashedly chauvinistic about where they live. Perhaps you'll see a resident of laid-back Little Five Points sporting a T-shirt reading "30307: It's not just a ZIP code—it's a way of life." Or you may hear someone reciting the motto, "Gwinnett is great." On the other hand, just a few years ago, an amusing car dealer's commercial featured potential buyers asking plaintively about his location, "Where's Loganville?" That small city is now in the middle of fast-growing Gwinnett County, and few have to wonder about the location of the formerly small farming community.

Wherever they call home, residents will find their neighborhood more than just a place to hang their hats and pick up their mail. It provides a refined sense of focus, bringing a manageable, human scale to urban life. To be one person among more than four million in a 20-county area of 6,150 square miles is overwhelming; to be one among a few thousand in a friendly neighborhood is to feel a sense of community.

Because so much of Atlanta life is organized around communities, and neighborhood names are widely used to identify locations, it's worthwhile for tourists as well as new residents to spend a few moments becoming familiar with the metro area's many distinct districts. In this chapter, we'll explain some of the parts of town you'll probably hear people talking about every day. Some of them have funny names; you can be forgiven if you snicker the first time you hear someone talking about Buckhead or Cabbagetown. Some, such as Inman Park, Grant Park, and Ansley Park, have names that honor community leaders who helped make Atlanta a great city.

The truth is that whether you prefer to live in a high-rise condominium or a gated country-club community, a downtown loft or a lofty mansion, you'll find what you're looking for in Atlanta if you're willing to be persistent and flexible.

As you begin to look for an Atlanta address, the first question to answer is a basic one: Do you prefer to live inside or outside I-285? Your answer to this question will be determined as much by your lifestyle and goals as where you work and play. Do you want to make your home far from the noise and hustle of the city, or right in the thick of everything? In this chapter, we'll talk about the city neighborhoods first, followed by a brief overview of the close-in metro counties. Space permits us to offer only an overview of Atlanta's neighborhoods, so we'll also suggest several ideas to aid you in further research.

Birth and Rebirth

Atlanta's city seal bears two dates: 1847, when the city was chartered, and 1865, when it began to rise from the ashes of the Civil War. In the same way, many Atlanta neighborhoods have a fascinating story of birth, decline, and renewal. In the 1960s and much of the '70s, Atlanta was widely perceived to be in big trouble. Once-proud areas, such as Inman Park, had badly declined. Peachtree Street in Midtown gained national attention as a bustling hippie hangout where drugs were sold openly. Adult bookstores and movie theaters were abundant. Shocked visitors returned from the city describing it as something akin to the Sodom of the South. Charging that the "sorry, no-good, cowardly" city government was not able to control lawbreakers, flamboyant segregationist Gov. Lester Maddox threatened in 1969 to call out state troopers to restore order.

Racial issues, which took on new importance in the 1960s and '70s, had always been important in Atlanta politics, and black people had long accounted for a very large minority of the city's residents. Atlanta's earliest black citizens were former slaves who, having been forced to build the city's fortifications during the Civil War, returned here to begin their new lives as free persons once peace was restored.

Then came the race riot of 1906, in which white mobs, enraged by inflammatory newspaper accounts of black "outrages" against white women, went on a rampage that lasted nearly a week, murdering blacks in the streets of downtown Atlanta and burning black homes. Image-conscious Atlanta got some very bad publicity as the riot was reported around the globe. And in the wake of it, the progressive city passed some very unprogressive legislation. In 1910 the city council passed a law requiring all restaurants to serve one race only. In 1913 Atlanta became the first Georgia city to legislate segregation in residential areas.

However, during the civil rights era, Atlanta integrated without much of the violence and rancor that tore apart many other Southern cities. Atlantans understood the importance of living up to Mayor William B. Hartsfield's famous remark, when he proudly dubbed Atlanta "the city too busy to hate." President Kennedy singled the city out for praise as its schools peacefully entered the era of integration. But beneath the veneer of cooperation, Atlanta was in turmoil. The end of residential segregation sent many affluent whites fleeing to the suburbs north of Atlanta and beyond. Newspaper articles warned of the creation of an all-black city surrounded by all-white suburbs. In 1975 the *Atlanta Journal-Constitution* published a mournful series of articles decrying Atlanta as a "City in Crisis." (Although a complete racial polarization did not come about, the white flight of the 1960s and '70s left central Atlanta with a solid black majority.)

But even as many once-fashionable areas spiraled into seemingly endless decline, something remarkable happened. In the late 1970s and early '80s, Atlanta began to attract new residents who were eager to live in an integrated city. When these visionaries looked at the dusty old mansions and rundown bungalows along Atlanta's tree-lined streets, they saw not inevitable decay but dazzling opportunity. One by one, Atlanta's historic neighborhoods began to awaken as if from a dream. Freed from the backward practices of segregation, Atlantans—whose city had always been multiracial—now began to integrate it, block by block and street by street.

This is not to say that Atlanta is entirely integrated: Segregated housing patterns are still quite evident today. The south side remains home to more blacks than whites; the north side, to more whites than blacks. But there are blacks who live on the north side just as there are whites who live on the south side. And in the in-town areas where the two halves of the city come together, black and white Atlantans, as well as those of other races and nationalities, live, learn, work, play, and worship together with an ease that would have been thought impossible just a few decades ago.

In this chapter we'll discuss neighborhoods in the northeast, northwest, southwest, and southeast sections of town. On the north side, Peachtree Street and Roswell Road divide east and west; on the south side, Capitol Avenue divides east and west. On the east side, Edgewood Avenue and Boulevard Drive divide north and south; on the west side, Martin Luther King Jr. Drive divides north and south.

Insiders' Tip

Many neighborhoods inside the city limits of Atlanta are going through dramatic revivals. One significant example is the East Lake neighborhood near the Bobby Jones Golf Course. A few short years ago this was home to East Lake Meadows, a housing project so violent and crime-ridden that even the police were afraid to enter it alone. Today the project buildings have been torn down, and a very pleasant (and safe!) mixed-income housing development has taken its place.

As you read about Atlanta's neighborhoods, keep the following points in mind: It's not uncommon for one street to be claimed informally by two different neighborhoods, which can be a little confusing. Also, the same name may be used for a neighborhood and for its primary park. For example, Candler Park is the name of a city park, the neighborhood around it, and the area's MARTA station. Many neighborhoods are served by a nearby MARTA station; those without a rail station are served by MARTA buses.

Let's begin with a brief roundup of some of the interesting neighborhoods inside I–285.

The price information listed here was compiled with the assistance of the *Atlanta Journal-Constitution* and several metro-Atlanta real estate agencies.

Neighborhoods in the City

Downtown

There was a time in the last decade when Atlanta's Downtown district was home to only banks, businesses, Rich's and Macy's main stores, and a small handful of decent places to eat. What a difference an Olympics can make!

The city's 1996 efforts to spruce up and restore an aging business district, anchored by the Five Points intersections of Marietta, Peachtree, and Decatur Streets, not only attracted new entrepreneurs but also captured the attention of a new wave of urban pioneers. Abandoned office buildings, stores, even old apartments took on new life as lofts whose main attraction was their location near Centennial Olympic Park, Underground, and hundreds of employers. As residents returned, so did the restaurants, the corner coffee shops, and, to a limited extent, the shopping conveniences usually found in residential neighborhoods. Areas once deserted after 6:00 P.M. now are places where residents jog, walk their dogs, and stroll to dinner. Not far from Five Points, just beyond the park, the warehouse area of Castleberry Hill has become one of the hottest loft markets. Former industrial complexes have been revitalized as the Nexus and King Plow Arts Centers, which include studio and residential space for artists, a theater, and an upscale restaurant. And the city council has formed a loft development task force to facilitate the renovation of old Downtown properties into modern living and working spaces.

Initially, most of Downtown's restored living space was rented as apartment-lofts. But in the last 3 years, the majority of the units, boasting high ceilings, oversize windows, hardwood floors, and exposed pipes, have been converted to condominiums, selling from about $150,000 to more than $500,000.

Northeast Atlanta

Joel Hurt was a civil engineer, a developer, and a visionary. In 1887 Hurt hired James Forsyth Johnson to design Atlanta's first garden suburb after the fashion of famed landscape architect Frederick Law Olmsted. Inman Park's name honors civic leader Samuel M. Inman. Since Inman Park was 2 miles east of Five Points, an important part of Hurt's plan was the building of the city's first electric trolley line, which began service from downtown to 963 Edgewood Avenue on August 22, 1889. The restored original Trolley Barn, (404) 521-2308, at that address is now a popular rental hall for weddings and other events.

The plan for Inman Park's 189 acres included broad streets along which were planted coastal Georgia live oak trees. Though such trees had never been known to survive in Atlanta, many of these giants still tower over the neighborhood today. Many prominent Atlantans lived in Inman Park, including Coca-Cola founder Asa Candler, whose Callan Castle stands at the corner of Euclid Avenue and Elizabeth Street, and Hurt himself, who lived at 167 Elizabeth Street.

Inman Park peaked as a fashionable address around the turn of the 20th century. Soon, the public's taste began to turn away from Victorian architecture, and the neighborhood began to lose its wealthy residents to other, more opulent develop-

Inman Park is listed on the National Register of Historic Places. PHOTO: ATLANTA CONVENTION & VISITORS BUREAU

ments such as Druid Hills and Ansley Park. The neighborhood declined in prestige and was considered little better than a slum by the 1960s, and its darkest hours occurred when some fine homes were knocked down to make way for two highways (though they were later halted before construction began). The amazing transformation—symbolized by the neighborhood's butterfly logo—began in the late '60s when determined Atlantans began to revitalize the area.

Today, Inman Park is listed on the National Register of Historic Places and is home to former Atlanta Mayor Bill Campbell. Homes in Inman Park range from bungalows in need of work to fully restored Victorian mansions, and prices reflect this: Homes start at $200,000 and go up to $850,000. The district's annual springtime festival draws thousands of visitors and is one of the most popular of Atlanta's many neighborhood festivals. Lively Little Five

Points, the eclectic shopping district between Inman Park and Candler Park, helps nearby areas attract new residents as well as visitors. The Inman Park/Reynoldstown MARTA station serves this area.

East of Little Five Points is Candler Park, which was once part of the independent town known as Edgewood. The neighborhood's centerpiece is Candler Park, a hilly green space with a public golf course; it's named for Asa Candler, who donated the land for recreation. In the early days of the automobile, the area gained popularity as a residence for Atlanta commuters. Though Candler Park lacks the grand Victorian mansions that grace Inman Park, the area has many pleasant homes both large and small. Homes here have been selling from $190,000 to more than $400,000.

Similar homes may be found in Lake Claire, which is just east of Candler Park and Clifton Road along McLendon Avenue. And despite the name, there is not a lake here. In general, the blocks north of McLendon are further along in their revitalization than those south of McLendon. If you're lucky enough to be here in the spring, take a drive up steep, dogwood-lined Claire Drive, a much-photographed example of Atlanta's floral glory. Residents of the neighborhood host an annual "Tour of Funky Homes" and invite the public into some of their more unusual renovations and expansions. Candler Park and Lake Claire are served by the Edgewood/Candler Park MARTA station. Home prices start in the $200,000s and climb into the $400,000s.

Throughout much of the 1980s, neighbors in Lake Claire, Candler Park, and Inman Park waged a fierce battle in the courts, in the media, and sometimes through bulldozer-blocking direct action to prevent construction of the Presidential Parkway. The roadway was to have linked Ponce de Leon Avenue with the Downtown Connector via the Carter Presidential Center, but residents protested the big road's impact on the area's cherished parks and laid-back lifestyle. Even though the huge pylons that were to have held the big road were already built, residents prevailed. The renamed Freedom Parkway has a 35 mph speed limit and bike and jogging trails, and it stops at Moreland Avenue, instead of crossing the neighborhood to join Ponce.

Directly north of Candler Park along Ponce de Leon Avenue is one of Atlanta's most famous neighborhoods, 1,400-acre Druid Hills. Fresh from developing Inman Park, Joel Hurt hired renowned landscape architect Frederick Law Olmsted, designer of New York's Central Park, who was then in Asheville designing the grounds of the Vanderbilts' Biltmore Estate, to lay out the neighborhood. Olmsted worked on preliminary plans but died before he could finish them. He left it to his sons Frederick Jr. and John Charles to complete his work. Olmsted's plans placed six elegant linear parks like a string of pearls along winding Ponce de Leon. (These parks too would have been severely impacted by the original Presidential Parkway.)

Druid Hills' many beautiful homes preside over broad lawns that are ablaze with seasonal colors in the spring and fall. The current St. John's Melkite Catholic Church, 1428 Ponce de Leon Avenue NE, was once the home of Asa Candler. Druid Hills' location beside Emory University helped preserve it even in the face of Atlanta's turbulent growth. The Druid Hills Historic District is listed on the National Register of Historic Places.

One of Druid Hills' most famous residents never actually existed—but her house does. Jessica Tandy won an Oscar for her portrayal of the feisty Druid Hills widow who is the title character in *Driving Miss Daisy*. The house that was the setting for the movie is at 822 Lullwater Road. Among the many other lovely homes here are architect Neel Reid's own residence at 1436 Fairview Road; the home of Walter T. Downing, another famous architect, at 893 Oakdale Road; and Boxwood, 794 Springdale Road, whose original owner, Charles Rainwater, designed the Coca-Cola bottle. Sales of Druid Hills homes have been between $500,000 and $2 million.

While we're on the east side of town, we'll touch on Decatur, 6 miles east of downtown Atlanta. Decatur is an independent city more than a decade older than Atlanta with its own fascinating history. It's home to Agnes Scott College and Columbia Theological Seminary. The Old DeKalb County Courthouse on the Decatur town square was built of Stone Mountain granite in 1917.

Ponce de Leon Avenue passes through the center of Decatur, becoming East Ponce de Leon. Another major east/west thoroughfare is College Avenue. Clairmont Road and Columbia Drive are big north/south routes. Decatur has areas of poverty and wealth as well as numerous transitional areas, and home values vary accordingly. In general, pricier housing is more likely to be found north of College Avenue than south of it. The south side, however, has many pleasant streets and areas, such as Winnona Park, that attract young homeowners looking for houses to improve. Home prices in Decatur can be as low as $250,000 or as high as $750,000 for a renovated property in a historic district. Decatur is served by the East Lake, Decatur, and Avondale MARTA stations.

One mile east of Decatur is another independent city, Avondale Estates. In the early 1920s patent medicine millionaire George F. Willis' idea for a totally self-contained residential development attracted national attention. Willis bought an existing small community, Ingleside, and over a period of four years transformed it into a world of its own, with parks, clubhouses, a lake, and a pool. Even so, the town as it stands today realizes about only one-third of Willis' elaborate original concept. While he worked on the giant carving at Stone Mountain, sculptor Gutzon Borglum, who was a friend of Willis, lived in a house at the corner of Berkeley and Kensington Roads.

In 1926 the Georgia Legislature designated Avondale Estates an independent city with its own mayor, city council, police, and sanitation department. The district's commercial buildings are in a Tudor style that suggests an English village; its dwellings include English medieval, Craftsman bungalows, Dutch Colonial- and Spanish Mission–style homes. Home prices here fall between $150,000 and $400,000. Avondale Estates is listed on the National Register of Historic Places. MARTA's Avondale and Kensington stations serve this area.

Now let's swing back west. As you travel north on Peachtree from Five Points downtown, the first substantial residential area you encounter is Midtown. Like Inman Park, it's about 2 miles from Five Points. And like Inman Park, it was the brainchild of a streetcar builder. Developer Richard Peters bought up 405 acres in the early 1880s with the idea of building a neighborhood and operating a streetcar line to it. Peters' son Edward built the showy Queen Anne–style home at the corner of Piedmont and Ponce de Leon in 1883; the house has been a restaurant, appropriately named The Mansion, since 1973.

Building in Midtown continued for nearly 50 years, and there is a commensurate range in architecture, from simple bungalows to fine Victorian mansions. But after World War II Midtown lost many residents to the suburbs, and some homes were converted to apartments and board-inghouses. In the late '60s and early '70s, Midtown went hippie in a big way; conservative people shunned the area and neighboring Piedmont Park, which was the site of numerous anti–Vietnam War protests.

By the mid-'70s, Midtown, like some other city neighborhoods, was turning a corner. Its solidly built homes, tree-lined streets, and convenient location convinced adventurous buyers of the area's underlying value. Gays, singles, and yuppie couples were drawn by Midtown's tolerance and urban charm and settled there by the thousands, many as homeowners who greatly improved their properties.

The recent rush to escape grueling daily commutes has made Midtown one of the city's hottest real estate markets. Empty office buildings, old storefronts, and an abandoned hotel, the Biltmore, have been refurbished as luxury condominiums, and are selling quickly to buyers willing to pay top dollar for the neighborhood's central location and proximity to arts, entertainment, and restaurant destinations. New condominiums are under construction on former vacant lots along Juniper, Piedmont, and Peachtree Streets. Even though they're far from completion, most have waiting lists of well-heeled buyers. Midtown prices run the gamut from $167,000 to more than $1 million.

Between Midtown and Druid Hills, Virginia-Highland grew and took its name from its central intersection: Virginia and North Highland Avenues. When it was first developed in 1916 as North Boulevard Park, the subdivision was another "streetcar" community, with a line that ran down North Highland to Ponce. Many of the houses are solid brick Craftsman structures with porches.

Virginia-Highland was damaged in the 1960s when the state tried to build an expressway, I-485, through the neighborhood. The road was eventually halted but not before homes were condemned and the community was disrupted. After that experience, Virginia-Highlanders took to jealously guarding their neighborhood against too much change. They keep a watchful eye, for example, on growth in the popular North Highland Avenue commercial district, whose restaurants and bars attract visitors from all over town. Virginia-Highland home prices range from $250,000 to well over $700,000.

North of Virginia-Highland is the Morningside/Lenox Park section. Similar in many ways to Virginia-Highland, this area's residents also had to battle the State of Georgia over plans to build the I-485 Expressway. Morningside dates from the post–World War I years. A former farming community, it was purchased and developed by M. S. Rankin and James R. Smith. Lenox Park got under way in 1932, the product of the architectural firm Ivey and Crook.

Many Lenox Park homes are built of stone and brick in Tudor and English Country styles. Morningside's homes are in a variety of styles, reflecting the influence of neighboring districts Virginia-Highland and Ansley Park. Morningside Elementary is one of the city's most highly regarded public schools. Home prices in Morningside and Lenox Park start at about $280,000 and go to $750,000.

North of Midtown is another of Atlanta's best-known neighborhoods: Ansley Park. Edwin Ansley launched this development in 1904. Unlike other early Atlanta neighborhoods, Ansley Park was designed as a community for automobile, not streetcar, commuters. The development was laid out by Solon Zachary Ruff, who had worked with the Olmsted firm in creating Druid Hills.

Ansley spent more than $500,000 to drain swamps and otherwise whip the neighborhood's 350 acres into shape. Six hundred home lots of varying sizes and numerous small parks were planned in the district. Many Ansley Park homes sit atop hills with broad lawns descending to the street. In several sections, houses that might have sat directly across from each other are instead separated by parallel streets flanking a hilly park. As a result, Ansley Park—though it is bordered by two of Atlanta's busiest streets (Peachtree and Piedmont)—is a district of almost pastoral beauty. It's listed on the National Register of Historic Places.

You'll find homes of various sizes here, including many fashionable mansions by famous architects, such as Philip Shutze,

Neel Reid, Walter Downing, and Henry Hornbostel, whose signature designs made an indelible mark on Atlanta's architecture. From 1924 to 1967, the Georgia Governor's Mansion was at 205 The Prado. Margaret Mitchell and John Marsh lived for a time in the apartments (now condos) at One South Prado and Piedmont Avenue. The Robert W. Woodruff Arts Center is nearby, as are the Colony Square complex and the Arts Center MARTA station. Before it was developed as Ansley Park, the entire district was part of the estate of George Washington Collier. Though it has been remodeled many times, the 1823 Collier House at 1649 Lady Marian Lane in the adjacent Sherwood Forest neighborhood is one of the oldest residential structures in Atlanta. Home prices in Ansley Park range from $450,000 to $2 million.

North of Ansley Park is another neighborhood that traces its origins to post–World War I enthusiasm and the growing popularity of the automobile: Brookwood Hills, developed by B. F. Burdette. The land (like Ansley Park) was owned by the Collier family; it was the site of the fierce Battle of Peachtree Creek during the Atlanta Campaign. Brookwood Hills has tennis courts, a community swimming pool, and many shade trees. It's listed on the National Register of Historic Places. Brookwood Hills home prices start in the low $450,000s and go as high as $1 million.

Peachtree Hills is north of Brookwood Hills. It was established after the Depression; most houses are of brick and frame bungalow-style construction. The neighborhood has many apartments and a pleasant community commercial district at Peachtree Hills Avenue and Virginia Place. Peachtree Hills home prices average around $350,000.

North of Peachtree Hills is Garden Hills, another pleasant neighborhood of tree-lined streets and solid homes, most of which were built in the 1920s and '30s. Developer Philip McDuffie laid out the area in accordance with the popular Frederick Law Olmsted aesthetics. To create more of a self-contained village, he called for two schools, a small commercial district, and some multifamily housing. His vision is reflected in the International School, the Garden Hills Elementary school, a thriving business district along Peachtree Road, and a community center with a clubhouse and a pool. Home styles in Garden Hills include American Colonial, Tudor, English Cottage, Georgian, and more. The neighborhood is on the National Register; home prices start at about $400,000 and go over the $1 million mark.

Between Peachtree Hills and Garden Hills is Peachtree Heights East, developed by Eurith Rivers (who became Georgia's governor). Across Peachtree Road is its sister neighborhood, Peachtree Heights West, developed in the 1910s and '20s by Eurith Rivers and W. P. Andrews. Towering over many beautiful homes built by the city's leading architects is the high-rise Park Place condominium, Atlanta home of musician Elton John. Much of Peachtree Heights West is listed on the National Register of Historic Places. Home prices in the two neighborhoods run anywhere from $500,000 to more than $4 million.

Northwest Atlanta

Buckhead, the city's famous district with both northeast and northwest addresses, is an area where districts and neighborhoods overlap. As we just discussed, Brookwood Hills, Peachtree Hills, and Garden Hills are each distinct neighborhoods, but they are all claimed by Buckhead, as are Peachtree Heights and Collier Hills, which we'll discuss in a moment. As

Antebellum-inspired architecture is prevalent throughout the city. In spring many Buckhead homes are surrounded by floral splendor. PHOTO: ATLANTA CONVENTION & VISITORS BUREAU

defined by the Buckhead Coalition leadership group, Buckhead comprises all of Atlanta north of I–75, I–85, Peachtree Creek to Cobb County in the west, the city limits in the north, and DeKalb County in the east.

In the 1910s and '20s, Buckhead began to lure wealthy Atlantans who wanted more seclusion than was offered by such residential showplaces as Druid Hills and Ansley Park. Today Buckhead has a variety of home types and sizes, but when most people envision Buckhead real estate, they think of West Paces Ferry Road and the Tuxedo Park neighborhood. Along West Paces and the streets turning off it are homes of astonishing elegance and beauty, many that were built as summer retreats for Atlanta's wealthy families. This area is home to the Georgia Governor's Mansion and the Swan House, the opulent 1928 mansion that presides over the Atlanta History Center's grounds. Philip Shutze designed the Swan House and other area homes; Neel Reid also designed fabulous mansions in the area. Golf great Bobby Jones lived here; Anne Cox Chambers of the Cox media empire, one of the world's wealthiest women, still does. Windcrofte, at 3640 Tuxedo Road, was the home of Coca-Cola president Robert Woodruff. Tuxedo Park prices start at $700,000 and can go as high as $5 million. However, a custom-designed architectural wonder can cost as much as $20 million.

Northwest of central Buckhead and about 8 miles north of downtown is Chastain Park, named for former Fulton County Commissioner Troy G. Chastain. The popular park has a golf course, athletic fields, a crafts center, and an art gallery. Its best-known feature is its outdoor amphitheater, which holds nearly 6,000 people and presents some 60 popular and classical concerts between the spring and fall. The streets surrounding the park feature many fine homes. Chastain Park home prices run from $450,000 to $1.5 million.

Still on the west side, let's head back down Peachtree to Haynes Manor. Special attractions here are the Bobby Jones Golf Course, and the Bitsy Grant Tennis Center, named in honor of the Atlantan tennis champion. Jeweler Eugene Haynes created it by selling parcels of his own estate. Today, its houses sell from $700,000 to just more than $3 million. Vacant lots have sold for $900,000.

Immediately south of Haynes Manor is Collier Hills, which, along with Brookwood Hills on the other side of Peachtree, was the site of the bloody Battle of Peachtree Creek. Most of the houses here are in the traditional styles of the 1940s and '50s. Home prices range from $400,000 to $700,000. Homes here are extremely popular with young couples, singles, and families. A side benefit is that "souvenirs" of the battle are still found during landscaping and other renovations.

West of the I–75 interstate is a section of modestly priced neighborhoods that have been enjoying a renaissance. Home Park, built as a working-class neighborhood, has been attracting new interest in recent years, particularly among the fixer-upper crowd. The 1930s Berkeley Park, with its small frame cottages, has seen a resurgence of renovations and a bid to be listed on the National Register of Historic Places. The Bolton area along the Chattahoochee—although still a fairly gritty urban light industrial area—is also showing new signs of life as builders construct new homes on vacant land in the area.

Home prices run between $90,000 and $250,000.

Southwest Atlanta

Vine City is bisected by Martin Luther King Jr. Drive, where the addresses change from northwest to southwest. The district takes its name from Vine Street. It was home to African-American millionaire Alonzo Herndon, who built a stunning Beaux-Arts mansion at 587 University Place NW. Until his assassination, Dr. Martin Luther King Jr. lived with his family in the house at 234 Sunset Street NW.

Vine City has middle-class and poor areas; the area underwent much upheaval with the construction of the Georgia Dome. The district is served by the Vine City and Ashby MARTA stations. Between

Designing Atlanta

Some Northerners like to joke—but only around other Northerners—that what William Tecumseh Sherman did to Atlanta in the Civil War was urban improvement. In a sense, they're right.

Atlanta in the 1860s was more a frontier town and a railroad terminus than the gracious Southern seaports like Charleston or Savannah. There were plantations, but the depiction of Tara in *Gone With the Wind* was about as good as it got.

"Atlanta's architecture was, and to a certain extent still is, ruled by an alliance between privately controlled boosterism and traditionalist aesthetic tastes," writes Isabell Gournay in the *AIA Guide to Architecture in Atlanta.*

In the 19th and early 20th centuries, entrepreneurs, who favored traditional Victorian styles in their homes and neoclassical structures for their businesses, shaped Atlanta's architecture. Unlike Chicago or New York, there was very little cutting-edge architecture until the High Museum (see Close-Up "From Great Tragedy, Great Hope") was built in the 1960s.

Perhaps because Atlanta is such a new city, even by North American standards, preservation has taken a back seat to development. (It wasn't until after World War II that the city experienced significant geographical expansion and population growth.) All that is left of Atlanta's first skyscraper, the Equitable Building near Five Points downtown, are some columns outside the front door of its replacement, a glass-and-steel high-rise that carries the same name. There even was an attempt to demolish the fabulous Fox Theatre, a 1920s-era movie palace (see our Close-Up "Backstage at the Fox") until a public campaign in the mid-1970s spared it. That event may have triggered a keener interest in preservation.

Atlanta's skyline is the tower of the South. Largely designed by architect John Portman Jr., the spectacular view captures the southern heart and the urban advancement of this ever-growing city.
PHOTO: ATLANTA CONVENTION & VISITORS BUREAU

Today the oldest remaining downtown skyscrapers are the Flatiron Building, finished in 1897, and the ornate Candler Building, named for Coca-Cola Co. founder Asa Candler, built in 1906.

Two of Atlanta's three most noted architects, Neel Reid and Philip Shutze, both specialized in revivalist styles. Most of their work lives on in the Buckhead mansions of the early 20th century, with Shutze's Swan House, now a museum, as a standout. Shutze also designed The Temple, a domed, revivalist-style synagogue on Peachtree Street.

The third noted Atlanta architect, John Portman, is equally a developer. He is noted both for his hotels, which created the soaring lobby atrium design, and his office/retail complex at Peachtree Center. In 1967 Portman first used the atrium in his Hyatt Regency Hotel, Atlanta's first downtown hotel since the 1920s. He had begun his downtown redevelopment in 1961 with the Merchandise Mart, which helped launch Atlanta's position as a convention city.

Since then, dozens of skyscrapers have risen downtown and in the "new downtowns" of Midtown and Buckhead as the center of development has continued to move north. The rooftop restaurant on the Hyatt Regency, which once had a commanding view of the entire city, is now surrounded by taller buildings. Landmarks in Midtown include the One Atlantic Center, also called the IBM Tower, built in 1987, and the High Museum.

Buckhead's commercial appeal began in the 1950s with the often-enlarged and remodeled Lenox Square mall, still the largest urban mall in the Southeast.

Traditionalism still reigns in Atlantans' choice of home styles. Across the northern arc of suburbs, two-story brick and siding interpretations of Georgian, Victorian, or European styles are the most popular in the upscale subdivisions.

Vine City and West End is Atlanta University Center, whose six historically black colleges form the nation's largest center of African-American higher education. Housing prices range from $50,000 to $80,000.

West of Vine City is Mozley Park, which was the site of the Battle of Ezra Church during the Atlanta Campaign. A former Rebel soldier, Hiram Mozley, settled in the area after the war, became a doctor, and invented a patent medicine. Following his death, his estate was divided into various home lots and sold. The neighborhood grew up around the city park named for Mozley. In 1949 a black clergyman and his family braved the color barrier, and by the late 1950s the area was home to more minority residents than whites. Mozley Park home prices run from $45,000 to $100,000.

South of Mozley Park is West End. It was here, on the corner of Lee and Gordon Streets, that Charner Humphries opened his Whitehall Tavern alongside the Newnan-Decatur Road in 1835, two years before railroad surveyors drove in the "zero milepost" that marked the center of what became Atlanta. The area largely escaped destruction in the Civil War.

After the war, Col. George Washington Adair christened the area West End after the famous district in London. Adair ran a line of mule-drawn streetcars between West End and the present location of Midtown. Train service was also available to the central district, making the section a popular address for those employed downtown. West End's best-known resident was Joel Chandler Harris, the journalist who penned the Uncle Remus stories. His restored home, the Wren's Nest, is a National Landmark. West End is also home to Hammonds House, a pre–Civil War home that is now a museum of African-American fine art.

West End was adversely affected by the construction of I–20 and lost many residents to other neighborhoods, but it remains a vibrant community. The area's historic Queen Anne cottages and churches help provide stability. West End's annual neighborhood festival was established in 1975. The West End MARTA station serves the area. Home prices go from $90,000 to $250,000.

East of West End, Adair Park is named for Col. George Washington Adair. In addition to being a real estate developer and streetcar builder, Adair was a newspaper publisher, a train conductor, and a wholesale grocer. Adair went bankrupt in 1873 and again in 1877; however, upon his death in 1899, he left his sons a vast real estate empire. Today this integrated residential district is served by the West End and Oakland City MARTA stations. Nearby Capitol View and Capitol View Manor, once within a clear view of the gold-topped state capitol building, are regaining popularity with middle-income buyers who want close-in locations. Prices start in the $90,000s and go into the $200,000s.

Follow Cascade Road out of the West End area into one of the city's poshest areas. The Cascade Road corridor is home to many of the city and state's elite African-American families. This beautifully wooded area of rolling hills became a favored address with prominent black Atlantans after its desegregation in the 1960s. Large lots and wide streets are lined with sprawling brick ranches in neighborhoods dating from the 1950s. Nearby, new developments boast minimansions with the latest bells and whistles. Home-run king Hank Aaron's five-acre spread includes a lake and a tennis court. Homes prices here start in the $130,000s and go up to $1 million.

Southeast Atlanta

Just east of Capitol Avenue, the Summerhill section is deriving a lasting benefit from having the Olympics in its front yard. Once a thriving neighborhood populated principally by African Americans and Jews, Summerhill was decimated by the construction of I-20 in the 1950s. The exodus from the neighborhood was only exacerbated when a big section of it was condemned to make way for Atlanta–Fulton County Stadium. Community activists worked closely with the city to make plans for the Olympic Stadium, now Turner Field, and to attract new homeowners to the area. The neighborhood's incredibly convenient location—near the Downtown Connector and Downtown business district—have helped it attract a new wave of residents. Infill houses, as well as an upscale town house community, have helped pull buyers into the area. Summerhill home prices start in the $30,000s and go into the $200,000s for some of the new town house communities.

Bordering Summerhill to the east is Grant Park. Col. Lemuel P. Grant was a civil engineer who moved to the South to help build the Western & Atlantic railroad and later designed the 10-mile system of fences and forts that encircled Civil War Atlanta, passing directly through the present-day Grant Park (which now contains the only intact, albeit tiny, stretch of the defense line). Grant donated 100 acres of his land to the city in 1882 for use as a public park. Grant Park became a favorite playground for Atlantans, and a lovely Victorian neighborhood grew up around it. (Lemuel Grant's mansion on St. Paul Avenue, from which he reportedly watched the burning of Atlanta in 1864, was refurbished by private owners.)

Grant Park faltered following World War II due to suburban migration and the construction of I-20 through the area. As in many other in-town neighborhoods, however, discounted property values and the area's charming homes began bringing people back. Today Grant Park residents continue to restore the district, which contains small, moderate-size, and imposing homes, with prices ranging from $200,000 to the $420,000s. The neighborhood has been placed under the city's historic zoning ordinance to help protect the character of the architecture.

Directly north of Grant Park and across I-20, historic Oakland Cemetery stands serenely, a Victorian time capsule surrounded by a modern metropolis. Just east of Oakland on the other side of Boulevard is another reminder of days

The Fulton Bag and Cotton Mill has been turned into loft apartments. PHOTO: JOHN MCKAY

gone by: the Fulton Bag and Cotton Mill. The mill's 2,600 workers and their families, many of whom came to Atlanta from Appalachia, lived in the adjacent mill village. Developer George Adair originally named the development Pearl Park, in honor of his daughter, but over the years it gained, and retained, a less poetic name: Cabbagetown.

The mill closed in 1976, but many of its residents remained in their neighborhood and found other work in Atlanta. Winter Properties Inc. of Atlanta converted the giant mill structure into lofts, offices, and retail space. This project gained national attention in 1999 with the dramatic airborne rescue of a crane operator trapped high over an accidental fire during renovations. The widely circulated photo of Atlanta Fire Department Squad 4 firefighter Matt Moseley dangling over the raging fire wrapped protectively around crane operator Ivers Sims has become a dual celebration of the heroic spirit of our beloved firefighters and a re-

inforcement of the resurrection of our city from the wrath of flame. (It is worth noting that both Moseley and Sims are still doing their dangerous jobs, and Moseley has used his celebrated feat of heroism to bring awareness and support to his often underpaid and overworked fellow firefighters.)

Cabbagetown's streets are narrow, and its tiny houses are set close together. Here, as in other parts of town, good bargains on in-town homes have lured buyers. The King Memorial MARTA station serves this district. Cabbagetown home prices range from $70,000 to $180,000.

Directly east of Grant Park is Ormewood Park. It's one of the few remaining in-town areas with low-priced attractive housing for those who have been priced out of more established neighborhoods such as Midtown and Virginia-Highland. Small Craftsman cottages stand alongside more spacious infill housing. The Burns Club of Atlanta, a private social club, meets at 988 Alloway Place SE in a cottage that is a replica of poet Robert Burns' home in Scotland. Home prices in Ormewood range from $150,000 to $270,000.

Continue east along Memorial Drive into one of the city's most amazing real estate districts. The once run-down and dilapidated areas of East Atlanta, Kirkwood, and East Lake are teeming with newcomers intent on turning the area back into a thriving residential district. Their efforts have proved enormously successful. East Lake Village, a shopping district at the crossroads of Flat Shoals and Glenwood Avenues, is booming with coffee shops, restaurants, antiques shops, and funky stores. The restored East Lake Golf Course, a historic property that anchors the neighborhood of the same name, draws players from around the metro area. Once surrounded by crime-infested housing projects, East Lake is being rebuilt with mixed-income town houses and the energies of renovators who are buying the Victorian cottages around the greens. There's little left for under $100,000; the top price is about $300,000.

County by County

Whether you prefer to live in the center of everything or far from the maddening crowd, you'll find a wealth of options around Atlanta.

In the 1890s the advent of streetcars made it possible for people to live some distance from where they worked. In the 1900s the automobile accelerated that process, making more distant areas convenient to the Downtown business dis-

trict. After World War II, the interstate highway system created by President Dwight D. Eisenhower made it possible for Atlanta workers to commute from remote areas, some so remote they were a long day's buggy ride away in the previous century. This process, as we have seen, led to the virtual abandonment of some of Atlanta's original neighborhoods, which are now again attracting residents.

In this section, we'll briefly discuss the counties that make up the Atlanta metropolitan region. The real estate sales data evaluation was provided by the *Atlanta Journal-Constitution* and Steve Palm of Smart Numbers. The information represents home closings from January through December 2001. Population growth figures are from the 2000 census, updated portions of which were released in April 2002 and provided by the Atlanta Regional Commission.

Close-in Counties

Clayton County

Principal cities/towns/communities: College Park, Forest Park, Jonesboro, Lake City, Lovejoy, Morrow, Riverdale.

Total number of homes sold in 2001: 6,347, with an average price of $112,900.

Clayton County is home to Hartsfield Atlanta International Airport; it's also the fictional site of the mythical plantations Tara and Twelve Oaks in *Gone With the Wind*. Houses in Clayton range from modest starters to elegant homes in planned communities and on the shores of Lake Spivey. Spivey Recital Hall on the campus of Clayton State College has been lauded as a world-class venue and hosts a performance series featuring many greats in the fields of classical music, opera, and jazz. From 1990 to 2000, the population of the country grew by 36 percent to include well over 251,800.

Cobb County

Principal cities/towns/communities: Acworth, Austell, Kennesaw, Marietta, Powder Springs, Smyrna.

Total number of homes sold in 2001: 18,162, with an average price of $160,000.

Cobb County, Atlanta's big, powerful neighbor to the northwest, saw its population increase by 39 percent in the 1990s, with nearly 630,000 residents currently. It's home to more than 500 manufacturing firms including Lockheed Martin Aeronautical Systems Co., one of the state's largest industries, which employs 10,000, and to Dobbins Air Reserve Base, where Air Force One lands whenever America's chief executive visits Atlanta.

Cobb boasts an array of attractions, including Six Flags Over Georgia, White Water, and the Kennesaw Mountain National Battlefield Park. An additional boost to business is the Cobb County Galleria Convention Centre. The Cobb County and Marietta public school systems, along with several private schools, educate the county's youth. Thanks to organizations such as the Marietta/Cobb Museum of Art and Theatre in the Square, the arts are booming in Cobb.

DeKalb County

Principal cities/towns/communities: Avondale Estates, Chamblee, Clarkston, Decatur, Doraville, Lithonia, Stone Mountain, Pine Lake.

Total number of homes sold in 2001: 15,663, with an average price of $149,000.

The easternmost parts of Atlanta's city limits stretch into DeKalb County; it's named for Baron de Kalb, a German nobleman who fought alongside the Americans in the Revolution. DeKalb is home to one of the state's largest school systems, as well as Emory University, the U.S. Centers for Disease Control and Prevention, and the American Cancer Society's national headquarters. DeKalb is part of the MARTA system, affording its citizens dependable transportation all around the county and Atlanta. DeKalb's housing opportunities range from inexpensive apartments to the luxury of Druid Hills estates to country living in the shadow of Stone Mountain. DeKalb continued its nearly unrestrained growth in the 1990s. Although many parts of the county are considered "built out," its population increased by 24 percent to an astonishing 685,800.

Douglas County

Principal cities/towns/communities: Douglasville, Fairplay, Lithia Springs, Winston.

Total number of homes sold in 2001: 2,535, with an average price of $127,500.

Douglas County is bisected by I-20; its residents can make it to Downtown in about 20 minutes. There are 166 acres of county parks, 50 acres of Douglasville city parks, and the 2,000-acre Sweetwater Creek State Park. Two acute-care hospitals serve residents. The county's population increased 37 percent during the 1990s, but still totals only 98,200 residents in a relatively large area.

Fayette County

Principal cities/towns/communities: Fayetteville, Brooks, Peachtree City, Tyrone.

Total number of homes sold in 2001: 2,737, with an average price of $195,000.

Fayette County's per-capita income is among the state's highest. Priding itself on a balance of progress and preservation, the county has developed a master plan to direct growth well into the 2000s, which is badly needed to handle the amazing 55 percent growth rate in the 1990s. The current population is 97,300. In much of the county, one-acre minimum zoning is still in place for residential properties. The planned community of Peachtree City, incorporated in 1959, is favored by retirees, airport employees, and golf lovers (the town has 40 miles of pathways for golf carts, a favored local mode of transportation). I-85 gets commuters to downtown Atlanta with ease.

Fulton County

North Fulton: Principal cities/towns/communities: Alpharetta, Mountain Park, Roswell, Sandy Springs.

South Fulton: Principal cities/towns/communities: College Park, East Point, Fairburn, Hapeville, Palmetto, Union City.

Total number of homes sold in 2001: 22,013, with an average price of $178,000.

Fulton, which contains almost all of the City of Atlanta, is Georgia's most pop-

square-mile district are in every category, including farmhouses, luxury condos, apartments, and planned communities.

Gwinnett County

Principal cities/towns/communities: Buford, Grayson, Dacula, Duluth, Lawrenceville, Lilburn, Norcross, Suwanee, Snellville.

Total number of homes sold in 2001: 22,283, with an average price of $154,900.

The county's water towers beside I-85 have long crowed "Gwinnett is Great." And it turns out they weren't joking. For some years, Gwinnett has been one of the fastest-growing counties in the United States, with a growth rate of an astounding 79 percent in the 1990s, and a current population of 638,800. The giant Gwinnett Place Mall has been hugely popular with shoppers northeast of Atlanta, who once faced a long drive to reach major malls in Atlanta. Those willing to go a bit farther up I-85 shop at the palatial Mall of Georgia at the county's northern edge. The Gwinnett Civic and Cultural Center boasts a 1,200-seat performing arts theater.

Henry County

Principal cities/towns/communities: Locust Grove, Hampton, McDonough, Stockbridge.

Total number of homes sold in 2001: 5,571, with an average price of $135,000.

Atlanta metro area's second-fastest-growing area, Henry County saw its population more than double in the 1990s, with 138,700 residents and a decade-long growth rate of 134 percent. It's an accessible area with seven interchanges on I-75 that make it appealing to businesses such as Amazon.com, NEC Technologies, and BellSouth. Housing opportunities range from modest starter homes to lavish country club communities.

ulous county, with 840,000 residents and a growth rate of 25 percent. The city divides the county into northern and southern halves whose farthest reaches are 73 miles apart. Sales in the northern neighborhoods account for the bulk of the transactions in the county.

Major north Fulton businesses include Digital Equipment Corp., Equifax, American Honda, and AT&T. Housing opportunities range from apartments and condominiums to private estates and gated golf/tennis communities such as the Country Club of the South, Windward, and St. Ives. GA 400 provides north Fulton with direct access to Downtown, the interstate highways, and the airport.

South Fulton County's proximity to Hartsfield International Airport and its railroad infrastructure have made it a natural for commercial development: It has 12 industrial parks, the headquarters of Delta Air Lines and Chick-fil-A, a Ford plant, and the facilities of many other major companies. It's also home to the internationally renowned private school Woodward Academy in College Park. The 40,000-square-foot Georgia Convention and Trade Center near the airport can accommodate groups of up to 5,000. The Southeast's only velodrome in East Point is every cyclist's dream. Homes available in this 109-

Outlying Counties

Cherokee County

Principal cities/towns/communities: Ball Ground, Canton, Holly Springs, Nelson, Waleska, Woodstock.

Total number of homes sold in 2001: 5,499, with an average price of $155,880.

Cherokee takes its name from the Native Americans who once called the area home. Sixty percent of county residents commute to work in metro Atlanta, most via I-575 and I-75; most of them live along the county's south fringe close to these routes. Serious growth in Cherokee County began during the last decade, and the county is now home to 158,700 residents, with a growth rate of 74 percent. Homes are available at a wide range of prices. Canton is the site of a large marble finishing plant.

Coweta County

Principal cities/towns/communities: Corinth, Grantville, Haralson, Madras, Moreland, Newnan, Sargent, Senoia, Sharpsburg, Turin.

Total number homes sold in 2001: 3,072, with an average price of $133,450.

Coweta is west of Fayette in the southwestern corner of the metro area. The county saw its population increase by 70 percent during the 1990s, to now include just under 100,000 residents. Newnan has many antebellum homes that survived the Civil War and has often been used as the location for movies and TV shows. The 2,500-acre Shenandoah Industrial and Business Park is home to a Kmart distribution center and many other companies.

Forsyth County

Principal cities/towns/communities: Cumming.

Total number of homes sold in 2001: 4,773, with an average price of $209,900.

North of Fulton and Gwinnett, Forsyth County lies along the western side of Lake Lanier. The county has six interchanges on GA 400, which give it great access to the city and the interstate system to the south and to the mountains in the north. Forsyth is home to 21 industrial parks. Housing opportunities range from apartments to lavish mansions on the hilly shores of Lake Lanier. In the 1990s Forsyth was the state's growth leader, increasing its population by 150 percent to a high of nearly 140,000 residents.

> ## Insiders' Tip
>
> If you're a pet lover, you'll find yourself in good company in Fayette, Forsyth, and Cherokee Counties. More than 47 percent of the residents there included pets in their households.

This is additionally amazing when one considers the somewhat rough recent history of Forsyth County. It was the last county in the state to integrate, featuring exactly one black resident as recently as 1980, and being the reluctant host to the last major civil rights marches, led by Dr. Martin Luther King Jr.'s old battle lieutenant, the late Hosea Williams, in 1987 and 1988. The exceedingly rapid changes here have led some longtime residents to half-jokingly propose building a "wall" to keep growth confined to the southern half of the county.

Newton County

Principal cities/towns/communities: Covington, Mansfield, Newbern, Oxford, Porterdale.

Total number of homes sold in 2001: 2,476, with an average price of $115,500.

Newton County is bisected by I-20, which helps it attract big corporate players such as Mobil Chemical, Stanley Tools, and Bridgestone. Eight thousand students attend Newton's one high school, two middle schools, and eight elementary schools; there are also three nearby private schools. Its county seat, Covington, has a historic square and courthouse surrounded by antebellum homes. Oxford is the town where Emory University was born; the two-year arm of that school still operates there. Newton was founded in 1821 and has 85 churches and about 80,000 residents.

Paulding County

Principal cities/towns/communities: Dallas, Hiram.

Total number of homes sold in 2001: 3,658, with an average price of $127,150.

North of Douglas and west of Cobb is Paulding County, which is 20 miles from Atlanta on its east side and 40 miles away on its west side. Seventy percent of residents came here from elsewhere, and, though the county has more than 200 subdivisions, more than half of its land remains undeveloped. During the 1990s, growth burbled along at more than 99 percent, with nearly 102,000 people calling it home in 2002. Paulding is home to the concrete manufacturer Metromont and to Shaw Industries, the world's largest carpet maker.

Rockdale County

Principal cities/towns/communities: Conyers, Milstead.

Total number of homes sold in 2001: 1,748, with an average price of $131,700.

Rockdale County is bisected by I-20, which makes it just a 30-minute commute to downtown Atlanta. The county's population grew 34 percent during the 1990s, to now include more than 73,500. Rockdale has four major industrial parks and has attracted many international, particularly Japanese, companies: It's home to Maxell, which donated the cherry trees whose annual springtime display sparks a large festival in Conyers. Major U.S. firms here include John Deere and AT&T. The Georgia International Horse Park in Conyers hosted equestrian events during the 1996 Olympics.

Apartments

The metro area has thousands of apartments for rent at nearly every price level. Some areas, such as the Buford Highway in northeast Atlanta and the Chattahoochee River area in Cobb, have large concentrations of apartments. But you can also find apartments in areas such as Midtown and Garden Hills, which are best known for their single-family homes. The major sources of information on apartments for rent are the *Atlanta Journal-Constitution,* the *Marietta Daily Journal,* and the free, weekly *Creative Loafing.* Several free publications showcasing apartments for rent are available around town; they're listed with the real estate publications in our Media chapter.

If you'd like professional assistance in choosing your new Atlanta apartment home, call one of the following services.

Apartment Finders
2250 North Druid Hills Road
(404) 633-3331, (800) 278-7327

Not only will the experts at Apartment Finders help you find a place to rent, but they also provide tips on relocation, corporate apartments, and finding a roommate. The company lists more than 350,000 rental units, as well as houses and condominiums. Fees are paid by the rental property owners.

Apartment Selector
3000 Windy Hill Road, Marietta
(770) 956-0177

In business since 1959, this national company has offices across the metro area. Offering properties of all sizes in all areas, the firm provides free transportation for your apartment search seven days a week. All services are paid for by the property owner. To prepare for your move to Atlanta, call (800) 543-0536.

Apartments Today
11285 Elkins Road, Suite D-1, Roswell
(770) 664-4957

Call Apartments Today for free assistance in finding your new Atlanta address. This company can help you find a long- or short-term apartment to lease. Fees are paid by the owner.

Free Home Finder
3652 North Peachtree Road
(770) 455-1781

This service will drive you to view the properties of your choice. A free roommate match service and a newcomer kit are available. Free Home Finder will even pick you up at MARTA stations. All prices and sizes of apartments, furnished and unfurnished, are available.

Promove
3620 Piedmont Road NE
(404) 842–0042
Promove will help you get settled in the city by narrowing your choices to focus on what's really important for you. It will loan you color photos of prospective properties and answer your questions about living in the metro area. The firm maintains three Atlanta offices; its services are free to renters.

Real Estate Firms

Sometimes it seems as if there are no native Atlantans left in Atlanta. Although residents joke about it, it is true that the vast majority of Atlanta's population has arrived here from somewhere else. Couple the fair weather and job opportunities with the wide range of housing prices, and Atlanta is hard to beat.

Even though Atlanta real estate is priced more reasonably than that of many other cities, prices have risen steadily in the last 10 years, although there has been a downturn ever since the 9/11 attacks. And as traffic becomes more and more of a concern, prices for those communities and counties closer to the heart of the city have climbed. As an example, home shoppers frequently note that real estate in East Cobb is usually $10,000 to $20,000 more than comparable homes on the west side, where the access to the interstate system is less convenient. But on the positive side, Atlanta does offer, within a reasonable distance of Downtown, everything buyers could imagine in housing opportunities—from pastoral country estates to luxury high-rise condominiums.

Atlanta has a thriving real estate community with thousands of informed agents who are eager to assist you. Here's a small sample of metro area firms ready to help you in your relocation to Atlanta.

W. T. Adams & Co.
458 Cherokee Avenue
(404) 688–1222

This Grant Park–based company specializes in the in-town communities surrounding the historic neighborhood.

Century 21
3390 Peachtree Road
(404) 266–2121
The Century 21 agents have offices in nine metro counties, from the west side in Carroll County and across the northern arc. The national company frequently is applauded for its extensive relocation services.

Coldwell Banker–Buckhead Brokers
5395 Roswell Road
(404) 252–7030, (800) 989–7733
Despite the name, this firm covers the entire metro area with 10 offices. Its beginnings were in the Buckhead area. The firm offers all real estate services, including a home rental division. A call to the number listed previously will direct you to the regional office serving the area of your choice.

Coldwell Banker/Bullard Realty Co.
238 Stockbridge Road, Jonesboro
(770) 477–6400
This Henry County company has been a leading real estate agency on the city's southside for years. Agents are specialists in new and resale homes in the southern arc.

Coldwell Banker–The Condo Store
900 Peachtree Road
(404) 292–6636
Founded in 1993, this 45-agent-and-growing company is one of the few in the metro area that deals exclusively with condominiums, luxury high-rises, town houses, and cluster homes. A second office in Dunwoody opened in spring of '97.

Harry Norman Realtors
77 West Paces Ferry Road
(404) 233–4142, (800) 241–8263
More than a dozen sales offices covering the entire northern metro area have grown from this firm's beginnings in 1930, when Harry Norman's mother started the company. Relocation is one of

the firm's specialties. This service includes picking you up at the airport, making your hotel reservations, and other helpful assistance. The company also operates an office in Highlands, North Carolina, (800) 233-8259.

Metro Brokers/Better Homes and Gardens
750 Hammond Drive
(404) 843-2500

In 1997 the two dozen offices of Metro Brokers joined forces with the real estate services of Better Homes and Gardens to offer more programs for agents, education, and information networking—even subscriptions to the magazine! The brokerage has about 700 agents who help buyers find homes across the metro area, from north Fulton to Peachtree City and Newnan on the south side.

Northside Realty
6065 Roswell Road, Suite 600
(404) 252-3393, (800) 241-2540

With 800 sales associates in 24 branch offices, Northside is one of Georgia's largest independent real estate brokerages. In 1985 Northside was the first Atlanta real estate firm to sell more than $1 billion in residential real estate. That track record continues, with an estimated billion dollars in sales every year throughout the metro area and surrounding counties. NR Hotline, (404) 843-1800, open round the clock every day of the week, allows you to enter a five-digit access number shown on a property's yard sign and get detailed information on the property being considered.

Jenny Pruitt & Associates Realtors
990 Hammond Drive
(770) 394-5400

Another multilocation presence, this firm has three offices (in Buckhead, Cobb County, and Sandy Springs) that serve the entire metro area. Special divisions for rental, relocation, and new homes are provided. The corporate office, listed above, will put you in touch with the specific office you need.

RE/MAX
1100 Abernathy Road
(770) 393-1137

This company has about 55 individual franchises around the metro area. More than 2,700 agents handle new home sales, resales, and relocation services. RE/MAX independent agents are among the city's leaders in sales volume.

Education

For the last several years, state and local leaders have been taking a tough look at the state's educational systems. Out of their brainstorming, many positive changes have occurred. Thanks to the proceeds of the Georgia Lottery, more high school students than ever are attending state colleges and universities for free, and prekindergarten programs are preparing 3- and 4-year-olds to enter school as successful students. Many counties have explored and supported the idea of charter schools, privately managed neighborhood institutions where parents are intensely involved partners in their children's studies. In between, opportunities abound in a number of outstanding public and private schools and several top-notch colleges and universities, from Emory to Georgia Tech.

Public School Systems

The state's schools have seen significant improvement since Georgia established the Georgia Lottery for Education in 1992. Lottery revenues have helped fund instructional technology for Georgia's public schools, including 15 regional Technology Training Centers that provide teachers, principals, and administrators the chance to learn about, use, and experiment with new technologies. Lottery money has also funded the HOPE scholarship program and a popular voluntary prekindergarten program for 4-year-olds.

If you're enrolling children in Georgia public schools, be aware that the law requires them to be 5 years old by September 1 for kindergarten and 6 years old by September 1 for first grade. Younger children moving into Georgia who have already attended a public or accredited private school may enroll in Georgia schools provided the kindergartner is 5 years old by December 31 or the first-grader is 6 by that date. Parents planning to enroll children in school should contact the school superintendent's office in the county or city where they'll be living. Each system decides what credits to accept from transfer students. Parents or guardians usually need to request that records or transcripts be forwarded to a student's new school or system.

Students enrolling in public school must provide a certificate of immunization for measles, rubella, tetanus, diphthe-

Insiders' Tip

A handy resource for finding just the right school is *The Ultimate Atlanta School Guide,* a comprehensive statistical look at more than 17 public school systems as well as the larger private schools in the greater metro area. The information was compiled by education writers from the *Atlanta-Journal Constitution.* This 400-plus-page book tells you what schools service which ZIP codes, along with key information, such as enrollment, dropout rates, and standardized test scores. It's available for $21.95, and it is easily found in most larger metro area bookstores. Or see www.ajc.com/infostore. Call (404) 526-5668.

ria, polio, mumps, and whooping cough. Sixth-graders must have at least one additional dose of MMR (measles, mumps, rubella) vaccine. The county health department may issue medical exemptions for children who cannot be immunized for medical reasons or whose parents or guardians present an affidavit stating that immunization is against their religious beliefs.

Students at all grade levels entering the public schools for the first time must provide certification of eye, ear, and dental examinations. Students will also be asked to furnish a Social Security number. Parents who decline to provide the number may sign a statement to that effect, and their children will receive student identification numbers.

Atlanta Public Schools
210 Pryor Street SW
(404) 827–8000
www.atlanta.k12.ga.us

The City of Atlanta system serves about 57,000 students in 97 schools (69 elementary, 17 middle, and 11 high), where the student-teacher ratio is a bit over 15 to 1. It also has three adult education centers including Atlanta Area Technical School, a facility that provides post-secondary technical training in a variety of diploma programs including paralegal studies, dental assistant, computer programming, and electronics. The system operates five alternative learning programs, a Parental

Services Center, and an Adult Learning Center focusing on literacy that prepares adults for the General Equivalency Diploma (GED) examination.

In 1999 Southside High, Young Middle, and Morningside Elementary were named Georgia Schools of Excellence. (Schools of excellence receive the designation based on their performances over three years in a number of areas including leadership, teaching environment, curriculum and instruction, student environment, and parental and community support.)

Atlanta city schools benefit from intense community support. Atlanta Partners for Education, a joint program of the metro Atlanta Chamber of Commerce and the Atlanta Public Schools, provides for the development and maintenance of partnerships in which businesses, community organizations, governmental institutions, and other groups provide increased educational and enrichment opportunities for students in the Atlanta Public Schools. Partnerships help students increase self-esteem and achievement, as well as learn about the expectations and realities of the work world. Partnerships also boost school staff morale by providing educational opportunities and recognition. Other metro area school systems have instituted their own education partnership programs.

The Atlanta Magnet School Program offers 16 four-year programs for concentration in specific fields of study. Open to any Atlanta resident or tuition-paying noncity resident, the magnet programs encourage mature, self-motivated students to explore possibilities in the fields of their choice. Some magnets include on-the-job training and experience. The magnet schools focus on a significant range of occupation areas, such as the performing arts, international studies, communications, science and mathematics, financial services, information processing, and hospitality. Other subject areas include transportation, educational careers, engineering and applied technology, language studies, fashion retailing, entrepreneurship, and health care professions.

Atlanta public schools offer more than reading, writing, and arithmetic. PHOTO: FULTON COUNTY SCHOOLS

Cobb County Public Schools
514 Glover Street, Marietta
(770) 426-3300
www.cobb.k12.ga.us

This fast-growing suburban area across the Chattahoochee River from Atlanta has the second-largest school system in Georgia and the 30th largest in the U.S. Cobb has more than 100,000 students in 62 elementary schools, 21 middle schools, and 14 high schools. The system also has an Adult Education Center where adults 16 and older can take classes to improve their basic educational skills, work toward high school completion, or earn a GED. The pupil-teacher ratio varies by grade level and specific activity. In general, the ratio ranges from one teacher per 20 students to one teacher per 27 students. Almost 85 percent of Cobb graduates go on to college.

The Cobb County system has 13 National Schools of Excellence and 30 Georgia Schools of Excellence. There are four magnet programs open to all Cobb students by application and/or audition: a performing arts program; three math, science, and technology programs; and an International Baccalaureate program.

Special education programs, designed for all disabled students, include programs for children with special learning disabilities, health impairments, and emotional/behavioral disorders. Cobb County, along with the Marietta City Schools, participates in Partners in Education, a program coordinated by the Cobb Chamber of Commerce that matches businesses with schools to provide enrichment and incentives to students. Cobb also offers after-school programs in all elementary schools at a nominal cost. There are programs for gifted students, and there is one open campus school, Oakwood High in Smyrna.

Cobb County schools garner a significant share of honors, including numerous national and statewide awards for teaching excellence and school programs. Cobb County annually sends more than 100 students to the Governor's Honors program, a summer session for outstanding students held on a Georgia college campus.

DeKalb County School System
3770 North Decatur Road, Decatur
(404) 297-1200
www.dcss.dekalb.k12.ga.us

DeKalb's school district has an enrollment of approximately 98,000 students.

Exploring Science at School

New in the 2002–03 school year was the opening of two separate facilities in the Atlanta area, concentrating on bringing very technologically advanced, highly interactive lessons in aviation and space exploration to elementary and middle school–age students. The first to open, at the beginning of the school year, was the Georgia National Guard's Peach State STARBASE (Science and Technology Academics Reinforcing Basic Air and Space Education) Program, which targets at-risk fifth-grade students and is located in a specially built facility inside Dobbins Air Reserve Base. The second, opened early in 2003, is the Challenger Learning Center at SciTrek (see our Kidstuff chapter), which centers around a space shuttle mission simulation and is aimed at a general student population in the fourth to eighth grades.

The STARBASE program is a fully federally funded, National Guard Bureau–sponsored, and Georgia Department of Defense–staffed adjunct educational academy intended to increase the interest in, and abilities at, the maths and sciences in a student population that is in danger of falling behind in or dropping out of school. Participating schools (currently limited to Cobb County and Marietta City, due to space constraints) send 25 to 30 students at a time, one day a week for five weeks, to the facility at Dobbins. There they participate in student-centered, hands-on experiments and activities designed to boost their classroom lessons in math and sciences, as well as give them "real-world" experiences and lessons in positive decision making, high-ordered thinking skills, anti–drug use, and anti–gang participation issues. While at STARBASE, the student "cadets" explore Newtonian physics, basic algebraic and geometric concepts, aerodynamics, communications, teamwork-building skills, and logic problems. These lessons are applied in two major areas—learning to fly light to heavy

Students enjoy the flight simulation laboratory of the STARBASE program. PHOTO: JOHN MCKAY

aircraft in STARBASE's state-of-the-art flight simulation laboratory, and building and flying small model rockets.

Unfortunately, STARBASE is not open to the general public, and its 840 yearly student slots have all been taken up by Cobb County and Marietta City schools, with a lengthy waiting list for any slots that open up. Future plans call for a doubling or tripling of class sizes and opening up to more metro area schools.

The Challenger Center is based around a two-room simulator, consisting of a space station and Mission Control. Students take on the roles of astronauts, engineers, and scientists in order to complete assigned missions. They learn and apply navigational skills, build a probe, and work at various stations essential to actual missions, including life support, robotics, and communications. Their two-hour missions are filled with tasks and realistic dilemmas that build problem-solving, critical thinking, and communication skills. Halfway through, the mission requires a crew exchange so everyone has an opportunity to experience both Mission Control and the space station.

The Challenger Learning Center is intended for 18 to 36 students, not including two to four adults per group. School-based missions will be run twice each day: 9:00 to 11:00 A.M. and noon to 2:00 P.M. Monday through Friday. Missions will also be run after school hours upon request by youth groups, Scout groups, and similar organizations. The cost of each mission is $500, which includes teacher training, pre- and post-visit materials, admission to the museum, and the mission itself. The Challenger Center plans to open to the general public sometime in mid- to late 2003. Call (404) 522–5500, ext. 347, or check on their Web site, www.scitrek.org, for more information.

DeKalb's 83 elementary schools, 19 high schools, and 16 middle schools make it one of the largest school operations in Georgia. Statistics from the 1987–1993 school years showed DeKalb's per-pupil expenditures as consistently higher than the state average; in the 2001–02 school year, $6,622 was spent on each student. Eighty-two percent of DeKalb students continue their education past high school.

In the DeKalb system, elementary schools for the most part extend through the seventh grade, with high schools serving grades eight through 12. The county is moving to a middle school system, with 16 middle schools operating as of the 2002–03 school year. There is full-day kindergarten in every DeKalb elementary school and 80 prekindergarten programs.

Students in DeKalb enjoy a student-teacher ratio that averages 25 to 1 system-wide; of course this does vary on grade level. More than 60 percent of teachers and administrators hold a master's degree or doctorates.

DeKalb's magnet school program for students with special interests and abilities offers bountiful opportunities. There are schools for high achievers, math, science and technology, computer education, the performing arts, writing, and more than a half-dozen foreign languages, including Russian, Japanese, and Chinese. A special feature operated by the county school system is Fernbank Science Center. This museum, classroom, and woodland complex is on 65 acres of old-growth forest. It also houses the nation's third-largest planetarium. The telescope in its observatory is the largest in the world dedicated primarily to public education. Each year, the STT Program (Scientific Tools and Techniques) gives nearly 200 ninth- and 10th-grade students the opportunity for independent study in science and math. (For more information on Fernbank, see our Kidstuff and Attractions

schools. As with the surrounding metro counties, Fulton is in the midst of a building program for new schools, to help relieve the serious overcrowding in some of the northern arc schools. The communities represented are rural, suburban, and urban; students have the opportunity to interact with and develop an understanding of a variety of people. The student-teacher ratio averages from 18 to 26 students per teacher systemwide.

Fulton County schools' curriculum stresses academic achievement and success. Local option sales taxes passed in 1997 provided five years of funds for extensive renovations in every Fulton County school and the construction of 18 new schools. College Park Elementary School is the first in Georgia to offer a year-round schedule. Mimosa Elementary is a state pilot site for Japanese language instruction. The system provides comprehensive programs for exceptional children including those with mental and behavioral disorders, high academic talent, physical limitations, and learning disabilities. School counselors implement developmental guidance programs to help students maximize their potential.

Fulton's elementary schools offer after-school child care, and half-day and full-day summer enrichment programs. Selected middle schools offer after-school enrichment programs as well as intramural physical education activities. Fulton County high schools offer a broad range of extracurricular activities including athletics, honor societies, career awareness opportunities, and recreational programs. Four high schools offer magnet programs to help students interested in concentrating their studies in mathematics and science, international studies, or visual and performing arts. More than 80 percent of Fulton graduates continue their education. Fifteen Fulton County schools are Georgia Schools of Excellence; four are National Schools of Excellence. Fulton's honors include: Georgia Educator of the Year in numerous curricula and the Presidential Award Winner for Excellence in Science Teaching. In early 2000 four of the system's schools were ranked in the country's top 500 by *Newsweek* magazine; the

chapters.) Special education classes serve approximately 11,000 children with special needs in specific areas, including learning disabilities, hearing, vision, speech, and emotional disorders. Unique in the Southeast, and one of only a handful in the country, is DeKalb's International Center. Established in 1985, the center acts as liaison between schools and the 9,500 international language students and their families, who represent 160 countries and 66 language groups.

Fulton County Schools
786 Cleveland Avenue SW
(404) 763–6820
www.fulton.k12.ga.us

Besides Atlanta, the county seat, nine other incorporated cities lie within Fulton's boundaries: Alpharetta, Roswell, Mountain Park, College Park, Hapeville, East Point, Fairburn, Palmetto, and Union City. The Fulton County school system serves students in these cities as well as the unincorporated areas of the county.

More than 72,000 students from diverse backgrounds attend Fulton County's 48 elementary, 15 middle, and 11 high

College Board has presented the system with an Award in Excellence for advanced placement courses.

Gwinnett County Public Schools
52 Gwinnett Drive, Lawrenceville
(770) 963–8651
www.gwinnett.k12.ga.us

In fast-growing Gwinnett, public school student enrollment is projected to reach well above 147,000 by September 2007. One example of this north metro county's booming growth is North Gwinnett High School, which had 1,700 students in the 1999–2000 school year, 2,200 in the 2000–01 year, and enrolled more than 2,500 in the 2001–02 year! Currently, 92 schools serve more than 123,000 students, who enroll according to cluster attendance zones. (A cluster is a geographical area containing three to four elementary schools, one or two middle schools, and a high school.)

Gwinnett provides educational opportunities through its vocational education center, special education center, community schools program, and Gwinnett Technical Institute, the state's largest vocational/technical school. With more than 14,000 employees, the school district is one of the largest employers in the county.

The student-teacher ratio averages 22 to 1. Currently, 68 percent of Gwinnett's teachers have at least a master's degree. All grades and all schools offer gifted education programs; the system also offers enrichment opportunities in such areas as art, music, foreign language, drama, and debate. Extracurricular activities include athletics, service and social clubs, Odyssey of the Mind, and many academic teams. Each elementary school offers a full-day kindergarten program.

Gwinnett's students and educators are recognized regularly for outstanding achievement. Thirteen Gwinnett schools have been named National Schools of Excellence; 37 are Georgia Schools of Excellence. Gwinnett students, educators, and schools are recognized regularly for outstanding achievement in academics and in extracurricular areas.

Insiders' Tip

The Gwinnett County school system is one of the fastest-growing public systems in the nation.

About 87 percent of graduates continue education. All high schools offer advanced placement courses, joint enrollment with area colleges, and work/ study programs.

Public School Resources

Georgia Department of Education
(404) 656–2800
www.doe.k12.ga.us

For the past few years, the state legislature and the governor's office have been deeply involved in education issues, leading to some sudden and sometimes unexpected changes in the way our schools operate. The state offices maintain a Web site with detailed information about educational systems as well as individual schools. Test results, personnel profiles, even attendance data is included.

Private Schools

A sizable number of educational facilities in the metro Atlanta area flourish apart from the public school system. Curricula range from traditional liberal arts programs to those designed for the gifted or the learning disabled.

We don't have the space to evaluate each of the metro area's many private schools, which number somewhere in the neighborhood of 100. As with the public schools, we offer an overview, presenting a sampling of schools by county. For further information, a very good source is the *Atlanta Journal-Constitution*'s comprehensive *The Ultimate Atlanta School Guide*, updated yearly and available in most area bookstores for $21.95, or directly from the AJC at (404) 526-5668. Be assured whatever your child's needs—academically gifted, learning disabled, developmentally delayed, and all shades in between—the Atlanta area schools stand ready with an appropriate program.

Two other useful resources for learning more about Atlanta-area private schools are the Georgia Independent Schools Association, (770) 227-3456 or www.gisa2.org, and the Georgia Association of Christian Schools, (706) 549-2190 or www.gacs.org.

Cobb County

Shreiner Academy
1340 Terrell Mill Road, Marietta
(770) 953-1340
www.shreiner.com

This eight-acre facility, with a pool and performing arts center, was founded in 1980 for preschool through grade eight. The accelerated curriculum focuses on traditional academics. With about 300 students, the school features foreign language and computer instruction, among many other offerings. Preschool for 2-year-olds and summer camps are also offered. The student-teacher ratio is about 15 to 1 in the elementary and preschool classes; it's 10 to 1 in the middle and high school.

The Walker School
700 Cobb Parkway N, Marietta
(770) 427-2689
www.thewalkerschool.org

Since it opened in 1957, this independent day school has focused on a college prep program for its students. The more than 1,000 students served are from 4-year-old kindergartners through 12th graders. The student-teacher ratio is about 14 to 1. Campus features include three libraries, two gyms, four computer centers, an auditorium, and six science labs. After-school care is available. The school's student-produced literary magazine, *The Pegasus,* has received awards from the National Teachers of English and Columbia University. From 1997 to 1999, 21 percent of the graduating class received recogni-

tion from the National Merit Scholarship Corporation.

Whitefield Academy
1 Whitefield Drive
(678) 305-3000
www.whitefieldacademy.com

This Christ-centered preparatory school was founded in 1997 with 96 students in grades six through 12. Since then, it has grown to more than 400 students. The facility continues to expand to accommodate a growing student body committed to intellectual development, positive relationships, and physical fitness.

DeKalb County

The Friends School of Atlanta
121 Sams Street, Decatur
(404) 373-8746

Approximately 135 students from 4-year-old kindergartners through eighth graders attend the Friends School. The focus is on each child's individual skills and needs. The school, with a student-teacher ratio of 13 to 1, also offers after-school care and summer programs.

Marist School
3790 Ashford Dunwoody Road NE
(770) 457-7201
www.marist.com

This private Catholic college preparatory school educates 1,032 students in grades seven through 12. Founded in 1901, Marist was originally in downtown Atlanta but relocated to its present 57-acre campus in 1962. Owned and operated by the Society of Mary, a Roman Catholic religious order of priests and brothers, the Marists and their board of trustees have made a commitment to maintain diversity by limiting Catholic admissions to a maximum of 75 percent. The remaining 25 percent is open to students of other faiths. The staff includes 82 full-time classroom teachers plus administrators, librarians, guidance counselors, and campus ministers. More than three-quarters of the staff hold advanced degrees. About 20 advanced placement classes are offered.

The Paideia School
1509 Ponce de Leon Avenue
(404) 377–3491
www.paideiaschool.org

Founded in 1971, Paideia (a Greek word for "community of learning") is an independent, nonsectarian school committed to having a racial, socioeconomic, and intellectual cross section of students. The school serves families with children ages 3 through 18. Paideia's philosophy is based on the belief that school can be informal and individualized yet still educate well. In addition to teaching basic skills and content areas, the school promotes development in art, music, and physical education. About 870 students are enrolled, with a student-teacher ratio of 12 to 1.

St. Martin's Episcopal School
3110-A Ashford Dunwoody Road NE
(404) 237–4260
www.stmartinschool.org

Christian-oriented academic excellence characterizes this school, founded in 1959, for more than 600 preschool to eighth-grade students. The student-teacher ratio is about 10 to 1 in elementary and middle grades; early childhood classes have a ratio of 8 to 1. St. Martin's is part of an adopt-a-school program with Oglethorpe University, whose students work as teacher apprentices and aides in the after-school program. After-school care is offered until 6:00 P.M.

St. Pius X Catholic High School
2674 Johnson Road NE
(404) 636–3023

As the Catholic high school of the Atlanta Archdiocese, this 42-year-old school offers three levels of instruction: accelerated, college prep I, and college prep II. The philosophy, based on faith and religious belief, is to help students develop individual potential, to build the community, and to foster service to others. A traditional class structure serves more than 1,000 students in grades nine through 12; the student-teacher ratio is about 16 to 1.

Yeshiva Atlanta
3130 Raymond Drive
(770) 451–5299
www.yeshivaatlanta.org

Founded in 1969, Yeshiva is an Orthodox Jewish high school with an enrollment of about 130 students in grades nine through 12. The traditional class structure is split, with students spending half-days in Judaic/Hebraic studies and half-days in general studies. The student–teacher ratio is about 12 to 1. The 50,000-square-foot facility sits on a 10-acre site.

Fulton County

Atlanta International School
2890 North Fulton Drive
(404) 841–3840
www.aischool.org

In 1984 members of Atlanta's business and international community formulated a plan to offer area students the same international educational opportunities as those found in the world's leading cities. Their idea gave birth to the Atlanta International School, where students from kindergarten through high school are exposed to the cultures of the world.

In 1985 AIS held its first classes for 51 students in a rented schoolhouse in Buckhead. Two years later, the school moved to a larger facility in the area, but just 10 years later, the student body had out-

> ## Insiders' Tip
> Many teachers prefer to teach in private schools. Even though the pay is less than in public schools, private schools are seen as having better classroom discipline and a freer academic environment.

grown the site. In 1995 the school took up permanent residence at its present location, where six science labs, fiber-optic wiring, computer facilities, a library, gym, and ball fields are part of the property.

Today, AIS enrolls about 800 students from 60 countries. Beginning in the early grades, students are immersed in dual language courses in either French, German, or Spanish. With 15 students per class, the student-teacher ratio is 8 to 1. The school is accredited by the Southern Association of Colleges and Schools, the European Council of International Schools, and the International Baccalaureate Organization.

Galloway School
215 West Wieuca Road NE
(404) 252–8389
www.gallowayschool.org

This Buckhead school was founded in 1969 by Elliott Galloway on the principle that children need to learn the values of common decency and dignity along with academics, the arts, physical fitness, problem solving, and collaborative skills. Serving approximately 740 students from age 2 through grade 12, the school sits on a hill overlooking Chastain Park. Galloway has more than 95 faculty members, more than half of whom have advanced degrees. Within the past several years, almost all the interior spaces in the original hand-hewn brick main building were extensively renovated. An attached classroom building contains 15 classrooms, a multipurpose room, and school offices. A three-story, 16-classroom building and a gymnasium/fitness center were completed in 1996.

Greenfield Hebrew Academy
5200 Northland Drive NW
(404) 843–9900
www.ghacademy.org

Founded in 1953, the Hebrew Academy offers a child-centered traditional approach in a curriculum specially designed for the school. About 600 students attend classes in prekindergarten through eighth grade. The first part of the day is spent doing traditional classwork; the afternoon is devoted exclusively to Judaic studies and the Hebrew language. Science and com-

puter labs, music, and art centers are part of the facilities. The student-teacher ratio for the upper grades is 19 to 1; the numbers are slightly lower for the elementary school.

Heiskell School
3260 Northside Drive NW
(404) 262–2233
www.heiskell.net

This nondenominational Christian school was founded in 1949 with a traditional class structure. The school is based on the belief that a child's home, church, and school should complement each other. The approximately 360 students served range in age from 2 years old to eighth grade. The student-teacher ratio is 12 to 1. United States history and academic excellence are stressed.

Holy Innocents' Episcopal School
805 Mount Vernon Highway
(404) 255–4026
www.hies.org

The fourth-largest independent school in the Atlanta area, Holy Innocents' has approximately 1,300 students ranging in age from 3 years through 12th graders. The school opened in 1959 with the mission of providing students with an enriching program guided by Judeo-Christian principles. The 33-acre campus includes a worship space, fine arts facility, and sports fields. The student-teacher ratio averages 10 to 1.

Lovett School
4075 Paces Ferry Road NW
(404) 262–3032
www.lovett.org

On a picturesque 100-acre setting along the Chattahoochee River, Lovett aims to develop the whole child in all aspects of academic, arts, and athletic programs by concentrating on the student's intellectual, physical, spiritual, social, and emotional growth. This college-prep school was founded in 1926 and serves about 1,512 students ranging in age from 4 through 12th graders. After-school care is available. The student-teacher ratio is approximately 10 to 1.

Pace Academy
966 West Paces Ferry Road
(404) 262–1345
www.paceacademy.org

Pace Academy was founded in 1958. About 825 students in kindergarten through 12th grade study in an atmosphere of caring and personalized attention. The school's stated philosophy is "to have the courage to strive for excellence." The traditional college prep curriculum includes advanced placement classes and honors classes.

One hundred percent of Pace Academy seniors go on to higher education. An extensive service learning program fosters good citizenship and community outreach. The school's 25-acre campus is anchored by a Tudor-style home built in 1931, dubbed "the Castle," which houses administrative offices. The student-teacher ratio is 10 to 1.

Trinity School
3254 Northside Parkway NW
(404) 231–8100
www.trinityatl.org

Founded in 1951, Trinity School is an elementary and preschool with 480 students, from 2-year-olds to sixth graders. In addition to a challenging academic program, Trinity emphasizes the ethical values of the Christian religion and its Jewish heritage as well as respect for different backgrounds. Spanish, art, music, values education, physical education, and technology are key parts of the curriculum. Summer camp and after-school programs are available. The student-teacher ratio is about 9 to 1.

The Westminster Schools
1424 West Paces Ferry Road NW
(404) 355–8673
www.westminster.net

Founded in 1951, Westminster educates about 1,740 students from pre-K through 12th grade with a rigorous academic program based on Christian philosophy. Westminster has a 171-acre campus with 16 tennis courts, a natatorium and an outdoor pool, four gyms, and six playing fields. The traditional curriculum is col-

lege preparatory, while the school's mission statement conveys its philosophy: Christian commitment, whole person development, and excellent education. In grades five through 12, the average class size is 14. In classes with younger children, the average is 9.

Woodward Academy
1662 Rugby Avenue, College Park
(404) 765–8262
www.woodward.edu

Woodward was founded in 1900 by Col. John Charles Woodward as Georgia Military Academy. In the mid-1960s, the school dropped the military focus, went coeducational, and was renamed in honor of the founder. The curriculum is college prep with a traditional structure. The diverse student population of 2,850 studies on three campuses. The Woodward-Busey campus in Riverdale hosts the prekindergarten through sixth-grade crowd; a third campus in north Fulton County is for grades prekindergarten through grade six. The main campus, which also offers pre-K through sixth grades, sits on about 65 acres and has more than 30 buildings, including a state-of-the-art science center, and a library with approximately 200 Internet connections. Woodward also has a natatorium, five indoor basketball courts, and football, track, and practice fields. Woodward has third-generation students from some Atlanta families and many alumni employed on campus. Woodward transports more than 1,000 students by bus daily.

Approximately 60 percent of Woodward's faculty members have at least a master's degree. The student-teacher ratio is approximately 18 to 1.

Gwinnett County

Country Brook Montessori School
2175 Norcross-Tucker Road, Norcross
(770) 446–2397

An academic preschool and grade school founded in 1983, Country Brook Montessori School serves approximately 200 children ranging in age from 1 through 12. One of many Montessori schools in the metro area, Country Brook has a staff trained in the Montessori curriculum, which supports full development of children in all aspects. The student-teacher ratio is 11 to 1 for students ages 6 to 9; it's 16 to 1 for students ages 9 to 12.

The variety of extracurricular activities available includes art, Spanish, gymnastics, music, and computers. Country Brook has a hot lunch program and enrichment programs before and after school for enrolled children. Country Brook opens at 7:00 A.M. and closes at 6:30 P.M.

Greater Atlanta Christian School
1575 Indian Trail, Norcross
(770) 243-2000
www.greateratlantachristian.org

After planning for seven years, this school opened in 1968 to offer a traditional class structure for children in kindergarten through grade 12. The average class size is 19. One hundred percent of the students pursue higher education. More than 1,615 students are enrolled on the 74-acre campus. After-school care is available for kindergarten through eighth grade.

Special Schools

Approximately 40 institutions exist for students with special needs beyond the public school system or private school programs. These needs encompass a wide range of physical, mental, and emotional needs. For more information, call the United Way of Metropolitan Atlanta at 211 or (404) 614-1000 for a listing of more than 2,000 community organizations, including many that deal with human service needs. County school boards also are a good source for referrals. A multitude of Atlanta agencies and organizations exist to lend assistance.

Atlanta Speech School
3160 Northside Parkway
(404) 233-5332
www.atlantaspeechschool.org

The Atlanta Speech School was founded in 1938 by the Junior League of Atlanta. It was based in a building the League bought with money raised at a ball to mark the opening of *Gone With the Wind*. The school housed the first audiology clinic in the area, which continues to provide evaluation of all kinds of communication disorders. Today, 211 students attend nursery, kindergarten classes, and grades one through six. Speech pathologists and reading specialists work in each classroom.

The Howard School
1246 Ponce de Leon Avenue
(404) 377-7436
www.howardschool.org

Founded in 1950, the Howard School specializes in programs for students with language and learning disabilities. More than 280 students, from age 4 to 18, attend classes at the Ponce de Leon campus in Druid Hills and on the north campus, 9415 Willeo Road, in Roswell. The focus in both locations is to provide students with a challenging and nurturing environment to help them understand their own learning styles. Classes usually have fewer than 10 students; student to teacher ratio is approximately 5 to 1.

Learning Disabilities Association of Georgia
P.O. Box 1337, Roswell 30077
(678) 461-4471

This organization has 10 councils throughout the state that provide support group services to families of children and adults with learning disabilities.

The Frazer Center
1815 Ponce de Leon Avenue NE
(404) 377-3836
www.thefrazercenter.org

Classes for children from 6 weeks to 5 years are designed for those who are moderately to severely developmentally delayed, those with multiple handicaps, and those with neuromuscular and musculoskeletal disorders. The average class size is 15. The center also provides vocational and community living skills training for adults 18 and older. Supported employment for adults is also available. The center serves Fulton and DeKalb Counties.

Special Needs Resources

**Atlanta Alliance on Developmental
Disabilities (AADD)
828 West Peachtree Street, Suite 304
(404) 881–9777
www.aadd.org**

AADD is a nonprofit United Way agency dedicated to improving the lives of Atlanta citizens with developmental disabilities. Staff and volunteers of AADD provide practical skill training, recreation, and community participation for consumers as well as advocacy for their interests. AADD also promotes community education and greater acceptance of people with developmental disabilities.

**Emory University Psychological Center
1462 Clifton Road NE
Suite 235 Dental Building
(404) 727–7451**

A component of Emory University's Department of Psychology, this center offers diagnostic and therapeutic services for educational, emotional, and neuropsychological difficulties in children, adolescents, and adults. The center offers psychotherapy with fees on a sliding scale as well as a broad range of testing services including IQ, achievement, neuropsychological, personality, and learning disabilities assessments.

Colleges and Universities

Atlanta's richly varied colleges and universities make it a magnet for students and teachers from around the world. Here we have institutions specializing in a wide range of studies from engineering, law, and medicine to religion, art, and fashion design.

Beyond their own academic programs, Atlanta's colleges and universities give their students the broader benefits associated with life in a major city that is home to people from practically every culture. The Atlanta environment yields great possibilities for enhancing education through arts and cultural events, interaction with the business world, the resources of other area schools, and daily exposure to people from all walks of life.

The following is a brief look at some of Atlanta's institutions of higher learning.

**Agnes Scott College
141 East College Avenue, Decatur
(404) 638–6000
www.agnesscott.edu**

Six miles east of downtown, Agnes Scott College is a private, four-year liberal arts college for women. Founded in 1889 by Decatur Presbyterian Church, it was named for the mother of industrialist and developer Col. George Washington Scott, whose $112,000 gift to the school was the largest contribution to education ever made in Georgia at that time. In 1907 Agnes Scott became one of Georgia's first accredited colleges and universities.

Today, Agnes Scott's 910 students come from 42 states and 31 countries. The college boasts an 10-to-1 student-faculty ratio; the average class size is 15; 100 percent of the tenured full-time faculty hold doctorates; 60 percent are women. About 20 percent of students are adult women returning to college to complete degree work. Approximately 90 percent of students live in campus dorms. The library maintains extensive collections relating to Robert Frost, who visited the college 20 times, and Catherine Marshall, alumna, class of '36.

The 100-acre campus is involved in a master renovation and expansion program. The college's many fine Gothic- and Victorian-style buildings are surrounded by broad lawns, old trees, and brick walks. Portions of 20 movies, commercials, and TV shows have been filmed here, including *A Man Called Peter, Fried Green Tomatoes,* and, most recently, *Scream II.*

Insiders' Tip

If you're new to the area, take an adult education class. It's a great way to meet new people in the area.

The Art Institute of Atlanta
6600 Peachtree Dunwoody Road NE
100 Embassy Row
(770) 394–8300
www.aia.artinstitutes.edu

The Art Institute of Atlanta was founded in 1949 as the Massey Business College, and was renamed in 1975. It offers associate of arts degrees in culinary arts, fashion marketing, interior design, Web site administration, photographic imaging, graphic design, computer animation, multimedia, and video production, and a bachelor of fine arts degree in interior design and graphic design. Diploma programs are offered in advertising design, commercial photography, and residential interiors. The school has programs for professionals in the above fields who want to update or acquire new skills.

In June 1999, the college moved to a new location in the northern suburbs. The institute's five-story, 115,000-square-foot facilities include IBM and Macintosh computer labs, a multicamera video studio, a computer animation lab, audio and video production and editing studios, photography studios, an interior design resource library, and teaching kitchens and a dining lab that doubles as a high-end teaching restaurant open to the public. Some 2,100 students attend classes here.

Atlanta College of Art
Woodruff Arts Center
1280 Peachtree Street NE
(404) 733–5001
www.aca.edu

Founded in 1928, Atlanta College of Art offers a four-year program leading to a bachelor of fine arts degree. As a founding member of the Woodruff Arts Center, ACA is the only art college in the United States that shares a campus with three major arts organizations: the High Museum of Art, the Alliance Theatre, and the Atlanta Symphony Orchestra. Woodruff Arts Center is in Midtown and is served by the Arts Center MARTA station.

Of ACA's 425 students, about 150 are housed on-campus in the six-story Lombardy Hall. The college has 23 full-time and 50 adjunct professors; the student-faculty ratio is 12 to 1. Each year, some 2,000 adults and children participate in the college's community education programs. ACA's facilities include studios, darkrooms, a sculpture building with a wood shop and foundry, a 400-seat auditorium, and a 3,850-square-foot gallery that is open to the public free of charge.

Atlanta Metropolitan College
1630 Metropolitan Parkway
(404) 756–4000
www.atlm.edu

A coeducational, nonresidential institution, Atlanta Metropolitan College was founded in 1974 and today has more than 2,000 students. The college's 83-acre campus includes wooded areas and a lake.

AMC offers programs leading to associate's degrees in arts, science, and applied science. The college offers extensive developmental studies programs for students requiring help with basic English, math, and reading skills, and it has a cooperative program with Atlanta Area Technical School.

Bauder College
Phipps Plaza, 3500 Peachtree Road NE
(404) 237–7573
www.bauder.edu

Insiders' Tip

If you are looking for a career field with possibly one of the highest needs in the Atlanta area, look into the Art Institute of Atlanta's Culinary Institute. The CI graduates about 80 well-trained chefs per year, and Atlanta alone has more than 8,000 independent restaurants clamoring for their services!

A college in a mall? It sounds too good to be true, but Bauder's "campus" is also home to Saks Fifth Avenue, Lord & Taylor, and Parisian. The college was founded in 1963 and offers associate of arts degrees in fashion merchandising, business administration, interior design, and fashion design. Theoretical knowledge and applied skills are emphasized and provided through a variety of teaching techniques.

Atlanta itself is an important part of the students' education: The college is at one of the Southeast's leading fashion malls in a city that's a regional design and wholesale center—home to the Atlanta Apparel Mart, the Atlanta Merchandise Mart, and the Atlanta Decorative Arts Center, the second-largest freestanding design center in the nation.

Bauder has dormitory apartments, for female students only, 2 blocks from the college. About 500 students are enrolled. The student-teacher ratio is about 18 to 1.

Columbia Theological Seminary
701 South Columbia Drive, Decatur
(404) 378–8821
www.ctsnet.edu

Founded in South Carolina in 1828, Columbia Theological Seminary relocated in 1925 to a 57-acre campus in Decatur. Affiliated with the Presbyterian Church (USA), Columbia has about 600 students working toward master's (divinity, theological studies, theology) and doctoral (ministry, theology) degrees. The student-teacher ratio is about 12 to 1.

Centered in Biblical, historical, and theological disciplines, Columbia's curriculum also includes innovative course work in international education, theology and media, clinical pastoral education, urban ministries, evangelism, and spiritual formation. The school attracts clergy and laypersons from across the nation to its seminars, retreats, and continuing education programs. Its center for Asian ministries provides exchange programs and educational opportunities for Korean-American churches.

DeVry Institute of Technology
250 North Arcadia Avenue, Decatur
(404) 292–7900
www.devry.edu

DeVry/Atlanta, established in 1969, moved to its own 22-acre campus in 1985 and now has more than 3,500 students. The average age of students is 28; 20 percent receive military benefits.

The institute confers bachelor's degrees in accounting, business administration, computer information systems, electronics engineering technology, technical management, and telecommunications management, and an associate's degree in applied science in electronics. DeVry's students are eligible for the state's Tuition Equalization Grant and HOPE scholarship program. The school boasts a student-to-computer ratio of 6 to 1 and reports that more than 97 percent of graduates who actively pursue employment find jobs in their chosen field within six months of graduation. The school also offers some of its programs at a branch campus in Alpharetta, where the average student age is 30.

Emory University
1380 South Oxford Road NE
(404) 727–6123
www.emory.edu

Emory had just 15 students when it began back in 1836; today more than 11,600 (representing all 50 states and 105 nations) are enrolled there. In addition to the 631-acre Atlanta campus, Emory has a two-year division, Oxford College, in Oxford, Georgia, about 35 miles east of Atlanta.

The undergraduate student-faculty ratio is 10 to 1. About 30 percent of students live on campus in residence halls and apartments. Emory's five libraries house more than two million volumes.

In 1980 Emory received the assets of the Emily and Ernest Woodruff Fund; the $105 million gift was the largest ever given to a philanthropically supported institution up to that time, and during the next dozen years its value more than quintupled. Since 1990 Emory has increased the size of its physical plant, building or acquiring more than 1.6 million square feet. Especially notable is the Michael C. Carlos Museum on campus (designed by famous architect Michael Graves). The Carter Center is an interdisciplinary arm of Emory. Emory University Hospital is a nationally known medical facility (and a favorite of ailing celebrities).

Georgia Institute of Technology
225 North Avenue NW
(404) 894–2000
www.gatech.edu

Georgia Tech's reputation extends light years beyond its 330-acre campus west of the Downtown Connector near Midtown. In a 2003 ranking, *U.S. News and World Report* named Tech the ninth-best public university in the nation, fourth in graduate engineering, sixth in undergraduate engineering, and the top school in the nation for industrial engineering programs.

During the 1996 Games, Tech was known to people around the world as the Olympic Village. Its 10,000-seat Alexander Memorial Coliseum hosted all 12 medal events in boxing. At the brand-new aquatic center, the water polo pool (seating capacity: 4,000) was the site of all aquatic events except the finals, which were held in the shaded, 15,000-seat aquatic stadium. The village's population included about 15,000 athletes and officials.

Immediately after the Olympics, Tech hosted the 1996 Paralympic Games for physically challenged athletes, using many of the same facilities the Olympics used.

Tech gained seven new residence halls as a result of Olympic construction. (Oddly enough, these are not the new buildings most visibly allied to the campus; the tall dorm buildings between Tech and the Downtown Connector are occupied by Georgia State University students.)

Georgia Tech was established in 1885 and has fared especially well in the past 20 years. More than 15,000 students are enrolled in six colleges: architecture; computing; engineering; sciences; management; and the Ivan Allen College of Liberal Arts. The student population is 70 percent male; 90 percent of freshmen rank in the top 10 percent of their high school class.

Georgia Perimeter College
3251 Panthersville Road, Decatur
(404) 244–5090
www.gpc.edu

Georgia Perimeter College, formerly DeKalb College, has approximately 24,650 students divided among four campuses: Decatur, Clarkston, Lawrenceville, and Dunwoody. There is also a center with classrooms and a library in Conyers. Students work toward two-year associate's degrees in arts, science, and applied science.

The average age of the students is mid-20s; under the college's flexible schedule, classes are offered in the day, evening, and on Saturdays, allowing students to earn their degree while fulfilling their responsibilities of work and family. A special College on TV program allows participating students to view classes and earn credits with a minimal number of visits to a campus.

Two-thirds of students work more than 20 hours a week and attend college part time. Since Georgia Perimeter College, then DeKalb College, first held classes at its original Clarkston campus in 1964, more than a half-million students have passed through the system.

Georgia Perimeter College is the third-largest college in the University System of Georgia, which includes all of the state-assisted institutions.

Georgia State University
1 Park Place S
(404) 651–2000
www.gsu.edu

In downtown Atlanta just east of Five Points, GSU is the second-largest institution of higher learning in Georgia and the largest urban university in the Southeast. GSU has its own MARTA rail station, used daily by about 10,000 students, faculty, and staff. The university has a total of more than 27,000 students.

There are 50 academic departments at GSU, divided among six colleges: arts and sciences, business administration, education, health sciences, law, and public and urban affairs. There are 150 student organizations on campus, an award-winning student newspaper, *The Signal,* and a popular 100,000-watt student radio station (WRAS 88.5 FM).

Until the fall of 1997, GSU had no dormitories. But after the Olympics, the four dormitories adjacent to Georgia Tech (built at a cost of more than $85 million) were turned into GSU Village. The dorms now house 2,000 students as well as a post office, gym, and fitness center and 24-hour security, parking, and unlimited free access to MARTA. In addition GSU's physical education complex was remodeled to host the Olympic badminton competition. Work was completed in early 1996 on the renovation of the long-vacant Rialto movie theater (just south of the Central Library) into a concert hall for GSU's performing arts groups, as well as entertainers from around the country.

Keller Graduate School of Management of DeVry University
250 North Arcadia Avenue, Decatur
(404) 298-9444
www.keller.edu

Founded in Chicago in 1973, Keller's MBA program has grown to become the seventh largest in the country. In 1987 Keller acquired the DeVry Institute system. Keller's Atlanta center opened in 1993; today the school operates 18 centers in eight states.

Telecommunications management is the newest of the eight concentrations offered in Keller's MBA program. Keller also offers master of human resource management and master of project management programs. The programs are geared toward working adults, who often find it easy to continue their studies at another

Keller center if they are transferred out of Atlanta. In addition to the main campus, Keller has a northside facility at Perimeter Center and an Alpharetta campus that opened in the fall of 1997.

Kennesaw State University
1000 Chastain Road, Kennesaw
(770) 423-6000
www.kennesaw.edu

Some 14,000 students attend classes at Kennesaw State, which was founded in 1963 as part of the state's University system. Today, it's nationally recognized as an innovative, teaching-oriented university, offering a wide variety of undergraduate studies in the arts, sciences, education, nursing, and business, as well as graduate degrees in business, education, accounting, professional writing, nursing, and public administration. In addition, the school sponsors many free theater, dance, and arts activities for the general public.

The campus is off I-75 at exit 117, 10 miles north of Marietta. Enrollment includes many traditional and nontraditional students. The average student age is 27.

Life University
1269 Barclay Circle, Marietta
(770) 424-0554
www.life.edu

Founded with 22 students in 1974, Life College at one time was the single largest chiropractic college in the world and has the world's largest chiropractic library. It has 15 buildings, and peaked in the 1990s with more than 4,000 students and 265 faculty members. The campus also boasts a historic village of log structures dating from the 1790s that were moved to the school from around the Southeast; it's free and open to the public seven days a week during daylight hours.

Life confers the degrees doctor of chiropractic, bachelor of business administration, bachelor of science in nutrition for the chiropractic sciences, bachelor of science in nutrition for dietetics, and master of sport health science. The college has more than 50 service, social, and fraternal clubs, and many sports teams, including nationally ranked basketball, track, and rugby teams.

As of early 2003, Life University has lost its accreditation from the Council on Chiropractic Education, effectively putting a halt to its primary mission. The Southern Association of Colleges and Schools (SACS), the most important regional accreditation agency, granted Life a one-year probationary accreditation in December 2002, keeping the nonchiropractic college courses open for at least that length of time. Life has filed suit in court challenging these issues, and the best advice we can offer is to check with Life's Web site or the local news agencies for the final outcome.

Mercer University
Cecil B. Day Campus
3001 Mercer University Drive
(770) 986–3000
www.mercer.edu

The second-largest Baptist-affiliated institution in the world, Mercer University was founded in 1833 and is based in Macon, Georgia. It has been rated one of the top 15 schools in the South by *U.S. News and World Report* for 13 consecutive years. The 335-acre Cecil B. Day Campus in Atlanta is known as Mercer's Graduate and Professional Center, although it also offers undergraduate programs. Approximately 1,200 full-time and 800 part-time students at the Atlanta campus study programs including pharmacy, business and economics, education, and engineering. The university offers off-campus centers in Douglas County and Covington, as well as at Grady Hospital and the Georgia Power Co.

Oglethorpe University
4484 Peachtree Road
(404) 261–1441
www.oglethorpe.edu

Named for the founder of Georgia, James Edward Oglethorpe, Oglethorpe Univer-

Insiders' Tip

HOPE, Helping Outstanding Pupils Educationally, is one of the three educational initiatives funded by the Georgia Lottery. The program provides recent high school graduates and other eligible residents with financial assistance for degree, diploma, or certificate programs at Georgia public or private institutions. Students with 3.0 cumulative grade averages can receive public college scholarships that include tuition, mandatory fees, and a book allowance up to $100 per quarter. Students need to reapply for each academic year. In keeping with its name, HOPE offers a second chance for students whose grades may slip after 45 credit hours. Sophomores may continue their education at their own expense, then reapply for HOPE assistance if they've earned a 3.0 cumulative average by the end of sophomore year.

sity was founded in 1835 by Georgia Presbyterians to train ministers. It was originally located near Milledgeville, at that time the capital of Georgia. During the Civil War, the university's students became soldiers, its buildings became barracks and hospitals, and its endowment became worthless Confederate bonds. The college closed in 1862 and tried unsuccessfully to reorganize in Atlanta during Reconstruction.

Oglethorpe University was rechartered in 1913; two years later the cornerstone was laid for the present 118-acre campus, whose layout and Gothic Revival architecture were inspired by Corpus Christi College, Oxford, England, the honorary alma mater of James Oglethorpe.

The university's 1,225 students hail from 37 states and 31 nations; 50 percent are from Georgia. The student-faculty ratio is 13 to 1; 95 percent of faculty members hold terminal degrees. Internships are available in all of the school's 28 undergraduate and three graduate academic majors.

The International Time Capsule Society is headquartered at Oglethorpe, and there, behind a great steel door, lies the "Crypt of Civilization." This time capsule was considered the finest ever developed when it was sealed in 1940. Its contents include a machine to teach English, a quart of Budweiser, a coffeemaker, and a Lionel train. It's not yet time to begin lining up for your place at the capsule's unsealing—check our *Insiders' Guide* for A.D. 8113!

Southern Polytechnic State University
1100 South Marietta Parkway, Marietta
(770) 528–7281
www.spsu.edu

Approximately 4,000 students study for their bachelor's and master's degrees at this school, founded in 1948 as the Southern College of Technology. The student population, from 35 states and 82 countries, attend day, evening, and continuing education classes in 16 science programs. Master's programs include computer science, construction, engineering technology, management of technology, software engineering, technical and professional communication, and quality assurance. The student-teacher ratio is 20 to 1.

Atlanta University Center

Atlanta University Center is a consortium of six historically black colleges in southwest Atlanta. Together, the six colleges form the largest predominantly African-American private institute of higher learning in the nation. Although the six institutions share a library and cooperate in many areas, they remain distinct from one another. The following is a look at Atlanta University Center's six member colleges.

Clark Atlanta University
223 James P. Brawley Drive
(404) 880–8000
www.cau.edu

Clark Atlanta University was formed in 1988 through the consolidation of Atlanta University, founded in 1865, and Clark College, founded in 1869. CAU is one of only two private, comprehensive, historically black universities in the nation offering programs of instruction and research from bachelor to doctorate degrees.

CAU's approximately 4,800-member student body is 70 percent female. The university provides on-campus housing for 1,800 students. The student-faculty ratio is 16 to 1. Several of CAU's dormitories provided the setting for Spike Lee's movie *School Daze*. CAU operates the popular jazz radio station WCLK 91.9 FM.

Clark Atlanta's 5,000-seat stadium was one of two venues used for hockey competition during the Olympics. A 470-bed dormitory, built for use by the Atlanta Committee for the Olympic Games, houses students.

CAU was also the official institution for the Olympic Host Broadcast Training Program, which trained 1,200 college students to work with national and international professional journalists during the Games. More than $2 million of the program's state-of-the-art digital equipment

Harkness Hall is the main administration building for Clark Atlanta University.

PHOTO: CLARK ATLANTA UNIVERSITY

was donated by Panasonic Broadcast Television Corp.

Interdenominational Theological Center
700 Martin Luther King Jr. Drive SW
(404) 527–7700
www.itc.edu

Established in 1958, the Interdenominational Theological Center is made up of six separate seminaries: Gammon Theological Seminary, United Methodist, founded in 1872; Charles H. Mason Theological Seminary, Church of God in Christ, founded in 1970; Morehouse School of Religion, Baptist, founded in 1867; Phillips School of Theology, Christian Methodist Episcopal, founded in 1944; Johnson C. Smith Theological Seminary, Presbyterian Church USA, founded in 1867; and Turner Theological Seminary, African Methodist Episcopal, founded in 1894.

ITC's approximately 400 students come from 32 states and seven nations. ITC offers master's (divinity, Christian education, and church music) and doctoral (ministry, theology, and pastoral counseling) degrees.

Since its formation in 1958, ITC has graduated more than 25 percent of all trained black ministers in the world. ITC's James H. Costen Lifelong Education Center was used as Olympic housing during the 1996 Games.

Morehouse College
830 Westview Drive SW
(404) 681–2800
www.morehouse.edu

Established as Augusta Institute in Augusta, Georgia, in 1867, this college relocated to Atlanta in 1879, where it was first known as Atlanta Baptist College and then, in 1913, as Morehouse College.

Today, Morehouse is the nation's only predominantly African-American, all-male liberal arts college. Its 3,000 students represent 42 states and 15 foreign countries; more than half graduated high school in the top 20 percent of their class. Of its more than 200 faculty members, almost 95 percent of assistant professors and above hold doctorate degrees. Morehouse confers bachelor of arts and bachelor of science degrees in 35 major areas of study.

Morehouse's most famous alumnus was Nobel laureate Dr. Martin Luther King Jr.; Morehouse is also where filmmaker Spike Lee spent his School Daze. Fourteen Morehouse men have gone on to serve as president of a college or university. Morehouse's 6,000-seat arena was the site of early rounds of men's and women's basketball competition during the Olympics.

Morehouse School of Medicine
720 Westview Drive SW
(404) 752-1500
www.msm.edu

Morehouse School of Medicine began with 24 students in 1975; today it has approximately 200 students. The 205-member faculty includes many off-site community physicians who work with interns and students. MSM confers the four-year doctor of medicine degree, the Ph.D. degree in biomedical sciences, and a master's degree in public health.

Residency programs have been established in family medicine, internal medicine, preventive medicine, psychiatry,

Historic Graves Hall, built in 1889, was the first building on the campus of Morehouse College.
PHOTO: MOREHOUSE COLLEGE

obstetrics, gynecology, and surgery. In conjunction with testing services to be performed, the Atlanta Committee for the Olympic Games provided $1 million to help MSM establish a research laboratory to study sports performance–enhancing drugs.

Morris Brown College
643 Martin Luther King Jr. Drive NW
(404) 220–0270
www.morrisbrown.edu

In 1881 Morris Brown College first held classes for 107 students in a wooden building at the corner of Boulevard and Houston Street. Its name honors the memory of the second consecrated bishop in the African Methodist Episcopal Church; the college was founded through the generosity of the members of Big Bethel AME on Auburn Avenue.

Its faculty members take pride in motivating not only average and better-than-average students but also those considered to be high risk. Today, more than 2,000 students pursue degrees in more than 40 areas of study. The student-teacher ratio is about 36 to 1.

Morris Brown's 15,000-seat Alonzo Herndon Stadium was the site of the finals in men's and women's hockey during the Olympics and the 2002 film *Drumline*.

In December 2002, Morris Brown lost its accreditation from the Southern Association of Colleges and Schools (SACS), the most important regional accreditation agency, primarily due to concerns about Morris Brown's financial situation. The school has filed an appeal with SACS, stating that it believes this situation may be resolved over time; the best advice we can offer is to check with Morris Brown's Web site or the local news agencies for the final outcome.

Spelman College
350 Spelman Lane SW
(404) 681–3643
www.spelman.edu

Founded in 1881, Spelman College is one of the oldest U.S. institutions dedicated to the education of African-American women. Recent years have brought new recognition to the long-respected school: Spelman has repeatedly made the top 10 list of U.S. women's colleges and the top 10 Southeast colleges in *Money* magazine's "Best Buys" issue. In 1997 the magazine ranked Spelman as the very best buy among historically black colleges. Highly acclaimed Dr. Johnetta B. Cole, who declined an offer to serve as U.S. secretary of education for the first Clinton administration, resigned in June 1997 after 10 years at the helm. During Dr. Cole's tenure, Oprah Winfrey donated $1 million to Spelman's capital fund and praised "the extraordinary legacy of Spelman College and Dr. Johnetta Cole." Dr. Beverly Daniel Tatum is the president.

Spelman has just more than 2,100 students and a student-faculty ratio of 12 to 1. More than 83 percent of full-time faculty have doctorate or other advanced degrees. Nearly half the students are engaged in some form of community service; 37 percent major in math or the natural sciences. Upon graduation, 45 percent of Spelman women continue their studies.

Resources
Southern Association of Colleges and Schools
1866 Southern Lane, Decatur
(404) 679–4500
www.sacs.org

Call this association if you need help trying to decide which college to attend. It can provide information on schools throughout the region.

Teaching in Georgia

Nearly every public school in Georgia requires most, if not all, teachers to possess a current Georgia Teaching Certificate; at this time, no national or other state certification is recognized as absolutely equivalent. Certification requires at least a bachelor's degree and a certain number of professional education course credits, along with passing a formal examination known as the Praxis II. Recent new requirements include criminal background screening and demonstrated computer competency. The professional (called "clear renewable") certification currently issued is good for five years and has some continuing education requirements for renewing; Georgia has not issued permanent or "life" certifications since the 1970s.

The agency responsible for issuing certifications is the Georgia Professional Standards Commission, Certification Section, (404) 657-9000. It has an unusually good Web site at www.gapsc.com, which contains about anything right on-line you would want or need to know in order to get your certification, including all the necessary forms and the latest legislative developments (hint: the 2003 session was quite heavy on education issues!). The GPSC also has information for out-of-state teachers looking to transfer their license to Georgia. The Educational Testing Service is responsible for the certification exam itself, which is the same one used by 34 other states, and it also has an unusually useful and complete site at www. ets.org/teachingandlearning.

Georgia is also blessed with an excellent recruitment office run by the Georgia Department of Education. Its primary asset to teachers looking for work is the TeachGeorgia site, at www.teachgeorgia. org/gadoe/RecruitHome/nsf/welcome. Along with lists of schools and their openings, TeachGeorgia has an on-line resume service, which will both alert you via e-mail the moment a position in your field becomes available and forward your resume to that school system.

One thing to remember is that private schools are often willing to hire uncertified teachers, even if public schools will usually not even grant them an interview.

Insiders' Tip

Test results that are available through the Department of Education are a school's overall marks in standardized tests, such as the Iowa Test of Basic Skills. Individual student test results are not released.

This is especially true with the current teaching shortage, which is projected to last quite some time in certain high-needs fields (like math, science, and special education), and grow worse as Atlanta's population continues to boom.

A sign that this is indeed a "teachers market" is the fact that one metro county school system continues to have more than 1,000 openings well after the halfway point in the 2002–03 school year, and that another metro system is offering multi-thousand-dollar "sign-on" bonuses for certain fields. Another sign of the times is that yet a third metro system announced that it would need at least 3,000 more teachers for the 2003–04 school year, assuming that its student population did not exceed projections and that only the usual percentage of teachers quit or retired!

Health Care

We hope you'll be healthy and happy during your stay in Atlanta. But if you happen to get sick or injured, we can help take care of you. As a regional center for health care and research, the Atlanta area offers high-quality health care and enviable accessibility.

The Atlanta metropolitan area boasts a wealth of top-notch doctors and medical facilities, which says a lot about the desirability of the Atlanta area as a place to live. It also reflects the steady stream of new doctors, nurses, and allied health professionals graduating from the many training centers in the metro and surrounding areas.

Local medical students train at Emory University's School of Medicine and Morehouse School of Medicine, while future pharmacists study at Mercer University's Southern School of Pharmacy. Nursing programs are offered at Clayton State College and University, DeKalb College, Emory University, Georgia State University, Kennesaw State University, Morris Brown College, and Oglethorpe University. The Medical College of Georgia Schools of Medicine and Nursing in Augusta and the Mercer College of Medicine in Macon are within a three-hour driving distance of the city.

Because Atlanta is a national center in medical research, residents have the opportunity to participate in many clinical research trials that evaluate new treatments.

Numerous major medical organizations have headquarters in Atlanta. Foremost in this category is the Centers for Disease Control and Prevention (CDC), an agency of the U.S. Public Health Service. A major research facility with programs taking place in the Atlanta headquarters and field stations, health departments, and other facilities throughout the world, CDC is an institution dedicated to promoting health and quality of life by preventing and controlling disease, injury, and disability.

The American Cancer Society's national headquarters coordinates and supports the state and county divisions of this, the largest voluntary health agency in the world. Although no research takes place at this office, the staff administers and supports the society's national research programs taking place at various venues throughout the country.

The Arthritis Foundation national headquarters coordinates research and offers nationwide, community-based services including self-help courses, exercise classes, support groups, and instructional videotapes. The foundation provides educational brochures and booklets for the public and publishes a national bimonthly consumer magazine, *Arthritis Today*.

Yerkes Regional Primate Research Center at Emory University is the oldest scientific institute dedicated to primate research. Yerkes Main Station facility specializes in biomedical research; the 117-acre Field Station studies primate social groups.

Georgia Institute of Technology Research Institute is one of the country's premier bioengineering programs producing advances in prosthetics and engineered assistance for the disabled. Tech's Medical Informatic Research Group, part of Georgia Tech's Graphics, Visualization, and Usability Center, is exploring ways in which computer science methods and techniques can help solve problems in medicine and biomedicine.

The Carter Center, a separately chartered, independently governed part of Emory University, counts Global 2000 among its many other programs and initiatives. Global 2000 is a coalition of governments, corporations, individuals, and organizations that addresses global environmental, agricultural, economic, and public health concerns. Among its other accomplishments, Global 2000 has been instrumental in helping to eradicate Guinea worm disease and in building a modern center for the design and manufacture of artificial limbs in China. The Task Force for Child Survival and Development, headquartered at the Carter Center, addresses issues of immunization, malnutrition, disease control, and child advocacy.

Since there are 50 or so medical facilities of varying sizes within the four-county area we focus on, and dozens more within close range, we can't do justice to their multispecialty programs in one chapter. We are, instead, providing an overview. Consider our thumbnail sketches the tip of the iceberg, and know that whatever your medical or mental health need, skilled and dedicated health care professionals in the Atlanta area are ready to serve you.

The major HMOs also have facilities throughout the metro Atlanta area in ever increasing numbers: You'll find their main numbers listed in this chapter so that you may call to locate offices and/or affiliated physicians close by.

The metropolitan Atlanta area has a number of strategically located trauma centers. A rating of Level I trauma care indicates the hospital offers the most extensive, immediate, and round-the-clock services for emergency, life-threatening needs. A Level II rating indicates 24-hour capability for surgery and specialty care. A Level III rating means these services, surgery and specialty care, are usually available within 30 minutes to an hour.

We present hospitals within the perimeter of I–285 as being in the City of Atlanta and list those outside the Perimeter by county.

Hospitals

Atlanta

Atlanta Medical Center
303 Parkway Drive NE
(404) 265–4000
www.atlantamedcenter.com

Formerly known as Georgia Baptist Hospital, the facility near downtown Atlanta was renamed when it was purchased by Tenet Healthcare Corp. of Santa Barbara, California. The medical center has grown over nearly a century to more than 467 beds and approximately 2,500 employees. The facility offers the services of more than 500 physicians. The medical center is affiliated with the Medical College of Georgia and boasts a highly sought-after residency program.

The general acute-care institution has several centers of excellence, including heart, cancer, orthopedics, obstetrics, and gynecology. The medical center has a 30-bed neonatal intensive care unit.

The cancer center, in the Mary Thompson Way Building at 345 Boulevard, employs a multidisciplinary approach to cancer care. The center supports cancer patients by providing treatment, education, counseling, and research.

The medical center offers such highly technical services as laser angioplasty for the treatment of heart disease. The center's nationally renowned cardiac rehabilitation program offers comprehensive physical, occupational, and speech rehabilitation therapies.

Atlanta's first hospital-based aeromedical service is based at Atlanta Medical. LifeFlight program transports patients from accident sites and other medical facilities and is fully staffed for extreme emergencies. The medical center has a Level II trauma unit. It also offers the Transportation Express, a free ground transport system between the primary

Insiders' Tip

The oldest hospital-based helicopter ambulance service in the southeastern United States is LifeFlight, based at the Atlanta Medical Center (formerly the Georgia Baptist Hospital).

care locations and the main campus. Equipped for handicapped patients in wheelchairs, the shuttle operates Monday through Saturday for stable patients who don't need medical care while in transit. Family members and friends may use the service to visit patients.

Children's Healthcare of Atlanta
www.choa.org

Created in 1998, Children's Healthcare of Atlanta merged two of the metro area's three children's hospitals, Egleston and Scottish Rite. The separate names live on, however, at the two original hospitals, Egleston on the Emory University campus in DeKalb County and Scottish Rite in Sandy Springs in the hospital complex known locally as "Pill Hill."

In addition to the hospitals, Children's Healthcare of Atlanta operates more than 25 satellite centers throughout the metro area.

Even though they have combined, each hospital retains its history and identity.

Children's Healthcare of Atlanta at Egleston
1405 Clifton Road NE
(404) 325-6000

Founded in 1916 as Egleston Children's Hospital, the 235-bed facility's top pediatricians treat more than 100,000 children each year at the hospital and neighborhood centers. As a major referral center for the Southeast, the system has several nationally recognized programs, including the AFLAC Cancer Center at Egleston Hospital and the Emory Egleston Children's Heart Center.

The hospital provides comprehensive pediatric care ranging from the diagnosis and treatment of ear infections to that of complex diseases. Egleston physicians also perform heart surgery and organ transplants. As a clinical, teaching, and research institution, the hospital offers all subspecialties in medical care. It enjoys a Level I rating for pediatric trauma care.

Egleston excels in several areas, including treatment of cystic fibrosis, care for brain tumors, orthopedics, medical-psychiatry patients, and premature infants.

A little fun helps the staff at Children's Healthcare of Atlanta at Egleston treat a young patient.
PHOTO: CHILDREN'S HEALTHCARE OF ATLANTA AT EGLESTON

Numbers to Call

For emergencies requiring ambulance, police, or fire departments • 911
AID Atlanta • (404) 872–0600
Georgia Dental Association • (404) 636–7553
Georgia Hospital Association • (770) 955–0324
Georgia Psychological Association • (404) 351–9555
Georgia Poison Center • (404) 616–9000
Georgia Registry for Interpreters for the Deaf • (404) 299–9500
Medical Association of Atlanta/Academy of Medicine • (404) 881–1714
Medical Association of Georgia • (404) 876–7535
CDC National AIDS Hotline • English (800) 342–AIDS • Spanish (800) 344–SIDA
   Hearing Impaired (800) AIDS-TTY
Mental Health Association of Metropolitan Atlanta • (404) 527–7175

Egleston's Children's Advocacy Center disseminates injury prevention messages through billboards, newspapers, magazines, television, and radio. Egleston is headquarters for SAFE KIDS of Georgia, a statewide coalition focusing on injury prevention. Each year, more than 500 heart surgeries are performed at Egleston. It is the state's only pediatric facility to perform a full range of pediatric transplants and kidney dialysis.

Children's Healthcare of Atlanta at Scottish Rite
1001 Johnson Ferry Road NE
(404) 256–5252

This north Atlanta multispecialty pediatric center opened in 1915 as a small facility for indigent, disabled children. Since then, the facility has grown into a premier children's medical center, equipped to provide general pediatric care as well as advanced subspecialty care.

Scottish Rite is strongly committed to children's health, welfare, and development. Pediatric advocacy programs include the Scottish Rite Child Care Fund, which offers financial aid; the Child Advocacy Center, the only hospital-based center in Georgia for child victims of sexual abuse; "Immunize Georgia's Little Guys," a coalition of businesses, organizations, and individuals dedicated to raising the state's immunization rate for children aged 1 to 24 months; and various community education and parenting programs

aimed toward keeping children healthy.

Scottish Rite's 24-hour pediatric emergency/trauma center is staffed with private-practice pediatricians. The center has 24 exam rooms, including two pediatric trauma rooms and two X-ray suites. Two helicopter landing pads and two covered ambulance bays provide direct access for critically injured or ill children. Child-size equipment and an emergency staff trained to minimize pain and fear ensure an atmosphere of compassionate, competent care. The emergency center has a computerized diagnostic system for hard-to-diagnose cases.

Specialty areas at Scottish Rite include the Hematology/Oncology Center; the Asthma Education Center; the Pulmonology Function, Sleep Disorder, and Bronchoscopy Laboratories; the Children's Epilepsy Center; and the Center for Craniofacial Disorders. Scottish Rite also has an extensive orthopedics program and comprehensive inpatient and outpatient rehabilitation units for children recovering from severe head and spinal cord trauma.

DeKalb Medical Center
2701 North Decatur Road, Decatur
(404) 501–1000
www.drhs.org

Since 1961 DeKalb Medical Center has provided the community with a variety of diagnostic, treatment, and prevention services. The 523-bed, acute-care medical center has a medical staff of more than 1,000 physicians representing more than 40 specialty areas.

The medical center's programs and services include a 24-hour emergency department offering trauma triage and chest pain emergency center services, extensive wellness and health promotion programs, and comprehensive cardiology and critical care services. Its surgery center was the first in Atlanta to be fully equipped with fixed video surgery capabilities.

Other specialties include an extensive cancer program approved by the American College of Surgeons and family-centered maternity services featuring comfortable maternity suites, a Level III neonatal intensive care unit, and specialized perinatology services for high-risk pregnancies. DeKalb Medical Center also offers a full array of rehabilitation and occupational health programs and a variety of behavioral health services.

DeKalb Medical Center is part of the Promina Health System, an alliance of hospitals and numerous other primary and urgent care facilities. Among the other hospitals in the Promina system are Gwinnett Medical Center, Piedmont Hospital, and Southern Regional Medical Center.

Emory Crawford Long Hospital
550 Peachtree Street NE
(404) 686–4411
www.emoryhealthcare.org

This hospital's name honors Dr. Crawford W. Long, the Atlanta surgeon who first used ether as anesthesia. Part of Emory Healthcare, the 583-bed hospital offers a 24-hour emergency department and more than 600 board-certified or board-eligible physicians on staff, and more than 2,000 employees.

Situated off the I–75/85 Downtown Connector (exit 100), Crawford Long provides easy access for those in the central business district and Atlanta's downtown convention and tourism zone.

Crawford Long offers a wide spectrum of services: pulmonary medicine, thoracic and cardiovascular surgery, gastrointestinal medicine, gynecology and obstetrics, oncology, international travel medicine, plastic and reconstructive surgery, and

neonatology. Additional services include outpatient surgery and radiology, family-centered maternity care, a menopause center, and in-vitro fertilization. The hospital's nationally recognized Carlyle Fraser Heart Center, now part of the Emory Heart Center, is dedicated to the prevention, diagnosis, and treatment of heart and lung disorders. It also has a Level III neonatal intensive care unit and a two-chamber hyperbaric oxygen unit.

Crawford Long was one of the first facilities in Georgia to have a cancer program approved by the American College of Surgeons. The hospital pioneered a treatment for prostate cancer called cryosurgery, which offers a shorter recovery period than traditional methods.

Volunteer international interpreters, who together speak more than 25 languages, assist patients and physicians. Crawford Long also provides speakers to business and civic organizations and offers many wellness, health information, and screening programs.

Emory University Hospital
1364 Clifton Road NE
(404) 712–7021
www.emoryhealthcare.org

In March 1904, Wesley Memorial Hospital, Emory Hospital's predecessor, opened with 50 beds in a downtown Atlanta mansion that Union Gen. William Tecumseh Sherman's army spared during the Civil War. When the hospital needed bigger quarters in 1922, Coca-Cola founder and philanthropist Asa G. Candler donated a 275-bed facility on the hospital's current site on the Emory University campus. Today, the university-owned, nonprofit institution has 587 beds, including 484 beds in the main facility, 56 in the Center for Rehabilitation Medicine, 47 beds for psychiatric treatment in the Uppergate Pavilion, and 12 beds in an NIH-funded Clinical Research Center.

The hospital is one of the nation's largest centers for heart surgery and angioplasty and a referral center of choice for the most difficult cardiac cases. Emory's innovative Chest Pain Center provides 24-hour care to individuals experiencing symptoms of a heart attack. The center offers immediate access to cardiology experts without a physician's referral.

Emory has a multiple organ and tissue transplantation program that includes heart, heart-lung, lung, heart-kidney, liver, kidney, kidney-pancreas, bone, bone marrow, cornea, and sclera transplantation. The hospital also leads in the neurosciences, especially in the surgical treatment of aneurysms, brain tumors, and movement disorders such as Parkinson's disease.

Although it's considered a general acute-care facility, Emory Hospital doesn't provide maternity or pediatric services.

The hospital is part of Emory Healthcare, which also comprises Emory Crawford Long Hospital, the Emory Clinic, and affiliates such as Wesley Woods Geriatric Center. Emory Healthcare also participates in a joint venture with Nashville-based Columbia/HCA to run an additional seven hospitals and five surgery centers in metro Atlanta. Those hospitals are Cartersville Medical Center in Bartow County, Dunwoody Medical Center, Eastside Medical Center, Metropolitan Hospital in Atlanta, Northlake Regional Medical Center in Tucker, Parkway Medical Center in Lithia Springs, and Peachtree Regional Hospital in Newnan.

Grady Memorial Hospital
80 Jesse Hill Jr. Drive SE
(404) 616–4307
www.gradyhealthsystem.org

This hospital, opened in 1892, is named for Henry W. Grady, a visionary Atlantan who promoted the progressive philosophy of the "New South." In the heart of Downtown, Grady Memorial functions primarily to meet the health care needs of medically indigent residents of Fulton and DeKalb Counties.

The hospital offers emergency care to anyone requiring it. Grady has four emergency centers, including Atlanta's only and very highly rated Level I trauma center that provides round-the-clock care in surgery, anesthesia, and specialized services such as neurosurgery and obstetrical surgery.

Grady's Georgia Poison Control Center stays open 24 hours a day, staffed by physi-

cians, registered nurses, pharmacists, and certified poison information specialists. The Rape Crisis Center provides a 24-hour hot line, examinations, and medications as well as individual, family, and group counseling.

Grady's Burn Center is one of the nation's largest. The National Institutes of Health named Grady's Sickle Cell Center a National Center of Excellence. Grady has also been praised for its TB control and tracking program and for having the most comprehensive AIDS program in the nation. The hospital also operates a Regional Perinatal Center for high-risk mothers, a Diabetes Detection and Control Center, and a Teen Center with programs to help teens postpone sexual involvement.

Grady is affiliated with the Emory University and Morehouse Schools of Medicine. It serves as a major training and research center and offers patients the latest advancements in various medical fields. The Grady Health System comprises many components, among them: Hughes Spalding Children's Hospital; five comprehensive community health centers; two women's and children's health centers; and a 400,000-square-foot pavilion of outpatient care centers, women's health services, and the neonatal intensive care nursery. The hospital also operates a 24-hour nurse advice line at (404) 616–0600.

Hughes Spalding Pediatric Hospital
35 Jesse Hill Jr. Drive SE
(404) 616–6600
www.gradyhealthsystem.org/hughspalding. htm

Founded in 1892 under the auspices of Grady Memorial Hospital, Hughes Spalding became a freestanding hospital in 1992. Hughes Spalding offers a full range of primary and acute-care pediatric services for children from infancy to 18 years of age.

Specially trained pediatric physicians, nurses, and staff members offer advanced pediatric expertise in areas such as respiratory care, physical therapy, diagnostic radiology, laboratory services, and social services. Hughes Spalding's Emergency Care Center offers round-the-clock service in an urgent care center and in a walk-in clinic for patients with less urgent needs. Hughes Spalding uses nearby Grady Memorial for specialty pediatric care in a variety of fields including dermatology, ophthalmology, otolaryngology, genitourinary, and pediatric surgery.

Northside Hospital
1000 Johnson Ferry Road NE
(404) 851–8000
www.northside.com

Northside Hospital is a 444-bed, nonprofit, full-service community hospital serving the north Atlanta community. More than 1,700 physicians from a variety of fields staff the hospital, which cares for more than 100,000 patients annually.

With more than 16,800 babies born at Northside each year, the hospital ranks first in the nation among community hospitals in the baby delivery business. The hospital provides a Perinatal Diagnostic Unit as well as a High-Risk Perinatal Unit for women who must be hospitalized during high-risk pregnancies.

The hospital's Breast Care Center houses state-of-the-art equipment, and Northside's staff includes surgeons who are nationally known for treating complicated gynecological conditions. Staff surgeons helped pioneer videolaparoscopy, a technique that dramatically reduces recovery time for many operations. Northside opened Atlanta's first outpatient surgery center more than two decades ago.

Northside's Institute for Cancer Control features an American Cancer Society Information Center. Here patients find out about a program in which former cancer patients spend time with current patients and the "Look Good . . . Feel Better" program, which offers consultations on how to cope with the physical changes brought on by chemotherapy and radiation.

ScreenAtlanta, Northside Hospital's mobile health screening unit, fosters cancer's early detection by bringing education and low-cost screening procedures to the community. At the request of businesses and other organizations, the ScreenAtlanta van travels throughout metro Atlanta, offering tests for lung function, cholesterol, and diabetes as well as computerized cancer risk assessment and information on breast, testicular, oral, skin, and colorectal cancer. The mobile mammography van provides mammograms.

Northside offers a variety of support groups and classes addressing such topics as parenting, children's issues, adolescence, divorce, assertiveness skills, stress reduction, and communications skills. The hospital's Recovery Center focuses on programs and groups for adults and adolescents whose lives have been affected by alcohol and/or drug abuse.

Northside operates a sleep disorders center and a 24-hour major emergency department. For minor emergencies, Northside's Health Express, open Monday through Friday from 11:30 A.M. to 8:00 P.M., eliminates long waits.

Insiders' Tip

All metro Atlanta area emergency dispatch centers are now equipped with "Enhanced 911," which instantly provides the dispatcher with location and caller information before they even answer the call. A side benefit of this is that a police officer will respond to any 911 call made where the caller is unable or unwilling to speak to the dispatcher, to ensure that everything is okay.

Piedmont Hospital
1968 Peachtree Road NW
(404) 605–5000
www.piedmonthospital.org

On a ridge nicknamed "Heartbreak Hill" by the approximately 50,000 runners who pant up it during the annual Peachtree Road Race, Piedmont Hospital sits on historically significant land. It was at this Civil War site that troops from Confederate General William Hardee's Corps unsuccessfully assaulted Union General Joseph Hooker's Corps during the Battle of Peachtree Creek. A stone monument on the property commemorates that struggle.

Throughout most of this century, Piedmont Hospital has mirrored the growth of the Buckhead district it calls home. Founded as a 10-bed sanitarium in 1905, Piedmont now has 458 beds for acute care and a 42-bed extended care/skilled nursing care facility on its 26-acre site. More than 3,000 employees and a medical staff of more than 800 physicians offer care in every major category of medicine.

Piedmont Hospital offers obstetrics and women's services at the maternity and women's center, a breast health center, and a prostate center. The Fuqua Heart Center of Atlanta at Piedmont provides cardiology and cardiovascular surgery services including open heart surgery. Piedmont also boasts the Sports Medicine Institute/Reconstructive Joint Center of Atlanta. Injured players from Atlanta's professional sports teams go to Piedmont for their sports-related medical procedures.

At Piedmont's Neuroscience Institute, neurosurgeons perform gamma knife surgery, a technique that uses sharply focused gamma radiation to treat many brain tumors and vascular malformations without incision. Gamma knife procedures take about half a day, and patients can often resume normal activities the next day.

Among its other services, the hospital offers oncology, an inpatient rehabilitation unit, and the Katherine Murphy Riley Outpatient Diagnostic Center. The T. Harvey Mathis Rehabilitation and Fitness Center includes the Piedmont Hospital Health and Fitness Club for employees and members of the community.

The hospital's Level III 24-hour emergency department features a fly-in helipad atop the building.

In 1994 Piedmont Medical Center, Inc. became a founding partner of the Promina Health System.

Saint Joseph's Hospital of Atlanta
5665 Peachtree Dunwoody Road NE
(404) 851–7001
www.stjosephsatlanta.org

This is Atlanta's first hospital, established in 1880 by the Sisters of Mercy. A private, not-for-profit, 346-bed facility, it counts cardiac care, cancer care, and orthopedic care as three specialty areas. Medical staff includes more than 700 physicians. St. Joseph's moved from downtown to its present location on "Pill Hill" in 1978, and has been almost continuously renovating and expanding since then.

Well established as a regional referral hospital, Saint Joseph's provides outreach health care to the medically underserved and working poor through the Mercy Mobile Health Care Program.

Saint Joseph's has scored a number of firsts in cardiac care, among them, the first in the Southeast to perform open-heart surgery. Saint Joseph's features one of the busiest cardiac catheterization programs in the country; the hospital staff includes a heart transplantation team. Annually it performs more than 2,000 open-heart procedures.

The Specialty Center for Cancer Care & Research at Saint Joseph's houses the Community Clinical Oncology Program, which coordinates nearly 100 clinical trials investigating various therapies for cancer and cancer prevention.

The hospital's orthopedic program provides joint replacement surgery and shoulder and knee reconstruction. Last year, the hospital opened the Specialty Center for Wellness & Rehabilitation Care. The center provides various rehabilitation services for conditions such as voice and swallowing problems and incontinence. Outpatient hospital services include a breast health center and surgery. Saint Joseph's coordinates vascular and gastrointestinal services and has a fully staffed, 24-hour emergency department.

South Fulton Medical Center
1170 Cleveland Avenue, East Point
(404) 305–3500
www.sfmed.org

South Fulton Medical Center is a 465-bed hospital that provides a wide spectrum of medical services to the south metro Atlanta area. Located in East Point, the hospital is easily accessible from I–85 and I–75. It is part of the Tenet health system.

SFMC services include a breast health center; a primary care center; a free physician referral and health information service; maternity care, complete with a Level II special care nursery; oncology; and cardiology. SFMC's rehabilitation center is the only facility of its kind south of I–20 for strokes, brain injuries, and bone fractures. The hospital also provides wellness and community outreach programs, nuclear medicine and MRI, and inpatient and outpatient surgery.

SFMC's emergency room is the designated receiving center for Hartsfield Atlanta International Airport. To meet the area's growing need for primary care physicians, South Fulton Medical Center has placed physicians specializing in internal medicine, family practice, and OB/GYN in satellite offices throughout the south metro area.

Southwest Hospital and Medical Center
501 Fairburn Road SW
(404) 699–1111
www.swhosp.com

Southwest dates to 1943, when the Society of Catholic Medical Mission Sisters established the Catholic Colored Clinic in response to a lack of adequate medical care in south Atlanta. By 1974, governance of the hospital had passed to a board of trustees, with an official name being bestowed in 1975. Southwest proudly proclaims its status as one of only six institutions of its kind in the nation that is owned, governed, and managed by African Americans.

The 125-bed hospital's medical staff includes more than 200 physicians. In 1981 Southwest formed an affiliation with Morehouse School of Medicine for clinical training and services. The facility's primary care center specializes in the treatment of children and adolescents.

Southwest offers cardiopulmonary services, a certified mammography program, maternity care, nuclear medicine, a gastroenterology lab, an intensive care unit, physical therapy, ultrasound, and outpatient surgery. The radiology and laboratory departments perform diagnostic procedures. Southwest also has a 24-hour emergency department. In 1997 it became an affiliate partner of Emory Healthcare.

VA Medical Center–Atlanta
1670 Clairmont Road, Decatur
(404) 321–6111

For our visitors and new residents who are veterans, this federally owned hospital provides general acute care in addition to a wide range of other services. With 173 beds in its general medical and surgical facility and 100 beds in the nursing home care unit, the VA Hospital is well prepared to provide patients with quality medical care.

Affiliated with the Emory University School of Medicine, the VA Hospital carries on a broad-based research program with more than 73 investigators who participate in research projects focused on AIDS, Alzheimer's disease, cancer, infectious disease, and many other health concerns.

The hospital's Atlanta Rehabilitation Research and Development Center on Aging conducts research to identify the rehabilitative needs of older veterans, especially those with disabilities.

Special services include cardiac catheterization, open-heart surgery, and

---

Insiders' Tip

The Cecil B. Day Alzheimer's Disease Pavilion at Wesley Woods Geriatric Center is considered one of the leading facilities in the country for researching this terrible, debilitating condition.

prosthetics programs for veterans with complex amputations. Clinical programs offer substance abuse and post-traumatic stress disorder treatment, gynecology, and gerontology, to name a few.

Wesley Woods Geriatric Center at Emory University
1821 Clifton Road NE
(404) 728–6200
www.emoryhealthcare.org

Wesley Woods Geriatric Hospital, on the Emory University campus, is part of Emory Healthcare. The facility has four 25-bed units, each housing a different geriatric specialty service: acute and long-term acute medicine, psychiatry, neuropsychiatry, and rehabilitation. Each specialty also sponsors outpatient assessment and treatment clinics.

Wesley Woods, Inc., the corporate umbrella of all the Wesley facilities in Georgia, has created a network of apartment and cottage residential retirement facilities throughout the state. In Atlanta, Asbury Harris Epworth Towers, Branan Towers, and Wesley Woods Towers give senior citizens affordable housing options that feature a variety of floor plans, nutritious meals, planned activities, transportation, and other services. Wesley Woods Towers also offers assisted living apartments. Budd Terrace offers long-term nursing care with 236 beds.

Wesley Woods' Cecil B. Day Alzheimer's Disease Pavilion is recognized as the preeminent center for Alzheimer's disease in the state. The hospital's geriatric neurologists and psychiatrists diagnose and treat patients with memory loss, movement disorders, sleep disorders, suspected dementia, and other complex psychiatric and behavioral problems.

The Aging Helpline is staffed by Wesley Woods personnel. Call (404) 778–7710 for specific information.

Atlanta Specialty Hospitals

Hillside Psychiatric Hospital
690 Courtenay Drive NE
(404) 875–4551

Founded in 1888, Hillside is Atlanta's oldest social service agency. Its various roles demonstrate great flexibility in responding to the changing needs of the community.

Originally founded as a home for needy children, today Hillside is a licensed psychiatric hospital serving children and adolescents from ages 10 to 18. The 61-bed facility offers individualized psychotherapy as well as group and family therapy.

Hillside's licensed special education program enables youngsters to continue their schooling. Diagnostic services for severely emotionally disturbed patients are available. With both open and closed facilities, Hillside provides the appropriate setting for a wide range of needs.

The hospital's excellent programs are designed to return the whole child to a well state. Activity therapy, art therapy, horticulture therapy, and speech and language therapy, administered by members of Hillside's 120-employee staff, contribute to a child's progress. Twenty-four-hour nursing and an extensive aftercare program are part of Hillside's comprehensive treatment.

The hospital has created a therapeutic foster care program for children who are ready to leave Hillside but who do not have community or family resources available to them. These children can continue to receive a variety of Hillside services while living in the community with foster families.

Kindred Hospital Atlanta
705 Juniper Street
(404) 873–2871
www.kindredhealthcare.com

Kindred Hospital is a licensed long-term acute-care hospital specializing in extended care for the medically complex patient. Particular focus is on pulmonary services for the ventilator-dependent patient. Most patients transfer from other acute-care hospitals' intensive care units.

A full range of medical services is available to Kindred patients, including renal dialysis, orthopedic care, and diagnostic radiology. Psychiatric treatment and support groups address the psychological needs of patients.

Kindred is a regional referral center. Patients come from a five-state area. Three hundred employees staff this 72-bed hospital.

Laurel Heights Hospital
934 Briarcliff Road NE
(404) 888–7860
www.laurelheightshospital.com

This licensed psychiatric hospital has more than 100 beds and approximately 150 employees on staff. Laurel Heights' intensive residential treatment program provides long-term care for young people ages 4 to 17 and their families. In a highly structured environment, with 24-hour supervision and various modalities of therapy, youth with emotional and behavioral problems learn to take responsibility for their choices in life. Year-round schooling by accredited teachers is also made available so that their general education will not be neglected.

Shepherd Center
2020 Peachtree Road NW
(404) 352–2020
www.shepherd.org

Shepherd Center (formerly known as Shepherd Spinal Center) in Buckhead is a private, not-for-profit hospital specializing in catastrophic care. The hospital treats people with spinal cord injury and disease, acquired brain injury, multiple sclerosis, and other neuromuscular disorders and neurological problems. In 2002 it was ranked in the top 20 for Best Rehabilitation Hospitals by *U.S. News and World Report*.

Serving the Southeast since 1975, the 100-bed specialty hospital offers a continuum of health care services ranging from intensive care through acute rehabilitation and subacute care to outpatient services.

The center houses the largest model spinal cord injury program in the country and a 20-bed brain injury unit. The National Multiple Sclerosis Society designated Shepherd the official Southeastern Multiple Sclerosis Center. The hospital's MS center treats 1,300 patients and participates in clinical research, including the Shepherd/Harvard Multiple Sclerosis Research Initiative.

Urology specialists at Shepherd diagnose and treat male potency and fertility disorders. They have expertise in treating continence-related problems.

Shepherd also has a fully accessible fitness center with a 25-yard pool, weight room, track, and gym. A variety of fitness programs as well as arts and crafts classes are open to people of all abilities.

Clayton County

Southern Regional Medical Center
11 Upper Riverdale Road, Riverdale
(770) 991–8000
www.southernregional.com

Southern Regional Medical Center, operated by the Promina Health System, is a 406-bed, acute-care hospital and the largest facility on the metro area's south side. The medical center provides a continuum of services, from inpatient and critical care to rehabilitation and home health.

The emergency department handles more than 70,000 patients a year in the 34-bed, acute-care facility. All the unit's nurses are trained in advanced cardiac life support, and many are certified in neonatal, pediatric, and trauma specialties. The cardiac unit handles heart catheterization and implantation of pacemakers. And a community care center reaches out to the community to provide ambulatory, primary care for minor acute illnesses and stable chronic illnesses. Clayton County residents may obtain services on a sliding fee scale.

The medical center also operates RiverWoods, a private, nonprofit psychiatric center. It is the only substance abuse and psychiatric treatment center on the south side. Among its services are crisis intervention and assessment, observation, aftercare, and inpatient and outpatient services.

Referral Services

Virtually every hospital has a phone service, usually nurse-staffed, to provide physician referrals or to give general health information. You'll probably choose a physician based on your needs, your location, and, in some cases, your health insurance policy requirements. We list a sample of the available help lines.

Atlanta Medical Center • (404) 265–3627
Children's Healthcare • (404) 250–5437
DeKalb Medical Center • (404) 501–9355
Emory Health • (404) 778–7744
Georgia Academy of Family Physicians • (404) 321–7445
Medical Association of Atlanta • (404) 881–1714
North Fulton Regional Hospital • (770) 751–2600
Northside Hospital Doctor Matching • (404) 851–8817
Promina • (404) 541–1111, (770) 541–1111
St. Joseph's Hospital Physician Referral Service • (404) 851–7312

Cobb County

Emory-Adventist Hospital
3949 South Cobb Drive, Smyrna
(770) 434–0710
www.emoryadventist.com

A joint venture of the Emory Healthcare system and Adventist Health System/Sunbelt Health Care Corp., Emory-Adventist is an 88-bed, general-care hospital with an additional 12 beds in a transitional care unit. It has a 24-hour emergency center, surgery, occupational health services, MRI, lithotripsy, and home health services. It is a Christian facility that cares for the needs of the whole person.

Ridgeview Institute
3995 South Cobb Drive, Smyrna
(770) 434–4567, (800) 329–9775
www.ridgeviewinstitute.com

Established in Smyrna in 1976, Ridgeview Institute is a private, nonprofit behavioral health care system that provides treatment for children, adolescents, and adults with psychiatric and addictive problems. The facility's comprehensive continuum of care includes intensive inpatient, partial hospitalization, and outpatient treatment options designed to keep costs down and promote a prompt return to job, family, and community.

Special services at Ridgeview include the Impaired Professionals Program and the women's center. Respond, Ridgeview's mobile assessment team, provides free psychiatric and addiction assessment and referral services. The Respond mobile assessment team offers telephone consultations within 10 minutes and on-site evaluations, when needed, within one hour, seven days a week, 24 hours a day.

One of a minority of hospitals in the country not owned or managed by a health care corporation, Ridgeview has treated more than 30,000 patients. Ridgeview is also committed to professional and community education and offers monthly services for clinicians, support groups, and a family learning series to the community.

WellStar Cobb Hospital
3950 Austell Road, Austell
(770) 732–4000
www.wellstar.org

Part of the Cobb County–based WellStar Health System, the 302-bed hospital serves one of the fastest-growing areas in metro Atlanta. The hospital's women's center provides innovative single-room maternity care, neonatal intensive care, and many other services. The hospital's 24-hour emergency department includes

A young patient tells her doctor where it hurts.

PHOTO: CHILDREN'S HEALTHCARE OF ATLANTA

senior adults. Kennestone Women's Center is a 153,000-square-foot facility for the care of women and children, including maternity care, a neonatal intensive care unit, and a women's heart program.

WellStar Windy Hill Hospital
2540 Windy Hill Road, Marietta
(770) 644-1000
www.wellstar.org

Another member of WellStar Health System, the 115-bed Windy Hill Hospital has recently transitioned to a long-term acute-care hospital for patients needing institutionalized care for at least 25 days continuously. Windy Hill Hospital also offers a surgical and diagnostic center for outpatient procedures.

In addition to the three hospitals in Cobb County, WellStar also operates facilities in Douglas and Paulding Counties.

DeKalb County

Dunwoody Medical Center
4575 North Shallowford Road
(770) 454-2000
www.emorydunwoody.com

Dunwoody Medical Center is a fully accredited, 168-bed general medical-surgical hospital. It belongs to the joint venture of Columbia/HCA and Emory Healthcare.

Dunwoody Medical Center's new women's pavilion features 10 labor/delivery/recovery rooms, 28 postpartum rooms, and a neonatal intensive care unit. The same nurse cares for the mother and her baby to assure continuity of care and provide maximum educational opportunities.

Other women's services include working women's mammography, with Saturday appointments and on-site interpretation. The endometriosis care center focuses on the diagnosis and treatment of endometriosis. Routine procedures include ultrasound and advanced laparoscopic surgery.

Outpatient surgery, a new cardiac catheterization lab, an educational program for diabetics, and sports medicine specialists are just a few of the many ser-

a fast-track area for minor illness and injury, a chest pain center, and trauma triage. The children's emergency center is a service of South Cobb Hospital and Children's Healthcare of Atlanta at Scottish Rite.

WellStar Kennestone Hospital
677 Church Street, Marietta
(770) 793-5000
www.wellstar.org

Licensed for 539 beds, this is the largest WellStar hospital. Kennestone's full range of services includes a 24-hour emergency/trauma center, advanced laparoscopic and orthopedic surgery, and cardiology services. The hospital also has an oncology center, diagnostic center, and sleep center.

Health Place is a wellness and fitness center on Kennestone's campus. It offers classes and ongoing health programs, including a comprehensive cardiac rehabilitation program. Children's Healthcare of Atlanta at Egleston center at Kennestone offers after-hours pediatric care for minor illnesses and injuries. Atherton Place is a senior living community for independent

vices the medical center provides. Dunwoody Medical Center's 24-hour emergency services department is a Level III trauma center.

Fayette County

Fayette Community Hospital
1255 Highway 54 West, Fayetteville
(770) 719–7000
A nonprofit subsidiary of Piedmont Medical Care Center, the parent organization of Piedmont Hospital and a partner of Promina Health System, Fayette Community Hospital opened in late 1997. With a 100-bed capacity, the 141,000-square-foot facility offers a full range of services including medical, surgical, critical care, diagnostic, laboratory, and 24-hour emergency care.

An FAA-approved helipad is also located at the hospital. Comprehensive outpatient services and outpatient surgery as well as respiratory care and physical therapy are also available.

An 80,000-square-foot professional building occupied by board-certified/qualified physicians is adjacent to the hospital. The hospital and professional building are located on 28 acres on Highway 54, just west of Sandy Creek Road.

Fulton County

North Fulton Regional Hospital
3000 Hospital Boulevard, Roswell
(770) 751–2500
www.northfultonregional.com
As a Level II trauma center, North Fulton Regional provides seven-day, 24-hour, in-house anesthesia and operating room coverage. Since 1983, the 167-bed hospital has offered general acute care to the rapidly growing areas north of metro Atlanta, including Roswell, Alpharetta, and Cumming.

Nearly 900 employees and a medical staff of some 400 physicians provide support to patients in this full-service medical/surgical community hospital owned by Tenet Healthcare Corp. Treatment for major illnesses, such as cancer and heart problems, is part of North Fulton's pro-

grams. The hospital's women's health center delivers some 1,100 babies annually, and a neonatal intensive care unit tends to the needs of infants born preterm. The hospital also provides care in the areas of nuclear medicine, orthopedic services, diagnostic radiology, and renal dialysis.

Individualized treatment in the Renaissance Rehabilitation Center focuses on progressive care that enables patients to return to normal life quickly. North Fulton offers special sports medicine programs, a pain control center, and a sleep disorder center.

North Fulton provides outpatient surgery procedures in addition to a fully staffed emergency room. The hospital's ongoing series of health education programs is designed to raise the level of health awareness in the community. These are augmented by periodic screening programs and support groups.

Gwinnett County

Founded in 1959, the Gwinnett Hospital System (GHS) was established as a nonprofit health care organization to provide high-quality medical care to its neighbors. In 1994 GHS became part of the Promina Health System.

Gwinnett Medical Center
1000 Medical Center Boulevard
Lawrenceville
(678) 442–4321
www.gwinnetthealth.org
Opened in 1984, Gwinnett Medical Center is a 190-bed, acute-care hospital offering all general medical, surgical, and diagnostic services. The center also provides cardiac catheterization, lithotripsy, and magnetic resonance imaging services.

Gwinnett DaySurgery, on the Gwinnett Medical Center campus, houses the GHS Laser Institute. This facility specializes in some of the most advanced outpatient laparoscopic and laser surgeries available regionally and is the site of national physician and nurse training.

Centrally located in the county, the center houses a Level III 24-hour emergency department that is the trauma triage center for Gwinnett County. The

Scottish Rite Children's Emergency Center at Gwinnett Medical Center serves pediatric emergency cases. It is part of the Promina Health System. As of this writing, an expansion project is under way.

Gwinnett Women's Pavilion
550 Medical Center Boulevard, Lawrenceville
(678) 442–5600
www.gwinnetthealth.org

The 34-bed Gwinnett Women's Pavilion, on the 120-acre Gwinnett Medical Center campus, opened in 1991. It's metro Atlanta's first freestanding hospital for women.

Gwinnett Women's Pavilion offers maternity, diagnostic, and educational services to women of all ages. The diagnostic center provides mammography, ultrasound, and osteoporosis screenings. Experienced health care professionals staff a 30-bed neonatal intensive care unit.

Joan Glancy Memorial Hospital
3215 McClure Bridge Road, Duluth
(678) 584–6800
www.gwinnetthealth.org

This 90-bed general hospital offers medical, surgical, diagnostic, and 24-hour emergency services. Thirty of the hospital's beds are dedicated to the Glancy Rehabilitation Center, established in 1988.

At the Rehab Center, accident and stroke patients get the training and therapy they need for independence. The Glancy Rehabilitation and Sports Medicine center offers outpatient services.

A new facility, opened in 1995, expanded the hospital's services. At Joan Glancy's Howell Station campus on Pleasant Hill Road, the Glancy Outpatient Center provides full-service outpatient surgery and laboratory and imaging services with the latest in convenience amenities.

SummitRidge
250 Scenic Highway, Lawrenceville
(678) 442–5858
www.gwinnetthealth.org

This 72-bed facility is part of the Gwinnett Hospital System. The hospital provides psychiatric and chemical dependency treatment for adults and adolescents.

Services include inpatient, partial hospitalization, and outpatient care as well as aftercare programs. Supported by a free, confidential assessment and referral service, assistance is provided 24 hours a day. SummitRidge's community services include education programs for schools and other groups, seminars, and support groups.

Emergency Medical Services

Atlanta boasts some of the oldest true EMS (Emergency Medical Services) units in Georgia. Grady Memorial Hospital EMS was transformed in 1973 from a "taxi for the sick," first operating in horse-drawn carriages in 1892, to an "emergency room on wheels," able to perform nearly every lifesaving treatment right on the scene of an accident or sudden illness. Metro Ambulance Service (no longer in business) followed in the late 1970s with the first helicopter ambulance service in Georgia, operating from its headquarters near downtown Marietta, and staffing its Bell JetRanger helicopters with former Vietnam War Dustoff pilots and combat medics.

The concept of an "emergency medical service" was born in the late 1960s, at the famed ShockTrauma Unit at the University of Maryland Medical Center in Baltimore. A visionary physician named R. Adams Cowley looked at the battlefield work that was then being done in Vietnam, using helicopters to rapidly move wounded soldiers to treatment facilities, and at the never-seen-before problems that cropped up while dealing with critically wounded people. His pioneering theories and practices developed into the system we are now blessed with, one that is designed and implemented with one thought in mind: to get to a critically injured person and begin stabilizing treatment within one hour of the injury.

This short period of time, known to paramedics and physicians as the "Golden Hour," is, for very obscure and not fully understood reasons, a critical limit within which certain treatments must be done if a seriously injured person is going to survive more than a few days or hours (if this is not done, then really weird and lethal conditions like "liver shock" show up a few days later). To address this need, starting in the mid-1970s a new form of "ambulance driver" emerged. Initially known simply as emergency medical technicians (EMTs),

these specially trained rescuers pioneered a wide variety of medical practices adapted to use on the streets, as well as a whole new industry centered around tools designed to rapidly access injured people in wrecked automobiles (such as the famed "Jaws of Life," universally known to the professionals as a Hurst Tool). A popular TV show of that era, Emergency!, gave most folks their first glimpse into this emerging new world of professional rescue response.

Today, to make a really long story short, ambulances in Georgia are divided into two large groups: emergency and non-emergency. Emergency ambulances are all a part of the statewide 911 emergency dispatch system, and are staffed by at least two well-qualified and nationally certified medics, with at least one being a highly trained paramedic (the highest "rank" one can obtain in the EMS world), and are required to carry more equipment than most smaller emergency rooms contain, as well as a wide variety of specialized light rescue gear. Non-emergency ambulances still carry a modest amount of modern emergency equipment but are used exclusively for routine transport of bed-bound patients, usually to and from doctor's appointments and hospital treatments. In addition, most fire departments have one or two EMTs or paramedics on each crew, most metro fire departments also have dedicated fast response and heavy rescue units, and every police officer is trained to provide at least basic emergency medical care.

Insiders' Tip

Fire department engines and ladder trucks are frequently the first responders seen at accident scenes, but they are not there (usually) for their fire-suppressing capabilities. Nearly all firefighters in the state of Georgia are certified at least as EMS First Responders, and many carry EMT or even paramedic certifications as well. The well-dispersed status of metro firehouses means that they are also frequently the closest responders to any given emergency scene.

Activating the emergency medical system anywhere in the Atlanta area is an exercise in utter simplicity: pick up any telephone and dial 9-1-1. It is invariably a free call, and sophisticated phone company computers automatically route your call to that area's emergency dispatch center. This might sound like we're stating the obvious, but with five area codes, 22 emergency dispatch centers, more than 25 EMS systems, and nearly 30 fire departments in a more than 6,000-square-mile area, it is by no means a simple task! The emergency dispatcher will ask you a long series of questions, trying to glean every available bit of information from you about the injured person and the emergency situation, but this by no means is delaying the ambulance response. As soon as the dispatcher gets the location of the emergency (sometimes just by looking at a special type of caller ID on their computer screens), they will send out the nearest ambulance. The rest of the information they get from you is relayed by either radio or computer link to the ambulance while it is en route.

This brings up our last point about the EMS—when you place that 911 call, it puts an entire integrated system into operation. In every Atlanta area location, the closest available fire department unit will respond (to provide the quickest-possible available qualified personnel, and to give the sometimes shorthanded ambulance crews some extra help), the local police will respond to provide scene security, as well as traffic and crowd control, and if the situation calls for it, special hazardous materials or heavy rescue units will respond along with the ambulance. The paramedic acts as a sort of manager of the situation, organizing all the responding units as needed, contacting his base hospital's emergency room physicians for orders and consultation on treatments needed in the field, and ordering patient transportation to the closest medical facility appropriate to handle their needs (Note: Very frequently, this definitely does not mean the closest hospital!) If the patient's condition is critical, a helicopter ambulance may be requested to provide faster transportation to a high-level trauma center.

To give you an idea of what abilities these EMS professionals have using just a single example, every emergency ambulance in Georgia by state law must carry all of the same equipment any hospital emergency room has to deal with heart attacks, and at least one paramedic trained and certified to use it right in the patient's own living room—exactly what Dr. Cowley envisioned more than 40 years ago. EMS is bringing the emergency room straight to the patient's location, instead of the other way around.

Special Needs and Services

AID Atlanta
1438 West Peachtree Street NW
(404) 870–7700
www.aidatlanta.org

This is Atlanta's largest HIV/AIDS service agency. AID Atlanta offers complete health services, financial assistance, HIV testing, prevention, and education.

HMOs in Atlanta

Aetna U.S. Healthcare • (770) 346–4300 • www.aetnaushc.com
BlueChoice • (404) 233–1649 • www.ahpi.org
Cigna • (800) 526–5481 • www.cigna.com
HealthStar-Georgia • (770) 396–1009
Kaiser Permanente • (404) 261–2590 • www.kpga.org
Meridian Medical Group • (770) 436–2222
United Health Care • (404) 982–8900

Atlanta Care Center
4840 Roswell Road, D-100
(404) 262–2273
www.atlantacare.com

This abortion alternative facility is not a clinic, although it does provide pregnancy testing. In addition, Atlanta Care offers counseling, support, and adoption referrals.

Hospice Care

Atlanta is blessed with a number of facilities offering alternatives in cases of life-limiting illness. Counseling services for the patient and family in bereavement are helpful. The services offered vary from hospice to hospice.

Here are some points you may want to consider when selecting a hospice. Ask if the institution is Medicare/Medicaid certified and if it accepts private insurance. Many hospices have a 24-hour emergency service line. Inquire about a specific hospice's membership in national certifying organizations as well as the types of licenses it holds.

Haven House at Midtown
244 14th Street NE
(404) 874–8313

Located in an old, restored home, Haven House accepts any terminally ill patient to inpatient hospice or home hospice care. There is also a day care program where folks can come and drop off their loved ones while they work. Haven House has 19 beds and offers full medical nursing services. Patients remain under the care of their own physicians, who work with the hospice's medical director. Insurance coverage includes Medicaid and Medicare; Haven House also has a fund available to indigent patients. It's staffed 24 hours a day, seven days a week.

Hospice Atlanta
1244 Park Vista Drive
(404) 869–3000
www.hospice-atlanta.org

Patients, including children, with a six-month life expectancy or less are eligible for care at Hospice Atlanta. Operated by Visiting Nurses Association, the facility has a 36-bed, two-story building and three cottages, each with 12 beds. In-house laundry service and three meals a day are provided to patients. There are also family rooms and kitchens as well as individual kitchenettes in each cottage for family members who wish to make and store food for family members. The kitchen staff is on call 16 hours a day. Medicare, Medicaid, indigent funding, and all standard insurance companies are accepted.

Northside Hospice
5825 Glenridge Drive NE, Building 4
(404) 851–6300

Affiliated with Northside Hospital, the hospice is a Medicare-certified offshoot that provides care to terminally ill patients in their homes. A multidisciplinary team approach is utilized that combines nursing, social service, home-health aides, a chaplain, and volunteers. Services include 24-hour nursing seven days a week and a bereavement follow-up for the family within 13 months of a death. Medicare or commercial insurance is filed.

Walk-In Clinics

In the Atlanta metro area, some but not all urgent care centers are affiliated with hospitals. In such centers, if the situation requires, patients are quickly transported to the hospital's main facility. All urgent care centers offer immediate care for a wide variety of needs, often with extended hours.

Atlanta

FamilyCare Centers
5019 LaVista Road, Tucker
(404) 501–3270
1045 Sycamore Drive, Decatur
(404) 501–4270

All of the FamilyCare Centers treat minor illnesses and injuries and are affiliated with DeKalb Medical Center. Each is staffed by a physician, an RN, X-ray technologist, and lab technicians. The centers are open from 8:00 A.M. to 11:00 P.M. Monday through Friday and 10:00 A.M. to 6:00 P.M. weekends and holidays. FamilyCare files most insurance claims as well as Medicare and accepts all credit cards.

Grady Health System
Center Hill
(404) 699–0509
DeKalb/Grady, 30 Warren Street SE
(404) 377–9301
Boatrock, 5838 Boatrock Road SW
(404) 616–1820
Northwest, 1247 Bankhead Highway
(404) 616–2265
South DeKalb, 2626 Rainbow Way SE
(404) 241–1866
Southwest, 2600 Martin Luther King Jr. Drive SW
(404) 696–0506
Lindbergh Children's Center
2581 Piedmont Road NE
(404) 842–0046
Lindbergh Women's Center
2581 Piedmont Road NE
(404) 842–9810
W.T. Brooks, 1636 Connally Drive, East Point
(404) 761–7121

In addition to Grady Memorial and Hughes Spalding Pediatric Hospitals, the Grady Health System also operates numerous neighborhood centers throughout the metro area.

Northside Health Express
1000 Johnson Ferry Road NE
(404) 851–6762

In the emergency room at Northside Hospital, Northside Health Express provides minor emergency care from sore throats to minor lacerations and extremity injuries. A nurse practitioner sees patients first, and if they need further evaluation, the emergency physician sees them. Hours of operation are from 10:00 A.M. to midnight, seven days a week. Most insurance plans, including Medicare and Medicaid, are accepted, as are credit cards.

Beyond Atlanta

Children's Healthcare
1371 Church Street Extension, Marietta
(770) 425–0752
Fayette Community Hospital
1265 Highway 54, Fayetteville
(770) 719–5750
4850 Sugarloaf Parkway, Lawrenceville
(770) 513–0746

In addition to Egleston and Scottish Rite hospitals, Children's Healthcare of Atlanta operates numerous clinics and urgent care facilities throughout the metro area, including the above locations.

WellStar Health System Neighborhood Healthcare Centers
1010 Johnson Ferry Road, Marietta
(770) 579–7930
3805 Cherokee Street, Kennesaw
(770) 426–5665
3600 Sandy Plains Road, Marietta
(770) 977–4547
2890 Delk Road, Marietta
(770) 955–8620

These urgent care facilities, which are part of the WellStar Health System, do not accept ambulance patients. Each is staffed by in-house physicians who utilize on-site X-ray and laboratory facilities. The centers are open seven days a week from 8:00 A.M. to 8:00 P.M. Most insurance plans are accepted, as are all major credit cards.

Alternative Medicine

Nontraditional medicine has been gaining followers throughout the nation at a remarkable rate, and Atlanta is no exception. If one were to go by the number of health stores in a mile radius, it would seem that we are avid believers, and with Atlanta's burgeoning Asian population, it is not at all surprising that acupuncture is particularly popular (although you'd be hard-pressed to locate a practitioner from the telephone directory).

For specific practitioners in alternative medicine, we suggest you call the referral numbers at the end of this section. And for your edification, we offer the following overview of some of the most popular alternatives to traditional medical doctors.

Acupuncture

Five thousand years ago, the principles of acupuncture evolved and became part of Chinese culture. But it wasn't until 400 B.C. that the practice became a written treatise called the Nei Ching. Traditionally, acupuncture rebalances energy-Qi-life's energy, which travels through the body along meridians or channels. When the Qi is obstructed due to life's disturbances, including climatic changes, diet, lifestyle, and stress, blockages are formed in the body consisting of the buildup of lactic acid and carbon monoxide, which manifest themselves by stiffness, pain, and disease. Using sterile and disposable stainless steel needles as thin as a hair and heat-producing materials along acupoints, the blocked meridians are unblocked.

The best way to find an acupuncturist is to ask a chiropractor for a referral.

Aromatherapy

Like acupuncture, aromatherapy has a history as old as the ages. In fact, Cleopatra used herbs as a birth control method and plant oils to seduce her legions of admirers. When she wanted a particular potion, she sent couriers throughout her lands to dig up the herbs she needed. We Atlantans have it a lot easier, with health-food stores in almost every strip shopping center carrying plant oil extracts in bottles of just a few ounces. And in case you have your doubts about the efficacy of aromatherapy, ask an employee at a health-food store for excerpts from recent University of Cincinnati, Duke University, and University of Arizona studies that seem to suggest Cleopatra knew more about such things than modern medicine. Some of the more popular herbal aromas include eucalyptus for colds, peppermint and ginger for upset stomachs, and lavender for relaxation.

Chiropractic

Chiropractic is a holistic approach to health care, stressing the patient's overall health. It recognizes that many factors affect health, including diet, exercise, rest, environment, and heredity.

Chiropractors use drugless, nonsurgical treatment to stimulate the body's natural recuperative abilities. Chiropractors use X-rays, orthopedic, physical, and laboratory tests, but the emphasis is on spinal analysis. Treatment often involves manual adjustment of the spinal column. Also common are light, water, massage, ultrasound, electric, and heat therapy. Chiropractors do not perform surgery or prescribe drugs.

Homeopathy

Samuel Hahnemann, a doctor of medicine in the early 1790s, became frustrated with orthodox medical practices, in particular the bleeding and subsequent death of Emperor Leopold II of Austria. In place of standard, for the times, medicine, Hahnemann evolved a method for treating disease based on a doctrine for ascertaining the curative powers of drugs, and he called this method "homeopathy" in an essay published in 1796.

The Organon of Rational Therapeutics, his detailed exposition, instructions, and philosophy of homeopathy, was first published in 1810. An edition of this monumental work appeared in 1921, almost a century after Hahnemann's death.

Homeopathy was practiced widely in Europe, particularly after French premier Guizot, when asked in the mid-1800s by the allopathist/apothecarian community to ban such treatment, instead noted that if homeopathy was "a valueless method," it would collapse on its own accord. But if it was truly an advance of traditional medicine, it would spread. Homeopathy is currently a worldwide practice.

Referral Agencies

The following referral agencies are offered as a starting place for nontraditional health care services.

Georgia Council of Chiropractic
(770) 428–7351
www.georgiachiropractic.org

Homeopathic Academy of Naturopathic Physicians
(503) 761–3298
www.healthy.net/pan/pa/homeopathic/hanp/index.html

National Center for Homeopathy
(703) 548–7790
www.healthy.net/nch

The Informed Choice (cosmetic surgery)
(404) 812–7077
www.theinformedchoice.com

Spas

OK, so spas probably aren't what you think of immediately when you hear "health care." But with your busy life, destressing is essential, and what better way to rid the body and soul of built-up toxins, grease and grime, anger, and anxiety than to lie back, relax, and receive a wide range of massages, facials, body treatments, and aromatherapy at one of the many salons in and around Atlanta?

The office, the kids, and the boss just disappear as muscles unwind while the massage therapists skillfully soothe away the stress. Try a therapeutic body wrap or body polish. Treat your feet to reflexology, a massage technique designed to de-stress your whole self by manipulating pressure points on your tootsies.

If you need these services to stay sane, start saving now because spa treatments are not inexpensive. Pricing is as diverse as the facilities, and many spas offer samplers and full- and half-day packages that combine several services. Holiday packages are especial bargains, and if you bring friends with you, ask for a discount.

Spa Château Élan offers one-night sleepover packages, and a luxury week can cost as much as a year's tuition at the local community college. But you'll feel like a million when you go home!

Atlanta

Dermess Skin Care Center
3726 Roswell Road NE
(404) 261–5199
Yin & Yang, 721 Miami Circle NE
(404) 233–6241

Therapeutic complexion and skin repair treatments are the specialty at Dermess. And you can also go bronze with their safe tan treatment. Peels, waxing, and an extensive product line are also available.

Jolie the Day Spa & Hair Design
3619 Piedmont Road NE
(404) 266–0060
www.joliethedayspa.com

Noelle offers a selection of half- and full-day spa packages, including a couples' day and a relaxation day for men and women. Choose from a variety of spa treatments, including therapeutic and full body massages, aromatherapy mud wraps, seaweed cellulite treatments, and repechage four-layer facials. In addition, Noelle provides hair design, scalp treatment, permanent waving, hair relaxing, and hair coloring.

Natural Body
www.naturalbody.com
1402-2 North Highland Avenue NE
(404) 872–1039
5975 Roswell Road, Suite 225
(404) 255–9699
4300 Paces Ferry Road
(770) 319–9001
2385 Peachtree Road, Suite A3A
(404) 869–7722

Natural Body's diverse array of spa services includes glycolic, sea algae, and aromatherapy rejuvenation facials; manicures, pedicures, and other hand and foot treatments; herbal wraps; body massages; steam therapy; and Dead Sea mud treatments. Several spa treatment combinations are offered.

Aside from the standard spa treatments of massage and facials, Natural Body's Rejuvenation Bars offer Chinese elixirs served in small mixed-drink glasses, which can fortify, enhance, or relax you. Clients get the drinks gratis as part of their treatment; visitors can purchase them.

Spa Forever Young
4279 Roswell Road NE, Suite 602
(404) 250–9698

This spa's European- and Oriental-trained staff help you repackage yourself to bring out your natural beauty. Forever Young offers a variety of facial treatments, body massages, body polishes, and herbal wraps. They also provide nail care, hair removal, lash and brow tinting, and makeovers.

Spa Sydell
www.spasydell.com
Buckhead Plaza, 3060 Peachtree Road NW
(404) 255–7727
Cumberland Mall, Cobb Parkway NW,
south of I–285/75 in Cobb County
(404) 255–7727
Perimeter Square West
1165 Perimeter Center West
(404) 255–7727
Pleasant Hill Square
2255 Pleasant Hill Road, Duluth
(404) 255–7727
10593 Old Alabama Road Connector,
Alpharetta
(404) 255–7727

The most well known of the Atlanta-originated spas, this company owned by the Harris family offers glamorous settings. Sydell Harris, respected for her charitable activities as well as her graciousness, is much in evidence. Specialties of the house include massage for two, a day at the spa which includes lunch from some of the best restaurants in the city, makeup consultations and hairdos, and gift certificates in handsome maroon packaging. Spa Sydell has rubbed, oiled, and otherwise pampered most of the glitterati in town as well as visiting Hollywood and sports stars.

The Buckhead location has been expanded to 6,500 square feet. Spa Sydell's other locations offer the full range of treatments for body and face, wraps, hair removal, manicures, and lash and brow tinting.

Beyond Atlanta

Repose Day Spa
8610 Roswell Road NE
(770) 587-0480
www.reposedayspa.com

Repose, in Loehmann's Plaza, offers a number of spa services including facials, exfoliation treatment, hand and foot therapy, waxing, herbal body wrap, and sea salt body polish treatments. A day of pampering package is available.

The Spa at Château Élan
Haven Harbour Drive, Braselton
(678) 425-0900
www.chateauelan.com

This spa, modeled after a European health spa, is part of the popular Château Élan complex, which is about an hour's drive northeast of downtown Atlanta. This is the only spa in the metro area where you can stay overnight, for several nights, or for a whole week. The Spa at Château Élan offers a number of spa packages that entitle you to various spa services as well as meals and accommodations. Or just enjoy a day at the spa; choose one of their prepared packages or design your own.

Besides a full range of spa treatments and services, the spa has a sauna, steam room, whirlpool, and exercise equipment. You can get an individual fitness assessment as well as a personalized exercise prescription. Outdoor types will enjoy the nature trails for hiking and biking. A 14-month, $2 million enhancement program was completed in July 2002. This includes 14 themed guest suites as well as new men's and women's locker rooms. A custom nail salon is part of the new addition. See more about Château Élan in our Accommodations and Day Trips and Weekend Getaways chapters.

Media

The same industry—transportation—that made Atlanta the business capital of the South also made it a regional media center. Along with bullets and beans, those early trains brought news from distant parts, news for which there was an eager and ever-growing audience.

Prior to the city being razed during the Civil War, four regular newspapers were joined by three Tennessee papers whose staffs took refuge in Atlanta and continued publishing. During Reconstruction, Atlanta struggled hard to get on its feet. During those days, Northern newspaper reporters wired dispatches back home, making it clear that the bold young city was doing much more than sulking and nursing its wounds. Here's how one newspaper writer described our furiously rebuilding city to his readers in the North:

"From all this ruin and devastation a new city is springing up with marvelous rapidity. Men rush about the streets with but little regard for comfort or pleasure, and yet find the days all too short and too few for the work at hand. Atlanta seems to be the center from which this new life radiates; it is the great Exchange, where you will find everybody if you only wait and watch."

Media coverage like this helped Atlanta build its reputation as a Southern city focused on the future, not the past. This image was reinforced by national and international media reports from the great cotton expositions of 1881, 1887, and 1895.

To some degree, postwar Atlanta had the media to thank for setting the city on a course toward modernism. The visionary young newspaperman Henry Grady used his editorship of the *Atlanta Constitution* as the pulpit from which he preached the doctrine of a "New South" building its economy on industry, not just agriculture.

In 1922 the *Atlanta Journal* launched the South's first commercial radio station, WSB-AM. (The call letters were later claimed to stand for "Welcome South, Brother.") The 100-watt station's studio was on the newspaper building's fifth floor; its antenna was on the roof. Auto tycoon Henry Ford and movie star Rudolph Valentino were among early visitors to the tiny station. In 1948 WSB-TV, the first television station in the South, went on the air.

As technology improved, so did Atlanta's presence on the national and international media scenes. Now programming that originates here is beamed 24 hours a day to every part of our nation and all over the world.

Atlantans and visitors to the city can take advantage of a dizzying range of media possibilities, including the morning and afternoon daily newspapers, 13 television stations broadcast over the air (including four with extensive daily local news coverage), plus dozens of radio stations and scores of magazines, weekly and monthly newspapers, and small newsletters.

Atlanta can be a boomtown for those interested in becoming part of the media: Writers can get a jump start on their careers by offering their skills to any number of free press outlets; on-air talents can hone their skills on public access stations; and screen performers will find numerous opportunities to do ad agency work. In fact, the economic impact of the film and video industry in Georgia is substantial. Since the Georgia Office of Film and Videotape was created in 1973, more than 360 theatrical and made-for-TV movies have been filmed in our state. Of these, more than 180 were filmed, entirely or in part, on location around Atlanta. *Drumline, Sharky's Machine, Freejack, Basket Case III, The*

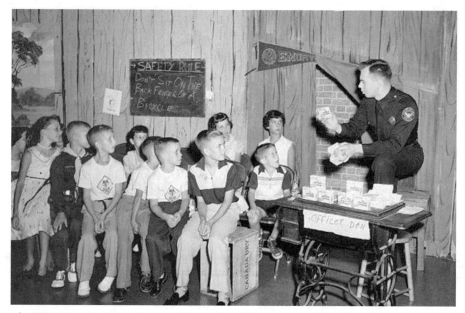

The WSB-TV set of Atlanta's beloved children's show, "The Popeye Club," with "Officer Don," in 1956. PHOTO: COURTESY OF THE TRACY W. O'NEAL PHOTOGRAPHIC COLLECTION, SPECIAL COLLECTIONS DEPT., PULLEN LIBRARY, GEORGIA STATE UNIVERSITY

Oldest Living Confederate Widow Tells All, and *Road Trip* were among them. *Scream II* used Atlanta and its environs as a backdrop; Denzel Washington and a cast that included hundreds of local extras filmed *Remember the Titans* in and around town.

Two of the best-known made-in-Atlanta movies are Spike Lee's *School Daze,* which was filmed on the campus of Atlanta University Center, and the 1989 Oscar-winner for best picture, *Driving Miss Daisy,* which includes scenes of Druid Hills, Little Five Points, The Temple on Peachtree Street, and other recognizable locations.

In Atlanta you'll never lack for something to read, listen to, or watch. The following is a roundup of the city's best-known media outlets as well as lots of smaller ones. Whether you're visiting Atlanta or relocating here, you'll find our media to be a nonstop resource of information on the city's life.

Television

Turner Broadcasting System Inc.
One CNN Center
Marietta Street at Techwood Drive NW
(404) 827-1700

Turner Broadcasting System, the mega company that owns *The Wizard of Oz,* the Atlanta Braves, the Atlanta Hawks, Space Ghost Coast-to-Coast, World Championship Wrestling, *Gone With the Wind, The Jetsons,* CNN and Headline News, Sport-South, the Goodwill Games, *Yogi Bear, The Shawshank Redemption, Johnny Quest,* and *Huckleberry Hound* (this list could fill the whole book!), remains a major media player even after the merger of the company with Time Warner and the more recent merger with media-giant American Online.

Turner Broadcasting System Inc., prior to the sale, employed 8,200 people worldwide. The company entered the television business with the purchase of a single Atlanta UHF television station in 1970. Turner had moved to Atlanta in 1963 and quickly turned around his family's failing billboard company. In 1976 Channel 17 became the first cable superstation when its signal began beaming from a satellite 23,000 miles out in space. WTBS SuperStation had fewer than 700,000 subscribers, who were treated to a mixed bag that included old movies and TV shows, Atlanta Braves baseball (TBS bought "America's Team" in 1976), and commercials for odd products such as Slim Whitman records and a kitchen-full of peelers, slicers, and dicers. Today it's America's top-rated 24-hour basic cable service.

When Turner launched CNN in 1980, detractors scoffed at the world's first 24-hour, all-news network. In the years since, its U.S. subscriber base has grown from 1.7 million to more than 77 million, and CNN has shown the world everything from the War in Iraq to O. J. Simpson's car chase.

Through the years, TBS continued to launch networks (Cartoon Network, Headline News, Turner Network Television, Turner Classic Movies) and acquire subsidiaries (Castle Rock Entertainment, Hanna-Barbera Cartoons Inc., New Line Cinema). Turner Entertainment Company also owns more than 3,300 film and TV titles, including *Gone With the Wind, The Wizard of Oz, King Kong, Casablanca, Ben Hur* (1926 and 1959 versions), and *Citizen Kane.*

TBS founder Ted Turner was hailed as "prince of the global village" by *Time* magazine when it named him Man of the Year in 1991. In September 1995, after lengthy negotiations, Time Warner bought TBS for $7.5 billion. The resulting mega-corporation is the world's largest entertainment company; Turner, as vice-chairman and Time Warner's largest single individual shareholder, has kept Atlanta as the capital of the Turner empire.

See our Attractions chapter for information about the guided tour offered at CNN Center.

The Weather Channel
300 Interstate North Parkway
(770) 226–0000
www.weather.com

When they want to get the latest on hurricanes, floods, or earthquakes—and when they just want to know what to wear to work—more than 93 percent of U.S. cable households can check the Weather Chan-

nel. The world's only 24-hour, continuous-coverage network devoted exclusively to the weather is headquartered in northwest Atlanta.

The Weather Channel reports local, regional, national, and international weather conditions and runs a forecast specific to the viewer's local area every eight to 10 minutes around the clock. There are also regular reports such as the Weekly Planner (:20 past the hour) and International Weather (:11 past the hour). The channel's "weathertainment" shows focus on phenomena such as tornadoes and flooding.

As conditions warrant, the channel adds regular reports on fall foliage, heat or cold waves, holiday weather, and beach forecasts.

The Weather Channel really shines when the weather acts up. Its forecasters meticulously track the path of big storms, often giving far more detailed information about their progress than other news sources. Frequently the channel has a crew beachside bravely beaming live video as a hurricane makes landfall. (We have frequently wondered if that crew had "won" or "lost" the argument for who went there!)

The Weather Channel was launched in 1982, the brainchild of John Coleman. The weather forecaster on ABC's *Good Morning, America,* he served as the network's first president. The Weather Channel has generated an operating profit since 1985. It's owned by Landmark Communications Inc. in Norfolk, Virginia.

People TV
190 14th Street NW
(404) 873–6712
www.peopletv.com

Radicals railing against the government; drag queens twirling batons or lip-synching to Connie Francis; teens discussing the challenges facing youth today: You may find all this and more on People TV (Public Access Cable 12).

The 1980 franchise agreement between the City of Atlanta and its cable supplier provided for the creation of a public access cable TV channel, on which ordinary citizens can have their own programs shown free of charge. Atlanta's channel is a leader in the field of urban public access channels. Originally part of the cable company, public access is now a separate, private, nonprofit organization, called People TV, founded in 1986.

Through the facilities of People TV, Atlanta residents can take low-cost classes in video production, television directing, and editing. Once certified, they can use the channel's professional equipment, or use home equipment, to produce their own shows.

There are few rules as to the content of the shows; freedom of speech applies. Pop star RuPaul began his show biz career on People TV on *The American Music Show,* one of the longest-running public access shows in the United States.

Major Local TV Stations and Their Network Affiliates

Atlanta's WSB-TV gave the South its chance to marvel at the newfangled "radio with pictures" on September 29, 1948. A string of "firsts" followed: WSB-TV provided the South's first telecasts of professional football, local election results, and church services (Christmas at First Presbyterian Church, 1948). The station was also the first in the South to broadcast a network show in full color, on February 16, 1954.

Television caught on with Atlantans, and more stations followed quickly. WAGA-TV began broadcasting in March 1949; WXIA-TV switched on in 1951. WAGA-TV is one of the top three Fox affiliates in the United States and home to one of the nation's highest rated 10:00 P.M. newscasts. WATL-TV is the nation's No. 1 affiliate of WB, the Warner Bros. Network (it still carries Fox's kids' programming). Tribune Broadcasting's station WGCL is the home of CBS in Atlanta. WUPA has been associated with UPN since 1995. With more than 1.77 million TV households, Atlanta is the nation's 10th-largest TV market.

Following is a listing of the television stations whose broadcast signals reach most of the metro area.

WAGA Channel 5 (Fox)
WATC Channel 57 (Community Television Inc.)
WATL Channel 36 (WB)
WGCL Channel 46 (CBS)
WGTV Channel 8 (Georgia Public TV/PBS)
WHOT Channel 34 (USA Networks)
WHSG Channel 63 (Trinity Broadcasting Network)
WPBA Channel 30 (PBS/Atlanta Board of Education)
WPXA Channel 14 (PAX TV)
WSB Channel 2 (ABC)
WTBS Channel 17 (Time Warner/Turner Broadcasting System)
WUPA Channel 69 (UPN)
WXIA Channel 11 (NBC)

Insiders' Tip

Three of the four major network stations (WSB-2, WAGA-5, WXIA-11) have "traffic" helicopters up during rush hours each day (which are getting longer, and longer...), so it is a very good idea to take a quick peek before leaving to see if any major problems have cropped up (all three usually swarm over the site of bad accidents). Many radio stations provide varying levels of traffic reports as well, but the best seems to be WSB-FM, 98.5, which practically turns over its entire broadcast to extensive coverage during the rush hours.

Radio

You can tune in to any kind of music in Atlanta and have commentary in almost as many languages including Spanish, Greek, and country (well, it is like another language to some of us). And if talk radio is your addiction, you can get your fix or have a fit over Rush Limbaugh, and be nagged by Dr. Laura, on WGST. Check out Atlanta's own homespun demagogues like Neal Boortz (WSB) or consumer maven Clark Howard (WSB), who not only helps resolve all your purchasing snafus but also announces the best airfare deals before they are published. (Prior to becoming a radio celeb, Howard owned a travel agency and his know-how in this area is astounding. But don't look to him for cushy, high-end vacation tips: He's a nut for a bargain. He suggests driving to Birmingham, Alabama [two hours away], to save $50 on airfare if Hartsfield and Delta aren't cooperating with his budget.) All of our talkers, by the way, accept call-ins and have special numbers for that purpose.

Several "alternative" stations are clustered at the left, public portion of the FM band. These include college radio (WRAS, WCLK, WREK), the local National Public Radio affiliate and classical station (WABE), and a community-operated station with diversified programming from reggae to bluegrass (WRFG "Radio Free Georgia").

WSTR "Star 94" is dedicated to playing the Top 40; WNNX "99X" introduces the city to the latest in new rock. Several stations play recent releases in specific musical areas. Numerous stations program oldies or easy listening rock and jazz.

The following listing will guide you through the dials. You'll find that some of these stations come in loud and clear throughout Atlanta at all times; at night, some even reach distant states. Others, however, are so weak they're receivable on one side of town but not the other. Switch around, pick your favorites, and set the dial for hours of enjoyment.

Contemporary

WBTS 95.5 FM (Dance/Top 40)
WBZY 96.7 FM (Alternative Rock)
WMXV 105.7 FM (Classic Hits)
WPCH 94.9 FM (Light Rock)
WSB 98.5 FM (Adult Contemporary)

Christian

WAEC 860 AM (Contemporary Christian)
WAFS 920 AM
WALR 1340 AM (News/Talk)
WAOK 1380 AM (News/Talk)
WDCY 1520 AM (Gospel)
WDPC 1500 AM (Gospel)
WGUN 1010 AM (Inspirational Talk)
WNIV 970 AM/1400 AM (Contemporary Christian/Talk)
WPBS 1050 AM (Gospel)
WSSA 1570 AM (Gospel)
WTJH 1260 AM (Gospel)
WWEV 91.5 FM (Contemporary Christian)
WVFJ 93.3 FM (Contemporary Christian)
WYZE 1480 AM (Gospel)

Classical

WABE 90.1 FM (NPR/Classical/Atlanta Board of Education)
WJSP 88.1 FM (NPR News/Classical)

College Radio

WCLK 91.9 FM (Jazz/Soul; Clark Atlanta University)
WOTA 540 AM (Alternative; GA Perimeter College)
WRAS 88.5 FM (New Rock; Georgia State University)
WREK 91.1 FM (Diversified; Georgia Tech)

Community

WRFG 89.3 FM (R&B, Rap/Hip-Hop, International, Reggae, Blues, Bluegrass)

Country

WKGE 1160 AM (Adult Standards/Oldies/40s–60s)
WKHX 101.5 FM
WMLB 1170 AM (Adult Standards/Oldies/40s–60s)
WTSH 107.1 FM
WYAY 106.7 FM

Jazz

WJZZ 107.5 FM (Smooth Jazz)

Kids

WDWD 590 AM (Radio Disney)

Latin

WAOS 1600 AM
WAZX 1550 AM
WFTD 1080 AM
WPLO 610 AM
WXEM 1460 AM

News/Talk

WCNN 680 AM (Sports/Talk)
WDUN 550 AM (News/Talk)
WGST 640 AM (News/Talk/Falcons Football)
WQXI 790 AM (Sports Talk)
WSB 750 AM (News/Talk/Braves Baseball/
   Hawks Basketball)

Oldies

WLKQ 102.3 FM (1950s–80s Oldies)

Rock

WKLS 96.1 FM (Album-oriented Rock)
WNNX 99.7 FM (New Rock)
WZGC 92.9 FM (Classic Rock)

Top 40

WSTR 94.1 FM (Contemporary Hits)

Urban

WALR 104.1 FM (Adult R & B)

WHTA 97.5 FM (Hip-Hop, Rap)
WVEE 103.3 FM (Urban Pop/Rap)

Publications

Daily Newspapers

Atlanta Daily World
145 Auburn Avenue NE
(404) 659–1110
www.zwire.com

Founded in 1928, *Atlanta Daily World* is the oldest African-American newspaper in Atlanta. Published twice weekly, the paper boasts a circulation of 45,000 readers who enjoy its coverage of local, national, and international news.

The *Atlanta Journal-Constitution*
72 Marietta Street NW
(404) 526–5151
www.ajc.com

The *Atlanta Journal-Constitution* is the city's morning daily.

The *Atlanta Constitution* was established in 1868. In its early years, *Constitution* staffers of note included editor Henry Grady (whose forward-looking "New South" philosophy helped energize and inspire the ruined region after the Civil War), Joel Chandler Harris (author of the Uncle Remus stories), and poet Frank Stanton (who became poet laureate of Georgia).

Insiders' Tip

More than 40 years ago, WJCC-AM radio out of Commerce, Georgia, offered country music fare hosted by a college kid named Bill Anderson. It was therefore fitting that for the station's 40th anniversary Bill Anderson, now a country singer, was brought back to honor the occasion. The Grand Ole Opry star performed at the local high school football field that was just a hog holler away from the building where he used to spin records. The town of Commerce also changed the name of the street where the station sat from Little Street to Bill Anderson Boulevard. WJCC now plays gospel and Americana tunes.

The *Atlanta Journal* was founded in 1883. In 1912 the *Journal* became the first Southern newspaper to publish its own Sunday magazine. As a staffer, Margaret Mitchell wrote 129 articles (under the by-line "Peggy Mitchell") during her four-year tenure at the magazine. Other well-known writers whose work appeared in the magazine included *New Yorker* founder Harold Ross, golfing legend Bobby Jones, humorist Will Rogers, and novelist Erskine Caldwell.

In 1939 the *Journal* and its radio station WSB were bought by James M. Cox, former three-time governor of Ohio and the Democrats' 1920 presidential nominee against Warren G. Harding. His granddaughter, Anne Cox Chambers, succeeded her father, James M. Cox Jr., in 1974 as chair of the combined Atlanta Newspapers (the business entity publishing the two papers, which merged in 1950). The two papers moved into their present nine-story downtown headquarters in 1972.

The Sunday paper hits the stands on Saturday afternoon; it carries extensive real estate listings and classified ads (job-seekers, take note) and includes valuable grocery coupons. Thursdays are devoted to Food and Home and Garden; Friday's "Weekend Preview" is a handy guide to planning your free time. The same stories, and more, are on the paper's Web site, www.ajc.com.

Fulton County Daily Report
190 Pryor Street SW
(404) 521-1227
www.fcdr.com

Daily Report is Georgia's only daily newspaper of law and business; it was established in 1890. The official legal newspaper for Fulton County, it runs legal and public notices and trial court calendars. The decisions of the Georgia Appellate Court are reported in full text in daily editions and in a weekly Friday supplement. *Daily Report* is of interest primarily to lawyers, but its matter-of-fact reportage on the often-shocking details of criminal, divorce, and civil court cases can be compelling.

Gwinnett Daily Post
166 Buford Drive, Lawrenceville
(770) 963-9205
www.gwinnettdailyonline.com

Gwinnett Daily Post, owned by Gray Communications Systems, has a circulation of 65,000 thanks primarily to Charter Communications and Benchmark Communications, who purchase a subscription for each of their viewers. In exchange, the paper develops a news and entertainment channel, G-Net, for the cable companies.

Both the *Gwinnett Daily Post* and G-Net cable are devoted primarily to features of interest to local residents. G-Net's programming includes a "Newsmakers" series as well as a "Hospital/Health Care" segment, which are cablecast repeatedly throughout a week.

Marietta Daily Journal
and Neighbor Newspapers Inc.
580 Fairground Street, Marietta
(770) 795-3000
www.mdjonline.com

Founded in 1865, *Marietta Daily Journal* is published every morning of the year. Its coverage favors local Cobb County news, but it also reports on state, national, and international events. The same company publishes the Wednesday–Sunday *Cherokee Tribune* and the 29 Neighbor editions in 11 counties, which are delivered free of charge to homes in targeted districts of the metro area. CEO Otis A. Brumby Jr. is the grandson of Thomas M. Brumby, whose chair company, founded in 1875 and still in existence, made the classic Brumby rocker a fixture on Southern verandas.

General-Interest Periodicals

Unless otherwise noted, most free papers in Atlanta are found in front of or in stores and clubs that cater to the kind of people the publication wishes to reach. For example, sports bars and health clubs have sports-oriented publications and health and environment tabloids. Other publications, such as *Creative Loafing* and the apartment and real estate magazines, have their own boxes or racks. Still others are simply piled high in front of shops. Call the publication to find distribution information.

Atlanta Citymag
277-B East Paces Ferry Road
(404) 231–5433

Published eight times a year, *Citymag* features fashions and lifestyles with plentiful photos. Information on art galleries and events is included. Look for *Citymag* at area newsstands.

Atlanta Magazine
1330 West Peachtree Street
(404) 872–3100
www.atlantamagazine.com

Atlanta retains its status as the monthly most closely associated with our city. It was initially an organ of the Atlanta Chamber of Commerce. Through the years, *Atlanta* has had many manifestations, including a stint as an investigatory and literary outlet for our finest writers. The magazine has won 150 awards from city, regional, and national groups. Along with coverage of where and what to eat, you'll also find articles profiling local political, social, and business leaders and an occasional feature on Georgia-grown celebrities such as Amy Carter and Braves pitcher John Smoltz. Currently, the editorial and advertising content is aimed squarely at the upper end of the income brackets; the coverage of Buckhead to points north is extensive, while that of the relatively poorer southside gets barely a nod of recognition. Its roots as an organ of the Chamber of Commerce are evident as well, with the very slick layout and design, but sometimes biting articles about city institutions are startling reminders that it is both independent and sometimes driven to more in-depth reporting.

Atlanta Now
233 Peachtree Street NW
(404) 521–6600
www.atlanta.com

This slick bimonthly is published by the Atlanta Convention and Visitors Bureau and is the city's official tourists' guide. Features include a two-month calendar of upcoming happenings and in-depth information on selected events. You'll also find maps, restaurant features, and food listings. It's available for free in various locations around the downtown convention district.

Creative Loafing
750 Willoughby Way NE
(404) 688–5623
www.atlanta.creativeloafing.com

Begun in 1972 by Deborah Eason and produced in her living room on the proverbial shoestring, *CL* is Atlanta's best-known free paper. The publishers have successfully brought the *Creative Loafing* name, concept, and format to readers in Greenville, South Carolina; Charlotte, North Carolina; Savannah, Georgia; and Raleigh, North Carolina. Each issue of *CL* is full of political opinion from local media celebs, truly objective restaurant reviews, gallery openings, and theatrical productions. The classifieds are a good place to look for an apartment or house rental. The "Telly" keeps you up-to-date with the daily scheduling on the tube, and the "Cuisine" department gets you "two-fer" restaurant coupons and discounts. "Soundboard," the paper's centerfold, tracks live music in the clubs. Distributed every Wednesday on store racks and from green street boxes, the Atlanta tabloid has a circulation of 140,000.

The company also publishes two local editions: *Gwinnett Loaf* and *Topside Loaf*, both based at 6659-E Peachtree Industrial Boulevard in Norcross. Each focuses on activities and events in the northern suburbs.

Guide to Georgia
1655 Peachtree Street NE, Suite 1004
(404) 892–0961

The free monthly *Guide to Georgia* is available from state Welcome Centers, at convention and visitors bureaus, and in many hotels. Its chapters report on upcoming events of interest in Atlanta and throughout Georgia from the mountains to the sea, including exhibits, performances, festivals, and more. A sports calendar details the month's pro and major college schedules.

Hudspeth Report
4920 Roswell Road NW, Suite 45B-209
(404) 255–3220
www.thehudspethreport.com

Focusing primarily on Buckhead and northside pubs and sport bars, this free monthly paper is aimed at the partying younger set rather than those seeking fine dining advice. But with a rapidly changing nightlife scene you need a scorecard to keep up with what's what—and the *Hudspeth Report* gives you one every month. You'll find lists of openings, closings, and long-term survivors as well as restaurant menus from some establishments, so you can decide what you want before you get there. The paper also includes movie briefs, reports on galleries and exhibits, and a night-by-night calendar of entertainment and sports happenings. Publisher Ron Hudspeth is a longtime fixture in Atlanta's nightlife scene, and what goes in this publication is most often from hard-won firsthand accounts. Around town, Ron is remembered fondly as the "flip side" of the late and sorely missed Lewis Grizzard, when they both had columns in the *Atlanta Journal-Constitution* during the 1970s and '80s.

Special-Interest Periodicals

African-American

Atlanta Tribune
875 Old Roswell Road, Roswell
(770) 587–0501
www.atlantatribune.com

Established in 1987, this monthly newsmagazine is geared toward affluent African-American professionals and entrepreneurs. Its metro area coverage includes corporate and professional news, plus reports on business, careers, technology, and wealth. The magazine has some 32,000 subscribers, and a weekly local cable show, *Inside the Atlanta Tribune.*

Arts/Creative Art Papers

Art Papers
P.O. Box 5748, Atlanta, GA 31107
(404) 588–1837

Now the Southeast's primary critical art journal, *Art Papers,* by the Atlanta Art

---

Insiders' Tip

Restaurant aficionados should pick up the Thursday *AJC* and the weekly *Creative Loafing* (new issues available every Wednesday) for the restaurant reviews, but must be aware of the three major local food critics' particularities. The *AJC*'s John Kessler has never given an "A" rating to any establishment, so far as we are aware, and tends to pick out the very high-end, bleeding-cutting-edge fusion and nouveau places to rate. *CL*'s Cliff Bostock is the most fun to read and leans very heavily toward low-end Asian in-town fare. *CL*'s Elliott Mackle is the most middle-of-the-road of all three, tending to choose mid-range independents and writing very balanced reviews of them.

Worker's Coalition, was founded in 1976 as a four-page, typewritten newsletter. These days the bimonthly tabloid-size magazine provides a forum for the exchange of ideas among artists, art organizations, and others in the arts community. Each issue carries in-depth articles on a topic of interest (such as art in an era of diminishing government funding), artist interviews, news briefs, commentary, and an extensive section reviewing exhibits of note throughout the Southeast and beyond. *Art Papers* has received numerous awards for excellence from public and private agencies, including the Andy Warhol Foundation for the Visual Arts; Georgia Governor's Award for the Arts; and the Mary Ellen LoPresti Award for Excellence in Publishing.

Art Papers is available at museums, bookstores, galleries, and cafes around town.

Oz
3100 Briarcliff Road NE, Suite 524
(404) 633–1779

Self-described as "the journal of creative disciplines," *Oz* tracks trends in advertising, marketing, and media. A free, bimonthly magazine, it includes an associations listing and calendar of events of interest to those in creative fields.

Business and Enterprises

Atlanta Business Chronicle
1801 Peachtree Street NE, Suite 150
(404) 249–1000

The *Chronicle* was established in 1978. Since then it has kept track of who's winning and losing and what's coming next in Atlanta's turbulent business world. More than 28,000 readers each week turn to *Atlanta Business Chronicle*. It has been recognized both regionally and nationally, winning recently both the Green Eyeshade Award from the Society of Professional Journalists and the Gerald Loeb Award for Excellence in Business Writing.

Issued weekly on Friday, the *Chronicle* may have a pullout section on real estate, banking, or hospitality. Throughout the year everything from retail to health care will have a section. The paper also produces special supplementary publications, such as *Who's Who in Atlanta, The Book of Lists,* and *Metro Market Reports,* which gives an economic overview of each major county or business corridor. It also provides focus reports on golf, catering, and other topics—all helpful info for marketing. In fact, these lists are also available on computer disks.

The *Chronicle* is highly pro-business (no surprise there) but occasionally steps into the political arena, too. The mayor, city council, and other government officials have felt the *Chronicle*'s scrutiny; investigatory articles have won Chronicle writers awards. Not even sacred cows are safe: Editorially, the *Chronicle* opposed efforts to salvage "The Dump," the Peachtree Street apartment house, now a museum, where Margaret Mitchell wrote *Gone With the Wind* (see our Attractions chapter).

Atlanta Small Business Monthly
6129 Oakbrook Parkway, Norcross
(770) 446–5434

Atlanta Small Business Monthly caters to the needs of small-business owners and man-

Insiders' Tip

When you ride MARTA, pick up a copy of the *Rider's Digest*. This 8½ x 11 sheet of paper, folded down to a handy pocket size, lists the latest info on schedule changes, new routes, and even dates of art exhibits, films, and other public events and how to get there. MARTA also has a Speaker's Bureau. Call (404) 848-5167 for more information.

agers. Articles profile Atlanta business leaders and cover issues such as successful meetings, strategic career moves, and purchasing equipment, insurance, and desktop software. *Atlanta Small Business Monthly* is sent free to your office or is available by subscription, a practice the publishers hope will catch on.

Catalyst
3379 Peachtree Road, Suite 300
(404) 888–0555
www.catalystmagazine.com

Aimed at young entrepreneurs and working professionals age 24 to 45, *Catalyst* focuses on professional and personal success. Regular departments include interviews with leading area CEOs, how to grow a company, leadership skills, and finance. Circulation is about 15,000.

Georgia Trend
5880 Live Oak Parkway, Suite 280, Norcross
(770) 931–9410
www.georgiatrend.com

Founded in 1985, this monthly details business activities throughout the state rather than concentrating on metro Atlanta activities and people. A circulation of 50,000 includes copies sent free of charge to area business execs. Look for reports on real estate, politics, and Southern stocks, plus features on moneymakers, media, and sports moguls. Call to be added to the mailing list.

Home Decor

Atlanta Homes & Lifestyle
1100 Johnson Ferry Road, Suite 595
(404) 252–6670

Beautiful Atlanta homes large and small fill the pages of *Atlanta Homes & Lifestyle.*

Eight times a year, the magazine takes its readers through fabulous metro homes and gardens. Article topics include home restoration, shopping for decor, art, and vacation getaways. Subscribers also receive four editions of *Second Home,* a showcase of Southern vacation getaways and must-have items to outfit them richly. Look for *Atlanta Homes & Lifestyle* at local newsstands.

Veranda
455 East Paces Ferry Road NE, Suite 216
(404) 261–3603

Remember those high-toned Sugarbakers, the fictional Atlanta sisters who ran their own decorating firm in the hit TV sitcom *Designing Women?* Well, if they actually existed, you can be sure they'd subscribe to *Veranda,* "the gallery of Southern style." This lush 300-page color publication practically drips elegance from every page. Extensive photo layouts showcase the lovely homes of the affluent, while the many ads proffer an array of items and services for the well-heeled. Each of the bimonthly issues will make your coffee table proud.

Worship and Spirituality

Atlanta's spiritual community is as diverse as its population from around the country and the globe. In addition to its traditional Bible Belt congregations, you'll find most Christian denominations, Jewish, Muslim, Hindu, and Buddhist faiths as well as smaller organizations practicing in the metropolitan area.

The city's proclivity for the graceful melding of cultures displays itself in churches for Vietnamese Catholics, Hispanic Seventh-Day Adventists, Chinese Baptists, and Korean Presbyterians. The city is home to a number of mosques and Buddhist and Hindu temples. A cluster of Russian Orthodox, Eastern Orthodox, and Coptic churches give their members an opportunity to practice traditions and rituals.

Community efforts toward interfaith action are commonplace. Three downtown churches jointly celebrate Palm Sunday with a procession of members bearing colorful banners and palms, accompanied by hymns and music from all three liturgies. The original buildings of these churches—Trinity Methodist, Central Presbyterian, and The Shrine of the Immaculate Conception—shared salvation from Gen. William Tecumseh Sherman's torches because of the persuasive powers of Father Thomas O'Reilly, the shrine's pastor. Ecumenical efforts among Atlanta's synagogues, temples, and churches include building community centers, operating homeless shelters, and working to promote harmony among Atlanta's citizens.

The most famous church in Atlanta is Ebenezer Baptist Church on Auburn Avenue. The Rev. Martin Luther King Jr., the famed civil rights worker and Nobel Peace Prize-winner, preached there, as did his father, the Rev. Martin Luther King Sr. The church is part of the King Historic District and is adjacent to the King Center.

Besides the Ebenezer Baptist, you'll find other influential, predominately African-American churches along and near Auburn Avenue, the historical setting of thriving entrepreneurship among African Americans. Churches in this area include the Wheat Street Baptist Church, Big Bethel AME Church, which was founded in 1847 by slaves, and many others. Big Bethel is the oldest predominantly African-American congregation in the metro area. In 1870 church members formed the Daughters of Bethel Benevolent Society. Cited by W. E. B. Dubois as one of the first examples of economic cooperation among blacks, the Daughters cared for sick and aging ex-slaves. In 1880 the first public school classes for black children were held in "Old Bethel," the church the congregation used before building Big Bethel.

Another noted place of worship is The Temple, the area's best-known synagogue and home to a Reform congregation, on Peachtree Street. It was the site of the infamous 1958 bombing, which became the topic of the book *The Temple Bombing* by Melissa Fay Greene. The incident, blamed on Ku Klux Klan and neo-Nazi sympathizers, came at a time when racial integration was being implemented in the South. It challenged Atlanta's violence-free reputation and

> **Insiders' Tip**
> Avoid the far right lane of traffic on Peachtree Road during Sunday morning hours as it officially becomes a parking lane for the overflow crowds from the clusters of churches on this main thoroughfare.

helped create a civil rights alliance between Jews and African Americans. The bombing also was mentioned in the play and movie *Driving Miss Daisy*. The building was designed by noted Atlanta architect Philip Shutze. Other prominent synagogues in the Atlanta area include Ahavath Achim (Conservative), Or VeShalom (Sephardic, traditional), and Beth Jacob (Orthodox). There is also the Chabad Outreach Center for Hasidic studies.

In Buckhead, the Episcopal Cathedral of St. Philip stands on a majestic rise above Peachtree Road. This congregation dates back to 1847, and the current cathedral was built in 1962. The church is the headquarters for the Episcopal Diocese of Atlanta.

Across the street, you'll find the Catholic Cathedral of Christ the King, headquarters for the Roman Catholic Diocese of Atlanta. Bishop Gerald P. O'Hara blessed and laid the cornerstone for the cathedral in 1937. Farther north on Roswell Road, Peachtree Presbyterian Church is the nation's largest Presbyterian congregation with more than 12,000 members.

In addition to those denominations, several others, including Methodists, Seventh-Day Adventists, Baptists, and Lutherans, have regional headquarters or offices in Atlanta. In addition, numerous Christian and Jewish organizations, as well as mission, business, and youth religious groups, are based here.

Greek Orthodox followers meet at Cathedral of The Annunciation. Each fall, the church stages an elaborate Greek festival (see Annual Events and Festivals) to raise money to support church activities.

The Religious Society of Friends, more commonly known as the Quakers, meets in Decatur. True to its heritage of involvement in civil rights, it provided a meeting place during the height of the integration movement in the '60s for Martin Luther King Jr., Andrew Young, and high school students who later peacefully integrated the schools in Atlanta.

Atlanta's gay community supports several congregations whose primary ministry is to lesbian and gay Christians. Among them are First Metropolitan Community Church of Atlanta, All Saints Metropolitan Community Church, and Bet Haverim synagogue.

Churches are an integral part of Southern culture, but Atlanta's diverse population seeks spiritual comfort in a variety of ways.

Atlanta Masjid of Al-Islam, an Islamic congregation, is one of several in the metro area. Baha'i followers meet in Stone Mountain, and Zen Buddhist meditation is practiced at the Frazer Center in Atlanta. Students and followers of Tibetan Buddhism established a center in northeast Atlanta in 1991, at the behest of the Dalai Lama of Tibet himself. The Drepung Loseling Institute, now affiliated with the Department of Buddhist Studies of Emory University, attracts regular visits from both the Dalai Lama and other noted monks and teachers.

Of course this is just a sampling of the options available. For a more complete list of Atlanta's worship opportunities, check the *Atlanta Journal-Constitution*. The newspaper publishes a "Faith and Values" section on Saturday where you can find articles and advertisements for services. In addition, the "freebies" newspaper racks in front of most bookstores, grocery stores, and urban markets have a host of religious-oriented announcements, newsletters, booklets, and even full-length newspapers, such as the monthly New Age publication *Aquarius*. The fact that Atlanta sits in the very "buckle" of the Southern "Bible Belt" assures that one should not have any problem at all in finding an appropriate place of worship.

Index

A

Abbett Inn, 69
Abbey, The, 84
Abernathy Arts Center, 189
Abigail's Victorian, 69
Academy Theatre, The, 219
accommodations
    Airport, 58–59
    Barrow County, 59–60
    bed-and-breakfasts, 65–70
    Buckhead, 53–56
    Clayton County, 60
    Cobb County, 60–61
    DeKalb County, 61–62
    Downtown, 47–50
    Fulton County, 62–63
    Gwinnett County, 64
    Hall County, 64
    Midtown, 50–53
    Northeast Expressway/Emory,
        56–57
    Northwest Expressway, 57–58
Actor's Express, 219
African-American History Month, 202
African restaurants, 81
Agatha's—A Taste of Mystery, 219
Agnes & Muriel's, 72
Agnes Scott College, 353
Agnes Scott College Tree Tour, 237
AID Atlanta, 380
Aikido Center of Atlanta, 253
air travel, 16–26
Alfred Tup Holmes, 251
Aliya/Ardavin Gallery, 231
Alliance Française d'Atlanta, 42–43
Alliance Theatre Company, 219–20
alternative medicine, 383–84
American Adventures, 187
American Express Championship, 280
American-Israel Chamber of
    Commerce, 43
American Pie, 103
American restaurants, 72–81, 103–6
American Roadhouse, 72
Amicalola Falls State Park day
    trip/weekend getaway, 285–86
Amsterdam Walk, 135

Amtrak, 26
amusement parks, 187–88
Anis, 88
annual events, 201–15
Ansley Inn, 65
Ansley Park Home Tour, 210
Anthony Ardavin Gallery, 231–32
Anthony's, 84–85
antiques stores, 137–40
Apartment Finders, 338
Apartment Selector, 338
Apartments Today, 338
APEX Museum, The, 149
Appalachian Outfitters, 260–61
Arbor Place, 132–33
Archibald Smith Plantation Home, 183
Architectural Book Center, 145
architecture, 330–31
area codes, 2
Art Institute of Atlanta, The, 354
Art Papers, 395–96
arts
    arts centers and venues, 229–31,
        234–35
    child-oriented, 189–91
    dance, 217–18
    galleries, 231–34, 235
    museums, 224–25, 227–29, 234
    music, 217–18, 224
    theater, 218–21, 223–24
ART Station, 189–90
Arturo's Piano Bar, 125
Asher, 107
Asheville, North Carolina day
    trip/weekend getaway, 313–15
Asiana Garden, 95
Asian Square, 41
Asti's Terrace Lounge, 117
astronomy, 243
Athens day trip/weekend getaway,
    294–96
Atkins Park, 72
Atlanta Airport Hilton and Towers, 58
Atlanta Alliance on Developmental
    Disabilities (AADD), 353
Atlanta Astronomy Club, 243
Atlanta Ballet, 217

Atlanta Ballet, The—*The Nutcracker,* 214
Atlanta Beat, 282
Atlanta Boardsailing Club, 245
Atlanta Botanical Garden, 149–51, 195
Atlanta Botanical Garden Country Christmas, 214
Atlanta Braves, 263–65
Atlanta Broadway Series, 220
Atlanta Business Chronicle, 396
Atlanta Care Center, 381
Atlanta Celtic Festival, 205–6
Atlanta Citymag, 394
Atlanta Civic Center, 229
Atlanta Climbing Club, 247
Atlanta Club Sport, 243
Atlanta College of Art, 354
Atlanta Contemporary Art Center, 229
Atlanta Costume, 142
Atlanta Cyclorama and Civil War Museum, 151–53
Atlanta Daily World, 392
Atlanta Dogwood Festival, 203
Atlanta Downtown Travelodge, 47
Atlanta Fair, 202
Atlanta Falcons, 269–71
Atlanta Farmers' Market, 143
Atlanta Fish Market, 97–98
Atlanta Flying Disc Club, The, 260
Atlanta Greek Festival, 210
Atlanta Hawks, 275–76
Atlanta Hilton and Towers, 47
Atlanta Hispanic Chamber of Commerce, 43
Atlanta History Center, 153–55
Atlanta History Center Candlelight Tours, 214
Atlanta Homes & Lifestyle, 397
Atlanta International Museum of Art and Design, 43, 185, 224
Atlanta International School, 43, 349–50
Atlanta Jazz Festival, 206
Atlanta Journal-Constitution, The, 185, 392–93
Atlanta Journal-Constitution Barbecue Fest, The, 210–11
Atlanta Lawn Tennis Association (ALTA), 258–59
Atlanta Magazine, 394
Atlanta Marathon, 282
Atlanta Marriott Century Center, 56
Atlanta Marriott Marquis, 47–48
Atlanta Marriott Northwest, 60

Atlanta Marriott Suites Midtown, 50
Atlanta Medical Center, 365–66
Atlanta Metropolitan College, 354
Atlanta Motor Speedway, 243–44, 280–81
Atlanta Now, 394
Atlanta Opera, The, 217–18
Atlanta Passion Play, 202–3
Atlanta Preservation Center Walking Tours, 155–56
Atlanta Public Schools, 342
Atlanta Renaissance Hotel Downtown, 48
Atlanta Rings in the New Year, 215
Atlanta Rowing Club, The, 254
Atlanta Silverbacks, 282–83
Atlanta Ski Club, 256
Atlanta Skydiving Center, 256
Atlanta Small Business Monthly, 396–97
Atlanta Speech School, 352
Atlanta State Farmers' Market, 143
Atlanta Steeplechase, 283
Atlanta Symphony Orchestra, 218
Atlanta Thrashers, 278–79
Atlanta Track Club, 255
Atlanta Tribune, 395
Atlanta University Center, 359–62
Atlanta University Center football, 274–75
Atlanta Virtuosi Foundation, Inc., 43
Atlanta Virtuosi's Hispanic Festival of the Arts, 209
Atlanta Whitewater Club, 261
attractions
    Atlanta, 149–76
    Cobb County, 176–79
    DeKalb County, 179–83
    Fulton County, 183–84
    fun freebies, 185–86
    Gwinnett County, 184–85
Au Rendez Vous, 88
auto racing, 243–44, 280–81
Avenue East Cobb, The, 133
Azteca Grill, 112

B
Babette's Cafe, 85
Bacchanalia, 76
Backstreet, 121
Bangkok Thai, 102
Bar, 117
Baraonda Caffé Italiano, 92
Bar at the Palm, The, 117

Bar at the Ritz-Carlton Buckhead, The, 117
Barbecue Kitchen, 99
barbecue restaurants, 90–91, 99–102, 113–14
Barefoot Sailing Club, 255
Barking Dog Theatre, 220–21
Barnes & Noble, 144
bars, 117–27
baseball, 263–69
Basil's Mediterranean Cafe, 89
basketball, 275–78
Bass Pro Outdoor World, 249
Bauder College, 354–55
Beach at Clayton County International Park, The, 188
beaches, 188–89
Bear on the Square Mountain Festival, 203
Beautiful Restaurant, The, 99
bed-and-breakfasts
    Atlanta, 65–68
    beyond Atlanta, 69–70
BellSouth Classic, 279
Beluga, 118
Bender Fine Arts, 232
Bennett Street, 138
Bentley's Bed and Breakfast, 66
Best of Atlanta Party, The, 202
Beverly Hills Inn, 66
billiards, 244
bi-planing, 244
Birmingham, Alabama day trip/weekend getaway, 315–16
Bitsy Grant Tennis Center, 259
Black Mountain day trip/weekend getaway, 315
Blind Willie's, 124–25
Blue and Gray Bed and Breakfast, 69
Blue Ribbon Grill, 72
Blue Ridge Grill, 76–77
Blue Willow Inn Restaurant, 113
boardsailing, 245
Bobby Jones, 251
Bone's, 79
bookstores, 144–46
Borders Books & Music, 144
bowling, 245
Brandyhouse, The, 118
Brasserie Le Coze, 88
Brasstown Bald day trip/weekend getaway, 286–87
Bridgetown Grill, 81
British American Business Group, 43

Brooklyn Cafe, 110
Brunswick Lanes, 245
Brushstrokes, 145
Buckhead Bed & Breakfast Inn, 66
Buckhead Billiards, 244
Buckhead Bread Company & Corner Café, 72–73
Buckhead Diner, 77
Buckhead Road Runners Club, 255
Buckhead shopping district, 135–36
Bulloch Hall, 183
buses, 11–16, 24

C

Cabbagetown Grill, 73
Caddy's Sports Bar, 128
Cafe Sunflower, 102–3, 114
Cafe Tu Tu Tango, 87
Cafe 290, 126
Cajun restaurants, 101–2, 106
Calcutta, 90
California Pizza Kitchen, 92
Callanwolde Fine Arts Center, 185, 229
camping, 246–47
Candler Park, 250
Candler Park & Lake Claire Music & Arts Festival, 211
Canoe, 77
canoeing, 247
Capitol City Opera Company, 218
Caramba Cafe, 95
Caribbean restaurants, 81
car rentals, 23
Carter Presidential Center, 156–57
Casbah, The, 81
Catalyst, 397
Cathedral Antiques Show, 201–2
Cathedral of St. Philip, 145
Centennial, 249
Centennial Olympic Park, 157–58, 188
Center for Puppetry Arts, 191, 221
Centro Norcross, 41
Century 21, 339
Challenge Rock Climbing School, 247
Chamblee Antiques Row, 138
Chapter 11, The Discount Bookstore, 144
Charis Books & More, 145
Charlie's Tradin' Post, 249
Chastain Memorial Park, 237
Chastain Park Amphitheater, 229–30
Château Élan, 59–60
Château Élan Golf Club, 251–52

Chattahoochee Avenue Warehouse, 136
Chattahoochee Nature Center, 183–84, 195, 237
Chattahoochee River, 237–38
Chattanooga, Tennessee day trip/weekend getaway, 316–19
Cheesecake Factory, 73
Chequers Seafood Grill, 113
Cheshire Bridge Road NE, 138
Cheshire Motor Inn, 50–51
Chick-fil-A Charity Championship, 279
ChickiBea, 141
children, activities for. See kidstuff
Children's Healthcare, 382
Children's Healthcare of Atlanta at Egleston, 366–67
Children's Healthcare of Atlanta at Scottish Rite, 367
Children's Healthcare of Atlanta Christmas Parade, 215
Chili Cook-Off, 211
Chili Pepper, The, 118
China Inn, 110
Chin Chin, 81
Chinese restaurants, 81–83, 110
Chops, 79
Chopstix, 81–82
Christmas at Callanwolde, 214–15
Christmas Lights, 215
churches, 398–99
Churchill Grounds, 121
City Club Marietta, 249–50
City Gallery East, 232
City Grill, 77
City Lights Dance Club, 127
Civilized Traveller, The, 145
Civil War Encampment, 210
CJ's Landing, 118
Clark Atlanta University, 359–60
Clark Atlanta University Art Galleries, 224
Clark Atlanta University football, 275
Clarkesville day trip/weekend getaway, 287–88
Classic Bi-Plane Rides Inc., 244
climbing, 247
Cloudland Canyon Park, 246
clubs, 117–28
CNN Center, 129, 158
Cobb Community Transit, 16
Cobb County Parks & Recreation, 259
Cobb County Public Schools, 343
Cobblestone, 250

Coca-Cola Excursion, 158–59
Coca-Cola Roxy, 230
Coco Loco, 95
Cokesbury Books and Church Supplies, 145
Coldwell Banker–Buckhead Brokers, 339
Coldwell Banker–Bullard Realty Co., 339
Coldwell Banker-The Condo Store, 339
College Park Recreation Department, 256
colleges/universities, 353–62
Colonnade, The, 99
Columbia Theological Seminary, 355
Columbus day trip/weekend getaway, 299–300
comedy clubs, 127–28
Comfort Inn, 64
Confederate Cemetery, 176
Connell Gallery, 232
consignment shops, 141–42
Consignshop, 141
Continental restaurants, 83–87, 107–9
Conyers Cherry Blossom Festival, 203
Costumes Etc., 142
costume stores, 142
Cotton Club, The, 120
Cotton House, The, 139
Country Brook Montessori School, 351–52
Courtyard by Marriott, 64
Courtyard by Marriott Atlanta Airport North, 58
Courtyard by Marriott Atlanta Airport South, 58
Courtyard by Marriott Cumberland Center, 57
Courtyard by Marriott Midtown, 51
Courtyard by Marriott Roswell, 62
Courtyard Downtown Atlanta, 48
Courtyard Marriott Buckhead, 53
Cowboy's Dance Hall, 126
Cozumel Mexican Restaurant, 112
Crabapple Corners, 139
Crawford W. Long Museum, 185
Creative Loafing, 394
cross-cultural restaurants, 87
Crowne Plaza Powers Ferry, 57
Crowne Plaza Ravinia, 61–62
Crystal Blue, 147
cultural diversity. See international goods/services
Cumberland Island day trip/weekend getaway, 308

Cumberland Mall, 129–30
currency exchange, 40
cycling, 248

D
Dahlonega day trip/weekend getaway,
    288–89
Dailey's Restaurant and Bar, 77
Dalton day trip/weekend getaway,
    289–90
dance, 217–18
Dance City Ballroom, 118
Dante's Down the Hatch, 87, 118
Dark Horse Tavern, 125
Darwin's, 126
Daughters of the British Empire,
    43–44
Dave and Buster's, 126, 127, 244
Davidson-Arabia Mountain Nature
    Preserve, 195
Dawat Indian Cafe, 110
Days Inn Atlanta/Downtown, 48
Days Inn-Midtown Peachtree Street, 51
day trips and weekend getaways
    Amicalola Falls State Park, 285–86
    Asheville, North Carolina, 313–15
    Athens, 294–96
    Birmingham, Alabama, 315–16
    Black Mountain, 315
    Brasstown Bald, 286–87
    Chattanooga, Tennessee, 316–19
    Clarkesville, 287–88
    Columbus, 299–300
    Cumberland Island, 308
    Dahlonega, 288–89
    Dalton, 289–90
    Eatonton, 298–99
    Ellijay, 290–91
    Gainesville, 291–92
    Helen, 293–94
    Jekyll Island, 308–9
    Macon, 300–302
    Madison, 296–98
    Okefenokee Swamp, 302–4
    Pine Mountain, 304–6
    Savannah, 309–11
    Sea Island, 311
    St. Simons Island, 311–12
    Tybee Island, 312–13
    Warm Springs, 306–7
Decatur Arts Festival, 206
decorator item stores, 137–40
DeKalb County Parks &
    Recreation, 259

DeKalb County School System, 343,
    345–46
DeKalb Farmers' Market, 41–42,
    142–43
DeKalb Medical Center, 367–68
DeKalb-Peachtree Airport, 25
Dermess Skin Care Center, 385
Deux Plex, 122
DeVry Institute of Technology, 355
dick and harry's, 107
Dining Room, The, 85
di Paolo Cucina, 111
Discovery Mills, 133
Dixieland Fun Park, 198
Dixie Speedway, 281
Dominick's, 111
Dong Khanh Restaurant, 103
Don Juan's, 95–96
Doubletree Guest Suites, 62
Doubletree Hotel Atlanta
    Buckhead, 53
Doug's Place, 113–14
Downwind Restaurant and Lounge, 73
Dreamland Barbecue, 114
driving rules and customs, 9–11
Druid Hills Home and Garden
    Tour, 203–4
Drury Inn and Suites, 60
Dunwoody Medical Center, 376–77
Dunwoody Nature Center, 195–96
Dusty's Barbecue, 99–100

E
E.A.R.L., 125
Eastern National Park & Monument
    Association Book Store, 145
Easter Sunrise Services, 204
Eatonton day trip/weekend getaway,
    298–99
EATS, 80
Echo Lounge, 125
Eclectic Electric, 232
Eddie's Attic, 127
Eddie's Trick & Novelty, 142
E D's Gourmet Records, 146
education. *See* schools
1848 House, 107
Einstein's, 73
El Azteca, 96
Ellijay day trip/weekend getaway,
    290–91
El Toro, 96
Embassy Suites Atlanta Airport, 59
Embassy Suites Atlanta/Buckhead, 53

Embassy Suites Galleria, 57
Embassy Suites Perimeter Center, 62
Embers Seafood Grill, 113
emergency medical services, 378–80
Emory-Adventist Hospital, 375
Emory Conference Center Hotel, 56
Emory Crawford Long Hospital, 368
Emory Inn, 56
Emory University, 355–56
Emory University Hospital, 368–69
Emory University Psychological
    Center, 353
Encore Bistro and Club, 122
English restaurants, 87–88
Eno, 85
equestrian events, 283–84
ESPN Zone, 128
Euclid Avenue Yacht Club, 124
Evans Fine Foods, 100
Express Bowling Lanes, 245

F
Fado Irish Pub, 87–88
Fairfield Downtown Atlanta, 48
Fairfield Inn, 60
Fairlie Poplar Artworks, 232
Fallin Gate, 66
FamilyCare Centers, 382
Famous Pub and Sports Palace, 128
Fandangles, 120
Fantastic Finds, 141
Fantastic Fourth Celebration, 207
FAO Schwarz, 199–200
farmers' markets, 41–42, 142–43
Farwax Records, 146
Fat Matt's Rib Shack, 100, 122
Fayette Book Shop, 146
Fayette Community Hospital, 377
Fay Gold Gallery, 232–33
Fellini's Pizza, 92
Fernbank Museum of Natural History,
    159, 191–92
Fernbank Science Center, 160, 192, 345
Festival of Trees, Festival of Lights, 215
festivals, 201–15
field hockey, 248
Final Touch Gallery & Books, 144–45
Fish Hawk, The, 249
fishing, 248–49
Flea An'Tique, A, 139
flea markets, 137–40
Flying Biscuit, 103
Flying Machine, 127
Flying Pig, 100

Food Studio, The, 77–78
football, 269–75
foreign goods/services. *See* interna-
    tional goods/services
Four Seasons, 51
Fox Theatre, 160–63
Fräbel Studio, 226–27
Frankie's Food, Sports, and
    Spirits, 128
Fratelli di Napoli, 92
Frazer Center, The, 352
Free Home Finder, 338–39
freeways, 3–7
French restaurants, 88–89
Friends School of Atlanta, The, 348
Fright Fest, 211
Full Moon Records, 146–47
Fulton County Airport-Brown
    Field, 26
Fulton County Daily Report, 393
Fulton County Parks &
    Recreation, 259
Fulton County Schools, 346–47
Fuzzy's, 101

G
Gainesville day trip/weekend getaway,
    291–92
Galerie Timothy Tew, 233
Galleria Specialty Mall, 130
galleries, art, 231–34, 235
Galloway School, 350
Gaslight Inn, The, 66
George's, 125
Georgia Book Store Inc., 145–46
Georgia Council for International
    Visitors, 44
Georgia Department of Archives and
    History, 163–64
Georgia Department of Education, 347
Georgia Dome, The, 271–73
Georgia Field Hockey Association, 248
Georgia Games, 284
Georgia Governor's Mansion, 164
Georgia Institute of Technology, 356
Georgia International Horse Park,
    283–84
Georgia Lighting, 138
Georgia Perimeter College, 356
Georgia Renaissance Festival, 204
Georgia Shakespeare Festival, 207, 221
Georgia's Historical Markers, 164
Georgia State Capitol, 164–65
Georgia State Soccer Association, 257

Georgia State University, 356–57
Georgia State University basketball, 278
Georgia Tech basketball, 276, 278
Georgia Tech football, 273–74
Georgia Tech's Robert Ferst Center for the Arts, 230
Georgia Trend, 397
German American Chamber of Commerce, 44
Glenn Memorial Auditorium, 230
Goethe-Institut Atlanta, 44
Golden Glide Roller Skating Rink, The, 256
golf, 249–52, 279–80
Good News Café, 73–74
Good Ol' Days, 103
Goodwill Industries of Atlanta, 140
Grady Health System, 382
Grady Memorial Hospital, 369
Granada Suite Hotel, The, 51
Grand China, 82
Grand Hyatt Atlanta, 53–54
Grant Park, 238
Grant Park Tour of Homes, 211
Greater Atlanta Christian Bookstore, 146
Greater Atlanta Christian School, 352
Great Gatsby's Auction Gallery, 138–39
Greek restaurants, 89
Greenbriar Mall, 130
Greenfield Hebrew Academy, 350
Green Manor, 103–4
Greenwoods on Green Street, 104
Greycourt Bed and Breakfast, 67
Greyhound Bus Lines, 26
Groundhog Day, 202
Guide to Georgia, 395
Gwinnett County Parks & Recreation, 259–60
Gwinnett County Public Schools, 347
Gwinnett Daily Post, 393
Gwinnett Historic Courthouse, 184
Gwinnett Medical Center, 377–78
Gwinnett Place, 133
Gwinnett Women's Pavilion, 378

H
Hachi Hachi, 111–12
Hambidge Center, 234
Hamilton's, 108
Hammonds House Galleries and Resource Center of African-American Art, The, 225

Hampton Inn Atlanta, 48–49
Hampton Inn Atlanta Airport, 59
Hampton Inn/Atlanta Buckhead, 54
Hampton Inn Atlanta Cumberland, 57
Hampton Inn North Druid Hills, 56
Hampton Inn Six Flags, 60
Hampton Inn Stone Mountain, 62
Hand-Me-Ups, 141
Hanger, The, 126–27
Hard Rock Café, 120
Harry Norman Realtors, 339–40
Harry's Farmers' Markets, 42, 143
Hartsfield Atlanta International Airport, 16–25
Haru Ichiban, 112
Hashiguchi Jr., 94
Have a Nice Day! Cafe, 118
Haveli Indian Cuisine, 90
Haven House at Midtown, 381
Hawthorn Suites Hotel Atlanta-Northwest, 60–61
health care
    alternative medicine, 383–84
    emergency medical services, 378–80
    HMOs, 381
    hospice care, 381
    hospitals, 365–78
    hotlines/helplines, 367
    referral services, 375, 384
    spas, 384–86
    special needs and services, 380–81
    walk-in clinics, 382
Heartfield Manor Bed and Breakfast, 67
Heaven Blue Rose, 235
Heiskell School, 350
Helen day trip/weekend getaway, 293–94
Herndon Home, The, 165–66
Hibernian Benevolent Society, 44
HiFi Buys Amphitheatre, 230
Highland Inn, The, 51–52
Highland Tap, 79, 125
High Museum of Art, 185, 190, 222
High Museum of Art Folk Art and Photography Galleries, 227
High Museum of Art Woodruff Arts Center, 225, 227
highways, 3–7
Hi Life Kitchen & Cocktails, 108
Hillside Psychiatric Hospital, 373
Hill Street Warehouse, 135
Hilton Garden Inn, 62–63
Himalayas Indian Restaurant, 90–91

history
Civil War, 28–32
early settlement, 27–28
Reconstruction, 32–34
20th century, 34–38
HMOs, 381
Hobbit Hall, 200
hockey, 278–79
Hoedown's, 122
Holiday Inn Atlanta Airport North, 59
Holiday Inn Atlanta Roswell, 63
Holiday Inn Atlanta South, 60
Holiday Inn at Lenox, 54
Holiday Inn Downtown Atlanta, 49
Holiday Inn Select Decatur, 56
Holiday Inn Select Perimeter
Dunwoody, 57
Holyfield's New South Grill, 108
Holy Innocents' Episcopal School, 350
Homewood Suites Atlanta-
Cumberland, 57–58
Horizon Theatre Company, 221
horseback riding, 252–53
Horseradish Grill, 78
Hospice Atlanta, 381
hospice care, 381
hospitals
Atlanta, 365–74
Clayton County, 374
Cobb County, 375–76
DeKalb County, 376–77
Fayette County, 377
Fulton County, 377
Gwinnett County, 377–78
hotels. See accommodations
Hotlanta River Expo, 209
hotlines/helplines, 367
Howard School, The, 352
Hsu's at Peachtree Center, 82
Hudgens Center for the Arts, 235
Hudspeth Report, 395
Huey's, 101–2
Hughes Spalding Pediatric Hospital,
369–70
Hyatt Regency Atlanta, 49, 120
Hyatt Regency Suites Perimeter North-
west, 61

I
Ice Forum, 198, 253
ice skating, 198, 253
Ichiyo Art Center, 230
Imagine It! The Children's Museum of
Atlanta, 192–93

Imperatori Family Karate Center, 253
Imperial Fez, 81
Independence Day, 208
Indian Delights, 91
Indian restaurants, 90–92, 110
Inman Park Spring Festival, 204
Interdenominational Theological
Center, 359–60
International Farmers' Market, 143
international goods/services
educational, cultural, and busi-
ness organizations, 42–45
exchanging currency, 40
foreign language/music radio
programs, 45
international malls, 40–42
interstates, 3–7
Ippolito's Family Style Italian
Restaurant, 111
Irish restaurants, 87–88
Irish Social and Information Club, 44
Italian restaurants, 92–94, 110–11
Iwase, 146

J
Jackson Fine Art, 233
Japan-America Society of Georgia, 44–45
Japanese Chamber of Commerce of
Georgia, 45
Japanese restaurants, 94–95, 111–12
JapanFest, 210
Java Jive, 80
Jekyll Island day trip/weekend getaway,
308–9
Jenny Pruitt & Associates Realtors, 340
Jewish Theatre of the South, 221, 223
Joan Glancy Memorial Hospital, 378
Joe's Crab Shack, 98
Joey D's, 108
Johnny Mercer Exhibit, 185
Johnny's Hideaway, 118
Jolie the Day Spa & Hair Design, 385
Jomandi Productions, 223
Jose's Mexican Restaurant, 112
Junkman's Daughter, 141
J.W. Marriott Hotel at Lenox, 54

K
Karma, 120
Kaya, 122
Keller Graduate School of Manage-
ment of DeVry University, 357
Kennesaw Mountain National Battle-
field Park, 176–77, 239

Kennesaw State University, 357
kidstuff
    amusement parks, 187–88
    art classes, workshops, and activi-
        ties, 189–90
    museums, 191–95
    nature activities, 195–98
    recreation, 198–99
    shopping, 199–200
    theater, 191
    water parks and beaches, 188–89
Killer Creek Chophouse, 105
Kindred Hospital Atlanta, 373–74
King & I, 102
King-Keith House Bed & Breakfast, 67
King Plow Arts Center, 230–31
King Week, 201
Korea Town Mall, 41
Krysalis, 148
Kurt's, 108

L
La Bamba Restaurante Mexicano, 96
La Fonda Latina, 96
Lagerquist Gallery, 233
La Grotta Buckhead, 93
Lake Lanier Islands, 184, 188, 246
Lake Lanier Islands Stables, 252–53
Lakewood Antiques Market, 139
Lamps N Things, 139
Lanier Sailing Academy, 255
Lasershow, 206
L'Assiette, 108
Latin American Film Festival, 213
Latin restaurants, 112
Laurel Heights Hospital, 374
Laurel Park, 239
League of United Latin American
    Citizens, 45
Learning Disabilities Association of
    Georgia, 352
Lee's Golden Buddha, 82
Legacy Golf Links, 250
Lenny's Bar, 125
Lenox Square, 130
Leopard Lounge, 122
Le Saint Amour, 88–89
Lickskillet Farm Restaurant, 108
Life University, 357–58
Lighting of Rich's-Macy's Great
    Tree, 213
Limerick Junction, 125
limousines, 25
Linda's Riding School, 253

Liquid Assets, 118
Little Five Points shopping
    district, 136
Little Gardens, 109
Little General Playhouse, 191
Little Saigon, 41
Little Szechuan, 82–83
LongHorn Steakhouse, 105
lounges, 117–27
Lovett School, 350
Lowe Gallery, 233
Lulu's Bait Shack, 118

M
Macon day trip/weekend getaway,
    300–302
Madison day trip/weekend getaway,
    296–98
magazines and newspapers, 392–97
Maggiano's Little Italy, 93
Magnolia Restaurant and Tea
    Room, 104
Malibu Grand Prix, 198–99
Mall at Peachtree Center, The, 131
Mall of Georgia, The, 133
malls, 129–34
Mama's Country Showcase, 127
Mambo Restaurante Cubano, 96
Mandarin House, 110
Mansion, The, 85–86
Manuel's Tavern, 74–75
Marcia Wood Gallery, 233
Margaret Mitchell Exhibit, 185–86
Margaret Mitchell House and
    Museum, 166–67
Marietta Bluegrass Festival, 206
Marietta/Cobb Museum of Art, 234
Marietta Conference Center and
    Resort, 61
Marietta Daily Journal, 393
Marietta History Museum, 177
Marietta National Military
    Cemetery, 177
Marist School, 348
Marriott Perimeter Center, 62
MARTA, 11–16, 24
martial arts, 253
Martini Club, 122–23
Martin Luther King Jr. Center for Non-
    violent Social Change, 168–69
Martin Luther King Jr. National His-
    toric Site, The, 169
Martin Luther King Jr. National Holi-
    day, 201

Mary Mac's Tea Room, 100
Masquerade, 123
mass transit, 11–16, 24
Masters, The, 279
Masters Economy Inn Six Flags, 63
Max Lager's, 75
McCollum Airport, 26
McKendrick's Steak House, 105–6
McKinnon's Louisiane Restaurant and
    Seafood Grill, 98
media. See news media
medical care. See health care
Mediterranean restaurants, 89
Memorial Arts Building, 222
Mercer University, 358
Metro Brokers/Better Homes and
    Gardens, 340
Mexican restaurants, 95–97, 112
Mexico City Gourmet, 96–97
Miami Circle NE, 139
Michael C. Carlos Museum, 227–28
Mick's, 75
Microtel Inn & Suites, 64
Mirror of Korea, 95
Mi Spia, 111
Mitchell, Margaret, 30–31
Mittie's Tea Room, 104
MJQ Concourse, 123
Modern Primitive Gallery, 233
Montreaux Atlanta International
    Music Festival, 209
Morehouse College, 360–61
Morehouse College football, 275
Morehouse School of Medicine,
    361–62
Morningside Farmers' Market, 143
Morris Brown College, 362
Morris Brown College football, 275
Morton's of Chicago, 79
motels. See accommodations
Mountasia Family Fun Center, 199
Mt. Fuji Japanese Steak House and
    Sushi Bar, 112
Mumbo Jumbo, 120
museums, 191–95, 224–25,
    227–29, 234
music, 217–18, 224
Music at Emory, 218
Music Midtown Festival, 206
music stores, 146–47
Mystery Valley, 251

N
Nan's Upscale Resale, 141–42

Nantahala Outdoor Center's
    Chattooga Outpost, 261
National Black Arts Festival, 208–9
National Historic Preservation
    Month, 206
Natural Body, 385
nature activities, 195–98
neighborhoods
    Downtown, 323
    Northeast Atlanta, 323–28
    Northwest Atlanta, 328–29
    overview/history of, 320–23
    Southeast Atlanta, 332–34
    Southwest Atlanta, 329, 331–32
    See also real estate
New Age shops, 147–48
New Sheraton Garden Buckhead,
    The, 54
news media
    newspapers and magazines,
        392–97
    radio, 391–92
    television, 388–90
newspapers and magazines, 392–97
New York Pizza Exchange, 111
nightlife
    bars, clubs, and lounges, 117–27
    Buckhead, 117–19
    comedy clubs, 127–28
    Downtown, 119–21
    Midtown/Little Five Points/
        Virginia-Highland, 121–25
    outside in-town Atlanta, 125–27
    overview of, 115–17
    sports bars, 128
Nikolai's Roof, 86
Nino's, 93
Noah's Ark Rehabilitation Center
    Inc., 196
Norcross Station Cafe, 104
North Atlanta Road Club, 248
North DeKalb Mall, 131
North Fulton Golf Course, 251
North Fulton Regional Hospital, 377
North Georgia Premium Outlets, 135
Northlake Mall, 131
North Point Mall, 133
Northside Health Express, 382
Northside Hospice, 381
Northside Hospital, 370
Northside Realty, 340
Northside Tavern, 123
Northwest Atlanta Hilton, 61
Northwoods Plaza, 41

O

Oakland Cemetery, 169–71
Oasis Cafe, 89
Oglethorpe University, 358–59
Oh Maria!, 97
Okefenokee Swamp day trip/weekend
	getaway, 302–4
Oktoberfest, 212
Old Courthouse on the Square, 179–80
Old Garden Inn, 69
Olympic-style events, 284
Omni Hotel at CNN Center, 49
103 West, 83–84
Orient at Vinings, The, 83
Otherside, The, 123–24
Outdoor Activity Center, 196
outlet stores, 134–35
Outwrite, 146
Oz, 396

P

Pace Academy, 351
Pad Thai, 102
Paideia School, The, 349
paintball, 253–54
Palm Restaurant, 78
Panola Mountain State Conservation
	Park, 239–40
Pano's & Paul's, 78
Pappadeaux Seafood Kitchen, 106
parks, 237–42
parks and recreation departments, 245
Park 75, 86–87
Paschal's Motor Hotel, 49
Paschal's Restaurant, 100
Pastis, 109
PATH Foundation, 240
Peach Bowl, 275
Peach Bowl Parade, 215
Peachtree Golf Center, 199
Peachtree Road Race, 207–8, 281–82
People TV, 389–90
Perimeter Mall, 134
Petite Auberge, 89
P.F. Chang's, 83
Philips Arena, 277
Phipps Plaza, 131
Phoenix and Dragon, 148
Picket Fences, 139
Piedmont Hospital, 371
Piedmont Park, 240–41
Piedmont Park Tennis Center, 259
Pilgreen's Restaurant and Lounge, 79

Pine Mountain day trip/weekend
	getaway, 304–6
Pinetree Plaza, 41
Pittypat's Porch, 100–101
pizza restaurants, 92–94, 110–11
Player's Billiards, 244
Play It Again, 142
Plaza Fiesta, 41
Plaza Latina, 41
Polo Club of Atlanta, 284
Pricci, 93–94
Pride of Dixie Antique Market, 139–40
Prime Outlets at Calhoun, 135
private schools
	Cobb County, 348
	DeKalb County, 348–49
	Fulton County, 349–51
	Gwinnett County, 351–52
Promove, 339
Providence Outdoor Recreation
	Center, 247
Psycho Sisters, 142
Public House Restaurant and Bar,
	104–5
public schools, 341–47
public transit, 11–16, 24
Puckett's Restaurant, 114
Punch Line, 127
Puppetry Arts Festival, 213

Q

Q-Zar, 199

R

R. Thomas Deluxe Grill, 75
racquetball, 254
radio, 45, 391–92
Radio Free Georgia, 45
Radisson Airport, 59
Radisson Northlake, 57
Rafters Neighborhood Bar &
	Grille, 128
Raiford Gallery, 235
Raja Indian Restaurant, 91–92
Ramada Inn and Conference
	Center, 52
Ray's on the River, 98–99
Razzoo's Cajun Café, 106
real estate
	apartments, 338–39
	Cherokee County, 336–37
	Clayton County, 334
	Cobb County, 334–35

Coweta County, 337
DeKalb County, 335
Douglas County, 335
Fayette County, 335
Forsyth County, 337
Fulton County, 335–36
Gwinnett County, 336
Henry County, 336
Newton County, 337
Paulding County, 338
real estate firms, 339–40
Rockdale County, 338
See also neighborhoods
recreation
astronomy, 243
auto racing, 243–44
billiards, 244
bi-planing, 244
boardsailing, 245
bowling, 245
camping, 246–47
canoeing, 247
child-oriented, 198–99
climbing, 247
cycling, 248
field hockey, 248
fishing, 248–49
golf, 249–52
horseback riding, 252–53
ice skating, 253
martial arts, 253
paintball, 253–54
racquetball, 254
roller skating, 256
rowing, 254
running, 254–55
sailing, 255–56
skiing, 256
skydiving, 256
soccer, 257
swimming, 257–58
tennis, 258–60
ultimate frisbee, 260
walking, 254–55
white-river rafting and tubing,
260–61
Red Top Mountain Park, 246
Regency Suites Hotel, 52
relocation. *See* neighborhoods; real
estate
RE/MAX, 340
Renaissance Atlanta Hotel-
Concourse, 59
Renaissance PineIsle Resort, 64, 252

Renaissance Waverly, 58
Rendezvous, 126
Repose Day Spa, 386
Residence Inn by Marriott Buckhead,
54–55
Residence Inn by Marriott-
Midtown, 52
resorts. *See* accommodations
restaurants
African, 81
American, 72–81, 103–6
Atlanta, 72–103
barbecue, 90–91, 99–102, 113–14
beyond Atlanta, 103–14
Cajun, 101–2, 106
Caribbean, 81
Chinese, 81–83, 110
Continental, 83–87, 107–9
cross-cultural, 87
English, 87–88
French, 88–89
Greek, 89
Indian, 90–92, 110
Irish, 87–88
Italian, 92–94, 110–11
Japanese, 94–95, 111–12
Korean, 95
Latin, 95–97, 112
Mediterranean, 89
Mexican, 95–97, 112
pizza, 92–94, 110–11
seafood, 97–99, 113
Southern, 90–91, 99–102, 113–14
steak houses, 79, 105–6
Thai, 102, 114
vegetarian, 102–3, 114
Vietnamese, 103
Rhodes Hall, 171
Rialto Center for the Performing Arts,
The, 231
Ridgeview Institute, 375
Rio Brava Cantina, 97
Ritz-Carlton Atlanta, The, 49, 120
Ritz-Carlton Buckhead, The, 55
River Birch, 69
Riviera Club, 120–21
Road Atlanta Panoz Racing School,
244, 281
Robert C. Williams American Museum
of Papermaking, 190, 228
Robert West Woodruff Arts Center,
222, 231
Rocky's Brick Oven Pizzeria, 94
Roland Center, 41

roller skating, 256
Rolling Stone Press, 233
Rose and Crown, 88
rowing, 254
Royal Thai Cuisine, 114
running, 254–55, 281–82
Ru San's, 95
Ruth's Chris Steakhouse, 106

S
sailing, 255–56
Saint Joseph's Hospital of Atlanta, 371
Salvation Army, 140
Sambuca Jazz Cafe, 119
Sanctuary, 119
Sandler Hudson Gallery, 234
Savannah day trip/weekend getaway,
    309–11
schools
    colleges/universities, 353–62
    private, 347–52
    public, 341–47
    special needs, 352–53
    teaching in Georgia, 362–63
Science Fiction & Mystery, 146
SciTrek, 171–72
SciTrek: The Science and Technology
    Museum of Atlanta, 193–94
Scott Antique Market, 140
Scottish Highland Games and Gather-
    ing of the Clans, 212–13
Sea Island day trip/weekend getaway,
    311
Seeger's, 78
Serenbe Bed and Breakfast, 69–70
7 Stages, 218–19
Shakespeare Tavern, The, 223
Shannon Southpark Mall, 134
Sharon's House of Lamps & Shades, 140
Sheep to Shawl Day, 204–5
Shellmont Bed & Breakfast, 67
Shepherd Center, 374
Sheraton Atlanta Hotel, 50
Sheraton Colony Square, 52
Sheraton Galleria, 58
Shiki Japanese Restaurant, 112
Shillings on the Square, 105
Shipfeifer on Peachtree, 89
shopping
    antiques, decorator items, and flea
        markets, 137–40
    bargain/outlet shopping, 134–35
    books and periodicals, 144–45
    child-oriented, 199–200

consignment shops, 141–42
costumes, 142
districts, 135–37
farmers' markets, 41–42, 142–43
international malls, 40–42
malls, 129–34
music, 146–47
New Age shops, 147–48
special-interest book shops,
    145–46
thrift stores, 140–41
vintage wear, 141
Showcase Eatery, 105
Shreiner Academy, 348
Shrine of the Black Madonna, 146
shuttle services, 25
Sia's, 109
Signature Shop & Gallery, The, 234
Silver Comet Trail, 241–42
Silver Grill, 101
Singles Outdoor Adventures Club, 243
Six Flags Over Georgia, 177–78,
    187–88
Six Flags White Water Atlanta,
    178, 189
60 Polk Street, 70
skiing, 256
skydiving, 256
Slocum's Tavern & Grill, 113
Smith's Olde Bar, 124
soccer, 257, 282–83
Solomon Projects, 234
Son's Place, 101
Sotto Sotto, 94
South City Kitchen, 101
Southeastern Conference Champi-
    onship Game (football), 275
Southeastern Expeditions, 261
Southeastern Flower Show, 202
Southeastern Railway Museum,
    184–85, 194
Southern Association of Colleges and
    Schools, 362
Southern Athletic Club, 254
Southern Bicycle League, 248
Southern Center for International
    Studies, 45
Southern Christian Leadership Confer-
    ence National Office, 172
Southern Christmas, A, 213–14
Southern Museum of Civil War and
    Locomotive History, 178–79
Southern Off-Road Bicycle
    Association, 248

Southern Polytechnic State University, 359–62
Southern Regional Medical Center, 374
Southern restaurants, 90–91, 99–102, 113–14
South Fulton Medical Center, 372
Southlake Athletic Club, 254
Southlake Mall, 134
South of France, 89
Southwest Hospital and Medical Center, 372
Spa at Château Élan, The, 386
Spa Forever Young, 385
Sparkles, 256
spas, 384–86
Spa Sydell, 385
special needs schools, 352–53
spectator sports
    auto racing, 280–81
    baseball, 263–69
    basketball, 275–78
    equestrian events, 283–84
    football, 269–75
    golf, 279–80
    hockey, 278–79
    Olympic-style events, 284
    running, 281–82
    soccer, 282–83
Spelman College, 362
Sphinx, 148
Spivey Hall, 224
sports. See recreation; spectator sports
sports bars, 128
sports clubs, 242–43
Springbrook Golf Course, 251
Springfest, 207
Spring Folklife Festival, 205
SpringHill Suites by Marriott, 63
Springvale-East Bed & Breakfast, 67–68
Spruill Center for the Arts, 190
Squid Roe, 113
St. Martin's Episcopal School, 349
St. Patrick's Day, 203
St. Pius X Catholic High School, 349
St. Simons Island day trip/weekend getaway, 311–12
St. Vincent de Paul, 140
STARBASE Program, 344–45
Star Community Bar, 124
steak houses, 79, 105–6
Stefan's, 141
Stone Mountain Golf Course, 252

Stone Mountain Park, 180–83, 199, 242
Stone Mountain Park Family Campground, 246
Stone Mountain Tennis Center, 260
Stone Mountain Youth Soccer Association, 257
Stoney River Legendary Steaks, 106
Street of Dreams, 210
streets, surface, 7–9
StudioPLUS, 64
Studio 211, 235
Sugar Magnolia, 68
Suite Hotel at Underground, The, 50
Summerfield Suites, 55
Summerfield Suites Hotel, 63
SummitRidge, 378
Sunday in the Park, 213
Sun Dial Restaurant and Lounge, 79
Sundown Cafe, 97
Sun Valley Beach, 189
Surin of Thailand, 102
Sweet Auburn Heritage Festival, 211
Sweetwater Creek State Park, 242
swimming, 257–58
Swissôtel Atlanta, 55–56
Synchronicity Metaphysical Dynasty, 148

T
Tabernacle, The, 231
Taco Mac, 75
Tall Tales, 145
Tanger Factory Outlet Center, 135
Tap Room, The, 121
Taste of the South, 207
taxis, 24
Telephone Museum, 186
television, 388–90
tennis, 258–60
Thai restaurants, 102, 114
theater, 191, 218–21, 223–24
Theater Emory, 223
Theater of the Stars, 223
Theatre Gael, 223
Theatre in the Square, 224
Theatrical Outfit, 223–24
Thrift House of the Cathedral of St. Philip, 140–41
thrift stores, 140–41
Tongue & Groove, 119
Tophat Soccer Club, 257
Tortillas, 97
Tour Championship, The, 279

Tour of Southern Ghosts, 212
Tower Records, 147
Town Center at Cobb, 134
trains, 11–16, 24, 26
transportation
    air travel, 16–26
    car rentals, 23
    commercial trains and buses, 26
    interstates and highways, 3–7
    limousines, 25
    local driving customs, 10–11
    mass transit systems, 11–16, 24
    rules of the road, 9–10
    shuttle services, 25
    surface streets, 7–9
    taxis, 24
Trinity Arts Group, 234
Trinity School, 351
Tucker Youth Soccer Association, 257
TULA Arts Center, 231
Turner Broadcasting System Inc.,
    388–89
Turner Field, 265–69
TV, 388–90
Tybee Island day trip/weekend
    getaway, 312–13

U
ultimate frisbee, 260
Uncle Tai's, A Chinese Bistro, 83
Underground Atlanta, 131–32, 172–73
Unicorn Place Vegetarian Cuisine, 114
Unity Bookstore, 148
universities/colleges, 353–62
University of Georgia basketball, 278
University of Georgia football, 274
Uptown Comedy Corner, 127–28
U.S. 10K Classic and Family Sports
    Festival, 209

V
V. Reed Gallery, 235
Value Village, 141
VA Medical Center-Atlanta, 372–73
Van Gogh's Restaurant, 109
Varsity, The, 80
vegetarian restaurants, 102–3, 114
Veni Vidi Vici, 94
Veranda, 397
Vesperman Glass Gallery, 234
Vibes, 147
Victoria Bryant Park, 247
Vietnamese Cuisine, 103
Villa Christina, 111

Village Inn Bed and Breakfast, 70
Vinings Jubilee, 132
Vinny's on Windward, 109
Vinocity Wine Bar, 75–76
vintage wear stores, 141
Virginia Avenue at North Highland
    Avenue shopping district, 137
Virginia Highland Inn, 68
Virginia-Highland Summerfest, 207
Vortex Bar & Grill, 76

W
WalkAmerica, 205
Walker School, The, 348
walk-in clinics, 382
walking, 254–55
Walking Club of Georgia, 255
Warm Springs day trip/weekend
    getaway, 306–7
water parks, 188–89
Wax N Facts, 147
Weather Channel, The, 389
weekend getaways. *See* day trips and
    weekend getaways
WellStar Cobb Hospital, 375–76
WellStar Health System Neighborhood
    Healthcare Centers, 382
WellStar Kennestone Hospital, 376
WellStar Windy Hill Hospital, 376
Wesley Woods Geriatric Center at
    Emory University, 373
Westin Atlanta North, 63
Westin Peachtree Plaza, The, 50, 121
Westminster Schools, The, 351
Westview Cemetery, 173
W.H. Reynolds Memorial Nature
    Preserve, 196–97
Wherehouse Music, 147
Whitefield Academy, 348
white-river rafting and tubing, 260–61
Whitlock Inn, 70
W Hotel Atlanta, 62
Wildfire Paint Ball Games, 253–54
William Breman Jewish Heritage
    Museum, 228–29
Williamson Brothers Bar-B-Q, 114
Windsong Sailing Academy, 255–56
Wingate Inn, 61, 63
Woodward Academy, 351
Woody's Famous Philadelphia Cheese-
    cakes, 80
World Bar, The, 119
World of Coca-Cola Atlanta, 173–74
Wrecking Bar, The, 139

Wren's Nest, The, 174–75, 194–95
W.T. Adams & Co., 339
Wuxtry, 147
Wyndham Garden Hotel Perimeter
    Center, 63
Wyndham Garden Hotel-Vinings, 58
Wyndham Midtown, 52–53

Y
Yellow Daisy Festival, 209–10
Yellow River Game Ranch, 197

Yeshiva Atlanta, 349
Y-Knot Sports Bar, 128

Z
Zab-E-Lee, 102
Zesto Drive-In, 80–81
Zoo Atlanta, 175–76, 197–98

About the Authors

John McKay

John is an Atlanta native, historian, and social studies teacher. He is very active in his church and lives north of Atlanta with his wife, Bonnie.

Bonnie McKay

Bonnie is a native of Albany, Georgia, a registered nurse, and serious amateur chef. She is very active in her church and Bible studies and lives north of Atlanta with her husband, John.